FROM THE FOLKS WHO BROUGHT YOU THE WEEKEND

Also by Priscilla Murolo

The Common Ground of Womanhood

Also by Joe Sacco

War Junkie

Safe Area Goražde

Palestine

FROM THE FOLKS WHO BROUGHT YOU THE WEEKEND

AN ILLUSTRATED HISTORY OF LABOR IN THE UNITED STATES

Priscilla Murolo and A.B. Chitty

Illustrations by Joe Sacco

THE
NEW
PRESS

NEW YORK
LONDON

Requests for permission to reproduce selections from this book should be mailed to:
Permissions Department, The New Press, 120 Wall Street, 31st floor, New York, NY 10005.

Excerpt from "Brother, Can You Spare a Dime?," words by E.Y. "Yip" Harburg, music by Jay Gorney, copyright © 1928 (renewed 1955) by Harms, Inc. U.S. rights controlled by Gorney Music and Glocca Morra Music. Reprinted by permission Akerman, LLP.

Published in the United States by The New Press, New York, 2018
Distributed by Two Rivers Distribution

ISBN 978-1-62097-448-3 (pb)
ISBN 978-1-62097-449-0 (e-book)
CIP data is available.

The New Press publishes books that promote and enrich public discussion and understanding of the issues vital to our democracy and to a more equitable world. These books are made possible by the enthusiasm of our readers; the support of a committed group of donors, large and small; the collaboration of our many partners in the independent media and the not-for-profit sector; booksellers, who often hand-sell New Press books; librarians; and above all by our authors.

www.thenewpress.com

Book design and composition by Bookbright Media
This book was set in Times New Roman and Gloucester MT

Printed in the United States of America

2 4 6 8 10 9 7 5 3 1

Contents

List of Illustrations

Preface to the Revised Edition

When this book's first edition went to press in 2001, the United States was not officially at war, both the Democratic and Republican parties favored reforms that would make the country more welcoming to immigrants, and most of the American labor movement agreed with John Sweeney's declaration a few years earlier that "We don't need any new programs. We just need to do what we've been doing even better."[1] Today, a seemingly endless "War on Terror" has U.S. troops on the move or on alert around the globe, xenophobia has become a core element in national politics, and labor activists of every stripe are experimenting with new programs. For all of these reasons, it seemed time to add fresh chapters to *From the Folks Who Brought You the Weekend*.

In addition, we felt keenly the need to update the old chapters, not only to correct mistakes and introduce newly discovered information but also to add citations, which would require a lot of research in historical documents. In the revised edition, every chapter is accompanied by notes that identify the origins of direct quotations and by a bibliography of our main secondary sources. We hope this will make the book a more effective springboard for readers who wish to do their own research on the topics we cover. After adding these bibliographies, we decided to dispense with the lengthy list of suggested readings included in the first edition. Today, the list would be twice as long and mostly redundant since the Internet makes it easy to track down good reading on labor history.

With regard to themes, the biggest difference between this edition of *From the Folks* and its predecessor is that we now look more closely at U.S. labor history's international dimensions. Both corporations and labor movements are today global affairs. This is hardly a brand-new development, but in the late 1990s, when our research for the book began, it was new enough that we did not fully recognize its significance. This time around, we've tried to rectify that weakness by devoting an entire chapter to globalization and by making global history a more prominent element in other chapters.

We owe some new acknowledgments. Thanks to Marc Favreau, our editor at The New Press, for giving *From the Folks* a second life. Thanks to Sarah Scheffel for exceptionally astute copyediting, to Terry Buck for meticulous proofreading, and to Emily Albarillo for expertly shepherding the book to publication. Thanks to Pauline Watts and Sarah Lawrence College for the Get It Done Award that gave Priscilla time to work on the book. Thanks also to Priscilla's graduate students and colleagues in the Union Leadership and Activism program at the University of Massachusetts; the experience and insight they have so generously shared have made a profound impact on our thinking about labor issues both present and past. We are incalculably grateful to Amanda Kozar for tracking down obscure sources, proofreading the manuscript, making sure the documentation is in good order, and steering us away from diction that would not register with readers considerably younger than ourselves. Cheers as well to Nick Thompson, who helped us review galley proofs before they went to press. For inspiration galore and numerous challenges to our old-fashioned assumptions, we are indebted to our family: our sons Tony and Max Schultz, our daughter-in-law Nicole Daro, and our grandchildren Sadie and Manny Daro Schultz, whose first sentences included "Union busting is disgusting."

All three of the people to whom we dedicate the book—David Montgomery, Martel Montgomery, Meridith Helton—are now gone from this world. We think of them every day and hope our work will honor their memory.

Yonkers, New York

April 2018

Foreword and Acknowledgments from the First Edition

Why this book now? For two reasons, mainly. When we started this project in 1998, no comprehensive survey of U.S. labor history for the general reader had appeared for more than a decade. Recent scholarship had added new dimensions and many details to the story of working people in America. It was past time to compile these insights into a new general history.

Also, the labor movement itself had changed—most dramatically in the 1995 election of the "New Voice" slate to the leadership of the American Federation of Labor-Congress of Industrial Organizations. This change reflected a belated recognition that the labor-government-management accord achieved after the Second World War had already been scuttled by both corporations and government, that without reorientation to new economic and political realities unions and the federation itself could become as irrelevant as any boss or banker might wish, and just wither away. Compared to the men they succeeded, the new generation of leaders had different ideas about the role of organized labor in society. These ideas are not new: they are revivals and developments of labor traditions that had long been subordinated to the demands of the scuttled accord of the Cold War era. It was a good time to look again at these traditions.

As we began drafting the story, a third reason appeared and became clearer as we continued. Even a casual look at American history reveals how much of what we learn and teach in school is just not true. Sometimes these misreadings are errors of fact—the extent of the U.S. war in the Philippines at the turn of the last century is one example. More often they are errors of omission—the African American role in the Civil War, for example. Mostly they concern perspective: looking at historical events from the bottom up alters our understanding of historical agency and causation. Adopting the perspective of people organizing to achieve common goals gives an account of historical events that is truer, and surely more useful.

Compared to conventional labor history, we tried mainly to be more inclusive in terms of "workers" and "working peoples' movements," and to incorporate as much recent research, historiography, and events as we could. Almost none of the material comes from our own research. We found an abundance of materials—in fact, too much. To keep the narrative from expanding beyond our publisher's mandate, or our control, we had to exclude more than we could include at every turn. There are some interesting books we did not write. We did not write a comprehensive account of trade unions, their internal affairs, or their complicated relationships with one another in and out of federations. We did not write a history of work, nor a history of labor and capital. We did not write a history of labor politics. These would be good and use-ful books. We also tried to keep from straying too far into major reinterpretations of American history, perhaps with mixed results. That would be a great book too, but beyond our ambition, and probably our competence.

Besides, for us the significance of the past is found in the present, and the present moment is full of rapid changes, even surprises. We are hopeful for the future, but certain of very little. We do know that in the past people have always found a way to struggle to make life better for themselves and their posterity. We know their struggles have generally been effective in proportion to the range and depth of the solidarity of their movements. We know the incessant and implacable adversary is privilege, legiti-mated by law, custom, and popular ideology, which never yields without challenge, to which democracy is anathema. We side with democracy. We write for the people who work too hard for too little, whose families and communities are hostage to the greed and arrogance of the same privilege that deforms our humanity and threatens our common welfare. We write for the people who can change history.

Our debts to historians and activists are too numerous to list. Our publisher, André Schiffrin and The New Press, and our editors, first Matt Weiland, then Marc Favreau, encouraged our work. Copyediting by David Allen helped to reconcile inconsistencies and force clarification. A Flik grant from Sarah Lawrence College gave Priscilla some money for travel. Feedback from students in labor history courses at Sarah Lawrence, the Midwest Summer School for Women Workers, and summer workshops spon-sored by Hospital and Health Care Workers District 1199 in Ohio, West Virginia, and Kentucky sharpened the analysis and the narrative. Friends and comrades like Kim Scipes, David Cline, and Gideon Rosenbluth helped us at particular points. Without the intellectual, emotional, and logistical support of Mary Reynolds, associate director of the Graduate Program in Women's History at Sarah Lawrence College, this book most likely would never have appeared.

We dedicate this book to three people. David Montgomery has been our personal intellectual guide to American labor history. His life and work combine the long view with mastery of historical detail and with activism to a degree all too rare in the profession of history. Martel Montgomery, David's wife, has been our good friend, steadfast and practical in seeing the possibility of change for the better, constant in her conviction that the principles by which we work for social justice apply with equal force to our everyday lives. Finally, our student and friend Meridith Helton learned labor history and then lived it, long enough at least to realize a personal dream work-ing for the union victory at the Fieldcrest Cannon mills in North Carolina. She died too suddenly and too soon, leaving us with an indelible and fiery memory of beauty, youth, and energy, love of music, adventure, and life, and passion for justice. She and her generation carry our hopes and quiet our fears. They have already started making our history.

Yonkers, New York
January 2001

FROM THE FOLKS WHO BROUGHT YOU THE WEEKEND

1

Labor in Colonial America: The Bound and the Free

The New World looked much like paradise to European voyagers in the fifteenth and sixteenth centuries. Christopher Columbus's first expedition (1492–93) took him to the Bahamas, Cuba, and Hispaniola, the island now shared by Haiti and the Dominican Republic. Claiming all of them as colonies for Spain's king Ferdinand and queen Isabella, Columbus described these islands as modern-day Edens in his report to the crown. He found Hispaniola especially breathtaking: "In that island . . . there are mountains of very great size and beauty, vast plains, groves, and very fruitful fields, admirably adopted for tillage, pasture, and habitation. The convenience and excellence of the harbors in this island, and the abundance of rivers, so indispensable to the health of man, surpass anything that would be believed by one who had not seen it . . . and moreover it abounds in various kinds of spices, gold, and other metals." The island's inhabitants seemed "exceedingly liberal with all that they have; none of them refusing any thing he may possess when he is asked for it, but on the contrary inviting us to ask them."[1]

Such impressions were not confined to the balmy Caribbean. In the 1580s, Englishmen hoping to colonize the rougher shores of today's North Carolina thought they had found an Eden on Roanoke Island. There, wrote Arthur Barlowe, "The earth bringeth forth all things in abundance, as in the first creation, without toil or labor."[2] Thomas Harriot forecast a happy relationship with Roanoke's natives, whose desire for "friendship & love" seemed certain to imbue them with "respect for pleasing and obeying us."[3] These were stock images in the earliest reports from European colonists in the Americas.

Many also told of astonishingly rich mineral deposits, which caught Europe's attention above all else. These rumors began with Columbus, who announced at the end of his first voyage that the islands he had claimed would supply Ferdinand and Isabella with "as much gold as they need."[4] The islanders would presumably be happy to serve it up. In fact, Caribbean gold deposits fell far below Columbus's estimates, and only brutal force could make mine slaves out of the region's natives, a collection of tribes known in retrospect as the Arawaks. The islands he likened to paradise in 1492 soon became hellholes where Spain enforced its rule with troops, heavy armaments, and attack dogs as the Arawaks were literally worked to death harvesting gold. The same befell Puerto Rico, Jamaica, and other islands that came under Spanish control in later years. By the 1530s, the Caribbean's goldfields had been stripped bare; the Arawak population had dwindled from about 10 million to a few thousand at best; and a new cycle of misery had begun as colonists turned from mining to cultivating sugarcane using captive laborers from Africa as well as the Americas.

Dreams of mineral wealth in the New World remained alive and well thanks to Spain's conquests of the Aztec empire in Mexico (1519–21) and the Inca empire in Peru (1532), both exceptionally rich in gold and silver. For decades to come, colonists throughout the Americas would dig for ore before getting down to the more mundane business of farming. Over the long haul, however, agriculture—the production of cash crops for European markets—proved more lucrative than mining; and so did the commerce in slaves, who raised the lion's share of colonial crops.

These developments vindicated Columbus's first impressions of the New World in one respect. Though the soil did not teem with gold and the people would not volunteer for servitude, the profits Europe extracted from American enterprises fully met his expectations. Many nations partook of the wealth: Portugal, England, France, and Holland joined Spain as major colonial and slave-trading powers, and their proceeds fueled economic growth throughout Europe.

Commerce across the Atlantic was not an entirely new phenomenon. Pre-Columbian journeys both to and from the Americas may have been numerous to judge from fragmentary evidence such as Roman coins found in the Americas, Inuit harpoon heads unearthed in Ireland and Scotland, and ancient Mayan sculptures that bear faces with African features. The Norse voyages described in Icelandic sagas are confirmed by archeological evidence of a short-lived settlement in Newfoundland in the early eleventh century, and timber from the region was shipped to Greenland for another 300 years. Columbus himself found evidence of commerce between Africans and Americans: Arawaks sometimes used spearpoints made from guanine, an alloy of gold, silver, and copper developed and used in West Africa, where it was also called guanine. The Arawaks said the alloy had come from dark-skinned traders. Columbus's son Ferdinand reported that his father met people "almost black in color" in what is now eastern Honduras; the Balboa expedition to Panama reportedly encountered a "tribe of Ethiopians."[5]

While transatlantic travel and trade predated Columbus, colonial ventures were something new. Unlike their predecessors, the voyagers of 1492 and after came from societies that had developed military technology to unprecedented levels during the Christian Crusades to seize the Holy Land from Muslims in the eleventh through thirteenth centuries. The new tools of war went hand in hand with the certainty of entitlement to any and all lands inhabited by non-Christians. And just as merchants had bankrolled the Crusades in return for trade monopolies, the men who pioneered Europe's colonization of the New World combined Christian piety with a keen eye for business opportunities.

Exploiting the colonies was never a simple matter, however. European monarchs gave giant tracts of American land to favorite courtiers, explorers, military men, and merchants, but land by itself could not make the recipients rich. It seldom contained precious metals; when it did, someone had to mine the ore. Contrary to Europeans' first impressions, moreover, the soil would not feed people without cultivation, let alone yield cash crops. To make a colony pay, its proprietors had to acquire and control a labor force.

Though colonial labor systems differed from place to place and changed over time, bondage was invariably their linchpin. Slaves, indentured servants, and other captives vastly outnumbered wageworkers, and the latter enjoyed few civil liberties beyond the enviable right to quit an unbearable job. For free laborers as well as the unfree, subordination was the central fact of life. Yet both groups repeatedly challenged their masters' authority. The things they endured and the ways they resisted form the core themes of colonial labor history in territories that are now part of the United States.

Legacies of Conquest

Spaniards were the first to colonize land that would be incorporated into the United States. They explored Florida in the early 1500s, hunting for gold and for Indian captives to work in Caribbean gold mines. By 1565, when Spain claimed Florida as a colony, Spanish expeditions had also explored much of what is today the southwestern United States and had established outposts as far north as Virginia and Kansas. By the mid-1700s, the Spanish frontier in North America was confined to southern latitudes but stretched all the way from Florida to California. Free laborers—Spaniards, Native Americans, Africans, and many people of mixed ancestry—were part of the workforce on this frontier. They included artisans, domestic servants, cotton sharecroppers, and herders on cattle and sheep ranches. Native American servitude was the mainstay of Spanish colonies, however, and fairly common in the sections of North America controlled by England and France.

In the late 1500s, the Spanish crown forbade the outright enslavement of indigenous people, but other forms of Native bondage remained legal, and slavery was often practiced despite the law. From Florida to California, Spain's North American colonies were dotted with missions established by Franciscan friars working to convert Indians to Christianity. This project proceeded on an especially large scale in the colony of New Mexico, established in 1598. By 1629, there were fifty Franciscan missions in the colony, and a reported 86,000 Pueblo Indians had been baptized. The majority of the converts lived in the mission settlements, where men, women, and children spent most of their waking hours at labor under the friars' supervision. Mainly, they raised crops and livestock, not only feeding the settlement but also producing surpluses that the friars marketed for consumption in America or for shipment to Spain. Mission industries expanded as time went on and grew especially large in California. By the early 1800s, the products included butter, tallow, hides and chamois leather, maize, wheat, wine, brandy, vegetable oils, and textiles. While Spanish law did not define mission Indians as slaves, neither were they free to come and go as they wished. Floggings awaited those who failed to do their assigned work, missed the compulsory religious services, or otherwise broke the friars' rules. Soldiers guarded the missions not only to keep rebellious Indians out but also to keep the converts in.

Still, many Indians preferred mission life to their treatment under secular Spanish rule. In New Mexico, colonists regularly violated the law by sending Navajo and Apache captives into slavery in Mexico's mines. Outside the missions, Pueblo peoples labored under the *encomienda* system in which recipients of royal land grants collected tribute from the land's inhabitants. Under this system, the Pueblos produced maize, cotton blankets, and hides for export to Mexico or Spain. Tribute in the form of forced labor was prohibited by the crown, but *encomenderos* habitually ignored that rule.

In both New Mexico and Florida, colonists also foisted *repartimiento* and *rescate* on native peoples. The system of *repartimiento de indios* drafted Indians for labor on public works projects—unloading ships, transporting supplies, and building and repairing roads, bridges, and fortifications. By law, the draftees served for limited terms, labored only on public projects, and received fair compensation. In practice, colonial officials often extended service beyond the legal term, dispensed with wages, and compelled *repartimiento* workers to labor for private businesses and households. *Rescate* was practiced in all Spanish colonies: Indians taken captive by other Indians were ransomed and bound over for domestic service in colonists' households. Technically these *indios de depósito* were not slaves, and did not pass their condition to their children. But they could be bought and sold, and some were sold into outright slavery in Mexico.

In New Mexico unbaptized Indians—especially women and children—were often seized and sold as domestic slaves in violation of the law. Officials tolerated the practice on the theory that it "civilized" the slaves; but like all forms of slavery, this one was more likely to barbarize the masters. In 1751, the wife of Alejandro Mora complained to authorities in Bernalillo, New Mexico, that he mistreated the Indian woman Juana, a slave in the Mora household. The investigating constable found Juana covered with bruises and burns, her ankles raw from manacles, her knees festering with sores. Mora had broken her knees to keep her from running away and periodically reopened the wounds with flintstone. Juana gave this testimony:

> I have served my master for eight or nine years now but they have seemed more like 9,000 because I have not had one moment's rest. He has martyred me with sticks, stones, whip, hunger, thirst, and burns all over my body. . . . He inflicted them saying that it was what the devil would do to me in hell, that he was simply doing what God had ordered him to do.[6]

Mora protested that he was only looking out for Juana's welfare. He had raped her, he said, only to test her claim to virginity, and he had tortured her only to keep her from becoming a loose woman. Authorities removed Juana from the Mora household; that was her master's only penalty.

English and French colonists enslaved indigenous people too, though never in the same numbers as did the Spanish. In the 1620s, Virginians sold Indian survivors of the Second Anglo-Powhatan War into slavery in the West Indies; in 1637, Indian survivors of the Pequot War in New England were enslaved in Bermuda. During the Tuscarora and Yamasee Wars (1711–15), Englishmen and their Indian allies captured and enslaved natives of the Carolina interior. In 1731, the French in Louisiana rounded up most of the surviving Natchez nation for sale to West Indies plantations. And while English and French colonies typically sent Indian captives to the Caribbean, quite a few were enslaved on the mainland. About a tenth of the slaves in French Louisiana were Indians, mostly women assigned to domestic work. French settlers in Detroit bought Pawnee, Osage, and Choctaw captives and held them and their descendants as slaves for most of the 1700s. A census of South Carolina in 1708 counted 3,960 free whites, 4,100 African slaves, 1,400 Indian slaves, and 120 indentured whites. In New York in 1712, about a quarter of all slaves were Indians. A census of Kingston, Rhode Island, in 1730 counted 935 whites, 333 African slaves, and 223 Indian slaves. By the late 1700s, Indian and African slaves had amalgamated to the point that census takers did not distinguish between the two, instead listing all slaves as "colored."[7]

Indigenous people also labored for Europeans in relationships that did not involve bondage. Many hunted and trapped for pelts to sell to colonial fur traders. Since Native Americans valued commodities differently than Europeans, they often failed to get market value for their goods. From the mid-1600s onward, some New England Indians were wage earners, working as farmhands, domestics, whalers, or construction laborers. This movement into wage work—a pattern that would eventually extend across the continent—reflected the losses of land that undermined Native Americans' ability to live without hiring out.

In 1742, the Seneca leader Canassatego spoke to Pennsylvania officials on behalf of the Iroquois nations: "We know our lands are now become more valuable. The white people think we do not know their value; but we are sensible that the land is everlasting, and the few goods we receive for it are soon worn out and gone. . . . Besides, we are not well used with respect to the lands still unsold by us. Your people daily settle on these lands, and spoil our hunting. We must insist on your removing them, as you know they have no right to settle."[8] In this instance and countless others, colonial authorities failed to remove the squatters, and Indians' economic independence eroded.

Indentured Labor in British Colonies

Indentured workers—commonly called "servants"—were a key source of labor for British colonies. They planted the first crops at the Jamestown colony founded in Virginia in 1607, Britain's first permanent settlement in what is now the United States. Twelve of them were aboard the *Mayflower* when it brought the Pilgrims to Plymouth, Massachusetts, in 1620. By the time the American Revolution broke out in the mid-1770s, more than half of all European immigrants to the colonies had entered as indentured servants. Estimates put their proportion at 60 to 77 percent. In the 1600s, the vast majority came from England as individuals, and the males far outnumbered the females. The next century saw a large influx of Irish and German families, and the gender ratio grew more even.

Until the 1660s, most Africans who came to British North America arrived as indentured workers too. The first twenty, at least three of them women, landed in Jamestown on a Dutch ship in 1619. Over the next forty-odd years, many hundreds of black indentured servants entered Britain's mainland colonies, from New England in the north to the Carolinas in the south. The majority came from England, Spain, or Portugal, where Africans had lived for two generations or more; others came from the West Indies.

Indenture placed workers in bondage for a limited term—typically three to five years, though some served considerably more time. What had promised to be a short term might stretch into a long one. Magistrates customarily extended the terms of servants hauled into court for fleeing their masters or otherwise breaking the law. For the duration of the indenture, they were their masters' property, and many were repeatedly bought and sold before their terms expired.

Mostly they were put to hard labor, clearing land and plowing new fields, cultivating crops that required constant work, draining swamps and building roads, laundering and cooking, hauling heavy loads. A man with special skills might enjoy lighter duty as an artisan's helper. That was the lot of William Moraley, an apprentice watchmaker back in England and for three years the servant of a New Jersey clockmaker who purchased him fresh off a ship that docked in Philadelphia in 1729. Craftwork was seldom the whole of a servant's assignment, however; in addition to cleaning time-pieces, Moraley herded livestock and labored in an iron foundry. He was fortunate in that the clockmaker beat him only once, as a punishment for trying to run away. Other masters had less self-control. Writing from Maryland in 1756, Elizabeth Sprigs told her father in London of repeated floggings: "I one of the unhappy Number, am toiling almost Day and Night . . . and then tied up and whipp'd to the Degree that you'd not serve an Annimal."[9]

Despite reports of such abuses, a great many people indentured themselves volun-tarily in return for transportation to the New World and, they hoped, better opportu-nities than Europe offered. The volunteers signed indentures with labor contractors who paid for their passage and then sold them to American employers. Because there was room to haggle, men and women indentured under this arrangement served rela-tively short terms. But quite a few servants had no choice in the matter. Some were English convicts sentenced to servitude in the colonies. Others were destitute children kidnapped off the streets of England's seaports or ordered into indenture by colonial authorities. Still others were debtors bound by law to work off their obligations to creditors. For these groups—especially convicts and children—terms of up to four-teen years were not at all uncommon.

Indentured servants faced the hardest times during the early decades of colonial settlement. Newcomers routinely succumbed to the deadly fevers that struck the colo-nies every summer. And the "seasoned" servants who had survived their first sum-mers were far from safe, especially the thousands indentured to tobacco planters in the Chesapeake region of Virginia and Maryland. Nearly two-thirds of these workers died before their indentures ended. Following an Indian attack that killed 347 James-town residents in March 1622, the Virginia Company in England inquired into the fate of the 700 people in the colony as of spring 1619 and the 3,570 immigrants who had arrived since then. A head count showed that just 1,240 remained alive. Some of them probably envied the dead. As one starving servant wrote to his parents in 1623, "I thought no head had beene able to hold so much water as hath and doth dailie flow from mine eyes."[10]

Endurance had its rewards. On fulfilling the term of service, each worker except for the convicts and debtors received "freedom dues"—a sum of money, a parcel of land in some colonies, and perhaps other things too, such as clothing, tools, a horse or a cow. In theory, the dues would turn released servants into proprietors of American farms, craft shops, or other small businesses. In reality, such happy endings were rare. Surviving records suggest that, of all the people indentured in British North America between 1607 and 1776, just 20 percent went on to self-employment in the colonies or newborn United States. About half did not outlive their indentures; most of the rest became wageworkers or paupers or returned to their countries of origin.

In the mid-1700s, the indenture system developed a new twist as shipping merchants devised a scheme that forced many thousands of free immigrants into terms of servitude. Recruitment agents commissioned by the shippers visited European towns and depicted America as a land where no one worked hard and everyone got rich. People who signed up for transport to this paradise were promised a cheap fare and easy credit if they could not afford the full price. By the time the passengers arrived in America, nearly all were in debt to the ship's captain, who had levied surprise charges for tariffs, duties, and provisions. Nobody could leave the ship without first clearing accounts, and no sooner was that announced than entrepreneurs came on board with offers to redeem people who signed indenture contracts for themselves and their children. Exhausted and frightened, the captives often agreed to exceptionally long terms of service. Most of these immigrants, known as "redemptioners," came from Ireland or Germany.

One eyewitness to their predicament was Gottlieb Mittelberger, whose *Journey to Pennsylvania* (1756) publicized the miseries he had seen. In 1750 Mittelberger left his home in the Duchy of Württemberg and joined a party of fellow Germans sailing for Philadelphia. The ship was so crowded with families and so poorly stocked with food that over half the passengers died in transit, their debts to the captain devolving to their kin. Desperate to leave the vessel when it finally docked, the survivors were ready to sign virtually any indenture contract. Adults committed themselves for terms of three to six years if they were lucky, six to twelve if their spouses were too sick to work or had died at sea. Minor children were bound over by their parents, or the ship's captain in the case of children orphaned during the voyage. Those between ten and fifteen years old were sold into service until age twenty-one. The youngest, who could not by law be sold, were given away to anyone who promised to maintain them.

One of a handful who had paid in full for his passage, Mittelberger escaped indenture, but he saw what awaited his less fortunate shipmates. As a schoolteacher in rural Pennsylvania, he watched "soul-drivers" march lots of fifty or more redemptioners into the backcountry and sell them into labor on farms where they were "beaten like cattle." Returning to Württemberg in 1754, he published his book in hopes that it would persuade fellow Germans to remain at home: "Let him who wants to earn his piece of bread honestly and who can only do this by manual labor in his own country, stay there rather than come to America."[11] Such warnings had little if any impact. As the century wore on, redemptioners arrived in Philadelphia in growing numbers—by 1770 at an average rate of twenty-four shiploads a year.

Slavery

In 1505, a Spanish ship carried a cargo of captives from West Africa to Hispaniola, inaugurating one of the most hideous and profitable business enterprises in world history. Over the next centuries, the transatlantic trade in African slaves would grow to gigantic proportions and involve merchants and shippers from virtually every European and American seafaring power. By the time the trade ended in the late 1860s, an estimated 12.5 million Africans had been forced onto ships bound for the Americas, and about 10.7 million of them had survived the journey. South America and the Caribbean were the primary destinations; fewer than 400,000 of the captives disembarked on the North American mainland, but some who first landed in the British Caribbean wound up in Britain's mainland colonies or, later, the United States.

British colonies in North America enslaved Africans almost from the beginning, as did the Dutch colony of New Amsterdam (which became British New York in 1664). As black indentured servants arrived in the early and mid-1600s, so did black slaves, though not yet in large numbers. The Dutch West India Company transported them to New Amsterdam as early as 1626. Others arrived in Boston in 1638 and in Connecticut the following year. Some indentured servants meanwhile became slaves in fact if not in name. Starting in the 1640s in Virginia, colonial courts used lifelong bondage as the punishment for black servants who fled their masters.

The decisive turn toward slavery came in the later 1600s, with Maryland and Virginia taking the lead. In 1663, Maryland's lawmakers declared all of the colony's black residents slaves for life and imposed the same status on all persons henceforth born to enslaved women. In 1670, Virginia condemned all Africans entering the colony to slavery, and a 1682 law extended the sentence to all offspring of enslaved women. Thus started a juggernaut. By 1710, every colony had passed laws that enslaved Africans and their descendants as well as Native American captives. Georgia, founded in 1732 with a charter that outlawed slaveholding, reversed that stand in 1750. Between 1700 and the start of the American Revolution in 1775, the number of slaves in British North America rose from about 25,000 to 500,000, about 90 percent of them laboring in the southern colonies of Maryland, Virginia, Georgia, and the Carolinas.

Slavery expanded in northern colonies too. By the mid-1700s, nearly every wealthy family in northern port cities owned household slaves, up to a third of the artisans in these cities used slave labor in their shops, and grain farmers from Pennsylvania to southern New England were replacing indentured servants with slaves. In Philadelphia and New York City, slaves constituted 20 percent of the whole labor force in artisan shops and did an even larger share of the work in maritime trades such as shipbuilding and sail making. In some grain-producing counties in northern New Jersey, New York's Hudson Valley, and Long Island, slaves far outnumbered free workers. The major slaveholding colony north of Maryland was New York, whose enslaved population rose from 9,000 in the 1740s to almost 20,000 in the 1770s. New England's 16,000 slaves as of 1770 were concentrated in Connecticut, Massachusetts, and Rhode Island, but some 2,000 worked in the more sparsely settled areas to the north.

The merchants and shippers of Newport, Rhode Island, became the leading North American participants in the transatlantic slave trade. Other cities whose ships regularly bore down on Africa included Providence, Rhode Island; Salem and Boston, Massachusetts; and Portsmouth, New Hampshire. While southern colonists dealt mostly with British slave traders, Yankees dominated the business in northern ports and shipped up to 10 percent of the slaves arriving in southern ports in the 1700s.

Africans' experience en route to America is vividly described in *The Interesting Narrative of the Life of Olaudah Equiano*, the autobiography of a former slave published in 1791. Born in 1745 in the Essaka province of Benin, Equiano was kidnapped at age ten or eleven, passed from hand to hand, and finally sold to a trader on the Guinea coast, where in 1757 he was carried aboard an English slave ship bound for Barbados. To guard against a revolt, crewmen placed the adults in iron chains and allowed just a few captives at a time to leave the hold and breathe fresh air on deck. Then, when the ship got under way, all were put below. As Equiano later wrote,

> The stench of the hold, while we were on the coast, was so intolerably loathsome, that it was dangerous to remain there for any time; but now that the whole ship's cargo were confined together, it became absolutely pestilential. The closeness of the place, and the heat of the climate, added to the number in the ship, being so crowded that each had scarcely room to turn himself, almost suffocated us. This produced copious perspirations, so that the air soon became unfit for respiration, from a variety of loathsome smells, and brought on a sickness among the slaves, of which many died. . . . The shrieks of the women and the groans of the dying rendered it a scene of horror almost inconceivable.[12]

Such was the setting on every slave ship, and Equiano recounted incidents that also typified the voyage. Beatings and force-feeding awaited those who refused to eat, for the same business logic that prompted slave traders to jam-pack their ships made them anxious to keep the cargo alive. When captives nearing death were brought on deck for resuscitation, some threw themselves overboard; two men on Equiano's ship succeeded in drowning while a third was rescued and flogged.

When the ship docked in Bridgetown, Barbados, merchants and planters came on board to inspect the captives, who were then taken ashore and penned in a yard. Several days later, Equiano remembered,

> We were sold after the usual manner, which is this:—On a signal given, such as the beat of a drum, the buyers rush at once into the yard where the slaves are confined, and make choice of that parcel they like best. . . . In this manner, without scruple, are relations and friends separated, most of them never to see each other again.[13]

The West Indies sugar planters who bought most of Equiano's companions rejected him, just twelve years old and frail "from very much fretting,"[14] so he and a few others in similar condition were transported to Virginia. There, he was sold to an English ship's captain and began a twenty-year maritime career during which he managed to purchase his freedom.

Some others enslaved in British North America gained their liberty through self-purchase, manumission, lawsuits, or flight. Until the American Revolution, however, such deliverance was rare. Of the nearly 5,000 "free colored people" in the colonies on the eve of the Revolution, the majority were freeborn descendants of indentured women, both black and white, or of noncaptive Indians. They were free by virtue of that ancestry, not because of soft spots in the fortress of slavery.

Slavery's tenacity reflected its economic value to the colonies, which exploited slaves' minds and muscles in remarkably elaborate ways. The typical slave of the colonial era was a field hand raising tobacco, rice, or indigo on a southern plantation; this was the most common labor for the men, women, and children. But slaves worked in many other capacities too. They tilled land on the giant estates that lined the Hudson Valley and on many a small farm from New Hampshire to Georgia. Their labors on southern plantations encompassed carpentry and blacksmithing, leather tanning and shoemaking, bricklaying and plastering, spinning woolen thread, weaving cloth, and sewing clothes. In northern colonies, they could be found in virtually all skilled trades, from maritime crafts to goldsmithing, printing, and cabinetmaking. Every colonial port counted slaves among its sailors and dockworkers. In many white households—rural and urban, northern and southern—enslaved women fetched water, hauled firewood, cooked meals, scoured kitchens, tended infants and children, and saw to other chores.

In addition to a wide variety of labor, slaveholders demanded deference. Nothing better illustrates this than the 1701 court case in which a Massachusetts slave identified only as Adam sued his master John Saffin for reneging on a 1694 promise to free him in seven years. Saffin's defense was that Adam had been "intollerably insolent, quarrelsome and outrageous," daring to work at his own pace, talk back when insulted, and resist beatings.[15] Though the jury sided with Saffin, Adam won his freedom in 1703 by appealing the decision to the colony's Superior Court. His appeal and indeed the original lawsuit would have been impossible outside of New England; elsewhere, slaves had no rights to sue or testify against whites.

In this context, assault, homicide, and rape became part and parcel of slavery; and while slaves on southern plantations were the most vulnerable to abuse, others were scarcely immune. New Jersey slaves were flogged to degrees that shocked the indentured servant William Moraley. "For the least Trespass," he wrote, "they undergo the severest Punishment . . . and if they die under the Discipline their Masters suffer no Punishment, there being no Law against murdering them."[16] A British visitor to colonial South Carolina recorded the following in his diary: "Mr. Hill, a dancing-master in Charles-Town, whipt a female slave so long, that she fell down at his feet, in appearance dead: when, by the help of a physician, she was so far recovered as to show some signs of life, he repeated the whipping with equal rigor, and concluded the punishment with dropping scalding wax upon her flesh—Her crime was, over filling a tea-cup!"[17] A New Englander who hobnobbed with Charleston's most prominent men was astonished to hear them speak with "no reluctance, delicacy or shame" about molesting women in the slave quarters.[18]

The most common forms of abuse, however, were starvation and overwork. In the 1990s, preservationists blocked the construction of a skyscraper atop the "African burial ground" in the oldest part of New York City and reburied the unearthed remains of over 400 people whose skeletons testified to slavery's grueling toll on black bodies.[19] The majority of the dead were children twelve and under, half of them infants. The adult skeletons showed lesions on shoulder, arm, and leg bones where muscles had been torn away by strain, and some showed circular fractures at the base of the skull, a sign that excessively heavy loads had been carried on the head. One skeleton belonged to a boy about age six who died in the early 1700s. Though his remains indicated that he had been malnourished and anemic from birth, the anchor points on his arm bones revealed that his muscles had been unusually well developed from lifting, and the many healed fractures in his neck showed that his head, too, had borne large weights. Whatever disease or trauma ended this child's life, it is fair to say that he was worked to death.

Free Labor

Although bondage lay at the core of colonial labor systems, the numbers of free men and women hiring out for wages steadily increased. This workforce included free immigrants, former indentured servants, Native Americans pushed off their lands, the lucky few who made their way out of slavery, and descendants of all these groups. Wage earners were a minority among free people, most of whom made a living through a family farm, a family craft shop, or some combination of the two. Almost from the start, however, the colonies were home to at least some wageworkers, and by the early 1700s wage labor was a fast-rising trend in British North America, especially in its coastal cities and towns.

The largest sectors of the wage-earning labor force were sailors, journeyman artisans, women and girls employed as domestic workers or in cloth and clothing production, and men and boys who plowed fields, hauled freight, and performed other back-breaking jobs that fell under the heading "common labor." Except for the journeymen, whose craft skills won them higher wages than the rest, these workers belonged to the poorest segments of free society. Though nearly all earned substantially more than their European counterparts, their lives were scarcely enviable by free Americans' standards.

Single women with dependent children got the worst of it, often trudging from place to place in search of a job that would pay enough to feed and shelter their families. Their chances of finding one were so slim that the overseers of Connecticut, Massachusetts, Rhode Island, and numerous towns in other colonies barred single mothers from settling down unless they relinquished the right to solicit help from local charities. Starting in the mid-1700s, agencies such as Boston's Society for Encouraging Industry and Employing the Poor opened cloth and clothing "manufactories" where destitute women and children worked for a pittance, just enough to keep them alive.

Most women wage earners escaped such dire circumstances, as did the majority of sailors and common laborers; but very few were comfortably situated. Domestic workers and farmhands typically lived with their employers, toiling sixteen hours a day or more in return for a tiny cash wage plus room and board. Even in Philadelphia, North America's most prosperous city in the late colonial era, sailors and common laborers almost never found steady jobs. Those who did earned about £50 per year—£10 less than a family of average size needed to survive in Philadelphia. To make ends meet, the wives and children of male wage earners often hired out too.

Workers' troubles in some occupations went beyond hard labor and low pay. Many sailors lost their lives at sea; many more suffered from what they called "Falling Sickness"—dizziness caused by recurrent beatings at the hands of their ships' officers.[20] Domestic workers sometimes faced physical abuse as well. In 1734, a group of them announced in the *New-York Weekly Journal* that "we think it reasonable we should not be beat by our Mistrisses Husband[s], they being too strong, and perhaps may do tender women Mischief."[21]

For all of these reasons, most free people did everything in their power to build lives that did not revolve around wage work. More often than not, they succeeded. Just as wages were higher than in Europe, alternatives to wage earning were more plentiful.

Family farming was by far the most common alternative; it occupied well over half of free people, both black and white. Land to the west of the well-established settlements was cheap enough for a great many people to buy. Others obtained acreage as part of their freedom dues or squatted on land the colonies had reserved for Native Americans. A good number of people rented farms, especially in Massachusetts, New Jersey, New York's Hudson Valley, and interior Pennsylvania and Maryland. Though farming was a family affair, it was also a commercial venture in most cases. Nearly every household marketed products such as corn, butter, and woolen goods; many also produced cash crops for export—tobacco in southern colonies, wheat in New England and the mid-Atlantic region. In the Northeast, where winter brought farmwork to a halt for several months each year, numerous households filled the time with craftwork, chiefly leather tanning and shoemaking. Farm families were often hard-pressed, even destitute, the landowners as well as the tenants. "Inconsiderable persons," the colonial elite called them.[22] Even so, they lived and worked without a boss breathing down their necks; therein lay the great attraction of farming.

Craftwork in cities and towns offered another route to independence, an astonishingly fast route by European measures. In Europe, an artisan spent many years preparing for self-employment as a master of his craft. First, he completed a seven-year apprenticeship, serving under a master craftsman in return for room and board; then he worked a long stint as a journeyman, perfecting his skills as he slowly saved money to finance a shop of his own. In America, it was easy to find shortcuts, for the craft guilds that oversaw the system in Europe almost never took root in the colonies. Absent guild oversight, few apprentices put in a full seven years. Some served less time by mutual agreement with their masters; others reneged on their apprenticeship contracts and ran away, eluding the law by moving to a different colony. Skilled labor was in such short supply that almost anyone with a few years of apprenticeship under his belt could get work as a journeyman, and journeymen usually earned enough to finance swift transitions to self-employment. In Philadelphia, journeymen earned slightly or substantially more than £60 a year depending on their crafts.

Benjamin Franklin's story exemplifies artisans' mobility. Born in 1706 in Boston, he was a candlemaker's son who at age twelve undertook an apprenticeship in printing—a much more prestigious craft, not far below silversmithing at the very top.

His master was his older brother James, whom Ben contracted to serve for seven years. By all accounts the boy learned quickly, but James's foul temper made it a difficult apprenticeship; so in 1723, two years before his contract expired, Ben ran away to Philadelphia, where he passed himself off as a journeyman and soon opened a printshop of his own. By 1748, he was sufficiently rich to retire from the shop and give himself full time to the almanac writing, political activity, and scientific experiments that would make him one of the most famous Americans of the eighteenth century.

The unregulated craft system could also undermine the very advantages it bestowed. By the mid-1700s, some trades were so crowded with master craftsmen that bankruptcies were common in slack times. Some masters lowered costs by retaining fewer journeymen and more apprentices—more than they could train in all aspects of the craft. Others turned to slave labor or imported out-of-town journeymen to glut the local job market and thus reduce wages. For the time being, though, such problems were confined to certain trades in certain locales. Most practitioners of most crafts still had good reason to believe Ben Franklin's adage, "He that hath a Trade, hath an Estate."[23]

This "he" was frequently a she. While midwives practiced a prestigious, wholly female trade, many more women engaged in male-dominated crafts, from silversmithing on down. Excluded from formal apprenticeships, they acquired craft skills by working in shops owned by their fathers, husbands, or other male kin. Virtually every master craftsman counted on women's assistance; it took more than his own labor and that of male employees to make the shop pay. A handful of women opened crafts shops of their own. In Baltimore, for example, Mary Minskie and two male assistants made metal corset stays and men's and women's clothing. But the vast majority of master craftswomen were widows carrying on their husbands' businesses—women like Ann Smith Franklin, who ran James Franklin's printshop for twenty-three years following his death.

Unruly Labor

The first labor rebellion in colonial North America preceded the establishment of permanent colonies. In the summer of 1526, about 500 Spaniards and 100 enslaved Africans made camp near the mouth of the Pee Dee River in what is now South Carolina. That November the slaves rose up, killed most of their captors, and escaped to nearby Indian settlements. The Spanish survivors retreated to Hispaniola; the Africans stayed on. Over the next 250 years, North America saw many more acts of resistance by colonial laborers, both bound and free.

Slaves and indentured servants frequently challenged authority in much the same ways Adam defied John Saffin. "Stubborn, refractory and discontented," in the words of Connecticut's colonial officials, they paced their work as they saw fit, objected aloud to insults, and refused to march dutifully to whipping posts.[24] Many took aim at their masters' property, breaking tools, injuring farm animals, setting fire to houses and barns. Some took aim at the masters themselves, along with anyone who got in the way. In 1678, the Englishman Thomas Hellier, indentured on a Virginia plantation called Hard Labour, axed to death his master, his mistress, and a woman servant who tried to assist them. In 1747, the Comanche Pedro de la Cruz led his tribesmen in an armed raid on the New Mexico town where he had been enslaved. In 1771, two African slaves in New Orleans were arrested for flogging their master and burning his hayloft. Stories of such incidents appeared in colonial newspapers on a fairly regular basis.

For both slaves and indentured servants, however, the most common form of resistance was flight. Newspapers carried column upon column of advertisements describing runaways and promising rewards for their capture and return. In British colonies, which were more thickly settled than those of France or Spain, most of the fugitives got caught. As one indentured Pennsylvanian wrote, "'Tis certain that nothing is more difficult than for a Slave or a Servant in *America* to make his Escape without being retaken, because the Master spares no Expence for that Purpose."[25] The penalties for apprehended runaways included whipping, branding, and the amputation of an ear. But attempts at escape continued nonetheless, inspired by the fact that some people managed to get away for good. Those who beat the odds typically found refuge among Native Americans or by fleeing to French or Spanish territory.

In Spanish Florida, escaped slaves from the Carolinas founded a town of several hundred in 1739. Located just north of Saint Augustine, surrounded by stone walls, and guarded by a town militia about 100 strong, this settlement—known as Fort Mose (short for Gracia Real de Santa Teresa de Mose)—became a barrier against British invasion as well as a beacon for runaways. In 1740, when an army of South Carolinians marched into Florida, their defeat at Fort Mose persuaded them to retreat. Welcoming new arrivals from the Carolinas and, later, Georgia too, the town survived until Spain ceded Florida to Britain in 1763 and Fort Mose's residents moved to Cuba.

Resistance to servitude also took the form of armed rebellion. Colonial records describe the suppression of hundreds of plots by would-be rebels, including indentured servants in Maryland in the 1650s, an alliance of Indian and African slaves in Massachusetts in 1690, slaves in French New Orleans in 1730 and 1732, about 150 slaves and 25 white allies in New York City in 1741, and the Pueblos in Spanish New Mexico in 1784, 1793, and 1810. If authorities exaggerated some plots and entirely dreamed up some others, their suspicions are understandable. Experience proved time and again that bondage begat revolts.

The largest by far occurred in New Mexico in August 1680, when 17,000 Pueblos rose up against Spanish demands for tribute under the *encomienda* system and for Indian conversions to Christianity. A model of strategic planning, this offensive mobilized Pueblos from over two dozen far-flung villages that spoke at least six different languages and widely varied dialects, many of them mutually unintelligible. The revolt also seems to have won strong support from the tens of thousands of baptized Pueblos laboring for Franciscan missions. By October, the rebels had driven every Spaniard out of New Mexico, and only a few hundred Pueblos from the missions had joined the exodus. Spain did not retake the colony until 1693 and never reestablished the *encomienda*. Following a smaller Pueblo uprising in 1696, the colonists also softened their demands for religious conversion and for labor from mission Indians and *repartimiento* draftees.

Slaves and indentured servants in British colonies launched scores of smaller-scale revolts that made up in daring what they lacked in size. The early 1660s ushered in thirty years of unrest in Virginia. Both slaves and servants fled their masters in record numbers. Authorities discovered plots for armed rebellion by servants in York County in 1661, a confederation of slaves and servants in Gloucester County in 1663, and slaves in the Northern Neck region in 1687. Bands of fugitive slaves staged repeated raids on plantations in various counties in 1672 and again in 1691. In 1682, when planters' overproduction of tobacco plunged the colony into a depression, slaves, servants, and impoverished free people laid waste to the tobacco crops on plantations throughout Gloucester County.

For Virginia's elite, the most frightening of all the uprisings in this period was Bacon's Rebellion in 1676. It began that spring as a revolt by backcountry farmers, most of them former servants working land they had received as freedom dues. In April some 500 farmers united behind the tobacco planter Nathaniel Bacon to wage war on neighboring Indians, in flagrant violation of their treaties with the colony's royal governor. By summer Bacon's troops were also plundering wealthy planters' property, and in September they attacked the colonial capital in Jamestown, where hundreds of slaves and indentured servants joined the uprising. Within days the rebels had burned Jamestown to the ground and fanned out into the surrounding countryside to loot plantations. Chaos reigned for the rest of the year, with slaves and servants fighting on long after Bacon died of dysentery in late October and the farmers started to trudge home.

Following Bacon's Rebellion, the large planters of coastal Virginia and nearby Maryland rethought their labor policies. The indenture system seemed terribly risky now that former servants had inaugurated a mass revolt in which black and white fought side by side. Slavery might prove safer, as long as slaves could be isolated from poor whites. To secure their dominion, the planter elite would henceforth purchase as many slaves as possible, use indentured workers only in a pinch, and try to minimize contact between the two. Colonial officials meanwhile criminalized marriage across the color line and granted servants certain rights and protections denied to slaves: the right to own property, for example, and protection from dismemberment as a penalty for insubordination. As other British colonies institutionalized slavery, they, too, passed laws designed to eliminate common ground between servants and slaves. Labor revolts that united black and white were soon a thing of the past.

Both slaves and servants continued to resist bondage, however, and especially bold mutinies broke out in New York, South Carolina, and Florida following its transfer to England's hands. In April 1712, about twenty-five slaves in New York City—including two Native Americans and a visibly pregnant black woman—armed themselves with guns, clubs, and knives, set fire to a building on the northern edge of town, and attacked the men who came to fight the flames. Soldiers garrisoned in the city quickly rounded up the rebels, save for six who chose suicide over capture; and fifty more slaves were arrested on the suspicion that they had helped to plan the revolt. In the end, twenty-one people were executed in gruesome ways designed to terrify potential rebels into submission.

The South Carolina rebellion began in the town of Stono on September 9, 1739, when about twenty slaves led by an Angolan named Jemmy seized guns and powder from a warehouse and set out for Spanish Florida, waving flags, beating drums, and shouting "Liberty."[26] About sixty more slaves soon joined the column, which attacked every plantation in its path and killed about twenty-five whites along the way. A militia detachment tracked down the rebels in a matter of hours but failed to stop their march for another ten days. While most of them were eventually killed or captured, as many as ten or fifteen got away.

In Florida, in summer 1768, a revolt erupted among Italian and Greek immigrants indentured to ten years' labor on an indigo plantation at New Smyrna on the colony's Atlantic coast. The plantation's British proprietors had recruited them with promises of comfortable lodgings, a half-share of the crop, and their own acreage as freedom dues. Arriving at New Smyrna in June and July 1768, the immigrants found an arid wilderness of uncleared land, severe shortages of food and shelter, and epidemics of gangrene and scurvy. On August 18, some 300 rebels led by Carlo Forni of Livorno, Italy, helped themselves to firearms from the plantation storehouse and locked up their English overseer. About 100 of them then crowded onto the only ship at the settlement's dock and set sail for Cuba. The British navy soon intercepted them, but a few of the rebels, including Forni, escaped in a rowboat and remained at large for another four months. The only fatalities stemming from this revolt occurred when Forni and one of his lieutenants were captured and beheaded by British authorities. Back at New Smyrna, the deaths were many; close to 900 workers had succumbed to disease by 1773. Four years later, the survivors deserted en masse, and the African captives who replaced them ran away in droves. By 1783, when Spain snatched Florida back from Britain, the plantation lay in ruins.

Free workers resisted subordination in ways that sometimes paralleled those of slaves and indentured servants. Save for the sailors, wage earners in British North America almost never staged strikes. Historians have so far discovered just a few exceptions to this rule—work stoppages in 1663 by fishermen in northern Massachusetts (now Maine) whose employer had withheld their earnings, in 1684 by the carters who hauled dirt from New York City's streets, in 1770 by the city's barrel makers, and in 1768 by its journeymen tailors. But wage earners repeatedly joined with others from the lower and middle classes to protest harms imposed from above. Most of these protests took place in cities, and Boston saw an especially large share. In 1713, when the city's grain supplies dwindled and its food prices soared, some 200 hungry Bostonians ransacked the ships and warehouses of a merchant exporting corn to the West Indies. In 1747, a crowd of several thousand armed with clubs and swords stopped a British commander from press-ganging Boston seamen into compulsory service in the Royal Navy. A city official who vigorously backed this riot's suppression soon lost his house to arson as hundreds gathered in the street, hollering, "Let it burn."[27]

On a more mundane level, free workers asserted their rights to dress and amuse themselves in ways the elite deemed inappropriate. As often as they could afford, they wore bits of finery such as a handkerchief, a garment of brightly colored chintz, or a collar of fine linen. Many workingmen and more than a few of the women congregated in taverns in their spare hours. Some showed up at entertainments intended for the gentry. All of this the upper classes abhorred. No less a body than the Massachusetts General Court denounced wage earners for desiring clothes "altogether unbecoming their place and rank" and for frequenting "taverns and alehouses where they idled away their time."[28] An important issue underlay such petty complaints. The elite resented free workers' liberty to do as they wished in at least some corners of their lives; and that was the very thing the workers valued most.

Nowhere was this more evident than in their responses to destitution, a constant danger for all wage earners save craft journeymen. From the mid-1600s onward, town officials in Massachusetts had the authority to expel "idle and unprofitable persons" who could not find steady wage work yet refused to volunteer for the security of indentured service.[29] They scavenged, begged, engaged in petty crime, squatted on other peoples' land, searched endlessly for a few days' work here and there—anything to avoid bondage for themselves and their children. Officials who tried to intervene met strong, sometimes violent resistance. In 1715, a sheriff served an eviction notice on a squatters' camp in Schoharie County, New York; Magdalena Zeh and her women neighbors attacked him with rakes and hoes, rode him out of the camp on a rail, and dumped him on the road back to Albany. In later decades, city governments opened poorhouses where the destitute could work in return for bed and board in strictly regimented dormitories. No one went there voluntarily; instead, authorities filled the dormitories with people who were too weak to flee. Philadelphia's poorhouse reported in the 1770s that inmates arrived "emaciated with Poverty and Disease to such a Degree that some have died in a few days of their Admission."[30]

Women sometimes resisted subordination in another way too: they fled their husbands. English law, which applied in the colonies, defined a wife as her husband's chattel. Whatever he desired, she should desire. Whatever wages she earned, property she obtained, or children she bore belonged to him. He was entitled to her labor in the household and entitled as well to give her "reasonable chastisement,"[31] meaning any physical punishment that did not inflict permanent injury or death. Most wives seem to have worked out tolerable domestic arrangements nonetheless, but quite a few did not. The same newspaper columns that described runaway slaves and servants also described runaway wives, warning that anyone who assisted these women would be prosecuted "with the utmost severity."[32] Such ads were placed by free men of all stations, from merchants and planters to silversmiths, tailors, bricklayers, and sailors.

Labor organizations were few and far between in colonial America and confined to men in skilled trades. Master craftsmen founded a handful of guilds. The largest, chartered in 1724, was the Carpenters' Company of Philadelphia, which regulated the prices master carpenters charged their customers, the wages they paid to journeymen, and their treatment of apprentices. But guilds had a minuscule impact on the helter-skelter American craft system, for they operated city by city and in a tiny minority of trades. Local benevolent societies sprang up in a somewhat larger number of trades. Encompassing masters, journeymen, and sometimes apprentices, these societies provided members with sick benefits, small loans, and assistance in times of dire need.

Journeymen occasionally formed ad hoc organizations in order to make demands on employers, as when the Journeyman Caulkers of Boston suddenly appeared in 1741 to announce that its members would no longer work for promissory notes. More commonly, master craftsmen came together to stop production in protest of statutory caps on the prices they could charge. Masters of all crafts subject to price controls—carters, coopers, bakers, chimney sweepers, and others—took part in such actions. The courts routinely convicted them of conspiracy, and black craftsmen in particular risked more brutal retaliation. Rage sufficient to spawn violence permeated the *South Carolina Gazette*'s report in 1763 that Charleston's black chimney sweepers "had the insolence by a combination amongst themselves, to raise the usual prices, and to refuse doing their work, unless their exorbitant demands are complied with—*Surely these are evils that require some attention to suppress.*"[33]

Among wage earners, sailors were by far the most militant. They included men of all colors and some women who went to sea disguised as men. They displayed a legendary contempt for wielders of arbitrary authority, from constables to kings. Several thousand of them became pirates, whose declared purpose was to "*plunder the rich.*"[34] And no one outshone sailors when it came to labor solidarity, for shipmates were quite literally all in the same boat. They frequently quit a ship en masse, refusing to leave port on vessels that were undermanned or in poor repair. They also staged numerous strikes, not only in port but also at sea. Safety was often the issue. In 1719, the crew of the *Hanover Succession*, sailing from Charleston to London, tired of pumping seawater out of the ship's leaky hold and refused to work until the captain agreed to return to port. In other instances sailors struck to protest floggings, to stop captains from changing the itinerary once a ship was at sea, or to demand time off when they reached the next port. Work stoppages are called strikes on account of sailors; they would "strike"—that is, lower—a ship's sails when they were no longer willing to work.

On the eve of the American Revolution, the vast majority of people in the colonies that would form the United States lacked rights enjoyed by the colonial elite. Slaves, indentured servants, apprentices, women of all stations, free men without property: none had the right to vote and hold office. Together, they made up at least 90 percent of colonial society, and most of them were poor as well as politically disfranchised. Therein lay the heart of the "labor problem" from labor's point of view. It was a problem shared by bound and free workers and one that both groups were determined to solve.

2

The American Revolution

On July 4, 1776, the Continental Congress in Philadelphia unanimously adopted the Declaration of Independence, announcing to the world that thirteen North American colonies intended to throw off British rule and found a new nation based on republican government. Penned by a committee headed by Thomas Jefferson of Virginia, this document was designed to stir souls:

> We hold these truths to be self-evident, that all men are created equal, that they are endowed by their Creator with certain unalienable Rights, that among these are Life, Liberty, and the pursuit of Happiness.—That to secure these rights, Governments are instituted among Men, deriving their just Powers from the consent of the governed—That whenever any Form of Government becomes destructive of these ends, it is the Right of the People to alter or to abolish it, and to institute new Government, laying its Foundation on such Principles, and organizing its Powers in such Form, as to them shall seem most likely to effect their Safety and Happiness.[1]

There, in plain language, was the spirit of the American Revolution.

The declaration's signers came late to that spirit. American colonists had been at war with Britain since April 1775, when Massachusetts militiamen opened fire on the British army; and the war's outbreak followed more than a decade of anti-British protests by common people, especially artisans and wageworkers in coastal cities. Wealthy colonists had sometimes sponsored and supported these protests but had also viewed them with alarm. Then, when they finally came around to the revolutionary program, they commandeered the movement.

Jefferson was one of the wealthiest slaveholding planters in North America, and the declaration's other signers were well-to-do planters, lawyers, and merchants. They believed that the right to self-government belonged to people like themselves—white men of substantial means. But such men could not win a war or found a nation without rallying common people, whose quarrels with the British regime had to do with privilege based on wealth and rank as well as royal prerogatives and imperial edicts. This prompted the founding fathers to place their signatures on a document that proclaimed ideals much more egalitarian than their own.

Nowhere did egalitarianism burn more brightly than among working people. Building on over a century of colonial labor rebellions, both the free and the unfree fought for "Life, Liberty, and the pursuit of Happiness" in many ways that the gentlemen of the Continental Congress did not appreciate. And these struggles grew all the more contentious after Britain's defeat, when men of wealth constructed a republic that reneged on democratic ideals.

From Resistance to Independence

Britain's empire in North America reached its zenith in 1763, when protracted wars with France and Spain ended in a treaty that gave the British control of all lands east of the Mississippi River. No one could have guessed that just twelve years later, American colonies would take up arms against the mother country; but the seeds of that revolt had already been planted, for Britain's imperial wars bankrupted its treasury. To meet the costs of empire, the British Parliament sought to squeeze more revenues from the colonies, touching off protests that led inexorably to revolution.

The first round of protests took aim at the Stamp Act of 1765, which required that legal documents and other printed materials bear a stamp purchased from British agents. Marriage licenses, land deeds, indenture agreements, commercial contracts, playing cards, books and newspapers, handbill advertisements: all of these and more became subject to the new tax. To add insult to injury, moreover, revenues from the Stamp Act financed Britain's colonial army and administrative apparatus—the very power structure that kept Americans under Parliament's thumb.

Anger at this arrangement sparked militant resistance, mainly among working people in major seaports. Men from the maritime trades organized demonstrations that swelled with artisans, common laborers, housewives, and children, and sometimes targeted the property of British officials. In New York City, sailors and other maritime workers formed the anti-British Sons of Neptune and staged what observers called an "insurrection" against the Stamp Act.[2] In Boston, the shoemaker Ebenezer McIntosh led a crowd of 2,000 workingmen that demolished the local stamp agent's office and vandalized his home.

Some members of the wealthy and middle classes joined the movement against the Stamp Act. In Boston, Newport, New York, and other cities, protest committees called the Sons of Liberty included merchants, lawyers, doctors, ministers, shopkeepers, and master craftsmen along with larger numbers of wageworkers. Other gentlemen, fearful of British reprisals, supported protests behind the scenes. These were fragile alliances, however, for common people's anger at Britain's heavy hand routinely fueled anger at the rich as a whole. Less than two weeks after Boston workingmen attacked the stamp agent's office and home, a second crowd ransacked the mansion of Massachusetts's lieutenant governor. In Newport, workingman John Weber led Stamp Act protests whose participants said such radical things about redistributing wealth that the city's merchants—who had hired Weber to organize the demonstrations—soon demanded his arrest.

Assaults on the rich persisted even after Parliament caved in to American protests and repealed the Stamp Act in March 1766. That May, in New York City, a crowd turned out to jeer at the fancy attire and manners of people attending the opening of an expensive new theater. Before the night was out, the demonstrators had torn down the theater and burned the debris—"to the Satisfaction of many at this distressed Time," a local newspaper reported, "and to the great Grievance of those less inclined for the Publick Good."[3]

With the Stamp Act gone, Parliament soon turned to a new plan for taxing the colonies. The Revenue Act of 1767 imposed tariffs known as the Townshend Duties on key goods Americans imported from abroad: paint, lead, glass, paper, and tea. Rebellious colonists responded with a "nonimportation" movement, a boycott of all goods from Britain. A wide network of boycott committees—called Sons of Liberty, Regulators, Associators, or Liberty Boys—extended from New Hampshire to South Carolina and from major cities to the backwoods. Merchants and shopkeepers who sold British merchandise were denounced as public enemies and often tarred and feathered too.

Women played crucial roles in the boycott by producing alternatives to British imports. They brewed herbal drinks and "rye coffee" as substitutes for tea; replaced paint with homemade whitewash; and virtually eliminated the colonies' dependence on British textiles by spinning gigantic volumes of cloth from wool, flax, and hemp. Hundreds of local women's committees—often called the Daughters of Liberty—organized spinning bees and promoted patriotic slogans like, "It is better to wear a homespun coat than to lose our liberty."[4] In Kinderhook, New York, when a man scolded a spinning circle for meddling in politics, the women stripped off his clothes, covered him with molasses and flax down, and sent him on his way.

Equally worrisome to colonial officials were the town meetings taking place in community after community, especially in New England. In 1768, customs commissioners in Boston sent the following report to higher-ups in Britain: "At these meetings, the lowest Mechanics discuss upon the most important points of government, with the utmost freedom, which being guided by a few hot and designing men become a constant source of sedition. Men of character avoid these Meetings . . . and they could not oppose any popular measure without being exposed to insult and resentment."[5]

As the boycott movement gained momentum, Britain enlarged its army in North America, stationing most of the reinforcements in New York City and Boston, the movement's most militant centers. The soldiers liked to supplement their meager pay by moonlighting in waterfront jobs. Local workers competed for the same jobs, which grew ever harder to find once the boycott of British imports curtailed commercial shipping. Tension mounted, punctuated by occasional fistfights, until pitched battles erupted in 1770. In January, workers and soldiers in New York City slugged it out in a two-day street fight known as the Battle of Golden Hill. Push came to shove in Boston that March, when British troops brawled with rope makers who had insulted a soldier looking for work. Two days later, on the night of March 5, a crowd of workingmen taunted soldiers from the same regiment, who suddenly opened fire. Five workers were killed and another six wounded in what colonists called the Boston Massacre.

The dead were stevedore Crispus Attucks, sailor James Caldwell, rope maker Samuel Gray, apprentice leather maker Patrick Carr, and apprentice ivory turner Sam Maverick. Attucks—a former slave of African and Native American ancestry—had been a member of the Sons of Liberty and a leader of the crowd. Ten thousand Bostonians marched in the martyrs' funeral procession, and the dead were commemorated in many surrounding towns. Well into the nineteenth century, much of Massachusetts celebrated March 5 as the premier holiday in honor of the American Revolution.

On the very day of the Boston Massacre, well before the news reached London, Parliament rescinded the Townshend Duties except for the tax on tea. With that, the nonimportation coalition began to fragment. Merchants wished to resume the lucrative trade with Britain. Well-to-do families had tired of giving up imported luxuries. And as much as colonial elites might resent British rule, most distrusted the "mob" of common people who clung to a boycott abandoned by the upper classes.

In fact, this so-called mob mounted well-organized resistance to the British. While the gentry vacillated, the movement spread. In New York City, Philadelphia, and Charleston, South Carolina, master craftsmen and journeymen formed mechanics' associations to press the boycott cause in colonial assemblies and councils. In November 1772, a Boston town meeting established the Committee of Correspondence to communicate with other cities and coordinate resistance. Within a few months, identical committees had been authorized by town meetings and popular assemblies in every colony. The committees' leaders typically came from the ranks of master craftsmen, professionals, or the handful of wealthy men still loyal to nonimportation, but small farmers, journeymen, and other wageworkers made up most of the rank and file.

The committees carefully planned direct-action protests, breaking British laws in orderly ways. A prime example was the famous Boston Tea Party of December 1773, in which squads of men boarded British ships, dumped their cargo of tea into the harbor, and left without claiming any booty. That winter, similar "tea parties" took place in other ports, and though jobs were scarce, workingmen in Boston and New York City conformed to strict boycotts on labor for the British army. When General Thomas Gage called for workers to build military fortifications in Boston, no one from that city stepped forward, and later efforts to recruit New Yorkers failed as well. In the end Gage had to import carpenters and bricklayers from as far away as Nova Scotia.

If organization and discipline strengthened the resistance movement, so did British reactions to the Boston Tea Party. To punish Massachusetts, Parliament passed a series of laws known in America as the Intolerable Acts. They closed Boston Harbor to all trade; forbade communities throughout the colony to hold more than one town meeting a year; allowed British officials indicted for crimes in Massachusetts to stand trial elsewhere; and authorized the British army to quarter troops in colonists' homes. These statutes ignited resistance in every part of Massachusetts, whose citizens stockpiled weapons, formed local militias, and held town meetings in defiance of British orders. Expressions of sympathy poured forth from other colonies, and committees of correspondence grew in size and number as they collected food, clothing, and money for the blockaded Bostonians. The new forces included members of the wealthy classes, not only merchants but also Virginia's big planters, who forged an anti-British alliance with that colony's poor whites.

For six weeks in fall 1774, representatives from every colony but Georgia gathered in Philadelphia for the first Continental Congress, which hammered out a common program for resistance. Though most of the delegates were men of wealth, the militant spirit of popular protests carried the day. The Congress launched a Continental Association, which decreed a total embargo on trade with Britain—no imports, no exports—and called for the formation of local committees to enforce the ban. By the end of the year, embargo committees and anti-British militias had sprung up in all colonies, and the association was forging them into a national movement.

Outright war began on April 19, 1775, when Massachusetts militia companies fought the British troops General Gage had sent to seize a colonial arsenal in Concord. Within days, militiamen closed in on Boston, besieging Gage's forces. In a matter of weeks, militia units from Connecticut, Rhode Island, and New Hampshire went to aid the siege, and another band of New Englanders routed British troops from Fort Ticonderoga in upper New York.

In Philadelphia, the Second Continental Congress laid plans to spread the fight. The delegates issued a formal declaration of war against Britain and authorized the creation of the Continental Army to be commanded by the Virginia planter George Washington. But when they debated the question of American independence, caution prevailed. Their declaration of war explicitly rejected independence, and another resolution implored Britain's King George III to reconcile with the colonies.

As the war continued, however, popular rage at Britain reached new heights, and radical agitators channeled that sentiment into support for independence. The most influential agitator was the journalist Thomas Paine, a former artisan whose plain language and democratic politics struck a deeply responsive chord among common people. In January 1776, Paine published a fifty-page pamphlet titled *Common Sense* that argued for an independent America under republican government. Readers snapped up more than 100,000 copies, and *Common Sense* was even more widely discussed; the literate read it aloud to people who could not read it for themselves. Echoing Paine, the Declaration of Independence signaled the Continental Congress's conversion to an agenda that the rank and file of revolutionaries had already embraced.

Not all common people backed the cause. Contemporaries estimated that about one-third of free colonists favored independence, another third opposed it, and the rest stayed neutral. Only in New England and Virginia did the revolution have majority support. On the whole, it was more popular among the laboring and middle classes than among the elite, but local resentments sometimes produced countercurrents. In 1771, the North Carolina militia had crushed the Regulator movement, in which backcountry farmers rallied to stop judges and land speculators from confiscating the homesteads of tax delinquents. When the Regulators' wealthy enemies later endorsed the revolution, much of the backcountry chose the other side. Revolutionary sentiment among large landowners had the same effect on many tenant farmers in New York's Hudson Valley and poor whites in the Eastern Shore district of Maryland.

For slaves—about 20 percent of the colonial population in 1775—the war fueled hopes for their own independence, and that repeatedly placed them at odds with white

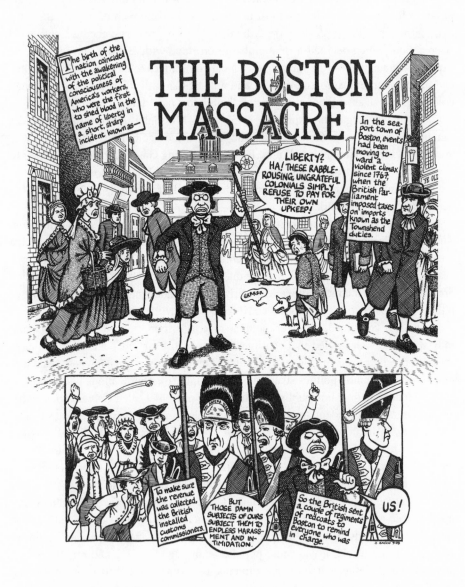

revolutionaries. The contradiction had been brewing since the days of the Stamp Act protests. Charleston, South Carolina, had imposed martial law for a week after slaves echoed white protestors' shouts of "Liberty." The crowd of Boston artisans led by Ebenezer McIntosh had excluded all blacks so as not to encourage their insubordination. By the time the Revolutionary War began, a rising tide of conspiracies, mutinies, and petitions for freedom had made clear that slaves stood ready to fight for whichever side offered better possibilities for emancipation.

Black men both enslaved and free served in the New England militia units that mobilized against the British in spring 1775 and in the Continental Army's earliest regiments. All of these troops were volunteers. Slaves usually enlisted with their owners' consent and always with the understanding that military service would render them free. That crack in the edifice of slavery agitated the Continental Congress, whose unity in support of the war rested on an agreement that it would not liberate slaves. In February 1776, following months of debate among congressmen and military commanders, George Washington ordered that free black men who had already served could reenlist in the Continental Army but that no other black or Indian soldiers would be accepted. By summer, militia laws in the various colonies had been amended to exclude all but white men.

As Continental leaders debated black enlistment, slaves in Virginia made a bid for emancipation under British auspices. In November 1775, the colony's royal governor, Lord John Dunmore, issued a proclamation promising freedom to all slaves who belonged to American rebels and bore arms for Britain. In the few weeks that elapsed before Continental troops drove Dunmore from the mainland, some 700 slaves made their way to his camp near Norfolk. About 1,000 more later managed to reach his ships anchored off Virginia's shore, and in summer 1776, when he sailed to Staten Island, slaves from New York and New Jersey reinforced his black regiment. By the end of the war, tens of thousands of escaped slaves—men and women alike—would serve Britain's army as soldiers or workers behind the lines.

Native Americans fought for both sides too, though most would have preferred to stay neutral. From Pequot towns in New England to Catawba villages in South Carolina, Indians in the heartlands of white settlement joined the revolution's troops in 1775 and resisted exclusion the following year. But the vast network of Indian communities on the colonies' frontiers spurned overtures from both the Continentals and the British. As the Seneca leader Kayashuta explained, "We must be Fools indeed to imagine that they regard us or our Interest who want to bring us into an unnecessary War."[6] In the end, though, few frontier communities could avoid the fight. Combatants from both sides penetrated more and more of Indian country and tolerated no neutrals. Forced to choose, many communities split into opposing camps, but most people sided with Britain, which pledged to uphold Indian claims to ancestral land that the colonists had time and again tried to grab.

The Declaration of Independence pointedly ignored the revolution's incongruities: that slaveholders shouted for liberty; that black and Indian volunteers for the cause had been turned away; that the Continental Congress still sought allies among frontier Indians who did not wish to fight; that republican values ran deeper at the revolution's grassroots than among its official leaders in Congress. Thomas Jefferson's committee revised its first draft of the declaration to delete the charge that King George disgraced himself by abetting slavery and the slave trade. The final draft's bill of grievances climaxed with the complaint that he incited "domestic insurrections" (a euphemism for slave revolts) and courted military assistance from "merciless Indian Savages." To defend slavery and condemn Indians contradicted the statement that "all men are created equal," but this was a political document, not a treatise on logic. If the congressmen thought themselves more equal than most—"the aristocracy of virtue and talent," as Jefferson later put it—they also knew that the revolution could not succeed unless masses of commoners regarded it as their own.[7]

The People's War and the Gentlemen's Republic

As Tom Paine observed in 1792, "The Independence of America, considered merely as a separation from England, would have been a matter but of little importance, had it not been accompanied by a Revolution in the principles and practice of Governments."[8] Common people, who bore the brunt of the war with Britain, took part in the political revolution as well. The elite remained in command, however, and concessions to those below were not evenly distributed.

After the Continental Congress declared independence, the rebel colonies—now members of the United States of America—began to draw up constitutions for state government. Virtually all of the men involved in this process agreed that politics should remain a male affair and that governments should be elected. But there was no consensus as to how much political power should belong to ordinary men as opposed to men of the elite.

Pennsylvania fashioned the most democratic constitution, adopted in summer 1776. It gave all taxpaying freemen the right to vote and hold office, created a unicameral legislature to be elected every year, and authorized the governor to do little more than execute the legislature's decisions. Except in emergencies, legislators could not pass a bill into law unless its text had first been distributed for discussion by the general public. In 1777, when small farmers in upper New York broke away to form the new state of Vermont (not formally part of the United States until 1791), they wrote a constitution modeled on Pennsylvania's.

By and large, however, conservatives dominated the states' constitutional conventions and strictly limited democracy. In Maryland and Virginia, for example, planters preserved their political clout by instituting prohibitive property qualifications for both voters and officeholders and by setting long intervals between elections. In New York and Massachusetts, merchants and lawyers drafted constitutions that provided for powerful governors and bicameral legislatures in which assemblies chosen by the whole electorate (male taxpayers) shared lawmaking with senates elected only by men of wealth. New Jersey was the only state that enfranchised women—as long as they were unmarried and met the same stiff property requirements as men.

Whatever their formal rights to take part in politics, both men and women of the lower classes made their voices heard. When wartime shortages pushed food prices through the roof, popular protests forced every state north of Maryland to enact price controls. Angry crowds of women meanwhile raided the storerooms of merchants and shopkeepers guilty of price gouging or suspected of hoarding necessities. In port cities, sailors and craft journeymen struck for pay hikes to meet the rising cost of living. In 1779, militiamen in Philadelphia assaulted the home of a prominent lawyer opposed to price controls and even wheeled up a piece of artillery before they were dispersed by a unit of light cavalry. The countryside was also in turmoil. Many tenant farmers stopped paying rent and joined with small freeholders to appropriate land owned by wealthy men who sided with Britain.

Slaves fled their masters in unprecedented numbers, 30,000 in Virginia alone, according to Thomas Jefferson's estimate. Petitions for freedom poured into state courts and legislatures, often echoing the Declaration of Independence. One petition presented in Massachusetts in January 1777 argued that slaves "have in common with all other Men a Natural and Unali[en]able Right to that freedom which the Gr[e]at Parent of the Un[i]vers[e] hath Bestowed equalley on all M[a]nkind."[9]

Quite a few fugitive slaves joined the Continental Army, whose color bars disintegrated as the fighting dragged on. The turning point came in 1777, when Congress scrambled to reinforce the military. American diplomats stepped up efforts to win European allies and eventually brought France, Spain, and Holland into the war. Various blends of diplomacy and coercion yielded Indian allies from the Delawares, Tuscaroras, Penobscots, and other frontier nations. Mainly, however, Congress looked to the states. Starting in January 1777, each had to supply the army with a certain quota of regular troops. Unlike state militiamen, who enlisted for three to twelve months, the regulars served for three years. Volunteers for such duty were so scarce that state recruiters usually welcomed one and all, ignoring legalities as to who could and could not serve.

Every state soon instituted a military draft, which ushered in more drastic changes in the army's makeup. While the draft laws typically ordered that only white men should be conscripted, that did not determine who actually served. A man who was summoned could send his slave, his indentured servant, his apprentice, or any paid substitute to take his place. Many draftees did just that, and many a town hired outsiders to substitute for its residents, if only to keep the local militia intact. By the end of the decade, the Continental Army bore little resemblance to the volunteer force that had mustered in 1775. Most of the soldiers were now conscripts or their stand-ins. Master craftsmen, journeymen, and small landowners—the core of the old army— were now outnumbered by lowlier groups: common laborers and landless farmers along with apprentices, indentured servants, and slaves.

The enlistment of bound workers pitted private-property rights against the public need for troops. Numerous petitioners called on Congress to stop military recruiters from inducting bondsmen without their masters' consent or compensation. A county committee in Cumberland, Pennsylvania, protested on the grounds that "all apprentices and servants are the property of their masters and mistresses, and every mode of depriving such masters and mistresses of their property is a violation of the rights of mankind."[10] Jonathan Hobby of Concord, Massachusetts, sued the army to return a teenaged slave who had enlisted while Hobby was out of town. Military judges agreed that Hobby's property rights had been violated but declined to rule on his suit. Congress waffled too, ordering the military to return runaway bondsmen at their masters' request but ignoring the routine violations of this order. The sharpest controversies arose over state laws on the enlistment of slaves. Northern and middle states quickly approved this practice once Congress assigned troop quotas. Maryland's legislature followed suit, but only after three years of debate and failure to meet its quota. Virginia, the Carolinas, and Georgia resisted to the bitter end, though they allowed black freemen to substitute for white conscripts. From the late 1770s until the fighting ceased, emissaries from Congress and General George Washington badgered these states to raise slave battalions. Every request was, to quote one of Washington's aides, "drowned by the howlings of a triple-headed monster in which prejudice, avarice and pusillanimity were united."[11]

A different spirit prevailed among the army's rank and file, in which men of every color soldiered for meager pay almost always in arrears. There were a few all-black regiments. Enlistees from Indian towns sometimes signed up in groups and formed their own squads. But most units were fully integrated, and they all merged in battle, with common soldiers of every description fighting side by side. The Massachusetts rosters included Ben Russell, a white apprentice printer from Worcester; Ezekiel Brown, a white schoolmaster from Concord who was fresh out of debtor's prison; Cesar Perry, a free black laborer from Bristol County; Charlestown Edes, a black slave from Groton; and the farmer Daniel Nimham, a Wappinger Indian elder from Stockbridge who died in battle near New York City. At least one woman was also part of this mix: Deborah Samson, a white woman from Middleborough who grew up as an indentured servant and, at age twenty-one, went off to war under the name of Robert Shurtleff. In other colonies, too, some women disguised themselves as men and joined the revolutionary troops.

Up to 20,000 women served the army in other ways. Most were soldiers' wives or widows, sometimes with children in tow. Since the Continental Army did not provide family allowances, poor women often had little choice but to follow the troops and work for rations. They served as cooks, seamstresses, laundresses, and nurses, and in the heat of battle, quite a few fought. The most famous was Mary Hays McCauley, who earned the nickname Molly Pitcher by carrying water to soldiers on the front lines. When her husband fell, she took his place as a cannon loader. Though General Washington regarded women "camp followers" as a nuisance, he was known to assign them to cannon crews when he ran short of men.

Tensions between the troops and their commanders ran high throughout the war. From the moment they took charge, Washington and his corps of officers complained about undisciplined foot soldiers. General Perisfor Frazer, a rich farmer from the outskirts of Philadelphia, thought the New Englanders especially hard to handle. As he wrote to his wife in July 1776, "among them there is the strangest mixture of Negroes, Indians, and Whites, with Old Men and mere children which together with a Nasty lousy appearance, makes a most shocking Spectacle, no man was ever more disappointed than I have been in respect to them."[12] The three-year enlistments instituted in 1777 were supposed to help officers whip the army into shape; but recruits who entered under the draft proved even more unruly than their predecessors. Several times in 1780, units from Pennsylvania and New Jersey mutinied over short rations and pay, and the ringleaders were executed on Washington's orders.

If ragtag troops were hard to govern, they nonetheless defeated the world's foremost imperial power. Of the 200,000 troops who fought Britain, about half served in local militias. Assembling at need, harassing the enemy with sniping fire, they made every British expedition costly. But Continental regulars endured the heaviest combat, casualties, and privations; the victory belonged first and foremost to them.

The fighting ended suddenly in October 1781, when British troops in Virginia were trapped between American and French forces. That winter Parliament voted to abandon the war, and in 1782 British troops withdrew from all states, accompanied by some 30,000 former slaves who had assisted them in the war. In the Treaty of Paris, signed in 1783, Britain formally recognized American independence and transferred to the United States all territory east of the Mississippi, south of the Great Lakes, and north of Florida. Slavery, Indian land rights, and other issues Congress had sidestepped in the Declaration of Independence would now come sharply to the fore.

Settlers and speculators rushed into the northwestern frontier, snatching land from the revolution's Indian allies as well as those who had sided with Britain. To restore law and order, Congress made the thefts legal. By 1790, treaties signed at gunpoint had deprived Indians of nearly all their land between Lake Ontario and the Ohio River. Back east, Indian veterans of the Continental Army did not fare much better. Debts incurred when the men were away compelled many households to sell off their land. Massachusetts rescinded Indians' right to self-government, putting their towns under the authority of white overseers. In the space of a few years, the new republic made explicit the principle that Indians were not "created equal," not even those who had bled for the revolution; and hardly anyone save for Indians themselves disputed that injustice.

Servitude became a more contentious issue. Master craftsmen pushed for stricter laws to control apprentices, who absconded even more frequently than during the war. Starting in 1783, state after state stiffened the penalties for runaway apprentices and anyone who abetted them. In most cases, however, the new statutes also extended republican rights to apprentices, stipulating that they could not be bound to labor beyond age twenty-one and spelling out procedures by which they could sue their masters for cruelty or neglect.

The indenture of European immigrants came under fire too. Right after the war, societies to protect indentured servants from abuse sprang up in New York, Maryland, and Pennsylvania. German immigrants, many of whom had arrived as redemptioners, were especially active in this cause. In 1784, one group in New York City proposed to pay off the indentures of a shipload of new immigrants and condemned the "traffick of White People" as a British custom at odds with "the idea of liberty this country has so happily established."[13]

Movements against slavery gathered on a larger scale, inspired by republican ideals, religious fervor, and the emancipation of several thousand black war veterans. In northern states, slave trading was outlawed and slavery itself edged toward extinction. Vermont had set the example in 1777, abolishing slavery under its constitution. In 1783, New Hampshire did the same, and Massachusetts courts ruled slavery illegal. Elsewhere in the North, freedom came at a snail's pace under gradual emancipation laws enacted by Pennsylvania (1780), Connecticut (1784), Rhode Island (1784), New

York (1799), and New Jersey (1804). Designed to reconcile slaves' rights to liberty and masters' rights to property, these statutes freed enslaved women's future offspring but only after they reached ages ranging from eighteen to twenty-eight.

In the southern states slavery expanded, despite opposition from several quarters. During the 1780s, some slaveholders in the upper South voluntarily freed their slaves. By the early 1790s, local societies to promote manumission had formed statewide networks in Delaware, Maryland, and Virginia. No southern legislature moved to abolish slavery, however. Nor did manumission societies spread to the lower South or even win many followers in their home states.

From Delaware to Georgia, the great majority of slaveholders sought to increase holdings depleted in wartime. They tracked down runaways, purchased the slaves southern states had confiscated from people who sided with Britain, imported tens of thousands of captives from Africa or the Caribbean, and enslaved some free blacks kidnapped from as far north as Massachusetts. In other cases masters reasserted claims to slaves freed during the war so that they could substitute for white conscripts.

These efforts more than offset freedom's progress in the North. By 1790, the free black population reached almost 60,000, up from just a few thousand at the start of the revolution; but slaves numbered about 698,000, compared to 500,000 in 1775. Some 658,000 slaves lived in the South, a little over 100,000 in Maryland and in each of the Carolinas. The largest slaveholder by far was Thomas Jefferson's Virginia, where the census of 1790 counted 292,627 slaves.

Although political conflicts over slavery would loom larger than all others in decades to come, the most explosive issue in the postwar era was a debt crisis that wreaked havoc on family farms. When American ports reopened to British trade, wartime shortages and inflation gave way to peacetime gluts and depression. Small farmers were the hardest hit, for agricultural prices were the first to fall. By 1786, many farms were so heavily mortgaged that their owners stood on the brink of bankruptcy, and to make matters worse, merchants who had earlier extended credit now demanded that customers pay their accounts in full. In state after state, farmers pressed legislatures to lower taxes on farmland, suspend debt collection, abolish imprisonment for debt, and ease the depression by issuing large sums of paper money.

The movement grew especially ferocious in Massachusetts, where lawmakers resisted the debtors' demands. In August and September 1786, many hundreds of armed farmers—most of them veterans of the Continental Army—seized courthouses to suspend debtors' trials. Daniel Shays, a captain during the war, emerged as the uprising's leader. That fall he organized 1,000 men to march on Boston, where merchants spent $200,000 to raise a private militia that turned back Shays's troops. In January 1787, they regrouped to besiege the Springfield armory but this time suffered a decisive defeat. Rural uprisings were also suppressed in New Hampshire, New Jersey, Pennsylvania, Maryland, Virginia, and South Carolina.

In the wake of these rebellions, the wealthy classes moved to consolidate their political power. From late May to mid-September 1787, delegates from every state but Rhode Island held a closed-door convention in Philadelphia. George Washington chaired the gathering, whose participants came from the revolutionary elite. They included ambassadors, high-ranking military officers, Continental congressmen, and the revolution's financiers. As far as the public knew, the delegates would merely amend the Articles of Confederation that had established a national government during the war. Instead, they wrote an entirely new Constitution of the United States.

The Constitution divided the government into legislative, executive, and judicial departments, each authorized to curb action by the others. On the legislative side there was a bicameral U.S. Congress, made up of the House of Representatives and the Senate. Delegates to the House would be elected every two years by voters who met the minimum qualifications to cast ballots for their state legislature; and the number of seats apportioned to each state would depend on the size of its population. The senators—two for every state regardless of population—would be chosen by state legislatures and serve six-year terms. The president and vice president would be chosen every four years by appointees to an "electoral college" in which each state had as many votes as it had seats in the House and Senate. From the Supreme Court to lower courts, federal judges would be selected by the president (subject to Senate approval) and serve indefinite terms.

Unlike the Articles of Confederation, the Constitution empowered the national government to levy taxes and tariffs, pay the war debt, regulate commerce, coin money and set its value, standardize bankruptcy laws, and otherwise look out for businessmen's needs. New prohibitions on the states outlawed actions demanded by indebted farmers. No state could issue its own money, allow debts to be paid in anything but gold and silver coinage, or make laws that impaired contracts such as mortgages and loans.

Southern planters won a favorable compromise when the Philadelphia convention debated whether slaves should be counted for the purpose of apportioning seats in the House of Representatives. Under the "three-fifths clause," 60 percent of the slave population was factored in and southern states got many more seats than they would have possessed otherwise. The Constitution also stipulated that states could import slaves from overseas for the next twenty years. Another clause obligated every state to return runaway slaves to their owners.

By summer 1788, the Constitution had been ratified by the required quorum of states, whose voters elected special conventions to debate the pros and cons. The patchwork of state restrictions on voting rights placed these proceedings in the hands of men who owned property—at least enough to make them taxpayers. This did not guarantee agreement, however. More often than not, ratification won by a nose.

While the wealthy generally endorsed it, state officials anxious to preserve their powers often came down on the other side. Popular radicals divided, many backing the Constitution as a means to solidify the republic, many others rejecting it as a yoke on democracy, and some waffling back and forth. Urban artisans championed ratification as the key to prosperity; a national government empowered to tax imports could protect American industries from foreign competition. Small farmers mounted the most resolute opposition, fearful that the new government would tax them into bankruptcy. As one Massachusetts farmer charged, the rich expected "to be the managers of this Constitution . . . get all the power and all the money into their own hands, and then they will swallow up all us little folks like the great Leviathan."[14]

When the Constitution became law, cities across the country celebrated with parades that included everyone from merchants and lawyers to apprentices and common laborers. The longest procession took place in Philadelphia on July 4, 1788; it was led by local dignitaries, regiments of the Continental Army, and a marching band. Some 17,000 people turned out, and artisans formed more than forty contingents representing their various crafts. But riots were brewing in rural Pennsylvania; just one week earlier, a band of farmers near Wilkes-Barre had kidnapped a judge involved with land speculators. In other states, too, the backcountry was as angry as the cities were joyous.

In spring 1789, the new government took command, with George Washington as president, both houses of Congress controlled by the well-to-do, and a great many citizens wary of or outright opposed to this concentration of power. That fall Congress proposed a series of constitutional amendments aimed at "extending the ground of public confidence in the Government."[15] Ten of these provisions, known as the Bill of Rights, were subsequently ratified by the states and added to the Constitution in December 1791. The First Amendment declared that Congress would not abridge popular rights to religious freedom, to free speech and a free press, to peaceful assembly, or to petition government to redress grievances. Other amendments guaranteed rights to bear arms, to protection from unwarranted searches and seizures, to trial by an impartial jury, and to other safeguards against abuse by criminal and civil courts.

So ended the American Revolution, with the Bill of Rights pledging to protect the many from persecution by the governing few. For forty years both the presidency and Congress belonged to the revolutionary elite and their protégés. In the 1790s, they split into rival parties, the Federalists backed by merchants and financiers, and the Democratic-Republicans favored by planters, farmers, and artisans. By the mid-1820s, the Federalists had collapsed into the Democratic-Republicans, whose rival sectors would regroup as the Democratic Party and the Whigs. These factional divisions and redivisions were intensely acrimonious, but no matter how federal elections turned out, certain basics remained the same: a coalition of planters and urban businessmen ran the government; federal policies fostered slavery, industrial development, and national expansion; and the U.S. Army was perpetually at war with Native Americans resisting encroachment on their land.

Republican Legacies

In 1794, Independence Day gatherings outstripped anything the nation had seen since the Philadelphia parade of 1788, and this time their tone was more defiant than triumphant. In city after city craftsmen came out to damn the reigning Federalist Party, cheer Democratic-Republicans, and celebrate the Fourth of July as a day for artisans to assert their rights as citizens. These sentiments resonated with broader patterns. In years to come working people of all sorts challenged oppression on republican grounds, defining liberty and equality not as privileges or prizes but as inherent rights. But shared ideals did not necessarily beget solidarity in a political system increasingly open to white men, closed to other free workers, and tyrannical toward slaves.

The Federalists of the 1790s enraged masses of Americans by ruling like British aristocrats. National and state legislators repeatedly held secret sessions and passed laws written in such arcane language that the general public could not decipher their meaning. In 1792, Congress enacted a militia law that authorized the states to draft men into service. In 1794, President Washington sent some 13,000 militiamen into Pennsylvania's backcountry to crush popular resistance to a federal tax on whiskey, which farmers distilled from their excess corn. In 1798, Congress tried to silence anti-Federalists with a Sedition Act that made it a crime punishable by fine and imprisonment to publish statements that subjected the government to "contempt or disrepute."[16] The Federalists constructed a legal system based on British law, which hamstrung wageworkers by treating labor unions as criminal conspiracies.

The earliest American unions emerged in the 1790s. They were established by white craft journeymen, starting with Philadelphia shoemakers in 1792. Other pioneers included tailors in Baltimore and printers and cabinetmakers in New York City. In the early 1800s, the movement spread to carpenters, masons, and tailors in New York; shoemakers in Baltimore and Pittsburgh; and printers in seven cities from Boston to New Orleans. Condemning employers for "depriving free men of their just rights,"[17] unionists aimed to carry republican self-government into the workplace—to regulate wages and hours of labor, to secure jobs for union members, and to keep others out of union shops. Whenever they made progress on these goals, they were hauled into court and convicted on charges of conspiracy. Long after the Federalist Party was a dead letter, the jurists it had appointed and the legal doctrines it had embraced undercut union organizing.

Politics offered a clearer field. In the mid-1790s, white craftsmen, seamen, and farmers joined with some well-to-do dissidents in a large network of political clubs that soon merged into the Democratic-Republican Party headed by Thomas Jefferson. The clubs championed causes the aristocratic Federalists despised: extensions of voting rights, an end to closed-door lawmaking, the establishment of public schools. They held dinners to honor the French Revolution of 1789–99, circulated radical pamphlets such as Tom Paine's *Rights of Man* (1791–92), and in 1800 helped to propel Jefferson into the presidency.

Jefferson's election ushered in twenty-four years of Democratic-Republican administrations headed by Virginia planters and widely supported by white workingmen. In some respects democracy advanced. Federalists slowly lost their hold on state and local governments, which began to provide for public education and to increase the portion of public officials that was elected rather than appointed. By 1825, all but three states (Virginia, Rhode Island, and Louisiana) granted voting rights to every white male citizen, and all but two (South Carolina and Delaware) chose presidential electors by polling voters instead of state legislators. White servitude receded as the white electorate expanded. State and local courts stopped enforcing indenture contracts for craft apprentices. The indenture of European immigrants died out as state lawmakers eliminated imprisonment for debt and thus liberated redemptioners from debt bondage.

Jeffersonian democracy did not expand women's rights, however. As under British rule, the legal system gave husbands absolute title to their wives' personal property, including any wages they earned. As in the past, husbands could legally subject their wives to beatings that did not cause irreparable bodily harm. As white men gained wider access to the ballot, moreover, women were left behind. They even lost what little ground they had gained in New Jersey, where Democratic-Republican lawmakers disfranchised women in 1807.

Industrial development added to women's subordination in some ways while liberating them in others. The earliest U.S. factories—textile mills in northern states—recruited a white workforce largely composed of women and girls. Some mills hired whole families, and in such cases male heads of household received the wages for all of their kin. By the 1820s, however, it was more common for textile manufacturers to staff their mills with young unmarried women, especially farmers' daughters. Mill jobs regimented their lives. They worked at least twelve hours a day, six days a week, and resided in company-owned boardinghouses that imposed strict rules regarding curfews, bedtimes, church attendance, and so forth. But their wages went into their own pockets, and that gave most mill women a greater sense of independence than they had ever before known.

As one worker later recalled about newcomers to the mill complex in Lowell, Massachusetts, "After the first pay-day came, and they felt the jingle of silver in their pockets . . . their heads were lifted [and] their necks seemed braced with steel."[18] While many women sent money to their families, just as many spent their earnings on themselves, buying new clothes, saving up dowries, sometimes sending themselves to school. A mill worker in Lowell wrote in a letter to her cousin that she intended to use her savings to attend Oberlin College in Ohio rather than behave like a "dutiful girl" and "place the money in father's hands."[19]

Mill women's independent spirit sparked labor protests as well. In December 1828, several hundred women left their stations at a cotton factory in Dover, New Hampshire, and paraded through town to protest new rules that fined workers for lateness and forbade them to talk on the job. In February and March 1834, some 800 women at Dover's Cocheco mill struck against a wage reduction and the company's demand that they pledge not to organize. To publicize their struggle, the strikers staged a parade that resembled Fourth of July celebrations. Accompanied by a brass band, the marchers waved flags, set off firecrackers, and shouted their determination to resist "the shocking fate of slaves."[20]

If slavery shocked some white Americans, it flourished nonetheless. As agreed at the Constitutional Convention, Congress outlawed the importation of slaves as of January 1, 1808. By then, however, slaves numbered about 1 million; and new births together with illegal importations would double that figure by 1830. The free black population grew at a slower pace, from about 180,000 in 1808 to 320,000 in 1830.

Congressional policy on admitting new states to the federal union helped slavery spread far beyond its old strongholds. From the 1790s onward, admissions proceeded according to a quota system designed to equalize the numbers of slave states and "free states" (where slavery was either illegal or marked for death via gradual emancipation). Slaveholders thus controlled half of the U.S. Senate, where their spokesmen could derail legislation unfriendly to slavery. This arrangement almost broke down in 1820, when Congress debated the admission of Maine as the twelfth free state and Missouri as the twelfth slave state. Northerners in the House of Representatives vehemently objected to slavery in Missouri, which lay in territory earlier designated "free soil." In the end, however, conciliation carried the day. Under a plan called the Missouri Compromise, Congress agreed that Missouri could come in with slavery intact, that additional slave states would have to lie to the south of Missouri, and that slave states and free states would continue to join the union in pairs.

While politicians sought to reconcile slavery and liberty, rebellious slaves carried republican doctrines to more radical conclusions. In fall 1800, Virginia militiamen broke up an underground army of about 600 slaves and some free black workers poised to march on the capital city of Richmond. Their leader was a young blacksmith named Gabriel, one of the 5 percent of U.S. slaves who could read and write. He had worked in Richmond since 1798, identifying white abolitionists, mixing with white craftsmen active in the Democratic-Republican movement, and avidly following news from the island of San Domingo (Hispaniola), where slaves' successful war for emancipation had widened into a fight for national independence. Along the way he came to believe that a slave revolt in Virginia could spark a more general uprising. His army planned to enter Richmond behind a banner proclaiming "Death or Liberty" to rally support from many whites as well as the black populace, and to force the state government to complete the American Revolution by ending slavery and upholding equal rights for all.[21]

Gabriel and twenty-five of his lieutenants went to the gallows for daring to think such things possible. One of them told the court, "I have nothing more to offer than what General Washington would have had to offer had he been taken by the British and put to trial by them. I have adventured my life in endeavoring to obtain the liberty of my countrymen, and am a willing sacrifice in their cause."[22] Within a year some veterans of Gabriel's army regrouped under a ferryman named Sancho and laid plans for a rural uprising along Virginia's border with North Carolina, once again expecting help from poor whites. When authorities got wind of the project in spring 1802, another twenty-five bondsmen were hanged. Following these executions in Virginia, the American Revolution receded as a reference point for slave resistance. But republican ideals remained a rich source of inspiration thanks to events in San Domingo, where black revolutionaries overthrew French colonialism and founded the independent republic of Haiti in 1804—the second republic established in the Western Hemisphere and the first to abolish slavery.

In 1822, authorities in Charleston, South Carolina, hanged thirty-five men for inciting a plot to replicate what Haiti modeled. The mastermind was the carpenter Denmark Vesey. A former slave who had purchased his freedom in 1800, he was the only freeman in the conspiracy's inner circle. Like Gabriel, Vesey could read, and Charleston's slaves had long relied on him for news of Haiti. In 1821, when Haitian troops overcame a protracted Spanish effort to recolonize their country, he turned from education to organizing. As one recruit later testified, "He said, we were deprived of our rights and privileges . . . and that it was high time for us to seek our rights, and that we were fully able to conquer the whites, if only we were unanimous and courageous as the St. Domingo people were."[23] The result was the largest slave conspiracy in U.S. history. At least several thousand people took part; some said as many as 9,000.

While free African Americans seldom participated in slave rebellions, a great many shared Denmark Vesey's identification with Haiti. Starting in 1825, when France finally recognized Haiti's independence, free black communities in both northern and southern cities gathered annually to celebrate the Haitian revolution. To quote one speaker in Baltimore, Haitians' victory provided "an irrefragable argument, to prove to her enemies, that the descendants of Africa never were designed by their Creator to sustain an inferiority, or even a mediocrity, in the chain of beings."[24] That was a crucial point for free African Americans, whose rights before the law had steadily declined since the Constitution took effect.

Federal action set the stage for white supremacy at the state level. The immigration law of 1790 reserved naturalized citizenship for white people; the Militia Act of 1792 excluded black men from service; and in 1810, the U.S. Post Office stipulated that only whites could carry the mail. Congress repeatedly welcomed new states that deprived black citizens of fundamental rights, and it never censured old states for withdrawing rights previously extended.

Close to 60 percent of free African Americans resided in southern states, whose lawmakers enacted the harshest restrictions. Starting with Virginia in 1793, states across the South prohibited or severely limited the entry of free black people, ordered those already resident to document their freedom before local authorities, and treated all who did not comply as fugitive slaves. By 1810, every southern state but Delaware had barred free blacks from testifying against white people in court, and in 1811, Georgia denied them the right to jury trials. Northern states passed a hodgepodge of discriminatory statutes that in some cases rivaled the South's. By 1820, for example, most northern school systems were either segregated or entirely closed to black children; both Ohio and Illinois outlawed the entry of black settlers; and Massachusetts was the only northern state where an African American could serve as a juror.

In both the North and the South, black voting rights eroded too. As of 1800, with sixteen states in the union, all but Virginia, South Carolina, and Georgia enfranchised free black men on the same basis as white men. But over the next half century just one incoming state (Maine) gave black men equal access to the ballot, and nine older states took it away—often at the same time that they removed property restrictions on the white electorate. By the 1850s, black men could participate in politics in just five of thirty-one states: Massachusetts, Rhode Island, New Hampshire, Vermont, and Maine.

In free black communities, then, activism generally centered in churches and benevolent associations. Virtually all of them worked against slavery in some fashion, surreptitiously in the South and openly in the North. As the southern communities helped fugitive slaves make their way to free states, the northerners built a network of abolitionist societies—more than fifty by the late 1820s. Most of these groups were run by men, but a fair number were women's organizations like the Colored Female Religious and Moral Society of Salem, Massachusetts, whose members gathered to "write and converse on the sufferings of our enslaved sisters."

Black abolitionism was especially dynamic in Boston, whose General Colored Association agitated for racial equality as well as an end to slavery and worked tirelessly to knit free African Americans into a national movement. One of the association's leaders was David Walker, a tailor who galvanized black activists with his militant *Appeal to the Coloured Citizens of the World* (1829). Condemning all manifestations of white

supremacy and racism, this pamphlet called on black America to rebel against every violation of the republican doctrine that "ALL MEN ARE CREATED EQUAL!!"[25] and excoriated Thomas Jefferson for perverting that principle. The Boston abolitionists also included a pioneer for women's rights: Maria W. Stewart, a widowed domestic worker who became the first American-born woman to speak publicly in behalf of equality for her sex.

The most radical elaboration of republican ideals came from the printer Thomas Skidmore, a New York City labor activist who had grown up in an old Yankee farm family in Newtown, Connecticut. In 1829, Skidmore published a manifesto titled *The Rights of Man to Property!*, which proposed sweeping redistributions of wealth and power. The country belonged equally to every one of its people, Skidmore proclaimed, and "the same eternal and indissoluble rights exist for all."[26] Every form of servitude should be abolished; every man and unmarried woman—white, black and Indian—should get a 160-acre homestead to call their own; factories, railroads, and other industrial property should be collectively owned; every adult should have full and equal voting rights; and government should consist of "a great judicial tribunal of all our citizens sitting in judgment over and deciding for themselves."[27] Skidmore promoted this program through the New York Working Men's Party, which he helped to found in 1829. Less radical voices prevailed, however. Within a few months he and his handful of followers were pushed out of the party, and their independent efforts fell apart with Skidmore's death in 1832.

His ideas lived on in piecemeal form. Over the next three decades, working people took part in various movements for land redistribution, for the abolition of slavery, for the establishment of co-operative workshops, for racial equality, and for women's rights. But many more years would pass before large numbers came together, as Skidmore endorsed, to "oppose everything of privilege . . . in whatever shape it might present itself."[28]

3

Slavery and Freedom in the New Republic

On January 10, 1860, the Pemberton Mill, a cotton textile factory in Lawrence, Massachusetts, collapsed like a house of cards. Of the 670 workers buried in the rubble, 90 died and another 120 suffered severe injuries. Erected in 1853 at a cost of $800,000 and equipped with the latest in steam-powered machinery, the mill had been touted as the finest example of the vast northern textile industry, in which wageworkers wove cloth from the cotton grown by slaves. In many ways the Pemberton epitomized the nation as a whole, a grand edifice standing on shaky pillars.

The Constitution's ratification ushered in seventy years of national growth. Land purchases and seizures extended the United States across the continent, from Florida to California and from New England to the Pacific Northwest. The population swelled from about 4 million in 1790 to over 31 million in 1860. Each decade brought a larger influx of immigrants, mostly from northwestern Europe and the British Isles. Close to 600,000 people arrived in the 1830s, 1.7 million in the 1840s, 2.6 million in the 1850s. Cities increased in number and size. In 1790, there were just six municipalities with more than 8,000 residents; by 1860 there were 141. New York's population reached 1.2 million, Philadelphia's 566,000, and six other cities topped 100,000—Boston, Baltimore, Cincinnati, St. Louis, Chicago, and New Orleans.

Agriculture, industry, and commerce flourished as never before. Cotton plantations spread across the lower South from the Atlantic coast to eastern Texas; corn, wheat, hog, and cattle farming proliferated in the Midwest; merchant wealth funded an industrial revolution that centered in the North but penetrated other regions too. More and more commodities were produced in factories, not only textile mills but also iron foundries, machine shops, printing plants, sugar refineries, meatpacking houses, boot and shoe factories, and furniture works. To fuel iron furnaces and power machinery, coal mining expanded from about 50,000 tons of output in 1820 to 14 million tons in 1860. East of the Mississippi, a giant network of new canals, paved roads, and over 30,000 miles of railroad track linked farms, plantations, factories, and mines to distant markets for their products. By 1860, the United States was the world's fourth biggest industrial power (behind England, Germany, and France) and second to none in commercial agriculture. It produced two-thirds of the world's raw cotton and industrial goods valued at more than $1.8 billion, with cotton textiles in the lead.

The economy was unstable, however—recessions rolled around on a regular basis, including an especially sharp downturn that began in 1837 and lasted a full seven years—and injustice and inequality abounded as well. The 1860 census counted nearly 4 million slaves. Free workers and their dependents, about 12 million people in all, lived on wages that averaged under $1 a day. Restrictions on free African Americans were harsher than ever. Women of all colors still lacked political rights. Federal law still stipulated that only white immigrants could become citizens and required that they wait for five years. In addition to dispossessing Native Americans, westward expansion involved the seizure of 1.2 million square miles of Mexican land. Two ruling classes—the South's richest planters, the North's industrial capitalists—dominated their respective regions and jockeyed for control of the federal government. Both regarded labor as nothing more than a commodity. The planters' regime supported a thriving interstate slave trade, buying and selling an average of 7,500 people a year from 1820 to 1860. The Pemberton Mill's owners calculated the market value of lives lost in the collapse as $500 for male heads of household down to $50 for children and paid just that to the dead's survivors.

As oppression mounted, so did resistance. Working people asserted themselves through labor unions, political action, co-operatives, strikes, and countless challenges to slavery. As in the past, different groups of workers fought on different fronts. Inequality and plain bigotry divided women and men, white workers and workers of color, U.S. natives and immigrants, the free and the unfree. Amidst these divisions, however, a critical mass of people combined against slavery's expansion into new territories. By 1860, this "Free Soil" coalition realigned American politics, and the compromises that had once secured slavery's future frayed beyond repair.

"If You Can't Fight, Kick"

The planters' regime spared no effort to preserve and defend slavery. Only a third of the South's white households owned slaves in 1830, and the proportion fell to a fourth by 1860. For that very reason, the planter elite—the richest 1 percent who owned one-quarter of all slaves—ruled the region with a heavy hand, organizing southern life to serve the slaveholding minority. Yet they never managed to squelch the tradition of resistance exemplified by the Tennessee slave who advised her children, "Fight, and if you can't fight, kick; and if you can't kick, then bite."[1]

Planters' supremacy in the South and their influence in Washington, D.C., owed a great deal to the cotton boom. While other cash crops—chiefly tobacco, rice, and sugarcane—remained important in parts of the South, cotton production soared from about 100,000 bales in 1800 to 5.4 million bales in 1860. The South's wealthiest planters made their fortunes in this business, which also profited smaller planters, family farms, cotton brokers, cotton shippers, and slave traders. Northern capitalists had a big stake in the business too; many of them engaged in cotton trading, advanced loans to cotton planters, and invested in cotton textile factories. What served the planter elite thus appealed to a good portion of the white South and much of the North's ruling class.

At bottom, though, the planters' regime rested on force. Armed and mounted posses policed country roads every night, on the lookout for "disturbances" among the slaves. Sentries patrolled cities and towns. Enormous state militias—more than 100,000 strong in Virginia—drilled frequently and mobilized at the least sign of trouble. Free people likely to inspire slave unrest faced increasing suppression. By the mid-1820s, nearly every southern abolitionist had been expelled from the region or intimidated into silence. White workers ran afoul of the law when they tried to organize; the courts routinely crushed their unions and strikes. Free blacks, who by 1860 numbered about 250,000 in slaveholding states, were now subject to curfews, public whippings for giving the slightest offense to whites, automatic imprisonment for possessing abolitionist literature, and statutory exclusion from learned professions and the majority of skilled trades.

Thousands of state and local laws targeted slaves. They were forbidden to raise a hand against any white person, to assemble without white supervision, to buy or sell anything without their masters' permission, to leave a plantation at any time, to walk city streets after dark without written passes . . . the list went on and on. Most states made it a crime to teach slaves to read or write. By 1860, several states in the Deep South had prohibited manumission.

Whatever their knowledge of the statutes, every day reminded slaves of their status as chattel. The slave trade besieged family life, breaking up a quarter to a third of all marriages and snatching countless children from their parents. One of the first things adolescent girls learned about sex was that white men could rape black women with impunity; not a single slaveholding state defined such assaults as crimes. Attempts at book learning carried tremendous risks. As Hannah Crasson of Wake County, North Carolina, later remembered, "You better not be found trying to learn to read. Our marster was harder down on that than anything else."[2] Some masters forbade slaves to worship on their own. Mary Reynolds grew up on a Louisiana sugar plantation whose overseer lurked around slaves' cabins at night and threatened to "come in there and tear the hide off your backs" whenever he heard prayers or hymns.[3]

Labor conditions varied considerably. As plantations multiplied, more and more slaves were field hands working in large, tightly-supervised gangs. This system prevailed on the lower South's cotton plantations, the upper South's tobacco plantations, and the sugar plantations of Louisiana. But most slaves did other kinds of work. As late as the 1850s, roughly half were household servants, craftsmen, or field hands on farms too small to qualify as plantations (units with at least twenty slaves). Some of this group—mainly urban craftsmen and servants—hired out for wages, saw to their own maintenance, and paid their owners a weekly fee. Another 5 percent of slaves worked for industrial enterprises such as mines, railroads, and factories. While the vast majority of industrial slaves were owned or leased by the businesses that employed them, a few were hired for a wage. Not all plantation field hands did gang labor, moreover. The rice plantations of South Carolina, Georgia, and Louisiana used the task system, under which each slave got a daily assignment, worked with minimal supervision, and could stop once the job was done. Task labor was also the norm on the cotton plantations on the Sea Islands along the coasts of Georgia and South Carolina.

Whatever the setting, slaves who broke work rules risked physical assault from masters and mistresses, the overseers they hired, or the slaves they appointed as foremen or "drivers." Some of this violence was simply sadistic. One tobacco manufacturer whipped a teenaged girl to death as his wife burned her with an iron. The *Richmond Dispatch* congratulated a factory overseer for shooting a bondsman who left the premises without permission. Jenny Proctor, born on an Alabama cotton plantation, spent her childhood working under a relentlessly cruel driver: "The least little thing we do he beat us for it and put big chains round our ankles and make us work with them till the blood be cut out all around our ankles."[4]

By all accounts, though, most slaveholders took a businesslike approach to labor discipline and insisted that their agents do the same. A magazine popular among planters summarized the strategy: "Never fail . . . to notice the breach of an established rule, and be equally unfailing in punishing the offender justly, according to the nature and circumstances of the offence. Never inflict punishment when in a passion, nor threaten it; but wait until perfectly cool."[5] Solomon Northrup, a free New Yorker kidnapped into slavery in Louisiana, saw this strategy at work during picking season on a cotton plantation: "It was rarely that a day passed by without one or more whippings. This occurred at the time the cotton was weighed. The delinquent, whose weight had fallen short, was taken out, stripped and made to lie on the ground, face downwards, when he received a punishment proportioned to his offence. . . . The number of lashes is graduated according to the nature of the case."[6]

But slavery was more than a business, and work rules were not the only dictates slave masters enforced with the whip. In a decision issued by North Carolina's supreme court in 1852, Judge Frederic Nash observed that any hint of insolence on the part of a slave "violates the rules of propriety, and if tolerated, would destroy that subordination upon which our social system rests."[7] Masters promoted "propriety" by doling out countless punishments of the sort described here by Frederick Douglass, the abolitionist leader who had been a slave in Maryland:

> A mere look, word, or motion . . . are all matters for which a slave may be whipped at any time. Does a slave look dissatisfied? It is said, he has the devil in him, and it must be whipped out. Does he speak loudly when spoken to by his master? Then he is getting high-minded, and should be taken down a button-hole lower. Does he forget to pull off his hat at the approach of a white person? Then he is wanting in reverence, and should be whipped for it. Does he ever venture to vindicate his conduct, when censured for it? Then he is guilty of impudence,—one of the greatest crimes of which a slave can be guilty.[8]

These humiliations—like armed patrollers, draconian laws, and everything else that propped up the planters' regime—were designed to control slaves' minds as well as their behavior. To make the system run smoothly, slaveholders had to make emancipation unthinkable.

The effort failed. Slaves repeatedly thought, sang, and dreamed about freedom, and defiant hopes often sparked rebellious action. Both forms of resistance required personal courage. Both were also collective projects, deeply rooted in the families and communities slaves constructed outside the meticulously supervised world of work.

Labor from dawn to dark or longer absorbed most but not all of their waking hours. Work usually ended early on Saturdays, Sunday was virtually always a day of rest, and most people could squeeze some spare minutes from the remainder of the week. These spaces between the demands of work provided seedbeds for resistance.

Family life inspired and supported innumerable challenges to masters' authority. In Maryland, Harriet Ross (mother of the famous Harriet Tubman) refused to give her youngest child to the Georgia slave trader to whom he had been sold. An older son later described her response when the trader and her master came knocking late at night: "She ripped out an oath and said, 'You are after my son; but the first man that comes into my house, I will split his head open.' That frightened them, and they would not come in. So she kept the boy hid until the Georgia man went away."[9] In Virginia, John Jones Middleton left the plantation where he was repeatedly beaten and lived in nearby woods, his wife and children supplying him with food and harboring him in their cabin many a night. Such stories are plentiful in memoirs written or dictated by former slaves. The stories do not always have happy endings; but their sheer volume illustrates how deeply family love and loyalties undercut slavery's "rules of propriety."

Community was family writ large, centered in gatherings that broke the rules in both tacit and overt ways. With or without permission, slaves regularly came together for prayer and praise, for parties and dances, and for self-education. This united people who did not ordinarily cross paths at work: field hands and artisans, household servants and industrial laborers, slaves held by different masters, and sometimes free blacks as well. When it was impossible to congregate in the open, they met in secluded corners of the woods or in cabins with shutters closed tight. To facilitate safe travel to and from the meetings, they frequently strung grape vines across the roads to trip the patrollers' horses. Sometimes they confronted a patrol head-on. Betty Jones remembered one such incident in Virginia, when patrollers showed up at a cabin where a meeting was in progress: "Jack Diggs an[d] Charlie Dowal shoveled fire an[d] coals right out [th]e door on them de[v]ils. [Th]ey runned from [th]e fire an[d] we runned from them. Ain't nobody g[e]t caught [th]at time."[10]

These gatherings were subversive in other respects too. At parties slaves satirized masters and mistresses in songs, jokes, and imitations of their high-handed ways. Educational meetings took place at many a "midnight school" where a literate slave taught others how to read and write.[11] In Natchez, Mississippi, Milla Granson ran such a school for seven years and graduated hundreds of pupils, some of whom later forged travel passes and ran away to Canada. In their religious meetings slaves shared a faith starkly different from the gospel heard at the services and Sabbath schools masters arranged. There, every sermon echoed Ephesians 6:5: "Servants, be obedient to them that are your masters." But the underground slave church fostered a religion of liberation exemplified in the lyrics of spiritual songs such as,

> *O, gracious Lord! When shall it be,*
> *That we poor souls shall all be free;*
> *Lord, break them slavery powers—*
> *Will you go along with me?*[12]

An ethic of solidarity permeated all of these activities. Participants trusted each other to keep secrets from masters and their agents; they also fostered secrecy by nurturing the independent spirit slaveholders tried so hard to kill.

The Reverend Charles Jones of Georgia, a white clergyman determined to save slaves from the sin of disobedience, was constantly frustrated by their refusals to identify wrongdoers. "Inquiry elicits no information," he complained. "No one feels at liberty to disclose the transgressor; all are profoundly ignorant; the matter assumes the sacredness of a 'professional secret.'"[13] Solidarity was not seamless; every community had traitors and informants from time to time. But solidarity was sturdy enough to support a rich network of group activities that slaveholders did not control.

These activities shaded over into more radical challenges to masters' power and to slavery itself. At least 100,000 bondspeople escaped from slaveholding states between 1800 and 1860, and many more tried to get away. Other forms of resistance dating back to the colonial era continued as well: arson, vandalism, assaults on masters, guerrilla raids by bands of runaways, and armed rebellion. Nearly every year brought news of slave revolts or conspiracies. In addition to the efforts led by Gabriel, Sancho, and Denmark Vesey, the most famous incidents included an uprising in 1811 of some 500 slaves on plantations near New Orleans and a mutiny in 1841 by slaves on the *Creole*, who took over the ship as it carried them down the Mississippi River and eventually reached freedom in the Bahamas.

But nothing shook the planters' regime like the 1831 insurrection led by the field hand Nat Turner in Southampton County, Virginia. Turner, who had learned to read the Bible, often preached at religious meetings. He later told a lawyer who recorded his confession that the Holy Spirit had appeared to him in 1828 and said, "I should . . . fight against the Serpent, for the time was fast approaching when the first should be last and the last should be first."[14] On the night of August 21, 1831, he and five disciples armed themselves and set out on a crusade against bondage. Their first blows fell on Turner's master and his family, all of whom the rebels executed. As the group pushed on toward the county seat, a town named Jerusalem, more and more slaves joined the march. By the morning of August 23, when militiamen put them to flight, the rebels numbered about seventy and at least fifty-seven whites had been killed. Turner, who eluded capture for another two months, was hanged in Jerusalem on November 11. Nineteen of his comrades—including three freemen—had already been tried and hanged, and over 100 black residents of Southampton County had been massacred in retaliation for the revolt.

Following the Turner cataclysm, American slaveholders fortified the machinery of repression. There were more patrols, bigger militias, harsher pressures on abolitionists and free blacks, and more brutal penalties for slaves deemed impudent. Slave communities survived nonetheless, waiting for the time when they could successfully act on the hopes expressed in their song about the Old Testament's Samson: "If I had my way, I would tear this building down."[15]

Wageworkers' Activism

While cotton production dominated the South, manufacturing transformed the North. At the close of the American Revolution, about three-quarters of free people in New

England and the mid-Atlantic states lived and worked on family farms. By 1860, farm families made up just 40 percent of the population in these states, where nearly a million people now did industrial work. As manufacturing boomed, so did wage labor. Like slavery in the South, the wage system became the core institution of the northern economy, steadily supplanting other means of making a living.

Wageworkers came from various backgrounds. Some were the descendants of the eighteenth century's tiny wage labor force of maritime workers, domestic servants, and common laborers. Some others were former slaves or their descendants. Many were craftsmen from trades such as printing and shoemaking, where competition from factories was driving artisan shops out of business and foreclosing journeymen's routes to self-employment. Wage work also absorbed numerous immigrants, most of them people of Irish, German, or British descent. But by far the largest cohort of wageworkers were native-born men and women from farming districts plagued by land shortages, debt, and competition from midwestern agriculture.

Like slaves' labor, wage work varied in terms and conditions. Domestic servants—the biggest occupational group among women workers—usually lived in their employers' homes, got cash payments in addition to room and board, and had almost no time to themselves. Other wage earners typically worked twelve to fourteen hours a day with Sundays off, but pay arrangements differed from group to group. Women normally got one-half of what men earned for comparable work. Many miners and factory workers received at least a portion of their wages in goods from a company store. Like young women employed in textile mills, railroad and canal construction laborers were often paid partly in cash and partly in room and board. Some workers, such as carpenters, bricklayers, and blacksmiths, earned a set amount for each day on the job; garment workers, printers, cigar makers, and others received "piece wages" that depended on their output.

Manufacturing was a world of contrasts with regard to technology and the organization of production. By 1860, many industrial workers operated power-driven machinery in factories, but many more used hand tools and worked in small shops. Garment and shoe manufacturers still relied extensively on "outworkers": women, children, and sometimes whole families who sewed clothing or stitched shoes at home.

Job opportunities depended on workers' color, sex, and national origin as well as their levels of skill. Factory jobs were reserved for whites and the best-paying positions for men. Craft shops owned by whites typically employed white men only except in a few trades—printing, shoemaking, and tailoring—where white women might work alongside male kin. German and British immigrants, who usually arrived with craft skills, formed ethnic networks that gave them a leg up in the U.S. labor market. Newcomers from Ireland, most of whom lacked industrial experience, concentrated in unskilled jobs, and anti-Irish bigotry further limited their options. As one typical employment ad read: "WANTED—A GIRL to take care of children, and to do other household matters. No Irish need apply."[16]

In the end, though, color trumped nationality; all European immigrants found wider opportunities than African Americans. While Irish women clustered in domestic work, many had moved into factory employment by the 1850s, and Irish men had made inroads into crafts such as plumbing, carpentry, blacksmithing, and glassmaking.

Black women, on the other hand, were almost wholly confined to jobs as laundresses, domestic servants, or outworkers for garment shops. Black men worked mostly as construction laborers, stevedores, sailors, waiters, or cooks, and their small numbers in skilled trades had declined as immigrants poured in. In Philadelphia, for instance, the ranks of black mechanics (both master craftsmen and journeymen) dwindled from 506 in 1838 to 286 in 1849.

Wageworkers across the board shared certain problems: poverty and insecurity despite long hours of labor, bosses who continually drove them in hopes of getting more for less, and inequality under political and legal systems designed by and for the elite. In every sector of the workforce, activists addressed these issues through collective action, not only unionism but many other projects too. Mutualism had boundaries, however. Specific conditions of life and labor differed sharply for men and women, skilled and unskilled, citizens and aliens, white and black; and labor activism reflected these distinctions.

White citizens and white craftsmen in particular—workers with the most resources and options—were the first to form labor unions. In December 1827, Philadelphia's craft unions formed the Mechanics' Union of Trade Associations, the first U.S. labor organization that encompassed workers from various trades. The following summer its member unions founded another first: a local Working Men's Party that ran its own candidates for municipal and state office, calling on craftsmen to use the ballot box "to take the management of their own interests, as a class, into their own immediate keeping."[17] By the early 1830s, similar parties had appeared in at least sixty cities and towns, from Portland, Maine, to Washington, D.C., and as far west as Cincinnati. They called for improvements in public education, for an end to compulsory militia musters, for repeal of conspiracy laws applied to unions, and for other reforms beneficial to the laboring classes. The Democratic Party soon embraced enough of these causes to co-opt independent labor politics, but craftsmen continued to organize across occupational lines.

From 1833 through 1836, craft unions established central federations in thirteen cities, including New York, Boston, Albany, Pittsburgh, Louisville, and Philadelphia (where the Mechanics' Union had disintegrated along with the Working Men's Party in 1831). Coordinating efforts through the National Trades Union (NTU) founded in 1834, these new "city centrals" spawned labor newspapers, mobilized strike support, helped to build new unions, and championed reforms that workingmen's parties had endorsed. First and foremost, they agitated and organized to reduce the standard workday from twelve or more hours to ten. While the NTU petitioned the federal government to grant its employees the ten-hour day, local activists staged strike after strike demanding the same from their bosses.

The largest of these strikes occurred in June 1835, when the Philadelphia Trades Union organized unionists from seventeen different crafts to join a walkout initiated by Irish "coal heavers," who unloaded barges along the Schuylkill River. This was the first general strike in U.S. history and a resounding success. After three weeks the city council announced that municipal workers would henceforth work ten hours a day with no reduction in pay, and private employers quickly followed suit. Inspired by Philadelphia's example, that summer and fall craft unions across the mid-Atlantic states launched strikes for the ten-hour workday, and in most cases they won.

The National Trades Union was part of a wider uprising among white workers. As craft unions mobilized for the ten-hour day, women and unskilled men built their own organizations and struck for better pay. The women activists included tailoresses in New York City and Baltimore; shoe binders in New York, Philadelphia, and Lynn, Massachusetts; and textile operatives in Lowell. In June 1835, against the backdrop of Philadelphia's general strike, some 500 workingwomen from various trades formed a citywide federation—the Female Improvement Society—that won wage increases for seamstresses who sewed uniforms for the U.S. Army. Among unskilled men, no one outshone Irish canal workers when it came to militancy. They staged at least fourteen strikes in the 1830s, and in January 1834, clashed with federal troops sent to put down a strike on the Chesapeake and Ohio Canal in Maryland. New York City's docks became a hub of strike activity in 1834–36, when sailors, stevedores, and coal heavers walked off their jobs and Irish construction laborers stopped work on nearby projects.

Employers fought the labor movement by firing and blacklisting activists and by taking unions to trial. In 1835, in a case involving a shoemakers' union in Geneva, New York, the state's supreme court ruled that both unions and strikes were illegal conspiracies. In June of the following year, twenty journeymen tailors in New York City were convicted of criminal conspiracy for striking shops that had nullified wage agreements with the tailors' union and discharged union members. A crowd of 27,000, about a fifth of the city's adult population, jammed into City Hall Park to protest the verdict, and their fury reverberated through the labor press. A Philadelphia paper ran this statement by women affiliated with the Journeymen Cordwainers (shoemakers): "It is our prerogative to say what institution we will be members of, that being bequeathed to us by our forefathers—the toilworn veterans of '76 who nobly moistened the soil with their blood in defence of equal rights and equal privileges, that we, their descendants, might enjoy the BLOOD-BOUGHT LEGACY free and unmolested."[18] The law did not recognize workers' right to organize, however, and that threatened everything the labor movement had achieved.

Following the tailors' conviction, leaders of the National Trades Union debated their movement's future. Some endorsed political action with an eye to repealing anti-union laws. A more radical contingent favored co-operative production, calling for the establishment of craft shops collectively owned and managed by their workers. Within months, however, the debates were moot. In spring 1837, a financial panic among bankers and speculators ushered in a long depression, and mass layoffs quickly destroyed the National Trades Union, the city centrals, and nearly all unions.

Reforms the NTU had endorsed made some headway as the Democratic and Whig parties vied for working-class votes. In 1840, President Martin Van Buren endeared the Democrats to workingmen by instituting the ten-hour day for employees on federal construction projects. Not to be outdone, Whigs in command of the Massachusetts Supreme Court gave unionism a landmark legal victory in 1842. Overturning a conspiracy verdict against a bootmakers' union in Boston, the court ruled in the case of *Commonwealth v. Hunt* that workers had the right to organize and strike for "useful and honorable purposes."[19] These concessions had limited impacts, however. Unions were so few and weak during the depression years that labor conspiracy trials virtually disappeared, and workers could not force state governments to follow Van Buren's example.

As the depression deepened, many working people poured into the nation's first mass movement for abstention from alcohol. In 1840, six Baltimore craftsmen who had recently sworn off drinking formed the Washington Temperance Benevolent Society to convert other men to sobriety. This crusade spread like wildfire in white working-class communities. By 1843, Washingtonian lodges had sprung up across the Northeast, and they claimed an aggregate membership of 3 million. The great majority of members were workingmen, though men of other classes also took part and women organized Martha Washington auxiliaries. Unlike older temperance groups sponsored by employers and churches, the Washingtonians did not moralize about drinking. They opposed it on the very practical grounds that it made hard times more difficult. Their lodges and auxiliaries dispensed aid to the down and out, hosted a steady round of parties, picnics, and other amusements, and held weekly "experience meetings" where reformed drunks testified about the depredations of alcohol and their happiness as teetotalers.[20] When the economy recovered the movement faded, but its veterans would carry the temperance cause into many labor organizations.

The depression also fueled popular interest in projects that promised a refuge from capitalism. Workers and their families joined with middle-class reformers to establish new communities based on communal living, collective ownership of property, and equal rights for all members. The most radical experiment was the Northampton Association of Education and Industry, which operated a farm and a silk mill in Northampton, Massachusetts. Founded by abolitionists in 1842, the Northampton Association welcomed both black and white members, including fugitive slaves. It was governed by community meetings where everyone had an equal voice. By vote of the membership, the workday at Northampton was ten hours; wages were replaced by a system of subsistence allowances and profit sharing; and those who performed housework got the same pay as others. From 1843 through 1845, the ideas of Charles Fourier, a French socialist philosopher, inspired the establishment of twenty-six communes. The first Fourierist settlement—the Sylvania Association in western Pennsylvania—was a co-operative farm organized by craftsmen from New York City and Albany.

Except for those sponsored by religious sects like the Shakers and Mennonites, co-operative settlements seldom survived for more than a few years. The main problem was lack of capital; members could not come up with enough cash to build decent housing, equip farms and workshops, and tide everyone over until the commune was self-supporting. As one veteran of the Hopedale Community in Milford, Massachusetts, explained: "The rich and well-to-do derided our scheme . . . the poor, needy, and homeless eagerly applied . . . [and] less than a third of our reliable associates had sufficient money at command to meet their own family expenses—much less to help in housing and furnishing subsisting employment to others."[21]

While communes faltered, more simple co-operatives proliferated. The most common were consumers' co-operatives modeled on the Working Men's Protective Union founded by Boston craftsmen in 1845. Protective unions ran nonprofit stores where members could purchase food, fuel, and other necessities at reduced prices. They also functioned as mutual benefit societies, providing sick pay and old-age pensions. By the mid-1850s, workers organized close to 800 protective unions, mostly in New England and New York State but also as far west as Wisconsin.

Co-operative production gained a following too. Just before the depression, some craft unionists in Philadelphia, New York, and several other cities had set up their own workshops, but none of these projects had survived the economic collapse. Starting in the late 1840s, producers' co-operatives reappeared in greater numbers, most of them organized by reborn unions. Some co-operatives, such as the Journeymen Molders' Union Foundry in Cincinnati, were established by strikers as a temporary source of income but then developed a life of their own. Others had grander aims. In New York City, where unions in more than a dozen trades opened workshops in 1850, labor organizations throughout the city came together at the end of the year to form an Industrial Congress dedicated to the proposition that workers had "inalienable rights to Life, Liberty, and the fruits of their Labor [and] to the use of such a portion of the earth and other elements as are necessary for their subsist[e]nce and comfort."[22]

Another popular cause was the "land reform" campaign that called on the federal government to give public lands to families who wished to homestead in the West. This movement was the brainchild of George Henry Evans, an English-born printer, editor of labor newspapers, and former leader of the New York Working Men's Party and the National Trades Union. In 1844, he headed a committee of veteran labor activists that founded the National Reform Association to rally workingmen for political action on behalf of land reform. While would-be homesteaders flocked to the campaign, so did many more workers who viewed land reform as a way to improve life in the East. An exodus of homesteaders promised to reduce competition in eastern labor and housing markets; those who stayed behind would presumably enjoy higher wages, better labor conditions, and lower rents. By the late 1840s, legions of workingmen had joined the National Reform Association's local clubs, pledging to vote only for politicians who had agreed in writing that all public lands should be set aside "for the full and exclusive use of actual settlers," not wealthy speculators.[23]

Factory workers from Maine to Georgia meanwhile agitated for the ten-hour day. This loose-knit movement did not generate a national organization, but it enjoyed a de facto headquarters in the New England Workingmen's Association, founded by Massachusetts activists in 1844. Despite its masculine name, the Workingmen's Association included workers of both sexes, most of them employed in textile mills. They came together to fight for the ten-hour day, not only as an end in itself but also as the first step toward a new social order. As one of the association's organizers explained, shorter hours of labor would give workers sufficient time, energy, and learning to undertake a grand effort to remake American life. This message spread far and wide through the Massachusetts labor press, read by mill workers across New England and in other regions as well.

In contrast to craft unions of the 1830s, the ten-hour organizations of the 1840s and 1850s sought to decrease the workday through political reform. They organized petition drives and mobilized voters to demand that state lawmakers prohibit private industry from employing anyone more than ten hours a day. A number of legislatures yielded to the pressure. New Hampshire passed a ten-hour law in 1847, as did Pennsylvania and Maine in 1848 and, over the course of the 1850s, six more states

(New Jersey, Connecticut, Rhode Island, Ohio, Georgia, and California). Loopholes rendered these statutes unenforceable, however. They allowed for individual contracts to extend the workday beyond ten hours, and factory managers routinely ordered workers to sign such contracts or find other jobs. In Massachusetts, textile corporations had such a stranglehold on the legislature that ten-hour bills never even came up for a vote.

Some ten-hour activists took up other issues too. Nowhere was their agenda more elaborate than in the Lowell Female Labor Reform Association (LFLRA), the biggest of several women's organizations in the New England Workingmen's Association. Members of the LFLRA organized a temperance group and a Fourierist club, raised money for the Society for the Abolition of Capital Punishment, and sent aid to Ireland during the Great Famine. Their newspaper, the *Voice of Industry*, promoted these causes along with protective unions and land reform; and, in sharp contrast to most of the labor movement, the LFLRA both condemned slavery and championed women's rights.

Solidarity and Fragmentation

The labor movement that emerged after the depression was more diverse than the movement of the 1830s and less cohesive. Printers, machinists, building trades workers, and cigar makers organized national craft unions, the first of which was the National Typographical Union founded in 1852. For the most part, however, union building was a local affair. Labor conventions and federations generally paid much more attention to issues like land reform, ten-hour legislation, and worker co-operatives than to organizing on the job. That was invariably the case at the National Industrial Congresses that convened annually from 1845 through 1856 and brought together unionists, land reformers, co-operationists, and assorted radicals. In 1850, forty-six organizations in New York City formed a local federation also known as the Industrial Congress. In addition to trade unions, participating groups included land reformers, mutual-benefit societies, consumers' and producers' co-operatives, Christian labor reform groups, and lodges of German socialists. They tried in vain to construct a common program, and the federation fell apart in less than two years.

Divisions on the basis of sex, nationality, and color permeated the labor movement as well. Women were mostly excluded or treated as men's underlings and helpmeets. While foreign- and native-born workers co-operated in some parts of the movement, natives in other parts were hostile to immigrants. Black workers were the ultimate outsiders, commonly targets of violence as well as exclusion. Many white labor activists embraced the movement to abolish slavery, but many more did not.

Women active in the movement demanded new rights for their sex. "You have been degraded long enough," the *Voice of Industry* told its female readers in 1846. "Resolve that you will think, reason, judge, love, hate, approve, and disapprove, for yourselves, and, at your own volition; and, not at the dictation of an other."[24] Most of all, the Lowell Female Labor Reform Association urged workingwomen to defy the notion that social activism was unwomanly. Sarah Bagley, the association's president, declared at a meeting of ten-hour organizers: "For the last half a century it has been deemed a violation of woman's sphere to appear before the public as a speaker; but when our rights are trampled upon and we appeal in vain to legislators, what shall we do but appeal to the people? Shall not our voice be heard and our rights acknowledged. . . ?"[25] One of Bagley's co-workers, writing under the name Julianna, urged mill women to rally under the motto "EQUAL RIGHTS or death to the corporations."[26]

Although New England's factory operatives sent no delegates, some other workingwomen attended the nation's first women's rights convention, which met in Seneca Falls, New York, in July 1848. Among the participants was the nineteen-year-old Charlotte Woodward, an outworker who sewed deerskin gloves for leather shops in Seneca County. She dreamed of becoming a typesetter but could not find a printer willing to teach a woman the trade. "I wanted to work," she later wrote, "but I wanted to choose my task. . . . That was my form of rebellion against the life into which I was born."[27] As the convention closed she put her name to a Declaration of Principles that updated the Declaration of Independence: "We hold these truths to be self-evident: that all men and women are created equal. . . ."[28]

Workingwomen's organizations had voiced such sentiments as early as 1831, when Sarah Monroe, the president of New York City's Tailoresses Society, chided workingmen for making light of a wage strike by her union. In a speech reprinted by the labor press, she asked, "if it is unfashionable for the men to bear oppression in silence, why should it not also become unfashionable with the women? or do they deem us more able to endure hardships than they themselves?"[29] In many cases workingmen actively supported women's militancy. During the strike wave of the mid-1830s, journeymen's unions backed women strikers, and women and men struck jointly in Philadelphia's shoe and textile factories. A decade later the ten-hour campaign in western Pennsylvania's cotton mills was punctuated by rip-roaring strikes of women operatives who rallied male friends to help. In 1845 and again in 1848, the strikers tore down factory gates and stormed in to oust workers who had remained on the job. Hundreds of men showed up to cheer these actions and dissuade police from stepping in. "Let 'em hit one of them gals if they dare—and we'll fetch them out of their boots!" one man told the *Pittsburgh Journal*.[30]

Chivalry was one thing; comradeship another. Even the most generous workingmen did not generally accept women as equals, and many craftsmen were profoundly disturbed by women's very presence in industrial jobs. The National Trades Union, whose locals supported many a women's strike, excluded women's unions and voted at its 1835 convention to oppose "the multiplying of all description of labor for females."[31] The shoemaker William English, head of Philadelphia's city central during its general strike for the ten-hour day, appealed to workingwomen to restrict their hours of labor in order to create more and better-paying positions for men. What nature intended, he said, was that men be the breadwinners so that women could devote themselves to housework, each generation of females training the next for the "sober duties of wives, mothers and matrons."[32]

In 1836, the NTU appointed a committee on female labor that echoed English. In its report to that year's convention, the committee urged journeymen's unions to help workingwomen organize for better labor conditions, but only as a stopgap, to "first curb the excess before we destroy the evil." The ultimate goal, the report insisted, should be women's removal from workshops and factories. Since workingwomen were "very blind to their real interest," they had so far failed to recognize the beauty of that goal, and so it was imperative that union men enlighten them. Every woman had to be informed that "her labor should be only of a domestic nature" and that taking industrial work was "the same as tying a stone around the neck of her natural protector, Man."[33]

When craft unions regrouped in the late 1840s and early 1850s, their posture toward women was much the same. They defined female industrial labor as an evil and proposed as a solution that workingmen receive a "family wage" sufficient to keep the womenfolk at home. A handful of unions helped to organize sister locals of workingwomen. The Journeymen Tailors of Cleveland admitted women in 1850 in return for their support of a union strike. That same year, the Journeymen Cordwainers in New York City established a local for women workers who were relatives of union men. Otherwise craft unions excluded women, as did most of the National Industrial Congresses.

There were moments of unity. Women and men co-operated closely in the New England Workingmen's Association, whose constitution specified that male and female branches of the organization enjoyed equal rights and obligations. President Sarah Bagley of the Lowell Female Labor Reform Association presented an address at the first National Industrial Congress in 1845. Women took part in the land reform movement under the auspices of the National Reform Association.

The most celebrated example of labor solidarity between men and women was the Great Shoemakers' Strike of 1860, in which some 20,000 shoe workers in factory towns across New England stopped work for six weeks to enforce demands for better pay. The strike was led by journeymen's unions but included a good many women, those who did outwork at home as well as those employed in the factories. The women were especially active in Lynn, Massachusetts, where they staged the strike's most widely reported parade. On March 7, two weeks into the strike, about 600 women braved a snowstorm to march through town with banners proclaiming, "American ladies will not be slaves," "May revolutions never cease while tyranny exists," and "Weak in physical strength but strong in moral courage, we dare to battle for the right, shoulder to shoulder with our fathers, husbands, and brothers." Male strikers marched behind the female contingents, and they too called for solidarity, their banners emblazoned with slogans like "As brothers we meet you. Our cause is just."[34] Townspeople came out to cheer the parade, and strikers from other shoe towns sent delegations.

This show of unity masked a split, however. As a journeyman from nearby Beverly observed, the men were striking "not as citizens and men merely but as heads of families,"[35] and in that spirit they had requested that the women restrict their pay demands so that male strikers might win more. Outworkers had readily agreed; since most lived in family households whose men worked in the shoe factories, they stood to benefit from a higher male wage. But there was resistance from factory women, most of them entirely self-supporting and about half from out of town. Just days before the parade on March 7, factory women had angrily abandoned the strike when outworkers reduced the high female wage demands earlier approved at a mass meeting. Strikers in other towns experienced the same division in less dramatic forms. Working women related to male shoe workers ardently supported the strike while most of the rest merely sat it out. If the

Great Shoemakers' Strike epitomized labor solidarity between men and women, it also revealed the boundaries of solidarity centered in the family.

Another fault line among working people divided native-born white Protestants from Catholics born in Europe. Labor campaigns of the 1840s and 1850s coincided with and in some instances blended with an anti-immigrant movement that especially targeted Irish Catholics. During the depression, nativism surged under the auspices of the American Republican Party, which was founded in 1841 and had major branches in New Orleans, Charleston, Boston, New York, Newark, Philadelphia, and St. Louis by late 1843. The party's platform called for immigrants' exclusion from politics. Public offices, it contended, should be reserved for native-born citizens, and immigrants should have to wait twenty-one years before they could file for naturalized citizenship and gain the right to vote. The party also charged that Catholicism—Irish Catholics in particular—caused most of the poverty, crime, and political corruption that plagued American cities. These arguments attracted a fair number of Protestant workingmen, especially those from skilled trades that employed few immigrants. In 1844, American Republican candidates swept municipal elections in New York City, and a wave of anti-Irish riots in Philadelphia claimed more than thirty lives.

A year later the party had sharply declined, but nativism flourished in new fraternal orders of white, native-born Protestants. While some were founded and led by men of the elite and mostly attracted genteel members, other nativist fraternities had working-class roots. The most popular was the Order of United American Mechanics (OUAM), born in Philadelphia in 1845 and quickly established in other cities in both the North and the South. Craft journeymen made up the great bulk of OUAM members, though master craftsmen with small shops joined as well. American Mechanics helped each other find jobs; promoted abstinence from alcohol, profanity, gambling, and sexual vice; and maintained a mutual insurance system that provided sick, unemployment, and death benefits. They also boycotted immigrant-owned businesses, pledged not to work with immigrant labor, and gathered on patriotic holidays to proclaim Protestant America's superiority to Catholic nations. Some of the journeymen's unions that sprang up in the 1840s and 1850s recruited their charter members from OUAM lodges or kindred groups.

Immigrants also built unions and in some big cities became the labor movement's driving force. The Laborer's Union Benevolent Association—organized in 1843 by Irish workingmen on New York City's docks and construction sites—became the country's biggest labor organization, with 6,000 members in 1850. By then, New York's craft unions were largely composed of Irish, German, and British immigrants, and the same pattern prevailed in all of the North's major cities. In 1849, British coal miners in Schuylkill County, Pennsylvania, established the country's first miners' union, one of many U.S. labor organizations founded by veterans of radical reform campaigns led by the Chartist movement in England. Many German unionists had radical backgrounds too; the most militant were the "Forty-Eighters," who had taken part in Germany's failed democratic revolution of 1848. Irish immigrants often had old-country experience in the radical Society of Ribbonmen or secret associations like the Whiteboys, which waged a guerrilla war against British colonialism. Infusing the American labor movement with new traditions of struggle, immigrants also expanded its awareness of struggles abroad. Native- as well as foreign-born labor activists attended mass meetings to congratulate British workers when Parliament passed a ten-hour law in 1847, to hail the revolutions that swept across Europe in 1848, and to express solidarity with Irish resistance to British rule.

In factory towns, on the other hand, immigrants and natives generally kept their distance from each other. That was especially true among workers in New England's cotton mills, where Irish Catholics became the largest ethnic group over the course of the 1850s. Unions born of the ten-hour campaign had mostly died out by the start of the decade, and working conditions were deteriorating. Yankee workers often blamed the decline on the Irish, who entered the mills at substandard pay and worked at speeds the Yankees had resisted. Sometimes employers recruited Irish strikebreakers. In 1851, mill overseers in Amesbury and Salisbury, Massachusetts, brought Irish immigrants to town to replace local people on strike over an elongation of the workday. For the most part, however, Irish workers replaced Yankee women departing for better jobs, and complaints against them were nothing more than bigotry dressed up as a grievance.

Some of the loudest complaints came from conservative quarters like the *New England Offering*, a journal edited by a former mill worker, largely written by Yankee operatives, and subsidized by textile companies. In July 1849, Eliza Jane Cate—author of several popular stories that celebrated Yankee workers like herself—turned her attention to the Irish immigrants who were a growing presence in the mills. She predicted that wages would fall on account of poor work by the Irish and that they would humbly submit to reductions "since they have little energy, few aspirations to be ministered unto by their gains, and . . . little of the home sentiment."[36] That was the gist of all nativist thinking: attribute character flaws to immigrants; then blame those alleged flaws for whatever was going wrong.

In the mid-1850s, a new nativist political movement gathered across the country, and garnered especially enthusiastic support in Massachusetts. In 1852, nativist fraternities organized the American Party, often called the "Know Nothings" because its founders disclaimed knowledge of the secret societies to which they belonged. The party's national platform replicated that of the American Republicans, but local Know Nothings often linked nativism and anti-Catholicism to other causes. In Massachusetts, where they endorsed labor reform, abolitionism, and women's rights, Know Nothings swept the state elections of 1854, winning the governorship, every seat in the state senate, and all but a few in the assembly. Once in power, they fired immigrants from state jobs, excluded them from the state militia, formed a committee to investigate Catholic convents, and instituted a literacy test for voters. They also enlarged the public school system, required that industrial workers under fifteen attend school several months of the year, abolished imprisonment for debt, granted property rights to married women, and passed resolution after resolution against slavery.

Conditions in the mills meanwhile continued to worsen, all the more swiftly after the economy slipped into a depression in 1857. In 1859, about 500 women—all immigrants and mostly Irish—struck several Lowell mills to protest wage cuts. None of the Yankee women supported the strike, and the low wages remained in force.

The most persistent and pernicious division among American workers was the color line. Not a single federation of labor unions included both black and white workers. The National Trades Union was entirely white and not by happenstance; its member unions and city centrals admitted whites only. Black activists were invited to a National Industrial Congress exactly once, in 1851, and the white Mechanics' Assembly of Philadelphia stormed out in protest.

A fair number of white workers supported the movement to abolish slavery. In upstate New York, the workingmen's parties of the early 1830s included antislavery planks in their platforms. Later that decade, craft journeymen provided the lion's share of signatures on the petitions that New York City's abolitionists sent to Congress. Mill workers in Lowell organized a Female Anti-Slavery Society in 1832, and twenty years later abolitionism had a large following in factories throughout New England. After touring the region in 1852, an organizer for the American Anti-Slavery Society reported that, "factory operatives *felt* the truth of the declaration that the Northern capitalist was close akin to the Southern slaveholder, and that the design of the Slave Power and Money Power is to *crush both black and white*."[37] German labor radicals also took strong stands for abolition. In San Antonio, Texas, the Forty-Eighter Adolph Douai published the Deep South's only abolitionist newspaper, until a proslavery mob ran him out of town in 1856.

For the most part, however, white workers were indifferent or hostile to abolitionism. Many argued that reform should begin at home, that white labor should focus on its own grievances. Some were put off by antislavery agitators who regarded the wage-labor system as a model of social justice. William Lloyd Garrison, the Boston editor who became the country's most prominent white abolitionist, alienated legions of working people in the 1830s when he asserted that all free men in America had equal opportunities to rise in the world, that workingmen's lowly state reflected nothing more than their own deficiencies, that those who blamed inequality on the rich and powerful were peddling a "pernicious doctrine."[38] In the 1850s, abolitionism's association with the Know Nothings alienated immigrants. Worker opposition to abolitionism also stemmed from desires to preserve the Democratic Party, whose core constituencies were workingmen in the North and slaveholders in the South. The Democratic press encouraged worries that slaves' emancipation would undermine white workers by flooding the job market with new competitors.

At bottom, anti-abolitionism rested on the same hard-core racism that made race riots part of the American landscape. Rioters often directed their fury at antislavery activists and symbols. For eight full days in July 1834, white mobs in New York City attacked antislavery meeting halls, stormed the home of a wealthy white abolitionist, and rampaged through black neighborhoods. Between 1832 and 1849, Philadelphia saw five major riots in which white workingmen invaded black districts to club and stone residents and destroy the churches and other buildings where abolitionists gathered. The Philadelphia riot of 1842 commenced with an assault on a black parade in honor of Britain's emancipation of slaves in the Caribbean.

In free black communities, abolitionism was the most vibrant social movement. In Boston, New York, Philadelphia, Cincinnati, and other northern cities with substantial black populations, antislavery work went hand in hand with agitation for equal voting rights, for the right to serve on juries, and for the desegregation of public schools and

SLAVE and WORKER

transportation. Black abolitionists also engaged in direct action to liberate fugitive slaves who had been apprehended. In 1833, an armed crowd in Detroit stopped a sheriff and his deputies from returning a Kentucky fugitive to his former master. In 1836, a group of women barged into a Boston courthouse and rescued two women fugitives. Starting that same year in New York City, many communities formed "vigilance committees" to harbor fugitive slaves, organize direct action on their behalf, and defend them in the courts.[39]

Black and white activists co-operated in the Underground Railroad, a clandestine network that helped up to 50,000 slaves escape to freedom. The railroad's best conductor was Harriet Tubman. Born a slave on the Eastern Shore of Maryland around 1820, she ran away to Pennsylvania in 1849 and became a hotel waitress in Philadelphia and Cape May, New Jersey. During the 1850s, she made thirteen trips back to Maryland, led out about seventy slaves, and inspired many more to escape on their own. Most of the people she rescued were members of her extended family.

In the workplace, as in unions, the color line was rigidly enforced. In 1838, Frederick Douglass arrived in New Bedford, Massachusetts, the center of the U.S. whaling industry and home to mariners of all colors from all over the world. The black community numbered over 1,000 in a city of 12,000, and included not only African Americans but also West Indians and Africans from the Cape Verde Islands. Black men voted, the public schools were integrated, and abolitionism had broad support among whites. But when Douglass applied for caulking work at a shipyard, he was told that the white caulkers would strike rather than work alongside a black man.

Black and white workers did make common cause on some occasions. In 1835, for example, they went on strike together at shipyards in Baltimore and Washington, D.C. Racial clashes were more typical, however, especially between black workers and white immigrants. In 1842, Irish coal miners in eastern Pennsylvania violently drove black men out of the mines, and Philadelphia's coal heavers warned that a riot would ensue if their employers hired any black men. In 1853, armed black laborers replaced Irish strikers on the Erie Railroad. In 1855, brawls broke out between Irish longshoremen on strike in New York City and black men who went in to work. As Frederick Douglass observed of the longshore strike, "Of course, colored men can feel under no obligations to hold out in a 'strike' with the whites, as the latter have never recognized them. Their expectation and determination were not to allow them to work at all."[40]

Black workers organized local unions of waiters, barbers, sailors, and ship caulkers, and sometimes a black union co-operated with its white counterpart. In 1853 in New York City, white hotel waiters who had just organized a union sought the counsel of the Waiters Protective Association, a black union that had already won a raise. A black waiter named Peter Hickman told them, "Gentlemen, I advise you to strike . . . for $18 a month, and if the landlords of this city do not give it, that you turn out, and be assured that we will never turn in in your places at less."[41] When white waiters did strike, a second black union hastily formed and sent its members to take the strikers' places. The Waiters Protective Association denounced the new group as a tool of the hoteliers and supported the strike to the end.

Mostly, black and white unions were in conflict if they were in touch at all. One of the worst confrontations erupted among caulkers in Baltimore's shipyards, where caulking was traditionally a black trade. In 1850, members of a black caulkers' association virtually monopolized the work, but over the next decade shipyards hired more and more German and Irish caulkers, sometimes bringing them in when the association called a strike. In 1858, the immigrants organized a rival union whose mission was to make caulking an entirely white trade. The union's members assaulted black workers and petitioned the state legislature to bar them from the shipyards. As violence flared, the black caulkers' association was dissolved by court order, and employers recognized the white union.

The land reform movement also placed black and white communities at odds. By the late 1840s, many white supporters of the National Reform Association had taken the position that wageworkers were in a worse position than slaves—"infinitely more depressed, degraded, and hopeless," to quote a spokesman for the association's New York City branch.[42] A decade later, Benjamin Gratz Brown, a Missouri legislator elected on a land reform platform, made the point more bluntly in a widely reprinted speech that declared his commitment to "EMANCIPATION OF THE WHITE RACE" through "legislation for the protection and profit of white labor."[43] That was hardly a formula for solidarity across the color line, but it could work in unintended ways. Though many land reformers shunned or even opposed abolition, they found themselves on a collision course with slaveholders as Americans debated slavery's extension to the West.

Westward Expansion and Irrepressible Conflict

The nation's expansion to the Pacific coast started largely as a southern drive to acquire new lands for cotton and new states for slavery. The Deep South was mostly cleared of indigenous people in the 1830s. Choctaws, Chickasaws, Cherokees, Creeks, and Seminoles were relocated to "Indian Territory" in what is now Oklahoma. Resistance succeeded in only a few cases. In Florida, Seminole villages and sister communities of fugitive slaves fought off the U.S. Army in a seven-year war starting in 1835, and some escaped relocation. In North Carolina and Tennessee, some Cherokees got away in the winter of 1837–38, when U.S. troops rounded up 17,000 people for a forced march to Indian Territory.

In the 1820s, American cotton growers and land speculators established slaveholding settlements in Texas, a province of newly independent Mexico. They clashed with the Mexican government after it abolished slavery in 1829 and later enacted laws to stop the American expatriates from importing slaves under the ruse that they were indentured. In 1835 the Americans rebelled, and in spring 1836 at San Jacinto they defeated an army led by Mexico's president, General Antonio López de Santa Anna. Captured in battle, Santa Anna bought his release by ceding independence to the province. It became the slaveholding Republic of Texas, whose president Sam Houston had earlier been the governor of Tennessee. Almost immediately, Texas began to petition for annexation to the United States, and in 1845 it became the twenty-eighth state.

The next year Congress declared war on Mexico, and by fall 1847, U.S. troops occupied Mexico City. In return for peace, the Americans demanded the northern half of Mexico, from California to what is now western Texas. It was transferred to the

United States in February 1848 under the Treaty of Guadalupe Hidalgo. The treaty stipulated that Mexicans living on this land would be treated as full-fledged U.S. citizens. Very quickly, however, the Americans set up special courts that reviewed Mexicans' land claims and nullified them by the hundreds. In New Mexico, about 3.7 million acres were confiscated; in California, the Southern Pacific Railroad wound up with 11 million acres. In what would become Arizona (part of New Mexico until 1863), U.S. companies took over the copper and silver mines, bringing in white workers and a two-tier wage system, one rate for whites and a lower "Mexican wage" for people of color.

The sharpest changes occurred in California, the site of a gold rush. Just a week before the Treaty of Guadalupe Hidalgo was signed, a mechanic struck gold on a construction site at Sutter's Mill in the New Helvetia colony near modern-day Sacramento. New Helvetia belonged to the German-Swiss entrepreneur John Sutter, who oversaw a gigantic wheat farm, a distillery, a hat factory, a blanket factory, a tannery, and various other businesses. These enterprises employed indigenous men and women recruited from local Miwok and Nisenan settlements. The workers were paid in disks that could be redeemed for goods at Sutter's store and policed by his private army of 200 Indians commanded by German officers. Native Americans in California would face much worse than this after gold was discovered.

Gold seekers swarmed into California from all over the United States and Mexico and from Europe, Central and South America, Australia, and China. As soon as they arrived, they made a beeline for Indian country in the interior, where the gold had been found. Some native communities were massacred, many others pushed off their land. At first they survived through wage work in mines and on ranches, but before long most of them were displaced by the many unlucky gold prospectors who now needed jobs. In 1855, the U.S. Army forced California Indians onto five reservations where they would supposedly feed themselves by growing wheat, but the land suitable for cultivation was too little to support everyone. California's indigenous population fell from about 150,000 in 1848 to 30,000 in 1860.

The new Anglo-American elite in California dreaded Mexican resistance. In July 1856, Los Angeles raised four vigilante companies to safeguard against a revolution after an Anglo constable fatally shot a Mexican man whose guitar he had tried to repossess on behalf of a creditor and the Mexican community rose up in protest. Another alarm went out the following year when a young man named Juan Flores escaped from San Quentin prison, organized a band of more than fifty Mexicans, and skirmished with Anglo lawmen. Again, Los Angeles raised vigilantes. They chased the band for eleven days, finally captured Flores and most of his men, and hanged him and three others before delivering the rest to legal authorities.

Some Tejanos (Mexican Texans) took up arms as well. In 1859, Juan Cortina, son of a prominent ranching family in the Brownsville area, led some sixty guerrillas—mostly ranch hands—in a campaign to redress Tejano grievances. Proclaiming their "sacred right of self-preservation," the band freed Mexicans from the Brownsville jail, raided the stores of Anglo merchants, and executed four Anglos who had gone unpunished for killing Mexicans.[44] By the end of the year, Cortina had more than 1,000 followers. On December 27, they were defeated by the U.S. Army, but skirmishing continued into 1860 and Cortina was never caught.

The annexation of northern Mexico intensified the national debate over slavery. In 1848, the House of Representatives endorsed a proposal to ban slavery from the lands annexed under Guadalupe Hidalgo, but the measure failed in the Senate. That same year antislavery Democrats and Whigs broke away to form the Free Soil Party, which carried on the fight against slavery's extension. Growing numbers of white workers and farmers supported the cause in the name of land reform, demanding that western lands be set aside for poor homesteaders rather than speculators or, they now added, slaveholding planters. New York's senator William Seward hit the nail on the head in a famous speech on the rising discord: "It is an irrepressible conflict between opposing and enduring forces, and it means that the United States must and will, sooner or later, become either entirely a slaveholding nation, or entirely a free-labor nation."[45]

Congress tried vainly to put the conflict to rest with a package of laws known as the Compromise of 1850: California joined the federal union as the sixteenth free state, and the number of slave states remained at fifteen. New Mexico and Utah were recognized as formal U.S. territories without any prohibitions against slavery. Slave trading was banned from Washington, D.C., but not slavery itself. Congress pledged not to interfere with the interstate slave trade, and it passed a Fugitive Slave Act that commissioned federal marshals to hunt down runaway slaves and set up special courts to facilitate the re-enslavement of anyone who got caught.

In defiance of the Fugitive Slave Act, black communities' vigilance committees stepped up rescue activities, and more and more whites lent a hand. In one famous incident in 1851, abolitionists in the rural town of Christiana, Pennsylvania, battled a posse of slaveholders and federal agents who arrived with warrants for four runaways. Thirty-one blacks and five whites were arrested for this incident, which left a slaveholder dead and another seriously wounded. Just one person, a white man, was brought to trial, and a sympathetic jury found him not guilty.

Tensions escalated in 1854, when Congress passed the Kansas-Nebraska Act that called for "popular sovereignty"—each new state would decide for itself whether to be a slaveholding state or free. This plan enraged Free Soilers and antislavery factions among the Democrats, Whigs, and Know Nothings. In summer 1854, they came together to found the Republican Party. Advancing the slogan "Free Soil, Free Labor," the new party called for an end to slavery's expansion and to federal laws supporting its existence.[46] Warfare meanwhile erupted in Kansas; as it moved toward statehood under the popular-sovereignty plan, both slaveholders and abolitionists organized guerrilla bands to stamp out the opposition. In May 1856, violence penetrated the halls of Congress. A few days after the Republican senator Charles Sumner of Massachusetts publicly referred to slavery as a "harlot" eagerly embraced by the southern elite, South Carolina's Democratic congressman Preston Brooks used a heavy cane to beat Sumner almost to death on the floor of the Senate.[47]

In the South, slave resistance heightened. Group escapes, plots, and mutinies were reported in Missouri and Virginia in 1850; North Carolina, Texas, and Virginia in 1851; Virginia again in 1852; Louisiana in 1853 and 1854; and Maryland, Mississippi, and Louisiana in 1855. The momentum accelerated in mid-1856, against the backdrop of a presidential election in which slavery was the principal issue. In Tennessee, four slaves working in an iron foundry near Dover were sentenced to death for plotting insurrection, and 150 black men marched on the town in an attempt to free the prisoners. In North Carolina, fugitive slaves living in the swamps near Lumberton stepped up guerrilla attacks on slaveholders and fought off posses that tried to clear the swamps. By the end of the year, every slaveholding state but Delaware was rife with news of slave riots and conspiracies, some of which involved white abolitionists. Tejanos also aided rebel slaves. In September 1856, authorities in Colorado County, Texas, expelled Mexicans for helping to arm more than 200 slaves conspiring to revolt. In a letter to newspapers across the South, these authorities warned that "the lower class of the Mexican population are incendiaries in any country where slaves are held, and should be dealt with accordingly."[48]

In the North, the newborn Republican Party, which embraced the Free Soil cause, won substantial working-class support in 1856. Increasingly, white workers defined slavery and slaveholders as menaces not only to land reform but also to free labor. A Republican labor convention in Pittsburgh made the case at length in a pamphlet addressed to the workingmen of Pennsylvania. The heart of the argument was simple:

> In another section of our country exists a practical aristocracy owning Labor, and made thereby independent of us. With them Labor is servitude and Freedom is only compatible with mastership. They despise us. They call us "Greasy Mechanics," "Filthy Operatives" . . . and being gentlemen, no doubt believe what they say. . . . These aristocrats desire to extend [their] system over all the territories of the nation. To extend it over the territories is to give them supreme power in the government, and then they will extend it over us.[49]

This was not an unreasonable fear; some prominent defenders of slavery did suggest that in a better world all labor would be enslaved.

In 1857, the U.S. Supreme Court gave its seal of approval to slavery and further galvanized the opposition. The case involved a lawsuit by Dred Scott, a Missouri slave who claimed to be legally free because his owner had taken him into Illinois and Wisconsin, where slavery was prohibited. The court ruled against Scott, finding that he was not entitled to sue in federal court because slaves were not U.S. citizens. According to Chief Justice Roger Taney, free blacks were not citizens either. That question had been settled long ago, he wrote, for the republic's founders had made clear their conviction that all black people were "so far inferior, that they had no rights which the white man was bound to respect."[50] The Supreme Court now affirmed that opinion, and ruled in addition that federal laws to restrict slavery's spread were unconstitutional because they deprived slaveholders of property without due process.

Across the North, antislavery forces protested the Dred Scott decision; across the South, slave resistance continued. Then, on October 16, 1859, the white abolitionist John Brown—already notorious for the savagery of his guerrilla campaigns in Kansas—led a raid on the federal arsenal in Harper's Ferry, Virginia. After two days of fighting, Brown and his band of eighteen men, both black and white, were all killed or captured. The raid attracted national attention, as did the trials of the surviving participants, who were convicted of treason and sentenced to death. As John Brown awaited his execution, black communities throughout the North held meetings in honor of the "old man." A resolution passed in New Bedford, Massachusetts, was typical: "Resolved, that the memory of John Brown shall be indelibly written upon the tablets of our hearts, and when tyrants cease to oppress the enslaved, we will teach our children to revere his name."[51] More immediately, over the summer of 1860, at least eleven slave plots and insurrections led or abetted by whites were suppressed in Georgia, Alabama, Mississippi, and Texas. At least twenty slaves and a dozen white men were hanged or lynched in Texas alone.

Many Americans continued to hope that slavery's defenders and enemies could peacefully coexist. Many white workers remained loyal to the Democratic Party, which supported the popular-sovereignty doctrine and the Dred Scott decision. But votes from small farmers and workingmen were enough to elect Republican Abraham Lincoln to the presidency in 1860. The Republican platform called for a ban on the admission of slaveholding states; for the abolition of slavery in the District of Columbia, all U.S. territories, and American ships on the high seas; for the end of the interstate slave trade; for strict enforcement of the ban on importing slaves from abroad; and for slaveholders' exclusion from federal jobs at all levels, from local post offices to Capitol Hill.

Even before Lincoln took office, the South's planter elite organized insurrection, and slaveholding states began to secede from the federal union. By mid-April 1861, the country was at war. On his way to execution, John Brown had left behind a note predicting that the national crime of slavery "*will* never be purged *away*; but with Blood." Now that prophecy would be fulfilled.[52]

4

Civil War and Reconstruction

By the eve of the Civil War, slavery gripped more Americans, ruled more states, and produced more dollars than ever before. The federal government had protected it from the earliest days of the republic, but never more vigorously than in the 1850s. When Abraham Lincoln's election threatened this arrangement, the South's master class confidently decided to break away from the federal union of states.

South Carolina seceded in late December 1860. The rest of the lower South soon followed: Mississippi, Florida, Alabama, Georgia, Louisiana, and Texas. In February 1861, the secessionists founded the Confederate States of America, later joined by Virginia, North Carolina, Tennessee, and Arkansas. In his inaugural address that March, Lincoln declared secession unlawful and assured the South, "I have no purpose directly or indirectly to interfere with the institution of slavery in the States where it exists."[1] Confederate states could return to the union without reprisal and with full faith that slavery would stay intact. But things had gone too far for that.

In mid-April, the Confederates answered Lincoln by bombarding the U.S. garrison at Fort Sumter in Charleston's harbor. On April 15, the president called for volunteers to fight the Confederacy; within days, troops were skirmishing along its northern borders. Confederate leaders fully expected to win the war. Since slaves did much of the work, many white men were free to fight, and most had received military training in the large militias southern states maintained. The war had some powerful opponents in the North, whose bankers and merchants generally wanted peace and a resumption of trade with southern planters. Britain, whose giant textile industry depended on American cotton, seemed likely to side with the Confederacy. If the North had more men and factories to equip an army, the South's prospects still looked bright.

What the Confederates did not anticipate was that slaves would mobilize for the South's defeat. By running away, by sabotaging production, by working and fighting for the Union army, slaves doomed the Confederacy. Southern leaders did not foresee that, but Lincoln did when his Emancipation Proclamation, issued on January 1, 1863, declared that the Confederacy's slaves "henceforward shall be free" and ordered that freedmen be received into the Union's military forces.[2] Abolitionism surged in the North; by the end of the war, Congress had passed a constitutional amendment to eradicate slavery and the states were poised to ratify the measure. The Fifty-Fourth Massachusetts, one of the Union army's black regiments, meanwhile marched into Charleston, followed by columns of black civilians, and together they burned down the city's slave market.

These were the early scenes of a second American revolution in which the victory over slavery sparked other insurgencies. Southern freedpeople struggled to claim their rights as workers and citizens. Northern workers revived the labor movement and organized on the political front. The women's rights movement campaigned for female suffrage. Like the first revolution, however, this one was incomplete. More than fifty years would pass before the Constitution recognized women's right to vote, and most of the gains made by freedpeople and northern workers were soon wiped out.

The Civil War

The war defied the expectations of political and social leaders on both sides. Confederate and Union officials alike thought the war would be over in short order and involve minimal casualties. The fighting began in a festive atmosphere, with high-society Charleston toasting the bombardment of Fort Sumter and upper-class residents of Washington, D.C., driving their carriages out to northern Virginia to watch and cheer the early battles. At first, moreover, neither side identified the war as a conflict over slavery. The Confederacy claimed to fight for states' rights to independence; the Lincoln administration's only declared aim was to "save the Union."[3] Contrary to expectations on both sides, however, the war dragged on for four long years and the casualties were enormous. Against this backdrop, slavery's abolition became a central Union cause.

The Civil War was the bloodiest conflict in U.S. history. It claimed the lives of 618,000 troops and uncounted numbers of civilians, and it maimed hundreds of thousands more. New military technology—the Winchester repeating rifle and the Gatling revolving machine gun—produced some of this carnage. Military tactics— long-term bombardment and mass charges against defensive formations and fortifications—produced even more. Most died from the complications of mass warfare; two-thirds succumbed to disease, hunger, or sheer exhaustion. Military camps were rife with mumps, measles, malaria, and typhoid; prisoners of war were packed into stockades with little food and less care, and thousands of them died of starvation or disease. Yet out of this carnage came one of the most glorious chapters in U.S. history—the eradication of chattel slavery.

African Americans argued from the start that the Union's war against the Confederate secession could not be won unless it became a war against slavery. Likening slavery to a snake, Harriet Tubman warned Lincoln that it would "spring up and bite you ag[a]in . . . till you kill him."[4] Since the Confederacy's wealth and power rested on slavery, the Union would ultimately be compelled, in the words of Tubman's comrade John Rock, "to take slavery by the throat, and sooner or later . . . choke her to death."[5] With that idea in mind, free black men were among the first to form volunteer companies when Lincoln called for troops to fight the Confederacy. In the spring of 1862, Tubman herself went to the Sea Islands of South Carolina to work as a nurse to the 10,000 former slaves who had stayed behind when their masters fled the previous December.

The federal government dragged its feet. Fearful of alienating slaveholding states that had not seceded (Missouri, Kentucky, West Virginia, Maryland, and Delaware), it not only hesitated to throttle slavery but also refused to enlist black regiments during the opening years of the war. A handful of white regiments admitted black men, and a few light-skinned blacks enlisted by "passing" as white; but, for the most part, African Americans were turned away. As Union casualties mounted and Confederate victories multiplied, however, the Lincoln administration had no choice but to change its stand on slavery and the enlistment of black troops. Only then did the Union start to win the war.

This shift in Union fortunes on the battlefield galvanized abolitionists on the home front. Their movement swelled, as did their political clout. By the time the war ended in April 1865, Missouri, Maryland, and West Virginia had abolished slavery on their own, and more than a million northerners had signed petitions in favor of the Thirteenth Amendment, whose ratification at the end of that year would erase the last legal vestiges of slavery from U.S. soil.

Working people had a major hand in transforming the Union's war from a fight against secession into a fight against slavery. Slaves played the leading role. As soon as the war started, they seized every opportunity to flee from their masters and make their way to Union army camps. These refugees from bondage numbered about a half-million by the end of 1862. Military and government officials called them "contraband of war" or "contrabands."[6] The historian W.E.B. Du Bois has more aptly described them as participants in a "general strike" against the Confederacy—a strike waged not only by those who reached Union camps but also by the legions of people who were unable to escape bondage but weakened the Confederacy from within by engaging in slowdowns, arson, and other forms of sabotage.[7]

Though some of the refugees soon left military camps for northern cities, large numbers stayed on to work for the Union army as scouts, spies, construction laborers, stevedores, mariners, laundresses, and nurses. In some cases, they served as soldiers, even before federal policy authorized their enlistment. In recognition of this assistance, several Union generals declared the refugees free by military order, and in summer 1862 Congress proclaimed the freedom of all slaves who escaped from Confederate masters.

The fact that the so-called contrabands had proved a crucial military asset—and could be even more valuable if allowed to enlist as soldiers—was clearly on Abraham Lincoln's mind when he penned the Emancipation Proclamation. This document, which proclaimed the freedom of all slaves under Confederate rule, did not immediately change anyone's actual status, for it applied only to slaves in areas that the U.S. government did not control. The proclamation did have immense repercussions, however. It foreclosed the possibility that Confederate states would be brought back into the Union as slaveholding states—an arrangement the Lincoln administration had repeatedly offered in the early days of the war. The Emancipation Proclamation also turned the Union army into an army of liberation that dismantled slavery as it advanced into Confederate territory. Most important for the Union's military fortunes, the Emancipation Proclamation announced that the U.S. armed forces would henceforth welcome black men. They had previously fought in very small numbers, under the banners of white regiments; now they would form all-black regiments and fight en masse.

Following the Emancipation Proclamation, about 186,000 black men entered the U.S. armed forces; they made up nearly 35 percent of all troops enlisted by the Union during the final two years of the war. Of the black troops, about 134,000 (72 percent) had been slaves when the war began. African American regiments served in the war's most vicious battles and distinguished themselves for bravery under fire. Harriet Tubman again was exceptional. After a stint in Florida, where she nursed Union soldiers sick with dysentery, she returned to South Carolina and, from 1863 through 1864, headed a corps of scouts and riverboat pilots that supported guerrilla raids deep into Confederate territory. Dressed as a soldier, wearing trousers, and carrying a rifle, Tubman personally participated in many of these raids. The most famous took place on June 1, 1863, when she guided a foray up the Combahee River. As a Boston weekly later reported:

HARRIET TUBMAN

Colonel Montgomery and his gallant band of 300 black soldiers, under the guidance of a black woman, dashed into the enemy's country, struck a bold and effective blow, destroying millions of dollars worth of commissary stores, cotton and lordly dwellings, and striking terror into the heart of rebeldom, brought off near 800 slaves, and thousands of dollars worth of property, without losing a man or receiving a scratch.[8]

The actual numbers were 150 soldiers and 756 slaves. After she reconnoitered the area, Tubman insisted that the colonel lead the raid; he had fought alongside John Brown in Kansas. She herself gathered the fugitives onto the three gunboats used in the raid.

Conditions of service were much harsher for black soldiers than for their white counterparts. The Confederates summarily executed black prisoners of war; the most notorious incident, known as the Fort Pillow massacre, took place in April 1864 in western Tennessee. The federal government itself discriminated against black troops. Although military recruiters promised them the same pay as white troops—$13 a month plus $3.50 for clothing—they were in fact paid the same as black laborers—$10 a month less $3 deducted for clothing. The *Christian Recorder* printed a communication from a soldier in the Fifty-Fifth Massachusetts regiment:

Resolved, that even as the founders of our Republic resisted the British tax on tea on the ground of principle, so did we claim equal pay with other volunteers, because we believed our military and civil equality at issue,— and independently of the fact, that such pay was actually promised; and not because we regulated our patriotism and love of race, by any given sum of money.[9]

To protest the injustice, many black soldiers refused to take any pay at all. Some did more: Sergeant William Walker of the Third South Carolina Volunteers was executed for leading a group of protestors who stacked their arms, in effect going on strike. Congress finally granted retroactive equal pay to free black recruits in June 1864 and to former slaves in March 1865.

White workingmen also played an important role in the Union's war against slavery. From the start, the Union army was mainly composed of laboring men—small farmers and wageworkers. They made up the vast bulk of all adult males in northern society and an even larger proportion of those who signed up to fight the Confederacy when Lincoln called for volunteers. In some cases, members of local labor unions signed up as a group. The federal government estimated at the end of the war that up to 750,000 men had left industrial jobs for the Union army. Wage earners—both industrial workers and farm hands—served in higher proportions than any other sector of northern society and composed more than 90 percent of a great many Union regiments.

White workers in the North were by no means unanimous in opposing the Confederacy, however. That was quite clear in the federal elections of fall 1862; the Democratic Party, which advocated peace with the Confederacy, gained congressional seats as pro-war Republicans lost ground. During the months preceding Election Day, white workingmen in a number of northern cities had struck or rioted to protest the hiring of black men. The Democratic Party fanned these flames by declaring that Republicans planned to "turn the slaves of the Southern states loose to overrun the North and enter into competition with the white laboring masses."[10]

In the minds of many white workers, the Emancipation Proclamation proved such accusations correct. This fueled long-standing resentments against African Americans and the Republican Party, and tensions came to a head when the federal government instituted a military draft in March 1863. Draftees could avoid service by paying a $300 fee or by hiring others to take their places, and many rich men exercised these options. When poor men were drafted, however, they had no choice but to serve. In July 1863, anger at this inequity combined with racial hostility to spark a bloody four-day riot in New York City, where white mobs attacked the property of wealthy white Republicans and terrorized black communities with arson, assaults, and lynchings. Estimates of the number of people killed in the riots range from 400 to 1,000.

For the most part, however, northern workers supported the war; and their determination to see it through generally grew deeper and stronger after the Emancipation Proclamation was issued in January 1863. Pro-war Republicans swept most local elections in the fall of that year. Their success at the polls is largely attributable to the fact that the Union army scored significant victories once black men were allowed to enlist. Union victories also grew more politically inspiring now that the U.S. Army was an army of liberation.

As pro-war sentiment swelled, so did active opposition to slavery. This was partly in recognition of African Americans' crucial contributions to the Union's war but also a result of abolitionists' increased activity following the Emancipation Proclamation. Now that one of the Union's official aims was to dismantle slavery in the Confederacy—slavery's very heart—abolitionists became the war's most ardent supporters. They took the lead in organizing a gigantic network of Loyal Leagues, Union Leagues, and Equal Rights Leagues that coordinated and linked pro-war and anti-slavery agitation in both black and white communities. Steadily gaining momentum, this movement propelled Missouri, Maryland, and West Virginia to abolish slavery; launched the petition drive calling for an antislavery amendment to the U.S. Constitution; reelected Lincoln in the fall of 1864; enabled antislavery Republicans to sweep that year's congressional elections; galvanized support for the Thirteenth Amendment when it was sent to the states for ratification; and successfully pushed the outgoing Congress to established the Bureau of Freedmen, Refugees, and Abandoned Lands (known as the Freedmen's Bureau) to coordinate protection and services for freed slaves and to redistribute land that had been confiscated by the Union army.

In April 1865, the Confederacy collapsed like a house of cards. By the end of the year, the Thirteenth Amendment had been added to the Constitution, legally banishing slavery from U.S. soil. It was a breathtaking advance—downright unimaginable before the war—and though everyone who backed the Union's war contributed to the victory, it originated among slaves themselves. They were the first to see the war's revolutionary potential.

Much remained to be done. Returning north from her service in South Carolina, Harriet Tubman was forcibly removed from a train's passenger car by the conductor and three other white men, who refused to recognize her military pass. She rode from Virginia to New York City in a baggage car.[11] A convention of veterans from Iowa's Sixtieth U.S. Colored Infantry declared in October 1865, "that he who is worthy to be trusted with the musket can and ought to be trusted with the ballot."[12] Except for the New Englanders, black veterans of the Civil War went home to states where they could not vote.

Southern Reconstruction and Counterrevolution

The Confederacy's defeat raised two key questions. On what terms would the former Confederate states be readmitted to the Union? What would happen to the nearly 4 million African Americans who had been enslaved when the war began? The answers were closely related.

Southern life had turned upside down. A family story handed down through generations illustrates the pattern. Caroline Gordon, known as Caddy, was a field hand on a Mississippi plantation when she heard the news that the Confederates had surrendered. As her great granddaughter would later tell the family, "Caddy threw down [her] hoe, she marched herself up to the big house, then, she looked around and found the mistress. She went over to the mistress, she flipped up her dress, and told the white woman to do something. She said it mean and ugly. This is what she said: 'Kiss my ass!'"[13] Sometimes alone, but more often in groups, freedpeople across the South celebrated the Confederacy's defeat.

But the old order did not disappear. Andrew Johnson, the Tennessean who became the president after Lincoln's assassination on April 14, 1865, sought quick reconciliation with the former Confederacy. He pardoned most of the rebels, put them in charge of reconstructing state governments, and directed that the vast tracts of lands seized by the Union army be returned to the previous owners. To earn readmission to the Union, rebel states had only to ratify the Thirteenth Amendment and repudiate the Confederate debt. White southern leaders moved quickly. They drafted new state constitutions that included elaborate "Black Codes," which denied black men the right to vote and hold office, barred black children from public schools, and instituted labor laws designed to keep freedpeople at work under slave-like conditions. Under the Black Codes, for instance, freedpeople could be jailed for vagrancy if they did not sign year-long labor contracts with white employers, and failure to serve out the term of the contract constituted a criminal offense. By December 1865, ten of the former Confederate states (all but Texas) had met the president's requirements for readmission.

Freedpeople made the best they could of their limited liberty. They reunited with family members sold away under slavery. They sent their children to the "freedmen's schools" set up by the federal government. They petitioned Congress for equal rights as citizens. They moved to cities to find alternatives to plantation labor. They organized to improve their working conditions. On the New Orleans waterfront, black and white dockworkers joined together and successfully struck for higher wages, though the whites demanded and got even more. Some freedpeople managed to get farms of their own, often purchased with the discharge bonuses received by Union army veterans.

Violence against freedpeople became widespread; beyond the many beatings and murders of individuals, there were mass slaughters. In Memphis, Tennessee, on May 1–3, 1866, forty-six black men (mostly Union veterans) and two whites were killed by mobs that also torched much of the black community and raped several black women. On July 30, a white mob rioted in New Orleans, killing at least thirty-five black people and injuring more than a hundred. Both riots were suppressed by federal troops, not local police.

Congressional Republicans had had enough. A radical faction supported black equality under the law and opposed negotiations with former rebels. Moderate Republicans meanwhile feared that, when southerners returned to Congress, they would challenge protective tariffs (good for manufacturers but not for planters) and possibly press for a default on the Union's war debts (owed to northern financiers). If freedmen were enfranchised, moreover, they would surely vote for the Republican Party's candidates; that appealed to radicals and moderates alike. When the newly elected southern delegates showed up to take their seats in Congress, the Republican-controlled House and Senate turned them away.

Still, Reconstruction stalled. Congress failed to override President Johnson's veto of an act establishing military courts to prosecute the many violations of freedpeople's civil rights. Congress did override another veto to pass a Civil Rights Act (1866) that was the first federal law to embrace the principle that all U.S. citizens are entitled to equal protection under the law. Congress also passed the Fourteenth Amendment, which prohibited states from violating U.S. citizens' "privileges and immunities" and from failing to give every citizen "equal protection of the laws."[14] The Civil Rights Act was routinely ignored, however; and the Fourteenth Amendment failed to win ratification because it was rejected by the legislatures of every former Confederate state except for Tennessee.

Then the congressional elections of fall 1866 gave Radical Republicans decisive majorities in both the House and the Senate; and the following spring, when the new Congress took office, the era of Radical Reconstruction began. On March 2, 1867, overriding yet another presidential veto, Congress passed a new Reconstruction Act. The ten former Confederate states that had rejected the Fourteenth Amendment came under martial law. To rejoin the Union, these states were now required to allow black men to vote and hold office, exclude former Confederate officials from voting and holding office, and ratify the Fourteenth Amendment. Under this plan, about 1.3 million men became eligible to vote. About 700,000 of them were African Americans; the others were poor white men formerly excluded because they did not own land. The first elections held under Radical Reconstruction chose delegates to constitutional conventions that overhauled state governments from 1867 through 1869.

The new governments were the most democratic the South had ever seen. Freedpeople poured tremendous energy into grassroots politics, sometimes in alliance with poor whites, usually under the auspices of organizations known as Union Leagues, Loyal Leagues, or Republican Clubs. In the lower South, where black voters were often the majority, African American men were elected to local and state offices. Mississippi, Louisiana, and South Carolina sent black men to the U.S. Congress. In the presidential election of 1868, freedmen's ballots provided the margin of victory for the Republican candidate, General Ulysses S. Grant.

Reconstructed governments eliminated all property requirements for voting and holding office. They rescinded the Black Codes. They recognized labor's right to organize. They abolished imprisonment for debt. They built public hospitals, orphanages, and asylums. They created the South's first free public school systems. They ratified the Fourteenth Amendment (adopted July 1868) and also the Fifteenth Amendment (adopted March 1870), which prohibited states from depriving citizens of voting rights "on account of race, color, or previous condition of servitude."[15]

Black workers at last had some elbow room to organize for better wages and working conditions. In March 1866, field-workers on a Louisiana plantation stopped work when the proprietor was late paying monthly wages. Black "washerwomen" (as they called themselves) in Jackson, Mississippi, announced on June 20 that year that they would no longer work for less than $1.50 a day. Black stevedores in Savannah, Georgia, went out on strike in February 1867 to protest a new municipal tax imposed on them. In April, black stevedores went on strike in Richmond, Virginia, and Mobile, Alabama.

Radical Reconstruction had severe limitations, however. One was its failure to reclaim and redistribute the vast acres of farmland President Johnson had returned to the planters. Few freedpeople ever acquired their own farms; most became sharecroppers, sometimes on the same plantations where they had been enslaved, employed by the same men who had owned them before the war.

Sharecropping relied on debt and credit. Contracts ran a calendar year, bound an entire family, provided a small monthly wage, and promised landlords a share (onefourth to one-half) of the crop. On the annual day of reckoning, the landlord first deducted various levies against the proceeds—payments for seed, tools, and draft animals supplied by the landlord; money for goods and supplies purchased on credit; and fines for days missed on account of sickness, bad weather, or absence, and for disobedience or insubordination. After the deductions, the worker's share might amount to only a few dollars; sometimes the deductions were so large and the proceeds so small (because of a poor crop, a fall in prices for agricultural commodities, or just plain cheating) that the worker owed money to the landlord. A family that ended the year free and clear could look for a new, perhaps better contract with a different landlord, but families in debt had to stay put for another year. Arkansas sharecropper Henry Blake later recalled: "A man that didn't know how to count would always lose. He might lose anyhow. They didn't give no itemized statement. No, you just had to take their word. . . . If you didn't make no money, that's all right; they would advance you more. But . . . you better not try to leave and get caught. They'd keep you in debt. . . . If there was an argument he [the landlord] would get mad and there would be a shooting take place."[16] For some families, debt peonage continued for generations.

Radical Reconstruction entailed other compromises too. Public school systems, hospitals, asylums, and other institutions remained segregated by race. The color line in employment went unchallenged; like their northern counterparts, black southerners had fewer job opportunities than whites and earned lower wages for comparable work. Even education might not help; black women trained as schoolteachers often worked as laundresses or domestic servants, and men with college degrees frequently had to settle for manual labor.

Neither the Freedmen's Bureau nor the U.S. Army could stop the violence aimed at freedpeople. Organizations like the Ku Klux Klan and the Knights of the White Camelia unleashed a wave of arson, beatings, rapes, and murders targeting black political leaders and activists, schoolteachers, professionals like doctors and lawyers, independent farmers and small businesspeople, and anyone who organized unions, strikes, or other labor actions.[17] But trouble could come with little provocation. In the early 1870s, a witness from Georgia told a congressional committee about landlords' deployment of terrorism against sharecroppers: "If they have any difficulty with a [N]egro, he is reported to the Ku-Klux. I saw that, just about the time they got done laying by their crops, the Ku-Klux would be brought in upon them, and they would be run off, so that they [the landlords] could take their crops."[18] Violence became so common that sometimes whole communities were "lying out" at night—sleeping in the fields and woods to avoid the nightriders.[19]

By 1870, every ex-Confederate state had been readmitted to the Union. In 1872, an amnesty act restored electoral rights to most ex-Confederates. Following his reelection that year, President Grant appointed prominent white southerners to federal jobs and pardoned Klansmen convicted of violating freedpeople's civil rights. Congress meanwhile dismantled the Freedmen's Bureau, and planters and their allies set their sights on the Radical Republican state governments. Conservative Democrats—sometimes in alliance with white Republicans—had already come to power in several states in which white voters were the majority, and this pattern was quickly replicated in other mostly white states. The counterrevolution then turned to states where black men formed substantial political blocs, casting the lion's share of votes in many counties if not statewide. Using terror campaigns to keep African Americans from voting and election fraud to keep Radical Republicans from winning, Democrats came to power in states where Reconstruction had been most advanced: Mississippi in 1875 and South Carolina and Louisiana in 1876.

Freedpeople resisted heroically. Henry Adams—born a slave in Georgia in 1843, sold to a plantation near Logansport, Louisiana, and emancipated at the end of the war—served for three years in the Union Army, where he learned to read and write. Discharged in September 1869, he settled in Shreveport, where he worked as a rail-splitter, plantation manager, and faith healer. In 1870, he joined other black veterans to form "The Committee," whose 500 members organized Republican Clubs, advised freedpeople of their legal rights, distributed ballots at election time, and investigated fraud at the polling places, swindles by landlords, and terrorist attacks. Adams became president of Shreveport's Republican Club in 1874, which got him fired from his plantation job. That year's elections were accompanied by unprecedented "bulldozing"—assassinations, beatings, arson—and the Republican Clubs fell apart in the countryside. Adams and his committee tried hard to rebuild the clubs for the 1876 elections, but the local White League stepped up its terror, and the Democrats won easily.

Though they knew election fraud and voter intimidation were occurring, federal officials did not intervene. In 1874 Radical Republicans lost their hold on Congress, and the national party soon deserted freedpeople. By the time President Grant left office in March 1877, he had withdrawn federal troops from every ex-Confederate state except South Carolina and Louisiana. His replacement, the Republican Rutherford B. Hayes, completed the withdrawals in April.

The radical governments were replaced with regimes that legally subordinated African Americans and strictly controlled their labor. They directed funding away from public education and projects like poor relief. They stifled black political activity with violence and deceit, and drove many black officials from their positions—those who remained depended on white patronage. They passed statutes reminiscent of the postwar Black Codes, criminalizing unemployment ("vagrancy") and quitting a job before the end of a contract. They developed extensive convict-labor systems, leasing prisoners to work without pay for railroad, mining, and lumber companies. They refined sharecropping laws to make sure landlords received their profits whether or not crops brought enough money to cover workers' wages too.

Many freedpeople abandoned any hope of building a decent life in the South and organized to leave for some other place where, as one activist put it, "a man can enjoy his political opinions without being murdered."[20] Despite opposition from the Klan, associations promoting black emigration sprang up all over the South. In 1877, the committee established by Henry Adams and others became the Colonization Council and held meetings throughout the region. The next year violence against freedpeople in rural communities grew worse. Fifty-nine African Americans—Adams among them—went to New Orleans to testify about the terror, then could not return to their home parishes, where the White League had marked them for murder. In the spring of 1879, about 6,000 black residents of Louisiana, Mississippi, and eastern Texas migrated to Kansas by riverboat, joined the next winter by 3,000 to 4,000 more from Texas who came by wagon or rail. These migrants, who called themselves "Exodusters," settled in as farm laborers, railroad workers, miners, domestics, and laundresses. By 1880, about a third had acquired their own land.[21] Adams himself remained in New Orleans, advocating emigration until at least 1884.

Although aimed at freedpeople, the counterrevolution that ended Radical Reconstruction harmed all labor, not just in the South but in the nation as a whole. The de facto disenfranchisement of freedpeople—a large portion of working-class Americans—increased the employing classes' edge in both regional and national politics. Also, by giving American manufacturers a low-wage haven to run to, the repressive labor system of the "New South" would eventually discipline workers in other regions too.

"Up with the People"

As Reconstruction and counterrevolution wracked the South, labor struggles elsewhere in the country traced a parallel course. During the war years a wave of workplace organizing occurred in northern states as the economy boomed on war production and inflation hit rents and prices. Despite the occasional use of troops to break strikes against firms engaged in war-related production, wartime strikes for higher wages often succeeded in short order. Hundreds of local unions sprang up, citywide assemblies of unions reappeared, and about a dozen "national" unions connected locals in various cities. African Americans in Union states began to build a black labor movement; in 1862, black sailors in New York City formed the American Seaman's Protective Association—the first seamen's union in the United States.

Peace permitted an even broader effort. In November 1865, a mass meeting of workers in Boston approved this declaration:

> RESOLVED, that . . . we rejoice that the rebel aristocracy of the South has been crushed, that we rejoice that beneath the glorious shadow of our victorious flag men of every clime, lineage and color are recognized as free. But . . . we yet want it to be known that the workingmen of America will in future claim a more equal share in the wealth their industry creates in peace and a more equal participation in the privileges and blessings of those free institutions, defended by their manhood on many a bloody field of battle.[22]

Movements for greater democracy faced many obstacles, however. The postwar economy was unstable. Employers used imported contract labor (authorized by Congress in 1864) to replace strikers. Corruption pervaded government, nourished by profiteering in military procurement and by land speculation that mocked the Republican commitment to "free soil." After the Homestead Act of 1862 made millions of acres of federal land available to settlers, investors staked bogus claims to obtain land at bargain prices. This was only a small part of the grab. Between 1862 and 1864, Congress gave 70 million acres to three railroads—the Union Pacific, the Central Pacific, and the Northern Pacific—and turned over 140 million acres to states, which made their own bargains with investors.

Labor was itself divided, especially by widespread racial animosities, and organized actions often stopped at the color line. Some labor activists recognized the problem. The *Boston Daily Evening Voice*, founded in late 1864 by white printers fired for union activity, advocated labor solidarity irrespective of occupation and race. An editorial from October 15, 1865, shows a characteristic blend of principle and expediency:

> The workingman's success is simply impossible without united and harmonious action. If the machinist says to the wielder of the pick and shovel, I will not associate with you,—if you want better wages you must get it on your own hook; if the clerk says to the coal-heaver, between you and I there is a gulf fixed; or if the white man says to the black, I do not recognize you as a fellow workman; and these feelings prevail, there is the end of hope for the labor movement. . . . There are now four million of the [N]egro race about to enter the field of free labor. If we take them upon equal ground with ourselves in the contest for the elevation of labor, they become an ally; but if we reject them. . . . [t]he black man's interests and ours are severed. He that might have been a cooperator becomes an enemy.[23]

However desirable, even essential, interracial solidarity proved an elusive goal.

The history of the National Labor Union (NLU) exemplifies both the high hopes for radical change and the odds against achieving it. Founded in 1866 at a labor convention in Baltimore, the NLU drew together a large network of local and national unions of metalworkers, coal miners, clothing and shoemakers, construction workers, typographers, and others. The NLU supported union organizing, producer and consumer co-operatives, and political action for a range of goals: making eight-hour workdays the law in every state; reforming the banking, currency, and tax systems to benefit people of small means; abolishing convict labor; securing the distribution of public lands to homesteaders instead of speculators; and building a national labor party to work for these and other reforms.

William Sylvis played an instrumental role in the NLU's formation. Born in 1828, one of twelve children of a poor white wagon maker in rural Pennsylvania, he began an apprenticeship at the age of eighteen in a local iron foundry. When the foundry went out of business a few years later, he moved to Philadelphia, by then a married man with a family to support. In 1855, he joined Philadelphia's Stove Molders' Union and became one of its leading organizers. In 1859, he helped found the National Molders' Union, which collapsed at the outbreak of the Civil War when its members—including Sylvis—volunteered for the Union army. By 1863, he was back home, working to revive the National Molders' Union, which elected him president. A tireless activist, he traveled thousands of miles to organize molders in city after city, living on donations from members of the new locals. His union became one of the strongest in the country. In 1864, it stopped a New York City company from operating a foundry at Sing Sing prison with convict labor bought from the state for 40¢ a day per man—the molders' union's rate was $3 a day.

As a leader of the National Labor Union, Sylvis worked like a demon, sustained by strong views. He described capital as a "proud, imperious and dishonest" aristocracy that had seized control of the nation's government and was now "blasting and blistering" all that it touched.[24] Labor, on the other hand, was humanity's salvation: "the germ from which springs a nation's prosperity . . . the only true fountain from which the masses can draw social happiness . . . [and] the attribute of all that is noble and grand in civilization."[25] Therefore, he argued, "Let our cry be REFORM—down with a monied aristocracy and up with the people."[26]Alongside his commitment to unionism, Sylvis favored the establishment of workers' co-operatives, so that "we will become a nation of employers—the employers of our own labor."[27] Elected president of the NLU in 1868, he literally worked himself into the grave, suddenly dying shortly before the NLU's convention of 1869.

The NLU preached and sometimes practiced labor solidarity across gender and racial lines. Several women's unions participated, including the newly founded Daughters of St. Crispin, the female counterpart to the shoemakers' Knights of St. Crispin, and the first national union of women industrial workers. In 1868, the NLU held the first national labor convention to endorse workingwomen's organization and right to pay equity; it urged them to join existing unions, build unions of their own, and "use any other honorable means to persuade or force employers to do justice to women by paying them equal pay for equal work."[28]

The NLU never endorsed women's right to vote. Although its convention of 1868 did seat Elizabeth Cady Stanton from the Woman's Suffrage Association, relations with the suffragists were uneasy. Some women unionists—New York and Massachusetts branches of the Daughters of St. Crispin, for example—supported woman suffrage; others argued that workingwomen could better their lives more effectively by organizing unions than by agitating for the vote.

The early career of Augusta Lewis illustrates the complexity of gender relations under the NLU's auspices. After starting as a newspaper reporter, Lewis learned typesetting, and in 1867 went to work as a typesetter for the *New York World* newspaper. At the time, about 200 women worked as typesetters in New York City's printshops, but the National Typographical Union (NTU) barred them from membership. In December 1867, the NTU's Local 6 struck the *World* when it ordered employees to set type for other newspapers that the local was striking. The *World*'s women typesetters stayed on the job, and the paper hired more women to replace the men on strike. When the *World* settled with Local 6 in September 1868, most of the women were fired. Lewis quit in protest, and within days joined with a small group of women workers and prominent suffragists (including Elizabeth Cady Stanton and Susan B. Anthony) to start the New York Working Women's Association, dedicated "to act for the interests of its members, in the same manner as associations of workingmen now regulate the wages, etc., of those belonging to them."[29] A week later Lewis called a meeting of women typesetters to discuss unionism, and on October 13, 1868, the Women's Typographical Union was founded, with Lewis (not yet twenty-one years old) as president.

Lewis soon forged an alliance with the men's local. It supplied financial assistance and a meeting hall; in turn, the women boycotted employers who paid women less than men for the same work. In January 1869, when Local 6 went on strike for higher pay in book and specialty printshops, members of the Women's Typographical Union refused to work for these shops, and encouraged other women typesetters to shun them too. Susan B. Anthony saw a different kind of opportunity. Backed by the printshops' proprietors, she opened a training program in which women could quickly acquire enough skill to replace the strikers.

In June 1869, at the insistence of Local 6's leadership, the NTU chartered the Women's Typographical Union as an official local. And when Anthony went to the National Labor Union's 1869 convention as a representative of the New York Working Women's Association, Augusta Lewis prompted a challenge to her credentials, arguing that the association was not a true friend of organized labor. The convention declined to seat Anthony as a delegate. The following year, Lewis became the NTU's corresponding secretary—and the first woman to hold a national office in any U.S. labor union. Charged with investigating typesetters' working conditions, she reported at the union's 1871 convention that, although the NTU now admitted women, it did not treat them as the equals of union men. In fact, she declared, most of her union sisters believed "that they are more justly treated by what is termed 'rat' foremen, printers, and employers than they are by union men."[30]

Interracial labor solidarity was even more inadequate. The NLU's founding convention in 1866 closed with stirring words:

> What is wanted . . . is for every union to help inculcate the grand, ennobling idea that the interests of labor are one; that there should be no distinction of race or nationality; no classification of Jew or Gentile, Christian or Infidel; that there is but one dividing line—that which separates mankind into two great classes, the class that labors and the class that lives by others' labor.[31]

But beginning at this same convention, the NLU repeatedly called for Chinese immigrants' exclusion from the United States, charging that the Chinese were naturally submissive workers who could only undercut American wage standards and working conditions.

The movement against Chinese labor started in California, where it had been brewing since the 1850s, when white prospectors formed vigilante gangs to drive Chinese prospectors from the gold fields. In the 1860s, the Central Pacific Railroad hired 12,000 Chinese men to build the western run of the first transcontinental railroad. They were 90 percent of the company's construction workforce, and paid at two-thirds the going rate for white laborers. By 1870, close to 50,000 Chinese immigrants lived in California, 12,000 of them in San Francisco.

Eastern and southern employers also experimented with using Chinese immigrants to replace other workers. In 1870, when the Knights of St. Crispin (mostly composed of Irish immigrants) struck Massachusetts shoe factories for higher wages and the eight-hour day, the owner of a factory in North Adams fired the strikers and replaced them with Chinese workers brought in from San Francisco. An attempt to form a Chinese section of the Knights collapsed amidst mounting racial hostility, and the strike collapsed, too, in North Adams and nearby towns. Over the next few months, Chinese workers recruited by labor contractors on the West Coast also replaced white workers in a steam laundry in Belleville, New Jersey, and a cutlery factory in Beaver Falls, Pennsylvania. Black workers were affected too; some plantation owners in Louisiana and Mississippi tried replacing black workers with Chinese, though they found the Chinese all too quick to respond to mistreatment with mass protests.

Indeed, the NLU's stereotype of docile Chinese workers was quite inaccurate. In 1867, railroad laborers from China staged an exceptionally large and brave strike for a favorite NLU cause—the eight-hour day. Five thousand men blasting tunnels and laying track through the Sierra Nevada mountains downed their tools and reportedly told their boss, "Eight hours a day good for white men, all the same good for China men."[32] As white workers scabbed, the Chinese held out, and finally returned to work only after the Central Pacific blocked the wagons carrying food to the strikers' remote mountain camps.

The NLU was somewhat more hospitable to black workers. From the start, it endorsed black labor's organization, and by 1869 delegates from black labor associations were attending NLU conventions. Still, the NLU never built an effective alliance between black and white workers, and almost none of its constituent unions admitted black members.

Self-organization among black workers proliferated. In December 1869, Isaac Myers, leader of Baltimore's Colored Caulkers' Trade Union Society, joined other black labor activists and reformers in Washington, D.C., to found their own National Labor Union. The call for this convention had come out of the State Labor Convention of Colored Men of Maryland that met in Baltimore the previous July. State and local meetings convened in multiple states to select delegates and discuss issues to be addressed by the national federation. The response was most enthusiastic in the South, where especially large gatherings took place in Macon, Georgia, and Columbia, South Carolina. Like many of the local meetings, the Macon convention produced a network of local unions and the statewide Colored Mechanics and Laboring Man's Association.

Delegates from eighteen states came to Washington to establish the black NLU. They called for equality before the law, especially equal access to public schools and eligibility for jury service. They sought land for freedpeople. They endorsed the Republican Party as the best (though imperfect) safeguard for freedpeople in the South. But the organization's primary goal was to secure equal opportunities for black workers to work in skilled trades and manufacturing and to join labor unions. In an address to the nation, the founders explained that they hoped "by argument and appeal addressed to the white mechanics, laborers and trades unions of our country, [and] to our legislators and countrymen at large, to overcome the prejudices now existing against us so far as to secure a fair opportunity for the display and remuneration of our industrial capabilities."[33]

Compared to its white counterpart, the black NLU took a broader view of racial solidarity. Its founders were not immune to worries about competition from Chinese immigrants; the state labor convention in Maryland had called on Congress "to drive Chinese labor out of the country."[34] But the local meeting in Macon, Georgia, had unanimously passed a resolution "offering a welcome to the Chinese,"[35] and the national convention took the same stand: "With us, too, numbers count. . . . Hence, our industrial movement, emancipating itself from every national and partial sentiment, broadens and deepens its foundations, so as to rear . . . a superstructure capacious enough to accommodate at the altar of common interest the Irish, the [N]egro, and the

German laborer . . . the 'poor white' native of the South . . . the white mechanic and laborer of the North . . . as well as the Chinaman."[36]

The black NLU also addressed "the woman question," which arose at the local meetings preceding the national convention. The Newport, Rhode Island, meeting heard an appeal from an unnamed workingwoman who complained that "in all your deliberations, speeches, and resolutions, which were excellent so far as the men are concerned, the poor woman's interests were not mentioned or referred to."[37] The meeting responded by appointing a woman to Newport's delegation to Washington. Nevertheless, while some of the organization's activists (like the schoolteacher Mary Ann Shadd Cary) campaigned for votes for women, the federation never formally endorsed woman suffrage.

Isaac Myers and his comrades hoped to coalesce with the white NLU, but that never happened. Starting in 1870, the white network concentrated on building the National Labor Party, which fielded candidates in 1872. Black labor leaders and activists, staunch supporters of Radical Reconstruction in the South, remained committed to the electoral success of the Republican Party. That political difference militated against fusion. By late 1873, moreover, both of the NLUs had been debilitated by an economic depression that would last until the end of the decade. Its constituent unions decimated, the white NLU quickly gave up the ghost. The black NLU lingered, surviving into the late 1870s as a paper organization that endorsed Republicans running for public office.

Labor organizations everywhere faced harsh repression when the economy collapsed following the Panic of 1873. Five thousand businesses closed, unemployment soared, and employer resistance to unionism escalated under the direction of city-wide and industry-wide employers' associations. Countless locals and several national unions were entirely wiped out; the rest shrank sharply. In 1870, more than thirty national unions functioned, and union membership totaled about 300,000; by 1877, just nine national unions remained, and union membership had fallen to under 50,000. In the latter year only one-fifth of the U.S. labor force had steady, full-time work.

Employers took advantage of racial divisions among workers to procure scabs during strikes. In June and July 1874, white coal miners in southern Ohio's Hocking Valley struck against a wage cut, and mine owners imported black workers to replace them. The following October, the St. Bernard Coal Company in Earlington, Kentucky, recruited a mostly black scab force to replace white strikers. In April 1877, when black stevedores in Richmond, Virginia, struck against the Powhatan Company shipping firm because of a 25 percent wage cut, the company immediately hired forty white scabs, and police escorted them to work, dispersing a black crowd that had gathered to enforce the strike.

Where workers co-operated across the color line, they were stronger. In April 1873, black workers led a strike for four months' back pay by about a thousand trackmen—both black and white—on the Chesapeake and Ohio Railroad near Beckley, West Virginia. This was an exceptionally militant strike; the trackmen seized a switching station, wrecked a locomotive, and blocked tracks with stones and tree stumps. But hard times militated against interracial solidarity. In November 1873, with the depression under way, 200 black laborers working on a Chesapeake and Ohio tunnel project near

Richmond, Virginia, also struck for back pay, about two months' worth. Within days the company had replaced them with newly arrived Italian immigrants. The strike was lost, and the black strikers lost their jobs as well as their back pay.

Whose Government?

In the South, state and local governments could not bring force and law fully into the service of employers until Radical Reconstruction was brought down. In August 1876, black workers on the rice plantations in South Carolina's Combahee River district staged a mass strike for cash wages instead of chits redeemable at plantation stores. Ten strikers were tried before a black judge in Beaufort, South Carolina, and set free to the applause of supporters gathered in front of the courthouse. The planters finally agreed to pay cash wages, as required by state law. That fall's elections and the withdrawal of federal troops the following spring overturned Reconstruction in South Carolina and foreclosed any possibility for such victories in the future.

As the South descended into a long night of violent suppression of black activism, state and local governments elsewhere also rushed to repress labor unrest. During the hungry winter of 1873–74, labor activists in New York City organized mass meetings and demonstrations to demand public assistance to the unemployed. On January 13, 1874, thousands of men, women, and children rallied in Tompkins Square on the city's Lower East Side, expecting to be addressed by Mayor William Havemeyer. Instead, the mayor sent the police, who charged into the square without warning, clubbing right and left, as mounted officers chased down people fleeing through the side streets. Hundreds of demonstrators and bystanders were injured, and several were arrested and sentenced to prison terms for resisting arrest. The city's unemployed movement stalled and dissipated in the wake of this brutality.

In eastern Pennsylvania's Schuylkill County, the Philadelphia and Reading Railroad enlisted local courts in its assault on labor activists in the anthracite coal mines that produced fuel for the railroad's locomotives. The miners' union—the Workingmen's Benevolent Association—disintegrated in 1875 when it lost a bitter six-month strike against a 20 percent wage cut that the company had instituted precisely to send the union out on a limb. But the union's death was not enough for the railroad's president, Franklin Gowen. He wanted to get the grassroots activists, in particular Irish immigrants, whose fraternal lodge, the Ancient Order of Hibernians (AOH), he regarded as a front for criminal conspiracies. In 1873, Gowen hired James McParlan, an operative from the Pinkerton National Detective Agency, which specialized in suppressing labor activists and political radicals. McParlan's assignment was to pass himself off as an immigrant miner, join the AOH lodge in Schuylkill County, and find evidence that it harbored a terrorist group called the "Molly Maguires." According to Gowen, the Mollies were Irish miners who aimed to destroy American society by fomenting labor unrest and attacking the forces of law and order, and during the strike of 1875, he engineered the publication of newspaper articles that treated these allegations as gospel. While the Molly Maguires were almost surely a myth, a number of miners did likely belong to secret societies that had originated in Ireland to organize armed resistance to British colonialism and land grabs. Following the strike's collapse in July, armed conflict broke out in the anthracite fields, with Irish miners squaring off against company gunmen. There were deaths on both sides—including the murder of a twenty-year-old pregnant woman, fatally shot in the middle of the night by masked intruders who suspected her family of involvement with the Mollies. In 1876, James McParlan surfaced to accuse nineteen miners of murder, and the Philadelphia and Reading's gunmen—the Coal and Iron Police—arrested them. Gowen arranged to serve as prosecutor in several of the subsequent trials. Carefully screened juries—Catholics were summarily excluded—ignored the inconsistencies in McParlan's testimony, and all of the defendants were convicted. Their public hangings began on June 21, 1877, when ten men went to the gallows. One historian fittingly described this episode as "one of the most astonishing surrenders of sovereignty in American history."[38] The company flagrantly engineered the executions, and the government dutifully carried them out.

Mining communities in Schuylkill County had scarcely finished burying their dead when the Great Railroad Strike swept across the country, taking the railroad magnates by surprise. Since the start of the depression in fall 1873, railroad workers had absorbed wage cut after wage cut, amounting to a cumulative reduction of more than 60 percent. Their strikes had been broken up by Pinkerton operatives, and their fraternal brotherhoods blacklisted. When the Baltimore and Ohio (B&O) Railroad imposed yet another 10 percent cut on Monday, July 16, forty firemen and brakemen in Baltimore refused to work, and were quickly dispersed and replaced. The strikers gathered at Camden Junction outside the city, stopped a freight train, and were again dispersed by police.

But at Martinsburg, West Virginia, a couple dozen more firemen left their freight trains and a crowd gathered in support. When the mayor arrested three leaders, the crowd freed them. When the company tried to send out freight trains with new firemen, the brakemen walked off as strikers blocked the trains. On Tuesday, B&O officials called for help from Governor Henry M. Mathews, who ordered two companies of militia into Martinsburg. The militiamen refused to fire on the strikers, and the walkout spread to other junctions. By the end of the day 500 men were out, joined by 200 boatmen on the Chesapeake and Ohio Canal, and the freight blockade at Martinsburg had stalled seventy trains with 1,200 cars, many fully loaded.

The B&O suggested that Governor Mathews ask President Rutherford Hayes for help. The president complied: on the morning of Wednesday, July 18, some 400 federal troops—many just returned from South Carolina—left Washington and Baltimore for Martinsburg, riding a special train provided by the B&O. There the troops used bayonets to push back the crowds and manned two trains, one going in each direction. The next day thirteen trains moved, all operated by troops.

Still, the strike spread along the rail lines. On Friday, July 20, in Baltimore, militia companies were stranded at Camden Station, surrounded by an angry crowd. When the local militia in Pittsburgh refused to fire on crowds supporting the strikers, Governor John P. Hartranft ordered Philadelphia militiamen to the scene. Arriving on Saturday, they fired on the crowd, retreated into the Pennsylvania Railroad's roundhouse, then withdrew under fire after a blazing railroad car was rolled into the building. At least 40 civilians were killed in Pittsburgh as 500 cars, 104 locomotives, and 39 buildings went up in flames. At Johnstown, the troops were stoned. At Reading, on Tuesday, July 24, the militia company from Morristown threatened to fire on the company from Easton, then stacked their arms and refused to deploy against the citizenry. Three thousand federal soldiers were sent to Pennsylvania, and Governor Hartranft led troop convoys around the state for two weeks, ordering them to open fire on every crowd until it dispersed.

Within a week of the incident at Camden Junction, strikes had occurred on more than a dozen railroad lines, north to upper New York State, west to the Rocky Mountains, and south to Texas. Mass rallies took place in Buffalo, Albany, Trenton, Boston, and New York City. On Thursday, July 26, a rally of some 10,000 workers at the Halsted Viaduct in Chicago beat back the police sent to disperse them, and Secretary of War George W. McCrary ordered General Philip Sheridan to suspend his campaign against the Native Americans from the Lakota nation and take his troops to Chicago.

In St. Louis, Missouri, a general strike developed and lasted five days. Railroad strikers from St. Louis and from East St. Louis, Illinois, across the river formed a joint committee that represented workers from four different railroad lines and sent out delegations to spread the strike to local factories and shops. As business as usual ground to a halt, the committee called on Missouri's governor John S. Phelps to convene the legislature to pass laws enforcing an eight-hour day and prohibiting the employment of children under fourteen in factories or dangerous occupations; appealed to St. Louis's Mayor Henry Overstolz to arrange for the distribution of food to destitute families and promised that the unions would foot the bill; and volunteered to help maintain public order.

While hopes ran high in St. Louis, however, the strike was already starting to peter out. Martinsburg had been pacified by Thursday, July 19; the Baltimore uprising had ended by the following Monday; and Pittsburgh was subdued the next day, just as things were heating up in St. Louis. Both there and in Chicago, the strike was over by Saturday, July 28. Overall, more than 100,000 railroad workers—about half the total—stopped work on about two-thirds of the nation's lines, and troops occupied cities from Baltimore, Buffalo, and Albany to St. Louis and Chicago.

Aside from the slaves' wartime efforts to undermine the Confederacy, the railroad strike was the largest work stoppage in U.S. history. It had many notable features. Striking railroad workers were widely supported by other workers and their families. In his book on the strike—rushed into print in September 1877—Joseph A. Dacus, former editor of the *St. Louis Republican*, described many a scene like this one in Baltimore: "Women frenzied with rage, joined the mob and incited the men to stand firm in the fight."[39] Across the country, about 120 strikers and supporters were killed by state and federal troops, and the dead included women and children.

Both black and white workers participated in the strike. Many people in the Martinsburg crowd were black. Black and white coal miners together halted trains in the surrounding countryside. Black workers in St. Louis closed the canneries and docks; black boatmen stopped steamboats on the Mississippi; and when St. Louis strikers sent a five-person delegation to the mayor, it included one black man. In Galveston, Texas, the strike began with black tracklayers and construction workers, and won a 30 percent wage increase. But racial animosity prevailed in San Francisco; on July 24, a mass meeting to discuss news of the strike spawned a mob of young white men who rampaged through the city's Chinatown, wrecking laundries and other small businesses. Anti-Chinese riots continued two more nights, and one Chinese laundryman was killed.

The strike was finally suppressed by federal troops, who were mobilized when some state militia units proved sympathetic to the strikers. City and state governments meanwhile mobilized their own armed forces: regular police, special deputies recruited and armed for the emergency, and civilian patrols, often organized and armed by the railroad companies.

The speed and scale of government intervention on the side of the railroad barons showed clearly that, whatever the hardships of the workers and the merits of their complaints, labor unrest would be treated as pathological social disorder. Business leaders, and the politicians and journalists they employed, saw everywhere the specter of "Communism"[40]—the insurrectionary spirit of the Paris Commune of 1871, allegedly spread by immigrant revolutionaries who incited tramps and hooligans to destroy civilized society. The federal government clearly feared that the strike would blossom into a revolution. From Friday, July 20 through Sunday, July 29, President Hayes met daily with his cabinet to review the crisis and military deployments. Sailors and marines were ordered to Washington to protect the Treasury should it come under attack.

From the vantage of 1877, the hope with which labor activists had celebrated the Confederacy's defeat in 1865 seemed quite ironic and almost naive. They had looked forward to "a more equal share of the wealth"; now they endured repeated wage cuts. They had expected to enjoy "the privileges and blessings" of citizenship; now they were targeted by police riots, kangaroo courts, state militia, and federal troops. Labor had defended the republic on the bloody battlefields of the Civil War, only to see it seized by capital.

The second American revolution, like the first, was deeply inspiring and woefully incomplete. The Constitution was amended to abolish bondage and guarantee equality before the law—revolutionary advances that were thwarted and stalled but never wholly obliterated by the reactionary triumphs of the planters of the South and the industrialists of the North. Many working people still believed in the vision of America articulated in a poem written by a member of the National Molders' Union on the centennial of the Declaration of Independence:

> For though slaves in their eyes we now may seem to be
> Created by God for their pleasure alone,
> The day's not far distant, when we shall be free,
> And tyrants their unpitied downfall bemoan.
> Then gird on the sword in our glorious cause,
> Every lover of liberty—all who'd be free,
> And rescue thy children from Tyranny's jaws,
> Break the chains that now waits for the child at they knee.[41]

Whether workers united could actualize this ideal remained to be seen.

5

Labor Versus Monopoly in the Gilded Age

The economic crash of 1873 helped to douse the democratic revolution sparked by the Civil War. It also ushered in the Gilded Age, a quarter century of glittering riches for American capitalists and leaden poverty for masses of working people. Even more than in the past, politics and law protected class privilege and the accumulation of wealth.

The fortunes and influence of wealthy Americans exceeded anything the nation had ever seen. At the top of the heap stood a new group of monopoly capitalists like Jay Gould, whose empire included a slew of railroads and controlling interests in the Western Union Telegraph Company and several steamship lines. Gould was famous for more than his wealth. His corrupt stock transactions ruined so many people that he retained a phalanx of plainclothes police to protect him from assault and bomb-proofed his office in the Western Union headquarters near Wall Street. He bought a daily newspaper (the *New York World*) so the public could read good things about him. He stocked the greenhouse of his country estate with $40,000 worth of orchids, surrounded himself with European artwork, relaxed on a 230-foot yacht, and bestowed lavish gifts on state and federal lawmakers and judges. When he died in 1892, he left $77 million to his heirs. As for labor relations, he was legendarily dishonest—always ready to compromise with a union that backed him into a corner and then renege on the deal the very next day.

For the vast majority of workers and their families, the Gilded Age brought unceasing economic insecurity in an unstable national economy. The depression of 1873–78 was followed by a sharp recession in 1883–85, and another, deeper depression that stretched from spring 1893 through most of 1897. Even in the relatively good years between economic downturns, working people suffered repeated wage cuts and lay-offs. At the same time, government officials serviced the interests of their business friends. In 1886, the U.S. Supreme Court declared that corporations were entitled to the same protections guaranteed to citizens under the Fourteenth Amendment. State courts nullified laws that limited hours of labor, set minimum wages, or otherwise restricted employers' "rights." Judges routinely issued injunctions against workers' strikes, demonstrations, boycotts, and organizing drives.

"There are too many millionaires and too many paupers," observed the *Chicago Tribune* in 1884.[1] In 1890, the richest 1 percent of Americans had a combined annual income larger than the poorest 50 percent. Captains of finance and industry feasted at lavish banquets. The guests at one dinner puffed cigarettes wrapped in $100 bills; at another, rare black pearls were tucked into the oysters served as appetizers. Workers meanwhile scavenged for firewood. Bernardo Vega, a twentieth-century Puerto Rican immigrant to New York City, recalled family tales about his Aunt Dolores's life in New York during the winter of 1879–80: "The price of coal had gone up, and what made it worse was that it was hard to come by. . . . Every day she would go out with the children in search of firewood to heat the house."[2] Each summer, millionaires on their way to ocean-side mansions in Newport, Rhode Island, caught the night ferry from Fall River, Massachusetts. As the ferry pulled out, passengers could watch mill workers on the beaches, digging for clams to supplement their meager diets. Children of the rich grew up with ponies, private tutors, and grand tours of Europe. In immigrant ghettoes like New York City's Lower East Side, children lived in tenement flats with little daylight, less ventilation, and no running water. The census of 1880 counted more than a million wageworkers under sixteen years of age. While millionaires built grand homes modeled on European castles, many families had no shelter at all. In city after city, homeless people lined up every night to sleep in police stations.

The poet Walt Whitman saw the increase in capitalist wealth as "a sort of anti-democratic disease and monstrosity."[3] But to big businessmen and their apologists, the ascendancy of the rich was inevitable, natural, and ordained by God—the beneficent result of social evolution based on "the survival of the fittest."[4] The steel tycoon Andrew Carnegie wrote in 1889 that, "Individualism, Private Property, the Law of Accumulation of Wealth, and the Law of Competition" were "the highest result of human experience."[5] John D. Rockefeller Sr., the oil and mining potentate, declared in a lecture to Sunday-school students: "The growth of a large business is merely a survival of the fittest. . . . This is not an evil tendency in business. It is merely the working-out of a law of nature and a law of God."[6] William Graham Sumner, a professor of political and social science at Yale and a favorite lapdog of the rich, opined that "The millionaires are a product of natural selection, acting on the whole body of men to pick out those who can meet the requirement."[7]

Capitalists did not have to rely on natural law alone; they could buy favors from legislators and judges. State lawmakers passed a raft of anti-labor statutes that made picketing and strikes illegal and authorized corporations to deploy their own police in company towns. Anything an employer did to discourage unions (short of mayhem and murder) was a perfectly legal defense of his property rights; and should his actions on that front in fact kill or maim working people, he virtually never had to answer for the harm done.

Labor activists, on the other hand, were repeatedly indicted for conspiracy. Prosecutors did not have to prove criminal intent or deeds; under the law, virtually all forms of collective action by workers violated an employer's freedom to run a business in a profitable manner. In *Moore's v. Bricklayers' Union* (1890), the Supreme Court of Ohio ruled it illegal to make an employer conduct business according to union regulations. While conspiracy laws favored employers, conspiracy trials were inefficient weapons against organized labor. Trials took time; they required witnesses; and, most important, they left the verdicts to juries, whose members might sympathize with unions. In 1877, a new, more streamlined legal weapon appeared—the labor injunction, which was first applied to striking railroad workers. Injunctions had several advantages over conspiracy trials. They were issued by "equity" courts in which judges alone determined all issues of fact and law, and decided what actions constituted contempt of court. Labor injunctions prohibited any activity that might cause irreparable harm to employers' property, including both tangible possessions like machinery and buildings and intangibles like the right to hire and sell.

Against this backdrop, working people mobilized on a scale that caught the upper classes by surprise. Though the labor movement had been devastated by the depression of the 1870s, the insurgent spirit so evident in the Great Railroad Strike had not died out. Following that strike's defeat, the labor editor George McNeill had insisted that workers would regroup to continue resistance to a system in which "conscienceless cunning and miserly acquisitiveness are rewarded better than constructive ability or open-hearted integrity."[8] These words proved prophetic. The 1880s and 1890s saw unprecedented levels of organizing, militancy, and political action by working people—initiatives aimed first and foremost at curbing the corrupt power of monopoly capital.

Industrial Capitalism: Consolidation and Crisis

The Union's victory in the Civil War cleared the way for the swift expansion of American industry, and railroads drove the trend. The first transcontinental line was completed in 1869; by the late 1890s, more than 100,000 miles of new track had produced the largest rail system in the world. This massive construction rippled through feeder industries such as lumber, iron, and steel. Increased iron and steel production in turn swelled demand for coal. The railroad network meanwhile linked more and more producers to far-flung markets, prompting a tremendous boom in industrial and agricultural output. Metal mining (gold, silver, copper, iron) proliferated in the West. Farms and ranches occupied more and more land. The South planted about 9 million acres of cotton in the early 1870s and about 24 million by the late 1890s. Annual wheat production in the North Central states rose from 67 million bushels in 1869 to 307 million in 1899. Meanwhile, in the Rocky Mountain states, wool production zoomed from 1 million to 123 million pounds a year.

Much of the land newly devoted to farming and grazing came from the railroads. They sold vast amounts to small homesteaders and to agribusinesses like the Miller and Lux partnership that owned more than 1 million acres in California's San Joaquin Valley. About 150 million acres of the railroads' land had come from the government, which had taken it from Native Americans, by fiat or by deadly force.

Federal military campaigns against Native Americans did not stop during the Civil War. In 1863–64 in Arizona, U.S. troops destroyed Navajo sheep, cornfields, and orchards. Then, in 1864–66, they rounded up 8,500 starving Navajos for a "Long Walk" (in reality, more than fifty forced marches) to a prison camp in New Mexico, where they were held for two years before returning to their homeland under a new treaty. In November 1864, at Sand Creek, Colorado, soldiers overran a camp of Cheyenne and Arapaho, killing 450 people. Immediately after the war, Lakota people contested the construction of a road through their lands in the northern Great Plains (Montana and Wyoming); the five-year confrontation ended with their confinement to a reservation in Dakota Territory.

Indian wars continued throughout the Gilded Age. In 1870, the Modoc left their reservation in Oregon to return home to northern California, where they fought off the U.S. Army for a year until they were overpowered in 1873. The uprising's leaders were executed or imprisoned and the rest of the Modoc were exiled to Indian Territory (now Oklahoma). In 1871, Chiricahua resistance to reservation confinement started the Apache Wars in New Mexico and Arizona. They ended in 1886, when Geronimo's band was captured, imprisoned in Florida until 1894, transferred to Oklahoma, and finally dispersed to several small southwestern reservations in 1913.

In 1875, following a gold strike in the Black Hills on Lakota land, federal troops mobilized to protect white prospectors. War parties led by Sitting Bull, Crazy Horse, and others mobilized men from the Northern Cheyenne and Arapaho as well as the Lakota, and the combined forces killed or wounded more than half of the U.S. Seventh Cavalry at Little Bighorn in June 1876. By mid-fall, however, the army had sent in reinforcements and Congress had cut off the Lakota's food supplies, compelling them to give up the fight and cede the goldfields to the United States.

In 1877, when the Nez Perce community in Oregon's Wallowa Valley was ordered to relocate to Idaho, Chief Joseph led resisters on a three-month retreat towards Canada, but the army pursued and finally caught them. They, too, were interned in Indian Territory, which they called *eeikish pah*, the "hot place."[9] The survivors were transferred to Washington State's Colville Reservation in 1885.

Some relocations were accomplished without wars. Pawnee and Ponca from Nebraska, Comanche from Wyoming, Tonkawa from Texas—all were moved to Oklahoma. Some military campaigns against Indians had no goal other than cultural suppression. In 1890, soldiers harried the adherents of what whites called the "Ghost Dance," a ritual originated by the Northern Paiute visionary Wovoka that called on ancestors to help restore the world that colonization had destroyed.[10] In December 1890, campaigns against this ritual climaxed in the slaughter of a Lakota encampment at Wounded Knee Creek in South Dakota. The U.S. Army reported killing 146 people, though the actual number was probably closer to 400, mostly women, children, and old men. Congress awarded twenty Medals of Honor to soldiers who had perpetrated this massacre.

The federal government also seized Native Americans' lands by statute. In 1887, the General Allotment Act (known as the Dawes Act) divided tribal lands into individual holdings, assigning 160 acres to each head of a family and 80 to each unmarried adult. The government then bought unassigned land and opened it to settlers. In 1891–92, 3.9 million acres—parts of the Sauk and Fox, Pottawatomie-Shawnee, and Cheyenne-Arapaho reservations—were taken in Oklahoma alone.

The government's contempt for Native Americans had much in common with its attitude toward workers who challenged capital's authority. Just as strikers disrupted the industrial operations that fattened big business, Indian nations did their best to maintain traditional ways of life instead of flocking to wage work. That enraged authorities. In 1865, an army surgeon wrote home about his first encounter with the Shoshone people in the vicinity of Fort Bridger, Wyoming, one of the many places where colonization had destroyed ecosystems that once supported hunting. "If they won't work like other people," he declared, "they had better be exterminated. They are nothing but a nuisance and an obstruction to civilization. . . . Let them know that they too must earn their bread by the sweat of their brows instead of eking out a miserable existence by hunting."[11] The regiments later deployed against Lakota Ghost Dancers harbored similar feelings. Two weeks before the bloodbath at Wounded Knee, one of these soldiers wrote to his wife: "It certainly is time something be done; here we are pampering a lot of worthless loafing Indians."[12]

If none paid more dearly than Native Americans for industrial capitalism's swift growth, many other Americans suffered too. While the rail system expanded commerce, it also destabilized the economy. Different railroad companies established many parallel routes, especially in the industrial heartland that stretched from southern New England and the mid-Atlantic states through the Midwest. To steal business from rivals, these railroads repeatedly slashed the rates they charged for freight traffic in the heartland; and, to offset shrinking profit margins, they both jacked up rates in other regions and cut railroad workers' wages across the country. As the price of freight service fell, moreover, industrial firms expanded production in hopes of capturing new and faraway markets. Soon, they too were cutting prices, each vying for business by underselling competitors. To extricate themselves from these races to the bottom, railroads and manufacturers often formed combinations known as trusts or cartels, whose members agreed to fix prices and divvy up markets in an orderly fashion. In 1890 Congress outlawed these combinations with the Sherman Antitrust Act, but they had never been very effective in any case. Time and again, their members reneged on promises to co-operate, and brief periods of stability gave way to new price wars and market grabs. In manufacturing no less than the railroad industry, price wars meant wage cuts; and for workers employed by companies on the losing end, temporary or even permanent layoffs were not far behind.

Different regions developed unequally. Monopoly capitalists headquartered in the industrial heartland dominated development in the South and West. Southern and western farmers, usually served by a single railroad, paid top dollar to transport crops to market. This exacerbated other problems: the exorbitant interest charged by merchants who extended credit to cotton farmers; the sky-high fees wheat farmers paid to store their crops in grain elevators, often owned by railroads; and the decline in agricultural prices as production increased. (In 1896, the average price for farm products was half what it had been in 1870.) In the Cotton Belt and on the Great Plains, many family farms went bankrupt. Kansas alone saw 11,000 foreclosures on farm mortgages from 1889 through 1893. By 1900, more than a third of all U.S. farms were worked by tenants or sharecroppers rather than owners; debt peonage was increasingly common; and farmhands' wages remained exceedingly low. Agriculture played a central role in the national economy, with cotton the single largest export and grain products not far behind, but most of the people who produced this wealth were locked into poverty.

Monopolists also restricted industrialization in the South and West. Hampered by higher freight charges, the iron and steel industry centered in Birmingham, Alabama, and the cotton textile industry in the Carolina Piedmont region were not only smaller than their northern counterparts but also more exploitive, paying significantly lower wages and using more child labor. In 1896, 25 percent of textile workers in North Carolina were under age sixteen, compared to 5 percent in Massachusetts.

San Francisco was the West's only manufacturing center. Most of the region's economy was designed to supply eastern factories with raw or semi-processed materials: agricultural produce, lumber, cattle, wool, coal, and smelted metal ores. Western industries followed the boom-and-bust cycles of eastern manufacturing, further destabilizing a labor market already weakened by the seasonal nature of work in farming, ranching, logging, and railroad construction. Though labor was in short supply in the West and workers in most occupations averaged higher daily wages than their eastern counterparts, their employment was less stable, and many of them—mainly but not only single men—migrated from place to place in search of jobs.

The Working Classes

As industrial capitalism expanded, so did the ranks of wageworkers. By 1900, they numbered about 18 million, up from 6.7 million in 1870; together with their families, they added up to at least three-quarters of the U.S. population of 76 million. They came from ever more diverse backgrounds, and their working conditions varied tremendously. Indeed, Americans in the Gilded Age often spoke of the "working classes" instead of a single working class.[13]

Immigration was a key source of working-class growth and diversity. From 1873 through 1897, 10 million immigrants entered the United States, more than during the previous fifty years; and they came from more places than ever before. European immigrants still outnumbered the rest, but more and more people arrived from Italy, Austria-Hungary, Russia, and Poland, and, in smaller numbers, from Portugal, Spain, Greece, and parts of the Ottoman Empire, which stretched from southeastern Europe through the Middle East. Japanese as well as Chinese arrived from East Asia. In addition to English- and French-speaking Canadians, immigrants from the Western Hemisphere included Mexicans, Caribbean islanders, and Central and South Americans. Nearly all immigrants had one thing in common: they depended on wage work for their livelihoods during their first years in the United States, if not longer.

Some were fleeing ethnic persecution in their homelands. Armenians fled brutality at the hands of Ottoman Turkey. Jews from eastern Europe sought relief from Russia's Czarist regime, which attacked them with pogroms; barred them from owning land; and confined them to *shtetls*, Jewish towns in restricted zones.

Most immigrants came in search of better economic opportunities. Many planned to go back home once they had saved enough, and quite a few did. Plans often changed, however. In 1882, Mihailo Evanich's family in the Croatian village of Smisliak selected him to go to America to earn money to send home. He found work in the copper mines in Calumet, Michigan. A year later he brought over his wife to keep house for him and several of his co-workers. By 1891, the couple had decided to stay and set up a saloon, which they ran as a club for Croat and Slovene miners. Evanich was called "Mike Evans" by his foremen and became a citizen under that name.[14] Some immigrants came and went several times. From the 1890s into the 1920s, Elias Garza moved back and forth between Mexico and the United States, working at a variety of jobs—from meatpacking to railroad track maintenance—in Kansas, California, Texas, and Arizona.

Many immigrants moved from wage work to self-employment. Kinji Ushijima, who arrived from Japan in 1887, worked first as a potato picker but then became a labor contractor. By the 1910s, his business cultivated potatoes on 10,000 acres he had purchased or leased. John Starkku came from Finland in 1890, and for five years worked his way westward, taking jobs in mines and lumber camps and saving every penny he could. When he reached Oregon's Hood River Valley, he bought land and planted orchards.

Many more immigrants never managed to save much. This was especially true for women who had to make it on their own, with substandard female wages. In 1886, an Irish-born sewing machine operator told investigators from the Colorado Labor Bureau: "My parents live in Ireland and are entirely dependent on myself and sister for support. . . . I am a good seamstress and work hard. I do not take ten minutes at noon [for rest]; no matter how hard I try I can not make over $1 per day."[15] In 1884, Rosa Cassettari came from the Lombardy region of Italy to join her husband who worked in the iron mines in Union, Missouri. When they saved enough, he bought a brothel, but she refused to live there and moved to Chicago, where she supported her children by washing clothes and cleaning houses. She later recalled walking everywhere with her children, nearly freezing to death: "I never took the streetcar. We needed those five cents to eat."[16] She ended up a cleaning woman in the Chicago Commons, one of many "settlement houses" established by genteel reformers who reached out to the urban poor.

Immigrant groups generally clustered in particular occupations. Chinese men were the majority of migrant farm laborers in California in the 1880s and 1890s. Many Irish women entered domestic service. Slavic men worked mainly in coal mines, steel mills, and railroad maintenance. Italians and Russian Jews of both sexes tended to concentrate in the garment industry. Puerto Ricans and Cubans often worked in cigar factories in New York City and in Tampa and Key West, Florida.

A great many new additions to the wage-labor force came from within U.S. borders. As railroads penetrated the Southwest, more and more Mexican Americans went to work in railroad construction and maintenance, in mining, in large-scale commercial farming and ranching, as domestics in Anglo households, and as laundresses and seamstresses in mining and railroad camps. Laguna Pueblos built and maintained the section of the Santa Fe Railroad on their reservation in New Mexico. Mi'kmaq families from northern New England harvested potatoes in Maine and wheat in Wyoming, Montana, and Canadian Alberta and Saskatchewan. Ottawas in Michigan worked seasonally as fruit and berry pickers, as lumberjacks, and in service jobs in resort hotels. Kumeyaays and Luiseños held most of the stevedore jobs on the docks of San Diego, California, and also worked on farms and ranches as fruit pickers, cowboys, sheepherders, and shearers.

Ninety percent of African Americans lived in the South, where they slowly moved from sharecropping into jobs paying an individual wage. Their choices were severely limited; as of 1890, agriculture and domestic service employed the vast bulk of African American workers, 96 percent of the women and 85 percent of the men. Exceptions included stevedores and teamsters in New Orleans; iron foundry workers in Birmingham; brick makers in Richmond; coal miners in West Virginia, Kentucky, Tennessee, and Alabama; teachers in black schools; and clerical and sales employees of black-owned businesses.

The industrial heartland saw a steep rise in the ranks of wage-earning women. Wives took jobs when their husbands' pay stopped entirely or was too low to support a family; this was especially common in black communities. The numbers of working-class daughters earning wages rose even more sharply. Before the 1870s, only the poorest families had regularly put daughters out to work. During the Gilded Age, even relatively prosperous working-class households began to send their daughters into the labor market once they had finished grammar school (around age fourteen). Though they spent some of their pay on themselves, virtually all of these workers contributed most of their earnings to family coffers, sometimes to cover bare necessities and in other cases to finance small luxuries like parlor furniture or good clothes. The new "working girls"—the vast majority white and born in the United States—usually took jobs in factories or as saleswomen in department stores, but also included office clerks, schoolteachers, and custom dressmakers and milliners. Most earned wages until they married and became mothers, typically in their mid-twenties; those who did not marry usually remained wageworkers for life.

Income was unevenly distributed within the working class. Higher-paying skilled jobs belonged almost exclusively to American-born white men or male immigrants from northwestern Europe. For their households, living standards rose, often despite the roller-coaster economy. Thanks to falling prices, the cost of living declined even faster than employers cut wages in skilled trades.

Workers on every rung of the occupational hierarchy generally disdained those below. As Lucy Warner, an operative in a Connecticut cotton mill, wrote in 1891: "The teacher considers herself superior to the sewing girl, and the sewing girl thinks herself above the mill girl, and the mill girl thinks the girl who does general housework a little beneath her."[17] Stratification combined with the diversity of culture and language to divide the working class by color, ethnicity, gender, and occupation.

Resentments and conflicts repeatedly led to violence across racial and ethnic lines. The anti-Chinese movement accelerated. In October 1880, a white mob drove out the residents of Denver's Chinatown, lynching one man along the way. In 1881, Texas railroad workers—Tejanos and Apaches as well as whites—repeatedly assaulted Chinese co-workers. In 1882, Congress passed the Chinese Exclusion Act, barring the immigration of Chinese laborers for ten years. The violence continued. In September 1885, after Chinese and Welsh coal miners brawled in Rock Springs, Wyoming, a mob attacked the Chinese section of the mining camp, killing twenty-eight and chasing the rest into the wilderness. White "ouster committees" drove Chinese from Tacoma, Washington, in November 1885 and from Seattle the following February.[18]

African Americans and Mexican Americans faced continued discrimination and violence. More than 2,500 African Americans were lynched between 1885 and 1900, mainly in Mississippi, Alabama, Georgia, and Louisiana. White craftsmen barred black men from most skilled trades. In August 1897, some 1,400 white workers went on strike at the Fulton Bag and Cotton Mill in Atlanta to protest the hiring of twenty black women. From the 1870s through the 1890s, Mexican Americans were lynched in Texas, California, Arizona, and Colorado, and Anglo cowboys repeatedly raided Tejano towns such as Socorro and Tascosa.

Native-born white workers and immigrants from northwestern Europe often despised Slavs, Italians, and Russian Jews. Slavs were vilified as dumb and docile, though they were in fact quicker than most immigrants to organize and strike. In 1891, coal miners in Wheeling, West Virginia, walked off the job when their employer refused to fire Italians, and 500 boys employed in a New Jersey glass factory rioted when fourteen Russian Jews were hired. Even when people worked together in relative peace, social life was typically segregated by color and ethnicity.

Within working-class communities, different ambitions contended. For some people, personal advancement took precedence. Others hoped simply to endure the daily struggle for survival. But a critical mass of activists proposed collective remedies for common problems. They aimed to rally workers to defend their "natural and essential rights" and build a better world for one and all. As the labor editor John Swinton put it, workers united had "the power to establish, by peaceful means, an industrial community, under which neither the 'bloated millionaire' nor the abject starveling shall dishonor the country in which they dwell."[19]

Working people from different backgrounds and occupations had more in common than dependency on wages. Everyone was affected by the economic crises that defined the Gilded Age. Everyone saw how governors, legislators, and judges served the interests of the moneyed classes. Everyone beheld the arrogance of business spokesmen like John Hay, the corporate lawyer and Republican statesman who pontificated: "That you have property is proof of industry and foresight on your part or your father's; that you have nothing is a judgment on your laziness and vices, or on your improvidence. The world is a moral world, which it would not be if virtue and vice received the same reward."[20] Or, as the *New York World* declared—even before Jay Gould purchased it—"Men must be contented to work for less wages. In this way the workingman will be nearer to that station in life to which it has pleased God to call him."[21]

Working-class communities were also bound together by traditions of struggle and resistance. Leading labor activists often had a keen sense of the movement's history in the United States, from the National Trades Union of the 1830s and ten-hour-day agitation of the 1840s to the national labor unions of the Reconstruction era. These legacies blended with other militant traditions rooted in U.S. soil or imported from immigrants' homelands.

Black communities harbored a rich heritage of resistance to slavery and included many veterans of the Civil War and Radical Reconstruction. One of the younger activists who carried on this legacy was Ida Wells. Born in 1862 in Holly Springs, Mississippi, she attended a freedmen's school and went to work as a teacher at age fourteen, supporting herself and four siblings after their parents died of yellow fever. At twenty-two she moved to Memphis, Tennessee, where she taught school until 1891, when she was fired for writing about conditions in the city's segregated black schools. The following year, she published a report on the lynching of three black grocers and had to flee the South for her own safety. She continued to crusade against lynching, traveling and speaking widely in the United States and twice taking her campaign to Britain. Pausing only briefly after her marriage to Chicago civil rights activist Ferdinand Barnett, Ida Wells-Barnett organized black women in support of many causes, including women's right to vote.

Workingwomen sustained other activist traditions too. Like the mill workers who joined with genteel labor reformers to agitate for ten-hour laws in the 1840s, women trade unionists in Chicago came together with middle-class groups to form the Illinois Women's Alliance in 1888. The alliance campaigned for laws against sweatshops and child labor. Just as women had rallied behind the railroad strike in 1877, Mary Septek organized Hungarian coal miners' wives, mothers and sisters to battle scabs during a strike near Hazelton, Pennsylvania, in September 1897.

Mexican American resistance to Anglo domination continued in the Southwest and increasingly targeted corporate power and privilege. In 1887, in San Miguel County, New Mexico, Juan José Herrera and his brothers Pablo and Nicanor formed an underground organization known as Las Gorras Blancas ("The White Caps"), recruiting up to 1,500 members within a couple of years. They conducted a guerrilla campaign against the Santa Fe Railroad and cattle corporations, cutting barbed wire fences and torching company property. Las Gorras also rallied behind an insurgent political party, El Partido del Pueblo Unido.

In the tradition of Chinese railroad workers' 1867 strike for the eight-hour day, Chinese farmworkers organized against unequal pay. Fruit pickers in California's Santa Clara Valley went on strike in 1880, as did hops pickers in Kern County in 1884. In 1890, California newspapers reported that Chinese immigrants had formed a labor union that demanded $1.50 a day for work in orchards and vineyards.

Other immigrant groups drew on their own militant traditions, including German socialism; Bohemian (Czech), Italian, and Mexican anarchism; Irish resistance to English occupation; Jewish radicalism forged under Czarist persecution; Puerto Rican and Cuban rebellion against Spanish colonialism. The labor movement of the Gilded Age tapped into all of these legacies. And if labor organizations sometimes failed to unite even their own ranks, workplace and community solidarity provided bedrock for resistance to corporate assaults on labor and dominance of American life.

The Knights of Labor

The labor movement of the Gilded Age was as diverse as the working class itself. From 1881 through 1897, the United States saw more than 18,000 strikes for higher wages, the eight-hour day, union recognition, and other goals. Labor activists promoted their objectives in many different languages and accents, and they gathered in arenas ranging from trade unions to political parties, social clubs to revolutionary organizations, and neighborhood saloons to national conventions. At every point this movement challenged monopoly capitalists, but by the end of the era, the boldest initiatives had been crushed, and the prevailing spirit had retreated from audacity to caution.

The largest and most influential labor organization of the Gilded Age was the Noble and Holy Order of the Knights of Labor, founded in 1869 as a secret organization of garment workers led by the Philadelphia tailor Uriah Stephens. When Stephens stepped down in 1879, he was replaced by Terence Powderly, a railroad machinist who had recently been elected mayor of Scranton, Pennsylvania, on a labor reform ticket. The organization's secrecy, which protected Knights from blacklisting by employers, involved elaborate codes. The cryptic message "*****$6\frac{10}{8x}$/75" chalked on a wall meant "Knights Assembly No. 75 will meet at 8:00 p.m. on June 10."[22] Members gathered in local assemblies that included both "trade assemblies" organized by industry and "mixed assemblies" of people from various industries and walks of life. Locals reported to district assemblies; annual conventions known as general assemblies debated and adopted policy; and a general executive board oversaw the order between conventions. The Knights' basic principle was solidarity; their motto, "An Injury to One is the Concern of All."[23]

In 1881, the Knights went public, issuing a Declaration of Principles that began with an attack on monopoly:

> The alarming development and aggressiveness of great capitalists and corporations, unless checked, will inevitably lead to the pauperization and hopeless degradation of the toiling masses. It is imperative, if we desire to enjoy the full blessings of life, that a check be placed upon unjust accumulation, and the power for evil of aggregated wealth. This much desired object can be accomplished only by the united efforts of those who obey the divine injunction, "In the sweat of thy face shalt thou eat bread."[24]

The Knights regarded monopolists as monarchs in all but name. To quote George McNeill, a longtime labor activist among the leaders of Boston's district assembly:

> The railroad president is a railroad king, whose whim is law. He collects tithes by reducing wages. . . . He can discharge (banish) any employee without cause. He can prevent laborers from following their usual vocations. He can withhold their lawful wages. He can delay trial on a suit of law, and postpone judgment indefinitely. He can control legislative bodies, dictate legislation, subsidize the press, and corrupt the moral sense of the community. He can fix the price of freights, and thus command the food and fuel-supplies of the nation.[25]

If this "iron heel of a soulless monopoly" undermined democracy, so did wage labor, which forced workers into dependency on employers.[26] As McNeill wrote, "These extremes of wealth and poverty are threatening the existence of the government. In light of these facts, we declare that there is an inevitable and irresistible conflict between the wage-system of labor and the republican system of government,—the wage-laborer attempting to save the government, and the capitalist class ignorantly attempting to subvert it."[27]

The Knights proposed to replace the wage system with a "cooperative commonwealth" in which workers would be their own masters. Only then, proclaimed the Declaration of Principles, could they have "the full enjoyment of the wealth they create, sufficient leisure in which to develop their intellectual, moral and social faculties; all of the benefits, recreation and pleasures of association; in a word . . . the gains and honors of advancing civilization."[28]

This message had an exceptionally broad appeal. The order's membership climbed steadily—from 28,000 Knights in 1880 to 43,000 in 1882, 71,000 in 1884, and 110,000 by 1885. At the movement's peak in 1886, about 750,000 Knights gathered in more than 15,000 locals across the country, and only seventy counties had no assembly at all. Up to 200,000 more Knights belonged to assemblies founded in Canada, England, Ireland, Belgium, France, Italy, Australia, and New Zealand.

The Knights of Labor also became the most inclusive U.S. labor organization of the nineteenth century. The order welcomed into its antimonopoly coalition all of the "producing classes"—not only wageworkers but also housewives, farmers, clergymen, shopkeepers, doctors, writers, editors, and other professionals. Employers could join, too, if they had once been wage earners and now treated their employees fairly by paying good wages and observing the eight-hour day. The only groups summarily excluded were liquor dealers, stockbrokers, bankers, professional gamblers, and corporate lawyers.

The Knights formally admitted women in 1882, after women shoe workers in Philadelphia had organized their own assembly. In 1886, when women made up about 10 percent of the order's membership, the general assembly established a national women's department headed by Leonora Barry, an Irish-born hosiery mill operative who led a female trade assembly in Amsterdam, New York. Chicago's giant district assembly was headed by Elizabeth Rodgers, a housewife and mother of twelve children. The order was the first U.S. labor organization to endorse female suffrage, and its local assemblies hosted many lectures on women's rights.

The order also welcomed immigrants, translated its literature into various languages, and chartered numerous foreign-language assemblies—with one major exception. Although the New York City and Philadelphia districts tried to organize Chinese workers in 1886–87, western districts were deeply involved in the anti-Chinese movement, and the organization's national spokesmen often called for Chinese immigrants' expulsion from the United States. When Wyoming Knights led the mob that massacred Chinese in Rock Springs in 1885, Terence Powderly blamed the violence on Chinese evasion of the Exclusion Act.

Black-white co-operation in the Knights set a new standard, however. The order's *Journal of United Labor* declared in 1880 that, "We should be false to every principle of our Order should we exclude from membership any man who gains his living by honest toil, on account of his color or creed."[29] By 1886, African American Knights numbered at least 60,000. Black men and women made up about half the order's rank and file in Virginia, North Carolina, and Arkansas, and a third of the whole southern membership. Even after the Knights went public, black members in southern states often had to organize in secret. After touring the South, a member of the national executive board reported that, "It is as much as a person's life is worth to be known as a member of the Knights of Labor there."[30] Southern assemblies were sometimes integrated; Ida Wells, who attended a Memphis assembly in the late 1880s, reported that "everyone who came was welcomed and every woman from black to white was seated with courtesy usually extended to white ladies alone in this town."[31]

The order's most dramatic confrontations with the color line came in October 1886, when the general assembly met in Richmond, Virginia. A local hotel refused to accommodate Frank Ferrell, an African American official from New York City's District Assembly 49 and a member of the general executive board. The whole New York delegation boycotted the hotel in protest and lodged with black families. Soon after, when the delegation went to see a production of *Hamlet* at a local theater, Ferrell took a seat in the orchestra section, which had always been reserved for whites. These incidents enraged the local press; the *Richmond Dispatch* rounded up some of Virginia's white Knights to publicly chide the New Yorkers for discourtesy to their host city.

In the convention hall, the color line was a contentious issue from the first session onward. Virginia's governor Fitzhugh Lee came to the opening ceremonies to deliver greetings, but upon learning that Frank Ferrell had been assigned to introduce him, Lee refused to take the stage. Terence Powderly hastily worked out a compromise under which Ferrell introduced Powderly, who then introduced the governor. But Ferrell's very presence on the dais made clear the Knights' commitment to unifying black and white workers, and his words drove home the point. "One of the objects of our Order," he reminded the delegates, "is abolition of those distinctions which are maintained by creed or color."[32] Later, the convention passed a resolution that "the organization of the Knights of Labor recognizes the civil and political equality of all men, and in the broad field of labor it recognizes no distinction on account of color." At the insistence of delegates more conservative than those from District Assembly 49, however, this resolution concluded on an entirely different note, with a promise that the Knights did not aim to "interfere with or disrupt the social relations which may exist between different races in any part of the country."[33]

Some northern newspapers condemned that concession to what one Kansas daily called "the influence of lingering prejudice on the southern mind."[34] But, as the resolution's authors had hoped, the southern press approved, so much so that not even the *Richmond Dispatch* complained when hundreds of out-of-town delegates joined with about 2,000 local Knights—most of them African Americans—for an integrated march through the city and an afternoon of games and speeches at its public picnic grounds. That evening Richmond's black Knights held a banquet in honor of the delegates from District Assembly 49. The *Cleveland Gazette*, a black newspaper, offered this verdict on the convention: "Taking all things into consideration, time, place surroundings, etc., it is the most remarkable thing since emancipation."[35]

The Knights of Labor (K of L) sponsored social and educational programs, ran candidates for office in over 200 cities and towns in 1885–86, and sponsored hundreds of consumer and producer co-operatives. First and foremost, however, K of L assemblies functioned as labor unions. Many craft unions wiped out by the depression of the 1870s reconstituted themselves under the order's umbrella. Local assemblies frequently went on strike to force employers to negotiate wages and working conditions, and trade assemblies in the same industry frequently backed each other with sympathy strikes. Walkouts grew more common as the order expanded. Across the country, K of L strikes averaged about 450 a year from 1881 through 1884; and they numbered 645 in 1885 and more than 1,400 in 1886 and again in 1887. In 1885, a successful strike against wage cuts on Jay Gould's southwestern rail lines greatly boosted the order's prestige and attracted many new recruits.

The Knights' biggest campaign originated outside the order, in the Federation of Organized Trades and Labor Unions (FOTLU). The federation was a relatively small network of national craft unions not affiliated with the Knights, and it seldom did more than pass resolutions. But in September 1882, its central labor union in New York City staged a workers' holiday; instead of going to work, some 30,000 men and women marched for labor's rights. Labor Day parades henceforth became annual events in New York and other cities, including Cincinnati, Buffalo, and Lynn, Massachusetts. (This paved the way for Congress to declare Labor Day a federal holiday in 1894.) Many marchers carried placards and banners emblazoned with the slogan "Eight hours for work, eight hours for rest, eight hours for what we will."[36] Earlier campaigns for the eight-hour day had aimed at winning it through legislation, but FOTLU leaders like P.J. McGuire of the Brotherhood of Carpenters held that unionists should take direct action to shorten the workday. The FOTLU convention of 1884 resolved that "eight hours shall constitute a legal day's labor from and after May 1, 1886" and called on member unions to prepare for strikes to enforce this edict.[37]

The Knights' general executive board declined to endorse the plan, and Terence Powderly secretly ordered his lieutenants to discourage local and district assemblies from supporting it. But the eight-hour cause galvanized rank-and-file Knights. Assembly after assembly pledged support, and organizers built multitudes of new assemblies on the eight-hour platform. That accounted for most of the order's astonishing sixfold growth from 1885 to 1886.

The eight-hour movement generated tremendous optimism—more than enough to sustain the order through a crushing rematch with Jay Gould. In February 1886, Knights on his southwestern railroads struck to enforce a demand for union recognition. This time around, Gould refused to give in, and lawmen mobilized to smash the strike. Many workers were arrested; in East St. Louis, Illinois, seven were killed during a battle with militiamen and police. By mid-April, it was clear that the strike would be defeated—that monopolists like Gould could find the wherewithal to vanquish mass revolts. But the Knights' eight-hour assemblies continued to multiply, and their spirits still ran high. On the evening of April 29, more than 5,000 members of Baltimore's assemblies paraded through the city with K of L regalia, a brass band and drum corps, and placards bearing slogans such as "Our Cause Is Just, In God We Trust" and "The Past Is History, The Future Is Bright." The parade ended at the Concordia Opera House, where an overflow crowd heard speaker after speaker predict that a mass "boycott" of wage work would quickly usher in the eight-hour day.[38]

On Saturday, May 1, about 350,000 workers at more than 11,000 establishments across the country went on strike. In Chicago, 65,000 strikers staged weekend rallies and parades. Counterattacks began on Monday, when the city's police fired into a group picketing the McCormick Harvester Works and killed at least four workers. Anarchist leaders of Chicago's eight-hour coalition called a protest meeting, held the night of May 4 at Haymarket Square. A few thousand showed up, but the crowd had dwindled to a few hundred by the time policemen arrived to disperse the gathering, a little after ten o'clock. As the police entered the square, someone—the culprit has never been identified—threw a bomb that instantly killed one officer and wounded another sixty-six, seven of whom later died.

For several weeks police rounded up labor activists by the hundreds. Meeting halls and residences were raided; entire families were jailed; evidence of incendiary plots was seized—or manufactured when it could not be found. Newspapers reported daily on the police department's progress in tracking down the perpetrators. On May 27, eight anarchists—August Spies, Albert Parsons, Adolph Fischer, George Engel, Louis Lingg, Samuel Fielden, Oscar Neebe, and Michael Schwab—were indicted for conspiracy to commit murder. Their trial began on June 21.

Only two of the defendants, Spies and Fielden, had been present when the explosion occurred, but the prosecution did not care who actually threw the bomb. The accused had been indicted for their militant leadership of the eight-hour movement and for their association with anarchism. The trial was merely for show, its outcome a foregone conclusion. The defendants were tried collectively, so that evidence against one could be used to besmirch the whole group, and the trial was unfair in every imaginable way. In 1893, when Illinois's newly elected governor John Peter Altgeld pardoned the surviving defendants, he pointed to numerous wrongdoings on the part of the police, the court, and the prosecution, including the manufacture of evidence, manipulation of the jury pool, and subornation of perjury.[39] All eight defendants were convicted; Neebe was sentenced to fifteen years and the others condemned to death.

After the trial, trade unionists and social reformers campaigned far and wide for clemency or the pardon of the defendants. Albert Parsons's wife was especially active. A Texan of black, Mexican, and Native American ancestry, Lucy Eldine Gonzalez Parsons worked tirelessly for the amnesty campaign, speaking to 200,000 people in sixteen states and inspiring widespread support. John Brown Jr. sent each of the condemned men a basket of Catawba grapes and a letter of solidarity that quoted his father's statement shortly before execution: "It is a great comfort to feel assured that I am permitted to die for a cause,—not merely to pay the debt of nature, as all must."[40] Petitions on behalf of the Haymarket martyrs came from as far away as Russia; their supporters held mass meetings in London, Paris, and other European cities. Just days before the execution, Governor Richard Oglesby commuted Fielden's and Schwab's sentences to life in prison. The night before he was to be hanged, Lingg cheated his would-be executioners by committing suicide. On November 11, 1887, Spies, Parsons, Fischer, and Engel went to the gallows. Some 25,000 people marched in their funeral procession.

The eight-hour movement had already fizzled, and the Knights were now on the wane. Within a week of the Haymarket bombing, strikers across the country were straggling back to work, brutalized by police and vilified by the press as dupes of an incendiary plot. Terence Powderly and his general executive board joined the conservative chorus. Denouncing anarchism, they refused to contribute to the Haymarket defense fund, and they tried their best to stamp out militancy among the order's rank and file.

In October 1886, trade assemblies of meatpacking workers led a strike of 25,000 at Chicago's Union Stock Yard, which had adopted the eight-hour day that spring and now declared a return to ten hours. Powderly told the striking assemblies to go back to work; when they defied him, he threatened to revoke their K of L charters. Smelling blood, the company broke off negotiations and announced that it would no longer employ any member of the Knights of Labor. A week later the strikers conceded defeat, and the meatpackers' assemblies soon died out.

Following this debacle, a long series of strikes pitted rank-and-file Knights against their national leaders as well as corporate employers. Workers lost nearly all of these battles, and the Order of the Knights of Labor shrank almost as swiftly as it had grown. Membership fell from 750,000 in 1886 to 220,000 in 1888, 100,000 in 1890, and only 20,000 by 1896. For many years, the organization survived in some locales: a handful of northeastern cities, black communities in the rural South, and Mexican American communities in the Southwest. The very last K of L assembly—motion-picture projectionists in Boston—endured until 1949. But by the end of the 1880s, the order was no longer the most dynamic labor organization in the United States.

The American Federation of Labor

As the Knights of Labor declined, a new national labor organization came to the fore. The American Federation of Labor (AFL) was founded in December 1886 in Columbus, Ohio, at a convention called by the Federation of Organized Trades and Labor Unions. The AFL's founding president—reelected almost every year until his death in 1924—was the cigar maker Samuel Gompers, an English immigrant of Dutch-Jewish descent. An alliance of thirteen national craft unions, the newborn federation advanced two fundamental principles: "pure and simple" unionism (a focus on wages, hours, and working conditions rather than grand plans for social reform) and voluntarism (unions' strict reliance upon themselves and their members, not labor-friendly legislators or genteel social reformers).[41] Defining itself as a better alternative to the Knights of Labor, the AFL practiced what one historian has aptly called "prudential unionism," a defensive strategy that accepted the wage-labor system and tried to avoid government intervention in labor disputes.[42]

In some respects the young AFL took up where the Knights had left off. In 1890, the federation revived the eight-hour campaign, selected the Brotherhood of Carpenters to be the first union to strike for the cause, and urged all unionists to demonstrate in support on May 1. The business journal *Bradstreet's* reported that more strikes started that day than on any previous day on record, and the Carpenters won the eight-hour day for more than 46,000 members. "Sympathy strikes" like this characterized AFL style in the early years. Of the 7,500 strikes its unions staged from 1890 through 1894, nearly one in ten was a sympathy strike.

Otherwise, the federation sharply distinguished itself from the Knights. It did not run candidates for public office. In contrast to the order's centralized structure, the AFL executive council upheld the autonomy of affiliated unions. The council intervened only to mediate between affiliates disputing jurisdictions and to provide support for organizing drives and strikes. Critical of rank-and-file Knights' penchant for going on strike without adequate resources, the AFL also encouraged affiliates to set high initiation fees and dues so that union treasuries would be large enough to sustain members through long work stoppages. And the Knights' diversity gave way to homogeneity in the AFL, which focused on organizing highly skilled workers—those with the most social clout. The AFL's initial membership reflected the composition of skilled trades; it was overwhelmingly male, white, and descended from northwestern Europe. Of the thirteen founding affiliates, only the Cigar Makers International Union and International Typographical Union admitted women, and none included many workers of color.

By 1892, the AFL's founding unions had been joined by twenty-seven others, many of them formed by defectors from the Knights of Labor. Newcomers included the Boot and Shoe Workers International Union, the United Mine Workers, the National Union of Textile Workers, and the United Garment Workers. The "international" unions had some Canadian locals, but were headquartered in the United States. The textile, garment, and shoe unions all had substantial female membership, virtually all white. About a fifth of the United Mine Workers' members in the coal fields were black men.

AFL headquarters lent verbal support to women's organizing drives but seldom came through with much more. In May 1892, the executive council hired Mary Kenney, a bookbinder from Chicago, as the federation's first general organizer of women. That summer she toured northeastern cities, establishing female locals of bookbinders and garment workers in New York City, Albany, and Troy, and making contact with interested women working in a variety of trades in and around Boston. This increased white women's presence in the AFL. In October, however, the executive council abolished Kenney's post. Several prolonged strikes by male unions had recently decimated AFL coffers, and now that every penny counted, most of the council regarded outreach to women as an expendable luxury. In December 1893, the AFL hired a second woman organizer—the Boston typographer E. Frances Pitts—and she, too, was let go within a few months. A permanent post did not materialize until 1898, when Eva McDonald Valesh, former editor of a labor newspaper in Minneapolis-St. Paul, was hired into the dual job of union organizer and assistant editor of the AFL monthly, the *American Federationist*.

If outreach to women was a low priority, the AFL did generally welcome those who came knocking at its door. Women's unions were often chartered as "federal labor unions"—locals that did not belong to a national union but instead affiliated directly with the AFL. By the late 1890s, all but a handful of the federation's affiliated unions had amended their constitutions to allow for female membership, but many kept women out in other ways—through high initiation fees, for instance, or with special examinations for female applicants. In the federal labor unions and in the nationals, nearly all of the young AFL's women members were native-born whites or immigrants from northwestern Europe.

Male membership grew somewhat more diverse, thanks largely to the executive council's early policies on that front. The council hired male organizers fluent in Italian, Yiddish, Bohemian, Spanish, and other foreign tongues and translated union literature into multiple languages. The AFL convention of 1890 resolved to deny a charter to the National Association of Machinists, whose constitution included a whites-only clause. The following year, the executive council fostered the establishment of a rival group, the International Union of Machinists of America, whose founding meeting in New York City condemned racial exclusion and voted to affiliate with the AFL. Much the same thing happened in 1893, when AFL headquarters refused to charter the all-white Brotherhood of Boiler Makers and Iron Ship Builders and set up an alternate union that admitted black men.

Starting in 1891, the executive council employed black men as general organizers. The first was George Norton from the Marine Firemen's Union in St. Louis; within a year he was joined by James Porter from the Car Drivers' Union in New Orleans (an organization of streetcar motormen). In 1892, both men helped to lead strikes that transcended the color line. That spring, black workers on the St. Louis riverfront initiated a weeklong walkout that soon spread to their white counterparts and ended with wage increases across the board. In late October, black and white workingmen employed on the New Orleans docks launched a joint strike that culminated in an interracial walkout of 25,000 workers from forty-nine different unions. For four days, from November 7 through November 10, everything from printing offices to electrical plants to construction sites shut down tight as employers tried in vain to divide and conquer. Finally, they agreed to negotiate, and the dockworkers won their demands for shorter hours, higher wages, and overtime pay. As one local labor leader wrote to Samuel Gompers, the New Orleans strike was "the finest exhibition of the unification of Labor . . . ever had in this or any other city."[43]

The AFL's commitment to unifying workingmen always had boundaries, however, and they grew more restrictive over the course of the 1890s. From the start, the federation barred workers of Asian descent, and Gompers lobbied hard for extensions of the Chinese Exclusion Act when it came up for renewal in 1892 and again in 1902. By the latter year, AFL spokesmen were also calling for laws to limit immigration from eastern and southern Europe, and the federation's executive council no longer refused to charter national unions whose constitutions stipulated that only white workers could join. The policy on racially segregated locals had changed too. The executive council had initially defined them as a necessary evil that would disappear over time; black and white locals would presumably merge once white workers were educated away from what Gompers called "the ridiculous attempt to draw the color line in our labor organizations."[44] By the early 1900s, however, AFL headquarters regarded segregated locals as permanent arrangements and began to charter segregated labor councils in southern states.

From day one, moreover, the AFL's basic organizing strategy undercut its capacity to promote labor solidarity irrespective of color, nationality, and sex. The stress on craft unionism, together with hefty initiation fees and dues, inevitably distanced the federation from workers outside the skilled, relatively high-paying trades. A great many of those outsiders were native-born white men; but women, immigrants, and workers of color were all disproportionately confined to unskilled and semiskilled occupations, where craft unionism—not to mention expensive unionism—simply did not make sense.

Nor could the AFL strategy protect union craftsmen from assault by monopoly capitalists. Never was that more evident than when the Amalgamated Association of Iron and Steel Workers squared off against the steel baron Andrew Carnegie in the summer and fall of 1892. The Amalgamated admitted only the most skilled steel-workers. At Carnegie's mill in Homestead, Pennsylvania, less than a quarter of the 3,800 employees belonged to the union, whose agreement with the company placed the skilled men at Homestead among the best paid workers in the land. Determined to expand his power and profits, Carnegie decided that when the Amalgamated's contract expired on June 30, 1892, the Homestead mill would become a nonunion plant. To that end, Carnegie placed the mill's management in the hands of his lieutenant Henry Clay Frick, well known in western Pennsylvania for his hatred of unions and ruthless suppression of strikes.

As the Amalgamated's contract neared expiration, Frick announced the company's intention to cut union men's wages by an average of 22 percent. Then, on May 30, he issued an ultimatum: if the men did not accept the new wage scale by June 24, the company would no longer recognize their union. When the Amalgamated held firm, he went to war, shutting down the mill on June 30 and hiring the Pinkerton National Detective Agency to reopen it with scab labor.

Nearly all of Homestead's 11,000 residents rallied behind the Amalgamated. Unskilled steelworkers—mostly Slavic immigrants—joined union members in pick-eting the mill, as did many housewives and schoolchildren. In the wee hours of July 6, about 300 armed Pinkertons tried to sneak into the plant, traveling on barges that silently pulled up to the company's beach on the Monongahela River. But a patrol of workers had spotted the barges and sounded the alarm. As the Pinkertons landed, an angry crowd of Homesteaders streamed down to the beach, and both sides opened fire. The invaders surrendered after a daylong battle that killed seven workers and three Pinkertons.

When Governor Robert Pattison sent 8,000 militiamen to Homestead on July 12, the Amalgamated welcomed the intervention. A union spokesman declared, "On behalf of the Amalgamated Association I wish to say that after suffering an attack of illegal authority we are glad to have the legal authority of the state here."[45] The troops had arrived at Frick's request, however; they were there to safeguard the company, not the townspeople. By the end of the month, the mill was starting to produce steel with a force of scabs the Pinkerton agency had recruited in Pittsburgh. Militiamen escorted them to work.

The criminal justice system came to Frick's aid too. As the mill reopened, he orchestrated mass indictments of strike leaders on charges of murder, conspiracy, and even treason. This backlash gained momentum after July 23, when Frick was seri-ously wounded by Alexander Berkman, a young anarchist from New York City who had tried to assassinate him. Homestead's chief of police stepped up arrests of strikers on the pretext that local anarchists were plotting violence. By October, 185 criminal indictments had been issued, with some men charged four and five times. No one was convicted, but the legal battles decimated the union's strike fund.

In November, unskilled workers petitioned the Amalgamated for release from their pledge of support, and the union declared the strike over. The defeat shattered the Amalgamated, formerly one of the AFL's most powerful affiliates. Workers at Carn-egie mills in several other towns had walked out in sympathy with the Homestead strikers, and there, too, the Amalgamated lost union recognition. The union's membership fell from 24,000 in 1891 to 8,000 in 1895. Mills owned by the Carnegie Steel Company—later sold to J.P. Morgan and renamed United States Steel—would remain union-free for two generations.

In 1894, troops and courts combined to put down a mass railroad strike led by a new industrial union, whose members had come together regardless of skill. Craft organizations had done little for most railroad workers. Independent of the AFL, the five railroad brotherhoods (unions of engineers, conductors, firemen, brakemen, and switchmen) were even more exclusive and prudential. They ignored semiskilled and unskilled employees, tried to drive African Americans out of the industry, and seldom honored one another's strikes. Indeed, their leaders condemned strikes altogether. Their members' working conditions and pay were among the worst in the country. Each year, one trainman out of every hundred was killed on the job and another ten injured; in 1890, only engineers and conductors averaged more than $350 in annual wages. Small wonder, then, that in the fall of 1892, rank-and-file railroad workers met secretly in Chicago to plan "an organization built up of *'all classes'* of R.R. men."[46] This organization—the American Railway Union (ARU)—went public on June 20, 1893, its membership open to all white railroad employees except superintendents and corporate officials, with a national initiation fee and yearly dues of a dollar each. At the founding meeting, a proposal to admit black members had been defeated by a margin of 113 to 102. The ARU did admit white women, and supported equal pay irrespective of sex.

Eugene Debs, editor of *The Locomotive Firemen's Magazine*, became the ARU's president. After winning an eighteen-day strike against the Great Northern Railroad in April 1894, the union began to sign up new members at the rate of 2,000 a day. By June it was the nation's largest union, with 150,000 members in 425 lodges.

Among them were 4,000 workers who manufactured railroad passenger cars at the Pullman Palace Car Company complex in Pullman, Illinois, near Chicago. George Pullman ran a company town, keeping rents high while he reduced wages. When the ARU's Pullman lodges went on strike on May 11, 1894, he closed the plants. In June, the strikers appealed to the ARU's first national convention: "Help us make our country better and more wholesome. . . . Teach arrogant grinders of the faces of the poor that there still is a God of Israel, and—if need be—a Jehovah—a God of battles."[47] The convention authorized a boycott; beginning June 26, no ARU member would work on any train that included Pullman cars. When the railroad companies refused to detach the cars, the boycott became a general strike on the railways. Within three days, and despite opposition from the railroad brotherhoods, 150,000 strikers shut down eleven lines, to widespread sympathy fed by public resentment of the rail corporations.

Two days into the strike, U.S. Attorney General Richard Olney sought advice from Edwin Walker, counsel to the railroads' General Managers' Association. Walker recommended getting an injunction based on the Sherman Antitrust Act, a vaguely worded and rarely invoked federal law that supposedly took aim at trusts and cartels involved in interstate trade. On July 2, citing damage to interstate commerce and criminal conspiracy to obstruct postal service, the federal district court in Chicago enjoined all interference with rail operations, including any attempt to persuade a railroad employee not to work. The next day President Grover Cleveland dispatched federal troops to enforce the order. When they arrived in Chicago on Independence Day, riots broke out. Over the next few days, at least twenty-five civilians were killed, and the Illinois Central railroad yards went up in flames. Across the country, newspapers ran headlines like these from July 9: "No Truce with Anarchy" (*Boston Daily Globe*), "Soldiers Must Shoot to Kill" (*New York Times*), "Foreign Immigration a Menace" (*Washington Post*).[48] On July 10, Eugene Debs and other ARU officers were indicted for violating the injunction and immediately arrested as federal marshals and postal inspectors ransacked the union's headquarters.

An emergency committee called for a general strike in Chicago to begin the next day, but only 25,000 workers turned out. Many unions awaited the decision of the AFL's executive council, summoned by Gompers to a special meeting at Chicago's Briggs House hotel on July 12. The council contributed $1,000 to a legal defense fund, but agreed only to help Debs make an offer to call off the boycott if his members could return to their jobs. With that, the strike collapsed in Chicago, but it quickly spread westward, all the way to California. In the West, too, federal troops suppressed the strike, and authorities in Chicago saw to it that the ARU did not rebound there. Rearrested on July 17, Debs and other strike leaders were later convicted of violating the injunction, and the U.S. Supreme Court denied their appeal. Debs served six months; his fellow defendants three. By 1897, the ARU had all but disappeared; just two dozen delegates showed up at its national convention that June.

The Lessons of Defeat

The depression of 1893–97 hurt farmers and small businessmen as well as wageworkers, and resentment of monopoly capitalists' control of government spread far and wide. The People's Party—usually called the Populists—provided an opportunity to act. The party grew out of the Farmers' Alliances, which had preached agrarian organization against monopoly since the late 1870s, when the movement was born in Texas. The alliances had serious weaknesses; they tried to merge the contrary interests of small farmers and large planters, they tended to neglect sharecroppers and tenant farmers, and they practiced racial segregation. But the movement's convention of 1889 adopted the "St. Louis Program," which was both practical and audacious. It called for public ownership of the railroads, the breakup of large landholding companies, the abolition of national banks, the establishment of a graduated income tax, and the creation of federal "subtreasuries" that would lend money at nominal interest.

In 1890, "Alliancemen" entered electoral politics, gained control of many state governments in the South and Midwest, and won more than forty seats in Congress. At its first convention, held in Omaha, Nebraska, in July 1892, the People's Party expanded the Farmers Alliances' program to include "bimetallism"—a plan to increase the money supply by supplementing federal gold reserves with silver—and, in a nod to organized labor, called for a shorter workday and restrictions on immigration. In 1894, Populist candidates received 1.5 million votes, taking enough votes from Democrats to make Republicans the majority party.

Samuel Gompers did not think much of Populists, since their movement included employers. But the state governments they controlled were generally friendly to labor, and socialist trade unionists urged the AFL's executive council to declare independence from the two-party system and endorse the Populist challenge. At the federation's national convention in Denver in December 1894, the delegates adopted most of the socialists' program, but Gompers managed to defeat two crucial proposals: one for social ownership of the means of production and the other for independent political action.

While the AFL rejected the People's Party, the surviving assemblies of the Knights of Labor did not. The order had become a predominantly rural organization, its 75,000 members mostly in the West and South. The Knights sent delegates to the Populist conventions in St. Louis and Omaha.

Unfortunately, the Knights of Labor could no longer bring cross-racial solidarity to the movement. Though the order's overall membership declined after Haymarket, its black membership increased; in mid-1887, the Knights had more than 90,000 black members in the South, up from 60,000 a year earlier. That year 10,000 Knights—9,000 of them African Americans—went on strike in Louisiana's sugarcane fields. The strike was suppressed by lawmen and vigilante forces, and more than twenty-five black workers were killed. The order's general executive board declined to assist the strikers. By 1894, with radicals like Frank Ferrell long gone, the board had decided that the "Negro problem" could be solved only by deportation.[49] The southwestern Knights' Mexican American membership had also surged in the late 1880s, especially in New Mexico. In 1888, Juan José Herrera—founder of Las Gorras Blancas—was commissioned as a district organizer for the order and helped start more than twenty local assemblies of Los Caballeros de Labor in San Miguel and neighboring counties. But these assemblies never developed a working relationship with New Mexico's Anglo Knights and clashed repeatedly with the general executive board. When Herrera, his brother Pablo, and forty-five other Mexicans were indicted for Las Gorras activities, neither the board nor local Anglo Knights extended support. In 1891, Pablo Herrera (recently elected to New Mexico's territorial legislature) was expelled from the order for his connection to Las Gorras.

Racial exclusion undermined the Populists in both western and southwestern states. The Partido del Pueblo in New Mexico never developed ties to the national People's Party. In the South, a Colored Farmer's Alliance had formed alongside the white movement, and there were many attempts to confederate or merge the two. The white Populist leader Tom Watson argued for unity, telling Georgia farmers, "You are made to hate each other because upon that hatred is rested the keystone of the arch of financial despotism which enslaves you both. You are deceived and blinded that you may not see how this race antagonism perpetuates a monetary system which beggars you both."[50] But black activists could not count on white support. In 1891 members of Georgia's white Farmers' Alliance broke a cotton pickers' strike by members of the black alliance; Ben Patterson, the strike's thirty-year-old leader in Arkansas, was caught by a white posse and fatally shot. Tom Watson went on to build a long political career as an advocate of the Jim Crow system—a complex of new state laws and constitutions that required separation of the races and restricted black men's voting rights.

Desperate to recoup the losses of 1894, the Democrats began to echo the Populists' call for bimetallism and nominated Nebraska's William Jennings Bryan for president in 1896. A former congressman and popular orator, he had been stumping the country to speak in support of the proposal to monetize silver. After rancorous debate and division, the Populists also nominated Bryan for the presidency, though he did not endorse most of their program. Republican William McKinley swamped him at the polls, and the Populist moment passed.

Labor activists drew different lessons from the devastating defeats of the Homestead and Pullman strikes. Eugene Debs and his comrades saw the need for even greater solidarity. Samuel Gompers and many craft unionists concluded that it was futile to challenge the combined might of big business and government; judicious, "pure and simple" unionism worked best. Years later, Gompers said of the Briggs House conference: "The course pursued by the Federation was the biggest service that could have been performed to maintain the integrity of the Railroad Brotherhoods."[51]

The Populist failure in 1896 likewise offered contradictory lessons. Gompers favored cultivating those business and political leaders least hostile to labor. Debs concluded that workers had to "unite at the ballot box, not only to back up the economic struggle of the trades-union, but to finally wrest the government from capitalist control and establish the working class republic."[52] Others entirely rejected politics as a game wholly controlled by capital.

"How can the trade unions successfully combat the giant monstrosities of the closing years of the nineteenth century?" asked George McNeill in the AFL's monthly magazine in December 1896. If many people thought the labor movement defenseless against the "power of aggregate wealth," this veteran labor leader disagreed, and he proposed a plan for mounting a defense.[53] First, unions themselves had to aggregate, merging to form organizations that could organize whole industries and, through the AFL, coordinate strategies and share resources across industrial lines. In particular, McNeill argued, unions should pool money to support strikers, to finance pensions for disabled workers and those blacklisted in retaliation for their activism, and to organize the unorganized on a massive scale. Finally, the labor movement needed to build alliances with farmers and other small proprietors and to develop educational programs to rally the general population against monopolies. McNeill's article was widely reprinted and discussed. Several unions endorsed it and called on the AFL's leaders to convene a conference and get started. The federation's executive council ignored them.

6

Labor and Empire

In November 1897, the American Federation of Labor came out against the annexation of Hawaii. Four years earlier American sugar planters had deposed Queen Liliuokalani, set up a sham republic, and asked that it become part of the United States. Now the Senate debated the proposal. The AFL's *American Federationist* rebuked the scheme's advocates for "cover[ing] themselves with the mantle of patriotism." In reality, the *Federationist* asserted, the scheme was merely "corporate power . . . endeavoring to invade acquired, natural, and constitutional rights."[1] Twenty years later, Samuel Gompers, the AFL's premier spokesperson, would be a leading proponent of America's transformation into a world power. That shift took place in the context of a vast expansion of U.S. capitalism abroad and rapprochement between government and labor leaders willing to support the empire.

Empire Abroad and at Home

In 1898, the United States moved into the ranks of modern world powers by defeating the forces of Spain, one of the oldest European empires. The Spanish-American War's official purpose was to help Cubans free themselves from Spanish colonialism. The Cuban rebellion had been building for decades, and armed insurrection broke out in 1895. Many ordinary Americans sympathized with the rebels. So did U.S. businessmen, who had invested $50 million in Cuban sugar plantations and aimed to invest more once Spain was out of the picture. Early in 1898, President McKinley sent the battleship *Maine* to Havana Harbor to demonstrate American interest in Cuba; it blew up and sank on February 15, killing 266 sailors. U.S. newspapers, some of which had called for the acquisition of Cuba as early as the 1850s, screamed for a military reprisal. On April 20, Congress declared war on Spain. Fighting began on May 1 in the Philippines, where a rebellion against Spanish rule was already in progress. By the time the war ended in August, U.S. troops had also invaded Cuba, Puerto Rico, Guam, and Wake Island, and Congress had annexed Hawaii. John Hay, U.S. ambassador to Great Britain, called it "a splendid little war."[2] U.S. combat deaths totaled 379, although over 5,000 troops died from disease or poisoning by canned rations of rotted beef. Under the peace treaty, the United States acquired Puerto Rico, Guam, and the Philippines as colonies, and the U.S. military administered Cuba until an independent government was formed.

Puerto Rican patriots protested their island's treatment as spoils of war. As one pamphlet stated, "The voice of Puerto Rico was not heard. The idea that the Puerto Rican people might have something to say on the subject . . . was not even thought of. The island and its people were conveyed from one sovereign to another as a farm and its cattle are conveyed from a master to another."[3] U.S. governors abolished local councils, revised laws, and even changed the island's name to "Porto Rico"[4]—easier for English speakers to pronounce. In 1900, Congress made Puerto Rico an unincorporated territory, meaning that the United States controlled the island but did not recognize its inhabitants as citizens.

In the Philippines, also claimed as an unincorporated territory, the United States faced an armed movement for independence that controlled most of the archipelago. Under the leadership of Emilio Aguinaldo, the Revolutionary Congress wrote a constitution, and the Philippine Republic was inaugurated in January 1899. Within days, U.S. forces moved against the Republican army, commencing a three-year war that involved 126,000 American troops. On July 4, 1902, Washington declared the war won, but new rebellions gathered and fighting continued for another twelve years.

Expansion overseas was hardly a novelty. The United States had seized the island of Navassa from Haiti in 1858, purchased Alaska from Russia in 1867, and the same year planted its flag on Midway Island in the Pacific. But now expansionism had more momentum than ever before. A host of politicians, professors, clergymen, editors, and military leaders contended that empire building was essential to national stability.

The nation's industrial capacity significantly exceeded domestic demand; that had been a chief cause of depressions and deflation in the Gilded Age. U.S. Labor Commissioner Carroll Wright observed in the early 1890s, "It is incontrovertible that the present manufacturing and mechanical plant of the United States is greater—far greater—than is needed to supply the demand; yet it is constantly being enlarged, and there is no way of preventing the enlargement."[5] An overseas empire promised relief. As the historian Brooks Adams wrote in 1900, the "United States must provide sure and adequate outlets for her products, or be in danger of gluts more dangerous to her society than many panics such as 1873 and 1893."[6]

Imperialists also hoped that overseas military adventures would absorb popular energy. The *Atlantic Monthly* magazine endorsed war with Spain partly on the grounds that it would reduce social unrest: "Apostolic fervor, romantic dreaming, and blatant misinformation have each captivated the idle-minded masses. . . . These things all denote a lack of adventurous opportunities."[7] A sociology professor at Columbia University argued that, if Americans did not spend their "reservoir of energy" in overseas conquests, it would "discharge itself in anarchistic, socialistic, and other destructive modes . . . likely to work incalculable mischief."[8]

Racism bolstered expansionism. "Take up the White Man's burden," urged British writer Rudyard Kipling in a widely reprinted poem that welcomed the United States to the ranks of colonial powers ruling "new-caught sullen peoples" of Asia and Africa.[9] Theodore Roosevelt—Spanish-American War hero, McKinley's running mate in 1900, and president following McKinley's assassination in 1901—understood the Philippines war in similar terms. Speaking at a dinner in New York City, he asserted, "It is infinitely better for the whole world that . . . France should have taken Algiers, and that England should have taken India. The success of an Algerian or of a Sepoy revolt would be a hideous calamity to all mankind, and those who abetted it, directly or indirectly, would be traitors to civilization. And so exactly the same reasoning applies to our own dealings with the Philippines."[10]

Racist expansionism closely paralleled white supremacy at home. Quoting Kipling's poem, the *Atlantic Monthly* asked in an editorial, "If the stronger and cleverer race is free to impose its will upon 'new-caught, sullen peoples' on the other side of the globe, why not in South Carolina and Mississippi?"[11] In 1890, Mississippi had disfranchised most black men by imposing a literacy test on voters; in 1895, South Carolina had followed suit and instituted a poll tax as well. After the U.S. Supreme Court upheld the Mississippi restrictions in 1898, the disfranchisement of African Americans spread to Louisiana in 1900, to Alabama in 1901, and on across the South. Writing to the *Richmond Planet*, Battalion Sergeant Major John Galloway, a black soldier stationed in the Philippines, predicted, "The future of the Filipino . . . is that of the Negro in the South."[12] He was right. In 1901, the Supreme Court ruled that residents of the new U.S. colonies did not automatically enjoy rights and protections guaranteed by the Constitution.

Opposition to empire building was widespread at the turn of the century. Old-fashioned republicans despised colonialism; some racial purists fretted that colonial subjects might become citizens; businessmen worried about military costs; farmers dreaded competition from agricultural produce imported from the colonies. Labor unions played an active role in the anti-imperialist movement. Some unionists opposed wars of conquest on principle. Many more feared that militarism abroad would lead to repression at home.

Samuel Gompers denounced cheap colonial products and labor. In November 1898, he became a vice president of the Anti-Imperialist League, joining businessmen like Andrew Carnegie and politicians like Grover Cleveland. The league enrolled 500,000 members but failed to defeat McKinley's bid for reelection in 1900 and faded soon afterward. Criticism of expansion quickly disappeared from the labor press. In 1901, the *American Federationist* declared, "Never was labor better organized and alive to its interests than now, and never was America's foreign trade so stupendous as now."[13]

The American Federation of Labor had mixed relations with labor movements in the new colonies. In Puerto Rico, the Federación Libre de Trabajadores (FLT) accepted annexation to the United States and focused on winning an American standard of living for Puerto Rican workers. The AFL hired the FLT's founder, Santiago Iglesias, as an organizer in 1901. In the Philippines, the Unión Obrera Democrática Filipina rallied for independence. Suppressed by the U.S. military, it reorganized in 1903 and led a May Day march of 100,000 in Manila, demanding an end to U.S. occupation. For this the Unión Obrera was suppressed once again. In 1904, the AFL declined to organize Manila cigar makers for fear of abetting the movement for Filipino independence, which especially animated skilled workers. In Hawaii, white craftsmen from the U.S. mainland joined AFL unions, but these unions had nothing to do with Asian workers organizing on the sugar plantations.

In the wake of the Spanish-American War, the mainland economy flourished. The depression of the 1890s had ended by the time the war began; now the recovery turned into a boom. A wave of corporate mergers and acquisitions that had paused during the depression resumed and accelerated. Consortiums of financiers created holding companies beyond the reach of antitrust legislation. Between 1898 and 1903, thousands of firms were absorbed into ever-larger holding companies. The largest of all was United States Steel, formed in 1901 by J.P. Morgan of New York and Elbert Gary of Chicago after they bought a controlling interest in Carnegie Steel. Capitalized at $1.4 billion, U.S. Steel held 165 subsidiaries in a constellation of industries—steel, mining, shipping, and construction. Mergers and acquisitions reduced the ruinous competition of the Gilded Age.

Government regulated industry and commerce in business-friendly ways. The first federal regulatory agency—the Interstate Commerce Commission (ICC)—had accomplished virtually nothing since its establishment in 1887. Congress had authorized it merely to investigate freight railroads and make nonbinding recommendations as to the rates they should charge. In 1906, the ICC's powers expanded. Thanks to lobbying by manufacturers and merchants seeking predictable shipping costs, the agency now got jurisdiction over all interstate transportation, and its rulings on rates became binding unless overturned by the courts. A consortium of food companies lobbied for the Pure Food and Drug Act and Federal Meat Inspection Act; signed into law on the same day in 1906, they imposed product standards acceptable to manufacturers. Bankers designed the Federal Reserve System, established in 1913 to regulate finance. The Federal Trade Commission—set up the following year to regulate industrial corporations—was the brainchild of business magnates, most notably George Perkins of U.S. Steel.

Exports helped to sustain the business boom. The dollar volume of U.S. goods sold abroad increased by more than 50 percent between 1901 and 1914. Capital became an even more important export. As an economist pointed out in 1899, "The real opportunity afforded by colonial possessions is for the development of the new countries by fixed investments."[14] U.S. foreign investment—mostly in Latin America and Canada—more than tripled by 1914. Puerto Rican sugar production expanded under a monopoly of four U.S. corporations. The greatest prizes in the Philippines were the "friar lands," close to a half-million acres of estates abandoned by the Spanish Catholic church. The United States paid the Vatican for their titles and auctioned them off, mostly to American sugar planters.

The most vital U.S. import was labor. Immigration to the United States rose from 229,000 entries in 1898 to more than 800,000 in 1904, and averaged about a million a year over the next decade. The vast majority of immigrants now came from eastern and southern Europe, and arrivals from Asia, Latin America, and the Caribbean reached new heights. The result, to quote historian David Montgomery, was "nothing less than the ethnic recomposition of the American working class."[15] The so-called American worker—a descendant of northwestern Europe—became a relatively privileged minority of the labor force.

To native-born "old" Americans, the crowded immigrant ghettoes of modern cities looked like cesspools of vice and crime and a threat to social order. Proposed solutions came from many quarters. Old-fashioned evangelists and moral reformers campaigned to eradicate drinking, gambling, and prostitution. Newer ideas came from middle-class reformers who called themselves "progressives." Social workers in immigrant communities promoted vocational training, employment bureaus, and education in hygiene and American customs. Doctors, lawyers, social scientists, and other professionals advocated stricter housing codes and public sanitation. The impulse for reform ranged so widely that the age became known as the "Progressive Era."

Virtually every industrial state saw campaigns to ban child labor, regulate hours and conditions of work for women and teenagers, set standards for workplace safety and health, and create funds to compensate workers injured on the job. Beginning in Illinois in 1893, reformers in several states had lobbied successfully for labor laws to protect children and women in manufacturing, but these protections were often overturned in court or simply not enforced. When Congress took up child-labor legislation starting in 1906, southern textile manufacturers fiercely resisted it; but northern companies, already bound by state restrictions on child labor, supported federal action to reduce their southern competitors' advantage. While some business groups opposed laws requiring that workers be compensated for injuries, others joined the campaign in order to co-opt it. In 1911, the National Association of Manufacturers (NAM) wrote a "model" compensation law that restricted injured workers' claims. Within three years business lobbyists had persuaded twenty-five states to adopt the NAM formula.

Businessmen were also ambivalent about political reforms. "Good government" progressives challenged urban political machines like the New York Democratic Party's Tammany Hall, urged the appointment of experts as public administrators, and pushed to replace mayoral administrations with appointed commissioners or city managers. As the president of National Cash Register explained, such reforms were designed to put government "on a strict business basis."[16]

Businessmen and many progressives were less enthusiastic about democracy. To quote one business paper: "We have faith in popular opinion . . . when it is instructed, sober, moral, true. But we have no faith in popular opinion when it is rash, passionate, prejudiced and ignorant."[17] Common reforms aimed at regulating voting included literacy tests, registration far in advance of elections, and ballots supplied by election commissions instead of party clubhouses. Democratic reforms like ballot initiatives and recall elections were less widely adopted. Voter participation in elections fell from about 80 percent in the late nineteenth century to about 60 percent by 1920. The concept of democracy did not appear in the ideal government described by one prominent progressive businessman: "It is the work of the state to think for the people and plan for the people—to teach them how to do, what to do, and to sustain them in the doing."[18]

Separation of the races, especially in the South, was the most sweeping manifestation of the Progressive Era's obsession with social order. After the Supreme Court's decision in *Plessy v. Ferguson* (1896) upheld the constitutionality of racial segregation in Louisiana's railroad cars, white legislators in state after state enacted a myriad of laws that required the segregation of nearly every corner of southern life, from streetcars, theaters, housing, and cemeteries to brothels and the courtroom Bibles used to swear in witnesses. According to some southern progressives, segregation solved the problem of violence between races. Others thought it would stabilize white society. Progressive activist Reverend Edgar Gardner Murphy of Montgomery, Alabama, wrote that, "conscious unity of race is . . . better as a basis of democratic reorganization than the distinctions of wealth, of trade, of property, of family, or class."[19]

Segregation was not just a southern trend. In 1906, the San Francisco School Board assigned Asian American children to a separate public school, an order rescinded only after the Japanese government protested to President Roosevelt and agreed to restrict emigration to the United States. U.S. troops abroad carried Jim Crow with them, serving in segregated units with black regiments routinely placed under the command of white officers. When Afro-Caribbean workers were brought to Panama to dig the canal, Panamanian authorities segregated public facilities to please American sensibilities. Back in the United States, the federal government's commissioner of Indian affairs ruled in 1916 that people with one half or more Native American ancestry were not legally competent unless they passed a government review.

Philippine pacification was finally completed in 1914, and two years later Congress agreed to Filipinos' eventual independence. Aside from the purchase of the Virgin Islands in 1917, annexation had played out. The U.S. relationship with Cuba offered a better model. As promised, Cubans got independence in 1902. Their constitution—written under U.S. military occupation—gave the United States land for naval stations, a veto on Cuban foreign policy, and the right to send in troops at any time. American investment flowed into Cuba. This arrangement exemplified what became known as "dollar diplomacy": foreign policy designed to expand and protect U.S. corporations' investments abroad.[20]

Military interventions backed up diplomatic initiatives. U.S. forces joined other imperial powers in suppressing China's Boxer Rebellion in 1900 and stayed for almost thirty years. In 1903, U.S. warships backed a rebellion on Colombia's Isthmus of Panama in order to create a new government that would sign a canal treaty already prepared by lawyers in New York; eleven years later, the Panama Canal opened under U.S. control. To "protect American lives and property," U.S. troops occupied Cuba 1906–09 and again in 1917; Nicaragua almost continuously 1912–33; Mexico in 1914 and 1916–17; Haiti 1915–34; and the Dominican Republic 1916–24.[21] When Major General Smedley Butler looked back on his service in the Marine Corps in the Americas and China, he concluded, "I was a racketeer, a gangster for capitalism."[22]

Much as it needed troops, the empire needed workers just as badly. No one described this requirement better than Elbert Hubbard in his essay "Message to Garcia." Just before the war with Spain, Lieutenant Andrew Rowan of the U.S. Army had gone alone into Cuba's mountains to deliver a letter from President McKinley to the rebel general Calixto Garcia. In the March 1899 issue of Hubbard's magazine *The Philistine*, his tribute to Rowan became a meditation on the American working class. Employers, he wrote, could only be appalled by the average worker's "inability or unwillingness to concentrate on a thing and do it. Slip-shod assistance, foolish inattention, dowdy indifference, and half-hearted work seem the rule."[23] Even worse was the malcontent, "absolutely worthless to anyone else, because he carries with him constantly the insane suspicion that his employer is oppressing, or intending to oppress him. . . . He is impervious to reason, and the only thing that can impress him is the toe of a thick-soled No. 9 boot."[24] What civilization needed, Hubbard concluded, were diligent workers who would unquestioningly follow orders—workers who, like Lieutenant Rowan, could "carry a message to Garcia."[25] The essay so inspired American businessmen that they printed some 40 million copies to distribute to their employees.

The Labor Movement in the Progressive Era

The labor movement reflected the changing times. It coalesced around three organizational centers: the American Federation of Labor, the Socialist Party of America (SP), and a radical union known as the Industrial Workers of the World (IWW). The AFL—the first U.S. labor federation to survive a major depression—entered the twentieth century all the more committed to its "pure and simple" unionism based on craftsmen. Activists ignored or frustrated by the federation gathered in the SP and IWW. The three competed to lead American labor, each with a different program for winning better working conditions, richer lives, and social justice.

The American Federation of Labor focused on collective bargaining—contracts negotiated by professional representatives of well-funded unions of highly skilled workers, organized according to their separate crafts. The formula had weaknesses. In contrast to the federation's early years, craft unions now routinely crossed one another's picket lines and endlessly disputed jurisdictions. Salaried union officers and staff sometimes became grafters, offering employers sweetheart deals in return for bribes. Even squeaky-clean craft unions that were nominally open to less skilled workers charged dues beyond what they could afford. Attributing the AFL's survival to high dues, the federation's leaders also felt contempt for unions that rejected this strategy. According to the *American Federationist*, "Unions which are built upon the 'Cheap John,' low-dues idea . . . grow like mushrooms in the night and die for lack of that sustenance so necessary to their existence."[26]

To organize the unorganized, the AFL expanded its use of federal labor unions (FLUs) like those it had established for women workers in the 1890s. Originally conceived as a temporary stopping place for new recruits who would later join craft unions, FLUs now became permanent organizations for workers who did not fit into the AFL's craft structure. By 1913, they numbered about 800, and most of their members had no access to national labor unions on account of their occupations or their personal characteristics. Although Samuel Gompers described FLUs as "a splendid haven of protection," their proliferation as permanent organizations testified to craft unions' neglect of women, immigrants, and workers of color as well as the unskilled.[27]

As of 1910, about 73,000 women workers—less than 1 percent of the female labor force—belonged to any union. To recruit women into the AFL, Boston labor activists and reformers came together in 1903 to found the Women's Trade Union League, which subsequently spread to cities across the country. AFL leaders endorsed the project; but when national unions failed to charter locals organized by the league, the federation's executive council refused to press the issue or to charter the locals directly.

In 1900, only about 30,000 African Americans belonged to unions, two-thirds to the United Mine Workers (UMW). In Birmingham, Alabama, black workers were

active in the UMW, federal unions, and locals affiliated with national unions of barbers, plasterers, hod carriers, ironworkers, and others. Birmingham was exceptional,
however. In most cities the AFL had few or no black members.

The "new immigrants" from southern and eastern Europe were rarely skilled workers, and many AFL leaders considered them unfit for union membership and even for
admission to the United States. The federation lobbied Congress to test immigrants
for literacy, which would, according to Gompers, "shut out a considerable number of
South Italians and of Slavs and others equally or more undesirable and injurious."[28]
AFL opposition to Asian immigration and hostility to Asian American workers
continued unabated. In 1903, sugar beet workers in Oxnard, California, formed the
Japanese-Mexican Labor Association (JMLA), won a strike against a wage cut, and
applied for AFL membership. Gompers agreed to issue a charter but only if the union
would henceforth exclude Asians. When the JMLA refused to comply, he broke off
all relations.

The federation did charter a number of Latino locals in the Southwest. In California, AFL organizer Juan Ramírez helped migrant farmworkers near Long Beach and
San Pedro form La Unión de Jornaleros Unidos (FLU No. 13,097) in 1911. An independent union of Tejano railroad workers in Laredo became FLU No. 11,953 in 1905.
In El Paso, Texas, Anglo and Mexican American workers organized integrated locals
of the AFL's unions of typographers, painters, and carpenters; but these locals did not
include workers born in Mexico.

If prejudice begat AFL exclusiveness, so did thoughtful calculation by the federation's leaders. They believed that craftsmen could make steady headway with narrow craft unionism—"the line of least resistance," as an officer of the AFL's United
Garment Workers called it.[29] As the age of empire dawned, the AFL experienced a
growth spurt that seemed to confirm that formula's wisdom. By 1904, the federation
reported about 1,676,000 members in 120 unions, up from 265,000 members in 58
unions in 1897. Some national unions won contracts with employers' associations: the
Machinists with the National Founders' Association; the Typographical Union with
the Newspaper Publishers' Association; the United Mine Workers with bituminous
coal companies in the Central Competitive Field (Pennsylvania, Ohio, Indiana, and
Illinois).

The AFL also gained respectability by participating in the National Civic Federation (NCF), founded in 1900 to enlist employers, labor leaders, and prominent citizens to promote industrial peace. Gompers and United Mine Workers president John
Mitchell were charter members, along with industrial magnates like John D. Rockefeller Jr. of Standard Oil and Charles Schwab of U.S. Steel. The public was represented
by members of the elite—university presidents, Episcopal and Catholic bishops, and
retired U.S. president Grover Cleveland, now a trustee for the New York Life Insurance Company.

When 144,000 anthracite coal miners in the UMW went out on strike in 1902, the
National Civil Federation swung into action. Gompers and Mitchell stymied bituminous coal miners' plans for a sympathy strike, and NCF businessmen blocked the
coal companies' efforts to secure intervention by federal troops. President Roosevelt
ordered arbitration, which ended in a compromise that raised pay and shortened hours

but did not meet the strikers' demands for union recognition and the eight-hour day. While many miners protested the settlement, Gompers, Mitchell, and other AFL leaders hailed it as a vindication of "practical unionism."[30]

Even as they signed union contracts and hobnobbed with labor leaders in the NCF, employers never stopped searching for methods to contain and weaken unionism. One increasingly popular method was "scientific management," pioneered by Frederick Winslow Taylor at the Midvale Steel Works in eastern Pennsylvania. The eccentric son of a wealthy Philadelphia family, Taylor had left prep school to do industrial work at factories owned by his parents' friends. In the early 1890s, he became gang boss of Midvale's machine shop and set out to make it the most productive operation in the factory, indeed the world. The key, he decided, was to control workers' every move. First, he carefully analyzed the machinists' labor, dividing each task into a series of simple motions, all of which he timed with a stopwatch. Then he decreed the single "best way"[31] to perform each motion and demanded that workers strictly follow his decrees. Those who complied got higher pay; resisters were punished with fines, wage cuts, or dismissal. In 1895, Taylor began to publicize the Midvale experiments, and by the early 1900s, his scientific management system was winning a following among industrial employers.

What most attracted them was Taylorism's potential to marginalize craftsmen and their unions. Once craft labor was broken down into routine steps, the lion's share of industrial production could be reassigned to less skilled workers at lower pay, and craftsmen could be relegated to ancillary roles. Under old managerial systems, skilled men had dominated production. Their detailed mastery of the labor process empowered them to determine work methods and output quotas for themselves and their less skilled helpers. They could shut down their shops at will. But when craftsmen were isolated from semiskilled fabricators and assemblers and confined to tasks such as machine repair or tool and die work, they and their unions could hardly slow down production, much less bring it to a halt.

As scientific management undercut unions' clout on the shop floor, the National Association of Manufacturers tried to wipe them out with its Open Shop Drive, a "crusade against unionism"[32] launched in 1903. Within a year, the NAM established a Citizens' Industrial Association that worked with 247 employers' associations to distribute anti-union literature and compile blacklists of labor activists. The NAM worked also with the American Anti-Boycott Association, which specialized in taking unions to court. State and federal judges issued hundreds of injunctions against strikes, organizing drives, and other union activities. The U.S. Supreme Court extended the injunctions' reach in 1908, when it ruled that members of the Hatters Union of Danbury, Connecticut, were individually liable for financial damages to a hat company the union had slapped with a boycott.

The wave of assaults destroyed the AFL's momentum. Contracts lapsed and strike losses mounted. Unions all but disappeared from steel, meatpacking, and Great Lakes shipping. AFL membership fell by about 222,000 between 1904 and 1906, and the loss was not fully recouped for another half decade. Shrinkage exacerbated internal divisions. Jurisdictional disputes among AFL unions grew all the more acrimonious. Defending core constituencies, AFL headquarters and national unions abandoned those at the federation's margins; multitudes of FLUs collapsed along with all of Birmingham's black locals.

More and more critics of pure and simple craft unionism squared off against the AFL conservatives. The dissidents called for political action in conjunction with the Socialist Party and for campaigns to organize industrial unions—unions that welcomed all workers in a particular industry regardless of occupation or skill. The AFL already had some industrial affiliates—the United Mine Workers, the United Brewery Workers, the International Ladies' Garment Workers, and a few others. The sentiment for change was strongest in these quarters, but also grew in craft organizations such as the Typographical Union, the Machinists, and the United Brotherhood of Carpenters.

While AFL headquarters fought dissent tooth and nail, it also modified its policies to allow for political action within the two-party system. In particular, the federation sought to exempt labor from the Sherman Antitrust Act of 1890, whose ban on conspiracies to restrain free trade provided the foundation for most legal assaults on unions. In 1908, AFL spokesmen brought their cause to both the Republican and Democratic conventions. The Republicans recoiled; the Democrats gave it a lukewarm endorsement; and the AFL backed a presidential candidate for the very first time—Democrat William Jennings Bryan, who lost to the Republicans' William Howard Taft. Four years later, the AFL would back a victor as Democrats and a liberal Republican faction vied for labor's support.

This upturn in the federation's political fortunes was closely linked to the McNamara case, the most dramatic episode in the annals of the Open Shop Drive. In 1906, the National Erectors' Association joined the drive, confronting the AFL's Bridge and Structural Iron Workers. The Iron Workers fought back by dynamiting some eighty-seven steel structures built by nonunion labor. On October 1, 1910, twenty workmen died in an explosion that leveled the printing plant of the *Los Angeles Times* newspaper, a tireless champion of the open shop. The following spring, two men from the Iron Workers—James B. McNamara and his older brother John J., the union's national secretary-treasurer—were indicted for murder in connection with the blast. The brothers pled not guilty; and every branch of the labor movement, from archconservatives to revolutionaries, rallied in their defense. Then, on December 1, 1911, the McNamaras suddenly changed their pleas. Some said Samuel Gompers wept when he heard the news.

Many in the upper reaches of both the Democratic and Republican parties worried about the stability of a society in which unionists like the McNamaras—members of the AFL mainstream—resorted to violence. Accepting his party's nomination for reelection in 1912, President Taft denounced unions for "lawlessness in labor disputes."[33] Liberal Republicans broke away to form the Progressive Party and run Theodore Roosevelt on a platform that called for workplace safety standards, old-age pensions, an eight-hour day for women and teenagers, and other labor reforms. Democrat Woodrow Wilson endorsed workers' right to organize and carried the election with strong backing from the AFL.

Wilson's first year in office went badly for labor. Congressional bills to exempt unions from antitrust law were repeatedly blocked. In June 1913, the Justice Department indicted nineteen members of the United Mine Workers for conspiracy to organize the coal industry in West Virginia.[34] That September, in southern Colorado, the UMW launched a strike against Rockefeller's Colorado Fuel & Iron (CFI). Over 11,000 strikers and their families left CFI camps and set up tent colonies. Cheering them on was the veteran labor organizer "Mother" Mary Jones, then in her seventies and fresh out of jail for assisting a coal strike in West Virginia. The CFI battle wore on for months, with company guards and the state militia escorting scabs to work and harassing the strikers. On April 20, 1914, all hell broke loose. Militiamen and guards machine-gunned and torched the tent colony at Ludlow; twenty-one people were shot or burned to death, including eleven children. As the news spread, armed unionists poured into the region to defend the miners. Federal troops finally stopped the fighting in May, by which time sixty-six of the miners and kin had been killed. The strikers held out until December, then returned to work in defeat.

In the wake of the Ludlow massacre, Congress debated and eventually passed the Clayton Act. Amending the Sherman Antitrust Act, it stipulated that "the labor of a human being is not a commodity or article of commerce," that labor organizations should not be "construed to be illegal combinations or conspiracies in restraint of trade, under the anti-trust laws," and that workers were legally entitled to strike "by peaceful means" and urge others to do the same.[35] President Wilson signed the Clayton Act into law in October 1914. In the next issue of the *American Federationist*, Gompers called it "the Industrial Magna Carta upon which the working people will rear their structure of industrial freedom."[36] Prudent political action had apparently proved its value.

The bold political alternative shunned by the AFL was the Socialist Party, founded in 1901 by veterans of the Knights of Labor and the People's Party and by leaders of socialist organizations based mainly among German and Russian-Jewish immigrants. The SP aimed to use the ballot to build a new social order based on public ownership of industry and thoroughgoing democracy. Eugene Debs, former leader of the American Railway Union, was the party's chief spokesperson and its perennial presidential candidate. He had become a socialist while serving prison time for his role in the Pullman strike.

The SP organized a large network of locals and two national youth groups, the Young People's Socialist League for workers and the Intercollegiate Socialist Society for students. Starting in 1910, foreign-language associations—Italian, Finnish, German, Polish, Lithuanian, Yiddish, and others—joined the party as autonomous federations. By 1912, the SP published over 300 periodicals in many different languages.

Party members agreed on the electoral path to socialism but not much else, and SP headquarters in Chicago did not try to impose consistency. Urban members usually favored public ownership of land, while rural members generally thought land should belong to those who farmed it. Opinion on race and gender ranged from egalitarianism to outright bigotry. On the radical end of the spectrum was the West Indian immigrant Hubert Harrison, a brilliant writer and orator who became the party's most famous black organizer and a staunch partisan of its left wing. On the spectrum's opposite end stood Victor Berger, the Austrian-born leader of a strong socialist movement in Milwaukee, which elected him to six terms in Congress. Berger believed in white supremacy, reluctantly supported votes for women, and looked down on the

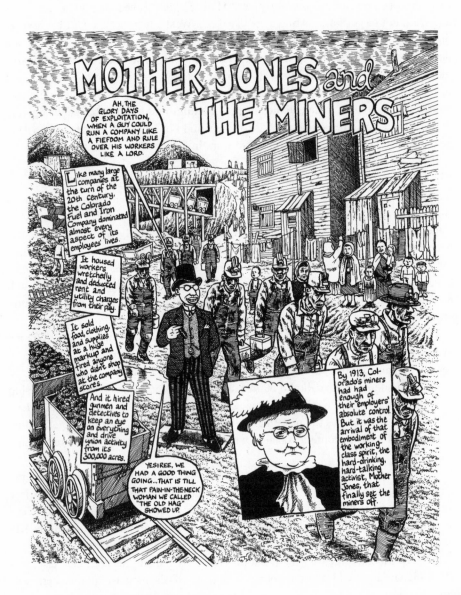

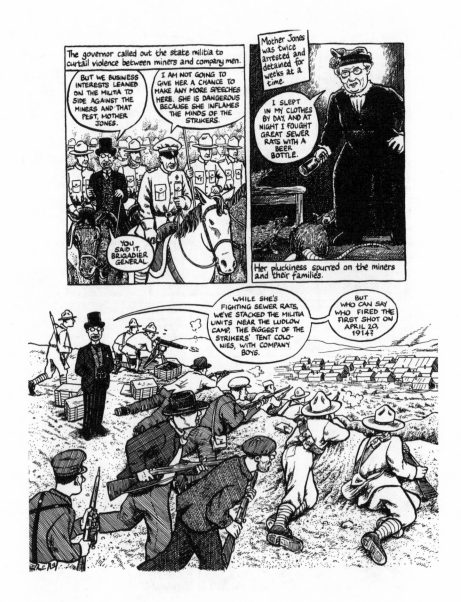

"new immigrants." New Yorker Morris Hillquit, another SP leader, was a new immigrant himself—a Latvian Jew who worked in garment shops and helped organize the United Hebrew Trades before he became a lawyer and socialist theorist. In St. Louis, Kate Richards O'Hare edited the monthly *National Rip-Saw* for 150,000 rural readers across the Midwest and drew crowds at "tent meetings" where farm families camped for days for talks and entertainment. O'Hare advocated birth control and woman suffrage, and accepted racial segregation. Another popular SP orator was George Washington Woodbey, a minister in the African Methodist Episcopal Church; he supported women's rights, called for unity among poor people of all races, and strongly opposed Asian exclusion. In Oklahoma, only whites could join the Renters Union of tenant farmers led by the Socialist J. Tad Cumbie. In southern Texas, party organizers such as Antonio Valdez and J.A. Hernández built interracial agrarian unions.

By 1910, the party had more than 3,000 locals. As of 1912, more than 2,000 Socialists held public office, and Eugene Debs won 6 percent of the vote in that year's presidential election. In 1914, Russian-born labor lawyer Meyer London became the party's second U.S. congressman, elected from New York City's Lower East Side.

The SP rejected "dual unionism"—the formation of radical unions to rival those of the AFL. Instead, the party's motto was, "Bore from within and capture the trade union movement."[37] Socialists joined AFL unions, became exceptionally dedicated members, and tirelessly promoted industrial unionism, organizing the unorganized, and political action in alliance with the SP. Socialists actively built industrial unions. In the winter of 1909–10, SP members like Lithuanian-born Pauline Newman played a central role in New York City's "Rising of the 20,000," a strike by women shirtwaist makers that won union recognition for the Ladies' Garment Workers. Party influence also extended to craft unions; Socialists led insurgencies that ousted conservative leaders from office in the AFL's unions of hatters, sheet-metal workers, and carpenters. In 1912, the Socialist Max Hayes of the Typographical Union challenged Samuel Gompers for the AFL presidency and got close to a third of the vote.

The party had a strong rural following among miners, railroad workers, and farmers, both tenants and small landowners. By 1910, the SP's largest state organization was in Oklahoma, and it was well established in Kansas, Minnesota, the Dakotas, Arkansas, and Texas. Socialist-led farmers' unions mobilized against landlords and bankers. In 1915, the North Dakota SP joined with dissident Democrats and Republicans to create the Non-Partisan League, which called for public ownership of banks and grain elevators, and elected dozens of its candidates to local and state offices.

SP speakers and publications identified socialism with American history and values. As its official platform declared, "The Socialist party . . . makes its appeal to the American people as the defender and preserver of the idea of liberty and self-government, in which the nation was born."[38] Employers' associations and business-minded civic groups replied with a barrage of literature that depicted socialism as an alien doctrine. AFL leaders loudly agreed.

Aside from this powerful opposition, the SP's mainstream strategy was itself problematic. Surveying the party's work in the AFL and electoral politics, labor radical Joseph Ettor concluded, "We tried, but the more we fooled with the beast the more it *captured us.*"[39] To serve the working class, or simply to remain in power, Socialist labor and public officials frequently placed immediately winnable goals above radical ideals. For example, the Socialist William H. Johnston, elected president of the International Association of Machinists in 1911, endorsed industrial unionism at AFL conventions but did not promote it in his own union, where he thought it would "cause unlimited trouble" by arousing jurisdictional quarrels with other unions.[40] Socialist efforts to "bore from within" the political system carried similar liabilities. The party stressed immediate reforms, defined as way stations on the road to a socialist future; but this program lost its radical edge when antisocialist progressives embraced many of the same reforms the SP championed.

The electoral focus could also distance the party from potential supporters. In 1910 the Oklahoma SP campaigned to block a state constitutional amendment designed to disfranchise most black voters, then pandered to race prejudice among white voters by running the segregationist J. Tad Cumbie for governor. This alienated black political clubs that had earlier vowed support for "our socialistic brethren."[41] Two years later—disfranchisement now in place—Socialists added a strong civil rights plank to their election platform and hired a black organizer, W.T. Lane of Kansas, to rally African Americans to support the SP. But, with disfranchisement enshrined in state law, electoral campaigns were no longer a viable means to mobilize black communities. Lane's organizing made headway only in coal towns, where Socialist activity centered in the United Mine Workers.

When Socialists confronted popular protest beyond the boundaries of unionism and electoral politics, they generally tried to redirect it. In February 1917, for example, thousands of immigrant housewives in New York City responded to soaring food prices by staging a consumer boycott, neighborhood demonstrations, and mass marches on both city hall and the Waldorf-Astoria Hotel, where the governor was rumored to be staying. Amidst the turmoil, the SP organized the Mothers' Anti-High Price League to lobby public officials. In their work with the league, Socialists repeatedly suggested that the boycotters would do better to support unions' efforts to raise wages and the SP's campaign for woman suffrage. Party strategists seldom recognized that working people could "vote" with collective action as well as ballots and "unionize" in communities as well as workplaces.

In contrast, the Industrial Workers of the World, often called Wobblies, thought the labor movement's future lay with the masses of workers denied the vote and excluded from the AFL. At the initiative of the Western Federation of Miners (WFM)—an independent union of metal miners—some 200 labor radicals convened in Chicago in June 1905. The WFM's secretary William ("Big Bill") Haywood welcomed them to "the Continental Congress of the Working Class."[42] Among the dignitaries on the platform were the Socialist Party's Eugene Debs and Mother Jones, the anarchist Lucy Parsons (widow of Haymarket martyr Albert Parsons), and the radical Catholic priest Father Thomas Hagerty, who had worked with the WFM and other unions in New Mexico. The convention adopted a constitution that began, "The working class and the employing class have nothing in common," and the IWW was born.[43]

Its founders disagreed on political action. Some promoted electoral work. Others advocated syndicalism—taking "direct action" on the job to build industrial unions until they were strong enough to launch a massive general strike through which workers would take over both industry and government. As Joseph Ettor put it, "If the workers of the world want to win, all they have to do is recognize their own solidarity. They have nothing to do but fold their arms and the world will stop."[44] Syndicalists prevailed at the IWW's 1908 convention, the others fell away, and Wobblies went forth to organize militant industrial unions under the auspices of the "One Big Union," the IWW.[45]

Best known for strike agitation and free speech campaigns, the IWW also staged lectures and debates and distributed pamphlets and periodicals in more than a dozen languages. Its *Little Red Songbook* included songs like "Solidarity Forever," written by the Wobbly newspaper editor Ralph Chaplin and today the anthem of American labor. IWW graphics, often contributed by avant-garde artists, made powerful appeals for labor unity and revolution and still sometimes appear in labor publications.

Wobbly agitators were dedicated, bold, and imaginative. "Big Bill" Haywood had organized miners for twenty years, always packing a gun. "Rebel Girl" Elizabeth Gurley Flynn, who mounted her first soapbox at age sixteen, traveled coast to coast as an IWW speaker. Black longshoreman Ben Fletcher organized across the South and led Philadelphia's Local 8 of the IWW's Marine Transport Workers Industrial Union; his trademark slogan was "All for one and one for all."[46] Joseph Hillström, born in Sweden as Joel Hägglund, arrived in the United States in 1902, tramped from job to job, joined the IWW around 1910, became a Wobbly organizer, and grew famous under the name Joe Hill as a writer of radical labor songs and poems. Frank Little, half-Cherokee, called himself the reddest Wobbly and the IWW's only true American; authorities in Fresno, California, once sent him to jail for publicly reading the Declaration of Independence.

Wobblies scrupulously practiced solidarity. As one of their circulars declared: "If you are a wage worker, you are welcome in the I.W.W. halls, no matter what your color. . . . ALL OF THE WORKING CLASS IN ONE BIG UNION."[47] They organized prostitutes along with other workers. They accepted unorthodox behavior; Marie Equi, an Oregon physician who became active with the IWW during a strike by immigrant women cannery workers, wore men's clothing and lived openly as a lesbian. IWW solidarity also crossed national borders. In 1911, when exiled Mexican anarchists invaded Baja California to fight the Diaz dictatorship, a hundred Anglo Wobblies joined them.

The IWW first gained national notice for its role in a 1909 strike at a U.S. Steel subsidiary in McKees Rocks, Pennsylvania. When the company cut pay, Slavic steelworkers went on strike and called in the Wobblies. Strikers and their wives battled state police for forty-five days; thirteen people were killed. After the Brotherhood of Railroad Trainmen, an independent union, refused to transport scabs, the company caved in. In 1912, the IWW's reputation grew with the "Bread and Roses Strike" in Lawrence, Massachusetts. In January of that year, 25,000 workers—immigrants from a dozen different ethnic groups—walked out of the city's textile mills to protest wage cuts. While the AFL textile union tried to quash the strike, the IWW organized "moving pickets" to foil injunctions and sent trainloads of strikers' children to safe havens in New York and other cities. After two months, the strikers won.

Militant solidarity was not always enough. In Merryville, Louisiana, during the winter of 1912–13, the IWW's Brotherhood of Timber Workers struck the Santa Fe Railroad's American Lumber Company, which had fired union members for testifying in defense of workers charged with murdering a company guard. Local farmers supplied the strikers with food. African Americans, Italians, and Mexicans hired as scabs joined the strike instead. In May, however, posses of lawmen and company guards attacked the town, ransacking homes, beating and arresting strikers, and killing a black organizer. The Brotherhood of Timber Workers was destroyed.

Local governments smashed other Wobbly efforts. In 1913, a strike by 17,000 rubber workers in Akron, Ohio, lasted a month. Police clubbed and arrested pickets, deputized vigilantes, broke up meetings, and ran Wobblies out of town. That same year the IWW supported 25,000 workers striking the silk mills in Paterson, New Jersey. Police arrested almost 3,000 pickets and killed two; the strike collapsed after seven months.

The IWW challenged local governments in more than twenty campaigns to claim free speech and assembly under the First Amendment. In 1909, when Missoula, Montana, tried to silence Wobblies with an ordinance against public speaking, the IWW called members and sympathizers into town and flooded the jail with free speechers. In Spokane, Washington, police detained more than 600 Wobbly speakers in November 1909. Several died from torture in the "sweatbox," where guards tossed prisoners back and forth between sweltering and freezing rooms.

Wobblies won many free-speech fights, but they remained prime targets for repression. In 1914, Salt Lake City police arrested Joe Hill for murder. The prosecution presented no motive, no eyewitness, and no connection between Hill and the victim, but still got a conviction. Shortly before his execution, Hill wired Bill Haywood, "Don't waste any time in mourning—organize."[48] The IWW scattered his ashes in every state except Utah; in Oregon, Dr. Equi performed the honors.

By 1915, the IWW had issued 300,000 membership cards in the United States; and like the Knights of Labor before them, the Wobblies had developed a presence overseas—in Mexico, India, South Africa, Sweden, Ireland, and other countries. But the U.S. locals had only about 15,000 active members and were highly unstable. Strikes brought in masses of recruits, but most dropped out after they went back to work. The locals—composed of workers from various industries and shops—were ill-equipped to deal with day-to-day conflicts on the job. After the strike defeats in Akron and Paterson, American Wobblies set out to build sturdier unions.

The new strategy came from the IWW's agricultural locals. In 1915, they merged to form the Agricultural Workers Organization (AWO) and adopted the "job delegate" system. Under this system, organizers in fixed locations directed hundreds of roving delegates, who settled workplace disputes while recruiting new members and collecting dues. With this system the AWO organized migrant wheat harvesters from Oklahoma into Canada, then branched out to other farmworkers and lumberjacks. By 1917, it had 70,000 members. Their dues funded AWO-style organizing drives among iron and copper miners west of the Mississippi, along with seamen and dockworkers in Atlantic, Gulf, and Great Lakes ports.

Repression continued. In 1916, police and company thugs savagely attacked striking IWW iron miners in Minnesota's Mesabi Range, and sheriff's deputies shot up a boatload of Wobblies at the town dock in Everett, Washington, killing six and wounding twenty-seven. Still, the IWW had at least 100,000 dues-paying members by 1918.

At their peaks, the IWW and Socialist Party combined were less than a tenth the size of the AFL, but Samuel Gompers and his lieutenants obsessively maneuvered to counter Socialists' influence and thwart Wobbly organizing. The *American Federationist* repeatedly printed attacks on the SP and IWW, most penned by Gompers himself. In 1912, he charged that Socialists were not genuine trade unionists but "fanatical . . . unscrupulous . . . vote-hunters."[49] After the Paterson strike, he declared the IWW "destructive in theory and practice."[50] Socialists and Wobblies responded in kind. The SP called the AFL's executives "misleaders" of labor and the "lieutenants" of the big businessmen in the National Civic Federation.[51] The IWW described the AFL as a nest of "union scabs"—members of craft unions that did not support other unions' strikes.[52] Meanwhile, the SP and the IWW came to loggerheads. In 1912, Victor Berger and Morris Hillquit got the Socialist Party's constitution amended to require the expulsion of members who opposed electoral activity or advocated illegal or violent methods of class struggle. In 1913, a party-wide referendum ousted "Big Bill" Haywood from the SP's national executive committee, and tens of thousands followed him out of the party.

By 1917, prospects nonetheless looked bright for syndicalists, political socialists, and AFL conservatives alike. The IWW was growing as never before; the SP was rebuilding through its foreign-language federations; AFL headquarters was celebrating Woodrow Wilson's second inauguration. But international developments had already started to shift the ground beneath their feet.

The Great War

By mid-August 1914, the great powers of Europe, along with their clients and colonies in the Balkans, the Middle East, and Africa, had divided into two camps and gone to war. By the time it ended in November 1918, the Great War between the Allies and the Central Powers had claimed 10 million lives in battle. Another 20 million people had died of war-related starvation or disease.

At first the United States declared neutrality, but there was considerable sympathy for the Allies—Britain, France, and Russia. Financiers like J.P. Morgan helped to fund their side of the war with close to $3 billion in loans and bond purchases. Businessmen joined politicians like Theodore Roosevelt in a "Preparedness Movement" that pressed for U.S. military intervention in support of the Allies. The American Defense Society and other patriotic associations held rallies for intervention and sponsored summer camps where young men could receive military training. Newspapers carried stories of war atrocities by the Central Powers—Germany, the Austro-Hungarian Empire, and the Ottoman Empire.

Still, many Americans opposed intervention. German Americans often sympathized with the Central Powers; most Irish Americans condemned any alliance with Britain; Russian Jews objected to aiding the czar. Pacifists meanwhile organized anti-intervention groups such as the American Union Against Militarism and the Women's Peace Party. Much of the AFL came out against intervention too. In May 1915, eight national unions headquartered in Indianapolis jointly condemned proposals for U.S. entry into the war. Their combined membership totaled about 900,000—almost half of the AFL's rank and file. In June, Labor's National Peace Council, based in Chicago, organized a countrywide labor coalition to demand strict neutrality, government ownership of munitions companies, and a ban on arms sales to the combatant nations. The many preparedness parades that took place during the spring and summer of 1916 met fairly widespread opposition from local unions and labor councils.

Employers and authorities alike took note. Strikes by munitions workers were blamed on German agents. Several leaders of Labor's National Peace Council were indicted for conspiring with a German officer to instigate strikes. When two of the defendants were convicted, the council fell apart. Police arrested AFL radicals Tom Mooney and Warren Billings for a bombing that killed ten people at San Francisco's Preparedness Day parade on July 22, 1916. Despite photographic evidence of Mooney's alibi, both men were convicted; they remained in prison for more than twenty years.

By 1917, Samuel Gompers supported intervention in the war. After President Wilson broke off diplomatic relations with Germany in February 1917, Gompers organized a summit meeting of labor officials. Invitees included members of the AFL Executive Council, national officers of seventy-nine AFL unions, and leaders of the five independent railroad brotherhoods. Gompers had left out the unions most staunchly opposed to intervention—independents like the Amalgamated Clothing Workers and AFL affiliates like the Ladies' Garment Workers, the United Mine Workers, and the Mine, Mill and Smelter Workers (formerly the Western Federation of Miners). At the summit, held on March 12 in Washington, D.C., he asked the assembled officials to issue a public statement that, although the labor movement preferred peace, "should our country be drawn into the maelstrom of the European conflict, we . . . offer our services . . . and we call upon our fellow workers and fellow citizens in the holy name of labor, justice, freedom and humanity, to devotedly and patriotically give like service."[53] Ruling revisions out of order and denying union leaders' requests to consult with members, he demanded and secured the statement's unanimous approval.

Just weeks later, on April 6, Congress declared war on Germany. The U.S. Army quickly expanded from 200,000 to over 4 million, including nearly 3 million draftees. More than 2 million American troops went to Europe, where close to 49,000 were killed in action and another 63,000 died of disease.

On the home front, the federal government took charge of the economy, allocating resources to war-related production, regulating its management, and taking direct control of communications and railroad systems. With the demand for labor soaring and immigration from Europe sharply curtailed by the war, industrial employers recruited new workers from the rural South, the Southwest, and Mexico. Some went to work in mining, lumbering, and wheat production or transportation; many more entered jobs in manufacturing. By the end of the war, about 500,000 African Americans, even more southern whites, and tens of thousands of Mexican Americans and Mexican immigrants had moved northward to the industrial heartland.

Soaring prices and the push for breakneck war production made 1917 the most strike-torn year in U.S. history to that date, with nearly 4,500 walkouts by over 1.2 million workers. The next year saw fewer strikes (3,353), but they involved just as many people. Workers knew that labor was scarce, that the government encouraged quick concessions to strikers in war industries, and that the owners of these industries were making windfall profits. They also believed that, if America was going to war because the "world must be made safe for democracy," to quote Woodrow Wilson, then democracy should extend into American workplaces.[54] In that spirit, many workers struck for the eight-hour day. As one of them later recalled, she and her shop mates in a Philadelphia hosiery mill saw no contradiction between supporting the war effort and asserting themselves through work stoppages. When local boys went off to the army, she remembered, "We laid down our tools and paraded with our boys to the railroad station, then ate our lunch when they were gone, and took the afternoon off to show our patriotism."[55]

Mobilizing industry, the government also mobilized public opinion on behalf of the war and backed up persuasion with repression. The Committee on Public Information flooded the country with pro-war press releases, advertisements, posters, movies, and some 75,000 speakers. The Espionage Act of June 1917 and Sedition Act of May 1918 meanwhile empowered the government to censor antiwar newspapers, ban antiwar literature from the U.S. mail, and jail antiwar speakers. About 900 people convicted under these laws went to prison; over 8,000 more were convicted of violating draft laws. The U.S. Justice Department coordinated with the American Protective League, a businessmen's group that reported disloyal activity—about 3 million cases of disloyalty by the war's end. Vigilantes took action as well, with groups like the American Defense Society dispatching patrols to break up antiwar gatherings.

Socialist Party leaders immediately condemned Congress's declaration of war and called for "continuous, active, and public opposition to the war, through demonstrations, mass petitions, and all other means within our power."[56] SP members ratified this stand by a margin of eight to one. A few thousand left the party, among them some prominent unionists like the Machinists' William Johnston and the Typographical Union's Max Hayes. In May 1917, Socialists joined with pacifists to launch the People's Council of America for Democracy and Peace. Opposing military conscription, defending civil liberties, and organizing against deteriorating labor conditions, it established branches in eighteen states by the end of summer 1917 and launched a Workmen's Council to mobilize antiwar sentiment in labor unions. The young Socialist A. Philip Randolph and his comrade Chandler Owen founded the monthly journal *The Messenger* to win African Americans to unionism, socialism, and opposition to the war. In the state and local elections of November 1917, the SP's candidates did well enough for Eugene Debs to declare, "The Socialist Party is rising to power. It is growing more rapidly at this hour than ever in its history."[57]

Antiwar agitation was drawing an increasingly harsh response, however. In early August 1917, the "Green Corn Rebellion"—an open revolt against the draft—erupted in Seminole County, Oklahoma. White, black, and Creek rebels cut telegraph wires, burned bridges, blew up oil pipelines, and declared their plan to march to Washington, D.C., feeding themselves on ripening corn along the way. Oklahoma police arrested 450 people, many of them SP members. At the end of August, a People's Council convention was banned from Minneapolis, then broken up by troops when it moved to Chicago. The War Department warned that it would suspend contracts at factories where unions endorsed the People's Council.

Subsequent measures targeted the Socialist Party itself. The U.S. Postmaster General banned SP publications from the mail. Federal agents ransacked the offices of

The Messenger, which the attorney general had identified as "by long odds the most able and the most dangerous of all the Negro publications."[58] The Justice Department indicted twenty-seven SP leaders under the Espionage Act; Eugene Debs was sentenced to ten years for making an antiwar speech in Canton, Ohio. Victor Berger was reelected to Congress, then convicted of speaking against the draft, so the House of Representatives refused to seat him. The SP grew in northeastern cities, especially in its foreign-language sections, but it suffered heavy losses in rural areas, where mail was often the only way the party could stay in touch with its rank and file. Average monthly membership dropped from about 80,000 in 1917 to 74,500 in 1918.

The most brutal repression fell on the IWW. Wobblies ridiculed fighting for any cause save for industrial freedom, but they did not mobilize against the war or even resist conscription in many cases. Instead, they focused on expanding the One Big Union. IWW members in northwestern lumber camps led a successful strike for the eight-hour day in summer 1917, and organizing drives continued among harvest hands, metal miners, lumber workers, stevedores, and merchant seamen. But the Wobblies' indifference toward the war provided no protection. Instead, their growing strength in strategic sectors of the economy made them a target. On July 12, 1917, in Bisbee, Arizona, where the IWW was leading a peaceful strike by copper miners, deputized vigilantes packed more than 1,200 strikers into railroad cattle cars, deported them to New Mexico, and left them in the middle of the desert. That same month, Frank Little went to Butte, Montana, where martial law had been declared when copper miners went on strike. On August 1, masked vigilantes seized Little, tied him to an automobile, dragged him to a railroad bridge, and hanged him. On September 5, 1917, federal agents raided IWW offices and homes in sixty-four cities. The Justice Department convicted 184 leading Wobblies of conspiring to obstruct the war effort. To quote "Big Bill" Haywood, who was sentenced to twenty years, "The Department of Justice had shook the organization as a bulldog shakes an empty sack."[59]

The AFL meanwhile flourished as Gompers campaigned to secure union support for the war, government support for union organizing, and labor participation in administrative agencies overseeing war production. The Federation's executive council rejected his proposal that it repudiate strikes for the duration of the war. Otherwise his campaign generally met with success. He set up the American Alliance for Labor and Democracy, which used funds from the Committee on Public Information to saturate the AFL with patriotic literature and organize chapters of unionists who pledged to support the war. Gompers also chaired the Labor Committee of the Council of National Defense, recommended unionists for government positions, and persuaded President Wilson to give unions and employers equal representation on the War Labor Board. The board's code of principles endorsed the eight-hour day, equal pay for men and women doing equal work, the right to a living wage, and the right to join a union.

During 1918, AFL membership rose by almost 40 percent, to 3.3 million. The United Mine Workers now represented close to 500,000 members (over 80 percent of all coal miners); the Carpenters and Machinists had more than 330,000 members each. By 1919, more than 1.8 million railroad workers belonged to AFL affiliates or the independent brotherhoods. Many of the new union members came from sectors of the workforce that the AFL and the railroad brotherhoods had declined to organize in the past.

Some of the new recruits were women. The Amalgamated Association of Street and Electrical Railway Employees protested the hiring of streetcar "conductorettes"; in Cleveland, the Amalgamated even struck over the issue. The Brotherhood of Railway Clerks recruited some 35,000 women, however, and the Machinists enrolled 12,500, who made up about 5 percent of the union's membership as of 1918. The International Brotherhood of Electrical Workers meanwhile recruited more than 20,000 women employed as telephone operators.

The "new immigrants" from eastern and southern Europe joined unions in unprecedented numbers. Chicago meatpacking workers—primarily Poles, Lithuanians, and Slovaks—poured into the Amalgamated Meatcutters and Butcher Workmen, which grew from 7,300 members in 1916 to nearly 63,000 by the end of the war. In March 1918, federal mediation brought pay increases and union recognition to the packinghouses. Inspired by this advance, AFL headquarters pulled together a committee of twenty-four national unions to organize the steel industry, where immigrants from eastern Europe also predominated.

Workers of color were less welcome. The AFL still excluded anyone of Asian descent. Unions in meatpacking and steel signed up Latinos, but in the Southwest, where their numbers were greatest, most AFL affiliates required that Spanish-speaking members be citizens and assigned them to segregated locals. For African Americans, AFL unionism could mean segregation, wholesale exclusion, or worse. In the pulp and paper mills of Bogalusa, Louisiana, the Carpenters recruited black and white workers into separate locals; in Key West, Florida, the union refused to admit black carpenters and thus prevented their employment on an army construction project. AFL organizers in steel signed up black workers in Cleveland and Wheeling but not in Pittsburgh, where white unionists were so hostile that the black community came to see them as the main obstacle to its advancement. The atmosphere was even more hateful in East St. Louis, Illinois. In May 1917, its central labor council sent out a letter calling for "drastic action" to rid the city of black migrants.[60] On July 1, when two policemen were killed in a gunfight in a black neighborhood, white workers mustered in union halls for a two-day rampage against African Americans. At least thirty-nine people were killed—shot, hanged, beaten to death—and many more burned out of their homes. Some 6,000 black residents fled the city.

The War's Aftermath

When the Great War ended on November 11, 1918, total union membership—in AFL affiliates, railroad brotherhoods, and other independents—topped 4 million. The Brotherhood of Railroad Trainmen expressed the spirit of the times: "The justice of the demand for a fairer share has been established; it took the war to do it, but it is not going to be given up now that the war has ended."[61] Organizing continued at full speed. By 1920, AFL membership stood at nearly 4.1 million, and total union membership exceeded 5 million. Almost 20 percent of industrial workers belonged to a union.

The years 1919–22 saw more than 10,000 strikes involving over 8 million workers—
more than 4 million in 1919 alone, a fifth of the labor force outside domestic work.
Strikes rolled through California citrus fields, southern cotton mills, Paterson's silk
mills, New England telephone companies, Bogalusa's pulp and paper mills, laundries in El Paso, cotton fields in Arizona, cigar factories in Tampa, and even Boston's
police force. In February 1919, Seattle became the site of the first citywide general
strike in U.S. history. What had begun as a shipbuilders' strike for a wage increase
mobilized more than 65,000 workers from occupations across the board; waitresses,
typographers, longshoremen, musicians, butchers, hotel maids, and others went out in
sympathy. They included members of AFL unions, Japanese workers in independent
unions, and a good many workers with no union at all. A general strike committee of
rank-and-file activists organized essential services such as garbage collection, saw to
the distribution of food and fuel, and kept the peace for five days, calling off the strike
only when troops neared the city. The shipbuilders still awaited their raise, but as
Seattle's central labor council explained, the strikers went back to work "feeling that
they had won"; they had demonstrated that workers could run a city on their own.[62]

Labor militancy swept through U.S. colonies as well. Against the advice of Samuel
Gompers, Puerto Rico's Federación Libre de Trabajadores staged wartime strikes in
the sugar and tobacco industries. Veteran labor radical Luisa Capetillo led a strike of
30,000 agricultural laborers on the eastern side of the island in 1918. In 1919, the FLT's
Partido Socialista Puertorriqueño (PSP) debated the issue of independence from the
United States but did not endorse it, deciding instead to return to the question after
Puerto Ricans achieved "the social democracy of labor"—universal adult suffrage
and legal recognition of workers' right to organize.[63] In the 1920 elections, the PSP
won nearly a third of the popular vote. In the Philippines, the Congreso Obrero de
Filipinas (COF) signed on to a no-strike pledge at the request of its allies in the Nacio-
nalista Party, which dominated the Filipinos' national legislature and movement for
independence. Even so, COF members struck the Manila Electric Railroad and Light
Company several times in 1919, and Domingo Simeon, the Congreso's secretary and
an official in the printers' union, was implicated in a fatal bombing intended to derail
a streetcar operated by scabs. In January 1920, a massive strike began on Hawaii's
sugar plantations, where Filipino and Japanese unions on Oahu led a work stoppage by
more than 8,000 field hands—70 percent of the plantations' workforce. The planters
used divide-and-conquer tactics to break the strike. They settled with Filipino leaders but held out against the Japanese union, as newspapers dubbed the strike a "dark
conspiracy to Japanize this American territory."[64] Finally, the planters hired Koreans,
Portuguese, and native Hawaiians to replace Japanese strikers, who gave up after six
months.

Stateside, labor activism expanded its political dimensions. Strikers demanded the
release of political prisoners, public takeovers of open-shop industries, and labor's
participation in the European peace talks that followed the Great War. The labor
movement also looked to independent political action. In January 1919, unions in New
York City formed the American Labor Party, which called for restoration of civil liberties, no more declarations of war except for those authorized by national referendum,
and "democratic control of industry and commerce, by those who work."[65] By 1920,

AFL unions and the railroad brotherhoods backed twenty-three state labor parties, which merged with agrarian organizations to form the Farmer-Labor Party that July.

Political realignment rippled through radical labor as well. Socialists who supported the Bolshevik Revolution in Russia broke away from the SP in September 1919 and formed two new revolutionary parties—the Communist Party (mostly immigrants) and the Communist Labor Party (mainly native-born activists). In 1923, they merged with other pro-Bolshevik factions to found the Workers' Party of America, later known as the Communist Party USA. Many Wobblies joined the new communist movement, among them "Big Bill" Haywood and, in later years, Elizabeth Gurley Flynn.

Radicalism and racial pride surged among black workers. Cyril Briggs and Richard Moore left the SP in 1919 to found the African Blood Brotherhood, dedicated to socialism and black liberation; by 1923, the brotherhood had 7,000 members, including a chapter of West Virginia coal miners. It fused with the Communists, attracted by the Bolshevik Revolution's support for self-determination on the part of oppressed peoples. Marcus Garvey's Universal Negro Improvement Association (UNIA) won a gigantic working-class following. Founded in 1914 in Jamaica to promote black pride and power, the UNIA had a half-million U.S. members by 1921. Black unionists inside the AFL attacked its failure to press affiliates to eradicate their color bars. At the federation's 1920 convention, David E. Grange of the Marine Cooks and Stewards Association shouted from the floor, "Do not pussyfoot, stand for the democracy the American Federation of Labor is supposed to stand for. It did not offend the dignity of any man to send the Negro into the firing lines in France."[66]

Far from ending with the war, government repression of radicals increased in the postwar years. The U.S. Justice Department established the Radical Division—headed by young J. Edgar Hoover—to compile dossiers on subversives. On the night of January 2, 1920, U.S. Attorney General A. Mitchell Palmer deployed federal agents in seventy cities across the country to arrest and detain 10,000 people the Justice Department had identified as seditious aliens. About 500 were deported; the rest turned out to be citizens, or immigrants without radical ties. State governments joined the hunt for subversives. New York's Lusk Committee began to investigate "un-American" activities in 1919; it was the first of many such initiatives. By 1921, thirty-two states outlawed "criminal syndicalism," which included a range of activities—advocating illegal labor tactics, distributing literature that encouraged them, or belonging to an organization that endorsed them. In 1923, California sent 164 Wobblies and Communists to prison. In Massachusetts Nicola Sacco and Bartolomeo Vanzetti, Italian immigrants active in Boston anarchist circles, were charged with killing two people during a payroll robbery, and despite sturdy alibis, they were convicted in July 1921 and finally executed on August 23, 1927.

Vigilante attacks on radicals proliferated. On November 11, 1919, the first anniversary of the Great War's end, members of the American Legion attacked the IWW office in Centralia, Washington; one legionnaire was killed and all of the Wobblies defending the office arrested. Among them was Wesley Everest, a lumberjack who had been drafted into the army during the war and served in a unit that harvested timber in Washington and Oregon. That night, the town's jail turned him over to a lynch mob that hanged him from a bridge outside of town and riddled his corpse with bullets. No one was charged with his murder. Seven other men who defended the IWW office that day got prison sentences of twenty-five to forty years.

Racial violence, too, undermined labor's surge. In the summer of 1919, race riots erupted in cities and towns across the country, with African Americans fighting off assaults on their communities. A five-day riot in Chicago halted cross-racial organizing in the packinghouses. Vigilantes meanwhile attacked interracial unionism. In Bogalusa, two AFL unions—the Carpenters and the International Timber Workers—brought black and white workers together to strike the Great Southern Lumber Company in 1919. The company organized and armed a Self-Preservation and Loyalty League to harass the strikers. On November 22, 1919, league members opened fire on Sol Dacus, the strike's most vocal black leader, killing him and four white workers who had come to his aid. African American labor unions were among the institutions besieged in 1921 when white mobs in Tulsa, Oklahoma, rampaged through the city's black community, looting and torching buildings and killing scores of people.

Racism even tainted the final victory of the woman suffrage movement. By 1917, both major parties endorsed votes for women, who had already been enfranchised by eleven states. With its 2 million members—from wageworkers and housewives to professionals and socialites—the National American Woman Suffrage Association was one of the largest women's networks in the country. In January 1918, the House of Representatives narrowly passed the Nineteenth Amendment for woman suffrage; after several defeats, the Senate passed it in June 1919. Fourteen months later, the deadline for its ratification by three-quarters of the states was fast approaching, and it was still one vote shy of the mark. At the eleventh hour, Tennessee's legislature approved the amendment by a razor-thin margin, persuaded by white suffragists who argued that enfranchising educated white women would help to preserve racial segregation.

Attacks on radicals and interracialism heralded a massive assault on all labor activism. After the War Labor Board was dismantled in June 1919, corporate America launched a new campaign for the open shop. The first target was AFL organizing in steel. By mid-1919, the steel drive had signed up about 100,000 workers, a quarter of the industry's labor force. When the companies began to fire union activists, organizers called a strike. It began on September 22; within a week, 365,000 men had walked out. U.S. Steel led the counterattack. It mobilized local and state courts and police departments, which deputized company guards and private detectives. Pickets were beaten, arrested, and jailed by the thousands, and twenty strikers were killed. Immigrants came under especially heavy assault. Casting the strikers as ignorant foreigners betraying the nation, steel executives published in pamphlet form the sermon of a conservative priest who called on English-speaking men to crush the strike by any means necessary: "You can't reason with these people. Don't reason with them . . . knock them down!"[67] Business clubs ran newspaper ads proclaiming that there was "no good American reason for the strike."[68] Reporters and editors across the country echoed the message. The *Pittsburgh Leader* called for the swift deportation of immigrant strikers who came into police custody. The *Los Angeles Times* denounced "revolutionists in the union labor movement" for stirring up "foreigners from whom the right of suffrage is withheld because they are not yet fit for it."[69] Samuel Gompers tried in vain to persuade his friends in government to impose arbitration. In January 1920, the steel strike and organizing drive collapsed in defeat.

Hostility toward immigrants took many other forms as well. It fueled the spectacularly unsuccessful experiment with the prohibition of alcohol, inaugurated in January 1920 under the Constitution's Eighteenth Amendment. Many advocates of prohibition had touted it as a means of controlling unruly immigrant communities, and the ban's enforcement was aimed disproportionately at immigrants. Immigrants were also subject to vigilante attacks. Coal miners in West Frankfort, Illinois, were on strike when rumors circulated in August 1920 that Italians had committed some local bank robberies and murders. Striking miners joined nativist mobs in a three-day rampage against foreigners and drove out hundreds of immigrants, including fellow strikers. Anti-immigrant sentiment passed into law at every level. An Alabama statute called for state inspection of Roman Catholic convents, said to imprison kidnapped Protestant girls. In 1913, California had barred Asian immigrants from owning land; now they were barred from leasing it. Federal immigration laws passed in 1921, 1924, and 1927 altogether excluded Asians and reduced arrivals from eastern and southern Europe to a few thousand a year. The annual number of deportations climbed from 3,600 in 1923 to 16,000 in 1929.

Employers still needed new workers, and Congress did not restrict immigration from the Americas or U.S. colonies. Filipinos on the U.S. mainland, mostly young men working in agriculture, rose in number from about 5,600 in 1920 to 45,300 in 1926. The numbers of Mexican immigrants in the border states expanded from 423,000 in 1920 to 1.2 million in 1930. Although they were not subject to restrictive quotas, immigrants who crossed the U.S.-Mexican border were expected to pay a tax of $8 each, plus a $10 visa fee—more than many of them could afford. Policing this system, the U.S. Border Patrol, established in 1924, helped to define a new category of employee, the undocumented worker.

That most AFL members were white U.S. citizens did not shield their unions from attack. Inspired by the steel strike's defeat, employers in industry after industry formed associations to destroy labor organizations. In Cleveland, San Francisco, Fort Wayne, and a slew of other cities, employers formed new associations to promote what they called the "American Plan"—an open-shop policy that wrapped itself in the flag. The National Association of Manufacturers proclaimed the union shop an affront to "the great Constitution of the greatest government on earth."[70] Other prominent men heartily agreed. "The Open Shop means liberty," wrote Elbert Hubbard; it "should have the sympathy of all good men," added William Howard Taft.[71] Compared to its turn-of-the-century predecessor, the postwar campaign for the open shop devoted much more attention to propaganda. It sent speakers to high schools and colleges; flooded clergymen and educators with open-shop literature; and seized every opportunity to take its message to the general public. Older methods of fighting unionism persisted, however. More than a hundred private detective agencies supplied employers with operatives who spied on workers, fingered the activists for dismissal, started fights at union meetings, beat up strikers—anything to disrupt labor organizing.

Unions fought back by every means available, including gigantic strikes by textile workers, railroad workers, and coal miners in 1922. But the hopes of 1919 had evaporated. The elections of 1920 gave Republicans the presidency and both houses of Congress. In tune with the political shift, the U.S. Supreme Court ruled in 1921 that the Clayton Act did not in fact protect labor unions from injunctions issued under the Sherman Antitrust Act. A short, sharp depression in 1921–22 threw close to a fifth of the nation's labor force out of work. Strike after strike went down to defeat, and unions were demolished or debilitated. By 1923, total union membership had dropped to about 3.6 million. Unions had disintegrated in meatpacking and textile manufacturing; the United Mine Workers and Machinists had suffered major losses; and the AFL had lost a quarter of its rank and file.

The 1920s also saw the passing of three men who had led important sectors of the American labor movement: Samuel Gompers, Eugene Debs, and "Big Bill" Haywood. Gompers went first. Already suffering from heart failure, he traveled to Mexico City in December 1924 for the Fourth Congress of the Pan-American Federation of Labor (PAFL), an organization the AFL initiated in 1918—with secret funding from the federal government—in hopes of extending U.S. influence on labor movements throughout the Western Hemisphere. Shortly after his arrival at the meeting, Gompers collapsed and was rushed back across the border. He died in San Antonio on December 13, at age seventy-four. The PAFL disintegrated in 1930, after the AFL endorsed calls for yet another U.S. military occupation of Cuba.

Debs died of heart failure at age seventy, on October 20, 1926. He had started his ten-year sentence for sedition in April 1919. Running for office as "Prisoner 9653," he had won over 900,000 votes in the presidential election of 1920; but following his pardon on Christmas Day 1921, he could not revive the Socialist Party. Its national membership continued to dwindle, and its clout in labor circles diminished virtually everywhere except in New York City's garment unions. Debs devoted his final years to the cause of world peace.

In 1921, "Big Bill" Haywood—convicted of sedition three years earlier—jumped bail while out on appeal and fled to the Soviet Union, where he advised the Bolshevik government on labor affairs. News from the United States was heartbreaking; the IWW became little more than a shadow, losing members to mechanization in mining, timber, and longshore work, and splitting in 1924 on account of a fight over central authority versus local autonomy. Haywood died in Moscow on May 18, 1928—felled by a stroke at age fifty-nine.

All three men lived long enough to see their organizations battered or broken entirely. Gompers came to trust the government that Debs hoped to take over and Haywood planned to smash; but that government turned on all of them—not all at once or with equal fury, but in the end without much differentiation. Corporations dominated the political landscape. Just as the military protected corporate interests abroad, lawmakers, courts, and police protected them at home. As the historian W.E.B. Du Bois observed in 1925, "Modern imperialism and modern industrialism are one and the same system; root and branch of the same tree."[72]

7

America, Inc.

The postwar depression gave way to a spectacular economic boom, one of the biggest in U.S. history. The boom was based on industrial production and business profits. Between 1924 and 1929, auto and steel output rose by nearly 50 percent; production of chemicals and electrical equipment by even more. Total pretax corporate profits increased by more than half, from $7.6 billion in 1924 to $11.7 billion in 1929. Profits financed more mergers and acquisitions. Over 300,000 industrial corporations operated as of 1929; but the largest 200—giants like U.S. Steel, Anaconda Copper, General Motors, and Westinghouse Electric—reaped more in profits than all the rest combined. Capital itself concentrated: more than 4,000 bank mergers and acquisitions took place between 1923 and 1929. Speculators did very well. Average stock prices nearly tripled between 1922 and 1929. By the latter year, there were 486 investment corporations—stocks and bonds their only assets—and new ones appeared at the average rate of one a day.

Many workers shared in this prosperity. Average wages rose modestly but steadily during the boom years, while the cost of food and other necessities remained relatively constant. Consumer credit magnified the purchasing power of personal incomes. People of even moderate means could buy goods from clothing to radios to vacuum cleaners to automobiles, all on installment plans. Homes, too; the best-paid workers found mortgages easier to get. More and more families could afford to keep their children in school past the eighth grade.

For the labor movement, however, times were lean. Corporations elaborated their campaign to undermine unionism, with the continuing collaboration of politicians, judges, and police. During the 1920s, state and federal courts issued 921 labor injunctions, about the same number issued 1877–1919. Police routinely arrested strikers—7,500 during a garment workers' strike in New York City in 1926; 2,400 during a textile strike in New Bedford, Massachusetts, in 1928. In major cities, special "Red Squad" police units surveilled and harassed labor radicals, identifying activists for employer blacklists and fingering aliens for deportation. Strikes were fewer and smaller and failed more often—in fact, almost always.[1] Most leaders of the American Federation of Labor (AFL) and railroad brotherhoods slid into a downright paralyzing conservatism, renouncing militancy and giving up on efforts to organize the unorganized. In spring 1929, William Green, Samuel Gompers's successor as the AFL's president, wrote in a letter to one of the federation's regional directors that the "appalling indifference of the workers themselves" ruled out the unionization of mass production.[2]

But even as Green penned these words, strikes for higher pay, shorter hours, and union recognition were starting to sweep through southern textile mills. And such uprisings, which occurred in other settings, too, were not the only cracks in corporate America's dominance during the boom years. Throughout that era, workers engaged in many forms of subtle resistance to corporate power as well as sporadic outbreaks of open defiance. If William Green failed to take these rumblings seriously, he was scarcely alone. The labor movement's decline combined with rising prosperity to persuade many observers that worker militancy lay on its deathbed. As 1929 drew to a close, however, the stock market went bust and prosperity gave way to a depression that would be the worst the United States had ever seen. By 1933—just a decade after the spectacular boom had begun—a third of the nation was destitute and, while unions were weaker than ever, the rumblings of discontent in working-class communities had grown too loud for anyone to ignore.

The Roaring Twenties

The 1920s are usually portrayed as a light-hearted time when flappers, bootleggers, and entertainers set the trends in American life. But big businessmen were the era's greatest celebrities. Reporters interviewed them, photographers pursued them, newspapers and magazines featured their thoughts on every topic from business and national and international politics to sports and culture. Economist Stuart Chase later observed of the boom years that the business magnate had become "the dictator of our destinies," replacing "the statesman, the priest, the philosopher, as the creator of standards of ethics and behavior," and reigning as "the final authority on the conduct of American society."[3]

In the workplace the employer ruled absolutely, his rights protected by courts and enforced by police or private operatives. But as immigration restrictions tightened, employers spent more on efficiency experts than on detectives. More and more firms adopted scientific management, not so much to break craft control of work but to get more work out of each employee. Likewise, they installed labor-saving machinery. Mechanization was better than immigrant labor, one business journal declared in 1923: "Machinery 'stays put.' It does not decide to go out on strike . . . go to Europe . . . or take a job in the next town."[4] New technology and designed workflow got assembly lines moving four times faster in 1928 than in 1918. In the period 1923–29, workers' average output in manufacturing rose by more than a fifth; in mining, it rose by more than a quarter. The Aetna Life Insurance Company's scientific management of clerical work raised the output of typists and billing clerks by as much as 50 percent.

The drive for productivity prompted new attention to employee welfare programs, designed, in the words of an American Telephone and Telegraph executive, "to help our workers get those worries out of their minds so they can come on the job 'rarin' to go.'"[5] Employers invested in workplace safety, lighting, and ventilation. They financed recreational and educational programs and medical services for employees (and sometimes their families too). They offered employees mortgage loans and stock options, and group insurance against illness, accident, and death. By 1929 more that 350 companies provided retirement pensions. Of course there were limits to employers' largesse. Only the biggest and most prosperous companies operated extensive welfare plans, and the most valuable benefits were the least common—a survey of large firms found that only a fifth offered stock options or pensions. Benefits were not equally distributed within the workforce. Highly skilled workers—the most highly paid—got the most generous array of extras.

This corporate benevolence was predicated on corporate control, typically described in benign terms. In May 1929, Charles Schwab—then president of Bethlehem Steel— told a gathering of steel executives that the industry's workers counted on them to provide "welfare, progress and happiness."[6] U.S. Rubber's chairman of the board put it more bluntly: "Management must lead."[7]

Nevertheless, some show of democracy could be expedient. Perhaps the most innovative feature of the corporate labor policies in the 1920s was the Employee Representation Plan (ERP), first developed by Colorado Fuel & Iron (CFI) immediately after its bloody defeat of the United Mine Workers in the strike of 1913–14. The War Labor Board later endorsed the concept, and by summer 1919, there were 225 ERPs. In early 1922, they numbered about 725. By the end of the decade, ERPs covered more than 1.5 million workers, most of them employees of industrial giants.

ERPs represented a new management philosophy: the "citizenship theory of labor relations," to quote one social scientist.[8] In contrast to unions, they promised workers the opportunity to help manage their workplaces without ever squaring off against their employers. The joint labor-management committees established under ERPs had very limited jurisdictions. They discussed employee welfare programs; developed schemes for improving efficiency and eliminating waste; and perhaps adjudicated minor disputes, grievances, and complaints about unfair dismissals. And not much more. As an immigrant coal miner who participated in CFI's representation plan later explained to investigators: "Under union, miners have educated men who no work for the company, but give all their time to take up grievances. Pretty hard for a man who works for the company to take up grievances because he afraid that if he make the boss mad, maybe he be fired, or given a bad place."[9] Indeed, Charles Schwab said of his company's ERP, "We discuss matters but we never vote. I will not permit myself to be in the position of having the labor dictate to the management."[10]

The concern for workers' well-being and the respect for labor rights expressed in welfare capitalism were supposed to demonstrate what one businessman described as "the employer's sincere belief that the interests of the employer and employee are mutual and at bottom identical."[11] If employers really believed this, however, they did not necessarily think that workers shared the conviction. Many companies with welfare programs required employees to sign contracts pledging that they did not belong to a union, would not join a union, and would neither strike nor encourage others to strike. By the late 1920s, over 1.25 million people worked under these "yellow dog contracts," and dozens of court injunctions directed union organizers to steer clear of these workers.[12]

Corporate clout in government reached such heights in the 1920s that it was hard to tell where business left off and government began. The Republican Party held the White House and dominated Capitol Hill throughout the decade. All three of the presidents elected in the 1920s were great fans of business. Warren Harding (elected in 1920, died in office in 1923) headed an administration famous for graft, corruption, and fraudulent sales of government property. Businessmen appreciated his strong support for protective tariffs and opposition to government regulation of business. Calvin Coolidge inherited the office from Harding and was elected in his own right in 1924, promising to lower both taxes and federal spending. Congress cut income taxes in half in 1926 and sharply reduced estate taxes; businessmen loved it. President Herbert Hoover, elected in 1928, had earlier worked as a mining engineer in China, Africa, and Latin America and had served both Harding and Coolidge as secretary of commerce. Hoover promoted trade associations and helped U.S. companies expand their overseas markets. Andrew Mellon, whose family was worth about $450 million, served as secretary of the treasury in all three administrations.

The Democrats were just as friendly to business, but less successful. In 1924, their nominee for the presidency was John Davis, chief attorney for the Morgan banking companies. Their candidate in 1928—New York's governor Alfred Smith—picked investor and General Motors executive John J. Raskob to chair his campaign and head the Democratic National Committee. Raskob, said to be worth $100 million (more than $1.4 billion in 2017 dollars) moved the party headquarters to the General Motors skyscraper in New York City.

Government took care of business in many ways. The Supreme Court voided minimum wage laws as unconstitutional, ruling that "in principle, there can be no difference between the case of selling labor and the case of selling goods."[13] The Justice Department gave up applying antitrust laws to corporations. The Bureau of Indian Affairs (BIA)—especially under Harding's secretary of the interior, Albert Fall— helped loot Native Americans' landholdings. After the Midwest Refining Company found oil in the San Juan district of the Navajo reservation in 1921, the BIA appointed a Navajo business council to sign oil leases. Its legality was quite dubious, so the next year the bureau held elections for a new tribal council, which signed the leases, even as the investigation of the scandal involving Teapot Dome (a navy-owned oil field opened to the Mammoth Oil Company) exposed Fall's regular receipt of cash gifts from oil companies. In the Oklahoma "Oilpatch," state courts adjudicated disputes over mineral rights on Indian Territory allotments. When a local banker became the court-appointed guardian of Choctaw orphan Ledcie Stechi, he received the income from leasing her twenty acres of oil fields, while she died of malnutrition.

U.S. foreign policy likewise promoted U.S. business. The State Department helped broker foreign loans to increase demand for U.S. exports. After U.S. banks lent $110 million to the German government, a host of U.S. corporations—including Ford, General Motors, General Electric, Standard Oil, Dow Chemical, the Du Pont gunpowder company—set up operations in Germany. The State Department's support for Wall Street's loans to foreign governments persuaded many Americans that the U.S. Treasury backed the foreign bonds, which helped to sell them. That turned out not to be true, but U.S. troops did stand ready to protect American investments overseas. From 1922 onward, marines were sent to China again and again. Occupation of the

Dominican Republic ended in 1924, but Haiti remained under U.S. control until 1934. In 1924 and 1925, U.S. soldiers went to Honduras to protect American property. In 1925, U.S. troops put down a general strike in Panama. In 1926, U.S. troops returned to Nicaragua, beginning a new series of interventions that continued until 1933.

In short, every level of government operated on the principle that whatever benefitted corporations would benefit Americans, one and all. In 1925, in a speech before the American Society of Newspaper Editors, President Coolidge declared that "the chief business of the American people is business."[14] The editors shortened it to "The business of America is business," and newspapers disseminated the slogan far and wide.[15]

Business values permeated society, spread by mass media and educational institutions. Colleges and universities expanded courses in business administration, accounting, marketing, and related subjects. High schools beefed up vocational curricula to match corporate labor requirements. Pamphlets and booklets furnished by corporations found their way into elementary schools' courses on science, personal hygiene, and social studies.

Media consolidated like other businesses. Newspaper chains such as the Hearst syndicate bought up or drove out independent publishers; by 1927, the chains controlled more than a third of newspaper circulation. Syndicated fare—advice columns, sports features, political cartoons, and editorials—dominated the news. In the radio industry, the government promoted consolidation. Broadcast radio debuted in 1920. By the end of the decade stations were broadcasting from cities all across the country, and one-third of U.S. households owned a radio set. Many early stations were run by churches, ethnic associations, and labor councils, each broadcasting as many hours and with as much power as it could afford. Once Congress created the Federal Communications Commission to regulate frequencies, wattage, and schedules in 1927, the best slots went to commercial stations.

The profit in media came from advertising, which expanded tremendously as companies competed to sell the huge volume of goods they produced. Besides manipulating fantasies and anxieties to create demand for products, advertising also promoted good work habits. According to the ad agency executive Bruce Barton, advertising's chief value lay in its capacity to "make people dissatisfied with the old and out-of-date and . . . send them out to work harder to get the latest model—whether that model be an icebox or a rug, or a new home."[16] Corporate public relations firms placed advertising in the news itself, using techniques pioneered during the Great War by the Committee on Public Information. For many corporations, a reputation for service to the community was at least as useful as brand-name recognition. Corporate donations to parks, recreation centers, libraries, churches, and Boy Scout and Girl Scout troops made effective advertising when reported as news. One investigator found that, in the *New York Times* issue of December 29, 1929, over half the stories were originated by press agents.

If business sometimes seemed to be a religion, religion sometimes resembled a business. One of the bestselling titles of 1925–26 was Bruce Barton's *The Man Nobody Knows*. The book portrayed Jesus as history's greatest corporate executive, who "picked up twelve humble men and created an organization that won the world."[17] Many churches deployed advertising and public relations techniques to recruit members and raise money.

Business values influenced some feminists. The National Women's Party (NWP) opposed protective labor legislation for women, echoing business's arguments that labor laws restricted individual freedom and that corporate executives understood that treating female employees well was good business. In 1929, when an ad man for the tobacco industry approached journalist Ruth Hale of the NWP, she recruited ten young women to march in New York City's Easter parade as they smoked cigarettes—"torches of freedom," they told reporters.[18] In the real world, women working for wages were mostly confined to low-paying, dead-end jobs. Many employers of office workers hired only single women and dismissed them if they got married.

Even bigotry became a business. One-time preacher William Simmons made his living promoting fraternal organizations to which he sold uniforms and other paraphernalia; in 1915, he started a new Ku Klux Klan, which grew to include about 5,000 members in Georgia and Alabama by the end of the war. In 1920, Simmons made a deal with two Atlanta-based public relations agents, Edward Clarke and Elizabeth Tyler. For 80 percent of each initiation fee, they would market the Klan. Clarke and Tyler hired paid organizers ("kleagles") and trained them in market research, teaching them how to study communities to determine which groups were most hated by white, native-born Protestants in that locale. Klan organizers would then vilify those groups—not only people of color, but also radicals, immigrants, bootleggers, Catholics, Jews, and Mormons. Kleagles sold a full range of KKK regalia and literature, and in 1923, they expanded the market by organizing a massive women's auxiliary. By mid-decade, Klan membership reached about 4 million, with chapters across the country and influence in both the Democratic and Republican parties. Enriched by shares of the proceeds, the Klan's national and regional leaders then turned on one another in a flurry of lawsuits and allegations of arson, blackmail, kidnapping, and murder. By the end of the 1920s, membership had fallen to about 40,000.

To the extent that operations like the Klan threatened social peace, many businessmen opposed them; financial considerations could restrain even virulent bigotry. Henry Ford hated Jews. In 1920–26, his *Dearborn Independent* newspaper (distributed nationally through Ford dealers) ran articles alleging that Jews were responsible for monopolies, Bolshevism, wars, foreclosures, political corruption, bootlegging, high rents, and short skirts. In 1925, Aaron Sapiro, an attorney for the American Farm Bureau, sued the *Independent* for libel. To avoid paying damages, Ford publicly repudiated his accusations, though his personal opinions did not change. He would later become a vocal admirer of the Nazi regime in Germany.

To some people, poverty seemed to be on the verge of disappearance in the 1920s, thanks to the acumen and benevolence of business. President Coolidge saw a divine plan at work, declaring "that the man who builds a factory builds a temple, and that the man who works there worships there."[19] Campaigning for the presidency in 1928, Herbert Hoover boasted that Washington's co-operation with Wall Street had brought Americans "nearer to the abolition of poverty, to the abolition of fear and want, than humanity has ever reached before."[20]

This might have been true for some, but certainly not for all. Just 5 percent of American households had accounts with stockbrokers. About a third of the nation's total personal income went to the richest 5 percent of the people. The top 10 percent spent half the nation's expenditures on health care, education, and recreation. Modern research suggests that half of all U.S. families in the 1920s had to skimp on necessities. In New York City, some 2 million people lived in substandard housing. Half of U.S. households lacked indoor flush toilets; a third lacked electric lights. Workplaces were dangerous; throughout the 1920s, deaths on the job averaged around 25,000 a year and work-related injuries 100,000 a year.

Average real wages (income adjusted for inflation) rose about 1 percent annually from 1923 through 1929. Some workers did better. Skilled construction workers in unions did very well: depending on their trade, their wages rose between 22 and 36 percent overall. Printers, paper makers, hosiery and knitting mill workers, and autoworkers all did better than average.

Others did worse. Wages for domestic work rose about 2 percent over the period. For women in manufacturing, wages hardly changed. Although real wages rose considerably for skilled railroad workers, they declined for their unskilled counterparts. Wages also declined in the textile, leather, glass, tobacco, and mining industries. Cotton textile workers were especially hard hit; their wages fell by more than 10 percent in the South and close to 5 percent in the North. Anthracite coal miners' wages dropped 14 percent between 1923 and 1929, while bituminous miners suffered a 30 percent drop. Agricultural workers' wages fell in the early 1920s and did not recover—they ended the decade at about the level of 1914.

Better hourly wages did not always translate to better annual income, moreover, because not all workers were steadily employed. The federal government was yet to tabulate unemployment statistics, but the national average among nonagricultural workers was probably about 7 percent. Local surveys showed some higher rates: 10–25 percent unemployment in Cincinnati's six poorest wards. Rising industrial productivity contributed to joblessness. While manufacturing output nearly doubled over the course of the 1920s, the industrial workforce in 1929 remained about the same size it had been in 1919, close to 8.6 million.

Mechanization also affected farmwork; tractor use increased by a factor of ten during the decade. New crop-management methods and greater reliance on fertilizers also increased farm productivity. But agriculture never recovered from the postwar depression, and overproduction just made the market worse. By 1929, average farm income per capita was little more than a third of the nonfarm average. Over the course of the decade about 13 million acres of farmland were abandoned, and by 1930 almost half the country's farmers were tenants and about half of family-owned farms were mortgaged.

Farmworkers suffered the most. A California grower described migrant farmworkers in 1920: "They camped along the roadside. . . . They did the cooking in the open, exposed to all the dust and filth that happened to pass. If there was no well water near, they drew their supply from a nearby stream—many times one that ceased to flow, but leaving enough in the holes for them to drink."[21] Child labor was common in the fields. In the Upper Midwest's beet fields—where harvest work was especially backbreaking—investigators found that about half the harvesters were under fifteen, and quite a few as young as six. The federal government's schools for Native American youth sent students to work in the Colorado and Kansas beet fields for wages as low as 9¢ a day. Children were especially useful to beet growers; the plants were thinned with a short hoe (declared illegal many years later). Beets were harvested with a hook-topped machete, which could pick and top the beet in a single swing. Experienced *betabelaros* usually had a permanent stoop in their backs, and often fewer than ten fingers.

Even prosperity could be deceptive. Some workers could afford to flee the city for a home in one of the proliferating suburban developments, but this material comfort had an underside. Many suburban communities barred home sales to people of color, Jews, and other racial and ethnic minorities, and Klan organizers recruited many suburbanites. Suburban households were often deep in debt for houses, cars, furniture, and appliances; consumer credit was easy to get but hard to pay off. Despite modern labor-saving appliances, surveys showed that housework and childcare required about the same amount of time in the 1920s as they had two decades earlier—about fifty-five hours a week—and some mothers, including more married women than ever before, had to work outside their homes to cover the bills.

The Labor Movement of the Twenties

For the labor movement, the 1920s were an era of defeat, retreat, and division. Total union membership fell from about 3.6 million in 1923 to 3.4 million in 1929; AFL unions had 2,769,000 members in 1929, 1.3 million fewer than in 1920. The losses were not evenly spread. The railroad brotherhoods and craft unions generally maintained their numbers. Building trades unions actually grew. But industrial unions in mining, mass production, and agriculture suffered enormous losses. The United Mine Workers—a half-million strong in 1920—had only 84,000 members in 1929. The Mine, Mill and Smelter Workers barely survived the decade, and the same was true of industrial unions in the clothing and textile industries. Unions of agricultural workers virtually disappeared.

Organized labor moved in increasingly conservative directions. In 1924, shortly before Gompers's death, the AFL had experimented with independent political action, endorsing the Progressive Party's presidential candidate, Senator Robert La Follette of Wisconsin. Gompers's successor, William Green—a United Mine Workers official who had served for more than a decade on the AFL's executive council—was less inclined to take chances. The *Chicago Tribune* aptly described him as a leader "whose other name is Caution."[22] AFL headquarters abandoned independent political action and discouraged militancy on the job. Co-operation with employers became a guiding principle, as it did for leaders of the railroad brotherhoods too. Labor spokesmen endorsed scientific management and other speed-up schemes. In return for union recognition, twenty rail unions dropped demands for permanent government control of the railroads and joined with railroad executives to draft the Railway Labor Act. Passed by Congress in 1926, the act set up a system of compulsory arbitration and presidential intervention that made legal strikes almost impossible.[23]

Labor leaders echoed businessmen's expressions of affection for capitalism. Some even became capitalists themselves, starting union-owned banks and other business ventures. The Brotherhood of Locomotive Engineers pioneered this experiment, sponsoring more than a dozen banks by the late 1920s, investing more than $60 million in real estate, and buying coal mines that employed nonunion labor. Other labor banks were started by the Amalgamated Clothing Workers, the Ladies' Garment Workers, the Brotherhood of Railway Clerks, and the New York State Federation of Labor.

Some union business was less respectable. By the outbreak of the Great War, labor racketeering was well established in the building trades in San Francisco, Chicago, and New York City. The racketeers worked closely with employers' associations. The associations rigged bids and divided up the work, and unions controlled by gangsters staged strikes to discipline would-be competitors or drive them out of the industry. In the 1920s, dynamite or arson often replaced strikes as the weapon of choice, and assassinations took place too. Labor racketeers also targeted workers. In New York City, for example, a rogue faction of the American Federation of Musicians retained a "business manager" whose cadre of "sluggers" terrorized musicians who failed to pay union dues. The city's garment unions meanwhile retained the notorious gangster Arnold Rothstein to furnish them with strong-arm men and bribe police not to assault picket lines. By the end of the decade, gangsters like Al Capone in Chicago and Dutch Schultz in New York entirely controlled some local unions, whose treasuries they fattened by selling "strike insurance" to employers and then raided to finance other criminal schemes.

Labor officials—like public officials—proved unable or unwilling to clean out these gangsters, sometimes sharing in the profits and in other cases accepting gangsterism as a necessary evil. In 1930, when the writer Louis Adamic published an exposé of labor racketeering in *Harper's Magazine*, an official of one of Chicago's largest AFL affiliates wrote to thank him for recognizing that strong-arm tactics were labor's last resort in the face of repression: "Capital has the court, always, to say nothing of its gunmen, police and soldiery. The economic 'game' in the existing system is loaded against us—and we behave as one does believing one has been roped in an unfair game."[24] The problem was that, once racketeers involved themselves in a union's operations, they never left of their own accord.

Labor radicals had not entirely disappeared. After the failure of the steel strike of 1919–20, William Z. Foster, a former Wobbly who had headed the multi-union committee to organize the steel industry, founded the Trade Union Educational League (TUEL). Funded by the Amalgamated Clothing Workers, the TUEL promoted industrial unionism in the AFL, amalgamation of the railroad brotherhoods, and independent political action and racial harmony throughout the labor movement. Starting in 1923, when Foster joined the Communist Party, Communists in the labor movement embraced the TUEL agenda. TUEL members and sympathizers were elected to office in a number of unions, including some districts of the United Mine Workers, and they won top posts in the Ladies' Garment Workers and the Fur and Leather Workers. Tens of thousands of workers went on strike under TUEL leadership, in New York's garment industry in 1926; in the silk factories of Passaic, New Jersey, that same year; and in the cotton mills of New Bedford, Massachusetts, in 1928. AFL leaders responded by expelling TUEL activists from their unions, and the banished insurgents started their own "red unions" among coal miners, garment workers, and textile workers. In

1929, the TUEL reorganized as the Trade Union Unity League (TUUL), which set out to build a left-wing labor federation to rival the AFL.

Radicals also maintained a foothold in labor education. Their best-known project was the Brookwood Labor College, a two-year residential school in Katonah, New York, that was founded in 1919. Brookwood students, who numbered about fifty a year, were mostly financed by unions, including the Mine Workers, Machinists, Ladies' Garment Workers, and several railroad brotherhoods. In 1928, the AFL ordered its affiliates to dissociate from the school, but Brookwood had already graduated hundreds of rank-and-file activists, and it stayed open until 1937.

Rank-and-file workers often resisted corporate power in surreptitious ways. Louis Adamic recalled his days as a factory hand in eastern Pennsylvania: "After the suppression of the organized radical movement in 1922 or thereabouts, there was perhaps as much radicalism among American workers as ever before." Now, however, it was expressed through individual actions; workers "wasted the bosses' time and material, thereby . . . diminishing the profits of employers, who, they believed, underpaid them."[25] At the Swift meatpacking plant in Chicago, women packing bacon secretly agreed to turn out no more than 144 packages an hour; they enforced the agreement by passing twisted, tattered bacon slices to anyone who tried to break the quota. Many workers had disparaging nicknames for their Employee Representation Plans or "forgot" to vote in elections for ERP committees.

Organizing drives and strikes emerged among workers neglected by the AFL and railroad brotherhoods. In 1925, black railroad workers employed by the Pullman Company turned away from their ERP and established the Brotherhood of Sleeping Car Porters and Maids under the leadership of A. Philip Randolph (by then no longer associated with the Socialist Party). The AFL refused to grant the brotherhood a national charter, instead consigning the members to federal labor unions; but that did not deter the union, even though twelve years passed before it won a national contract. In August 1927, immigrant workers from northeastern factories to southwestern mines went out on strike to protest the execution by electric chair of Nicola Sacco and Bartolomeo Vanzetti in Massachusetts. Their funeral in Boston drew 10,000 mourners.

Agricultural workers began organizing again in the late 1920s. In California, mutual benefit societies among Mexican farmworkers helped launch La Unión de Trabajadores del Valle Imperial and the Confederación de Uniones de Obreros Mexicanos. La Unión led 3,000 cantaloupe harvesters on strike in 1928. Reflecting its roots in *mutualistas*, the Confederación de Uniones not only organized in the fields but also set up libraries and a medical clinic. The Tejano labor activist Clemente Idar meanwhile organized beet field-workers in Colorado, Nebraska, and Wyoming into a multiethnic Beet Workers Association, affiliated with the AFL.

The labor movements in Puerto Rico and the Philippines entered politics and slipped into accommodation and corruption. In Puerto Rico, the Partido Socialista Puertorriqueño (PSP) made peace with conservative politicians and began to win elections, gaining considerable political patronage. Santiago Iglesias, founder of the Federación Libre de Trabajadores (FLT), became the colony's resident commissioner in Washington. The sugar industry still dominated the island, and the FLT failed again and again to win permanent contracts with the growers. The Great Depression began sooner—and lasted longer—in Puerto Rico than on the U.S. mainland, but when the PSP took over the island's department of labor in the early 1930s, its appointees showed little interest in wages and working conditions. In 1933, when the FLT finally won a sugar-industry contract for the next year's harvest, the terms were so bad the field-workers briefly went on strike against the agreement.

In the Philippines, an alliance with the government began to take a toll on the Congreso Obrero de Filipinas (COF). When Filipino field-workers in Hawaii went on strike in 1924, the COF supported them. But its founder Hermenegildo Cruz, now director of the Philippine Labor Bureau, conducted his own investigation and reported that labor conditions in Hawaii were satisfactory. His consistent support for the colonial government of the Philippines became so controversial that the COF unraveled, splitting in 1929 and surviving in name only after 1932.

Ethnic divisions continued to impede worker solidarity. In Hawaii, the planters discouraged labor organizing by recruiting many nationalities and giving each its own holiday: Chinese New Year; *Obon*, the Japanese Festival of Souls; and, for Filipinos, Rizal Day, in memory of Spain's execution of Filipino patriot Jose Rizal in 1896. On the U.S. mainland, workers of different races or nationalities worked side by side in a few big industrial enterprises—for example, the Ford Motor Company. Yet, even in the rare settings where interracial and interethnic solidarity developed on the shop floor, it ended at the factory gate. Virtually everywhere workers assembled off the job—in neighborhoods, in union halls, in clubs, in lodges, in places of worship—racial and ethnic separatism was the order of the day. Color lines held firm; immigrants gathered by nationality and subdivided by religion; U.S. natives descended from northwestern Europe stood aloof from everyone else. The very few exceptions were mainly confined to the labor movement's radical fringe. Led by the TUUL's National Textile Workers Industrial Union, southern textile workers organized into racially integrated locals and unleashed a wave of strikes in 1929; but such combinations of militancy and solidarity were very seldom seen in the late 1920s.

Depression and Protest

Organized labor's weakness in numbers and nerve helped set the stage for the Great Depression. While the Roaring Twenties saw gigantic increases in industrial output and home construction, unionism's decline severely restricted wage hikes and workers' ability to resist the speedups that helped limit the numbers of industrial jobs. The bottom line was that working people could not buy enough to sustain the system; earnings were simply too low and joblessness too common. By summer 1929, consumer spending had tapered off despite easy credit, home building had slumped, and manufacturers' unsold inventories had swelled to the point where many firms were cutting production and laying off workers. The U.S. economy was already teetering when the stock market crash of October 1929 pushed it over the edge.

Total national income fell from about $83 billion in 1929 to $40 billion in 1932. Working people got the worst of it. By January 1930, the unemployed numbered 4 million. By the end of 1932, 15 to 17 million people were jobless, about a third of the labor force. Millions more made do with part-time jobs. Unions lost about a half-million members.

Wages were cut. By 1933 average annual earnings decreased by 19 percent in transportation, 30 percent in manufacturing, 35 percent in mining, 42 percent in agriculture, and 48 percent in construction. There was little cushion; fewer than half of white working-class families had any savings in 1929, and those who did had just $336 on average. Workers of color had less.

Local governments and charities tried to provide relief, but their efforts were quickly overwhelmed. Encampments of homeless people sprang up on public or vacant land on the outskirts of cities across the country. Many households dissolved, their children sent to friends, relatives, or homes run by charities. Legions of desperate women kept themselves afloat, and sometimes supported whole families, by turning to prostitution. Hunger was common, and malnutrition encouraged the spread of diseases like tuberculosis and pellagra. New York City recorded ninety-five deaths by starvation in 1931. Despair flourished too; the city reported about 25,000 suicides in 1930–31.

The depression hit immigrants and people of color especially hard. Tejanos called the depression *La Chilla* ("the squeal") because it caused so much pain; in Texas an entire family could work all day picking cotton and make just enough to buy themselves a single meal. After the blizzard of February 1932, New York City hired 12,000 men to shovel the streets; Bernardo Vega recalled, "Many Puerto Ricans jumped at the chance to make some money . . . wrapped up in rags, their necks covered with old newspapers, swinging their shovels and shivering to the bone."[26] A 1932 report on the unemployed in Chicago's meatpacking district told the story of Rose Majewski, a Polish immigrant whose husband had abandoned her and their five children. Laid off from a janitorial job that had paid up to $21.50 a week, she got work cleaning chicken carcasses for $10–12 a week, but lost that job in June 1930 and could not find another. By 1932, she and her family lived in a converted barn on $5 a week from a private charity and a monthly box of food from the county welfare bureau.

In 1931, African Americans made up 17 percent of the national population but 33 percent of the unemployed. The disproportion was even more striking in cities like Charleston, South Carolina (49 percent of the population but 78 percent of the unemployed), and Pittsburgh, Pennsylvania (8 percent of the population but 38 percent of the unemployed). The autoworker Dave Moore recalled that black Detroiters were "living in cars and . . . going around to these markets where there was a possibility of food, picking up rotten potatoes, cutting the rotten off to salvage some part of that potato that may be good."[27] The journalist Marvel Cooke later wrote about her experience at one of the many "slave markets" in New York City where black women were picked up by housewives looking for domestic help: "I was part of the 'paper bag brigade,' waiting patiently . . . for someone to 'buy' me for an hour or two, or, if I were lucky, for a day."[28] Black men congregated at this same locale, 170th Street and Walton Avenue in the Bronx, where the going wage was often as low as 10–15¢ an hour. In Fayette County, West Virginia, the Union Carbide Corporation paid several thousand men—two-thirds of them African Americans—15–30¢ an hour to drill a tunnel through a mountain of silica, generating dust so damaging to their lungs that workers began to die on the job just two months after the project began in June 1930.

By the time the tunnel was finished in December 1931, hundreds had died and hundreds more would succumb after that; a company cover-up prevented an exact count. Union Carbide offered the widows of white men a lump sum of $1,000 and the widows of black men $600.

Immigrants were encouraged, even forced, to leave the country. By winter 1932–33, about a half-million Mexican nationals and their children had returned to Mexico. About 40 percent went voluntarily, often with the aid of workers' organizations like Detroit's Liga de Obreros y Campesinos. The rest were formally deported, chased out by vigilantes, or transported by charitable organizations that provided relief to Mexicans only when they agreed to exit the United States. Among the children and youth exiled to Mexico were many thousands of native-born U.S. citizens, targeted on account of their ancestry. On the West Coast a wave of anti-Asian agitation and violence hit Filipinos. In March 1934, Congress passed the Tydings-McDuffie Act, which capped immigration from the Philippines and paid the return fare for Filipino nationals living in the United States who promised never to come back.

For the first two years of the economic crisis, President Hoover and Congress insisted that relief was a local responsibility. Certain that the root of the problem was a loss of confidence on the part of businessmen, the Hoover administration organized conferences at which experts sought to persuade corporate executives that, if they would only resume production and stop cutting wages, recovery would be just around the corner. By 1932, it became clear that something more was required. Hoover proposed and Congress authorized the Reconstruction Finance Corporation (RFC), which funded some federal construction projects and made loans both to private companies for expansion—that is, job creation—and to local governments to help finance public relief. Congress also passed the Norris-LaGuardia Act, which barred injunctions against peaceful union activities, including strikes and pickets, and outlawed the yellow dog contracts in which workers had pledged never to join a union. None of these measures helped much. Unemployment continued to rise, local governments continued to run out of relief funds, and the labor movement continued to shrink.

In the early months of the depression, many corporations maintained their commitment to welfare capitalism, refraining from cutting wage rates, experimenting with job sharing to minimize layoffs, and providing loans and advances on pensions. But they could hold out for only so long. In 1931, wage cuts began in earnest, followed by mass layoffs and further cuts in wages and benefits. In 1930, the AFL's president William Green had received a gold medal from the Theodore Roosevelt Memorial Foundation in recognition of his efforts to curb labor unrest. Now he got a letter from an out-of-work machinist about to be evicted from his home: "The bankers and industrialists who have been running our country have proved their utter inability or indifference to put the country in a better condition."[29] Millions agreed.

One proposal for relief was government-sponsored unemployment insurance. AFL headquarters initially opposed the plan on the grounds that it would make jobless workers wards of the state. A growing number of national unions and state and local labor federations backed the plan, and it was endorsed nearly unanimously at the AFL's annual convention in November 1932, but years would pass before the government implemented such a plan.

For the most part, labor protests of the early 1930s took place outside the AFL unions. Worker revolts broke out in mass production, mining, and agriculture—sectors where unionism had taken the worst beatings in the 1920s. In May 1931, at a U.S. Rubber factory in Mishawaka, Indiana, 2,000 nonunion workers went on strike to protest wage cuts and speedups. In Tampa, Florida, Cuban-American cigar makers struck in 1931, after factory owners ousted the *lectores* that workers hired to read aloud to them so that the labor would be less tedious. In July 1932, nonunion workers protesting wage cuts shut down more than a hundred hosiery and furniture factories in North Carolina. The National Miners Union, affiliated with the Trade Union Unity League, led coal strikes in Ohio, West Virginia, Pennsylvania, and eastern Kentucky in 1931–32. In Illinois, the AFL's United Mine Workers (UMW) staged a four-month strike against wage cuts in 1932. When union officials endorsed a settlement, many strikers rejected it, and 18,000 UMW members broke away to form the Progressive Miners of America.

In January and February 1930, two strikes hit California's Imperial Valley, one among Mexican and Filipino field hands, the other among white workers in the packing sheds. TUUL organizers set up an Agricultural Workers Industrial League. When its most active organizers were convicted of criminal syndicalism, it regrouped as the Cannery and Agricultural Workers Industrial Union, which survived into 1935 and led twenty-four strikes, losing only three. January 1931 saw an uprising of 500 black sharecroppers in England, Arkansas. The following summer their counterparts in Tallapoosa County, Alabama, launched the Share Croppers' Union, which had about 2,000 members across the state by spring 1933 and 6,000 members a year later.

Worker militancy also spilled beyond workplaces, generating a widespread movement of the unemployed. Radical activists organized high-profile demonstrations like the Communist-led protests by more than a million jobless workers in major cities across the country on March 6, 1930, when protests took place in a host of European cities too. But the movement focused mainly on grassroots organizing around local struggles. In San Francisco, for example, Communists in the Kungyu Club—formed in the 1920s to support the Chinese Revolution—helped organize the Chinese Unemployed Alliance (CUA). Aiming its demonstrations at the most powerful Chinatown businessmen's group, the Chinese Consolidated Benevolent Association, the CUA called for housing and jobs. The Communist Party built a national network of neighborhood-based Unemployed Councils that pressed relief agencies for aid, and rallied to block evictions of families for not paying rent. Socialists built similar groups in Baltimore and Chicago. A.J. Muste from Brookwood Labor College led a group of its graduates in organizing Unemployed Citizens Leagues whose members used barter systems and labor exchanges to make ends meet.

Unemployed organizing sometimes shaded over into workplace organizing. On March 7, 1932, Detroit's unemployed councils joined with autoworkers affiliated with the TUUL in a mass "hunger march" in front of the Ford Company's River Rouge Plant in nearby Dearborn, Michigan.[30] Three thousand demonstrators demanded that Ford slow down its assembly lines and rehire laid-off workers. Police and company guards fired on the crowd, killing four and mortally wounding a fifth, who died several months later. Another sixty workers were injured.

The unemployed movement routinely organized across color lines, and its Communist-led sectors were especially active in defense of African Americans' rights. Unemployed councils rallied to support the nine young black men sentenced to death on false charges of rape in Scottsboro, Alabama, in 1931, and in defense of Angelo Herndon, a nineteen-year-old black Communist sentenced to death under Georgia's anti-insurrection law after he organized an interracial hunger march in Atlanta in 1932. Both struggles were successful, though justice was long in coming. Herndon was freed by the Supreme Court after a five-year legal battle, and the last Scottsboro prisoners were released in 1950.

Of all the protests that erupted in the early 1930s, none jolted the nation more than the Bonus March of 1932. Following the Great War, Congress had promised that the war's veterans would receive bonuses of $50–100 in 1945. In summer 1932, some 20,000 jobless veterans, organized in part by the left-wing Workers Ex-Servicemen's League, converged on Washington, D.C. Many were accompanied by their families. They set up tent cities and vowed to stay put until Congress authorized immediate payment of the bonuses. On July 28, troops commanded by General Douglas Mac-Arthur, with Colonel Dwight D. Eisenhower the second in command, dispersed the veterans and their families with tear gas, burned their encampment to the ground, and ran them out of town.

As the Bonus Marchers straggled home amidst a deepening depression, the ballad "Brother, Can You Spare a Dime?" by the radical songwriters Yip Harburg and Jay Gorney captured working people's mood:

> They used to tell me
> I was building a dream,
> And so I followed the mob.
> When there was earth to plow
> Or guns to bear,
> I was always there
> Right on the job.
> They used to tell me
> I was building a dream
> With peace and glory ahead.
> Why should I be standing in line
> Just waiting for bread?[31]

Anger at the Hoover administration and its business allies had been simmering since the depression began; now it reached a boil. The AFL remained neutral in the presidential election of 1932, which pitted Hoover against the Democrats' Franklin D. Roosevelt, an advocate of government relief programs and unemployment insurance. But while mainstream labor leaders proceeded with caution, the majority of Americans who went to the polls that year wanted a sweeping change. They elected Roosevelt by a hefty margin, and then waited to see if the new president would make a difference.

8

Labor on the March

When Franklin Roosevelt took office on March 4, 1933, the depression was deeper than ever. Jobless workers and their dependents numbered about 50 million; more than 5,500 banks had failed, wiping out many a depositor's life savings; cities and towns were starting to shut down public services for lack of funds; countless farm and home mortgages were in foreclosure; many businesses could no longer cover their payrolls. To meet the crisis, Roosevelt immediately summoned Congress to a special session that ushered in a recovery program known as the New Deal.

The New Deal was a mixed bag of reforms and emergency measures. It tightened government regulation of banks and the stock market. It created hundreds of thousands of jobs through public works projects. It revived state and local relief programs with massive federal grants that extended aid to some 27 million people—about a fifth of the nation's population—by 1934. Other New Deal initiatives included loans and subsidies to farmers; federal insurance of bank deposits up to $5,000; federal refinancing of home mortgages; the repeal of Prohibition by a constitutional amendment passed by Congress and quickly ratified by the states; and an Indian Reorganization Act that provided for Native American home rule, ended the compulsory allotment of tribal land to individuals, and allowed Indian nations to form corporations modeled on the 1922 Navajo Tribal Council.

The New Deal's centerpiece was the National Industrial Recovery Act (NIRA) of June 1933. The NIRA aimed to resuscitate industrial production and profits by eliminating cutthroat competition among rival firms. The federal government suspended antitrust laws and called on business leaders in major industries like steel, auto, textiles, and mining to draw up "codes of fair competition," which the president then signed into law.[1] Smaller industries soon followed suit, extending NIRA codes to 90 percent of the nonagricultural economy. The codes regulated prices, production quotas, product standards, and labor conditions.

A new federal agency, the National Recovery Administration (NRA), administered the program and touted it far and wide with parades, rallies, placards, and songs. The NRA's Blue Eagle insignia adorned goods marketed by companies in compliance with the program, providing a seal of approval for patriotic shoppers. Noncompliant companies could be prosecuted, but the government seldom pressed charges. It relied instead on negotiation and persuasion, seeking what Roosevelt called a "partnership in planning" with business.[2]

Workers, on the other hand, would have to fight to be heard. At the government's insistence, businessmen adopted industrial codes that banned child labor and established both minimum wages and maximum hours—typically a forty-hour workweek for at least $12 to $15. This certainly improved conditions in many workplaces, but in the absence of unions, employers hired and fired at will, sped up the pace of work, and kept wage scales close to the new minimums.

The New Deal's main concession to workplace democracy was NIRA Section 7(a), which declared that workers "shall have the right to organize and bargain collectively through representatives of their own choosing, and shall be free from the interference, restraint, or coercion of employers of labor, or their agents."[3] But it soon became apparent that corporate executives did not intend to obey this part of the law and that Washington would not force the issue. The New Deal showed time and again that a federal declaration of labor rights was merely a piece of paper. To fulfill its promise, working people had to take matters into their own hands. They did just that, with a dynamism that startled the nation.

From mid-1933 through 1934, about 2.5 million men and women went out on strike, and unions sprang up by the thousands, in workplaces where employers had once driven them out and in places where they had never operated before. These insurgencies gave birth to a new labor movement that would transform federal politics and policies, spark a rebellion in the American Federation of Labor (AFL), and bring to the bargaining table the country's most notoriously anti-union corporations. At the beginning, however, none of this looked likely. Washington was committed to a business-oriented New Deal, labor conservatives firmly controlled the AFL, and open-shop employers were gearing up for a new and final offensive.

Grassroots Unionism

In May 1933, a month before Congress enacted the NIRA, St. Louis witnessed a strike that foreshadowed battles to come. Some 1,400 women walked off their jobs in the city's nut-shelling plants to fight for a rollback of wage cuts, for equal pay for black and white workers, and for union recognition. None of these women had much experience in the labor movement. About three-quarters of them were African Americans, risking their jobs at a moment when black unemployment rates stood well above 50 percent. They belonged to a newborn local of the Food Workers Industrial Union (FWIU), affiliated with the Trade Union Unity League instead of the larger and stronger AFL. For all of these reasons, employers expected to win hands down, but the strike's grassroots character gave it surprising momentum.

Mass picketing buoyed the strikers' spirits and turned back scabs. Each plant had its own shop committee and picket captains chosen by the rank and file. The shop committees' chairwomen formed a central strike committee that organized mass meetings on a daily basis, and "flying squadrons" moving from plant to plant kept the picket lines in close touch with one another. Friends and family joined strikers on the lines and helped them build a support network that extended from unions to churches to civil rights groups. After just ten days, the strikers won a settlement that met their wage demands, including pay equity for black workers. And although employers still refused to recognize the FWIU, the wage victory galvanized its St. Louis branch. The nut shellers helped to organize other low-wage workers, strengthen the city's unemployed councils, and launch a militant campaign to desegregate public parks.

These patterns of struggle permeated the new labor movement that took shape during the New Deal's early years. Craft unions had become accustomed to defending only the interests of their highly skilled members and avoiding the risks of concerted action or solidarity with the masses of unskilled workers, who often belonged to stigmatized ethnic and racial groups. Now, grassroots industrial unionism—a marginal force since the early 1920s—took center stage. Its hallmarks were mass action, democratic decision-making, and do-it-yourself organizing that reached beyond workplaces and union halls to rally entire communities.

In the second half of 1933, union membership grew by 775,000—an astonishing figure given the depth of the depression. The surge continued through 1934, pushing the AFL's total membership over the 3 million mark, slightly higher than it had been in 1929. The federation's industrial affiliates recouped their crippling losses of the 1920s. By 1935, industrial unions represented more than a third of all union members, compared to a sixth in 1929.

Fresh recruits poured into unions old and new. As soon as the NIRA was enacted, organizers for the United Mine Workers sprang into action, using sound trucks, posters, and handbills to spread the message of Section 7(a): "The president wants you to join. . . ."[4] Miners grabbed membership cards as fast as the union handed them out, and many started locals without waiting for organizers to arrive. The UMW added 300,000 members and penetrated new territory in Kentucky and Alabama. The International Ladies' Garment Workers grew by 100,000, reviving its old strongholds in New York City and building new, predominantly Mexican American locals in Los Angeles and San Antonio. The Amalgamated Clothing Workers—now an AFL affiliate—signed up 50,000 new members. Black workers in Alabama's iron mines led an organizing drive by the Mine, Mill and Smelter Workers. More gains followed in 1934. By summer of that year, the UMW was more than a half-million strong; the United Textile Workers had over 300,000 members, up from 50,000 the year before; and the Amalgamated Association of Iron and Steel Workers had grown from about 5,000 to more than 100,000. Mass-production workers from other industries also pounded on the AFL's door. Mostly, they came in through federal labor unions (FLUs); by the end of 1934, the AFL had chartered more than 1,400 new federal locals. Their ranks included 100,000 autoworkers, 90,000 woodworkers, and 60,000 rubber workers.

Organizing accelerated on other fronts too. "Red unions" affiliated with the Trade Union Unity League (TUUL) enlisted at least 125,000 new members—coal miners in Gallup, New Mexico, steelworkers in Ohio, office workers in New York City, farmworkers in California. California's farmworkers also built ethnic unions such as the Filipino Labor Union and new branches of the Confederación de Uniones de Campesinos y Obreros. In Laredo, Texas, Mexican workers from different trades formed La Asociación de Jornaleros. Black and white sharecroppers and tenant farmers in the

Mississippi Delta founded the Southern Tenant Farmers' Union. Pork butchers in Austin, Minnesota, spearheaded the formation of the Independent Union of All Workers, which organized a range of workplaces in the Upper Midwest, from meat plants and department stores to beauty shops and gas stations. Professionals and highly skilled tradesmen formed unions such as the American Newspaper Guild, which First Lady Eleanor Roosevelt joined when she began to publish a newspaper column; the Screen Actors Guild, led by the movie stars Boris Karloff and Groucho Marx; the Mechanics Educational Society of America, founded by tool and die makers; and the Federation of Architects, Engineers, Chemists and Technicians, formed originally as a "United Committee" of unemployed civil engineers to protest wage standards under the NIRA's Construction Industry Code.

As unions expanded, so did community organizing under radical auspices. In New York City, the Communist-led United Council of Working-Class Women built tenant unions and staged rent strikes. The Birmingham branch of the Communists' International Labor Defense mobilized 3,000 to demand federal intervention to defend black communities against lynchings. The unemployed movement—spearheaded by Socialists as well as Communists—picked up momentum in cities across the country. By 1936 it was large enough to establish a national organization, the Workers Alliance of America.

The workplace organizing drives of 1933–34 spawned some 3,500 strikes, and unrest continued into 1935, which saw another 2,000. Strikes erupted in workplaces from factories to cotton fields, trucking depots to laundries, construction sites to office buildings; even among homeworkers, especially garment workers from New York to San Antonio to Mayaguez, Puerto Rico, where "inside" needleworkers employed in factories brought "outsiders" who sewed at home into a 1933 strike over piece rates. In Pennsylvania's Lehigh Valley, "baby strikers"—children working in garment shops for as little as 3¢ an hour—attracted national attention.[5]

Conflict was especially bitter in agriculture, where New Deal policies made labor conditions worse. To shore up the prices of farm produce, the government paid landowners to cultivate fewer acres. Sharecroppers and tenants found themselves evicted; field hands scrambled for fewer jobs; and farm wages fell, exempted from NIRA regulations. In 1933 alone, thirty-seven California farm strikes, most led by the TUUL's Cannery and Agricultural Workers, involved 50,000 workers; it was the largest strike wave ever seen by the state's agribusinesses. Strikers and their families set up tent colonies, pooled resources, maintained mass pickets despite brutal repression, and won better pay scales in twenty-nine of the strikes. In 1933–35, strikes also hit cranberry bogs in Massachusetts, cotton fields in Arizona and the Deep South, sugar plantations in Puerto Rico, orchards in the Pacific Northwest, and vegetable farms in Ohio, Michigan, and New Jersey.

Strikes by nonagricultural workers meanwhile swept through cities and towns in every part of the country. The peak came in mid-1934, when four exceptionally big uprisings grabbed headlines.

In April, workers in an AFL federal union at the Auto-Lite ignition-system factory in Toledo, Ohio, went on strike for union recognition for the second time in three months. When the company got an injunction and resumed production with scab employees, the Lucas County Unemployed League put half a dozen people on a picket line. More joined every day; by late May, there were thousands of pickets—enough to keep the scabs from leaving the plant. When the demonstrators defied the National Guard's orders to disperse, the troops attacked, killing two and wounding hundreds. For several days, fighting filled Toledo's streets. After the city's unions voted for a general strike, Auto-Lite accepted most of the strikers' demands.

Street fighting also broke out in San Francisco, where stevedores joined the AFL's International Longshoremen's Association (ILA) in search of higher pay and shorter hours for themselves and all other longshore workers on the West Coast. Negotiations produced no results, so on May 9, 1934, at 8:00 p.m., longshoremen walked out in every West Coast port and added a new demand: union-controlled hiring halls. Other maritime unions issued their own demands; sympathy strikes spread as far as Gulf ports like Mobile, Alabama. Two months into the strike, authorities moved to open the docks. On July 5—"Bloody Thursday"—police attacked the pickets in San Francisco, killing two and wounding more than a hundred. Local unions responded by calling a general strike. On July 16, 127,000 strikers shut down the city, everything from factories to restaurants to streetcars. Vigilante bands beat strikers and ransacked union halls, and the general strike collapsed after three days. But the longshore strike continued until rank and filers voted to accept federal arbitration. On July 30, strikers lined up on the waterfront and returned to work—all together, all at once. Arbitration gave the ILA most of its demands, and other unions also won improvements.

Minneapolis, too, saw a general strike in 1934. It stemmed from an organizing drive by Teamsters Local 574, which set out in 1933 to unionize the city's trucking companies. Led by a communist faction—Trotskyists, who opposed Stalinist policies in the Soviet Union—this organizing drive swelled the local's membership from no more than 75 to about 6,000. On May 16, 1934, they struck for union recognition, well prepared for a long battle. Organizations of farmers and the unemployed had vowed to support the strikers; strike headquarters included a commissary and infirmary; a women's auxiliary cooked for the pickets, treated them for injuries, and canvassed for donations. Just days after the walkout began, pickets came under attack by local police and deputized civilians, both company guards and members of an employers' association that called itself the Citizens Alliance. Fortified by sympathy strikers from the city's building trades unions, the pickets fought back with clubs and other weapons, and a protracted battle on May 22 left two deputies dead. With that, the trucking companies agreed to settle, but in mid-July they reneged on a promise to bargain with warehouse workers as well as drivers and loaders, so the strike resumed—this time with the participation of some 10,000 workers from the trucking companies and 35,000 sympathy strikers. By order of Local 574, the pickets were now unarmed, but that did not shield them from violence. On July 20, police sprayed buckshot over a picket line, killing two strikers and wounding sixty-seven. By the end of the month, 4,000 National Guardsmen occupied Minneapolis, but few trucks moved. Finally, on August 21, the Citizens Alliance accepted the strikers' demand for union recognition for drivers, loaders, and warehouse workers, and tens of thousands took to the streets for a twelve-hour celebration.

Along with these hard-fought victories in Toledo, San Francisco, and Minneapolis came a massive defeat for the nation's textile workers. NIRA standards were a joke in most of the textile industry. Workers flooded into the AFL's United Textile Workers with complaints about subminimum wages, hours longer than the standards allowed, and an insidious form of speedup known as the "stretch-out"—assigning each worker to run multiple machines.[6] UTW leaders proceeded with caution, but over the summer of 1934, rank and filers organized walkouts that spread from Alabama's cotton mills to textile factories throughout the South. Then, on August 18, an emergency convention of the UTW voted for a general textile strike to force employers to comply with the NIRA. Beginning September 1, more than 400,000 workers walked out, idling every kind of textile mill from Alabama to Maine; it was by far the biggest strike of the 1930s. Mass pickets and parades filled the streets of many mill towns. In some communities, like Durham, North Carolina, the strikers had such widespread support that they experienced no violence; but that was not the norm. During the strike's first week, at least nine pickets were fatally shot: one in Trion, Georgia, two more in Augusta, Georgia, and seven in Honea Path, South Carolina. By the time the strike ended on September 21, the violence had spread northward, with four strikers killed in Saylesville, Rhode Island, and a fifth in nearby Woonsocket. Despite these sacrifices, nothing was won. President Roosevelt promised to appoint a new NIRA committee to oversee labor relations in the textile industry and urged employers not to discriminate against workers who had taken part in the strike. With that, UTW leaders rushed to call off the strike. The new NIRA committee never materialized, however, and in the South thousands of workers who had taken part in the strike found themselves permanently blacklisted from the industry. Textile corporations continued to flout the NIRA.

The textile strike's defeat was merely the largest of many setbacks for the new labor movement, which saw more losses than victories. Grassroots unionism was immensely powerful, but it faced tremendous obstacles.

Federal officials gutted NIRA Section 7(a) through bogus interpretations of the law and lax enforcement. Corporations like U.S. Steel and General Motors rushed to establish new Employee Representation Plans (ERPs). Within months of the NIRA's passage, the number of workers covered by ERPs shot up from 1.25 million to double that figure. Employers persuaded the National Recovery Administration that these "company unions" were bona fide labor organizations that fulfilled workers' right under Section 7(a) to "organize and bargain collectively."[7]

When New Deal agencies favored workers, they could not enforce their decisions. As the strike wave rolled across the country, the government set up labor boards to adjudicate workplace disputes and established a National Labor Relations Board in July 1934. This board routinely interpreted the NIRA in favor of unions, but it lacked authority to enforce decisions. The final word remained with the National Recovery Administration, which almost always sided with employers.

AFL conservatives undercut the new labor movement as well. Just as the textile strikers scared the UTW's leadership, militant mass-production workers alarmed AFL headquarters. In March 1934, some 200,000 autoworkers were poised to strike against the open shop. The AFL's president William Green negotiated a truce that got them a new labor board, which promptly denied them union recognition. Steelworkers met a similar fate that summer, as did rubber workers the following year. Green and company also frustrated efforts to parlay FLUs in mass production into full-fledged industrial unions. The AFL's executive council invited craft unions to raid federal locals for their skilled members, leaving the less skilled—along with others rejected by the crafts on account of color, sex, or nationality—to fend for themselves. At the AFL convention of 1934, the Teamsters' president Daniel Tobin bragged that his 135,000 members were superior to "the rubbish that have lately come into other organizations," saying straight out the thoughts of nearly every craft union's national officials.[8]

Such attitudes did not go unchallenged. As the AFL's industrial unions like the United Mine Workers and the Amalgamated Clothing Workers revived, their leaders called for militant organizing in mass production. The TUUL amplified the chorus in the winter of 1934–35, when its radical unions dissolved and sent their members into AFL affiliates.

But labor leaders who lacked the will to organize retained the balance of power. By summer 1935, the AFL had so disappointed its new recruits in mass production that more than a half-million of them had dropped out. The exodus decimated the United Textile Workers, the Amalgamated Association of Iron and Steel Workers, and federal unions in auto, rubber, and other industries.

For its part, corporate America tried to deprive the new labor movement of popular support, force it to abandon mass action, demoralize its rank and file, and pick off its most militant leaders. Anti-labor propaganda portrayed every strike as a Bolshevik plot and every militant unionist as a violent agitator following orders from Moscow. Employers founded or funded a host of associations to spread the gospel: the American Legion (which received insurance and banking money), the Sentinels of the Republic (linked to Pew family oil interests), the American Liberty League (supported by General Motors executives), and organizations like the U.S. Chamber of Commerce and the Daughters of the American Revolution.

Employers mobilized support from state and local governments. Birmingham and Bessemer, Alabama, passed municipal ordinances against the possession and distribution of radical literature, which local judges interpreted to mean any union publication. Homestead, Pennsylvania, banned mass meetings; when Frances Perkins, U.S. secretary of labor, went there to talk with steelworkers in 1933, she had to meet them at the post office, on federal property. In July 1934, California authorities helped break the agricultural strike wave by arresting eighteen TUUL leaders for criminal syndicalism. Across the country, eighteen strikers were killed on picket lines during the second half of 1933; eighty-eight more over the next two years. More than 18,000 pickets went to jail in 1935.

Corporate and vigilante violence supplemented legal repression. In 1933, California's agribusinesses, banks, and utility companies started the Associated Farmers, which mobilized battalions of up to 2,000 goons to attack pickets and raid tent colonies. Hate groups stood ready to help. In 1934 the Ku Klux Klan revived in Dallas, Texas, to save America from labor radicals. A General Motors executive suggested to a colleague who faced a union drive: "Maybe you could use a little Black Legion. . . . It might help."[9] A midwestern offshoot of the Klan, the Black Legion killed at least ten auto-union activists in 1934–35. Corporations also relied on professional union busters. After 1933, big business spent an estimated $80 million a year on private detectives who specialized in anti-labor espionage and violence. More than 200 agencies furnished tens of thousands of operatives to companies including Chrysler, Standard Oil, Firestone, Westinghouse, Campbell's Soup, Quaker Oats, Montgomery Ward, Borden Milk, and Statler Hotels. Some corporations, like the Ford Motor Company and U.S. Steel, maintained their own in-house security forces.

While repression increased the risks of organizing and undermined many a strike, grassroots unionism persisted. Anti-communist propaganda failed to ignite a new "red scare," partly because it charged that Bolsheviks were behind the New Deal as well as the new labor movement, which meant that the Roosevelt administration declined to support the campaign. Moreover, the new labor movement's community networks were largely resistant to red-baiting. Even brutality could backfire. In Birmingham, Alabama, a metalworker took his eight-year-old son to see a union organizer who had been tortured by thugs employed by Tennessee Coal and Iron, a subsidiary of U.S. Steel. As the boy examined the wounds, his father instructed him: "Look at that, sonny. That's the company. That's what you got to learn to hate—and fight agin."[10]

Corporations' belligerence—their war on unions, countless infractions of NIRA rules, wild charges against the New Deal—played poorly with the general public too. The White House was flooded by letters demanding that the president control big business. Then, in May 1935, the Supreme Court voided the NIRA as a violation of the Constitution's limits on federal power, and the Roosevelt administration swiftly changed course. A second New Deal took shape, this one based on a government partnership with working people, not businessmen.

In a concession to popular anger at business magnates, Congress substantially raised federal taxes on corporations and wealthy individuals. It also passed the Public Utility Holding Company Act, breaking up gas and electric monopolies that charged exorbitant rates.

A new federal agency, the Works Progress Administration (WPA), greatly expanded public works programs to create more jobs. By early 1936, more than 3.4 million workers were on its rolls. Most worked on construction projects—roads, bridges, parks, recreation centers, and other public facilities. The WPA also organized the Federal Writers Project, the Federal Theatre Project, and other arts initiatives that employed writers, musicians, actors, and visual artists. It worked with the new National Youth Administration (NYA) to provide part-time jobs to penniless students so they could continue their educations. In the South, both the WPA and the NYA complied with Jim Crow, segregating workers by race and excluding black participants from supervisory positions; in the Southwest, the wages of Mexican Americans employed by the WPA averaged well under a third of the highest wages for whites. New Dealers in Washington forced state and local officials to abandon the common practice of reserving all public works jobs for whites, however, and they initiated a number of construction projects—schools, parks, hospitals, and housing complexes—that benefitted communities of color.

Another core component of the second New Deal addressed the free market's failures to give working people economic security, both short- and long-term. The Social Security Act established a national system of unemployment insurance, administered by the states and financed by a tax on employers. In addition, the act established pensions for workers, funded by taxes on both employers and workers; and it authorized federal grants to states to assist disabled individuals and destitute children along with their mothers. The Social Security system was not especially generous or fair. It excluded agricultural, hospital, domestic, and public workers; and these exclusions especially disadvantaged workers of color, who were disproportionately concentrated in agriculture and domestic jobs. Workers' pensions varied according to their income, replicating disparities in wages. When survivors' pensions became part of the system in 1939, they were subject to the same restrictions as pensions for workers. Although aid to children, their mothers, and the disabled was federally financed, local officials decided who did and did not receive assistance. In the South, black mothers and their children often found it impossible to secure benefits; officials simply funneled the women into domestic jobs in white homes—jobs whose pay during the Great Depression might amount to nothing more than hand-me-down clothes and leftover food. California's Republican governor instituted a "no work, no eat" policy under which anyone deemed fit for farmwork was expelled from relief rolls whenever growers needed field hands.[11] For all its stinginess and inequities, however, the Social Security Act represented a breakthrough. For the first time in U.S. history, the federal government took responsibility for delivering the security that capitalism could not provide.

The centerpiece of the second New Deal and its most important concession to the labor movement was the National Labor Relations Act, usually called the Wagner Act after its author, Senator Robert Wagner of New York, and signed into law on July 5, 1935. Whereas the NIRA's Section 7(a) had recognized unions' right to exist, the Wagner Act gave them protection. It established secret-ballot elections in which workers could vote whether or not to be represented by a union. It prohibited employers from interfering with organizing and specifically banned common modes of interference: threats, coercion, or restraint against an organizing drive; sponsorship of groups that claimed to be labor organizations (company unions); discrimination against union members in hiring, firing, layoffs, or job assignments; retaliation against workers who reported violations of labor law; and refusals to bargain with a union voted in by the workers. Finally, the Wagner Act established a new National Labor Relations Board (NLRB) to oversee the representation elections, hear and rule on complaints about violations of the act, and petition federal courts to enforce the board's rulings. One of the codas added that, "Nothing in this Act shall be construed so as to interfere with or impede or diminish in any way the right to strike."[12] Like Social Security, the Wagner Act disproportionately excluded workers of color; it did not cover agricultural workers, domestic workers, hospital workers, or public employees. From employers' standpoint, however, any protection for unionism was too much.

Big business despised the second New Deal and the Wagner Act most of all. The National Association of Manufacturers fought its passage with the biggest campaign in the history of corporate lobbying. When the Wagner Act became law, the American Liberty League challenged it in court, and many employers vowed to ignore it, waiting for the Supreme Court to declare it unconstitutional.

Workers struggling to organize mass production were cautiously optimistic. They had made gains without much help from the NIRA; more seemed possible now. But the AFL remained an obstacle, most of its leaders belonging to one of two camps:

those who preferred to ignore mass-production workers entirely and those willing to take in new dues-paying members so long as their own prerogatives and power would remain intact. Both groups doubted that mass production could really be unionized.

In fact, however, federal labor unions in mass production were on the move. They founded a national auto union in August 1935 and a rubber union the following month. They fought to keep their skilled members when poachers from craft unions came around. Something more was at stake than jurisdictional issues or contending theories about the merits of industrial unionism on the one hand and craft unionism on the other. At the most basic level, initiative confronted paralysis. As the labor journalist Len De Caux put it, "the will to organize" was the real issue. "The Old Guard," he observed, "was acting dog-in-the-manger over members nobody had."[13] The activists intended to build unions large and militant enough to beat the open shop; if craft conservatives blocked the way, they would have to be shoved aside.

More easily said than done; AFL officials had defeated many insurgencies. But this time around union leaders were not of one mind. John L. Lewis—president of the United Mine Workers, the nation's largest union—sided with the insurgents and was ready to lead an assault on the old guard, and the heads of a few other unions stood ready to follow. In October 1935, when delegates gathered in Atlantic City for the AFL's annual convention, the stage was set for a fight that would split the federation.

The Rise of the CIO

Convention debates between industrial and craft unionists grew more acrimonious than ever. Lewis and a few like-minded union leaders sponsored a resolution calling for unrestricted industrial union charters for mass-production industries. After hours of speeches pro and con, the convention voted the resolution down, 18,024 to 10,933, and the issue seemed settled. But delegates from the federal labor unions and the new auto and rubber unions kept rising to make their case, while President Green tried to silence them from the podium. When the Carpenters' president William Hutcheson interrupted a rubber worker, Lewis loudly objected. Hutcheson called Lewis a "big bastard," and Lewis decked him with a right-cross to the jaw.[14] That blow—later called "the punch heard round the world"—made clear that the dissidents could no longer be held in check.[15]

On November 9, 1935, Lewis and seven other leaders of AFL unions met to found the Committee for Industrial Organization (CIO) "for the purpose of encouraging and promoting the organization of the unorganized workers in mass production and other industries upon an industrial basis."[16] These men represented long-established organizations: the United Mine Workers, the Amalgamated Clothing Workers, the Ladies' Garment Workers, the Mine, Mill and Smelter Workers, the United Textile Workers, the International Typographical Union, the Cap and Millinery Workers, and the Oil and Gas Workers. But the catalyst for the CIO was the new labor movement. The grassroots uprisings that had persuaded Congress to pass the Wagner Act had also convinced Lewis and company that industrial organizing would pay off. And the dues paid by more than a half-million new members had so enriched the UMW and the garment unions that the CIO could fund organizing campaigns without any help from AFL headquarters.

The CIO started as eight unions whose membership totaled about 1 million. Two years later, there were thirty-two CIO unions with 3.7 million members, the vast majority covered by collective bargaining agreements. Most of the newcomers were mass-production workers in industrial unions, though other kinds of workers and organizations climbed aboard too. The Steel Workers Organizing Committee (later the United Steelworkers of America) had 550,000 members and contracts with all divisions of U.S. Steel. The United Mine Workers had 600,000 members. The United Auto Workers and United Rubber Workers—previously federal labor unions—had respectively 375,000 members and contracts with General Motors, Chrysler, and several smaller auto companies, and 75,000 members and contracts with Goodyear, Goodrich, and General Tire and Rubber. Other CIO forces included 400,000 textile workers; close to 500,000 members of various garment unions; 140,000 workers in electrical manufacturing; 130,000 in transportation and maritime unions; 120,000 in white-collar unions of retail workers, office workers, public employees, newspaper reporters, architects, engineers, and other professionals; and 100,000 woodworkers, from loggers to machine operators in furniture factories.

Rubber workers in Akron, Ohio, became the first to put the CIO on the map. In mid-February 1936, when the giant Goodyear tire plant announced layoffs, several hundred members of the newborn United Rubber Workers (URW) threw up a picket line. Within days, more than 14,000 Goodyear workers were out on strike. Their tactics typified grassroots unionism. Thousands of pickets—rubber workers from Goodyear and other companies, along with their families and neighbors—encircled the plant's eleven-mile perimeter day and night, even during blizzards. When Goodyear got an injunction, the URW and Akron's central labor council promised a general strike if the National Guard enforced the injunction. The guardsmen did not intervene. When police tried to tear down tents set up along the picket line, General Tire Company workers left their shop to help beat back the police. When the rubber barons organized a "Law and Order League" of vigilantes, the union organized a counterforce of workers who had served in the Great War.[17]

The strike was not just a local effort, however. Seasoned organizers from the CIO's founding unions converged on Akron to assist the URW. CIO headquarters donated to the strike fund. CIO researchers helped with publicity, digging up facts about Goodyear's profits and stock manipulation. CIO leaders let Goodyear and its customers know they risked national boycotts if violence broke the picket line. After a month, the company offered to shelve the layoff plan and bargain with the union. The strikers debated the offer at mass meetings and agreed to go back to work.

Both of the forces at play in the Akron victory contributed to CIO growth. Rank-and-file activists carried grassroots mobilization to new levels. The CIO and the unions that had established it poured staff and money into organizing the unorganized. Bottom-up and top-down efforts were powerful in combination, but not always a true partnership; grassroots activists and those from CIO headquarters had different approaches to building the labor movement.

The differences showed especially with respect to political action. When President Roosevelt ran for reelection in 1936, John L. Lewis knew his defeat would be disastrous for labor and vigorously campaigned for him. The AFL also endorsed Roosevelt, who appointed the Teamsters' president Daniel Tobin chairman of the Democratic

Party's National Labor Committee. With the AFL's old guard as the dominant force on that committee, Lewis joined with Sidney Hillman of the CIO's Amalgamated Clothing Workers to start Labor's Non-Partisan League, whose member unions—including a great many unaffiliated with the CIO—funneled $1.5 million into Roosevelt's campaign but did not endorse his party.

As they maneuvered to increase the CIO's influence in the White House, Lewis and Hillman faced a grassroots movement for an independent labor party. It had the support of five state labor federations, scores of central labor councils, and hundreds of locals in industrial unions, including Lewis's Mine Workers and Hillman's Clothing Workers. To contain this movement, Lewis gave the United Auto Workers $100,000 for organizing, contingent on their endorsement of Roosevelt. Hillman meanwhile oversaw the conversion of New York City's chapter of the Non-Partisan League into the American Labor Party, suggesting that the league would become the nucleus for a national labor party once Roosevelt was reelected. In the end, however, CIO headquarters did not follow through on that idea.

In 1936 Roosevelt won millions of working-class votes because of the second New Deal and its contrast with the Republicans' relentlessly pro-business platform. The president got over 60 percent of the popular vote, carrying every state but Maine and Vermont. Urban working-class voters—immigrants and their children as well as migrants from rural America—came to identify themselves as Democrats. African American support for the Republican Party evaporated as federal programs brought some relief to black communities. Black votes went to Roosevelt even though he failed to endorse a federal anti-lynching law opposed by southern Democrats.

The movement for independent political action survived in third-party initiatives in Wisconsin, Minnesota, California, and Washington. In New York City, the American Labor Party (ALP) became the majority party among East Harlem's Italian, Puerto Rican, and African American voters. In every congressional election from 1938 through 1948, the ALP's candidate, Vito Marcantonio (a former Republican), won the race to represent East Harlem in the U.S. House. For the most part, however, the ALP merely endorsed candidates fielded by other parties. National spokesmen for the CIO and its member unions remained firmly wedded to the two-party system.

As Lewis and Hillman stumped for Roosevelt's reelection, the CIO launched an organizing drive aimed at U.S. Steel, and here, too, a top-down approach held sway. Lewis appointed the United Mine Workers' Philip Murray as chairman of the Steel Workers' Organizing Committee (SWOC) and armed it with a war chest of $750,000. SWOC announced it would maintain "centralized and responsible control of the organizing campaign" and "insist that local policies conform to the national plan of action."[18] A staff of lawyers, researchers, publicity agents, and salaried organizers—few of them steelworkers—conducted a campaign based mainly outside the mills. These tactics were designed, in Murray's words, "to banish fear from the steel workers' minds."[19] They could join SWOC without paying initiation fees (or even dues after October 1936) and were not expected to talk up the union. Instead, SWOC staged national meetings where the CIO was endorsed by New Deal politicians and leading spokesmen for the various racial and ethnic groups represented in the mills. By the end of 1936, SWOC claimed more than 100,000 members, though the union was close to invisible on the job.

On March 2, 1937, after secret meetings with John L. Lewis (so secret that even Philip Murray did not know about them), U.S. Steel reached an agreement with SWOC. Workers flocked into the union, but it remained highly centralized. Murray appointed all regional and district directors and field organizers. The national office set local dues policies, prohibited strikes without permission, and reserved the right to expel anyone breaking that rule. Murray's directors—not local officers elected by members—negotiated and signed contracts.

Organizing in the automobile industry followed a very different course, moving from the bottom up. SWOC probably owed its victory at U.S. Steel to the autoworkers at General Motors (GM)—the world's largest corporation and bitterly anti-union. The United Auto Workers (UAW) had planned to begin a campaign in Cleveland and Detroit in January 1937, but after Roosevelt's reelection a series of spontaneous strikes quickened the pace. In November and early December 1936, when workers struck at GM plants in Atlanta and Kansas City, UAW leaders discouraged the actions as premature. Then, on December 28, one department at the company's Cleveland plant staged a sit-down strike, and the rest of the plant's 7,000 workers soon joined in, vowing to occupy their workplace until GM signed a national contract. On December 30, workers occupied GM's Fisher Plant No. 2 in Detroit. The next day, workers at Fisher No. 1 in Flint, Michigan, launched an action that became a national emblem of grassroots unionism. Following a lunchtime meeting, several hundred workers returned to Fisher 1, escorted guards and managers out of the plant, and settled in to stay. On January 3, 1937, with sit-downs spreading rapidly, UAW delegates met in Flint, composed formal demands, and declared a company-wide strike.

Workers' occupation of the Flint plant was exemplary in planning and discipline. Members of a shop committee patrolled to make sure no one damaged cars or machinery; drinking and gambling were forbidden. The UAW Women's Auxiliary—strikers' wives, sisters, mothers, daughters, and friends—began with fifty members on the second day of the strike and quickly grew to many hundreds. The women raised money, provided food and childcare for strikers' families, and walked on picket lines. Genora Johnson, wife of local union leader Kermit Johnson and a member of the Socialist Party, organized a Women's Emergency Brigade, whose members wore red berets and carried hammers, crowbars, and two-by-fours to demonstrations and pickets. A group of military veterans that called themselves "Union War Vets" served as bodyguards for strike leaders, pledging to protect them by any means necessary. Support came from outside Flint as well; even First Lady Eleanor Roosevelt contributed to the strike fund. As one striker later told the oral historian Studs Terkel, "It started out kinda ugly because the guys were afraid they put their foot in it and all they was gonna do is lose their jobs. But as time went on, they began to realize they could win this darn thing, 'cause we had a lot of outside people comin' in showin' sympathy."[20] The pickets in front of the plant numbered as many as 10,000, and the momentum in Flint inspired GM workers everywhere. By mid-January, seventeen of the company's plants and well over half its workforce were on strike.

The company refused to negotiate unless the occupied plants were vacated. In response, the UAW made plans to take Chevrolet Plant No. 9 in Flint. Spies reported the plan, however, and GM's security force positioned itself to prevent the occupation. Then, as union members and the Women's Emergency Brigade stormed Chevy 9, other

UAW militants walked into Chevrolet Plant No. 4, which made all the engines for the Chevrolet line. Half the plant's 4,000 workers joined the occupation. On February 3, 1937, after the governor refused to order troops to evict the strikers, GM finally agreed to negotiate. A week later the company recognized the UAW at the striking plants, dropped charges and lawsuits against the strikers, and agreed to submit other issues to a labor-management conference.

The victory at GM snowballed. The Chrysler Corporation signed with the union in April 1937, and by the end of the year the UAW had recruited 400,000 members. In Flint, it established a general union (UAW Local 156) that organized not only auto-workers but also grocery clerks, laundry workers, waiters and waitresses, and others. The sit-down tactic was widely copied. In the first two weeks after the Flint victory there were eighty-seven sit-down strikes in Detroit alone—in auto-parts plants, cigar factories, bakeries, and other workplaces. Over the course of 1937, about 300,000 workers staged a total of 477 sit-down strikes. The Flint victory also proved the strength of what Len De Caux, now editor of the *CIO News*, called "tumultuous democracy."[21] UAW locals were virtually autonomous; all of the union's officers were elected by the membership; and the radical Unity Caucus contended with the moderate Progressive Caucus for a decade.

Whatever their internal dynamics, all CIO unions fostered workplace democracy. Alfred Sloan Jr., chairman of General Motors, later recalled the fury of businessmen forced to bargain with the CIO: "Our rights to determine production schedules, to set work standards, and to discipline workers were all suddenly called into question."[22] Unions restricted employer prerogatives.

Unions could also impose restrictions on workers. Following the Goodyear victory, officers of the United Rubber Workers squared off against the many rank and filers who staged departmental sit-downs to protest unsatisfactory conditions. However effective on the shop floor, these "wildcat strikes"—strikes unauthorized by the union—undercut the URW's negotiations with Goodyear. To gain concessions from management, union officials had to be able to deliver labor peace. Union after union clamped down on wildcats once employers agreed to negotiate.

The Wagner Act cut both ways too. The National Labor Relations Board elections played a big part in the CIO's growth, and unions counted on board rulings to enforce protections stipulated by the Wagner Act. But employers broke the law more efficiently than the government administered it. Even after the Supreme Court upheld the Wagner Act in April 1937, the NLRB was so swamped by complaints about employer violations that unions could wait months for a ruling, or even years if the dispute went to the courts. Moreover, government help came at a price. No union could call on the NLRB—even for an election—without accepting its rules for union conduct, which prohibited strikes and boycotts in support of other unions.

Reliance on the NLRB also turned the CIO away from workers not protected by the Wagner Act. While it chartered two small unions of public employees, workers employed by the federal jobs programs received virtually no attention, even though they were clearly in a militant mood. From 1933 through 1939, they staged close to 700 strikes, most of them led by organizations of the unemployed. Farmworkers also got short shrift. In July 1937, local and regional unions of sharecroppers, farmhands, fishermen, and food processors started a new CIO union: the United Cannery, Agricultural, Packing and Allied Workers of America (UCAPAWA), which brought together 110,000 members, unprotected field-workers and protected plant-workers alike. Focusing on the organizing drives that seemed the easiest to win—drives that could culminate in an election supervised by the NLRB—UCAPAWA's central office supported farm organizing less and less and suspended it entirely in 1939. Domestic workers fared worse; the CIO did not even try to draw them in. As one unnamed union leader told a researcher from the YWCA, "The organization of household workers will come about as a sort of 'mopping up' process when we have the bulk of other women in unions."[23] But that was highly unlikely to happen anytime soon.

Still, the CIO advanced working-class solidarity in important ways. CIO unions welcomed men and women of every color, creed, and nationality. This solidarity had limits. Women workers did not hold leadership positions in proportion to their numbers in CIO unions; the same was true for people of color. CIO contracts left hiring decisions to employers, and seniority clauses perpetuated the effects of past discrimination in hiring and job assignments. Although mass-production unions claimed jurisdiction over everyone working in their industries, they rarely reached out to the legions of women who staffed company offices.

Nevertheless, women's ranks in U.S. unions expanded from about 200,000 in 1935 to 800,000 in 1940. The CIO and its National Coordinating Committee of CIO Auxiliaries meanwhile created a large and vital network of local and national women's auxiliaries in the UAW and other unions, including the Rubber Workers, SWOC, the National Maritime Union, and the Mine, Mill and Smelter Workers. The auxiliaries were active in many strikes. Violet Baggett, married to a Cadillac worker, joined a UAW auxiliary when her husband went on strike. In a letter to the UAW's newspaper, she wrote: "I'm living for the first time with a definite goal. I want a decent living for not only my family but for everyone. Just being a woman isn't enough any more. I want to be a human being."[24] In Detroit and some other cities, women's auxiliaries also took on housing and consumer issues.

Like their counterparts in the AFL, new members of CIO unions pledged "never to discriminate against a fellow worker on account of creed, color or nationality," but the CIO went much further than that.[25] Its unions adopted constitutions that outlawed exclusion, discrimination, and segregation. They fielded organizers from diverse backgrounds and published union literature in many languages. They reached out to working-class churches and community organizations irrespective of race or ethnicity. They worked with civil rights groups like A. Philip Randolph's National Negro Congress, the Southern Negro Youth Congress (based in colleges and universities), the American Committee for the Protection of the Foreign Born, the Committee for the Protection of Filipino Rights, and the Japanese American Democratic Clubs in several California cities. They supported projects like El Congreso de los Pueblos de Habla Español, founded under the leadership of Luisa Moreno, a Guatemalan-born organizer for UCAPAWA. El Congreso brought together more than a hundred Mexican American and Mexican associations to fight "against discrimination and deportation, for economic liberty, for equal representation in government, for the building of a better world for our youth," to quote the organization's eighteen-year-old executive secretary,

In December 1936, workers at one of General Motors' Flint, Michigan, factories began a sit-down strike to express their grievances to a company that refused to recognize any union. The action proved to be a watershed event in the story of American labor

THE FLINT SIT-DOWN STRIKE

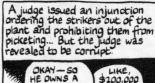

Josefina Fierro de Bright.[26] CIO unions also cultivated connections with the radical ethnic associations affiliated with the International Workers Order, like the Slovak Workers' Society, the Garibaldi-American Fraternity Society, and the Cervantes Fraternal Society.

Time and again, the CIO's rank and file united across racial and ethnic lines. When 200 black women from the Tobacco Stemmers' and Laborers' Industrial Union struck the Brown and Williamson Tobacco Company in Richmond, Virginia, roughly the same number of white women from the Amalgamated Clothing Workers joined the picket line. The Maritime Workers Industrial Union (predecessor to the National Maritime Union) signed up 3,000 Chinese sailors after agreeing to support their demands for equal pay and the right to go ashore in U.S. ports. When Chinese-American members of the Ladies' Garment Workers struck a San Francisco factory owned by National Dollar Stores, white salesclerks honored picket lines in front of the stores. Mexican and Russian Jewish women at the California Sanitary Canning Company in Los Angeles united to win a UCAPAWA strike. Filipino and Japanese workers came together to build strong UCAPAWA locals on Hawaiian sugar plantations. In Chicago, black, white, and Mexican workers mingled in SWOC and the Packinghouse Workers' Organizing Committee. Journalist Ruth McKenney wrote of white rubber workers in Ohio: "Men from the southern mountains, once fair bait for the savage program of the Ku Klux Klan, applauded the speeches of Jewish garment workers, cheered the advance of Irish Catholic transport workers, sat side by side in union meetings with Negro workers."[27]

This culture of solidarity owed a great deal to left-wing radicals, especially Communists. Although John L. Lewis had ruthlessly attacked leftists in the past, he hired many as CIO organizers, recognizing their militancy, discipline, and success at building interracial co-operation in the TUUL. When colleagues objected, Lewis responded, "Who gets the bird? The hunter or the dog?"[28] CIO leaders would presumably reap the rewards of the radicals' skill as organizers. Communists and their allies became leaders in their own right, however. They were elected to head many locals and some national unions, and solidarity made the greatest advances in these settings.

Corporations had their own brand of solidarity. The "Little Steel" companies—Republic, Youngstown Sheet and Tube, Inland, Bethlehem—planned in concert to block unionization and handed the CIO its first major defeat. Once U.S. Steel had recognized the union, SWOC turned to the industry's second tier, and called a strike against Little Steel in May 1937. Tom Girdler, Republic Steel's chief executive officer, organized the joint resistance. In Chicago, Cleveland, Massillon, Ohio, and other steel towns, strikers were gassed, clubbed, and shot, and thousands were jailed following confrontations with police or National Guardsmen. In South Chicago on Memorial Day (May 30), police attacked a gathering of Republic Steel strikers and their families, beating and shooting more than fifty men, women, and children. Ten died, all of them men; nine were the victims of gunshots and one was clubbed to death. Eight more workers were killed before the strike ended in defeat.

This violence was neither spontaneous nor accidental. The companies spent nearly $500,000 on weapons for use during the strike. Youngstown Sheet and Tube bought eight machine guns, 369 rifles, 190 shotguns, 450 revolvers, and 109 gas launchers—

plus 10,000 rounds of ammunition and 3,000 tear-gas canisters. Republic Steel bought more military supplies than any state or local police department in the country. So found the U.S. Senate's committee on civil liberties chaired by Wisconsin's Robert La Follette Jr. (son of the Progressive Party's 1924 presidential candidate). Opening its hearings in 1936, the La Follette Committee investigated corporate efforts to sabotage union organizing. Testimony documented the "Mohawk Valley Formula," a multi-step strikebreaking strategy devised by the Remington Rand typewriter company in upstate New York and promoted nationwide by the National Association of Manufacturers.[29] The formula combined elaborate propaganda campaigns with harassment and violence.

A faltering economy compounded the CIO's trials. In 1937, following a year of recovery, the Roosevelt administration cut government spending to balance the federal budget and reaped disastrous results. The recovery halted in mid-1937; by 1938 the depression was back in full force. In early 1938, Mexican American pecan shellers in San Antonio won a bitter strike—over a thousand strikers served time in jail—only to find themselves replaced by machines a few months later. Heavy industry was hit especially hard. Layoffs robbed the UAW of three-quarters of its members. SWOC and the United Rubber Workers were badly weakened. Though many CIO unions held steady and some even grew, the CIO claimed 200,000 fewer members at the end of 1939 than it had two years earlier.

Competition from the AFL helped shrink the CIO as well. The federation suspended CIO unions in 1936 and expelled them the following year. In May 1938, the Committee for Industrial Organization became the Congress of Industrial Organizations, an independent federation momentarily larger that the AFL, even though two of the CIO's founding unions—the Ladies' Garment Workers and the Cap and Millinery Workers—abandoned it at this juncture. (A third founder, the International Typographical Union, never got around to joining the CIO, but the AFL expelled it in 1938 for refusing to pay a "war tax" to fund fights against the CIO.[30]) Goaded into action, the AFL finally started organizing. Like John L. Lewis, some of its leaders hired radicals to get things rolling; now on the Teamsters' payroll, Trotskyists from Minneapolis organized 200,000 long-haul truckers in eleven states. Craft unions developed industrial divisions; the International Brotherhood of Electrical Workers (an electricians' union) started organizing production workers in electrical equipment factories. Customarily cautious unions grew bold; the Hotel Employees and Restaurant Employees (HERE) used a sit-down strike to win union recognition and increased wages and paid vacations for lunch-counter waitresses and salesclerks at Woolworth's five-and-dime stores in Detroit—the workers even got half-pay for the time they had been on strike. Some AFL organizing drives superseded long-standing color bars. In California, Filipinos and Mexican Americans belonged to a newly chartered Field Workers Union Local 30326; in Alaska, the Packers Union's first, second, and third vice-presidents were, respectively, Japanese, Chinese, and Mexican American.

CIO and AFL unions sometimes co-operated at the local level. In Detroit, for example, HERE formed an alliance with the UAW, and in Kenosha, Wisconsin, CIO locals belonged to the AFL's trades and labor council. Mostly, however, the two federations fought over members and contracts. These battles took place in a host of sectors, including meatpacking, the machine tool industry, trucking and warehousing, public employment, and woodworking, lumber, and paper mills. Often, the AFL's spokesmen promoted it as a conservative, even reactionary, alternative to the CIO. In a letter to his union's locals, the Machinists' president A.O. Wharton described the CIO as a "gang of sluggers, communists, radicals and soapbox artists, professional bums, expelled members of labor unions, outright scabs and the Jewish organizations with all their red affiliates."[31] As the CIO's ranks dwindled, the AFL's grew, from 3.4 million in late 1937 to over 4 million in late 1939, and its numbers surpassed the CIO's by more than a half-million by the end of 1940.

Beset on all sides, the CIO abandoned militant tactics like the sit-down strike after 1937. More and more, it relied on NLRB procedures and rulings to win contracts. In response, the AFL joined employers in pressing Congress to restrain the board's powers.

Whose America?

The government was not a dependable ally of working people. Businessmen and other conservatives called the economic downturn the "Roosevelt depression,"[32] arguing that the second New Deal undermined business confidence by legislating restraints on profitability. The Roosevelt administration blamed the downturn on a "general strike of capital,"[33] and John L. Lewis agreed. Both he and the president charged that businessmen had cut back investment to induce a depression they hoped would undo the Wagner Act and the rest of the New Deal. Whatever its cause, however, the renewed depression put Roosevelt and his political allies on the defensive.

After the economy slumped, just one major reform made it through Congress: the Fair Labor Standards Act (FLSA) of June 1938. The act put a floor on wages and a ceiling on hours—25¢ an hour and 44 hours per week, with time and a half for overtime—and provided for improvements that would take the standards to 40¢ an hour and 40 hours a week in 1940. It also outlawed the employment of children under sixteen in most occupations and under eighteen in hazardous occupations. As enacted, the FLSA was weaker than the law the president had proposed. Congressional amendments limited its coverage to workers engaged in interstate distribution or production, and exempted many groups, including farmworkers and agricultural processers, fishermen, domestic workers, and professionals. The AFL opposed the Fair Labor Standards Act—as it had always opposed minimum-wage legislation—on the theory that the minimum would become the maximum.

In the Democratic primaries of 1938, Roosevelt campaigned for New Dealers seeking to unseat conservatives (mostly southern incumbents), but few of the challengers won. In the general election, Democrats retained the majority in both the House and Senate, but New Dealers did not, and southern "Dixiecrats"—Democrats committed to the Jim Crow system—joined hands with Republicans to bring the New Deal to a standstill.

Ultra-right sentiment surged among businessmen in 1938–40, especially sympathy for the fascist experiments in Germany and Italy. Henry Ford and International Business Machine's president Thomas J. Watson accepted medals from the German government. A newly formed "League for Constitutional Government" churned out fascist literature addressed to the upper classes. Among the group's stalwarts was H.W. Prentis Jr., a leader of the National Association of Manufacturers, who lectured on the dangers of "more and more democracy," including primary elections, referendums, ballot initiatives, candidate recalls, direct election of senators, and the National Labor Relations Board.[34] In 1940, midwestern businessmen from Sears Roebuck, Quaker Oats, Hormel, and other companies helped to establish the America First Committee to oppose U.S. intervention against Hitler.

The CIO drew fire from every part of the conservative spectrum. The Ku Klux Klan's Imperial Wizard in Atlanta announced that his organization's primary target was now the CIO—"infested with Communism and seeking to organize the Negroes against the whites."[35] Nazi sympathizers in the Constitutional Educational League published the bogus booklet *Join the CIO and Help Build A Soviet America*, and the National Association of Manufacturers distributed 2 million copies. Father Charles Coughlin, the "Radio Priest" in Royal Oak, Michigan, whose weekly broadcasts reached up to 30 million listeners nationwide, blended praise for the AFL with attacks on the Roosevelt administration, the CIO, Communists, and Jews.[36] *The Labor Advocate*, the newspaper of the AFL's central labor council in Birmingham, Alabama, identified the CIO as "America's Public Enemy No. 1."[37]

In May 1938, the U.S. House of Representatives established the Committee to Investigate Un-American Activities, chaired by the Texas Dixiecrat Martin Dies, who solicited testimony from a steady parade of "expert witnesses" that included both AFL spokesmen and right-wing crackpots from other quarters. On August 13, 1938, the AFL's vice president John Frey named 284 CIO organizers as Communists, promised to name 230 more, and charged that they used sit-down strikes and mass picketing to train workers "for the day when the signal for revolution is given." On August 14, the front page of the *New York Times* proclaimed, "COMMUNISTS RULE THE C.I.O."[38] Later, Walter Steele, owner and editor of the *National Republic* magazine, went before the Dies Committee to testify about the Communist Party's outreach from the CIO to 640 organizations ranging from church councils and civil rights groups to the Boy Scouts and Camp Fire Girls. In May 1939, Dudley Pierrepont Gilbert, a New York socialite, told the committee that he was funding the organization of an underground army of Klansmen, Nazi sympathizers, and other right-wingers that would crush the revolution soon to be unleashed by Communists with the help of the CIO and Jewish financiers. The committee concluded that WPA writing projects and theatrical productions harbored subversives, identifiable as such because they were pro-union, antifascist, and opposed to racial discrimination. Defunded by Congress, the Federal Theatre Project closed in 1939. The Dies Committee also investigated charges that Communists controlled the La Follette Committee, which the Senate shut down in 1940.

Immigrants were especially suspect. In 1940, Congress passed and the president signed into law the Alien Registration Act, commonly called the Smith Act (because its main author was Virginia's Dixiecrat congressman Howard Smith). It required that all aliens—noncitizen immigrants—be fingerprinted, register with the U.S. Justice Department, and keep the government informed of their whereabouts. The act also made it a federal crime to advocate, advise, or teach the necessity or desirability of forcefully overthrowing local, state, or national government, or to belong to an organization with such a doctrine. In effect, it was a federal anti-syndicalist law.

If it was a crime to have revolutionary goals, many CIO members and allies were guilty. They aimed to reconstruct American life from bottom to top. As Len De Caux observed, "Now we're a movement, many workers asked, why can't we move on to more and more? . . . Why can't we go on to create a new society with the workers on top, to end age-old injustices, to banish poverty and war?"[39]

Radical ambitions went hand in hand with patriotism. Strikers celebrated victories by singing "The Battle Hymn of the Republic." Portraits of Abraham Lincoln adorned the pages of union newspapers and the walls of union offices. Labor activists routinely compared themselves to the patriots of 1776 and abolitionists like John Brown, Frederick Douglass, and Sojourner Truth. The Communist Party called on all opponents of fascism and war to defend the "life, liberty and pursuit of happiness of the American people" and the "sacred guarantees of our Bill of Rights."[40]

CIO-style patriotism included a clear-eyed recognition of injustice and a strong sense of obligation to correct it. In his memoir *America Is in the Heart*, Filipino immigrant and labor activist Carlos Bulosan declared: "We must interpret history in terms of liberty. We must advocate democratic ideas and fight all forces that would abort our culture. . . . We . . . understand the many imperfections of democracy and the malignant disease corroding its very heart. We must be united in the effort to make an America in which our people can find happiness."[41]

Unity required respect for the diversity among working people, a sentiment perhaps best articulated in "Ballad for Americans," written by radical composer Earl Robinson and lyricist John LaTouche for the Federal Theatre Project's 1939 musical production *Sing for Your Supper* and later turned into a hit recording by the world-famous singer, actor, and political activist Paul Robeson. In this cantata, the chorus sings about American history as the soloist replies and—in response to questions from the chorus—slowly reveals his identity:

> I'm the everybody who's nobody. . . . I am the et ceteras. And the so forths that do the work. . . . I'm just an Irish, Negro, Jewish, Italian, French and English, Spanish, Russian, Chinese, Polish, Scotch, Hungarian, Litvak, Swedish, Finnish, Canadian, Greek and Turk, and Czech and double Czech American. . . . I was baptized Baptist, Methodist, Congregationalist, Lutheran, Atheist, Roman Catholic, Orthodox Jewish, Presbyterian, Seventh Day Adventist, Mormon, Quaker, Christian Scientist—and lots more! . . . You know who I am . . . AMERICA![42]

For most CIO activists, this was patriotism: insistence on equal rights for every race and ethnic group, respect for their distinct cultures and contributions, unity on democratic grounds, and the belief that working people had a special claim on the nation because their labor had built it and still kept it going. As Carlos Bulosan wrote, "America is not a land of one race or one class of men. . . . We are all Americans who have toiled and suffered. . . . All of us, from the first Adams to the last Filipino, native born or alien, educated or illiterate—We are America!"[43]

Commitment to democracy also fostered international solidarity. The National Maritime Union honored picket lines in foreign ports, during a 1938 strike by Puerto Rican dockworkers, for example. East Harlem congressman Vito Marcantonio of the American Labor Party defended Puerto Rican nationalists prosecuted by the colonial government. New York City's Transport Workers Union had ties to the Irish Republican Army. CIO Communists promoted American-Soviet friendship.

The gravest international issue was the spread of fascism. Under the increasing influence of militarists, the imperial Japanese government imposed direct military rule on its Korean colony in 1931; the Japanese Army occupied Manchuria the same year and embarked on the conquest of China in 1937. Fascist Italy invaded Ethiopia in 1935 and Albania in 1939. Nazis came to power in Germany in 1933, annexed Austria in 1938, and Czechoslovakia the next spring, then invaded Poland in September 1939, provoking war with Britain and France. By the end of 1940, German troops occupied most of western Europe, and Italy and Japan had joined Germany in an alliance of mutual defense against any attack. The CIO opposed fascism and aggression. Its unions joined churches, women's associations, and civil rights groups in the American League Against War and Fascism, which lobbied against trade with fascist nations. The CIO worked with Chinese-American groups and the National Negro Congress to boycott goods from Japan. Communists spearheaded a Hands Off Ethiopia campaign.[44]

The Spanish Civil War got the most attention. In 1936, General Francisco Franco led a fascist military coup against Spain's republican government. During the three-year war that ensued, Franco's forces were assisted by troops, guns, and bombers sent in by Germany and Italy while the republican side received support from the Soviet Union. Labor activists were among 2,800 Americans who went to Spain to fight fascism, most as members of the Abraham Lincoln Brigade. Unions from both the AFL and the CIO supplied the republicans with food, clothing, medicine, and financial aid. Unlike the AFL, the CIO also denounced the U.S. government's embargo on arms shipments to Spain, and opposed Roosevelt's recognition of the Franco regime when the fascists finally won in 1939.

The CIO took aim at domestic fascism too. Its 1938 convention condemned the poll taxes used to rob African Americans of their voting rights. CIO officers and member unions joined with the American Committee to Protect the Foreign Born to urge repeal of the Smith Act. As an honorary member of the National Maritime Union, Paul Robeson declared at its convention of 1941, "We stand for mankind wherever it may suffer and wherever it may be oppressed. . . . As long as we are struggling for a better life, we have one cause."[45]

In 1940, the Great Depression was ending, the recovery based on government spending on military hardware. Roosevelt promised to keep the United States out of the wars raging in Europe and Asia, but his administration both expanded the U.S. arsenal and sent arms to Britain. Congress appropriated $16 billion for airplanes, warships, and other munitions. The CIO picked up momentum, growing to 4 million by the end of the year.

Roosevelt was reelected in 1940, but by a narrower margin than in 1936, beating Republican Wendell Wilkie by 5 million votes. John L. Lewis broke with other CIO leaders to oppose Roosevelt's nomination and endorse Wilkie in the general election. If the president was reelected, Lewis declared, he would know the CIO's rank and file backed Roosevelt, take it as a vote of no confidence in his own leadership, and resign as the CIO's president. When Roosevelt carried the election, Lewis kept his word, and Philip Murray of the Steel Workers Organizing Committee took his place at the CIO's helm. With the New Deal in retreat, Lewis gone, and the nation beginning to prosper but edging toward war, the labor movement headed into a new and uncertain era.

9

Hot War, Cold War

War-related production created a rising tide of employment that lifted the economy out of depression. Union leaders took key roles in the mobilization for war, and unions made dramatic gains, especially in mass-production industries. At the war's end, the Congress of Industrial Organizations (CIO) claimed 6 million members; its unions enjoyed new rights to representation and collective bargaining; and its leaders planned to use labor's political power to expand labor and civil rights and New Deal social programs. The postwar regime did have a place for organized labor, but it was not a central role, and it came with political requirements that undermined the labor movement. Union leaders' plans faltered, and even the reconciliation of the American Federation of Labor (AFL) and much of the CIO could not restore the movement's momentum.

In 1940, labor—like the rest of the country—was divided over preparations for war. After the Roosevelt administration allowed government contracts to go to companies that broke labor laws, John L. Lewis no longer trusted Roosevelt and joined with Communists to oppose any move to propel the United States into another war. Most union leaders opposed the peacetime military draft, which Congress passed by a one-vote margin in September 1940; but a few loudly endorsed it. In July 1940, as the draft bill made its way through Congress, Lewis advised unionists at the UAW's annual convention "not to be beguiled into war hysteria or a war state of mind."[1] Sidney Hillman of the Amalgamated Clothing Workers, the CIO's vice president, told the same gathering that America should prepare "to the hilt" and that "No man can be true to his union if he is disloyal to our country."[2] Hillman enjoyed Roosevelt's confidence and served on his National Defense Advisory Committee.

CIO unions meanwhile enrolled close to a million new members. At Ford, the United Auto Workers lined up endorsements from civil rights activists, and in May 1941, the union swept an NLRB election that pitted it against a breakaway UAW faction affiliated with the AFL. The first Ford contract stunned observers. It provided for a union shop, dues checkoff, seniority protection, grievance procedures, and the highest wages in the industry, all in return for a no-strike clause. In another surprising advance, the CIO's Steel Workers Organizing Committee shut down Bethlehem Steel's plant in Lackawanna, New York, in February, struck its plant in Bethlehem, Pennsylvania, in

March, and then went on to win one NLRB election after another. Youngstown Sheet & Tube and Inland Steel signed union contracts without asking for elections.

Some employers resisted. When strikes affected military procurement, company executives and War Department officials called for federal intervention. In January 1941 open-shop Allis-Chalmers fired union activists from a plant making turbines for the U.S. Navy, and UAW Local 248 walked out. Now co-director of the federal Office of Production Management (OPM), Sidney Hillman tried to mediate but failed. In March Roosevelt ordered the plant reopened, and the National Guard suppressed the picket line. The following month the local accepted a compromise.

The fight at North American Aviation in Inglewood, California, was more complicated. In April 1941, the UAW won an NLRB election at North American and demanded big wage increases. The company stalled and thousands of workers, led by UAW Local 683, began to picket the plant on June 5. Soon 11,000 workers were out on strike. UAW headquarters wanted no part of the action, which it had not authorized. Richard Frankensteen, director of the union's aviation division, denounced the strike as Communist-inspired, suspended Local 683's officials, and ordered its members back to work, as did the national CIO. The pickets refused to stand down, however; when local police lobbed tear-gas canisters at them, the pickets threw them back. Then, on June 9, the U.S. Army's Fifteenth Infantry Division moved in, breaking up picket lines, placing picket captains under military arrest, and occupying Local 683's offices. With that, the strike ended. Federal mediators later handed down a settlement that included substantial pay hikes, but Local 683 permanently lost its UAW charter. A new local, number 887, took its place.

These events displayed the increasingly bitter feuding between Communists and anti-communists in the CIO. During the national election of 1940, Roosevelt loyalists had been quick to charge their opponents with communist loyalties, and that year's CIO convention approved (with a no roll-call vote) the first of what *CIO News* editor Len De Caux called "anti-communazi" resolutions, which condemned communism, fascism, and other "foreign ideologies."[3] Shifts in the Communist Party's policies helped to fuel the fire. After Germany and the Soviet Union signed a nonaggression pact on August 23, 1939, the party became an outspoken opponent of U.S. involvement in any foreign war; but as soon as German troops invaded the Soviet Union on June 22, 1941, the party began to call for military intervention against fascism. However welcome the Communists might be as allies in this fight, the party's switch reinforced widespread suspicions that it followed orders from Moscow.

John L. Lewis maintained his antiwar position. In September 1941, he initiated a series of short strikes for union recognition in the "captive" mines, those owned and operated by coal-consuming corporations like U.S. Steel. More and more isolated within the CIO, he disaffiliated the United Mine Workers in 1942 and led the union's 600,000 members back into the AFL the following year.

Another labor constituency also criticized the mobilization for war. In December 1940, A. Philip Randolph of the AFL's Brotherhood of Sleeping Car Porters and Maids called for 10,000 black workers to converge on Washington, D.C., to protest racial discrimination and segregation in war industries, government employment, and the armed forces. By the following spring, over 100,000 people were ready to rally in the capital on July 1, 1941. When Roosevelt agreed to ban racial discrimination by military contractors, Randolph called off the march. His compromise angered most of his allies; they were even angrier at union leaders and Communists who put the fight against fascism abroad before the struggle for justice at home. Although the march did not take place, the March on Washington movement persisted until the late 1940s.

Labor leaders who co-operated with the drive toward war could sometimes get the government to help them with a union's internal affairs. In Minneapolis, Teamsters Local 544, led by Trotskyist communists from the Socialist Workers Party (SWP), threatened in mid-1941 to join the CIO. At the suggestion of the Teamsters' national president Daniel Tobin, the Justice Department invoked the Smith Act, raided the SWP's office in Minneapolis, and led a grand jury to indict twenty-nine party members or allies—most of them active in Local 544—for conspiracy to advocate overthrow of the government. Eighteen of the defendants were convicted, with sentences ranging from twelve to sixteen months. Tobin's lieutenant, Jimmy Hoffa, took over the local. Asking in vain that the U.S. Attorney General drop the charges, the American Civil Liberties Union observed that the government had "injected itself into an interunion controversy in order to promote the interests of the one side which supported the administration's foreign and domestic policies."[4]

On December 7, 1941—the same day a federal arbitrator announced the UMW would represent the captive mines—Japanese warplanes attacked the U.S. Navy's base at Pearl Harbor in Hawaii. The next day Congress declared war on Japan (and the judge in the trial of the Socialist Workers Party handed down sentences). Three days later, Germany and Italy declared war on the United States. Over the next three and a half years, the war touched every part of American life and transformed the labor movement. How these changes looked depended on where one stood; the view from union offices was rosier than the view from the shop floor.

America at War

For the United States the Second World War began and ended in the Pacific. After Pearl Harbor, Japanese troops—who already controlled French Indochina—overran Thailand and British, Dutch, and U.S. colonial possessions in Southeast Asia and the Western Pacific, from Singapore, Indonesia, and the Philippines to Attu and Kiska in Alaska's Aleutian Islands. With Great Britain and the Soviet Union facing Nazi conquest, the United States was almost alone in its war against Japanese expansion, and it came late to the European theater, which U.S. troops entered only after the Soviets had defeated the main Nazi force at Stalingrad in February 1943. Nevertheless, the European war against fascism shored up morale in the United States, sustaining the nation's vision of the war as a fight for democracy.

The Second World War dwarfed its predecessor, the Great War of the 1910s. The death toll was enormous—more than 50 million overall, more than 18 million in the Soviet Union alone. Compared to the First World War, U.S. losses were considerable, though mostly military: 322,000 combat dead, 675,000 wounded, and 124,000 captured, with more than 12,000 dying in captivity.

The nation mobilized on an unprecedented scale and at immense cost—$350 billion, about ten times more than the cost of the First World War. More than half the money was borrowed; the national debt quintupled. Corporate profits soared on the wings of cost-plus government contracts along with tax credits for building or retrofitting plants for war production. Unemployment virtually disappeared. Labor shortages in industrial centers drew many new workers from rural areas, especially the South and Southwest. War production penetrated some rural areas too. Navajo miners working on reservation lands on the Colorado Plateau extracted a thousand tons of uranium for the government's atomic bomb project. The president set the workweek at forty-eight hours, with hours over forty paid as overtime. More wageworkers made more money than ever before.

A host of agencies coordinated the effort. The War Production Board directed the conversion of civilian plants to military production; at General Motors, for example, autoworkers made antiaircraft guns while their counterparts at Ford produced B-24 bombers. The Board of Economic Warfare allocated rubber, petroleum, and other materials essential to the war effort. The Office of Price Administration (OPA) set maximum prices for manufactured goods, rationed scarce goods like sugar, coffee, and gasoline, and controlled rents in cities overcrowded with war workers and military personnel. Other agencies oversaw scientific research, transportation, housing construction, aid to allies, war information, and propaganda. The War Manpower Commission (WMC) coordinated both military conscription and the workforce in war production. By mid-1943, the WMC had frozen 27 million workers in jobs deemed critical to the mobilization for war.

Almost everyone supported the war. Families planted "victory gardens" to offset food shortages and bought government war bonds to help finance the war effort. Volunteers collected scrap metal, served on civil defense committees, organized blood drives, and wrote "victory mail" to cheer up the troops. Some opposition came from religious pacifists like the Catholic Worker organization and the Fellowship of Reconciliation, and from a few Socialists. More substantial opposition came from fascist groups like the Silver Shirts and the Christian Nationalist Crusade, though the Ku Klux Klan endorsed the war. Out of 10 million men drafted for military service, the Selective Service System classified just 43,000 as conscientious objectors and reported that about 350,000 tried to evade conscription.

Federal agencies working with civilian groups promoted patriotic sentiments with a gigantic propaganda campaign. Newspapers, magazines, posters, billboards, movies, and radio broadcasts celebrated the war as a battle for democracy and portrayed wartime America as a beacon of tolerance, fairness, and equality. But just as the war against fascism was also a war for empire, its impact on home-front democracy was ambiguous too.

Vastly increasing the demand for labor, it diminished gender, racial, and ethnic barriers in employment and advancement in the workplace. Urban communities of Native Americans expanded as more than 40,000 men and women left reservations to take industrial jobs. The press celebrated multiethnic co-operation at work; the *Detroit News* described a group of autoworkers with Slavic, Italian, and German surnames as an "All-American production team."[5] Congress relaxed restrictions on immigration.

In 1942 it initiated the Mexican Farm Labor Agreement (better known as the "Bracero Program"), which brought in Mexican guest workers to fill jobs in agriculture, and in 1942 it revoked the longstanding exclusion of immigrants from China. President Roosevelt promised U.S. citizenship and veterans' benefits to Filipinos who mobilized to fight the Japanese until American forces arrived. (Congress reneged on that pledge in 1946.) In the United States and the territories it still controlled, all men from eighteen to forty-five were subject to the military draft, irrespective of their citizenship status. Japanese Americans were expelled from the U.S. military immediately following Pearl Harbor, then admitted as volunteers and organized into all-Japanese units. African Americans, Filipino Americans, and Puerto Ricans from the island served in segregated units or job assignments. Of the more than 15 million people who went into the military, some 700,000 were black, 350,000 Mexican American, 142,000 Filipino, 48,000 Puerto Rican, 30,000 Japanese American, 19,000 Native American, and 12,000 Chinese American.

About 350,000 women joined the military. Most were assigned to duties traditionally cast as female, serving as nurses, typists, and so forth. There were, however, exceptions to this rule, most notably the Women Airforce Service Pilots (WASPs), who flew military planes from aircraft factories to stateside pilot-training bases and points of embarkation to the theaters of war. War production also gave women the opportunity to play new roles. The female labor force grew by more than 5 million during the war years, mostly in industrial and office work. Popular stereotypes like "Rosie the Riveter" portrayed the female war worker as a woman who had temporarily traded domestic life for a factory job while her man was away at war, and some women did in fact fit that profile. More commonly, however, women employed in defense plants had been wage earners before the war began and would remain so when it was over. The military mobilization changed their lives by giving them access to jobs that were formerly off-limits. White women previously consigned to the typing pool could now move into supervisory positions, or move from the assembly line to more highly skilled work. Women of color could at last leave domestic or agricultural work and enter industrial jobs. At the beginning of the war, for example, the U.S. automobile industry employed just 115 black women; a year later, about 5,000 black women belonged to the UAW.

For masses of black workers, the war had two fronts. The March on Washington movement led a "Double V" campaign, calling for victory over fascism overseas and victory over racism at home.[6] In August 1942, residents of St. Louis who had organized to march on Washington a year earlier marched instead on Carter Carburetor, whose 2,650 employees included not one black worker.

The Double V effort had an ally in the federal government's Fair Employment Practice Committee (FEPC), which monitored job discrimination. In 1942, the FEPC directed Allis-Chalmers and nine other companies to cease biased treatment of workers on the basis of race and religion. The War Manpower Commission investigated bigotry too, finding that twenty-two railroads and fourteen railroad unions discriminated against African and Mexican Americans. Some unions maintained color bars despite the pressures to abolish them. As of 1943, twenty AFL affiliates and independent railroad brotherhoods still excluded black members; another eight confined them to segregated locals. In 1944, when the FEPC ordered the AFL's Brotherhood of

Boilermakers to cease discrimination, the union charged that the agency was run by Communists.

Shifts in the color line triggered forceful reactions too. This was especially the case in Detroit. In June 1942, after the federal government built the Sojourner Truth Housing Project for the city's black workers, local and state officials had to send in police and the National Guard to protect the project's residents from violent harassment. In 1943, 25,000 white autoworkers at Detroit's Packard Motor Company walked off the job to protest black workers' placement in jobs traditionally assigned to whites. The strike ended four days later, when the UAW's president R.J. Thomas got the government to issue a back-to-work order and declared that the union would not object to the strikers' dismissal from their jobs. Two weeks after that, on June 20, 1943, Detroit exploded; thirty hours of racial violence left thirty-four people dead—twenty-five of them African Americans, mostly killed by police. The carnage did not end until 6,000 federal troops occupied the city.

Racism permeated the military too. During the summer of 1943, racial disturbances took place at bases around the country and overseas. When Walter White, head of the National Association for the Advancement of Colored People (NAACP), became a war correspondent, he was surprised to hear African American soldiers stationed in England speak about encounters with "the enemy"—until he realized that they referred to white GIs, who routinely abused their black counterparts.[7] Back in the United States, black newspapers reported nearly every week that a black soldier had been beaten or killed off base, usually somewhere in the South. White troops sometimes operated as racial vigilantes. In June 1943, rumors spread in Los Angeles that Mexican American "zoot suiters" (young men who wore a distinctive style of tailored suit) had beaten up members of the U.S. Navy. Gangs of servicemen, assisted by local civilians and police, retaliated by hunting "zooters"—African Americans and Filipinos as well as Mexicans—and stripping and beating any they caught.

The federal government itself committed the most massive wartime violation of civil liberties. In February 1942, President Roosevelt ordered the internment of Japanese Americans on the U.S. mainland—about 112,000 men, women, and children. Internment was impractical in Hawaii, where more than a third of the population—and an even higher proportion of the plantation labor force—had Japanese ancestry, but the authorities did declare martial law there, detaining 3,400 community leaders and closing Japanese newspapers, language schools, and temples. Some labor officials, such as A. Philip Randolph, joined social workers and church leaders in denouncing the internment. Louis Goldblatt of the California CIO Council warned against turning the antifascist struggle into a race war. But none of this had a discernable effect on federal policy. In fact, the government compounded its crime by persuading South American countries—chiefly Peru—to deport people of Japanese descent to the United States, where they too were interned, classified as hostages of war. The fighting in the Pacific followed a racial logic as well. Each side, Japan and the United States alike, defined the enemy as innately inferior, even inhuman, and soldiers imbued with that sentiment often preferred not to take prisoners alive.

The internment of Japanese Americans was the U.S. government's most glaring act of repression aimed at its own people, but it was not the only one. When the Nation of Islam came out against the war, the government suppressed its newspaper, *The Final Call*, and imprisoned its chief spokesperson, Elijah Muhammad. The leader of the Black Hebrew Israelite sect in New Orleans received a fifteen-year sentence for encouraging resistance to the military draft. About 6,000 conscientious objectors—most of them Jehovah's Witnesses—went to prison, and many of them served their time in solitary confinement on bread-and-water diets. Another 12,000 objectors were placed in "service" camps, where they worked without pay in jobs like firefighting.

With regard to labor relations, the war had a more salutary effect. As soon as the fighting started, most union leaders pledged not to strike for the duration. To resolve labor disputes, the Roosevelt administration established the National War Labor Board (NWLB), made up of representatives of labor, business, and government. To protect unions from losing members, the NWLB approved "maintenance-of-membership" agreements under which all employees had to belong to the union, new hires having fifteen days to join or be dismissed.[8] Under these arrangements, union membership in the United States more than doubled, reaching almost 15 million in 1945.

In May 1942, the Steel Workers Organizing Committee merged with the AFL's Amalgamated Association of Iron and Steel Workers to form the United Steelworkers of America (USWA), affiliated with the CIO. Immediately, the USWA began bargaining with "Little Steel," demanding higher pay to cover increases in the cost of living. In July 1942, the National War Labor Board okayed a 15 percent raise over the wage levels of January 1, 1941, and this became the pacesetter. The NWLB applied the same formula to all wartime wage demands. Unions could get around the standard by negotiating better nonwage ("fringe") benefits. The NWLB routinely approved union contracts that provided for improvements in paid holidays and vacations, travel and meal allowances, shift differentials, incentive pay, bonuses, insurance, and medical care.

The wartime detente with management gave progressive union leaders new opportunities to promote their social agenda. Unions campaigned against racism: the UAW endorsed the Double V campaign, the USWA pressed for federal prosecution of the Klan, and CIO unions in Los Angeles joined hands to protest housing discrimination, register Mexican American voters, and defend youths arrested for wearing zoot suits. Union officials also confronted white workers (like those at the Packard Company) who resented black workers' advancement. When a Chicago defense plant operated by the Bendix Corporation hired a black man into the tool room, a UAW steward declared, "He's coming here to work. Anybody who doesn't like it if a black person comes in this shop can leave right now. Turn in your union cards and get the hell out. Go."[9] In fact, nobody quit, and interracial solidarity went further. New friendships and new perspectives developed to the point where one of the plant's most vocal racists began to champion black workers' rights. And even after Bendix shuttered the plant at the end of the war, members of its UAW local continued to get together. As Sylvia Woods, a black activist in this plant, later recalled, "We could call a union meeting and bring in maybe seventy-five percent of our plant two years after it closed down. . . . I have seen people change. This is the faith you've got to have in people."[10]

Women workers of all races made headway in the wartime labor movement. Their numbers in unions rose from 800,000 in 1940 to 3.5 million in 1944, when they made up almost a quarter of total membership. Some unions responded with new initiatives. In 1944, women constituted 40 percent of the CIO's United Electrical, Radio and Machine Workers (UE) and a full third of its national staff. The union's complaints to the National War Labor Board forced General Electric and Westinghouse to pay women as much as men for the same work. Women represented 28 percent of UAW membership in 1944, and UAW locals hired women counselors to help female members with problems like childcare and sexual harassment. In the United Cannery Workers (UCAPAWA)—renamed the Food, Tobacco, Agricultural and Allied Workers (FTA) in 1944—more than half the shop stewards were women, two-thirds of the contracts required equal pay for equal work, and three-quarters of them allowed pregnant women to takes leaves of absence with no loss of seniority.

In the name of war production, some labor leaders promoted even more radical forms of workplace democracy. Together with the CIO's president Philip Murray, Walter Reuther of the UAW's General Motors division proposed industry councils in which unions would join with management to allocate resources and improve productivity. Conservatives in the U.S. Congress stymied the plan by placing labor on the defensive. In June 1943, they overrode President Roosevelt's veto of the War Labor Disputes Act (also known as the Smith-Connally Act, sponsored by Senate Dixiecrats Howard Smith and Tom Connally), which authorized the federal government to take over essential industries affected by or merely threatened by strikes and prohibited unions from contributing money to candidates in federal elections. The same Congress also voided NLRB prohibitions against "back-door" contracts that employers signed with AFL unions in order to block CIO organizing drives.[11]

To push back, the CIO set up the Political Action Committee (CIO-PAC) to marshal union support for Roosevelt, pro-labor candidates, and progressive legislation. Under Sidney Hillman's direction, CIO-PAC raised money and worked with progressive groups outside the labor movement, but its main campaign—developed after a careful study of the 1942 elections in industrial districts—was an effort to turn out the union vote. It lobbied legislators to allow military personnel to register and vote by mail. It also made special appeals to women and African Americans, urging them to build on wartime advances by supporting a revitalized New Deal. CIO-backed candidates did well in the 1944 primaries.

CIO-PAC was nominally nonpartisan, and it endorsed a few Republicans, but mobilizing labor support for Roosevelt was its central mission in 1944. Republicans loved to repeat the story that, before the president selected Harry Truman as his running mate, he directed his aides to "clear everything with Sidney."[12] In fact, Sidney Hillman's first choice for the job was the incumbent vice president Henry Wallace, a vocal advocate of unionism, racial equality, and self-determination for the colonized world. Despite Wallace's popularity with rank-and-file delegates to the Democratic National Convention, he was dumped in favor of Truman, the favorite of party bigwigs, who coaxed, pressured, and coerced delegates into voting their way. The general election's results fell far short of CIO-PAC's goals. Roosevelt was reelected and Democrats gained ground in Congress, but voters provided no mandate for strengthening the New Deal.

Differences between union leaders and members meanwhile undercut the labor movement. During the war years, production steadily sped up. At Kaiser Steel's shipyards, for example, it took workers about eighty days to build a cargo ship in 1942; by 1944, they needed only twenty-two days. As the pace of work quickened, industrial accidents proliferated; the U.S. Labor Department recorded more than 6.5 million of them during the war. Through 1943, in fact, accidents on the job claimed about 37,600 American lives—thousands more than the numbers who died in combat in the war's early years. Against this backdrop, union members filed multitudes of grievances about working conditions, and union leaders' pledge not to strike for the duration of the war made it exceedingly hard to get the problems resolved. Stella Nowicki, who worked at the Swift meat-processing plant in Chicago, saw the no-strike pledge's effect on her local of the CIO's United Packinghouse Workers: "Grievances were hung up without being settled or turned down because the company knew we couldn't do anything."[13]

In most unions, moreover, adherence to the no-strike pledge required suppression of rank-and-file job actions. Union members staged thousands of wildcat strikes during the war, most of them stemming from local grievances about working conditions. In 1944, the peak year for wildcats, the Labor Department counted 4,956 strikes involving about 2.1 million workers. Norm Bully, a Buick worker in Flint, Michigan, and head of the city's CIO council, recalled,

> The corporations were showing no sense of patriotism or loyalty and were contributing nothing. All the sacrifices were on the part of the workers. When real and pressing grievances arose and there was no solution and management hid behind the no-strike pledge, then people felt that they were justified . . . in forcing a settlement.[14]

Fisher Body sandblasters struck to get ten minutes paid cleanup time at the end of the shift. At Ford's River Rouge plant, assembly line workers walked out when the company removed their stools and then walked out again to protest bad ventilation. Members of UAW locals in southern Illinois struck when workers on leave for military service returned with medical discharges and were declared unfit for work. In all, about half of the UAW's membership took part in strikes in 1944, many striking in sympathy with workmates who were unfairly disciplined or discharged. In contrast, fewer than one in twenty members of the United Electrical Workers (UE) joined strikes that year. The UE was a "red union"; the UAW was not; and, in general, Communist union leaders were the quickest to crack down on anything that might disrupt the war effort.

Although the United Mine Workers had issued a no-strike pledge, John L. Lewis repeatedly defied it. To beat the Little Steel formula, he led more than 400,000 bituminous coal miners out on strike four times in 1943. Few union leaders could have imitated him even if they had tried. Lewis controlled the UMW from top to bottom, and he was a master of negotiation by showdown—utterly unconcerned that the coal strikes enraged the federal government and much of the American public. When the government threatened to replace the strikers with troops, the union retorted with its old adage, "They can't mine coal with bayonets."[15] Circumventing the National War Labor Board, Lewis bargained directly with Harold Ickes, Roosevelt's secretary of the interior, who granted the miners a wage increase of $1.50 a day.

Although the UMW occupied a uniquely advantageous position—its members supplied what was then the nation's most important fuel—Lewis's noncompliance with the wartime rules of labor relations made sense on a broader scale too. The NWLB's support for maintenance-of-membership agreements vastly increased the numbers of union members, and checkoff ensured that members' dues would be paid in full and on time. But these arrangements did not necessarily nurture workers' commitments to unionism or give them a sense of ownership of the unions to which they belonged, and the concomitant ban on strikes diluted unions' power on the shop floor. Worse still, the ban drove a wedge between union leaders and members of the rank and file. In theory, no-strike pledges increased unions' political clout by placing the government in their debt, but nothing guaranteed that labor would ever receive the balance due.

During 1944, the war turned in favor of the Allies. Germany was caught between massive Soviet armies and Anglo-American forces. They met at the Elbe River late in April 1945; Germany surrendered unconditionally on May 7, less than a month after President Roosevelt died. In the Pacific, Japanese forces were in retreat and the U.S. military was preparing for an invasion of Japan. Then, on August 6 and 9, American planes dropped nuclear bombs on Hiroshima and Nagasaki, instantly killing tens of thousands, with many more soon to die from burns and radiation. Japan stopped fighting on August 14 and formally surrendered on September 2. As the Allies occupied Poland and Germany they liberated camps where the Nazis had exterminated millions of Jews, along with Slavs, leftists, Romani people, and gay men.

The end of the war found the United States with the apparatus of a planned economy—the Office of Price Administration alone had 73,000 paid employees and 200,000 volunteers—and the specter of a postwar depression on the horizon. Military contracts were cancelled, and war workers laid off, including 4 million women pushed out of the traditionally male jobs they had filled during the war. Meanwhile, tens of thousands of U.S. soldiers staged demonstrations in Manila, Seoul, Paris, and Frankfurt, demanding to be sent home. Civilians and veterans alike believed that wartime sacrifices had earned them the right to equality, wider opportunities, and a better standard of living.

Congress had already passed the Servicemen's Readjustment Act, nicknamed the GI Bill of Rights, in June 1944. The act provided for subsidized home and business loans, student stipends and job training, unemployment benefits, life insurance, hospital care, disability pensions, burial allowances, and cash bonuses. It was the most generous package of benefits that war veterans—or any other ordinary Americans—had ever received. Like the relief programs funded by the Social Security Act, however, GI benefits were administered by local officials who discriminated against African Americans, Mexican Americans, and other people of color. Of the first 67,000 homes purchased with the help of the GI Bill, for example, more than 99 percent went to white families. Such disparities energized the civil rights movement of the postwar era.

The labor movement, too, readied itself for a fight; but while AFL leaders wanted the government out of labor relations, leaders of the CIO hoped to mobilize the nation behind a progressive agenda. The prospects for advances on the latter front looked promising since President Truman proposed to continue price controls, raise the minimum wage, legislate fair employment practices, expand compensation for the unemployed, and fund a national housing program. Businessmen, on the other hand, were mobilizing to dismantle not only wartime controls and regulations, but also the entire New Deal. The political contest started early. In August 1945, the UAW's vice president Richard Frankensteen won the nonpartisan primary for Detroit's mayoral election. The NAACP loudly cheered his victory over the incumbent Edward Jeffries, who had blamed black activists for causing the white race riot of summer 1943. If Frankensteen carried the general election, the NAACP predicted it would mean "better housing, more attention paid to employment problems of all citizens, new anti-discrimination ordinances and a more progressive administration."[16] None of this came to pass. Backed by city newspapers and business leaders, Jeffries told white Detroit that, with Frankensteen as the mayor, Communists would move black families into white neighborhoods and lower their residents' property values. In November, Jeffries won reelection by a wide margin. That same week, a labor-management conference convened by Truman broke up without reaching any agreement as to the ground rules for labor relations in peacetime.

The Postwar World

In the first twelve months after the war's end, more than 4,600 strikes took place across the country; over 5 million workers participated. Some cities saw general strikes. In January 1946, 10,000 people from thirty AFL and CIO unions rallied in Stamford, Connecticut, with placards reading "We Will Not Go Back to the Old Days"[17] after striking machinists were assaulted by state and city police. In February, a coalition of unions shut down Lancaster, Pennsylvania, for two days to stop police attacks on striking city transit workers. Later that month, in Houston, Texas, 20,000 members of the AFL's building trades unions organized a one-day strike in solidarity with municipal employees on strike for higher pay. In May, in Rochester, New York, 35,000 unionists from both the AFL and the CIO went on strike in solidarity with municipal workers demanding the right to organize. In November, the CIO's South Jersey Industrial Union Council mobilized its member unions for a "general sympathy holiday" in support of the American Newspaper Guild, which had launched a wage strike at the *Camden Courier and Post*.[18] In December, when department stores in Oakland, California, refused to negotiate with Retail Clerks Local 1265, about 130,000 workers staged a two-day solidarity strike that was "more like a revolution than an industrial dispute," to quote a complaint from the Teamsters' vice president Dave Beck.[19]

Mostly the postwar strikes focused on single industries and were led by industrial unions. The CIO's Oil Workers started the wave, striking on September 17, 1945, with the slogan "52 FOR 40 OR FIGHT," meaning fifty-two hours' pay for forty hours of work—in other words, a substantial raise above the restricted wartime wage.[20] Within days, 200,000 coal miners struck for union recognition, and 24,000 AFL lumber workers in the Northwest went on strike for higher pay. East Coast ports shut down for nineteen days as members of the AFL's International Longshoremen's Association struck to signal their rejection of a meager raise that their president-for-life Joseph Ryan had agreed to. An insurgent rank-and-file committee that generated the strike called for "a better and stronger ILA, without goons, kickbacks, and terrorism."[21] The International Association of Machinists launched a series of work stoppages in metal shops and the aircraft industry. The CIO's Textile Workers Union struck New England factories for 133 days, its Federation of Flat Glass Workers went out for 102 days, and Teamsters in the Midwest stopped work for 81 days. Four strikes mobilized huge numbers of factory workers: 200,000 in the auto industry, 300,000 in meatpacking, 180,000 in electrical manufacturing, and 750,000 in steel. Everyone wanted a raise.

Wage increases were central to CIO plans. Rising income for the working class would provide the consumer-purchasing power to sustain prosperity. Wartime profits were more than twice the prewar average, nearly the highest on record according to government economists, suggesting that employers could pay more without raising prices. Corporate analysts argued to the contrary that profits were so low any wage hikes would require the abolition of price controls.

The four mega-strikes resolved this disagreement, but not in ways that the CIO had envisioned. In the auto strike, the UAW took on General Motors; Walter Reuther, director of the union's GM division, demanded a 30 percent increase in hourly wages and challenged the company to open its books to prove that it could not afford the raise. GM refused to open its books and rebuffed Reuther's offer of arbitration. On November 21, 1945, the UAW shut down ninety-two GM plants in fifty cities, and on December 8 the union rejected President Truman's order to return to work. In January 1946 a presidential fact-finding panel calculated that the cost of living had risen 33 percent since 1941 and recommended that wages increase roughly half that amount—about 19.5¢ an hour at GM. Reuther accepted the deal, but the company rejected it, holding out for a rollback of government price controls. That same month, the United Electrical Workers struck GM, General Electric, and Westinghouse, demanding a 24 percent wage increase. Within a week, the United Steelworkers and both AFL and CIO packinghouse unions went on strike to enforce similar demands. To grease the wheels for settlements, the Office of Price Administration began authorizing price increases, and by mid-March the unions had national-pattern agreements in all four industries, with wage increases averaging 18–19.5¢ an hour. Price controls were on their deathbed, however, and corporations were poised to gouge consumers and then blame the gouging on unions.

Scoffing at the settlements that ended these four strikes, John L. Lewis called for larger raises for UMW members, plus employer contributions to the union's welfare fund. On April 1, 1946, some 400,000 coal miners struck to enforce the demands. The Truman administration seized the idled mines, exercising its powers under the Smith-Connally Act. When the Supreme Court upheld contempt judgments against the UMW and Lewis himself, he called off the strike; but the following year, when the mines returned to private control, their owners met the UMW's demands.

Truman cracked down on railroad brotherhoods too. When the Railroad Trainmen and the Locomotive Engineers issued a strike call in May 1946, 250,000 workers walked off the job, and U.S. rail traffic decreased from about 17,500 trains a day to a mere fifty. Truman responded by asking Congress for authority to draft the strikers into the military, and the walkout quickly ended, after just two days. For weeks, however, it reverberated in the national press, which generally congratulated the president for his toughness and seconded his recommendation that a joint congressional committee come up with plans to revise federal labor law.

If that dismayed the strikers, they could also find reasons to rejoice. While employers took out numerous injunctions against strike-related activities, they did not generally deploy the physical violence that U.S. strikers had faced so many times before. The New Deal and wartime labor regulations had established workers' right to organize and bargain collectively. Unions had proved their ability to defend and advance members' interests against the biggest corporations. Truman's crackdowns notwithstanding, organized labor now had friends at the highest levels of government and wielded unprecedented influence on American society and politics.

With all of this in mind, the CIO convention of 1946—which met in Atlantic City on November 18–22—united behind an exceptionally bold program for the postwar era. To this day, it remains the most radical agenda that modern American unions have ever embraced. The 600 delegates to the convention unanimously endorsed a long list of resolutions aimed at remaking American life in ways that would benefit not just union members but all working people. They called for the Wagner Act's extension to agricultural workers; for the Fair Employment Practice Committee's establishment as a permanent federal agency; for federal prosecution of lynching; for a federal law to eradicate state poll taxes and other impediments to voting rights; for enactment of federal laws to guarantee women's equality on the job and in society at large; for expansion of Social Security and veterans' benefits; for continuation of wartime controls on prices and rents; for massive federal investments in public housing; for a federally funded national health care system; for extension of public school systems to provide free education from nursery school through college; for a federal ban on injunctions against strikes; for federal laws to establish minimum health and safety standards in American workplaces; for a shutdown of the House Un-American Activities Committee; for "democratization of our armed forces" to remove unjustifiable privileges enjoyed by officers and reform the "unjust courtmartial system"; for a tax system that would reduce the burdens on low-income households and raise rates on windfalls enjoyed by companies with government contracts; for a planned national economy designed to maximize employment and take into account community welfare as well as corporate profits.[22] This is merely a sampling of the resolutions, which numbered close to fifty, each with multiple parts.

The convention addressed international affairs along with domestic issues. The resolution on foreign policy urged the U.S. government to sever diplomatic relations with fascist regimes in Spain and Argentina, to support self-determination and self-government for all colonized nations, to stop stockpiling atomic weapons, and to search for peaceful uses for atomic energy. "Above all," this resolution concluded,

> the common people of this country demand . . . friendship and unity among the three great wartime allies—the United States, Great Britain, and the Soviet Union. Failure to accomplish this necessarily means dissension and strife in the world and ultimate war. . . . Peace is not merely possible. In an atomic age it is indispensable to the continued existence of the human race. The people of this and every other nation on earth can accept—can envisage—no alternative.[23]

Doing its part to preserve the wartime alliance, the CIO had joined with the Trades Union Congress of Great Britain and the All Union Central Council of the Soviet Union to establish the World Federation of Trade Unions (WFTU), whose inaugural meeting took place in Paris in October 1945. The delegates gathered in Atlantic City enthusiastically reaffirmed the CIO's commitment to the WFTU.

Amid this exuberant consensus on behalf of social justice and world peace, just one note of disunity sounded. CIO president Philip Murray introduced a "Declaration of Policy" that asked delegates to endorse democracy, Americanism, and Franklin Roosevelt's "Four Freedoms" (freedom of speech and religion, freedom from fear and want), and to "resent and reject efforts of the Communist Party or other political parties and their adherents to interfere in the affairs of the CIO."[24] Communist-led unions made up a fifth of CIO membership, but only two delegates voted against the declaration, since its anti-communism seemed merely for show. In fact, it foreshadowed developments that would tear the CIO apart.

The federal government's plans for the postwar world differed profoundly from the CIO's, and nowhere was that more evident than with respect to foreign policy. In the final year of the war the British Treasury and U.S. Treasury Department oversaw the establishment of the International Monetary Fund to regulate exchange rates between different nations' currencies, and the International Bank of Reconstruction and Development (later called the World Bank) to finance rebuilding of highway systems, power plants, and other infrastructure that the war had damaged or destroyed. Emerging from the war as the world's most productive economy—with an infrastructure larger than ever—the United States dominated both institutions and used them to expand its influence overseas. The American dollar became the standard by which other currencies were evaluated, and nations seeking to borrow from the World Bank had to meet criteria determined by U.S. officials. The first loan, issued in May 1947, went to France, which received $250,000 after it expelled Communists from its coalition government. The following month, U.S. Secretary of State George Marshall announced a $16 billion plan under which the United States would fund the reconstruction of European countries that agreed to promote free trade and oppose communism. When the Philippines finally gained independence on July 4, 1946, Filipino tariffs and monetary policy remained under U.S. jurisdiction, as did the twenty military bases Americans had established on the archipelago. Connecting all of this was a single goal: expansion of foreign markets for U.S. corporations, lest their gigantic industrial capacity become a catalyst for depression.

The Soviet Union posed an obstacle to this imperative. Soviet troops had done the lion's share of fighting to halt the Nazi advance; communist parties everywhere had zealously supported and often led resistance to occupation by the Axis, and they now looked to the victorious Soviet Union for inspiration, guidance, and often direct instructions. A counteroffensive seemed essential to the promotion of American-style free trade. In 1946, the U.S. military set up the Strategic Air Command, whose only mission was to prepare to drop the new atomic bombs on the Soviet Union. In March 1947, President Truman inaugurated what came to be called the Cold War, announcing in a speech before Congress that the United States would henceforth base its foreign policy on containment of Soviet influence, suppression of communist movements around the world, and staunch support for all anti-communists. U.S. aid quickly poured into Turkey on the Soviet Union's southern border; into Greece, where a communist insurrection threatened a monarchy widely regarded as a puppet of Great Britain; and into a Chinese civil war in which the United States backed the losing side. In the early 1950s, U.S. troops helped the Filipino government overpower the communist-led Hukbalahap rebellion and fought a three-year war in Korea that ended as it had begun—in a stalemate between the communist regime that ruled the north and the anti-communist regime that ruled the south. Under the North Atlantic Treaty Organization (NATO), founded in 1949, the United States and the nations of western Europe pledged to mount a mutual defense should any one of them come under attack. Denied admission to NATO when it applied for entry in 1954, the Soviet Union formed its own Warsaw Pact with socialist nations of eastern Europe. Both organizations accumulated huge arsenals.

In addition to securing their markets overseas, the Cold War profited U.S. corporations by generating a never-ending demand for military hardware. In 1946, a steel industry journal had prophesied that "maintaining and building up our preparedness for war will be big business . . . for at least a considerable period ahead."[25] History certainly bore out that prediction. U.S. military spending climbed from $12 billion a year in 1950 to $40 billion in 1953, the bulk of it devoted to the development of nuclear weapons and the maintenance of U.S. bases around the world. In 1962, the magazine *Business Week* reported that 24,000 U.S. companies had defense contracts, which provided employment for 4 million American workers.

The Cold War was not just an international affair; it took aim at domestic targets too, the CIO chief among them. As soon as World War II ended, wealthy right-wingers stepped up donations to organizations such as American Action, dedicated to overturning the Wagner Act and opposing federal funding of housing and education, as well as fighting communism at home and abroad.

Corporate lobbyists meanwhile swarmed Congress. Their main achievement in 1947 was the Taft-Hartley Act (the Labor Management Relations Act, sponsored by the Republicans' Senator Robert Taft and Congressman Fred Hartley), which amended the Wagner Act to make it less protective of workers and unions. Taft-Hartley defined mass picketing and sympathy strikes as unprotected activity—activity for which workers could be fired. It placed new restrictions on secondary boycotts, protecting nothing beyond informational campaigns aimed at the general public. It banned closed shops and the unionization of supervisors, and it permitted states to ban union shops like those created by wartime maintenance-of-membership agreements. It held unions responsible for strike-related damages; prohibited strikes by federal employees; authorized the president to issue eighty-day injunctions against strikes deemed threatening to national health and safety; and established rules for NLRB oversight of elections to decertify or de-authorize unions. To undercut labor radicals, it also required that unions desiring NLRB protection have every officer above the level of shop steward file an affidavit swearing that she or he was not a Communist. As New York's congressman Donald O'Toole observed on the floor of the House, Taft-Hartley "was written sentence by sentence, paragraph by paragraph, page by page, by the National Association of Manufacturers."[26]

On June 23, 1947, a Republican-controlled Congress enacted Taft-Hartley over President Truman's veto. Outside the labor movement, quite a few Americans approved of the new law. Consumer prices had surged upward since controls were lifted in 1946, and corporate spokesmen laid the blame on organized labor. The postwar strike wave was fresh in the nation's memory, and many people had concluded it was only fair that the government rein in unions.

The U.S. Chamber of Commerce meanwhile fanned the notion that unionists and their supporters were deliberately sabotaging the nation's welfare. It mass-distributed a series of booklets—including *Communist Infiltration in the United States* (1946), *Communists Within the Labor Movement* (1947), and *Communists Within the Government* (1947)—that claimed to expose how Communists loyal only to the Soviet Union exerted control over the CIO, the NLRB, the U.S. Labor Department, and civic organizations friendly toward the labor movement. Acting on the chamber's advice and following a blueprint that it supplied, Truman established a "loyalty program" in 1947. It eventually covered more than 15 million people employed by government or by companies with government contracts. By 1948, six congressional committees were investigating the loyalty of government employees; the best known was headed by Wisconsin's Republican senator Joseph McCarthy. In 1953–54, fifty-one different committees took part in the hunt, and the House Un-American Activities Committee alone held 147 hearings. By then, nearly 30,000 people had been accused of disloyalty, and 10,000 had lost their jobs. Some also lost the right to vote, as well as unemployment, disability, old age, and veterans' benefits.

Taft-Hartley's passage and the loyalty program's establishment were opening acts in the largest and longest red scare in U.S. history. Beginning in 1948, leaders of the U.S. Communist Party were indicted, convicted, and imprisoned under the Smith Act. Legal restrictions on the left grew vastly more elaborate in 1950, when Congress passed the Internal Security Act (known as the "McCarran Act" for its principal sponsor, the Democratic Party's senator Pat McCarran of Nevada). Under this law, officers and members of some 600 peace, civil rights, labor, and other organizations thought to be influenced by the Communist Party had to register with the Subversive Activities Control Board. In 1953, two Communists—Julius Rosenberg and his wife Ethel Rosenberg—were executed for espionage on behalf of the Soviet Union, although authorities considered her innocent of direct participation. Communist Party membership dropped from its historic high of 80,000 in 1946 to about 3,000 in 1958, and its influence fell to just about zero.

Gay men and lesbians were also among the red scare's primary victims. Quoting one of his union's slogans, Revels Cayton of the CIO's Marine Cooks and Stewards explained, *"If you let them red-bait, they'll race-bait, and if you let them race-bait, they'll queen-bait. These are all connected. . . . "*[27] Twenty-one states passed new laws against "sexual psychopaths," a category that included not only rapists and other perpetrators of violent crime but also gay men and lesbians, who were said to be tainted by the same moral degeneracy that afflicted leftists.[28] In 1950 a congressional subcommittee declared that homosexuals were security risks—especially susceptible to blackmail by foreign agents—and in 1953 they were barred from federal employment. Organizing for legal and civil rights, gay men started the Mattachine Society in

1950 and lesbians established the Daughters of Bilitis in 1955. Harry Hay, a founder of the Mattachine Society and a former organizer for the CIO's Retail, Wholesale and Department Store Union, recalled that all five of the Mattachine founders were "union members experienced in working in underground unions. We took an oath that we would plead the Fifth Amendment before we divulged information of any sort about the group."[29]

In some respects the Cold War abroad benefitted democratic causes at home, for rivalry with the Soviet Union made U.S. government intensely anxious to enhance its image in the eyes of the world. The Jim Crow system—visible to anyone who read the international press or encountered the segregated U.S. military—damaged the nation's reputation in Asia, Africa, Latin America, and the Caribbean, where rebellions against white colonial rule were steadily gaining ground, often with Soviet support. President Truman took a remedial step in 1948, when he ordered the military's desegregation, and his administration went further at the end of 1952, when the U.S. Supreme Court was hearing arguments in *Brown v. Board of Education*. The Justice Department filed a friend-of-the-court brief that laid out the case's international implications: racial segregation's "adverse effect upon our relations with other countries," its usefulness to the Soviets as "grist for the Communist propaganda mills," and the threat it posed to "the effective maintenance of our moral leadership of the free and democratic nations of the world."[30] In 1954, less than an hour after the court's decision in *Brown v. Board* declared segregation unconstitutional, Voice of America—the government's global radio network—broadcast the story in thirty-four different languages. In 1957, when nine black students tried to enroll at the all-white Central High School in Little Rock, Arkansas, and the state's governor sent the National Guard to stop them from entering the school, newspapers around the world covered the story and U.S. embassies in country after country implored the State Department to do something to salvage the situation. Under pressure from Secretary of State John Foster Dulles, President Dwight Eisenhower deployed federal troops to enforce a desegregation order, and the State Department armed its diplomats with "Talking Points to Overcome Adverse Reaction to Little Rock Incident."[31]

As these events suggest, Cold Warriors' embrace of democratic causes had much more to do with appearances than with realities. Immigration policy changed, as did the government's relationship to colonies, but the fundamental inequities endured. The Immigration and Nationality Act of 1952 voided the 1790 law under which only a "free white person" could become a naturalized citizen and expanded the revocation of Chinese exclusion to cover all of Asia.[32] Under the new quotas this law established, however, immigration from each Asian country was capped at just 100 people a year. The law also authorized the government to deport resident aliens or naturalized citizens who joined or worked with the Communist Party, even if their association with the party had ended many years before. In 1952, Congress granted Puerto Rico commonwealth status, which empowered it to hold a constitutional convention and establish a republican government; but the island remained under U.S. sovereignty, its citizens subject to federal law but not authorized to vote in federal elections. Although Alaska and Hawaii became states in 1959, their indigenous peoples' status remained unsettled. On advice from the State Department, the Immigration and Nationality Act of 1965 abolished the discriminatory quotas that had advantaged Europeans over Asians and Africans, but it also imposed new restrictions: a ban on the entry of lesbian and gay immigrants and numerical limits on immigration from countries in the Western Hemisphere, which had not previously been subject to quotas.

Worst of all for democracy, the Cold War isolated and undermined the CIO's left-wing unions, most of which did not long survive the onslaught. Anti-communism was scarcely a new factor in the American labor movement, but the postwar confluence of the Taft-Hartley Act, the loyalty program, congressional hearings, and international conflicts—especially the Korean War, which killed more than 36,000 GIs—nurtured anti-communism as never before.

This disabled the CIO's first major organizing drive of the postwar era. In May 1946, it launched "Operation Dixie," a big push to expand unionism in the South. Directing the project was Van Bittner, who had earlier commanded the drive to unionize Bethlehem Steel. As Operation Dixie got rolling, Bittner announced that, "No crowd, whether Communist[s], Socialists, or anyone else, is going to mix up in this organizing drive."[33] The 200 organizers he fielded included no one known as a leftist, and the CIO's most conservative southern officials oversaw the campaign at the local level. The Food, Tobacco, Agricultural and Allied Workers and the Mine, Mill and Smelter Workers—left-wing unions that had established beachheads in the South—went to work on their own and scored significant gains, but the textile industry was the prize that Bittner had in mind. He designed Operation Dixie in ways he hoped would appeal to southern textile workers, virtually all of them white in the late 1940s and mostly conservative with regard to racial politics. Bittner had no intention of challenging the Jim Crow system—a fact he made clear by publicly rebuffing offers of assistance from a support committee headed by Harlem's congressman Adam Clayton Powell Jr. and from racial liberals in the Southern Conference for Human Welfare based in Birmingham. Almost all of the organizers employed by Operation Dixie were white and male, and they steered clear of leftists. Even so, they faced relentless red-baiting by textile bosses, by politicians, by the Ku Klux Klan, and by the AFL, which started a rival drive to unionize the mills. After Bittner died in 1949, his replacement—George Baldanzi of the CIO's Textile Workers Union—turned red-baiting in the other direction, aiming it at the AFL's United Textile Workers. In yet another twist, the CIO would use Baldanzi's own words against him in 1952, when he defected to the AFL and began to raid the CIO's textile locals. For all of these reasons, Operation Dixie never got far, although the CIO did not officially call it off until 1954.

As Operation Dixie's history suggests, by the late 1940s red-baiting did not require any grounds beyond opportunism on the part of the accuser; but there were genuine differences over policy that divided the CIO's left from the rest. These emerged during the presidential election of 1948. Both Truman and the Republicans' Thomas Dewey ran as Cold Warriors, and their platforms both called for civil rights legislation along with expansions of Social Security and federal spending on housing, health, and schools. Nearly all of organized labor's spokespeople came out actively for Truman and down-ticket Democrats—the movement's best hope for a repeal of Taft-Hartley. Right up to Election Day, pollsters confidently predicted that Dewey would win. Truman had lost popularity since the war's end, and two protest-party candidates further complicated his prospects. Senator Strom Thurmond, a conservative Democrat from South Carolina, ran as the candidate of the States' Rights Democratic Party, a newly formed group whose purpose was to preserve Jim Crow. That Dixiecrats could vote for one of their own diminished Truman's base in the South. He also faced an opponent to his left: Henry Wallace, nominated by a new Progressive Party and running as an opponent of the Cold War at home as well as abroad. Leaders of the CIO's left-wing unions were among his most ardent supporters. Philip Murray and Walter Reuther (now the UAW's president) publicly red-baited Wallace, their shrillness a testament to worries that the Wallace vote was throwing the election to Dewey. These fears proved quite wrong; although Thurmond carried four southern states, Truman beat his Republican rival by a comfortable margin—and Wallace came in fourth, with just 2.4 percent of the popular vote. As Murray and Reuther saw it, however, the leftists' support for Wallace was unforgiveable.

It involved three offenses: vocal opposition to U.S. foreign policy; divergence from two-party politics; and public deviation from policies agreed to by a majority of the CIO's executive board. In other times, any or all of these offenses might have been tolerated or punished in a relatively mild way. In the context of the Cold War and mounting anti-communism, they provided a warrant for banishment. Murray summarily fired leftists on the CIO's staff. Reuther, who had purged Communists from the UAW's staff as soon as he became the union's president in 1946, now oversaw the systematic expulsion of CIO unions led or significantly influenced by Communists.

The first target was the United Electrical Workers (UE), the CIO's third largest affiliate, with 600,000 members and contracts in force at more than 1,500 plants. Initially, the UE had refused to comply with the Taft-Hartley requirement that its officers file non-Communist affidavits with the National Labor Relations Board. This was not unusual immediately following Taft-Hartley's enactment. As a matter of principle, many labor officials of various political persuasions—even anti-communists such as Philip Murray—had declined to file. But that made their unions especially vulnerable to raids, for unless its officers' affidavits were all on file, a union would not be recognized as such by the NLRB. Taking advantage of this rule, three CIO unions—the UAW, the Communications Workers, and the Steelworkers—raided UE shops in 1948–49, winning NLRB elections in which the UE did not even appear on the ballot (since the NLRB did not consider it a certified union). In September 1949, the UE's annual convention voted to file non-Communist affidavits, but the raiding continued. In protest, the union withheld its dues to the CIO, and the CIO promptly expelled it, quickly chartering a new union—the International Union of Electrical, Radio, and Machine Workers (IUE)—to take over UE locals. Philip Murray himself met with Westinghouse and General Electric executives to plan the takeovers in their plants. President Truman sent personal regards that were mass distributed to electrical workers: "Please extend my cordial greetings to the officers and members of the IUE-CIO. I wish them every success."[34] In its official report on the UE's expulsion, the CIO's executive board entirely ignored these events. Instead, it asserted that the UE had revealed itself as a puppet of the Soviet Union and presented as evidence for that charge the union's opposition to the Cold War, support for Henry Wallace, and criticisms of the executive board.

Over the course of 1949 and 1950, the CIO expelled ten more unions: the United Farm Equipment and Metal Workers; the Mine, Mill and Smelter Workers; the Food, Tobacco, Agricultural and Allied Workers (FTA); the United Public Workers (UPW); the United Office and Professional Workers of America (UOPWA); the American Communications Association; the International Fur and Leather Workers Union; the International Longshore and Warehouse Union (ILWU); the International Fishermen and Allied Workers; and, finally, the National Union of Marine Cooks and Stewards. In each case, the process followed much the same pattern as it had for the UE; raids and red-baiting went hand in hand. As the expulsions multiplied, national union leaders such as Mike Quill of the Transport Workers and Joe Curran of the Maritime Union—both long associated with the CIO's left—abruptly changed course, denouncing old allies and purging Communists from their staffs. At the local level, CIO labor councils cut off left-led locals.

By amputating its left flank, the CIO lost its most diverse and imaginative unions and many of its most committed advocates of racial and gender equity. The FTA represented Mexican Americans, Filipinos, and African Americans, especially women. About half of the Marine Cooks and Stewards were black men, another quarter Asians, and a great many of its members gay. Mine Mill was mostly African American in the Southeast and Mexican American in the Southwest. In Hawaii, the ILWU had spearheaded the campaign that secured a "Little Wagner Act" to extend collective bargaining rights to agriculture, and it had unionized Japanese, Chinese, Filipino, Puerto Rican, Portuguese, and native Hawaiian field-workers.[35] Roughly 40 percent of the UE's members were women, and in 1946 it had prolonged its strike against General Electric rather than agree to a settlement that would have given the women smaller raises than men. Most members of UOPWA and UPW were white women, but UPW also represented black workers in federal cafeterias in Washington along with Afro-Caribbean laborers in the Panama Canal Zone. Left-led unions were the quickest to challenge racism in the workplace, the most deeply involved in civil rights campaigns in the larger society, and likely to go beyond others in creative responses to repression. The Marine Cooks and Stewards almost singlehandedly integrated employment on Pacific ocean liners; in New York City, members of four UE locals joined around-the-clock picket lines in support of housing desegregation; in Bayard, New Mexico, when strikers from Mine Mill were slapped with an injunction against picketing, their wives took over the line, held it for seven months despite harassment and mass arrests, and finally won the strike.

Despite their dynamism, most of the unions expelled by the CIO could not withstand what came after that: hundreds upon hundreds of raids by both AFL and CIO unions; scores of investigations by the House Un-American Activities Committee, which conducted hearings in cities across the country; and unremitting red-baiting in the press. In the end only the UE and ILWU survived as national unions, the UE much smaller than before and the ILWU limited to the West Coast and Hawaii.

The AFL and CIO raided each other as well, the CIO usually with less success. That, combined with the expulsions, took a big toll on CIO membership. After claiming 6.3 million members in 1946, the CIO could count only 4.6 million by 1954. Over the same period, the AFL grew from about 7 million to 10.2 million, and raids between its affiliates grew increasingly common.

Both federations threw themselves into the global Cold War. The AFL had come to this project in 1944, establishing a Free Trade Union Committee (FTUC) that helped the U.S. government promote anti-communist unions in Europe. In this, the AFL worked closely with the government's wartime Office of Strategic Services, which later became the Central Intelligence Agency, the FTUC's main source of funding when its work expanded in the postwar era. In 1949, as the CIO expelled its left, it also revised its international alliances, abandoning the World Federation of Trade Unions and uniting with the AFL and British Trades Union Congress to found a rival project: the International Confederation of Free Trade Unions (ICFTU), a multilateral offensive against left-wing labor movements, though never as militant as its U.S. participants wished. While no group matched the AFL when it came to enthusiasm for the Cold War overseas, the CIO scored a close second. During the Korean War, which began just as the last of the "red unions" were being ejected, the CIO not only applauded U.S. intervention but also joined hands with the American Legion and the U.S. Chamber of Commerce to sponsor petition drives against communism and raise money for Voice of America radio.

U.S. labor leaders' involvement in the Cold War had a significant impact on workers' movements overseas, especially though not only in the Americas. In 1954, for example, a strike wave hit the American-owned United Fruit plantations in Honduras. As the Honduran army arrested strike leaders, operatives rushed in from the Inter-American Regional Organization of Workers (ORIT), nominally an arm of the ICFTU but funded by the U.S. State Department. They promptly called off the strikes and set up a company union. In 1955, Juan Sáez Corales, a left-wing labor activist in Puerto Rico and a victim of the Smith Act, charged that the AFL and CIO had been brought to the island "to colonize the labor movement. Those organizations serve the interests of the Puerto Rican government and American employers who come to Puerto Rico to pile up more wealth."[36]

If U.S. labor's rank and file reaped rewards from movement leaders' co-operation with the Cold War, they incurred losses too. Co-operative unions were for the moment secure, but not influential enough to overturn Taft-Hartley. The labor movement supported liberal causes, but only within parameters set by the Democratic Party; the CIO's ambitious agenda of 1946 was not just abandoned but also almost entirely forgotten or dismissed as mere foolishness. Union members' pay outpaced inflation, but they lost ground with respect to union democracy and power in the workplace. Employers now insisted on elaborate grievance procedures that had to be exhausted before a union authorized a strike. Contracts granted management exclusive control over issues such as work rules, output quotas, and corporate policies regarding investment and disinvestment. Unionists could only watch when their plants ran away to the so-called right-to-work states that had exercised their prerogative under Taft-Hartley to outlaw the union shop. As a negotiator for General Motors told a reporter, "GM's position has always been, give the union the money. . . . But don't let them take the business away from us." Walter Reuther concurred: "We make collective bargaining agreements, not revolutions."[37] Deviations from this vision of unionism were ruthlessly suppressed.

"Big Labor"

By the early 1950s, the AFL and CIO differed mainly in the degree to which they tolerated what Mike Quill called the "3 Rs" of unionism: racism, raiding, and racketeering.[38] These were hardly insurmountable differences, but William Green and Philip Murray distrusted each other, so occasional talks about a merger never got very far. Then, in November 1952, both men died unexpectedly. Walter Reuther became the CIO's new president. The AFL selected George Meany, a one-time business agent for the United Association of Plumbers who had climbed up the ladder to become the AFL's secretary-treasurer in 1939—and boasted that he had never gone on strike or walked on a picket line. In June 1953, Meany and Reuther declared a moratorium on raiding and formed the Joint Unity Committee, which finally arrived at a merger agreement in February 1955.

Under the terms of this pact, individual unions would retain their jurisdictions and stop raiding one another; and the new federation would adopt the CIO's stricter policies against racial discrimination and labor racketeering. Meany would become the AFL-CIO president; Reuther would head an industrial department that included all CIO unions and thirty-five AFL unions, which together made up almost half of the new federation's membership; and the AFL-CIO Department of International Affairs would make the fight against communism its highest priority and would answer directly to Meany.

Meeting separately in New York City in early December 1955, each federation ratified the merger, the AFL without dissent and the CIO with just three nays. On December 5 they met together for the inaugural convention of the American Federation of Labor and Congress of Industrial Organizations (AFL-CIO), with 145 affiliated unions representing almost 16 million members—more than a third of the U.S. labor force outside agriculture. Meany and Reuther issued a joint statement that heralded the "unity of the labor movement at a time when the unity of all American people is most urgently needed in the face of the Communist threat to world peace and civilization."[39]

The AFL-CIO Executive Council quickly set up a new political operation, the Committee on Political Education (COPE), and developed a five-point labor policy agenda for the election of 1956: improve national defense, increase wages to strengthen the economy, guarantee civil rights, overhaul Taft-Hartley, and regulate pension and welfare plans. The Democrats' platform covered most of these demands, and the AFL-CIO endorsed their presidential candidate, Adlai Stevenson. COPE worked on getting union members to register and vote. Although Stevenson lost, Democrats captured both houses of Congress and 175 candidates strongly backed by labor won election.

Over the next decade, COPE supported and Congress enacted improvements in Social Security benefits and coverage, increases in the federal minimum wage, and raises for federal employees. In the presidential election of 1960, union support played a crucial role in Democrat John Kennedy's very narrow win over Vice President Richard Nixon. Returning the favor, Kennedy expanded unemployment insurance and issued a presidential order that established collective bargaining rights for federal employees. Lyndon Johnson, who assumed the presidency after Kennedy's assassination in 1963, called for repeal of the section of the Taft-Hartley Act that permits individual states to ban the union shop, but the measure failed in Congress. The AFL-CIO endorsed Kennedy-Johnson initiatives with regard to civil rights: the Twenty-Fourth Amendment, which eliminated poll taxes in federal elections, the Civil Rights Act of 1964, and the Voting Rights Act of 1965. Supporting Johnson's "War on Poverty" too, the AFL-CIO seemed a model of Cold War liberalism.

But racism festered on the inside. During the merger negotiations, the CIO's Mike Quill had suggested that the AFL's abolition of Jim Crow become a precondition for unity, but this idea had been voted down. When A. Philip Randolph protested the merger agreement's failure to set a deadline for desegregating AFL unions, George Meany insisted that the agreement's vague language—"at the earliest possible date"— was good enough and put George Harrison of the segregated Brotherhood of Railway Clerks in charge of the AFL-CIO's civil rights committee.[40] Meanwhile, a number of union locals in the South publicly endorsed the Jim Crow system, and the Virginia Federation of Labor held segregated conventions. The NAACP's Herbert Hill described before Congress how the International Ladies' Garment Workers Union confined Puerto Ricans and African Americans to the lowest-paid work. When the Negro American Labor Council—A. Philip Randolph's brainchild—seconded the NAACP's criticism of AFL-CIO racial practices, Meany had Randolph censured at the 1961 convention. When members of the Plumbers' Local 2 struck the Bronx Terminal Market to protest the hiring of one black and three Puerto Rican plumbers, Meany defended his old local.

Women were almost entirely absent from the AFL-CIO's leadership. In 1961, Bessie Hillman (Sidney Hillman's widow and a vice president of the Amalgamated Clothing Workers) told a conference of union women: "I have a great bone to pick with the organized labor movement in this country. In my opinion they are the greatest offenders as far as discrimination against women is concerned. Today women in every walk of life have bigger positions than they have in organized labor."[41] Not until 1980 did a woman join the AFL-CIO's national executive council: Joyce Miller, also a vice president of the Amalgamated.

Although the merger agreement pledged that the AFL-CIO would "protect the American trade union movement from any and all corrupt influence, and from the undermining efforts of Communist agencies," the latter got much more attention than did labor racketeering, which remained a constant threat.[42] Some employers got "sweetheart" deals, designed—as Gus Tyler of the Ladies' Garment Workers observed—"to give the union heads an income, to give the employer relief from a real union, and to give the workers nothing."[43] The increasingly large union welfare and pension funds opened new avenues for corruption. Senator John McClellan's Select Committee on Improper Activities in the Labor or Management Field commenced televised hearings in 1957. The most spectacular revelations tied the Teamsters' Dave Beck—now the union's general president—to extortion, criminal associations, and rigged elections of union officials. When the Teamsters' national convention replaced Beck with Jimmy Hoffa, himself implicated in sweetheart contracts and welfare-fund fraud, the AFL-CIO expelled the union. Hoffa did not quietly fade away. He made jurisdictional agreements with some AFL-CIO affiliates, raided others, and mounted an organizing drive in Puerto Rico. The Teamsters grew.

While corruption in the Teamsters generated the most headlines, the McClellan Committee also investigated the Hotel and Restaurant Employees, the Operating Engineers, the Allied Industrial Workers, the United Textile Workers, the Laundry Workers, and the Bakery and Confectionery Workers. Like the Teamsters, the laundry and bakery unions were expelled from the AFL-CIO. Self-policing did not satisfy Congress, however. In 1959 it passed the Labor-Management Reporting and Disclosure Act (the Landrum-Griffin Act, sponsored by the Dixiecrat congressman Phil Landrum and Republican congressman Robert Griffin). The new law imposed financial disclosure and fiduciary responsibilities on administrators of pension and welfare funds; set standards for electing union officers and disciplining locals; included a "Union Member's Bill of Rights" that detailed what a union owed its members (free speech at union meetings, for example, and a copy of the collective bargaining agreement); and banned convicted felons and Communists from union office for five years after their release from prison or separation from the Communist Party.[44] Though the AFL-CIO desired regulation of pension and welfare funds and had already banned felons and ex-Communists from office, it blasted Landrum-Griffin—partly based on the principle that government had no place in internal labor business and partly because Landrum-Griffin directed disputes about the law's application to the courts rather than the more labor-friendly NLRB. The AFL-CIO hoped that President Kennedy's election would prepare the ground for a thorough overhaul of the law, if not its nullification, but this did not come to pass.

If the McClellan hearings and Landrum-Griffin represented setbacks, the year 1960 opened with a significant win for the AFL-CIO, in particular for the United Steelworkers of America. In 1959, the USWA had begun negotiations for a new contract with multiple steel companies, arguing that increases in worker productivity and industry profits provided the basis for wage hikes. Steel executives opposed any wage increase and demanded changes in the work rules that limited management's ability to introduce new labor-saving machinery. In mid-July, the talks reached a stalemate and 500,000 steelworkers walked off the job; by the fall, steel-consuming industries such as auto manufacturing were slowing or shutting down. In October President Eisenhower invoked Taft-Hartley and set up a board of inquiry. When the board failed to broker a compromise, the Justice Department took out an injunction; the union went back to work in early November and waited for the injunction to expire. Finally, on January 5, 1960, Kaiser Steel agreed to the union's terms, and the other steel companies soon accepted a similar deal that provided for more generous health and pension benefits, a deferred wage increase, automatic cost-of-living adjustments, and no change in work rules. While the Steelworkers' 116-day strike demonstrated that union members had not forgotten how to flex their collective muscle, the battle's outcome testified as well to organized labor's social-political clout. Vice President Nixon himself had pressured the companies to settle for the Kaiser agreement, lest their recalcitrance cause a renewed strike that could send the nation's economy into recession. "Big Labor," as the press called the AFL-CIO, seemed no less powerful than big business or big government.[45]

That the three clashed did not preclude partnerships, which grew steadily more elaborate with respect to global politics and trade. The AFL-CIO Department of

International Affairs supplied the State Department with labor advisers assigned to foreign aid projects and with "Labor Attachés" who were posted at U.S. embassies and consulates around the world.[46] The Free Trade Union Committee continued its work. Still run by its founding director Jay Lovestone—a Central Intelligence Agency (CIA) asset who had become George Meany's closest adviser on foreign policy—the FTUC specialized in clandestine operations, collecting intelligence on labor activists overseas and funneling CIA money into the hands of those deemed reliably anticommunist and in favor of free trade.

In 1962, the U.S. secretary of labor, Arthur Goldberg, helped George Meany establish the American Institute for Free Labor Development (AIFLD), a government-funded initiative run out of the AFL-CIO. Its charge was to stop other nations in the Western Hemisphere from going the way of socialist Cuba. Until 1980, businessmen held a large portion of the seats on AIFLD's board of directors; they came from firms such as Pan American World Airways, United Fruit, and the chemical conglomerate W.R. Grace. Indeed, it was impossible to pinpoint just where AIFLD ended and corporate America began. "We are collaborating with the Council of Latin America which is made up of the primary U.S. business institutions that have activities in that area. Our collaboration takes the form of trying to make the investment climate more attractive and more inviting": so explained AIFLD's executive director William Doherty Jr., one of the AFL-CIO's many vice presidents.[47] In 1964, labor strikes instigated by AIFLD operatives helped to bring down British Guiana's socialist prime minister, Cheddi Jagan. That same year, AIFLD helped to install new leaders in Brazilian unions that had supported the populist president João Goulart, deposed by a U.S.-backed military coup. By 1965, all AIFLD operatives were CIA professionals. Several other international projects replicated the AIFLD model: the African-American Labor Center (established in 1964), the Asian-American Free Labor Institute (established in 1967), and the Free Trade Union Institute (established in 1977 to focus on Europe).

Rank-and-file members of the AFL-CIO heard virtually nothing about its international programs, but their ripple effects at home grew more and more evident. U.S. firms did in fact find increasingly alluring opportunities for investment overseas, in large part because U.S. labor's international programs did so much to undermine politically progressive unions and the governments they supported. The implications for working-class life in the United States would not fully manifest themselves until decades later, but a disturbing pattern had surfaced by the 1960s: even in good years, the national economy could not create enough jobs to employ everyone who needed work. Automation and mechanization contributed mightily to this problem and got considerable attention from union leaders and the national press. A more crucial factor seldom discussed was a vast increase in foreign investment by U.S. corporations and concomitant slowdown in their investment in the United States.

Unions and union towns were among the first to feel the impact. Organized labor's ranks stopped growing in the mid-1950s, and the proportion of the national workforce that belonged to unions entered a slow but steady decline. In Camden, New Jersey, and other cities once bustling with industry and labor activism, corporate flight began to produce wastelands of abandoned factories, crumbling homes, streets and vacant lots littered with trash, and the omnipresent stench of economic collapse. Black unemployment was close to twice the national average, and the tightening job market made it all the more difficult to challenge discrimination in hiring.

Year by year, moreover, the costs of maintaining an empire mounted. The defense budget jumped from an annual average of $40–50 billion in the 1950s to $70 billion by 1967. The numbers of young men drafted into the military climbed from about 112,000 in 1964 to 231,000 in 1965, the year President Johnson escalated U.S. intervention in Southeast Asia. Over a million more would be drafted before that long war came to an end. Of the 2.5 million American draftees and volunteers who went to Vietnam—and some 58,000 who died there—about 80 percent came from poor and working-class communities. Therein lay the most glaring evidence that the Cold War formula for social peace was dysfunctional.

10

The Sixties

According to legend, American workers opposed the radical movements that shook the nation in the 1960s. Widely reproduced news photos from the era show hard-hatted construction workers attacking long-haired antiwar demonstrators in New York City. From classrooms to barrooms, Americans invoke these stereotypes when they talk about the sixties. Workers are routinely cast as conservatives, and the radicals as youth out of touch with the working class.

The real story is more complicated. The turmoil associated with the 1960s ran through more than one decade. Politically speaking, the American "sixties" began in the mid-1950s and extended into the late 1970s. Much of the ferment centered on campuses, but insurgent movements and ideas also reverberated from rural communities to inner cities, from churches to the military, from factories to rock concerts, and from local school boards to national political conventions. Sixties activists did not all belong to the college-educated middle class; working people joined and sometimes led civil rights protests, antiwar demonstrations, feminist projects, gay and lesbian initiatives, and militant movements to empower people of color and poor people across the board. Some unions enthusiastically plunged into social activism, working with community groups and even radical students; and despite opposition from most labor officials, the unrest spilled into other unions as well. To a large degree, then, sixties movements were workers' movements. Their causes often polarized the nation, but the divisions did not fall neatly along class lines.

In the Spirit of Montgomery

More than twenty years after canceling the March on Washington in 1941, A. Philip Randolph led a new March on Washington for Jobs and Freedom on August 28, 1963. Endorsed by every major civil rights organization and the AFL-CIO Industrial Department, and sponsored by the Brotherhood of Sleeping Car Porters, the United Auto Workers, and the Negro American Labor Council, this march turned out some 250,000 people, including many thousands of union members. They heard Dr. Martin Luther King Jr. proclaim, "I have a dream that one day this nation will rise up and live out the true meaning of its creed: 'We hold these truths to be self-evident, that all men are created equal.'"[1] The civil rights movement pursued this dream through direct action. The rally in Washington capped a spring and summer of mass demonstrations across the South, with more than 20,000 arrested for protesting the Jim Crow system.

Direct action protests had been mounting since the mid-1950s, when black residents of Montgomery, Alabama, desegregated the city's buses. On December 1, 1955, riding home from her job as a department store seamstress, Rosa Parks was arrested for refusing to give up her seat to a white passenger. E.D. Nixon, an officer in the Brotherhood of Sleeping Car Porters, bailed her out. Both Parks and Nixon were longtime activists with the NAACP. A decade earlier, they had built a national campaign to demand justice for Recy Taylor, a black woman gang-raped by six white men who twice escaped indictment by all-white grand juries in Alabama's Henry County. Although that campaign did not meet its goal, the activist network at its core remained intact, and Nixon and Parks now mobilized it for another epic challenge to Jim Crow, this time statutory segregation. Her arrest on the bus furnished the spark. The next day she and Nixon organized a meeting to plan a community response. Out of this came a call for a one-day bus boycott on Monday, December 5 (as it happened, the same day the first AFL-CIO convention began).

The boycott was solid. That afternoon its organizers formed the Montgomery Improvement Association, chose the young Baptist minister Martin Luther King Jr. to head the group, and debated whether to extend the boycott. That night thousands of people gathered, "on fire for freedom," to quote a newsman who covered the meeting.[2] They demanded that the boycott continue until black passengers could ride the buses on the same terms as whites. For more than a year, black workers throughout Montgomery walked for hours or carpooled to and from their jobs. Some, including Rosa Parks and her husband, got fired; more than 100 boycott leaders were indicted; Martin Luther King was tried, convicted, and fined. Still, the boycott held, and expressions of support poured in from across the country as Parks and other participants went on the road to spread the word in co-operation with the National Negro Labor Council and other organizations of the African American left. Finally, in November 1956, the Supreme Court ruled that the law segregating Montgomery's buses was unconstitutional, and the city received a cease-and-desist order on December 20. The following day Rosa Parks took a seat at the front of a bus.

Over the next decade, the spirit of Montgomery swept through black communities across the South. In the first year alone, protests against segregation got under way in more than forty cities and towns. The Southern Christian Leadership Conference (SCLC), founded in February 1957 and headed by Martin Luther King, started several voter registration drives coordinated by the veteran NAACP organizer Ella Baker.

Beginning on February 1, 1960, in Greensboro, North Carolina, black students sat down at segregated lunch counters in southern cities and refused to leave until served. In April a conference pulled together by Ella Baker gave birth to the Student Non-Violent Coordinating Committee (SNCC). Starting in the spring of 1961, activists in the North dispatched interracial groups of "Freedom Riders" into the South to challenge segregation in interstate transportation facilities. That November, SNCC protests in Albany, Georgia, filled the city's jails. In spring 1963, Martin Luther King led a "children's crusade" in Birmingham, Alabama; and national television covered the mass demonstrations of elementary school and high school students dispersed by fire hoses and police dogs.[3] In 1964, SNCC organized a Freedom Summer voter-registration campaign in Mississippi.

Although youth often led the way, the movement was a family and community affair. As Sheyann Webb later recalled, "I asked my mother and father for my birthday present to become registered voters."[4] Webb, who turned eight in 1965, lived in Selma, Alabama, where a series of mass demonstrations for voting rights began in January of that year and culminated two months later in a fifty-four-mile march to the steps of the state capitol in Montgomery, where the marchers were greeted by a cheering crowd that included A. Philip Randolph and Rosa Parks.

Jim Crow was worst in rural Mississippi. In Sunflower County in the Mississippi Delta, African Americans were more than 60 percent of the population and less than 2 percent of the electorate. In August 1962, when SNCC came to ask who would like to register to vote, Fannie Lou Hamer, a third-generation sharecropper and the grand-daughter of slaves, raised her hand and began a career as a civil rights leader. She lost her plantation job and had to leave her home; white racists spit on her and shot at her. Police in Winona, Mississippi, once forced black prisoners in the town's jail to give her a beating that rendered her partially blind. She refused to back down, and helped launch the Mississippi Freedom Democratic Party (MFDP). In 1964, she and other MFDP leaders went to the Democratic Party's convention in Atlantic City to challenge the credentials of the official (and all-white) state delegation from Mississippi and take its place. When President Johnson learned the issue might be debated on the convention floor, he sent Vice President Hubert Humphrey to quash the challenge. Humphrey recruited Walter Reuther to pressure the MFDP and its allies to accept a compromise under which just two of its delegates would be seated alongside the whole segregationist delegation. Fannie Lou Hamer delivered the MFDP's reply: "We wouldn't come all the way from Mississippi to take two seats. . . . That was an insult."[5]

To Hamer, the vote was never the only goal. She also promoted the Mississippi Freedom Labor Union (MFLU), which was founded in January 1965 and quickly enlisted more than 1,000 members in at least six counties. That spring and summer the union mobilized plantation workers to strike for the eight-hour day at minimum wage, sick pay, health and accident insurance, equal employment practices, and an end to child and elder labor. This inspired similar strikes by cooks, maids, and custodians. When the strikes failed and the MFLU fell apart over the winter of 1965–66, Hamer started Freedom Farm, a co-operative that bought land to raise food for its members and cotton for cash.

Though the Democratic Party rebuffed the MFDP, the civil rights movement did win concessions from the Johnson administration. In July 1964, the president signed the Civil Rights Act, which prohibited discrimination by race, color, sex, religion, or national origin in voter registration, employment, public education, and public accommodations. In August 1965, he signed the Voting Rights Act, which barred states from using literacy tests and other devices to disenfranchise people of color and empowered federal officials to register voters turned away by local authorities.

Johnson also declared a War on Poverty. The new Office of Economic Opportunity administered programs assisting poor people, especially those excluded from relief and aid programs run by state and local governments committed to white supremacy. The Job Corps provided training and employment to youth from poor communities. Community Action Agencies funded social services provided by local civil rights projects. The federal government funded adult literacy programs and the Head Start program for preschoolers. The Elementary and Secondary Education Act of 1965 gave direct federal aid to local school systems for the first time, but only if they were racially integrated or desegregating in good faith. Fulfilling a promise that dated back to the New Deal, Congress passed the Medicare and Medicaid Act in 1965; Medicare subsidized health insurance for the elderly while Medicaid paid medical expenses for indigent households.

Civil rights activists faced brutal and sometimes murderous reprisals every step of the way. In 1956 racists in Montgomery bombed Martin Luther King's and E.D. Nixon's homes. In the early 1960s, white mobs assaulted SNCC sit-ins in multiple cities. In 1961 a Freedom Ride bus was firebombed outside Anniston, Alabama, and riders were beaten in Anniston, Birmingham, and Montgomery. In 1963, the Ku Klux Klan bombed a Birmingham church, killing four girls, ages eleven through fourteen. In Mississippi, two SNCC workers were shotgunned in Ruleville in 1962, activist Medgar Evers was assassinated outside his house in 1963, and three students were abducted, tortured, and killed at the start of Freedom Summer in 1964. Local and state police often collaborated with white supremacist vigilantes; like Fannie Lou Hamer's beating, the attacks on Freedom Riders in Alabama were carried out under police supervision. Activists and protesters were arrested and jailed by the tens of thousands.

The Civil Rights Act of 1964 intensified the fury. By October of that year, in Mississippi alone fifteen people had been murdered and thirty-seven black churches torched or bombed. Police killed protester Jimmy Lee Jackson outside Selma in February 1965. On March 7, when 600 civil rights activists tried to leave Selma to march to Montgomery, police intercepted them at the Edmund Pettus Bridge on the edge of town and turned them back with billy clubs and tear gas. Two weeks later a much larger crowd managed to leave Selma under the protection of federal troops, but that did not end the violence. On March 25, as the marchers dispersed from Montgomery and the troops stood down, Klansmen—one a paid FBI informant—shot and killed Viola Liuzzo, a white mother of five, daughter of a coal miner, and wife of a Teamsters business agent, who had come from Detroit in solidarity with the movement.

Amid the rising violence, black activists began to wonder if integration into the American mainstream was possible, or even desirable. Federal concessions seemed meaningless: voting rights were not yet enforced; the War on Poverty had hardly begun; the Justice Department had not suppressed white terrorism. Events in northern cities showed that intransigent racism and persistent poverty were not peculiar to the South. Fannie Lou Hamer recalled, "I used to think that if I could go North and tell people about the plight of the black folk in the state of Mississippi, everything would be all right. But traveling around, I found one thing for sure: it's up-South and down-South, and it's no different."[6]

In 1962 in Cambridge, Maryland, student protests against segregation at the movie theater and the skating rink roused local activists to demand desegregation not only in schools and hospitals but also in jobs and housing. In June 1963, the National Guard arrived in Cambridge to keep the peace and then stayed almost continuously for more than a year. That same month, black New Yorkers picketed a Harlem construction site to protest their exclusion from the building trades unions, and 3,000 black students in Boston stayed out of public schools for a day to protest segregation. Over the next school year hundreds of thousands of students staged similar protests in other northern cities. In March 1964, the Congress of Racial Equality (CORE) blocked traffic on New York City's Triborough Bridge to protest conditions in Harlem: substandard schools and public services, dilapidated housing, poverty, and police brutality.

The righteous anger fueling these protests found an exceptionally eloquent spokesperson in Malcolm X, a former railroad porter and petty criminal under the name Malcolm Little. While in prison for burglary, he joined the Nation of Islam, renounced his "slave name," and became one of the Nation's most charismatic ministers. From Harlem's Temple Seven, Malcolm X condemned American white supremacy in all its forms and called on African Americans to practice self-respect, self-defense, and self-determination. In 1964, he broke with the Nation of Islam. Inspired by Africans' anticolonial struggles and the multiracial composition of orthodox Islam, he founded the Organization of Afro-American Unity (OAAU) to promote political action as part of an international, multiracial movement against oppression. On February 21, 1965, he was gunned down at an OAAU meeting in Harlem.

The rage that Malcolm X tried to steer toward political action now burst out in a wave of urban rebellions. Over the summer of 1964, protests against police brutality had turned violent in Harlem, Brooklyn's Bedford-Stuyvesant section, Philadelphia, and other cities. In August 1965, in the Watts section of South Central Los Angeles, traffic police pulled over a twenty-one-year-old man and then arrested his mother for protesting his detainment; thousands of people gathered, forced the police to retreat, and began four days of rebellion. They took weapons from pawnshops and military surplus outlets, built barricades, and stoned police and firemen to shouts of "This is for Selma" and "Long live Malcolm X."[7] They targeted stores known for price gouging, easy-credit schemes, and rudeness to patrons, and spared libraries, schools and black-owned businesses. The National Guard cordoned off the zone and cleared it street by street. Property damage totaled more than $35 million; thirty-four people were killed, nearly 1,000 injured, over 4,000 arrested.

The summer of 1966 saw rebellions in forty-three cities, with eleven people killed and more than 400 injured. The following summer brought even more disorders. In July, a revolt in Newark, New Jersey, lasted six days and spread to nearby cities, including Paterson, Passaic, and Elizabeth. Less than a week later Detroit broke out in the largest black uprising of the century: eight days of violence by civilians, police, and National Guardsmen that was finally suppressed by federal troops. By the end of summer 1967, seventy-five major rebellions had claimed eighty-three lives.

As fires blazed in urban black ghettos, the southern civil rights movement shifted direction. In the summer of 1966, SNCC declared itself for "Black Power." The new slogan reflected the group's growing identification with African and Afro-Caribbean movements for national self-determination, but the commitment to Black Power also had deep roots in SNCC's work with Alabama sharecroppers in the Lowndes County

Freedom Organization (LCFO). The LCFO ran its own candidates for public office, outside the Democratic Party, and practiced self-defense. SNCC members were surprised to learn that the local activists owned guns; as one man explained, "You turn the other cheek, and you'll get handed half of what you're sitting on."[8] Organizing in Lowndes County also put SNCC in touch with the Deacons for Defense and Justice, a network of black war veterans centered in Bogalusa, Louisiana, that provided armed defense of black communities and, starting in 1965, SNCC. Like the LCFO's black panther insignia, the Black Power slogan electrified legions of civil rights activists, and the Deacons' assistance prompted SNCC to recalibrate its understanding of nonviolence to allow for violence that was defensive as opposed to retaliatory.

These developments drew criticism from the Southern Christian Leadership Conference. Martin Luther King publicly chided advocates of Black Power for abandoning a commitment to nonviolence at all costs. Behind the scenes, however, he mentored younger activists, and his wing of the movement charted an increasingly radical course.

In 1966, the SCLC opened its first campaign outside the South, joining Chicago civil rights groups to challenge discrimination in housing. In April 1967, King denounced the U.S. war in Vietnam and identified imperialism as the enemy of racial equality at home. That December the SCLC inaugurated the "Poor People's Campaign" dedicated to the radical redistribution of wealth. The project recalled A. Philip Randolph's speech at the March on Washington, where he insisted that justice would require more than civil rights legislation "in a society in which 6,000,000 black and white people are unemployed, and millions more live in poverty."[9] Or, as Fannie Lou Hamer later put it, "I've passed equal rights and I'm fighting for human rights . . . for all the people of this country."[10]

For Martin Luther King, the right to organize took center stage in spring 1968, when black sanitation workers in Memphis, Tennessee, struck for union recognition and SCLC leaders rallied in support. On April 3, King—who had many times spoken before labor audiences—gave his final speech at a meeting of the strikers, who belonged to Local 1733 of the American Federation of State, County and Municipal Employees (AFSCME). The next evening, King was assassinated in Memphis, and black communities erupted, their youth battling police in more than 100 cities with forty-six lives lost.

By the time of King's death, the movement he had helped launch in Montgomery was starting to stall. Vigilante attacks had ebbed, but police repression had reached new heights. In 1967, the FBI directed all of its twenty-two field offices to "disrupt, misdirect, discredit" black activists from a range of organizations, including SNCC, the Nation of Islam, the Southern Christian Leadership Conference, and others.[11] In February 1968, police in Orangeburg, South Carolina, fired on black students peacefully protesting at the town's segregated bowling alley, wounding twenty-eight and killing three. When Republican Richard Nixon entered the White House the following year, the FBI grew even more aggressive and the police more trigger-happy. Co-optation undermined the movement too. As black voters registered in greater numbers, the Democratic Party absorbed grassroots activism; its southern wing integrated under the control of the old establishment. But challenges to white supremacy were mounting outside the South, in communities where new organizations campaigned to empower the dispossessed.

Power to the People

In the late 1960s and 1970s, activism surged in poor and working-class communities. Many of the activists had got their start in groups backed by unions. Students for a Democratic Society came out of the Student League for Industrial Democracy, an old socialist organization subsidized by officials from the UAW, and other unions; CORE started with support from several unions including AFSCME, the UAW, and the Teamsters. SNCC had links to the Highlander Folk School, a worker education center started in 1932 in Tennessee, and also got financial support from the AFL-CIO's United Packinghouse Workers as well as from the independent United Electrical Workers and International Longshore and Warehouse Union. Many other community activists came from the anti-imperialist wing of the peace movement, which renounced anti-communism and explored variations on the Marxist doctrine that only the organized working class could achieve revolutionary social change. The slogan Power to the People captured the general mood; the phrase was borrowed from the African National Congress, which led the long struggle against white minority rule in South Africa.[12]

The Black Panther Party for Self-Defense, founded in 1966 in Oakland, California, combined radical politics and militant tactics with community service programs. The Panthers saw black America as a colony; their goal was self-determination, their first concern black communities' survival. They demanded housing, education, jobs, black men's exemption from military service, the release of black prisoners, black juries for black defendants, an end to police brutality, reparations for slavery and discrimination, and a plebiscite overseen by the United Nations to determine "the will of black people as to their national destiny."[13] Their community services ranged from schools and daycare to food pantries and medical clinics, with programs to address sickle-cell anemia and high blood pressure. They supported prisoners' families through transportation and emergency-cash grants, and collected clothing and shoes for school children. By 1969, their free-breakfast programs served 23,000 children in nineteen cities.

The Panthers also identified with African and Asian anticolonial and anti-imperialist struggles, recruited mostly young working-class women and men (especially veterans and ex-convicts), and monitored police activities by conducting community patrols, armed with guns and law books. By late 1968, the party had twenty-five chapters from coast to coast.

It quickly became the chief target of local, state, and federal police, coordinated by the FBI's Counterintelligence Program (COINTELPRO). By 1970, police had killed twenty-seven party members. While some of these killings occurred during gunfights between police and the Panthers, others had all the earmarks of carefully planned assassinations. In the wee hours of December 4, 1969, for example, Chicago police burst into an apartment on West Monroe Street and shot to death Fred Hampton, chairman of the party's Illinois chapter, who was asleep in his bed. Another party member, Mark Clark, was also killed in the raid, and four other Panthers (two men and two women) were seriously wounded; but Fred Hampton was clearly the target. The raid was initiated by the Cook County state's attorney's office and the FBI. At their request, an infiltrator had surreptitiously drugged Hampton before he went to bed that night and supplied the raiding party with a floorplan of the apartment that identified the exact location of his room. An exceptionally charismatic organizer, the twenty-one-year-old Hampton was the prime mover behind a new alliance between Chicago's Panthers and radical youth in the city's Latino and poor white communities. After riddling his body with bullets, police found that he was still breathing, so finished him off with two shots to the head. All of this came to light through a series of lawsuits and court cases that eventually compelled the city, county, and federal governments to pay damages for violating the victims' civil rights.

While no other group was targeted to the same degree as the Panthers, they were typical in some respects; other groups based in black communities adopted much the same combination of service, militant protest, and special attention to youth, whether students, workers, or unemployed and on the street. (Black youth unemployment, first measured in January 1972 at 37.1 percent, fell below 30 percent only twice during that decade.) In Newark activists associated with the writer and Black Power advocate Amiri Baraka—earlier known as Leroi Jones—ran political and cultural projects ranging from the Committee for a Unified Newark (CFUN) to youth groups, cultural centers, community schools, repertory companies, and co-operative stores. In Detroit, SNCC veterans and a local group called UHURU started the *Inner City Voice* monthly newspaper and the Republic of New Afrika, an organization that advocated establishment of an independent black nation-state in the Southeast. The Detroiters also campaigned against police brutality; their city's police force held the national record for the high rate at which it killed civilians.

A series of national conferences spun off organizations and other initiatives. The Black Power Conference held in Newark in 1967 generated CFUN and laid much of the groundwork for the Congress of Afrikan Peoples, born in 1970 and soon operating in fifteen cities. The Black Economic Development Conference that met in Detroit in 1969 spawned a national organization with the same name. The National Black Political Convention held in Gary, Indiana, in March 1972 was attended by about 10,000 activists and founded the National Black Assembly. In May of that year, some 30,000 people from a wide array of organizations gathered in Washington, D.C., in honor of African Liberation Day, and 30,000 more held simultaneous demonstrations in San Francisco, Toronto, and several Caribbean cities.

Only in the U.S. Census were "Hispanics" a unitary group. Although most Latinos spoke Spanish, their communities differed in origin and history. Puerto Rican migration to the U.S. mainland had soared after World War II, propelled by the island's high rate of unemployment and by recruitment on the part of mainland employers such as the National Tube Company's steel mill in Lorain, Ohio, and Carnegie Illinois Steel in Gary, Indiana. By the mid-1960s, more than a million Puerto Ricans lived in northeastern and midwestern cities. The largest community was in New York City, where the Young Lords Party started in 1969 (borrowing its name and organizational model from the Young Lords Organization previously established by Puerto Rican youth in Chicago). The Young Lords Party (YLP) advocated self-defense, socialism, and self-determination for the Puerto Rican nation, and it recruited workers, students, unemployed youth, and military veterans returning from Vietnam. Its first community project was street-sweeping in Spanish Harlem and the South Bronx, with brooms confiscated from the city's sanitation department; but the YLP soon organized free-breakfast and clothing programs for children, free medical testing for tuberculosis and lead poisoning, rent strikes, drug detox programs, and cultural activities including study groups, concerts, poetry readings, and art shows. Although most YLP members were Puerto Ricans, the party welcomed all Latinos and African Americans too. Branches appeared in East Coast cities from Boston to Philadelphia, and later in the Midwest, Puerto Rico, and southern California. Other Puerto Rican groups developed too, including La Unión Latina, Resistencia Puertorriqueña, and Puerto Ricans for Self-Determination. The pro-independence Partido Socialista Puertorriqueño, founded on the island in 1971, set up the first of many U.S. branches in 1973.

Puerto Ricans also joined El Comité, which emerged on Manhattan's West Side in 1970, growing out of a neighborhood softball team of factory workers and ex-gang members led by Federico Lora, a Vietnam veteran of Dominican ancestry. El Comité organized against urban renewal, moving squatters into condemned buildings and then daring the city to remove them by force, a tactic later imitated by many housing activists. In addition, the group agitated for better public education, health care, and daycare centers, and supported strikes by Latino workers. Dominican activism in New York and other U.S. cities had proliferated after the spring of 1965, when the U.S. Marines invaded the Dominican Republic to prop up a teetering dictatorship and the regime's most active opponents had to flee.

Like Dominicans, Haitian immigrants were often refugees from a U.S. client regime, in this case the murderous dictatorships of François Duvalier and his son Jean Claude Duvalier, known as Papa Doc and Baby Doc. Tens of thousands of Haitians fled to New York City after Papa Doc came to power in 1957. Proud of Haiti's standing as the second republic in the New World, the first black republic in the world, and the first republic to abolish slavery, Haitians were deeply affronted by U.S. society's color line. Seeing their residence in the United States as temporary, they tended to focus their political energies on ending repression and exploitation in their homeland. For example, the Organization of Patriotic Haitian Women, born in New York in the early 1970s, insisted that feminist demands be subordinated to the task of Haiti's liberation.

More than two-thirds of the Latinos in the United States were of Mexican origin, and the largest Latino movement took shape in their communities. Migration from Mexico continued, both documented and undocumented. The federal government's Bracero Program, based on a 1942 agreement between Mexico and the United States, oversaw over 4 million entries of guest farmworkers before it ended in 1964. In that same period many Mexicans came to work in the United States without government documentation, for visas cost money to obtain; and undocumented entries proliferated after 1965, when the new Immigration and Nationality Act capped immigration from Mexico at 20,000 people per year. Immigrants did participate in the Mexican American movement, but it was based mainly among people born in the United States. Like their African American and Puerto Rican counterparts, Mexican American activists moved from a civil rights agenda towards radical nationalism.

In 1959, in southern California, the Mexican American Political Association started to register voters and protest police brutality and discrimination in housing and education. A Texas group—the Political Association of Spanish-Speaking Organizations (PASSO)—formed in 1961. In 1963, in Crystal City, Texas, PASSO joined with activists from the Teamsters to back a slate of working-class Mexican Americans who took over the city council. That same year, the longtime community activist Reies Tijerina organized La Alianza Federal de Mercedes (Federal Alliance of Land Grants) to press claims for lands that Anglos had confiscated after the United States annexed northern Mexico in 1848. In 1966, La Alianza, with 20,000 members in New Mexico, Colorado, Utah, Texas, and California, turned from legal maneuvers to direct action. Alianza activists occupied the Kit Carson National Forest in northern New Mexico, and in 1967 the organization raided a local courthouse to free members from detention.

Such militant actions galvanized young campus and community activists. They began to call themselves "Chicanos," turning a disparaging term for working-class Mexican Americans into a badge of unity and pride, and started a host of new organizations.[14] The Brown Berets, founded in 1967 in East Los Angeles, recruited barrio youth and modeled themselves on the Black Panthers. In 1969 they joined the National Chicano Moratorium Committee, which staged mass protests against the U.S. war in Vietnam. The following year, the Partido Nacional de La Raza Unida (the National United Peoples Party) was established in southern Texas and quickly spread to other southwestern states, building an especially strong presence in Colorado and California. Committed to "struggles for self-determination of all oppressed peoples," to equality between men and women, and to the principle that "working people must struggle and organize on every front for complete industrial democracy," the party ran local candidates on platforms calling for community control of schools, police, and public services.[15] Many of these candidates were elected. In Denver, La Raza Unida worked closely with the local Crusade for Justice, which ran a school that encouraged Chicano pride and convened the first national conference of Chicano youth.

Black and Latino resistance to oppression reverberated in the prison population. Authorities reported sixteen inmate uprisings in 1970, organized by groups like the California Prisoners Union, which spoke for "the convicted class."[16] Inmates at that state's Folsom Prison staged a three-week strike demanding better conditions and treatment, including the minimum wage and the right to organize; they asked Panthers and Brown Berets to negotiate for them. In upstate New York's Attica prison, inmates' compulsory labor in the metal shop and other enterprises provided the state with more than $1 million a year in saleable goods; there, anger at exploitation and mistreatment boiled over in August 1971. More than half of the 2,200 inmates rose up, seized the facility, and took thirty-nine of the guards as hostages, demanding decent food and shelter, religious freedom, legal assistance, reading material, and fair wages for prisoners' work. After four days of negotiation, state troopers stormed the prison, killing twenty-nine inmates and ten guards.

Another prison made headlines when the organization Indians of All Nations occupied the abandoned federal corrections facility on Alcatraz Island in San Francisco Bay. Proclaiming their "right to use our land for our own benefit," the occupiers announced plans to transform the island's buildings into a center for Native American studies and spiritual practice, environmental research, and vocational training in Native crafts.[17] They held Alcatraz for nineteen months, from November 20, 1969, to June 11, 1971. Their claim to the island rested on a treaty that the federal government had broken many decades before, but even long-established treaty rights had come under attack. Between 1946 and 1960, Indian nations had lost over 3.3 million acres of land, and on reservations from Alaska to Florida, activists organized around issues like water rights, fishing rights, and land use.

A third of the country's half-million Native Americans lived off reservations, mostly in cities. In 1968, Native American ex-convicts in Minneapolis-St. Paul started community patrols against police abuse and founded the American Indian Movement (AIM), which popularized the slogan "Red Power" and called for a return to native traditions.[18] In 1972, AIM joined the pan-tribal Trail of Broken Treaties, which took a caravan of cars and trucks to Washington, D.C., and occupied offices of the federal government's Bureau of Indian Affairs. In 1973, Oglala Lakotas on the Pine Ridge Reservation in South Dakota called on AIM to help them stand up to a private militia working for the reservation's chairman Dick Wilson, who was violently fending off a popular movement to remove him from office. AIM mustered at Wounded Knee and withstood a ten-week siege by the U.S. Army, though two members were killed by crossfire. Targeted by COINTELPRO and racked by internal divisions, AIM faded as an organization, but Native American activism endured, especially around treaty rights and environmental threats to ancestral land.

Native Hawaiians also asserted claims to ancestral land, as well as demanding reparations for the coup that had toppled their government in 1893 and set the stage for Hawaii's annexation to the United States five years later. The movement targeted land seized by the U.S. military, especially 600,000 acres taken during World War II. In 1976, protesters occupied Kaho'olawe Island, used since 1941 as a dump for toxic waste and a site for testing bombs and other weapons. The protest forced the island's demilitarization and decontamination.

Asian American immigrant communities had long organized their own associations and service organizations, often dominated by businessmen and focused on just one ethnic group. Starting in the late 1960s, young activists—most of them born in the United States—built groups that crossed ethnic lines and gave birth to an inclusive Asian American movement. Street gangs organized self-help groups to fight inter-ethnic gang warfare as well as drug addiction. In Los Angeles, Filipinos formed Pagkakaisa and Samoans created Omai Fa'atasai, but the Yellow Brotherhood and Asian American Hardcore recruited members of all Asian nationalities. By 1969, self-help organizing in San Francisco gave rise to the pan-ethnic Asian Community Center, which ran a food co-op and summer programs for children.

Admiration for the People's Republic of China inspired some activists to create organizations like the Red Guards in San Francisco, East Wind in Los Angeles, and I Wor Kuen (Righteous and Harmonious Fists) in New York City. They combined political organizing with service projects such as medical clinics, breakfast programs, daycare, and language classes. I Wor Kuen also protested against the tourist buses that brought sightseers to gawk at Chinatown, and it generated the Chinatown People's

Association, a coalition that mobilized mass rallies against police brutality and for Asian workers' employment on the Confucius Plaza housing project built with federal funds.

Activism—sometimes explicitly racist—intensified in white working-class communities as well. In 1968, when Alabama's ex-governor George Wallace ran for president on a segregationist platform, his American Independent Party established chapters in the North and West as well as in the South. On Election Day, he garnered almost 10 million votes nationwide and carried five southern states (Georgia, Alabama, Mississippi, Louisiana, and Arkansas). That same year, Italian Americans in Newark's North Ward elected a white vigilante leader to the city council. In the mid-1970s, the mostly Irish American residents of South Boston organized ROAR (Restore Our Alienated Rights), which violently protested school integration. Like-minded groups emerged in several midwestern cities.

But interracial alliances developed too. The Congress of Italian American Organizations allied with black and Puerto Rican groups to push for open admissions at New York City's public colleges. Greeks and Arabs in Dearborn, Michigan, joined Native Americans and others in a community council to fight plans to tear down low-cost housing. Struggles against real estate developers in Honolulu brought together virtually every ethnic group on the island. Chicago's Black Panthers and Young Lords formed a "rainbow coalition" (Fred Hampton's phrase) with the Young Patriots from the North Side's white Appalachian community.[19] In the 1970s, Newark's CFUN united with local Young Lords behind a "community choice" slate and elected Newark's first black mayor. In cities across the country, tenants unions, parents associations, and other neighborhood groups organized across racial and ethnic lines as never before.

The most widely supported cause of the sixties was stopping the U.S. war in Vietnam. No one contributed more to working-class opposition to the war than the protesters who were also Vietnam veterans. Individual veterans started denouncing the war in 1965. In June 1966, three draftees stationed at Fort Hood in Killeen, Texas—a training center for troops on their way to Vietnam—became the first soldiers to refuse to take part in the war. The "Fort Hood Three"—Dennis Mora (Puerto Rican), James Johnson (African American), and David Samas (white, of Italian and Lithuanian ancestry)—delivered a powerful statement to the press: "We represent in our backgrounds a cross-section of the Army and America. . . . We have been in the army long enough to know that we are not the only GIs who feel as we do. . . . We will not be part of this unjust, immoral, and illegal war."[20] A year later, at a meeting in New York City, GIs who had returned from the war organized Vietnam Veterans Against the War (VVAW), the first antiwar veterans organization in U.S. history. In April 1971, VVAW mobilized 1,500 veterans to camp on the National Mall in Washington, D.C., in defiance of a Supreme Court injunction; 800 threw their service awards and combat decorations over the barricade erected to keep them away from Congress, and 1,000 veterans—many on crutches or in wheelchairs—led a half-million people marching against the war. By then some antiwar and Black Power organizations operated inside the U.S. military. In Vietnam, mutinies compromised combat operations, and soldiers stateside refused to deploy against protestors.

Ruling the country and orchestrating the war were widely regarded as jobs for men, and that kind of thinking about gender shaped radical movements too. Women invariably did crucial work for insurgent movements, but in virtually every organization, men ran the show. Women confronted this inequity by challenging male leadership, launching independent projects, and forming their own organizations.

The welfare rights movement exemplified these patterns. Protests by women welfare recipients proliferated in the mid-1960s, especially in black communities. By 1966, action groups had sprung up in seventy cities across twenty-six states. They gathered under the umbrella of the National Welfare Rights Organization (NWRO), the brainchild of middle-class civil rights leaders. Professional men staffed the organization's national office, and they repeatedly made policy decisions that properly belonged to the women on NWRO's elected governing board. In 1972, the women pushed the men out and installed a new executive director: Johnnie Tillmon, daughter of a sharecropping family in Arkansas who had moved to Los Angeles in the 1950s, gone to work in a laundry where she served as a shop steward for the Laundry Workers Union, and become a welfare recipient and activist after her health failed in 1963. In a press release, Tillmon summarized her organization's new direction: "NWRO views the major welfare problems as women's issues and itself as strictly a women's organization."[21]

In many other quarters women found ways to work with men and enjoy autonomy too. In Los Angeles, the Asian Sisterhood ran its own counterparts to the Yellow Brotherhood's youth projects, and the Chicano movement included the Comisión Femenil Mexicana, a women's rights group. In New York, women in the Young Lords insisted that the party add this demand to its platform: "We want equality for women, down with machismo and male chauvinism."[22] They also launched a women's union to press for daycare, family health services, and laws to stop doctors from sterilizing women under duress. Sterilization was a similarly central issue for Women of All Red Nations, affiliated with the American Indian Movement, the Latin Women's Collective that worked with El Comité, and the Women's Committee of the Black United Front in Brooklyn. In the South, black and white women married to men active in the United Mine Workers founded Alabama Women for Human Rights, which supported strikes and campaigned for daycare, health care, and prison reform.

If feminism developed rapidly, the gay and lesbian liberation movement appeared almost overnight. Early one Saturday morning (June 28, 1969), police began a routine roundup of patrons at the Stonewall Inn, a gay bar in New York City's Greenwich Village. A woman vigorously resisted arrest, and within minutes a crowd barricaded the police inside the bar and torched it. Just days later local activists formed the Gay Liberation Front, which described itself as "a militant coalition of radical and revolutionary homosexual men and women committed to fight the oppression of the homosexual as a minority group and to demand the right to the self-determination of our own bodies."[23] Gay and lesbian organizations numbered nearly 800 by 1973 and thousands by the end of the decade. They enrolled many working people—including sex workers—along with students, artists, and intellectuals. Some groups recognized multiple kinds of oppression and cultivated multiple sources of pride. These included Gay Youth, Third World Gay Liberation, Radicalesbians, Hispanos Unidos Gay Liberados, and the Young Lords Party's gay and lesbian caucus.

Inspired by all of these developments, people with disabilities forged a militant movement too. On April 5, 1977, about 500 people demonstrated at the Washington headquarters of the Department of Health, Education and Welfare (HEW), 200 of them picketing outside while the rest entered the building to stage a sit-in, with seventy-five protestors staying overnight. That same day saw demonstrations in front of HEW's nine regional offices across the country, along with sit-ins at the offices in New York, Denver, and San Francisco. While the other sit-ins soon ended, the action in San Francisco lasted for three and a half weeks, until HEW issued regulations that barred federally funded programs from discriminating against people with disabilities. Helping the San Franciscans hold their ground were supporters ranging from the Black Panther Party to local Teamsters. One protestor, confined to a wheelchair following an accident eight years earlier, summarized the spirit of the sit-in and, indeed, all sixties movements: "We are showing that we are a strong people, not weak. We are not going to take discrimination and oppression any more."[24]

The Sixties in the Workplace

The myriad causes that galvanized communities resonated at work too. Unions, union caucuses, and other worker organizations aligned with liberation movements in the larger society. By the late 1960s, a strike wave was rising, and labor leaders were facing increasingly militant dissent from below. Like its predecessors, this surge of labor activism centered on workplace rights, but it defined those rights more broadly than its forerunners had.

For many workers, organizing unions was a civil rights struggle. New York City's hospital workers—mostly black and Puerto Rican women—were excluded from protection under the Wagner Act, subject to state law that barred them from striking, and paid less than a living wage. In 1958 they started organizing under the auspices of Local 1199 of the Drug, Hospital and Health Care Workers, a small left-led union born in the 1930s. The campaign centered on the city's "voluntary hospitals" (private nonprofit institutions), and after one of them—Montefiore Hospital in the Bronx—signed a contract that greatly improved compensation and working conditions, the movement spread like wildfire. In 1959, some 3,500 nonprofessional workers from six different voluntary hospitals defied an order from the New York State Supreme Court and struck for the right to organize, demanding that their employers hold elections in which workers could vote for or against union representation. Civil rights leaders rallied support for the strike. So did the city's central labor council, whose president, Harry Van Arsdale of the International Brotherhood of Electrical Workers, relentlessly pressured the hospitals to negotiate and led a march of 700 local union leaders and activists to join one of the picket lines in Manhattan. The strikers meanwhile held out despite many arrests and constant harassment from city police. After forty-six days, management gave in, and the strikers accepted an offer that promised grievance machinery, wage increases, and other improvements, but not formal recognition of Local 1199 as the workers' bargaining agent. That omission set the stage for another strike, which took place in 1962, after several hospitals reneged on their promises. Again, the strikers faced arrests and harassment. Again, the civil rights movement and central labor council supplied crucial support; A. Philip Randolph, Harry Van Arsdale, and others united to exert so much political pressure that Governor Nelson Rockefeller stepped in to pledge that state law would be expanded to give hospital workers collective bargaining rights. After two months on strike, the workers attended a victory rally featuring speeches by Randolph, Malcolm X, and Roy Wilkins of the NAACP, and a message from Martin Luther King, who had been called to a demonstration in Georgia. Malcolm X summarized the struggle's lesson: "You don't get the job done unless you show the man that you're not afraid to go to jail."[25]

In late 1968, in Charleston, South Carolina, public hospital workers—mostly women, all black—formed Local 1199B, and in March 1969, they launched a strike described by Coretta Scott King, Martin Luther King's widow and a radical in her own right, as "the single most important issue facing the forces of progress in America."[26] The SCLC provided substantial support, and after 113 days, court injunctions against demonstrations, more than a thousand arrests, and the governor's attempt to break the strike by sending in the National Guard, the civil rights leader Ralph Abernathy could declare, "We have discovered a winning combination—soul power and union power."[27] Although the strikers won wage increases, grievance procedures, and a credit union, recognition for 1199B was not part of the settlement, and that demand remained unmet. The local survived as a civil rights initiative, however. Working with the SCLC to register black voters, it saw Charleston elect its first black city officials since Reconstruction, and 1199B's local leaders remained active in their communities for many years. In December 1969, Local 1199 became the National Union of Hospital and Health Care Employees, with branches in Maryland, North Carolina, Pennsylvania, Ohio, New Jersey, and Connecticut as well as New York and, for a short time, South Carolina.

Like hospital workers, farmworkers were excluded from coverage under the Wagner Act. In 1962, community organizers César Chávez and Dolores Huerta initiated the National Farm Workers Association (NFWA) in Delano, California. The NFWA organized in the *mutualista* tradition: self-help through mutual aid. By 1965 it had about 1,700 members. That year Filipino grape workers who belonged to the AFL-CIO's Agricultural Workers Organizing Committee (AWOC) called a strike in Delano, and its local leader Larry Itliong asked Chávez for help. The NFWA joined the grape strike and spread it far and wide. Organizers slipped into the fields to talk to workers, while loudspeakers mounted on cars and trucks blared appeals to join the strike. Women and children set up picket lines; Huerta credited their presence for the strikers' insistence on nonviolence. In August 1966, AWOC and the NFWA merged to form the United Farm Workers (UFW), a union closely allied with the Chicano movement and warmly embraced by other sixties radicals. When the growers refused to negotiate, the union organized a national boycott of grapes. Fanning out across the country, UFW members and staff went to union halls, churches, campuses, and community organizations to drum up support, and activists everywhere responded, picketing supermarkets that sold "scab grapes" and volunteering to spread the campaign.[28] The UFW achieved its first contracts in 1970, winning higher pay, union hiring halls, a ban on the use of toxic pesticides like DDT, and employer-funded health care, housing, and job-training programs.

While most UFW members were Mexican Americans or, in much smaller numbers, Filipinos, the union also recruited African Americans and immigrants from Arab nations. (The first UFW member killed on a picket line was Nagi Daifallah, a young Yemeni man shot by police in August 1973.) In its California stronghold, the union joined community struggles for bilingual education, food stamps, housing, and public health projects. Jessie Lopez De La Cruz, the UFW's first woman field organizer, looked at labor and community work in the same way: "The way I see it, there's more poor people than rich people. We're trying to get together, organize, stay together."[29] Inspired and often assisted by the UFW, committees to organize farmworkers emerged in Arizona, in Texas, and among migrant tomato harvesters in Ohio and Michigan.

Once the grape contracts were signed in 1970, the UFW turned to the lettuce fields. Growers countered by rushing to sign contracts with the Teamsters, who had earned a reputation for negotiating sweetheart deals with employers beyond the trucking industry. Throughout the lettuce campaign, then, the UFW was fighting two opponents, using strikes, demonstrations, lawsuits, and a national boycott of lettuce harvested under Teamster contracts. In 1973, when UFW's contracts with grape growers expired, they too reached out to the Teamsters. That reignited the grape strikes and boycott, which expanded to include Gallo wines. Finally, in 1975, after a number of UFW pickets had been killed, California passed an Agricultural Labor Relations Act modeled on the Wagner Act. It established an Agricultural Labor Relations Board to conduct elections for union representation and adjudicate charges of unfair labor practices. The UFW regained momentum, winning most of the elections in which it took part, and once that pattern was established, the Teamsters agreed to back off.

The Black Power movement had a strong workplace component too. In Boston, Pittsburgh, Chicago, and other cities, black construction workers formed independent unions to rival the AFL-CIO's building-trades affiliates. Harlem Fight Back (which started as the Harlem Unemployment Center in 1964 and changed its name to Fight Back four years later), developed the tactic of bringing busloads of unemployed black construction workers to a building site and shutting it down until their demands for a fair share of jobs were met. The group's founder and leader, James Haughton, a veteran of the Korean War, had earlier worked with the Negro American Labor Council and was active in the antiwar movement and the Congress of Afrikan Peoples. A handbill he distributed exemplified Fight Back's politics:

WE DON'T WANT

> Integration
> Public housing in white communities
> Welfare

WE DO WANT

> To rebuild America's slums
> Top-dollar construction jobs

Decent jobs and decent housing for Black and Puerto Rican
Americans[30]

Coalitions modeled on Fight Back later emerged in New York's Puerto Rican and Chinese communities. In the summer of 1969, demonstrations by black men demanding construction jobs shut down twenty major building projects in Pittsburgh, Chicago, and other cities.

Black workers also mobilized inside unions. After a wildcat strike against speedup in May 1968, black UAW members at Chrysler's Dodge Main plant in Detroit found themselves targeted for retaliation by management and abandoned by the union. They formed the Dodge Revolutionary Union Movement (DRUM), which forced the company to rehire most of the fired strikers. This victory inspired many more "revolutionary union movements" (RUMs) in Detroit-area auto plants, along with a few RUMs in other local workplaces: HRUM for health and hospital workers, UPRUM at United Parcel Service, and NEWRUM at the *Detroit News*. They fought against discrimination by unions and employers alike and for more worker control of labor conditions. In 1969, RUM leaders and community activists from the *Inner City Voice* newspaper founded the League of Revolutionary Black Workers, which developed ties with other black workers' groups such as United Black Brothers at the Ford plants in Mahwah, New Jersey, and Lexington, Kentucky, and the Black Panther Caucus at the General Motors plant in Fremont, California.

Hit hard by layoffs during a slump in the auto industry in 1969–70, the league turned toward community organizing; but black rank-and-file caucuses survived, pushing union officials in bolder directions. The Ad Hoc Committee of Concerned Negro Auto Workers got the UAW to stop opposing black candidates for local offices, and they began winning elections in black- and even white-majority locals. In September 1972, some 1,200 black members and officers of thirty-seven different unions met in Chicago to create a "forum for black militancy within the trade union movement," to quote AFSCME's secretary-treasurer William Lucy. The outcome was the Coalition of Black Trade Unionists.[31]

Latinos had a parallel organization, the Labor Council for Latin American Advancement (LCLAA), founded in 1973 in Washington, D.C., at a conference attended by union officers and staff. The United Steel Workers already had a Chicano Caucus, organized in 1971, with chapters in nine cities from California to Pennsylvania and 3,000 members in Los Angeles alone. New York City was another hub of activity, with the multi-union Spanish Labor Committee in the lead.

In Puerto Rico, government repression of student antiwar activists drove a new generation of radicals into the labor movement. Beginning in 1968, a strike wave swept the island. In 1971, forty independent unions formed the Movimiento Obreros Unidos (MOU). It favored Puerto Rican independence, opposed the island's exemption from the federal minimum wage, brought labor support to socialist May Day activities, and fiercely defended MOU unions' autonomy from the AFL-CIO. Since the MOU's strikes came under attack by the island's pro-statehood governing party, they fueled popular support for independence. In 1975 Puerto Rican authorities intensified their repression of the movement. The MOU's executive secretary, Federico Cintrón Fiallo, was charged with robbing a San Juan bank; held as a terrorist, with bail

MIGRANT LABOR'S HEROINE

set at $500,000; and later sentenced for criminal contempt for refusing to co-operate with a federal grand jury. Following this setback, sectarian squabbles and disruption by police combined to end the MOU's effectiveness.

Feminism, too, sank roots in the labor movement, with new organizations uniting women workers, both union members and others. In 1971, 600 women from twenty-four cities met in Washington, D.C., for the first national conference of domestic workers. They represented local groups formed since the late 1960s, mostly by black women with experience in the civil rights movement. These groups joined to establish the National Council of Household Employees, which lobbied for the extension of labor laws to cover domestic workers. Clerical workers meanwhile built more than a dozen citywide associations, such as Women Office Workers in New York, Women Organized for Employment in San Francisco, and Cleveland Women Working. In 1977, several of these groups came together to form the 9 to 5 National Association of Working Women, with a founding membership of 10,000.

Airline flight attendants, who had unionized at a number of airlines in the 1940s and 1950s, formed Stewardesses for Women's Rights (SFWR) in 1974. It used lawsuits, pickets, and the mass distribution of buttons, bumper stickers, and leaflets to attack what SFWR called "sexploitation."[32] This included employer regulation of flight attendants' hairdos, makeup, and weight, and airline advertising that depicted them as sex objects for enjoyment of male passengers. When ads for National Airlines invited businessmen to "fly" its attendants, SFWR distributed buttons that read, "Don't fly me. Fly yourself."[33]

With women in the lead, the labor movement gained a foothold in one sector of the sex industry: the eight big-city Playboy Clubs operated by the soft-core pornographer Hugh Hefner, publisher of *Playboy* magazine. In 1964, Myra Wolfgang, vice president of the Hotel Employees and Restaurant Employees (HERE) began to organize informational pickets of the club in Detroit, publicizing the fact that its servers—young women called "bunnies" because their skimpy uniforms included rabbit ears and puffy cotton tails—received no wages and were expected to share their tips with the house. By the end of the year, these women had a union contract, and by 1969 the bunnies in every other club had one too. Among their gains were wages, an end to mandatory tip-sharing, new rules that barred customers from touching the servers, and a strong system of shop stewards who taught the company that, as Myra Wolfgang put it, "bunnies can bite."[34]

Labor feminism also brought union women together across occupations. In 1971, San Francisco activists founded the Union Women's Alliance to Gain Equality (Union WAGE), whose mission statement declared: "Women's liberation must for the working women, begin on the job."[35] Based mainly in California, WAGE had outposts in the Pacific Northwest, the Midwest, and New York City. Members aided drives to unionize women workers, promoted the formation of women's caucuses, and campaigned to preserve and extend protective labor laws. In March 1974, more than 3,200 women unionists from across the country met in Chicago to launch the Coalition of Labor Union Women (CLUW). Led by the labor movement's highest-ranking female officials, CLUW lobbied for women's advancement on the job and in unions, for organizing drives aimed at women workers, and for legislation that addressed their needs.

By the late 1970s, it also endorsed women's reproductive rights, including access to abortion in accordance with the U.S. Supreme Court's decision in the case of *Roe v. Wade* (1973). CLUW's founding president was Olga Madar, who in 1966 had become the first woman to serve on the UAW International Executive Board; her successor, Joyce Miller from the Amalgamated Clothing Workers, joined the AFL-CIO Executive Council in 1980 as its first female member.

The movement against the U.S. war in Vietnam also had a labor contingent. The surviving "red unions"—the United Electrical Workers and the International Longshore and Warehouse Union—opposed the war from its inception; so did Local 1199 and a few other AFL-CIO unions with left-wing leadership. In 1966, progressive labor officials in New York City set up a trade union division of the peace organization Committee for a Sane Nuclear Policy. The following year, the division hosted a National Labor Assembly for Peace in Chicago, where 523 officers of fifty different unions discussed how organized labor could contribute to "bringing this savage war to a swift and just conclusion, so that we may devote our wealth and energies to the struggle against poverty, disease, hunger, and bigotry."[36] On October 15, 1969, when Vietnam Moratorium demonstrations took place in cities across the country, forty unions sponsored the protest in New York City, officers of the UAW and HERE spoke at the Detroit event, and a UAW leader presided over a gigantic rally in Los Angeles. After U.S. military incursions into Cambodia came to light in April 1970, many union leaders denounced them. Victor Gotbaum of AFSCME's huge District 37 in New York City headed the Coalition for Peace that mobilized a mass protest march in Washington, D.C., and fifty unions were among the sponsors of an emergency peace conference that met in Cleveland. In 1972, about 1,000 trade unionists from thirty-five AFL-CIO unions founded Labor for Peace.

Lesbian and gay rights also became labor issues, albeit on a smaller scale. As the gay and lesbian liberation movement gained momentum, union officials and rank-and-file activists who had long hidden their sexuality began to come out of the closet. Conservatives sometimes forced them out, exposing the sexual identities of gay and lesbian progressives running for union office. In 1969, this happened to Bill Olwell, a vocal opponent of racial segregation and the Vietnam War who was up for reelection as president of Retail Clerks Local 1001 in Seattle. Gary Kapanowski, a militant shop steward in UAW Local 212, experienced even worse in 1974, when he ran for the post of shop chairman at a bathtub factory on the outskirts of Detroit. Opponents engineered his arrest on morals charges and then blanketed the factory with flyers asking, "DO YOU WANT A FAGGOT TO BE YOUR CHAIRMAN OF THE SHOP COMMITTEE?"[37] As it turned out, most of Kapanowski's co-workers did in fact want him to head the committee. Both he and Bill Olwell handily won their races and stopped hiding their sexuality.

If outing gay and lesbian progressives was starting to lose its effectiveness as a tool for labor conservatives, more radical developments were afoot too: union members were starting to organize gay and lesbian caucuses, and unions were beginning to expand their agenda to incorporate gay and lesbian rights. Teachers led the way. In 1970 the American Federation of Teachers condemned employer reprisals against gay and lesbian teachers; in 1974 the Gay Teachers Association became a caucus in

New York City's United Federation of Teachers; and in 1975 the Gay Teachers Coalition in San Francisco joined with Bay Area Gay Liberation (BAGL) in a successful campaign to get the city's school board to expand its nondiscrimination policy to cover sexual orientation. That teachers were coming out of the closet generated a tremendous backlash from the political right. Nowhere was it more ominous than in California, where state senator John Briggs sponsored a ballot initiative that, if passed, would ban gay men and lesbians from working in the state's public schools as teachers, aides, counselors, or administrators. Early polls suggested that this initiative—Proposition 6—would win by a wide margin when it went before the voters in fall 1978. In fact, it lost by more than a million votes, thanks to a massive door-to-door "No on 6" campaign supported by gay and lesbian organizations, the Teamsters, the ILWU, the American Postal Workers Union, two statewide teachers unions, the California Nurses Association, and locals from the building trades, service sector, and public sector, along with the executive council of the California AFL-CIO.[38]

San Francisco saw the most productive labor-gay alliance of the 1970s. After the gay activist Harvey Milk mobilized support for a Teamsters boycott of Coors beer, the Laborers Union and the Building and Construction Trades Council joined the Teamsters to endorse Milk when he ran for the city's board of supervisors in 1975 and again in 1977, when he finally won. In 1976, BAGL's labor committee, which included activists from an array of Bay Area locals, held a press conference with twenty-two union leaders to announce that they would work together to defeat anti-union ballot measures and to guarantee that all union contracts barred discrimination on the basis of sexuality. The alliance met some setbacks and losses. In October 1975, when the AFL-CIO's annual convention met in San Francisco, BAGL activists unsuccessfully pressed the delegates to commit the federation to defending gay and lesbian rights; in 1978 Harvey Milk was assassinated by an ex-member of the board of supervisors. But history was clearly on the side of gay and lesbian rights. Some unions far beyond San Francisco—for example, AFSCME locals representing librarians in Seattle and bus drivers in Ann Arbor, Michigan—had negotiated contracts that included nondiscrimination clauses. Gay and lesbian caucuses were forming in more and more unions. By the early 1980s, the trend was so well established at the grassroots that support for gay and lesbian rights was becoming the norm among union leaders. In 1982, AFSCME's national convention endorsed the cause, and the union's secretary-treasurer, Bill Lucy, got a friendly hearing when he raised the issue in speeches before leaders of the AFL-CIO's building trades unions and industrial unions. In 1983, the AFL-CIO convention adopted a civil rights resolution that explicitly endorsed gay and lesbian rights; Bill Olwell, now a vice president of the United Food and Commercial Workers, was there to thank the delegates.

From the late 1960s through the 1970s, labor activists also rallied around health and safety issues on an unprecedented scale. In December 1968, members of the United Mine Workers in Montgomery, West Virginia, organized the Black Lung Association to campaign for a state law that would provide compensation for miners who contracted black lung disease (pneumoconiosis), caused by breathing coal dust. The campaign spread quickly. By February 1969, UMW members across West Virginia, Pennsylvania, and Ohio were staging mass strikes for compensation laws. Late that year Congress passed the Coal Mine Health and Safety Act, which set up a compensation program. The law also established new mine-safety standards, and the number of deaths from accidents and explosions dropped by half over the next decade. The black lung campaign inspired others: the Carolina Brown Lung Association worked to get compensation for byssinosis, a lung disease caused by cotton dust, and the White Lung Association fought for compensation for asbestosis, caused by the asbestos widely used in insulation.

In 1970, Congress established the Occupational Safety and Health Administration (OSHA), authorized to set workplace safety and health standards and monitor compliance. OSHA was not up to the task; in its first sixteen years it issued only eighteen health and safety regulations, and even at its most active inspected less than 2 percent of U.S. workplaces in any given year. In response, unionists joined health professionals and scientists in a network of committees, councils, and coalitions on occupational safety and health. These "COSH" groups developed local and state standards on workplace safety and health, and provided advice and training to shop stewards and other local union officers. Strikes over health and safety issues actually doubled in the first four years after OSHA's authorization.

Some unions made other allies in the struggle against toxic workplaces. In 1973 the Oil, Chemical and Atomic Workers (OCAW) won a strike against Shell Oil, thanks in part to a boycott of Shell products backed by environmental groups like Friends of the Earth and the Environmental Defense Fund and community organizations like the National Tenants Association and National Welfare Rights Organization. The following year Karen Silkwood, an activist in OCAW Local 5-283, began documenting radiation hazards at the Kerr-McGee plutonium processing plant in Oklahoma City. After she was killed while driving to meet a union health and safety staffer and an investigative reporter from the *New York Times*, OCAW organized environmentalists and Native American activists into the Sunbelt Alliance, which targeted the nuclear industry in the late 1970s and raised money for Silkwood's three orphaned children.

Inspired by sixties movements for social justice, unionism in the public sector expanded dramatically. In 1958, New York City's mayor Robert Wagner—son of the U.S. senator who had authored the National Labor Relations Act—issued an executive order that established collective bargaining rights for the city's public workers. In 1959, Wisconsin became the first state to legislate union recognition and collective bargaining in the public sector. Other cities and states followed suit, as did the federal government in 1962. At that point about one-tenth of all public employees belonged to unions; by 1973 the proportion had grown to 23 percent, and there was more expansion to come. By 1980, almost 36 percent of public workers belonged to unions; membership in public-sector unions totaled about 5.8 million; and these unions accounted for about 30 percent of all union members in the United States. The American Federation of Teachers, the American Federation of Government Employees, and the American Federation of State, County and Municipal Employees had become some of the largest unions in the land. Professional organizations like the National Education Association and American Nurses Association had added collective bargaining to their services, though they did not formally affiliate with the labor movement.

Although strikes by public employees were almost always against the law, they broke out repeatedly anyway—among hospital workers, teachers, office clerks, social workers, fire fighters, police, and others. The peak came at the end of the 1960s; the year 1968 saw 411 strikes by public employees, and 1969 saw 412. During the 1970s, things quieted down, but only a little; during that decade, the number of strikes in the public sector averaged 375 a year. Each victory encouraged other groups to take their grievances to the streets. Memphis sanitation workers won their 1968 strike when the city finally recognized their AFSCME local after Martin Luther King's assassination. Within months, black garbage collectors in St. Petersburg, Florida, and Atlanta, Georgia, launched strikes for recognition of AFSCME locals and won with support from the Southern Christian Leadership Conference as well as the strikers' communities.

The first national walkout by federal employees began on March 18, 1970, when postal workers in New York City staged a wildcat strike for higher pay. It quickly spread to Boston, Pittsburgh, Akron, Houston, and other cities. Within days, the strikers numbered 150,000, despite federal injunctions against the walkout. On March 23, President Nixon sent federal troops and National Guardsmen to move the mail in New York, and postal union officers across the country were hauled into court. The strike ended two days later, when the government agreed to negotiate; postal workers got substantial raises and the strikers got amnesty.

The postal walkout came at the crest of a strike wave that extended from 1968 into 1977. Counting both the private and public sectors, strikes numbered over 5,000 per year and involved an average of 2.5 million workers, with more than 3 million on strike in both 1970 and 1971. The trend penetrated places where walkouts had earlier been rare or entirely unknown, and not only in the public sector. In 1969, singers, musicians, and dancers struck New York's Metropolitan Opera Company. Book publishers saw their first strike since the 1930s when Harper & Row office employees walked out in 1974. In San Francisco's Chinatown, garment workers broke another long truce, striking the Jung Sai company in 1975. Higher pay was the most common strike demand, as military spending fueled inflation in living costs. But many strikes concerned issues of power, like union recognition and management prerogatives on the shop floor.

Women's battles for union recognition could be especially hard-fought, perhaps because employers were especially loath to be bested by "girls." In Detroit, clerical workers struck Fruehauf Trailer for six months in 1969–70; operatives at the Oneita Knitting Mills in rural South Carolina stayed out for six months in 1973; women played leading roles in the long struggle to unionize the J.P. Stevens textile mills in Roanoke Rapids, North Carolina, where workers began organizing in 1963, voted in the Amalgamated Clothing and Textile Workers Union (ACTWU) in an NLRB election held in 1974, and did not get their first contract until 1980. Some 4,000 Mexican American garment workers in El Paso, Texas, struck Farah Manufacturing from May 1972 into March 1974 in an epic battle for recognition of their ACTWU local. They won with the help of a Farah boycott backed by the AFL-CIO, a national network of community and campus activists, and overseas unions as far away as Sweden and Hong Kong.

If sexism reinforced employers' resistance to unionism, involvement in an organizing drive helped to liberate workingwomen from multiple constraints. Looking back at the end of the 1970s, one Farah striker told an interviewer: "For years I wouldn't do anything without asking my husband's permission. . . . Of course I don't do this anymore. . . . I was able to begin to stand up for myself, and I began to feel that I should be accepted for the person that I am."[39] Another Farah striker recalled, "I was a very insecure person way back then. I felt that I was inferior to my supervisors, who were at that time only Anglo. None of this affects me anymore. I have learned that I am an equal."[40] Crystal Lee Sutton, a rank-and-file leader of the campaign to unionize J.P. Stevens—and the inspiration for the popular movie *Norma Rae*—identified the ACTWU organizer Eli Zivkovitch as the first man she encountered who had modern ideas about gender, "like realizing that women had more worth in this world than just being a sex object. That women had brains and that they should use those brains. It was okay for women to do so-called men's work."[41] Which in this case meant organizing a union.

The most famous battle over managerial prerogatives was a strike by UAW Local 1112 at the General Motors complex in Lordstown, Ohio, in March 1972. Virtually all of the strikers were in their late teens or twenties, many had college experience, and a good portion had served in Vietnam. Their strike targeted the latest trend in industrial management: paramilitary shop discipline to enforce unprecedented production quotas. Though the strike lasted just three weeks and ended in a draw, it made national headlines as a youth revolt against dehumanizing work and struck a deeply responsive chord among the mostly young workers on the front lines of automated speedup.

Local 1112's president Gary Bryner said of the strikers, "They just want to be treated with dignity. That's not asking a hell of a lot."[42] To the extent that dignity meant simple justice and respect, the same could be said of all working people's insurgencies on the job and elsewhere. But in this era, demands for dignity came from so many different directions that they added up to a veritable revolution.

Backlash

In October 1974, a special issue of *Business Week* lamented the sense of entitlement that drove social unrest. The editorial declared, "Some people will obviously have to do with less. . . . Yet it will be a hard pill for many Americans to swallow—the idea of doing with less so that big business can have more."[43] To get its way, corporate America had launched a collective assault on what one task force called the "excess of democracy."[44] By the end of the decade, demands that working-class communities tighten their belts came from Washington as well as Wall Street. In 1979, Paul Volcker—newly installed as chairman of the Federal Reserve—told Congress that, "The standard of living of the average American has to decline."[45] A majority in both the House and the Senate most definitely agreed.

A chorus of business-friendly "experts" on public policy declared that the federal War on Poverty had at last been won. In fact, it had scarcely made a dent. The proportion of families living below the official poverty line dropped from about 11 percent in 1967 to 10 percent in 1973, but 23 million Americans still lived in poverty, including 10 percent of whites, 22 percent of Latinos, and 33 percent of black America. President Nixon nevertheless decided in 1973 to shut down the Office of Economic Opportunity, and the many community projects it had supported lost their funding.

The federal cuts had especially harsh consequences in cities, where business leaders instigated reductions in public services. In New York City investment bankers staged a coup by refusing to underwrite municipal bonds unless they could dictate the city's budget. A 1975 law drafted by businessmen transferred budgetary power from elected officials to an Emergency Financial Control Board authorized to remove officials who defied its edicts. By the time the board disbanded in 1978, New York City had laid off 25,000 public workers and gutted spending on schools, hospitals, sanitation, mass transit, libraries, parks, and recreation.

Reduced services followed tax cuts in cities and states around the country. The cuts were often engineered by business interests. In the late 1970s, businessmen from California to Massachusetts funded groups agitating for lower property taxes, directing their appeals at white homeowners who were all too ready to believe that the government was giving black and Latino communities too much money and attention. When tax cuts were voted in, big investors in commercial real estate reaped the lion's share of savings, and the poorest neighborhoods experienced the largest cuts in public services.

Sixties-style community organizing receded under the new regimes. Urban infrastructures crumbled first and worst in the predominantly black and Latino neighborhoods that had been on the front lines of protest. Keeping a family safe and healthy in these neighborhoods now required so much extra work and worry that most people, especially women, could take on little more. The diminished cadre of activists scrambled to create substitutes for defunded programs and services. Old coalitions faded as neighborhoods vied for shrinking resources, and more and more white families fled to the suburbs. Community sympathy for public workers and their unions sharply declined, making it almost impossible for them to resist layoffs, speedups, and the erosion of wages and benefits.

Workers in the private sector also lost ground. President Nixon tried to control inflation with a wage and price freeze instituted in 1971. The freeze on prices was widely ignored, inflation persisted, real wages were not just stagnant but falling by 1973, and corporate pressures on the federal government grew ever more intense. The Business Roundtable, founded in 1972 by the heads of General Motors, U.S. Steel, and other giant corporations, coordinated a national drive to control the legislative process. Corporate political action committees multiplied from 89 in 1974 to nearly 800 by 1978, and they poured massive sums into campaign financing as well as lobbying, investing in Republicans and Democrats alike. The investments paid off: during the recession of 1974–75, the federal government abandoned its usual attempts to stimulate the economy; instead, it cut spending. Unemployment soared to levels unseen since the end of the Great Depression—8.5 percent nationally and more than five times higher among young black and Latino workers. Strike activity diminished until the economy recovered in 1976.

Business's political offensive took aim at a labor movement racked by internal divisions since the advent of the sixties. The AFL-CIO Executive Council refused to endorse the March on Washington in 1963. The Mississippi AFL-CIO's support for desegregation cost its unions about a third of their membership between 1960 and 1966. Competition between the United Farm Workers and the Teamsters reverberated beyond agriculture; in 1975, Teamsters headquarters disbanded Local 888 in San Francisco after its chief officer joined a UFW picket line at a Safeway supermarket. Some 200 black and Puerto Rican labor leaders denounced New York City's United Federation of Teachers for its strike against community control of public schools in the fall of 1968.

Many thousands of workers brought complaints against unions to the Equal Employment Opportunity Commission (EEOC) established by the Civil Rights Act. The building trades repeatedly promised to desegregate but made negligible progress except when the government required integrated work crews on federally funded projects. Industrial unions drew almost as many EEOC complaints as the building trades. Feminists from Steelworkers NOW—a union caucus with loose ties to the National Organization for Women—joined black and Latino men in a lawsuit charging discrimination by the steel industry and the United Steelworkers. A 1974 settlement brokered by the EEOC set new rules for transfer, training, and promotion and obliged the union along with nine major steel companies to pay $30 million in back wages to groups disadvantaged under the old rules.

Divisions over Vietnam were especially acrimonious. Most union leaders supported the war. The AFL-CIO expanded international operations with the Asian American Free Labor Institute (AAFLI), founded in 1968 to aid the corrupt but anti-communist Vietnamese Confederation of Labor. Frustrated by George Meany's intransigence on the war, Walter Reuther took the UAW out of the AFL-CIO in 1968 and joined with the Teamsters in an Alliance for Labor Action. The alliance disappeared after Reuther's death in an airplane crash in 1970.

The Nixon administration prodded organized labor to attack the antiwar movement. In May 1970, as activists across the country were protesting the fatal shootings of student demonstrators at Kent State University in Ohio, conservative union leaders worked with White House operatives to orchestrate shows of support for the war. In New York City, these initiatives included a riot by construction workers, who beat protestors gathered on Wall Street, stormed City Hall to raise the American flag that stood at half-mast in honor of the dead at Kent State, and charged onto the nearby campus of Pace College, where they smashed windows and assaulted students. Peter Brennan, president of the New York City Building Trades Council and an especially vocal supporter of Nixon's policies was later rewarded with an appointment to the president's cabinet as secretary of labor.

The AFL-CIO made no presidential endorsement in 1972. The building trades and maritime affiliates led a Labor for Nixon campaign. Most industrial and public-employee unions joined with the United Farm Workers and the Coalition of Black Trade Unionists in supporting the liberal antiwar Democrat George McGovern.

The Cold War would guide the AFL-CIO's foreign policy for many years to come. In Chile, where the CIA helped General Augusto Pinochet overthrow the popularly elected socialist Salvador Allende in 1973, the AFL-CIO's American Institute for Free Labor Development (AIFLD) ran training programs for the truckers whose strike in 1972 inaugurated the CIA's destabilization of the Chilean economy. AIFLD also trained the maritime union leaders who gave Pinochet's soldiers the names of labor activists to add to their death lists. Such operations remained cloaked in secrecy, more to shield AFL-CIO leaders from critics at home than to fool anyone in Chile. In 1977, the AFL-CIO expanded its European operations by starting the Free Trade Union Institute to undermine socialist and communist unions in post-fascist Spain and Portugal.

Union democracy became an increasingly explosive issue during the long strike wave. Many of the strikes were wildcats, contesting the authority of employers and labor officials alike. In April 1970, Teamsters in the long-haul trucking industry rejected a new contract signed by the union's president and shut down the industry in a wildcat action that stretched from Los Angeles to New Hampshire. In May a thousand information operators at New York Telephone defied their union's orders and abandoned their switchboards to enforce demands for higher pay and more sick days. In June rebellious UMW members in Pennsylvania, Ohio, and West Virginia staged an unauthorized walkout to protest inadequate hospital and pension benefits and lax enforcement of the Mine Safety Act. In August 1973, UAW staffers wielding baseball bats escorted union members to work during a wildcat strike over poor safety conditions at Chrysler's Mack Avenue stamping plant in Detroit. Following the Arab-Israeli War of October 1973, 2,000 members of an ad hoc Arab Workers Caucus in the Detroit UAW organized a one-day strike against the union's investments in Israeli government bonds. In 1974, Mexican and Mexican American members of the Steelworkers violated directives from the union and struck for higher pay at Superior Fireplace in Fullerton, California, and against speedup at the Kennecott mines in Bayard, New Mexico. In July 1976, Chicana cannery workers in San Jose, California, struck against a contract negotiated by Teamsters Local 679.

Wildcats were instigated by or gave birth to dissident union committees and pressure groups. For more than six years before the San Jose strike, the Cannery Workers Committee had been pushing for rank-and-file participation and bilingual meetings in Local 679. The Superior Fireplace strike was supported by the Comité Obrero en Defensa de Indocumentados en Lucha and the Centro de Acción Autónoma-Hermandad General de Trabajadores, both of them organizations that defended Mexican workers' rights. After the wildcat strike by postal workers in 1970, the "Outlaw" committee led by Vietnam veterans organized in bulk-mail facilities in northern New Jersey. Teamsters United Rank and File, which started in Toledo, Ohio, after the wildcat strike of 1970, soon fell apart; but Teamsters for a Decent Contract, organized by long-haul drivers in 1975, became Teamsters for a Democratic Union the next year and began a long campaign to reform the union. Strikers who had their union's blessings sometimes formed independent committees too; the Farah strike, for example, generated Unidad Para Siempre, a rank-and-file effort to build a more militant and democratic local.

Like their counterparts in the Teamsters, activists in the United Steelworkers organized against bad contracts. In 1973 the Steelworkers' president, I.W. Abel, signed the no-strike Experimental Negotiations Agreement (ENA) with the major steel companies. Ed Sadlowski, president of the union's District 31 covering Chicago and northwestern Indiana, joined with other union officers to found Steel Workers Fight Back, both to dump the ENA and to alter the union's rules to give members the right to vote on contracts. To these ends, Fight Back concentrated on electing Sadlowski president of the Steelworkers, but the campaign failed to reach out to the many locals beyond basic steel and to rank-and-file activists challenging racial and gender inequities. In 1977, Sadlowski lost to Lloyd McBride, Abel's choice for successor, by about 9 percentage points.

One reform caucus took over a national union. Pennsylvania miner and black lung activist Jock Yablonski had challenged the notoriously corrupt Tony Boyle for the post of UMW president. On Boyle's orders gunmen murdered Yablonski and his wife and daughter on New Year's Eve 1969. At the funeral, mourners started Miners for Democracy, which won the 1973 election with a slate headed by Arnold Miller, a retired miner and leader of the Black Lung Association. Following this victory, Miners for Democracy disbanded—too early, as it turned out. The new leadership made little difference in the mines and wildcats resumed; the biggest took place in the summer of 1976, when 150,000 miners—almost every UMW member east of the Mississippi River—walked out to protest injunctions against wildcat strikers in West Virginia.

The strike wave receded in 1978, broken by an unemployment rate that stubbornly refused to fall below 6 percent even after the recession's end. Democrats had strengthened their control of Congress following Nixon's disgrace and fall in the Watergate scandal of 1974, and Democrat Jimmy Carter had taken the White House from incumbent caretaker Gerald Ford in 1976, but the AFL-CIO's political agenda ran into a business lobbying campaign that killed both labor-law reform and an increase in the minimum wage. Corporate America meanwhile scored several major accomplishments: cuts in federal aid to cities, deregulation of the airline and trucking industries, and tax reforms that lowered rates on personal income and capital gains and increased credits for investment.

Even so, U.S. corporations increasingly moved investments abroad. Between 1970 and 1980, their assets in other countries multiplied fivefold; and by the latter year almost a sixth of their profits came from overseas. In addition to buying out or buying into foreign companies, they opened entirely new facilities outside the United States, sometimes in order to improve their access to natural resources or international markets but more often than not in a continuing quest for cheap labor. The places that most attracted U.S. investment were Hong Kong, Taiwan, South Korea, Singapore, Malaysia, Thailand, the Philippines and, especially, Mexico. In 1966, the Mexican government inaugurated its Border Industrialization Program by opening an industrial park in Ciudad Juárez, just south of El Paso, Texas. Fourteen years later, plants operating under the program numbered more than 600 and could be found all along the U.S.-Mexican border.

In July 1978, surveying the wreckage that runaway factories had left behind, the UAW's president Douglas Fraser publicly announced his departure from the Labor-Management Group, which brought together leaders of the country's largest unions and corporations. His open letter of resignation charged that "leaders of the business community, with few exceptions, have chosen to wage a one-sided class war—a war against working people, the unemployed, the poor, the minorities, the very young and the very old, and even many in the middle-class."[46] In October 1978, Fraser hosted a conference attended by thirty unions—both independents and AFL-CIO affiliates—and seventy-one allied organizations that ranged from the NAACP, the National Farmers Union, and the Women's Political Caucus, to groups working on environmental issues, tax reform, and consumer protection. In January 1979, this "coalition of coalitions" founded the Progressive Alliance.[47]

The alliance fizzled; its leaders never agreed on a presidential candidate. Meanwhile, bad investments and worse marketing strategies had nearly ruined the Chrysler Corporation by 1979. The banks that came to the rescue demanded concessions from the UAW—mainly, a two-year wage freeze. Fraser lobbied for the package and joined Chrysler's board of directors to help restructure the company. Its unionized workforce fell by nearly half, to 57,000, and older plants like Dodge Main closed.

George Meany retired in 1979 and chose Lane Kirkland as his successor. After a brief stint in the merchant marine during the Second World War, Kirkland had trained for the U.S. Foreign Service, then taken an AFL-CIO staff position in which he did research on pensions and Social Security. Meany had made him a special assistant in 1960 and elevated him to secretary-treasurer of the AFL-CIO in 1969. Kirkland had spent the next decade cultivating relations with politicians and intellectuals who favored an all-out war against communism. The AFL-CIO's executive council unanimously ratified his ascent to the presidency, proving that labor conservatism had survived the sixties with its commitment to the Cold War intact and its hegemony in the AFL-CIO unscathed. But the world had changed irrevocably, and even conservative unionism was not at all secure in the new order.

11

Hard Times

In the presidential race of 1980, the Republicans' Ronald Reagan, a retired movie actor and former governor of California, beat the incumbent Jimmy Carter by more than 8 million votes. The Carter administration had entered the election beset by crises. In 1979, U.S. client regimes collapsed in Iran and Nicaragua, the Soviet Union sent troops to prop up its own clients in Afghanistan, and Iranian radicals seized the U.S. embassy in Tehran, taking fifty Americans hostage. The U.S. economy meanwhile entered a period of acute "stagflation"—a recession coupled with rising prices and sky-high interest rates. In addition, Carter oversaw deregulation of the airline, trucking, oil, and gas industries: all of this worrisome to unions in manufacturing, where mounting costs for transportation and fuel could only accelerate the trend toward corporate disinvestment in the United States. With all of this in mind, President William Winpisinger of the International Association of Machinists mobilized an effort to dump Carter as the Democrats' nominee and replace him with Senator Edward Kennedy, a more reliably liberal option. Rank-and-file union members generally liked the idea, but most union leaders—along with other party insiders—bent over backward not to offend the incumbent, and the Dump Carter–Draft Kennedy movement went down in defeat. The Republicans meanwhile expanded their appeal. To their usual base of businessmen who still resented New Deal reforms, they added a new coalition of white voters eager for economic relief through reduced taxes, frustrated by the U.S. loss in Vietnam, and resentful of the new rights won by women, gay men and lesbians, and people of color.

The AFL-CIO endorsed and campaigned for Carter, but this made little difference. Many people eligible to vote did not go to the polls at all; the voter participation rate fell from nearly 70 percent in 1964 to less than 60 percent in 1980. Over half of blue-collar voters and 43 percent of voters from union households picked Reagan, and the Republicans took control of the Senate for the first time since the election of 1952.

The new administration quickly established itself as an archenemy of militant labor, suppressing a national strike and destroying the union that launched it. The union was PATCO, the Professional Air Traffic Controllers Organization, whose members worked for the Federal Aviation Administration (FAA). Founded in 1968 as part of the surge in organizing by public employees, PATCO had earned a reputation for taking strong stands on labor conditions, air safety, and its members' right to strike, despite the fact that the federal government had long ago outlawed strikes by its own employees. Itching for a showdown, Reagan appointees at the FAA stonewalled in contract negotiations with PATCO in spring 1981. At the end of July, the union conducted a strike-authorization vote, and on August 3, about 13,000 air traffic controllers stopped work. Four hours into the strike President Reagan declared on national television that controllers who did not return to work within forty-eight hours would permanently lose their jobs. On August 5, he not only fired 11,345 workers who had defied the deadline but also banned them from federal employment for the rest of their lives. Burdened with heavy fines, PATCO soon went bankrupt, and on October 22 the Federal Labor Relations Authority took away its certification to represent workers. When President Bill Clinton took office in 1993, he lifted the lifetime ban on the strikers' federal employment, but PATCO never revived. Looking back on the union's demise, Donald Devine, Reagan's director of personnel management, stressed its ramifications beyond the public sector: "American business leaders were given a lesson in managerial leadership that they could not and did not ignore."[1]

Although they anticipated these ripple effects, labor leaders seemed unable to come up with a coherent counterstrategy. By the time Reagan lowered the hammer on PATCO, the AFL-CIO had already announced a "Solidarity Day" march and rally in Washington, and affiliated unions turned out almost a half-million members and supporters on September 19, 1981. They cheered the PATCO strikers, but their unions did not coordinate a fight to defend the union. When some leaders proposed nationwide actions, the AFL-CIO's president Lane Kirkland declared, "I personally do not think that the trade union movement should undertake anything that would represent punishing, injuring or inconveniencing the public at large for the sins or transgressions of the Reagan administration." Instead, the AFL-CIO focused on calling in favors from the Democrats it had helped to elect, pressing them to mount more vigorous resistance to Republicans' domestic agenda. In subsequent years, Solidarity Days became congressional lobbying blitzes—and Reagan's transgressions injured more and more of the public at large.

When it came to foreign policy, moreover, the AFL-CIO embraced Reagan's revival of the crusade against communism. Lane Kirkland spearheaded a high-profile initiative: support for the Polish labor union known as Solidarność ("Solidarity"), which emerged among shipyard workers in the fall of 1980 and recruited over one-third of Poland's labor force by fall 1981. This marked the first time since World War II that that a country aligned with the Soviet Union produced a labor movement that Communists did not control, and Poland's government tried mightily to suppress it. Kirkland countered by sending money, attending Solidarność's national congress in Gdansk in September–October 1981, and naming the AFL-CIO's Solidarity Day in honor of the Polish movement. Accompanying Kirkland to Gdansk was Irving Brown, described in the AFL-CIO's press release as the federation's "European representative"[2] but exposed more than a decade earlier as an operative for the CIA. Applauding Kirkland's work for Solidarność, the *Wall Street Journal* advised readers not to undermine the project by making an issue of the CIA's involvement.

Other AFL-CIO contributions to the Cold War were less public affairs, run quietly if not covertly by the federation's international institutes. In El Salvador, the American Institute for Free Labor Development (AIFLD) promoted land reform to defuse peasant support for leftist insurgents and paid union leaders to join the pro-government labor federation. After a U.S. military invasion overthrew Grenada's left-wing government in October 1983, AIFLD trained union leaders friendly toward the new regime aligned with the United States; and in 1984 the institute set up a labor federation allied with the government of the Haitian dictator Jean-Claude Duvalier. In Angola, the African-American Labor Center (AALC) joined with the U.S. government and the right-wing Heritage Foundation to back the anti-Soviet faction in a long-running civil war, and in South Africa, the AALC embraced the United Workers' Union of South Africa, which colluded with employers to undermine more progressive labor federations and secretly received funding from the apartheid government's security police. In the Philippines, the Asian American Free Labor Institute (AAFLI) backed the Trades Union Congress against the Kilusang Mayo Uno ("May First Labor Movement") that campaigned against the dictator Ferdinand Marcos and for the removal of U.S. military bases from the archipelago. In Fiji, the AAFLI paid labor unions to oppose the nation's ban on nuclear weapons. In 1983, the Free Trade Union Institute (FTUI)—established six years earlier to influence European labor affairs—began to administer U.S. grants to unions worldwide. Mostly, however, the FTUI now focused on eastern Europe, funding anti-communist unions and sponsoring opponents of the independent General Confederation of Trade Unions that emerged in the Soviet Union as it disintegrated in the early 1990s. The federal government financed virtually all of these efforts. In response to an inquiry from the U.S. Senate, the general accounting office reported, for example, that in the period 1980–94, some 87 percent of AIFLD's budget came directly from the government—the United States Agency for International Development—while another 10 percent came from the National Endowment for Democracy, a nonprofit organization created by Congress in the Reagan years and bankrolled by Congress ever since.

To judge by the decorations it handed out, the U.S. government felt profoundly grateful for the AFL-CIO's service in the Cold War. In 1989, President George H.W. Bush selected Lane Kirkland for a Presidential Citizens Medal. His fellow honorees that year included the right-wing pundit William F. Buckley, the Dixiecrat-turned-Republican senator Strom Thurmond, and assorted members of the national security establishment. In 1994, President Bill Clinton gave Kirkland an even higher award: the Presidential Medal of Freedom, which Reagan had bestowed on Irving Brown six years earlier. None of this benefitted the U.S. labor movement or the nation's working class, whose joint fortunes steadily declined.

Lean and Mean

The "Reagan Revolution" was not entirely revolutionary; for the most part, it intensified trends already under way. More businessmen and their friends came to Washington, and they brought with them more business habits. Some simply looted the public treasury. At the U.S. Postal Service's board of governors, for example, the newly appointed chairman steered consulting contracts to his friends while the new vice chairman took bribes from contractors. More damaging to the public welfare were the perfectly legal tax reforms that slashed rates on capital gains and corporate profits, reduced income taxes on high-income households by more than half by the time Reagan left office, and gave the masses of working families merely nominal relief. In fact, nearly half of all taxpayers saw their spendable incomes shrink, with the decrease in federal taxes more than offset by increases in state taxes, local taxes, and payroll taxes for Social Security and Medicare.

Businessmen continued to call for greater freedom to do as they pleased, and Reaganites happily obliged. Deregulation spread to the banking and communications industries. Federal enforcement of safety, environmental, and consumer-protection laws receded as the White House cut agency budgets and installed administrators hostile to the agencies' missions. In 1983, when three members of the U.S. Commission on Civil Rights complained about lax enforcement of anti-discrimination laws, the White House fired them. In one respect, however, the government grew more heavy-handed than ever; thanks largely to harsher penalties for nonviolent offenses, the number of prison and jail inmates in the United States climbed from 474,368 in 1980 to 1,148,702 in 1990, with African American communities disproportionately affected by the rush to incarcerate.

Another pillar of the Reagan program was steep reductions in federal disbursements for social welfare—not just cash grants to needy households but also school lunches, services for the homeless, and much more. Grants under the Aid to Families with Dependent Children program fell from an average $477 a month in 1980 to $374 in 1992, and applicants for disability pensions or food stamps were increasingly likely to find themselves denied. According to Reaganites, these cuts would eliminate deficit spending by the federal government, but that promise never panned out. Massive increases in military spending outstripped the cuts to social programs, the deficits rose year by year, and the national debt ballooned—by 1985, more than 12 percent of annual federal spending went to interest payments.

Nor did Reaganites' promises come true in the private sector, where deregulation and lower corporate taxes would supposedly make the whole nation rich. In reality, wages continued to stagnate, for business did not spend its windfalls as the administration's experts had theorized. Instead of opening new operations, companies were increasingly likely to invest in other companies, buying shares in rival firms, diversifying to protect themselves against losses in a single industry, or just shopping for profits. Corporate ownership was changing as well. More and more, corporate investment involved money that had been borrowed, and the lenders—banks, private equity firms, and other financial institutions—demanded mammoth returns on the money they had in play. A perfectly profitable operation might be shut down simply because financiers suspected they could do better elsewhere or make more by selling off a company's assets than by putting them to work. By the mid-1980s, for example, major airlines such as Eastern and Frontier were collapsing under piles of debt and starting to sell off their fleets. When manufacturing facilities closed their doors, it was usually because their corporate owners had decided to ship production overseas. In 1982, General Electric shuttered its most profitable small-appliance operation, which produced Hotpoint irons in Ontario, California. About a thousand members of the United Electrical Workers—most of them black or Latino women—lost their jobs as GE shifted Hotpoint production to Mexico, Singapore, and Brazil. Business services relocated too. By 1982, jobs in data entry were moving to Ireland and Barbados; six years later Filipino, Indian, and Scottish contractors were processing credit card slips, supermarket coupons, insurance and hospital records, and book manuscripts for U.S. companies. Still, manufacturing accounted for the vast majority of jobs shipped overseas.

That trend combined with others to restructure the American workforce. Changes in its gender composition were especially striking. Stagnant wages propelled married women into the labor market at rates never before seen in peacetime; in household after household, their earnings provided the essential counterbalance to shortfalls in men's wages. Larger numbers of women were raising families on their own, moreover. In the mid-1980s, about 11 percent of the nation's children were living in single-parent households, virtually always with their mothers. By the mid-1990s, that figure topped 25 percent, and over 60 percent of mothers with children under six had paying jobs. More and more families thus had to purchase prepared meals, childcare, home nursing, and other goods and services traditionally provided by housewives.

The service sector expanded to meet these new demands and expanded further as corporate bureaucracies and distribution networks grew more elaborate. As employment grew in services, it flattened or declined in agriculture, mining, and manufacturing. These job losses resulted from automation and other labor-saving innovations and from expanding imports as well as from restructured production chains and runaway shops. Between 1979 and 1993, the number of U.S. jobs in services increased by 38 percent, while jobs in the production of everything from food to fuel to manufactured items declined by 12 percent.

Many of the jobs lost were union jobs; most of the jobs gained were low paid and nonunion. Against that backdrop, economic arrangements that had bolstered the postwar middle class steadily disintegrated. In 1980, 71 percent of full-time employees at large and mid-sized companies had medical insurance fully funded by the employer; by 1993, just 37 percent enjoyed such benefits. Downsizing and closures destroyed expectations of continuous employment over a lifetime. Home mortgage foreclosures measured economic distress; between 1980 and 1995, they tripled to over 450,000 a year. More jobs became part-time, temporary, or both. From 1970 to 1990, as total employment increased by 54 percent, involuntary part-time employment increased 121 percent and temporary employment 21 percent. By 1993, Manpower Incorporated—which supplied a host of employers with low-wage contingent workers—had replaced General Motors (GM) as the country's largest private employer.

Many workers in the new jobs were themselves new to the United States. While the numbers of arrivals from Europe and Canada held fairly steady over the course of the 1970s and 1980s, immigration from Asia and Latin America nearly doubled and the inflow from Africa more than tripled. Many of the newcomers—those from Vietnam, Cambodia, and El Salvador, for example—were refugees from the consequences of U.S. foreign policy. Though largely concentrated in the service sector, immigrants also became a significant portion of the workforce in low-wage manufacturing sectors that did not provide job security. By the early 1980s, for example, immigrant women were 40 percent of employees in the electronic assembly plants of North Carolina, the Route 128 corridor in Massachusetts, and California's Silicon Valley. As one employer in Silicon Valley told a researcher about his plant's operatives: "Beats me how they survive. But . . . just how many options have they got? We take advantage of this."[3]

Job scarcity made it all the easier to take advantage. Toward the end of 1982, the rate of unemployment shot up to over 10 percent and stayed there for close to a year. It did not drop below 6 percent until the fall of 1987, and by 1991 it was once again on the rise. Joblessness spread unevenly by industry, race, and geography. In 1981, a third of all autoworkers and half of all steelworkers were unemployed. Since the last hired were the first fired, the history of racist hiring practices in both auto and steel made the layoffs especially damaging to black communities. In Detroit, for example, unemployment among black youth reached 70 percent in 1982. Among the employed, working conditions sometimes recalled scenes from the Gilded Age. In early 1981, while Reagan blamed high unemployment on women's insistence on going out to work, a reporter from the *New York Times* visited Union City, New Jersey, to interview an Ecuadoran mother of two who lived in a windowless basement and worked there for twelve hours a day, seven days a week, sewing skirts for 20¢ apiece.

In addition to damaging working conditions, high unemployment undercut challenges to racial and gender discrimination in the labor market. Sometimes of their own free will and other times under court order, union leaders had generally accepted affirmative action in hiring and training. But when it came to layoffs, they insisted on strict seniority—a longstanding union principle that in this case threatened to erase many of the gains made by workers of color in the 1960s and 1970s. Women's integration into skilled trades also hit a wall. In 1978 the Carter administration had adopted statistical goals for female employment on federally funded building projects; women were supposed to get 6.9 percent of the jobs as of the early 1980s. By 1989, however, women were nearing that goal in just one construction trade—painting, where they constituted about 6 percent of the workforce. In other trades, they had not gone above 2 percent, and in some cases women's presence was so small that the government did not bother to report the numbers. For the most part, federal agencies had stopped pressuring employers and unions to undo workplace discrimination on the basis of race or sex, and a series of judicial decisions handed down in the 1980s had made it harder for workers to win lawsuits that targeted discrimination.

In some communities, layoffs fueled an explicitly racist nationalism that blamed job losses not on the corporations that cut their workforces but on unfair competition from Japanese firms that had penetrated U.S. markets. "Buy American" became a favorite union slogan, but things did not end there. In Pontiac, Michigan—home to a faltering GM plant—a Chevrolet dealer devised a new publicity gimmick in the summer of 1980; supplying sledgehammers, he invited visitors to his car lot to pound an imported Toyota into the ground. Before long, smashing Japanese cars was a popular sport in many auto-producing towns. The United Auto Workers promoted its spread as labor-friendly Democrats engaged in Japan-bashing of their own. During a debate in the U.S. House of Representatives, Congressman John Dingle of Dearborn, Michigan, blamed the U.S. auto industry's woes on the machinations of "little yellow people";

Tip O'Neill of Massachusetts—speaker of the House—vowed to "fix the Japanese like they've never been fixed before."[4] In June 1982, in the Detroit suburb of Highland Park, hate led to murder. Two white men—one a plant superintendent for Chrysler and the other his out-of-work stepson—hollered racial epithets as they took a baseball bat to the head of Vincent Chin, a Chinese American they had mistaken for Japanese. Chin died four days later. His assailants were found guilty of manslaughter in a county court, which sentenced them to three years of probation.[5]

Republicans' expertise at playing the race card for their own purposes meanwhile undermined organized labor's political clout. While the AFL-CIO strongly backed the Democrats' Walter Mondale in the presidential election of 1984, Ronald Reagan won by nearly 17 million votes, and his share of votes from members of union households rose to 46 percent. A longtime opponent of civil rights legislation and raconteur of fantastical stories about African Americans' getting rich on welfare benefits, Reagan won the support of legions of white workers fearful about their children's futures as well as their own. His successor, George H.W. Bush, also presented himself as a defender of white America, most famously by running a campaign ad that featured a black man convicted of raping a white woman and attributed the incident to Democrats' coddling of criminals.

Still, the Reagan-Bush years saw some legislative progress for working people. In 1989 Congress passed a ninety-cent increase in the federal minimum wage, lifting it from $3.35 to $4.25 an hour as of April 1991. To stay even with inflation since the previous increase—which took place in 1981—the minimum should have risen to $5.05; but an inadequate increase certainly beat no increase at all. Much more significant was passage of the Americans with Disabilities Act (ADA), which became law in July 1990. Banning workplace discrimination against people with physical or mental disabilities, the ADA etched into federal law protections that unions had long sought in the contracts they negotiated, and the AFL-CIO was a prominent member of the coalition of organizations that lobbied for the act—a reform that corporations and business associations vigorously opposed. Labor lobbyists and others pushed successfully for the inclusion of protections for people with HIV-AIDS and those addicted to alcohol or drugs. The ADA was the biggest legislative victory for civil rights since the Voting Rights Act of 1965.

The Reagan-Bush years also saw a few advances for labor progressives seeking alternatives in electoral politics. Starting in 1981, rank-and-file unionists supported the socialist Bernie Sanders in four successful races for the mayoralty of Burlington, Vermont. When Sanders ran for Congress in 1988, the state AFL-CIO worked instead for the mainstream Democrat, who came in a distant third but with enough votes so that the Republican beat Sanders by a nose. Then, in 1990, union leaders lined up behind Sanders, who became the first independent socialist member of Congress in more than sixty years. In national elections, the most promising year was 1988, when the civil rights activist Jesse Jackson entered the Democratic Party's presidential primaries, where he was the only African American candidate and the only candidate running on an unabashedly pro-labor platform. The AFL-CIO made no endorsement, but Jackson's "Rainbow Coalition" got active support from unions with large numbers of black and Latino members—District 1199, for example, and the American

Federation of Government Employees—and from many black labor officials and activists from other unions. Jackson pulled 35 percent of the primary votes cast by members of union households. In the end, the party establishment closed ranks behind Governor Michael Dukakis of Massachusetts, and the Rainbow Coalition dissipated as an organized political force. It was one thing to challenge business as usual in a single city or congressional district and another thing to do it on a national scale.

Arguably, the 1980s were precisely the time to try something new, for the Reaganites could scarcely have been more hostile toward American unions. Until 1983, the administration failed to fill two vacant seats on the National Labor Relations Board, whose backlog of cases grew. When the appointments finally materialized, the corporate lawyer Donald Dotson became the NLRB's chairman, and on his watch it issued a string of decisions against unions. Some set entirely new precedents. In 1984, for example, the board ruled that employers need not negotiate with unions over plant closures, okayed the transfer of union work to nonunion contractors, and reversed decades-old doctrine to make it easier for employers to fire strikers. The Dotson-era NLRB upheld union charges in 55 percent of the cases, down from 85 percent in the 1970s, and some unions waited five years for a final decision. During the Reagan years, moreover, federal agencies routinely ignored the longstanding rule that contractors doing business with the government should pay "prevailing wages," which previous administrations had usually interpreted to mean union scale. In the early 1980s, the military and other departments stopped enforcing this requirement, and by mid-decade, nonunion contractors got almost all the work.

At the bargaining table, once-mighty unions found it impossible to score advances or even hold the line; concessions to employers became the order of the day. Concessions bargaining emerged in response to threats that an operation would shut down unless labor costs fell. Congress engineered the first big concessions agreement in the final year of the Carter administration, financing a rescue of the teetering Chrysler Corporation on the condition that the United Auto Workers would backpedal at the bargaining table. When rank and filers balked at the deal, UAW staffers billed it as the only option. As one told a Michigan local in 1981, "Those of you who don't want to take a wage cut, go out and find another job."[6] It was no idle threat; that same year, a Ford casting plant in Sheffield, Alabama, closed after workers there refused to accept a 50 percent cut in wages and benefits. But concessions developed their own competitive momentum. General Motors and Ford soon demanded concessions to match Chrysler's, the UAW agreed, and in 1982 the membership ratified contract modifications.

For employers, the logic of concessions went beyond efforts to contain payroll costs. In 1982, when *Business Week* surveyed corporate executives on the subject, 57 percent reported that they preferred concessions on work rules to wage cuts. Almost a fifth agreed with the statement, "Although we don't need concessions, we are taking advantage of the bargaining climate to ask for them."[7]

In the automobile industry, "flexibility" became the buzzword; management redesigned production to make it more malleable with regard to function, scheduling, and employment. Auto companies juggled just-in-time deliveries, adopted more standardized parts and processes, redistributed production to more competitive contractors, and constantly recalibrated as they devised new benchmarks for how cheaply and swiftly

production could take place. The best-known benchmark was Toyota's 57-second minute, which required that assembly workers stay in motion for 57 of every 60 seconds
they spent on the job. Traditionally, auto production had been calibrated to keep them
moving for 75 percent of the workday; Toyota now upped that to 95 percent, and other
auto companies quickly followed suit. Individual workers performed more tasks at a
faster pace. Factories continued to run round the clock, but contingent and part-time
employment increasingly replaced permanent full-time jobs. Another innovation in
the name of flexibility was management's demand that UAW locals compete with outside contractors. At Ford's facilities in Detroit, for example, locals accepted concessions rather than see work shipped to Toyo Kogyo, a Japanese firm in which Ford was
a major stockholder. By 1987, twelve of the twenty-seven locals at GM assembly plants
had agreed to speed up production, mostly by voiding work rules. Management called
the new regime "lean production," and a host of companies in meatpacking, communications, transportation, and other sectors adapted lean practices for their own use.

Steelworkers faced an especially harsh climate, as their industry was hit by
"dumping"—foreign companies' selling surplus production at or under cost—and
the steep costs of modernizing open-hearth furnaces to control air pollution. By
1982, steel mills in the United States were running at 40 percent of capacity, and
another 100,000 steel jobs had disappeared. At the bargaining sessions for that year's
Master Steel Agreement—the last industrywide contract in steel—the seven largest
companies demanded $6 billion in givebacks. The United Steelworkers consented to
$2.5 billion in cuts, as long as the companies would devote the savings to modern-
izing the mills; but the companies had entirely different plans. U.S. Steel diversified;
buying Marathon Oil and Texas Oil & Gas, it shed a third of its remaining capacity in
basic steel along with several fabricating and finishing mills. Armco shipped in semi-
finished steel produced overseas and shut down a Houston plant where union members
refused to process imported billets. In 1985, Wheeling-Pittsburgh Steel—owner of
six major facilities in Pennsylvania, West Virginia, and Ohio—filed for bankruptcy
and moved to cancel its union contract. In 1986, the same happened with the LTV
conglomerate, whose holdings in steel included Republic, Jones and Laughlin, and
Youngstown Sheet and Tube. When the Master Agreement ran out in summer 1986,
the union's negotiations with U.S. Steel—now known as USX—hit a wall, and 22,000
steelworkers engaged in a six-month work stoppage that the company called a strike
and the union called a lockout. In February 1987, just days after union members ratified a settlement that included wage concessions and the elimination of about 1,000
jobs, USX announced that it would close four of its steel plants and eliminate another
3,500 jobs. Mini-mills meanwhile proliferated; they used small electric arc furnaces
to make specialty items, mostly with nonunion labor.

By the mid-1980s, unions across the private sector had their backs against the wall.
In 1983, Continental Airlines replaced strikers with new hires; 12,000 drivers at the
Greyhound bus company took a 15 percent cut in pay and benefits after a seven-week
strike failed to keep buses off the road; and the Atari video game company shuttered
its U.S. assembly operations when the Glaziers and Glassworkers Union launched a
drive to organize the plant. In 1985, the Brotherhood of Maintenance of Way Employees and other railroad unions lost 2,000 jobs during a strike over combining positions

on the Maine Central Railroad and at the Portland Terminal. The next year brought more of the same. Over 150,000 members of the Communications Workers struck AT&T for almost a month, then settled for an agreement that provided modest raises in pay and benefits but also wiped out cost-of-living adjustments and made it easier for the company to restructure work and shed jobs. When flight attendants at Trans World Airlines went on strike over unequal pay, 5,000 lost their jobs, and the Supreme Court threw out a favorable settlement of their lawsuit about sex discrimination. At the Alcoa metals company, both the United Steelworkers and the Aluminum, Brick and Glass Workers called off strikes and accepted contracts that lowered pay and benefits. Major union contracts signed over the course of 1986 raised wages by an average of 1.2 percent; in manufacturing, the average was a 1.2 percent reduction—this midway through a decade that saw a cumulative inflation rate of almost 65 percent.

Much the same patterns prevailed as the 1980s wore on. At the end of 1986, Greyhound drivers launched another strike against reduced wages and benefits; settling with a new owner in February 1987, they accepted a decrease amounting to 22 percent. In Maine, the United Paperworkers, which had lost over 300 jobs during a 1986 strike at Boise Cascade, lost 1,200 more after the union shut down a sixteen-month strike at International Paper. In 1989, the unions representing pilots and flight attendants at Eastern Airlines ended an eight-month strike alongside co-workers in the International Association of Machinists. The company refused to rehire strikers and filed for bankruptcy. Over the course of this "lean and mean" decade, every Master Freight Agreement negotiated by the Teamsters covered fewer trucking companies than the agreement it replaced, and permitted more regional and local concessions. Lump-sum bonuses increasingly replaced raises, and more and more unions agreed to two-tier contracts that gave new hires lower pay and stingier benefits than the old-timers. Even the building trades unions—long regarded as the labor movement's aristocrats—felt the pinch. An ever-larger portion of major contractors operated as open shops, and an ever-smaller portion of construction workers were union members.

While job losses took a toll on unions' numerical strength in the private sector, so did concessions bargaining. As Tony Mazzocchi of the Oil, Chemical and Atomic Workers observed, "Workers can see you don't need a union card to hold up a white flag."[8] From 1980 to 1990, the total number of union members in the United States fell from about 20.1 million to 16.7 million, and the damage was even greater than these figures suggested, for they included the public sector, where unionism was still making fairly steady gains. Counting the private sector only, union membership fell by almost 28 percent, from 14.3 million to 10.3 million, and union density dropped from about 20 percent to a little under 12 percent.

More than fifty AFL-CIO affiliates now had fewer than 50,000 members and uncertain futures. Some union leaders thought mergers offered a solution. As one of the AFL-CIO's regional directors told the *Wall Street Journal* in 1985, "It's a hell of a lot quicker and cheaper to add members through a merger than it is to organize new members. . . . That's especially true when you're up against managements that will fight you tooth and nail."[9] During the 1980s, the AFL-CIO did indeed buttress its numbers by readmitting former affiliates, most notably the UAW in 1981 and the Teamsters in 1987. As individual unions shrank, however, they vied with one another to acquire new units, so mergers at that level could become a bitter business. Battles over independent associations of public employees were especially hard fought. For two years beginning in 1985, the American Federation of State, County and Municipal Employees (AFSCME) competed with National 1199, the Communications Workers, the Teamsters, and several other unions to absorb various groups of state employees in Ohio. AFSCME won many of these contests, but also lost some New Jersey locals to the Communications Workers and some Massachusetts locals to the Service Employees. Unions also competed in new organizing drives. In 1986, no fewer than nine unions—including the Steelworkers, the Communications Workers, the United Food and Commercial Workers, and AFSCME—sent organizers into a twenty-city campaign to unionize clerical workers employed by the Blue Cross-Blue Shield insurance network. The United Auto Workers, which already represented 3,000 Blue Cross clerks in Michigan, meanwhile organized clerical and technical workers at universities in the Boston area, and the Teamsters established a clerical-technical local at the University of Chicago. As these twists and turns indicate, the scramble for new members propelled many unions far beyond their original jurisdictions. The Service Employees absorbed the International Jewelry Workers in 1980; the Food and Commercial Workers took in the Barbers and Beauticians Union in 1982 and the Insurance Workers International Union in 1983. As of 1987, just 40 percent of the National Maritime Union's 25,000 members were deep-water sailors. In 1989, the Amalgamated Clothing and Textile Workers organized gravediggers employed by the Catholic Archdiocese of Los Angeles.

"The general state of labor in this country is vigorous, energetic," Lane Kirkland told the *New York Times* in 1986.[10] The view from the trenches looked considerably less rosy, but a growing cohort of local union officers, staffers, and activists, plus a few national leaders, was determined to meet the challenge. "There is something rising out there," said Jerry Tucker. Formerly an assistant regional director of the UAW's Region 5, Tucker was now helping to lead a "New Directions" movement inside the union. This initiative was one of many efforts to redirect a labor movement that seemed headed for the rocks.[11]

Fighting Back

The challenges to business as usual included resistance to concessions bargaining, innovative approaches to organizing the unorganized, experiments with new forms of community-labor alliances, and continuing efforts around causes that took center stage in the sixties: racial justice, women's liberation, gay and lesbian rights, and opposition to foreign policy that placed the crusade against communism above everything else. Running through all of this was commitment to the labor movement's internal reform. The challengers wanted more democracy in unions, more militancy on the part of labor leaders, and more effective deployment of resources. In short, the goal was revitalization, which much of the AFL-CIO's executive council seemed unable to imagine, let alone achieve.

Some unions adopted tactics reminiscent of the young CIO. The most successful of these efforts took place in UAW's Region 5, which covered eight south-central states from Missouri to Texas. In 1981, when Local 282 at Moog Automotive in St. Louis faced demands for concessions, the union devised an alternative to the strike that the company expected and was well prepared to crush. "Running the plant backwards," as they put it, the local's members worked without a contract, followed managerial directives to the letter, refused overtime, policed the plant for health and safety violations, gathered to demand on-the-spot remediation of unacceptable conditions, and formed a solidarity committee that organized informational picketing, lunch-break rallies, and public demonstrations.[12] Moog management retaliated with firings and suspensions, but workers stood firm and the solidarity committee soon included 100 of the plant's 500 workers. After six months, the company agreed to a contract that raised wages and benefits by more than a third and reinstated fired and suspended workers with back pay. Over the next few years, several other locals in Region 5 replicated 282's tactics and scored similar victories at the Schwitzer cooling-fan plant in Rolla, Missouri, and at the Bell helicopter and LTV-Vought aerospace plants in Dallas-Fort Worth. At LTV-Vought the struggle extended for fifteen months, from March 1984 through June 1985, and ended only after the union reached out to another UAW local at an LTV subsidiary in Indiana and set a strike deadline that coincided with the expiration of that local's contract.

Another long strike against concessions involved cannery workers in Watsonville, California, most of them Mexican American women. In 1985, two of the city's frozen-food processors—Watsonville Canning and Richard Shaw—demanded wage cuts and reductions in medical coverage. Three years earlier, Watsonville Canning had decreased wages; now it played leapfrog with Richard Shaw, each company seeking to undercut the other. The workers belonged to a notoriously inadequate union: Teamsters 912, one of several locals the International Brotherhood of Teamsters established in the late 1940s, as it forcibly replaced the left-led Food and Tobacco Workers in California's canneries. In 1982, the local's leaders had acceded to wage cuts with scarcely a complaint; this time, however, the companies were in for a fight. One difference was the presence of a radical caucus, composed mostly of Anglos and affiliated with the dissident network Teamsters for a Democratic Union (TDU). When workers at Watsonville Canning and Richard Shaw went on strike in September 1985, the TDU group mobilized supporters throughout northern California. On the ground in Watsonville, however, the strike belonged to Latina workers, their families, and their neighbors, who saw the companies' demands for givebacks as an Anglo assault on the Mexican American community.

The strike displayed both the strengths and the limits of this labor-community alliance. Unorganized cannery workers contributed to the strike fund; Catholic Social Services devoted its emergency housing fund to the strikers' needs; thousands of local supporters joined the picket lines and rallies, enduring constant harassment by police. In February 1986, Shaw strikers went back to work with a wage cut about half the size of the one the company had tried to impose. At Watsonville Canning, the strikers stayed out for another thirteen months. When the company hired replacements, not one striker crossed over. When it engineered a decertification election, the strike committee rounded up 914 of the original strikers—some of them from as far away as Texas and Mexico—to outvote the 848 scabs. When Watsonville Canning went broke and Wells Fargo bank sold it to the Rio Farms Corporation, the strikers made clear that, by buying the company, Rio Farms had also bought the strike. Negotiating with the new owners, Local 912 hammered out a deal that did away with medical benefits and told the strikers it was time to go back to work. Most of them refused. Now a wildcat action, the strike continued, with workers massing around the plant to keep it closed. Finally, in March 1987, the company revised its offer and the strikers accepted a partial victory: a new contract that included a concession on wages but kept medical benefits intact.

Fights against concessions included some heartrending defeats too. One unfolded in the copper towns of Greenlee County, Arizona, where mine workers, mostly Mexican Americans, belonged to thirteen different unions, the largest of which was United Steelworkers Local 616. When their coordinated contracts ran out the last day of June 1983, the unions offered to freeze wages except for cost-of-living adjustments (COLAs), and four companies accepted that deal. But Phelps Dodge Copper Corporation demanded staffing cuts and no COLA, and over 2,000 of the company's miners—members of Local 616—walked out a minute after midnight on July 1. Although strikes for new contracts had taken place many times before, decades had passed since the company had tried to stay open during a strike. Now Phelps Dodge got an injunction against union pickets and organized convoys under police protection to bring in office employees and supervisors to work the mines. To get around the injunction, the Morenci Miners Women's Auxiliary took over picket duty. When it became clear that the injunction applied to the Auxiliary too, the women replaced it with an independent group called Citizens for Justice and continued to hold mass pickets. Six weeks into the strike, the company began hiring permanent replacements for the strikers, and phalanxes of National Guardsmen and state police used tear gas to disperse the crowds that massed to block scabs from entering the mines. The fight was far from over, however.

The Phelps Dodge strike lasted for more than a year, with the women returning to the picket lines again and again. Citizens for Justice set up a food bank and clothing exchange for strikers' families; fought their evictions; organized relief following a flash flood; dispatched members to strike-support rallies in New York, Boston, and California; and buoyed spirits back home by hosting community celebrations of Cinco de Mayo and the strike's first anniversary. In the end, though, Phelps Dodge prevailed. By October 1983, its operations were fully staffed by replacement workers, and a year later the new workforce voted to decertify all of the unions representing Phelps Dodge workers. In 1986 the NLRB upheld the decertification.

A second high-profile defeat pitted the headquarters of the United Food and Commercial Workers against the union's Local P-9 in Austin, Minnesota. Established in 1979, the UFCW arose from the merger of the Retail Clerks International Union and the Amalgamated Meat Cutters, which had absorbed the United Packinghouse Workers a decade earlier. Negotiating with pork-processing companies in 1981, the new union had agreed to a forty-four-month wage freeze, but within two years the companies were imposing wage cuts. In 1984 Hormel and Company, one of the largest processors, used layoffs and the threat of a total plant shutdown to bully a UFCW local in Ottumwa, Iowa, to accept concessions that reduced members' compensation by 23 percent. Hormel then turned to UFCW locals at its other facilities and demanded that they match the givebacks. Local P-9, the union at Hormel's flagship plant in Austin, said no and prepared for a strike, which its members approved by a margin of more than ten to one.

By the time P-9 walked off the job in August 1985, it had in place a United Support Group that mobilized families, retirees, and Austin youth to picket the plant; set up legal-defense and relief funds; and organized a nationwide Adopt-a-P9-Family program and boycott of Hormel products. The local had also hired Ray Rogers, whose New York–based labor-consulting firm, Corporate Campaign, publicized both the strike and Hormel's ties to unsavory banks and corporations doing business with South Africa's apartheid regime. Once the strike was under way, donations and good wishes poured in from unions, farmers, and a wide range of organizations active around peace, social justice, and environmental issues. In April 1986, thousands of supporters joined the strikers for a series of mass demonstrations aimed at stopping Hormel from running the plant with scabs. After teargassing the demonstrators on April 11, police detained seventeen of them on charges of felony riot and also arrested both Ray Rogers and P-9's president Jim Guyette on charges of abetting a riot. Still, the strike remained strong, with even more supporters rallying in its defense.

Through all of this, UFCW headquarters in Washington, D.C., refused to back P-9. William Wynn, the union's president, and Lewie Anderson, director of its packinghouse division, instead condemned the strike in the name of labor solidarity, insisting that P-9 had betrayed other UFCW locals by resisting concessions they had accepted. By the time the April demonstrations began, Wynn had sent telegrams and letters to all of the P-9 strikers, ordering them back to work. When they defied the order, the UFCW imposed a trusteeship on the local; and, as the outsiders now in charge of P-9 systematically dismantled the strike's support apparatus, President Wynn campaigned against the boycott, urging union members to buy Hormel meat. In September 1986, the trusteed local signed a new contract that granted the company all of the givebacks it had sought, prohibited all boycott activity, and specified that strikers who had taken part in the boycott would not be called back to work.

While the fight against concessions emanated mainly from the rank and file and local officers, some national labor leaders embraced the cause too. The prime example of that pattern was Richard Trumka, president of the United Mine Workers. A third-generation coal miner in western Pennsylvania, Trumka had worked his way through college and law school and spent several years on the UMW's staff before becoming its president in 1982. His election surprised and dismayed the AFL-CIO's old guard, which regarded him as too radical, but UMW members voted for him two to one, and he did not disappoint them. In 1984, when the union started work on a new agreement with the Bituminous Coal Operators' Association, the A.T. Massey Coal Company—owned by the Fluor Corporation and Royal Dutch Shell—refused to bargain. That October the union struck Massey's operations in West Virginia and Kentucky, staying out until the NLRB ordered the company to bargain in December 1985. Over the course of the strike, the UMW built an alliance with South Africa's National Union of Mine Workers, which had its own disputes with another coal company half-owned by Royal Dutch Shell. This convergence generated an international boycott of

Shell that continued long after the Massey strike ended and won support from miners' unions and anti-apartheid activists around the world as well as labor progressives across the United States.

Trumka also presided over a protracted strike against the Pittston Coal Company when it reduced medical benefits for miners and their families and entirely rescinded the health plan for about 1,500 widows, retirees, and disabled workers. Like every corporation demanding concessions, Pittston claimed there was no alternative, but the union proved that wrong. The strike, which ran from April 5, 1989, to February 20, 1990, began as a mobilization of 1,700 miners and their families, who blocked the roads to Pittston's mines in Virginia, West Virginia, and Kentucky. Soon, however, some 40,000 miners were involved, staging sympathy strikes across eleven states. The strike's vital center was Camp Solidarity in a recreational park near Castlewood, Virginia; managed by a women's network that called itself the "Freedom Fighters," it sheltered and fed thousands of people who came to support the strike and trained them in civil disobedience. Another women's group, the Daughters of Mother Jones, staged regular pickets in front of Pittston's corporate offices in Lebanon, Virginia, and occupied the building for thirty-six hours a couple of weeks into the strike. Strikers themselves later occupied a coal-processing plant for four days as thousands of supporters ringed the plant so that police could not clear the building. Although the Pittston strike took a heavy toll on the UMW's treasury—in addition to paying strike benefits, the union was fined more than $60 million for encouraging civil disobedience—surrender was out of the question. As Trumka told a reporter midway through the strike, "People keep asking how long we can hold out. The answer: one day longer than Pittston."[13] When the strikers finally returned to work, they had a contract that fully restored the medical benefits the company had cut.

Public employees also organized against cutbacks, and on that front, unions' relations with surrounding communities played decisive roles. As governments at every level endeavored to lower or contain spending on public services and maintenance of infrastructure, workers in the public sector faced the age-old threat of layoffs for some and speedups for the survivors. Their unions—long accustomed to taking part in politics—responded with lobbying, strikes, and electoral challenges to Democrats who squared off against public employees. In the 1980s, outreach to community activists became another essential tool. In summer 1986, AFSCME's blue-collar locals in Philadelphia learned this the hard way, losing a strike that the mayor successfully portrayed as a betrayal of the public interest. Following the defeat, a new slate of leaders took over the locals' parent body, District Council 33, and strengthened its alliance with the white-collar locals in D.C. 47, which had already developed connections to justice movements that took on apartheid in South Africa, British occupation of Northern Ireland, and violations of workers' rights in Central America. Working together, D.C. 33 and 47 made common cause with civil rights advocates on the city council and worked with a host of local unions and community organizations to launch Philadelphians United to Save City Services. These efforts quickly derailed the mayor's plans to privatize trash collection and, over time, tied struggles in defense of city services to struggles in defense of city employees.

Unions' attention to issues of social justice was not only a way to secure allies;

it also mattered to the basic labor conditions of women and workers of color, who made up a large portion of public employees. In 1985, in Nacogdoches, Texas, Stephen F. Austin State University privatized 156 food service jobs, contracting them out to ARA Services (now known as Aramark). All of these jobs belonged to black women. As the courts had found in response to a lawsuit by the NAACP, the university had systematically confined black job applicants to janitorial and food-service positions. It now privatized the latter in hopes of stymying a campus organizing drive by the Texas State Employees Union (TSEU) and complicating black workers' legal claims to the back wages that an appellate judge had ordered the university to hand over. In the end, however, privatization strengthened the workers' hand, thanks to the tenacity and creativity of the TSEU and its parent union, the Communications Workers of America (CWA). Once the women were employees of ARA instead of a public agency, they became eligible to file for a union election supervised by the NLRB. Although two years passed before they were able to implement this right, TSEU-CWA steadily moved things forward by flooding the NLRB with appeals and grievances, by sending busloads of ARA workers and other union members to lobby at the state capitol in Austin, and, especially, by mobilizing ever-larger shows of community support in Nacogdoches. When the election took place in September 1987, the union handily won, but the company continued to stall. What finally turned the tide was a rally 3,000 strong that included contingents from the TSEU, CWA locals at several telephone companies, other unions across eastern Texas, the NAACP, and the National Organization for Women. City officials insisted that both ARA and the university settle with the workers, who got a contract and back pay from the lawsuit, too.

In the private sector, the most sustained union involvement in grassroots politics came out of struggles against plant closings. In New Bedford, Massachusetts, local government helped United Electrical Workers Local 277 stop Morse Cutting Tool from shutting down. In 1982, Morse's owner, the Gulf and Western Corporation, gave the union an ultimatum: agree to wage cuts or see the plant shut down. In response, Local 277 called a strike and set up the Citizens' Committee to Support the Morse Tool Workers. The committee then persuaded the city council to authorize the mayor to save Morse by any means necessary, including seizure of the plant by right of eminent domain. After thirteen weeks, Gulf and Western signed a new contract that did not include union concessions. When the company announced in 1984 that it would sell or liquidate Morse, the mayor again threatened to seize the plant, and Gulf and Western came up with an acceptable buyer.

The longest-running campaign around plant closings began in 1981, when labor and community activists in the Pittsburgh region came together to form the Tri-State Conference on Steel. Lobbying for extended unemployment benefits and a moratorium on home foreclosures, Tri-State also generated the Steel Valley Authority (SVA), authorized to buy abandoned plants and devise plans to reopen them. Shortly after its incorporation in 1986, the SVA sought to take over U.S. Steel's Dorothy Six blast furnace in Duquesne, where laid-off members of Steelworkers Local 1256 had winterized the furnace at their own expense and stood watch around the clock to make sure the company removed no machinery from the facility. Private investors declined to finance the deal, however, and the SVA's charter forbade public funding of its projects. Although the Save Dorothy campaign galvanized the Monongahela Valley's steel towns, it came to nothing. Nor did the SVA succeed in a later effort to help the United Electrical Workers save two railroad equipment plants owned by the American Standard conglomerate. There was one notable victory. In 1989, when Pittsburgh's only large bakery closed, the SVA joined with Bakery Workers Local 12 and community organizations to establish the City Pride Corporation. With funds cobbled together from the union, neighborhood groups, and private investors, City Pride built a state-of-the-art bakery and began deliveries of fresh bread in 1992. All told, though, the Pittsburgh region lost more than 100,000 manufacturing jobs during the 1980s.

Community mobilizations around plant closings sometimes stretched far beyond a single city or region. In 1990, when Green Giant moved a broccoli-processing operation from Watsonville, California, to the company's plant in Irapuato, Mexico, laid-off workers (members of Teamsters Local 912) joined with local supporters to form El Comité de Trabajadores Desplazados, which put into motion a transnational response. One prong was a boycott of Burger King, Alpo Petfoods, and other companies owned by Green Giant's parent corporation, the Grand Metropolitan conglomerate headquartered in London. El Comité also sent emissaries to talk with workers in Irapuato, where some of the Watsonville workers had family members. This laid the groundwork for an alliance between activists from Teamsters 912 and the Authentic Workers' Front (Frente Auténtico del Trabajo, or FAT), a militant Mexican labor federation. Together, they achieved a $2 million severance package for the workers in Watsonville and some toxic-waste cleanup at the Mexican plant. The Watsonville activists also supported FAT in an organizing drive to replace the do-nothing union ensconced at the Irapuato plant.

No matter how creative the response, plant closings caused workers irreparable harm. No severance package could make up for the loss of a union job. Nor did saving a single plant significantly slow the growth of the Rust Belt: a great chain of decaying industrial cities that stretched from northern New England down to the mid-Atlantic region and out to the Midwest and Great Lakes states.

While these developments invited worries about the labor movement's future, a rising tide of labor activism in immigrant communities offered reasons to hope. In New York City's Chinatown, Local 23–25 of the International Ladies' Garment Workers Union (ILGWU) had won contracts with clothing factories by going to the bosses; the workers, virtually all of them Chinese women, became ILGWU members without ever having much contact with the union. In summer 1982, the factories refused to renew their union contracts. Furious that no Chinese bosses had been included in the industry-wide bargaining, they told their workers that labor conditions were better settled within the Chinatown community, without interference from "the white man's union."[14] Local 23–25 did indeed fit that description; its officers and staff were white, did not speak Chinese, and scarcely knew the rank and file. When they called a rally to protest the bosses' intransigence, they expected a small response. In fact, hundreds of women stepped forward to make phone calls and distribute leaflets, and on June 24 about 20,000 walked off the job to attend the rally and then march through Chinatown. Within days most of the bosses had signed contracts with the union, and the holdouts gave up on June 29, when 20,000 gathered for a second rally and march. Following these events, Local 23–25 began to hire Chinese-speaking staff, train stewards from the Chinatown shops, and work with members, community organizations, and public agencies to establish the Garment Industry Day Care Center of Chinatown in late 1983. Rank-and-file leaders from this local meanwhile became important voices in New York's progressive movements, forming a Chinese committee in the local Coalition of Labor Union Women and going to city hall to protest police brutality and Chinatown's gentrification.

On the West Coast, too, new immigrants were mobilizing in ways that surprised old unions. In East Los Angeles, the Angel Echevarria Company employed about 200 undocumented immigrants from Mexico and Central America to manufacture Somma waterbeds, a nationally distributed brand. As the company's owner explained, he had sought out an undocumented workforce because "the illegal worked a lot harder."[15] Unions typically steered clear of these workers, regarding them, in the words of one AFL-CIO official, as "a labor pool that is . . . more docile than the American workforce."[16] In the mid-1980s, an organizer who had himself fled the Somoza dictatorship in Nicaragua persuaded the ILGWU to reach out to the company's workers, who gave the union a solid victory in an NLRB election held in January 1985. When Echevarria appealed the election, workers stenciled union slogans on their shirts, called in sick in groups, observed department-wide moments of silence, and left work an hour early one day to attend a mass held at the plant gate. When the company began firing them for disruptive behavior, they launched a boycott of Somma waterbeds, and more than 200 local stores soon dropped the brand. In November 1985, the company settled. In keeping with a ruling by the national NLRB under Donald Dotson, the contract did not require that Echevarria rehire the workers it had fired, but they urged ratification anyway, just to beat the boss.

By the late 1980s, quite a few unions had come to see immigrant workers—both documented and undocumented—as essential to the labor movement's revitalization. In 1986, the Service Employees International Union (SEIU) launched a Justice for Janitors campaign to unionize immigrants in the building services industry in Denver. Modeling itself on the United Farm Workers, Justice for Janitors (JfJ) did not organize by handing out union cards and filing for NLRB elections. Instead it used rallies, sit-ins, traffic blockades, and street theater to make janitors and their labor conditions visible to the general public and mobilized churches and community organizations to join the workers in demanding change. In 1988, JfJ arrived in Los Angeles, where it worked with SEIU Local 399 and a broad coalition of supporters to win a union contract for janitors in downtown buildings. Then the campaign turned to workers who serviced the Century City office complex in the Westside district, where police clubbed and arrested janitors and their supporters at an otherwise peaceful demonstration held on June 15, 1990. After that brutal spectacle, public pressure on the building services companies and their clients became irresistible, and the Century City workers got their contract.

That July, at the American Racing wheel factory in Los Angeles, 800 workers, mostly first-generation Latino immigrants, struck for three days to protest layoffs that had so sped up the pace of work that on-the-job injuries had become routine. These workers had no union protection until six months later, when they voted to join the Machinists and founded their own local. Looking back on this struggle, Macario Camorlinga, a Mexican immigrant who played a leading role, attributed the victory to rank-and-file control of the drive to organize: "The company tried to identify and isolate the leaders, but we were all leaders."[17] By the time American Racing workers joined the Machinists, residential dry wallers in Los Angeles had started to organize themselves into an independent Movement of Drywall Hangers, led by immigrants from El Maguey, a village in Guanajuato, Mexico. On June 1, 1992, they went on strike for an increase in piece rates and dispatched flying squadrons to shut down construction sites from the Mexican border to Ventura, just north of L.A. When the California Highway Patrol intercepted the squadrons, they sat down on the freeways; and when the U.S. Border Patrol raided picket lines in search of undocumented immigrants, the strikers did not scatter. Their employers capitulated in November, after learning that the Movement of Drywall Hangers planned to charge them with violating overtime provisions of the Fair Labor Standards Act. Some 2,400 drywallers then joined Carpenters Local 2361 and got a union contract in 1993. In 1995, about 2,000 framers did the same.

If immigrants' labor activism displayed the power of racial-ethnic solidarity, it also exemplified workers' capacity to transcend ethnic differences. As veterans of the Los Angeles movement often stressed, Latino immigrants from different nations—or different parts of a single nation—came to the United States with different life experiences, political allegiances, cultural traditions, and understandings of unionism. The same diversity could be found among immigrants from other regions of the world, and they too built pan-ethnic movements. In 1987, immigrant and U.S.-born union members in Los Angeles formed the Alliance of Asian Pacific Labor (AAPL), which mobilized union support for language rights, political participation, lawsuits against job discrimination, and other issues important to Asian communities. In addition, AAPL provided strike support and helped unions recruit organizers fluent in Asian languages. In 1992, it gathered with similar organizations based in San Francisco, New York, and other cities to establish the AFL-CIO's Asian Pacific American Labor Alliance.

In some cases, immigrants from virtually everywhere joined hands under the same union banners. A prime example of that pattern was Local 26 of the Hotel Employees and Restaurant Employees (HERE), an organization of 4,000 workers in Boston's hotels. The vast majority of the local's members were immigrants or children of immigrants; 60 percent of them were women; 60 percent were workers of color; they spoke no fewer than eighty-seven different languages and dialects; and they held jobs that ranged from housekeeper, laundry worker, and dishwasher to bartender, restaurant server, and desk clerk. Still, Local 26 became one of the country's most cohesive labor organizations after insurgents running on a union-democracy platform were swept into office in 1981. In 1982 contract bargaining was placed in the hands of a fifty-person negotiating committee whose make-up replicated the local's diversity in sex, race, ethnicity, age, and kind of work. The negotiators' committee reported to a contract committee that was 350 strong and equally diverse. The contract committee kept the whole local informed, translating reports into multiple languages. When the next contract came up in 1985, the negotiating committee expanded to 125 members and the contract committee to 500. During the contract talks of 1988, the local set forth its boldest demands yet and prepared for massive civil disobedience if employers refused to meet them. Over the course of the 1980s, as many unions lost ground in pay and benefits, Local 26 won steady wage increases, better medical coverage, a legal-services program fully funded by employers, and an employer-financed trust fund to help workers with the rising cost of housing. According to its president, Dominic Bozzotto, the union owed this progress to the members' inner strength: "If you've raised three kids to teenagers on no money, then taking on management is nothing. If you've got the courage to leave your country, leave your family, come to a new place where you don't know the language, then a strike is a walk in the park."[18]

Fortifying unions, immigrant workers also played a central role in the development of worker centers, a new form of organization. These community-based projects offered low-wage workers services of various sorts, from legal aid and English-language instruction to help in dealings with bosses and landlords and interfacing with public officials and unions. The first U.S. worker center, the Chinese Staff and Workers Association in New York City, began in 1979 as an effort to promote unionism among Chinese immigrants, evolved into an independent union of workers in several Chinese restaurants, and expanded its portfolio to address violations of labor law and anti-discrimination statutes in the restaurant, garment, and construction industries. Another pioneer worker center was La Mujer Obrera (LMO) in El Paso, Texas. Founded in 1981 by Mexican American women who had taken part in the Farah strike of 1972–74, LMO confronted the aftermath of plant closures by Farah and other large clothing manufacturers. Mobilizing the community around compensation and retraining for laid-off workers, the group also helped workers challenge wage theft and win union contracts in the smaller garment shops that remained in town. Other worker centers that emerged in the 1980s and early 1990s included Asian Immigrant Women Advocates in Oakland, Fuerza Unida in San Antonio, and Korean Immigrant Workers Advocates in Los Angeles.

Immigrant communities were not the only ones experimenting with new modes of organizing. Among the earliest worker centers was Black Workers for Justice (BWFJ) in North Carolina. The group was born in Rocky Mount in 1981, when black women employed at the local K-Mart organized to challenge racial and gender discrimination at the store. In 1982, labor and community activists from ten counties came together to establish BWFJ as a statewide organization dedicated to empowering black workers and protecting the working poor in a state with the nation's lowest rate of unionization. Instead of putting all of its energy into conventional organizing drives aimed at NLRB elections—which unions usually lost in North Carolina—BWFJ experimented with ways of representing workers as a union without official recognition from the government or the boss. In 1982, BWFJ joined with community activists in Wake County to fight "Toxic Terrorism" by the Koppers Corporation, a conglomerate whose wood-treatment plant in Morrisville polluted residents' well water.[19] In 1988, when the nonunion Schlage Lock plant near Rocky Mount announced plans to move operations to Mexico, BWFJ helped Schlage workers organize a committee that publicized their exposure to chemical hazards and fought for severance packages equal to those of the company's white-collar employees. In 1990, when the Amalgamated Clothing and Textile Workers Union (ACTWU) lost an election at the Goldtex dyeing plant in

Goldsboro and the company fired the union's most vocal supporter, Ina Best, BWFJ launched a national campaign for her reinstatement. In 1991, when a fire at the Imperial Foods poultry plant in Hamlet killed twenty-five workers and injured another fifty-five—all of them trapped behind locked emergency exits—BWFJ worked with the town's residents to expose the company's history of safety violations and secure the owner's indictment and conviction on charges of manslaughter.

Just over the state line, the Tennessee Committee on Occupational Safety and Health (TNCOSH) led a statewide campaign for "Right to Know" legislation that would require companies to inform both workers and surrounding communities about toxic chemicals used in industrial processes. The state AFL-CIO kept its distance from this project, in which TNCOSH allied with left-wing organizations such as the Highlander Research and Education Center, but rank-and-file unionists and some local officers embraced the campaign and the general public rallied in support. In 1985, Tennessee's legislature passed a Right to Know law—the first of its kind in the South.

Another outcome of the campaign and, indeed, all community-labor activism was that grassroots leaders developed new networks and momentum. In Knoxville, for example, the Right to Know struggle mobilized Luvernal Clark, a shop steward at the Allied Signal seatbelt factory. She went on to chair the Tennessee Industrial Renewal Network's committee on outreach to Mexican workers employed by U.S. companies that had moved operations south of the border, and she later became the first black woman president of ACTWU Local 1742.

In some cases, unions worked especially hard to cultivate rank-and-file leadership. This led to two high-profile victories at elite universities, first Yale and then Harvard. At Yale, blue-collar workers had been unionized since the 1930s, but five campaigns by different unions had failed to bring clerical and technical workers on board. In 1982, the blue-collar union—HERE Local 35—initiated a new campaign that relied on personal conversations instead of mass distribution of union literature and focused on building a large organizing committee rather than getting workers to sign union cards. By the time the drive went public in 1983, almost a fifth of the university's clerical and technical employees belonged to the committee. Despite Yale's elaborate efforts to derail the drive, their new union, HERE Local 34, won a narrow victory in an election held that May. With the university still determined to bust the union, efforts toward a first contract extended for twenty months and included a sixty-nine-day strike by both Local 34 and Local 35 in the fall of 1984; pressure from students, faculty, and a host of organizations in the surrounding community; and civil disobedience that led to mass arrests of union members and their supporters. At the end of January 1985, Yale finally signed contracts with both locals.

The Harvard Union of Clerical and Technical Workers (HUCTW) won an NLRB election in May 1988, after fifteen years of organizing and two lost elections along the way. Like Local 34, HUCTW built itself through one-to-one conversations, constructing social networks centered on the union, one of whose chief slogans was "We care about each other."[20] That method—described by proponents as a distinctly female way of organizing—so alienated HUCTW from its parent union, the UAW, that the two parted company in 1985, but the organizers doubled down on their strategy and AFSCME eventually stepped in to adopt HUCTW and fund the drive without trying to take charge. Flying under Harvard's radar, the union astonished the university's administrators by winning the election and surprised them again in negotiations by leading the way toward a contract that bore little resemblance to most collective bargaining agreements. Instead of defining work rules, grievance procedures, job classifications, or management rights, the contract established an elaborate system of joint worker-management committees and councils that met regularly to set policy and resolve conflicts on matters ranging from health and safety to the allocation of space. With regard to bread-and-butter issues, HUCTW made enviable progress. The first contract improved pensions and health coverage, inaugurated a childcare program, and provided for annual pay increases averaging almost 10 percent. The second contract, signed in 1993, brought another substantial raise and ironclad job security.

In the face of hard times, new approaches to organizing also emerged in the labor movement's mainstream. The International Brotherhood of Electrical Workers had long required that electricians in its construction division pass through four- or five-year apprenticeships before they became journeymen. In 1987, starting in Boston and Atlanta, the union implemented a bottom-up program in which organizers went to nonunion building sites to sign up new members, who then took no-fail exams that qualified them to join the union as anything from beginning apprentices to full journeyman. The United Food and Commercial Workers meanwhile began to avoid NLRB elections and win union recognition via pressure campaigns that included consumer boycotts and investigations of employers' violations of laws regarding wages, hours, health-and-safety conditions, waste disposal, pension management, and so on. In 1984, the Service Employees International Union welcomed into its fold the United Labor Unions established by ACORN (Association of Community Organizations for Reform Now), a national network of neighborhood organizations that branched out to organize in low-wage workplaces and won union recognition for home health aides in Chicago and Boston, fast food workers in Detroit, hotel workers in New Orleans, and rag processors in Philadelphia. Even AFL-CIO headquarters saw a need for innovation; in 1989, Lane Kirkland authorized the SEIU's president John Sweeney and the Steelworkers' president Lynn Williams to establish an Organizing Institute (OI) to recruit and train student activists, community advocates, and rank-and-file union members for employment as labor organizers. Whether or not they had passed through the OI, more and more organizers sought alliances with civil rights and feminist organizations, defining unionism as a commitment to racial justice and gender equality as well as labor solidarity.

Hard times also generated closer attention to a range of issues especially important to women. In the early 1980s, public employee unions began to bargain for a new kind of gender equity in compensation. Instead of calling for equal pay for men and women doing the same work, they sought wage equality based on "comparable worth"—the principle that people should be paid equally for very different jobs that required comparable levels of skill, responsibility, effort, and so on. In May 1988 the Coalition of Labor Union Women organized 40,000 unionists and their family members to converge on Washington to lobby for an "American Family Bill of Rights," including the right to a job, to a living wage, and to health care as well as to equal opportunity. The following year, CLUW widely distributed a guide for union negotiators titled *Bargain-*

ing for Family Benefits, and in the early 1990s, the UAW, AFSCME, and ACTWU published similar guides for their locals. By that time, most unions endorsed childcare for their members, but women's reproductive freedom was an entirely different matter. In 1989, when reproductive rights came up for discussion at the AFL-CIO convention, the discussion was so contentious that delegates referred the issue to the federation's executive council, which formed a committee to study the appropriateness of the labor movement's taking a stand and, six months later, quietly announced that it had decided to leave the question of abortion rights "to the consciences of individual members."[21]

Another divisive issue was women's integration into traditionally male occupations. The building trades were especially attractive since they offered engaging work and, when unions were in place, high pay. But men in the trades so resented women's presence that tradeswomen often wound up in exceptionally hostile work environments—"trench warfare," as one woman electrician aptly put it.[22] Pornographic photographs of women adorned many jobsites, and the men sometimes deliberately injured female co-workers. While building trades unions seldom took action on the women's behalf, tradeswomen's organizations sprang up to do the job. In the early 1980s, New York City's United Tradeswomen had some 300 members and a roster of activities that included a newsletter to expose unacceptable working conditions and agitate for enforcement of anti-discrimination laws; street protests to demand that construction contractors hire more women and crack down on sexual harassment; workshops on nuts-and-bolts topics such as health and safety hazards and how to form women's committees inside building trades unions; and group discussions that built solidarity by confronting divisions based on race and sexuality. For United Tradeswomen and the kindred groups that appeared in other cities, the core goal was to gird members to stay in the trades, and in that they often succeeded, though the combination of job scarcity and unwelcoming work environments precluded significant growth in tradeswomen's numbers.

Labor activists organizing for lesbian and gay rights made greater headway, despite the federal government's hostility to the cause in the Reagan-Bush era. In 1982, gay rights resolutions were adopted at AFSCME's national convention and at meetings of the AFL-CIO's departments of building trades and industrial unions. That same year, UAW's District 65 local at the *Village Voice* newspaper in New York City became the first U.S. union to win family benefits for unmarried domestic partners. The AIDS epidemic, which hit gay men with particular ferocity, made health coverage an especially crucial issue and steadily increased the pressure for partner benefits. Pressed by unions and employee associations, a number of public agencies and some private companies added domestic partners to their benefits coverage over the next decade. In 1993, HERE Local 26 secured partner coverage for workers in Boston's hotels.

Local and national networks linked activists from different unions and industries. On the eve of the National March for Lesbian and Gay Rights that took place in Washington on October 11, 1987, participating unionists gathered at an official reception hosted by the AFL-CIO. At the local level, activists from various unions came together in Boston, San Francisco, New York, and Salt Lake City to forge alliances between organized labor and the movement for lesbian and gay rights. In Boston, for example, the Gay and Lesbian Labor Activist Network (GALLAN) helped the city's building trades unions establish their jurisdiction over jobs on a construction project to enlarge a gay health clinic, and the unions generously supported a GAL-LAN fundraiser to benefit both the clinic's work in response to the AIDS crisis and the United Farm Workers' campaign to protect workers from exposure to pesticides. Larger networks formed as well. In 1991, a conference of union activists sponsored by the magazine *Labor Notes* spawned Lavender Labor, an international network to support gay and lesbian labor activists coming out of the closet at work and in unions; an SEIU women's conference that year produced a Lavender Caucus, which soon had chapters around the country; and 1994 saw the birth of Pride at Work, a national organization of lesbian, gay, bisexual, and transgender unionists that addressed workplace discrimination and harassment.

Other significant departures from business as usual involved matters of foreign policy. With regard to South Africa, the AFL-CIO's cold warriors parted company with the Reagan administration, which steadfastly supported the vehemently anti-communist apartheid regime. With progressives from the Coalition of Black Trade Unionists, the United Mine Workers, AFSCME, and the Steelworkers in the vanguard, virtually all AFL-CIO officials were vocally anti-apartheid by the mid-1980s. Testifying before Congress, Lane Kirkland called for an end to all U.S. investments in and trade with South Africa, and Kirkland's second in command—the AFL-CIO's secretary-treasurer Thomas Donahue—was among the many protestors arrested for demonstrating at the South African embassy. In 1990, when the South African revolutionary Nelson Mandela toured the United States as a spokesperson for the African National Congress (ANC), his itinerary included a session with the AFL-CIO's executive council—a watershed event for the council since Communists were an important component of the ANC.

With regard to Central America, support for Reaganite policies remained intact at AFL-CIO headquarters, but powerful opposition gathered elsewhere in the labor movement. In September 1981, Jack Sheinkman—ACTWU's secretary-treasurer and a longtime opponent of Cold War politics—organized the National Labor Committee in Support of Democracy and Human Rights in El Salvador (known as the National Labor Committee, or NLC). Its purpose was to stop U.S. aid to a right-wing Salvadoran regime infamous for violations of labor and human rights and to the right-wing "Contra" guerrillas seeking to overturn the socialist government of Nicaragua. William Winpisinger, the Machinists' president, and Douglas Fraser, president of the UAW, quickly signed on as Sheinkman's co-chairs, and by 1985 the NLC had recruited the presidents of twenty additional unions, including AFSCME, SEIU, the Communications Workers, and the National Education Association. They lobbied Congress, sent fact-finding delegations to Central America and published their reports, joined with churches and human rights groups to mobilize demonstrations against U.S. policy in the region, and sponsored U.S. speaking tours of Salvadoran unionists. Lane Kirkland actively opposed all of this, as did the American Institute for Free Labor Development, the AFL-CIO's department of international affairs, and the national presidents of several unions, most notably John Joyce of the Bricklayers and Allied Craftsmen and Albert Shanker of the American Federation of Teachers (AFT). In 1985 and again in 1987, acrimonious debates about foreign policy erupted at the AFL-CIO's annual convention and ended in compromise: in 1985, a resolution that called for peaceful settlements of conflicts in El Salvador and Nicaragua and did not address the issue of U.S. aid; in 1987, a statement of opposition to both U.S. aid to the Contras and Soviet and Cuban aid to Nicaragua's government. That so many union leaders had publicly defied AFL-CIO headquarters was no small thing, however, and the fissure penetrated labor's rank and file too. Although the NLC's most prominent spokespeople were union presidents, it also generated multi-union committees of local activists that sprang up in more than two dozen cities, and on April 25, 1987, up to 50,000 union members gathered in San Francisco and Washington to join mass protests against U.S. policy in Central America and South Africa.

Challenges to the labor establishment mounted on other fronts as well. Located in New York City but available to activists across the country, the Association for Union Democracy helped rank-and-file dissidents unseat corrupt union officials. Activists affiliated with *Labor Notes* magazine, published in Detroit, forged national networks of reformers in the Teamsters, the UAW, the AFT, and other unions. In the Chicago-Gary area, activists from the Steelworkers and other unions joined with progressive academics to start the Midwest Center for Labor Research, whose *Labor Research Review* offered reports on far-flung efforts to revitalize the labor movement. A dozen national union presidents were voted out of office in the 1980s, and the early 1990s saw an epoch-making upset in the Teamsters. In 1991, following a federal mandate that the union's national officers be directly elected by its members, the reformer Ron Carey—endorsed by Teamsters for a Democratic Union—became the union's general president and his slate swept the down-ballot races for secretary-treasurer and thirteen vice presidencies.

Turnover in leadership had important ramifications for union staff members, whose own unions grew more assertive. The oldest staff unions dated back to the early 1950s, but the trend gained momentum in the late 1970s and 1980s, when organizers and other staffers formed unions at some of the AFL-CIO larger affiliates, including in the AFT (1979), the UFCW (1979), and the SEIU (1983). Job security was a crucial issue, for both newly elected union officers and old-timers who feared they would be voted out of office tended to blame their troubles on the staff. As John Scally, a leader of the CWA's staff union explained, "Everything is political in a labor union. And this is *the* problem in the union establishment today. If a staffer doesn't make [the] boss look good, he's going to want someone else in the job. . . . And if he comes to suspect you're cozy with his opposition . . . watch out!"[23] Democracy became a sharper issue as well. Like Scally, many staffers had been rank-and-file labor activists before they went to work for a union. They resented the bureaucratic hierarchies that union officers tended to take for granted and resisted when officers expected staff to bear the brunt of budget cuts necessitated by losses in membership. These issues breathed new life into staff unions. In 1961 they had tried unsuccessfully to organize a joint council. In 1987 they tried again and founded the International Congress of Staff Unions, which had forty affiliates by 1990.

Union reform could take any number of turns. In hospital workers' District 1199 in New York City, the retirement of a president who had been in office for decades ignited a civil war that lasted for most of the 1980s, with rival factions accusing each other of racism, megalomania, and corruption. During the same period, National 1199 successfully merged its mainly white district in West Virginia with its predominantly black district in Ohio, building solidarity through carefully planned educational and social events where members learned to confide problems, share hopes, and amplify their voices in unison. In 1989, the UFCW's Lewie Anderson—who had earlier spared no effort to crush the P-9 strike—got fired from his position as director of the union's packinghouse division and reinvented himself as the leader of a reform group that agitated against concessions bargaining. Unless they were in touch with projects like the Association for Union Democracy, the Midwest Center for Labor Research, the *Labor Notes* network, or Anderson's group, dissidents in separate locals of the same union might never even hear about each other, for national leaders controlled almost all internal communications. Another obstacle to reform was skepticism from workers who thought of their unions as service agencies, not vehicles for mobilization. Like their counterparts in Boston and New Haven, HERE's locals in northern California became vibrant rank-and-file unions; but members did not immediately warm to the idea that contract enforcement should be a collective affair. Their initial response was, to quote one organizer, "Geez, service has just gone down the hill. . . . What do I pay my dues for?"[24]

If the labor movement's revitalization proved more complicated than many reformers had anticipated, one and all of them agreed that the movement could not regain lost ground without new leadership. By the mid-1990s, even high-level officers of national unions had begun to second that idea, pointing specifically at AFL-CIO headquarters. Revitalization at the movement's grassroots would clearly take a long time, but conditions were ripe for a coup at the top.

The More Things Change . . .

Reaganomics was finally discredited on "Meltdown Monday" (October 19, 1987), when stock values measured by the Dow Jones Industrial Average fell by more than 22 percent. Bills still had to be paid, however, and the plan in Washington was to balance the federal budget through deeper cuts in spending on social programs, revisions of the tax code to lower corporate rates, and greater deregulation of the marketplace, especially international trade and investment. Republicans and Democrats both embraced these business-friendly policies, which remained intact after the Democrat Bill Clinton was elected president in 1992.

That same year saw an astonishing labor victory in the small town of Ravenswood, West Virginia, where Steelworkers Local 5668 won an eighteen-month battle with the Ravenswood Aluminum Corporation, which produced metal sheets for manufacturers of beverage cans. Following a playbook that was becoming sickeningly familiar, the company broke off contract negotiations in October 1990, locked out 1,700 union members, and brought replacement workers into a plant surrounded by barbed wire, security cameras, and guards outfitted in military gear. Since decent jobs were scarce in the surrounding area, management expected that Local 5668's picket line would soon collapse and its members stream back to work without a contract, but in fact the line remained solid and just seventeen members crossed it. Staunch support from the community helped the local hold out, as did the United Steelworkers' readiness to finance workers' living expenses beyond those covered by unemployment benefits. But it was the union's corporate campaign that finally forced the company to capitulate. Coca-Cola, Anheuser-Busch, and other beer companies were put on notice that consumer boycotts would ensue if they continued to sell beverages in cans made of Ravenswood aluminum. Locked-out workers and their families successfully lobbied the state legislature to crack down on health and safety violations in the Ravenswood plant. Most effective of all was the union's exposure of the company's secret connections to Marc Rich, a billionaire commodities trader and hedge-fund manager who had fled the United States to escape trial on sixty-five counts of tax evasion, fraud, racketeering, and other charges. In addition to publicizing his stake in Ravenswood, the Steelworkers sent delegations to Europe and South America to pressure bankers and government officials not to do business with Rich. That was the last straw. In April 1992—reportedly at Marc Rich's command—Ravenswood Aluminum fired the CEO and two vice presidents who had engineered the lockout. In May, contract negotiations resumed as members of Local 5668 returned to work.

While all of organized labor celebrated this triumph, labor leaders injected a note of caution, pointing out that the United Steelworkers had a larger treasury than most unions and that Ravenswood's connection to the notorious Marc Rich made the company exceptionally vulnerable to a corporate campaign. As one labor researcher told the *Chicago Tribune*, "There's no question that this was a victory. . . . But on the other hand we can't expect it to mean the resurgence of the American labor movement."[25] Inspiring as the Ravenswood story was, then, most union officials looked to politics for the antidote to union busting by means of replacement workers. Bill Clinton, then the frontrunner in the Democrats' presidential primary, had pledged to support federal legislation to outlaw the hiring of replacements to break strikes or perpetrate lockouts.

Labor had miscalculated what a Democratic administration would deliver, however. Wealth trickled down only slightly better under Clinton than it had under Republican presidents. The recession that gripped the national economy in the early 1990s gave way to an era of record-breaking increases in the creation of new jobs. But almost 90 percent of the job growth took place in comparatively low-wage service industries while employment in manufacturing steadily waned. Real wages—earnings measured in terms of buying power—declined for most workers in the first half of the 1990s, and their rise in the second half of the decade did not even come close to making up the ground lost since the early 1970s. The proportion of Americans living in poverty—15.1 percent when Clinton took office—fell steadily over the course of his two terms as president; but it never dipped below 11.3 percent.

With regard to organized labor's political agenda, the Clintonites were long on talk and short on results. In the general election of 1992, Bill Clinton endorsed the North American Free Trade Agreement (NAFTA) scheduled to remove restrictions on investment and trade between the United States, Mexico, and Canada; but he also called for the incorporation of stronger protections for labor and the environment. While that caveat appeased labor leaders for the duration of the election season, the protections that later materialized lacked teeth. A side agreement on labor established national administrative offices to hear complaints about infringements on workers' rights and violations of minimum labor standards, but these agencies were empowered merely to recommend compliance with the rules, not to enforce it. The side agreement on environmental standards set up a similarly ineffective bureaucracy. Nor did Clinton follow through on election-year promises to promote enactment of a federal law to bar employers from hiring permanent replacements to take the jobs of strikers. Spokesmen for the AFL-CIO stood by the Democrats nonetheless. In the congressional elections of 1994, Lane Kirkland persuaded union officials to back Democrats irrespective of their stand on NAFTA, but many voters in union households seem to have had other ideas. For the first time in forty years, Republicans gained control of both the Senate and the House of Representatives.

Corporate attacks on unions rolled on. A study of organizing drives in 1993–95 found that one-third of employers fired workers for union activities, a sixth used electronic surveillance to monitor employees, and more than half threatened to close the plant if the union won. When the UAW sent organizers to ITT Automotive in Auburn Hills, Michigan, for example, the company parked thirteen flatbed trucks in front of the plant, each one loaded with shrink-wrapped production equipment and bearing a large hot-pink sign that read "Mexico Transfer Job."[26] It was not necessarily an idle threat; about 15 percent of companies whose workers elected a union did reduce operations or close entirely, and in many of these cases production relocated to Mexico. Organizing drives encountered other forms of intimidation too. In 1995, when the United Food and Commercial Workers and the Laborers' International Union launched a campaign to unionize poultry-processing plants in the South, agents from the Immigration and Naturalization Service raided several plants to round up immigrant workers who lacked documentation. At the Perdue plant in Dothan, Alabama, where most of the workers were African Americans, white supervisors draped a cross with union T-shirts and set it afire in the style of the Ku Klux Klan. In the NLRB election, scheduled for the very next day, the Laborers lost the vote 646 to 242.

Decatur, Illinois, became one of the fiercest battlefields of employers' crusade against unionism. Trouble had been brewing for some time at A.E. Staley Manufacturing, a corn syrup factory owned by the British conglomerate Tate & Lyle. In 1991 Staley's management insisted that United Paperworkers Local 7837 grant the company the right to schedule twelve-hour shifts, to subcontract work, and to eliminate many seniority provisions and grievance procedures. Instead of calling a strike, the local fought back with an in-plant campaign of working to rule and a corporate campaign targeting Staley's major customers. That same year the Caterpillar heavy-equipment factory in Decatur rejected a UAW contract offer that replicated a settlement with Caterpillar's competitor John B. Deere. UAW Local 751 called a partial strike, but returned to work in April 1992 and started its own in-plant campaign. In June 1993, after Staley workers joined a rally in support of the Caterpillar local, Staley locked them out. Almost a year later the UAW struck Caterpillar over unfair labor practices. Then, in July 1994—just days after local police used pepper spray and mace to break up a demonstration in front of the Staley factory—the Rubber Workers' Local 713 struck Decatur's Bridgestone Tire plant in response to the company's demand for sweeping concessions. The city became a veritable war zone, with massive marches, police assaults on protestors, and bitter conflict between strikers and scabs or replacement workers.

In February 1995, seventy Decatur strikers went to confront the AFL-CIO Executive Council at its annual meeting in Bal Harbour, Florida. They found it making arrangements for Lane Kirkland's resignation. The plan called for him to retire gracefully at the next AFL-CIO convention and for Secretary-Treasurer Tom Donahue to take his place. But developments in Decatur had persuaded some members of the council that a more radical change was in order. An alliance of leaders from the UAW, UMW, AFSCME, SEIU, Steelworkers, and Teamsters made their own nomination for Kirkland's replacement, selecting SEIU's John Sweeney to head a "New Voice" slate that also included the UMW's Richard Trumka for the post of secretary-treasurer and AFSCME's Linda Chavez-Thompson for executive vice president. Infuriated by the challenge Kirkland abruptly resigned in June 1995 and appointed Donahue the interim president so that he would enjoy the advantage of incumbency when delegates cast their votes at the upcoming convention, to be held in New York City, on October 23–26.

Just before the convention, the Labor Resource Center at Queens College of the City University of New York hosted a conference on the labor movement's future. Rank-and-file activists from across the country discussed the need for union democracy, membership diversity, political action, international co-operation, and more creative, energetic efforts to organize the unorganized. These were the central planks of the New Voice platform.

12

One Step Forward, Two Steps Back

Delegates to the 1995 AFL-CIO national convention numbered over a thousand—many more than ever before, thanks to new rules that vastly increased participation by state federations and local labor councils. In other ways, too, this convention was more open than its predecessors. Visitors were welcome; the meeting hall's entrance was lined with literature tables and display booths; leaflets from striking locals and advocates of independent political action circulated through the crowd; rooms had been set aside for impromptu caucus meetings; and, for the first time since the AFL-CIO merger forty years earlier, the federation's leadership would be chosen through a contested election.

Interim president Tom Donahue waged a vigorous campaign, matching the New Voice slate promise for promise, and his partisans sought to reorganize the AFL-CIO Executive Council so that their camp would control it no matter who won the election. In the end, however, the New Voice agenda prevailed. On October 25, the convention's third day, John Sweeney carried the presidential election, winning the votes of thirty-four unions that together represented 57 percent of the AFL-CIO's rank and file. By the time the final gavel fell, his running mates—Linda Chavez-Thompson for vice president and Richard Trumka for secretary-treasurer—had also been elected, and a compromise with regard to the executive council had expanded it both to make room for more Donahue loyalists and to increase participation by women and people of color, who would now make up more than a quarter of the council's members.

The new leaders took the helm of a bruised and bleeding movement. In Decatur, Illinois, Bridgestone workers had ended their strike in May, the United Auto Workers would give up the strike at Caterpillar in early December, and three days before Christmas, Staley workers would ratify the contract they had rejected three years earlier. There was one notable victory to celebrate. In mid-December 1995, about 33,000 members of the International Association of Machinists at Boeing aircraft factories in Seattle, Wichita, and Portland, Oregon, ended a two-and-a-half month strike that won a substantial wage increase and beat back the company's plan to shift the costs of medical insurance onto workers. On the whole, though, 1995 was a bad year. With losses mounting, strike activity declined to an all-time low. The number of workers covered by union contracts fell to 18.3 million, about a half-million lower than the figure for 1994. In the private sector, union density fell to 10.3 percent, a level unseen since 1930.

The New Voice victory gave labor activists reasons to hope nonetheless, for the Sweeney administration not only called for organizing the unorganized but also put a lot of money where its mouth was. The AFL-CIO budgeted $20 million for organizing in 1996 and $30 million the next year. It opened a degree-granting National Labor College whose curriculum stressed education for activism. It also established an organizing department, a workingwomen's department to harness feminist energies, a Union Summer program to rally college students sympathetic to the labor movement, and the Committee 2000 charged with transforming local labor councils and state federations into vehicles for union organizing and united political action. Given employers' disrespect for labor law, organizing drives aimed at winning NLRB elections one workplace at a time could only slow unions' shrinkage. To achieve growth, the New Voice team sought to establish organized labor as part of a broad movement in which unions made common cause with civil rights activists, feminists, progressive clergy, and others committed to social justice.

This was much easier said than done. For one thing, the New Voice vision of social justice rested to a large degree on nostalgia for a rosy past that other progressive forces did not necessarily recognize as their own. Time and again, John Sweeney called for a revival of the "social contract" that had shaped American life during the three decades that followed World War II—decades he described as an era when "business, labor, and government worked together to help all Americans move forward."[1] That this era had also witnessed racial segregation, sex discrimination, dire poverty in some communities, witch hunts against leftists, criminalization of gay and lesbian sexuality, and two imperial wars in Asia, got lost in AFL-CIO rhetoric, and that limited labor's relations with potential allies.

The idea that postwar arrangements could be revived seemed downright naive, moreover, since trends were swiftly moving in just the opposite direction. In 1990, the average pay of chief executive officers at the 500 biggest U.S.-based firms was about $2 million a year, eighty-four times the average for employees. Nine years later, the CEO average stood at $12 million, 475 times the blue-collar average. In the larger society, the richest 20 percent of families were taking an ever-greater share of total family income, with the very poorest families actually losing ground in real dollars and the top 5 percent scoring the biggest gains. By the end of the 1990s, income inequality had returned to the level of the 1930s—about 100,000 millionaires alongside 36 million people living in poverty (as defined by federal government standards that significantly undercounted the poor). More than 2 million of the adults in poverty worked full-time all year, and another 7 million for part of the year. As banks aggressively pushed unsecured credit with high interest rates, people displaced from employment, facing divorce or medical emergencies, or carrying expensive student loans went broke. Bankruptcy filings increased by more than a third in the second half of the 1990s. By 1997, one of every six families living on $25,000 or less a year paid 40 percent of their income in debt service.

Political trends exacerbated these problems. In a much-heralded concession to the AFL-CIO's calls for a higher minimum wage, President Bill Clinton's administration raised the floor from $4.25 an hour to $4.75 in October 1996 and then $5.15 in September 1997. Measured in buying power, however, $5.15 an hour fell well below the minimum wage of $3.35 that was in force when Ronald Reagan took office in 1981. Clinton's welfare policy meanwhile increased the volume of workers forced to accept the minimum. In 1996, to guard his right flank as he stood for reelection, Clinton signed into law a Republican bill that ended Aid to Families of Dependent Children—the welfare program born during the Great Depression, as part of the Social Security Act—and replaced it with Temporary Assistance for Needy Families (TANF). Under TANF, which went into effect in July 1997, welfare recipients had to leave the rolls after two years, and no one could receive more than five years of assistance over the course of a lifetime. By 2000, this policy shift reduced welfare rolls by more than half, but most former recipients remained in poverty, subsisting on Social Security benefits for the disabled, making do with subminimum pay in jobs held off the books, or working in the formal economy for the minimum wage.

Capitalism's globalization posed another threat, this one most evident to workers in comparatively well-paid industrial jobs. Lobbying for the North American Free Trade Agreement (NAFTA) in the early 1990s, Chrysler, Caterpillar, Siemens, and other manufacturing giants had promised that its implementation would expand their operations in the United States. Just as NAFTA's opponents had predicted, however, it shifted many manufacturing jobs to Mexico—more than a half-million of them by the end of the year 2000. The auto, electronics, textile, garment, and woodworking industries were all especially hard hit, and with them the unions that had built strongholds in these sectors.

If organized labor was embattled, however, and its rhetoric sometimes insular, the New Voice agenda attracted a wide variety of progressives to the AFL-CIO. Whatever their limitations, unionists typically had more practical know-how than their campus allies, more material resources than community activists, and more freedom to act than churches that eschewed politics to maintain their tax exemptions or than advocacy groups anxious to safeguard their funding from liberal foundations—in short, more clout than other progressive forces. New Voice rhetoric acquired broad appeal, moreover, when it turned from nostalgia for the past to aspirations for the future. John Sweeney's favorite slogan—"America needs a raise"—hit home in an era of wage stagnation, and his book by that name, published in 1996, envisioned a revitalized labor movement as the "core of a larger effort to achieve economic security and social justice" that "will unite working Americans, and all Americans of goodwill, across the lines of color, class, and culture that divide us today."[2] He earned a reputation for speaking truth to power, as in this widely quoted admonition to elites gathered in Davos, Switzerland, for the World Economic Forum of January 1999: "Our task is not to make societies safe for globalization, but to make the global system safe for decent societies."[3] For all of these reasons, the new AFL-CIO generally got a warm response when it reached out to progressives beyond organized labor, but that by itself could not turn things around.

Advances and Retreats

Union organizing among immigrant workers continued to make headway. In 1996 the Laborers' International Union organized asbestos-removal workers in northern New Jersey, most of them immigrants from Ecuador. The Justice for Janitors movement picked up momentum in Los Angeles, winning a countywide contract with major building owners and cleaning services after a three-week strike in April 2000, and then moving on to more than a dozen cities across the country, from San Diego to Chicago to Cleveland to Stamford, Connecticut. That same year, in Minneapolis, Local 17 of the Hotel Employees and Restaurant Employees (HERE) staged a two-week strike that won union contracts for more than 1,500 hotel workers, about a third of them recent immigrants from Bosnia, Somalia, Togo, Eritrea, Tibet, Vietnam, Korea, Mexico, or Central America. The strikers spoke close to twenty different languages, but as Kate Shaughnessy, an organizer for the union, observed, they had forged "unity in diversity."[4]

On other fronts, too, unionism made noteworthy advances. In September 1997, 10,000 passenger-service workers at US Airways voted to join the Communications Workers of America (CWA). In February 1999, 74,000 home health care workers in Los Angeles County voted by a margin of 90 percent to join the Service Employees International Union (SEIU). This election, which marked the biggest union organizing victory since 1937, capped an eleven-year campaign that had involved both outreach to workers and extensive lobbying to revise state labor laws to allow collective bargaining by home health aides. Salaried physicians employed by hospitals, public health departments, and corporate health maintenance organizations began to enter the labor movement's mainstream. The American Federation of State, County and Municipal Employees (AFSCME) absorbed the independent Union of American Physicians and Dentists in California along with the Federation of Physicians and Dentists in Florida. The SEIU took in the Committee of Interns and Residents and the Doctors Council that represented salaried physicians in New York City and established the National Doctors Alliance to organize new units there and in other cities. The United Food and Commercial Workers signed up doctors at the AmeriHealth network in northern New Jersey. A national survey conducted for AFSCME in early 2001 revealed that up to 90 percent of physicians working for health maintenance organizations favored unionization.

Opening up another new frontier, in 1997 workers in the sex industry established a union shop at San Francisco's Lusty Lady, a "peep show" whose customers paid by the minute to watch through a window as nude women danced. Sex workers in California had organized in the early 1990s, forming a short-lived union at a strip club in San Diego and coming together in San Francisco to challenge club owners' illegal classifications of dancers as independent contractors—a ploy that deprived them of employee benefits and even wages. Instead of paying dancers for their work, the owners demanded that they themselves be paid, charging "stage fees" that came out of the tips dancers earned from the clubs' customers. By the mid-1990s, dancers in San Francisco were meeting in the offices of SEIU Local 790, which had promised

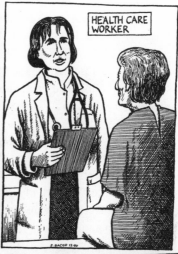

to assist their organizing, even though the union's national leaders disapproved of its involvement with sex workers. In 1996, women from the Lusty Lady club began to attend these meetings. Since their club was among the few that classified dancers as employees, their road to unionization was less cluttered than others, and they had grievances that only a union could resolve: racist scheduling practices that short-changed women of color with regard to stage time and the recent installation of one-way mirrored glass through which customers could photograph and film dancers without their consent. In August 1996, Lusty Lady employees voted fifty-seven to fifteen for union representation, and the following April they approved a first contract that provided for a union shop and applied wall to wall, raising the pay and guaranteeing the job security of all of the club's workers: dancers, bouncers, janitors, and cashiers. As word of this achievement spread, the Lusty Lady activists were inundated by inquiries from exotic dancers across the country, all of them eager for the advantages a union could offer. By 2002 the Las Vegas Dancers' Alliance was organizing in that city's strip clubs, and a year later it reported a membership of almost 1,000; but only at the Lusty Lady did dancers win a union contract. In 2003, when the club's owners decided to shut it down, employees formed a workers' co-operative and bought the operation, which they ran as a union shop. They were forced to close its doors in 2013, after Déjà Vu, a multinational adult-entertainment conglomerate, acquired the building where the Lusty Lady resided and drove it out of business by more than tripling its rent.[5]

The AFL-CIO seized a onetime opportunity when in 1998 the government of Puerto Rico lifted a longstanding ban on collective bargaining by government workers. A multi-union consortium persuaded 120,000 public employees to endorse collective bargaining in May 1999 and then filed for representation elections, the first of which took place in November, among public school employees. Cafeteria workers, who numbered about 10,000, voted to join the United Auto Workers. The American Federation of Teachers (AFT) gained more than 37,000 new members, whose Federación de Maestros de Puerto Rico became the AFT's second largest unit, second only to the one in New York City. Growth by absorption was not the same as growth through new organizing, however; the Federación de Maestros disaffiliated from the AFT just seven years after it joined.

The year 1999 saw two historic union victories in the South. In June, UNITE—the Union of Needletrades, Industrial and Textile Employees, established four years earlier through a merger of the International Ladies' Garment Workers and the Amalgamated Clothing and Textile Workers—won a representation election at the Fieldcrest Cannon mill complex in Kannapolis, North Carolina, where unions had been trying to organize textile workers since the 1920s and the Amalgamated had lost four NLRB elections since 1974. Adding 5,200 workers to UNITE's ranks, this election marked the largest-ever success for a southern organizing drive in the private sector. "It feels like we just organized G.M.," said the union's national director of organizing, Bruce Raynor.[6] Five months later, in November 1999, some 4,200 workers at the Avondale shipyard in Louisiana finally achieved union recognition—more than six years after they had voted under NLRB auspices for representation by craft unions affiliated with the New Orleans Metal Trades Council. Fieldcrest Cannon workers ratified their first contract in February 2000, and Avondale workers ratified theirs the following December.

Experiments with new forms of organizing multiplied in the late 1990s. In Redmond, Washington, just outside Seattle, contract employees at Microsoft formed the Washington Alliance of Technology Workers (Wash/Tech), which soon affiliated with the CWA. Angry about cuts to their retirement benefits, regular employees at IBM formed a national network called Alliance@IBM, which also joined the CWA. Both organizations launched publicity and lobbying campaigns to reform labor conditions in the high-tech sector. In California's Silicon Valley, the South Bay Labor Council not only became what one local politician described as "the most powerful political machine in the valley," but also established Together@work, a craft association for high-tech workers that offered pensions, health benefits, and a temporary employment agency.[7] In San Francisco, the International Longshore and Warehouse Union's Local 6 helped the independent Bike Messenger Association win contracts with two courier companies and file successful class-action lawsuits against employers who violated labor laws.

Under the Union Cities program, launched in 1997, the AFL-CIO fostered innovation on the part of local labor councils. Together@work, based in San Jose, got started this way, as did a wide range of initiatives in more than 150 other cities. These included multi-union organizing drives, recruitment and training of labor candidates for public office, and "Street Heat" projects in which dozens to hundreds of union members mobilized demonstrations whenever local workers confronted anti-union employers. The AFL-CIO's new national organizing department meanwhile inaugurated its own multi-union "geo projects"—geographically focused organizing drives. In Stamford, Connecticut, for example, the UAW, SEIU, HERE, and New England Health Care Employees District 1199 came together in 1998 to help each other unionize janitors, childcare and nursing home aides, retail employees, taxi drivers, municipal employees, and newspaper reporters. Less than three years later, some 4,500 workers had gained union recognition and first contracts, and their unions had joined with local clergy to elect labor-friendly candidates to the city council and school board and to help residents of the city's public housing turn back a plan to demolish their homes and instead win $15 million in renovations.

Strikes involving a thousand or more workers were few and far between. Until the early 1980s, they had numbered hundreds a year; in 1995, just thirty-one took place and that figure would soon go even lower—to twenty-nine in 1997 and seventeen in 1999. When big strikes did take place, however, they showed that workers united could still wield considerable power.

The most dramatic example unfolded in August 1997, with a fifteen-day strike by more than 185,000 Teamsters employed by the United Parcel Service delivery company. This battle took place at a major turning point in the union's history. At its helm stood Ron Carey, a former UPS driver who had risen through the ranks to become president of his local in New York City, gained a reputation as a militant and democratic leader, and won national office in 1991—the first time that Teamsters chose their general president by direct secret ballot as opposed to the wheeling and dealing of delegates appointed by local leaders. Once in office, Carey set about cleaning house in a notoriously corrupt union and deepened his relationship with reformers from Teamsters for a Democratic Union. The old guard took its revenge in February 1994, when Carey called the first national strike against UPS—a one-day walkout that few local leaders supported outside the Northeast and just a quarter of the workers joined. Within days, flyers charging that Carey had weakened the Teamsters began arriving in members' mailboxes. By 1996, when he narrowly won reelection as general president—by defeating Jimmy Hoffa's son James P. Hoffa, one of the union's in-house attorneys—Carey had placed more than sixty crime-infested locals under trusteeships and had become a constant target of charges that he himself was corrupt. Then, in spring 1997, just as negotiations for the next contract with UPS were getting under way, a grand jury began investigating charges that Carey's reelection team had illegally used union funds to finance the race against Hoffa, so the union's presidency was once again in doubt.

In light of that and workers' low participation in the strike of 1994, UPS management did not anticipate much of a fight. The company demanded a raft of concessions, offered a minuscule wage increase, responded to the union's demand for more full-time jobs with an offer to create 200 of them nationwide, and blithely informed customers that UPS would continue to operate in the event of a strike. But this was not 1994. Instead of relying on local leaders to build momentum for a strike, Teamster headquarters reached out to the rank and file through a survey to determine workers' chief contract demands (more full-time jobs, no subcontracting, substantial wage and pension increases, better safety provisions), a strike authorization vote (in which 95 percent endorsed a walkout), a host of local strike committees, and a strike website and hotline that disseminated the latest information. Teamsters for a Democratic Union went all out too. When the strike began on August 4, virtually every Teamster at UPS took part, the Independent Pilots Association whose members flew the company's planes refused to cross picket lines, and other unions across the country rallied to demonstrate their support. The strike also got warm support from the general public, who saw it, to quote one reporter, as a "revolt against the ruthless treatment of workers by so many powerful corporations."[8] After two weeks and two days and some $600 million in losses, the company gave up, agreeing to a contract that substantially raised pay, protected pensions, called for the creation of 10,000 new full-time jobs, required that work that had been subcontracted be offered to UPS employees, and obligated management to negotiate the maximum weight of packages that workers were expected to carry on their own. It was the largest work stoppage the United States had seen since the textile strike of 1934 and a brilliant victory in an age of setbacks.

Other strikers scored advances too. In August 1998, more than 100,000 telephone workers—members of the CWA and the International Brotherhood of Electrical Workers (IBEW)—beat back compulsory overtime with a two-day walkout at Bell Atlantic and a two-week walkout at USWest. In 1999, at Newport News Shipbuilding in Virginia, 9,200 members of United Steelworkers Local 8888 held out for sixteen weeks to win improvements in wages and pensions. The following year brought the largest white-collar strike in U.S. history, when the Society of Professional Engineering Employees in Aerospace (newly affiliated with the AFL-CIO's International Federation of Professional and Technical Engineers) led a forty-day work stoppage by 19,000 engineers and technical employees at Boeing, finally bringing their compensation into line with that of other union members at the company.

In the auto industry, a series of smaller walkouts showed that "lean" production dependent on "just-in-time" inventory could vastly strengthen the workers' hand when they went on strike. In March 1996, for example, 3,000 UAW members stopped work at a pair of General Motors brake plants in Dayton, Ohio. Within days, almost all of GM's North American assembly plants had suspended operations, and its parts plants were starting to shut down too. In January 1997, a mere 500 workers struck for union contracts at two seat factories operated by one of Ford's suppliers, and Ford quickly fell behind in production of its most popular light trucks. In January 2000, a strike in a single department at Chrysler Daimler's Jeep plant in Toledo, Ohio, lasted a matter of hours but nonetheless halted production at the whole plant and two others. In all of these cases and others like them, strikers won because their local actions had systemic ripple effects.

If successful strikes and organizing drives demonstrated the power of workers united, their unions still needed allies, and the New Voice administration devoted some of its best energies to forging or reinforcing partnerships between organized labor and other social movements. The new women's department succeeded in drawing unionists and feminists closer together. As part of the America Needs a Raise campaign, the AFL-CIO reached out to a wide range of community organizations to plan joint events in more than two dozen cities across the country. Alliances with campus activists proliferated as the federation supplemented the Union Summer program for college students with Legal Summer for students in law school and Seminary Summer for future members of the clergy; helped Union Summer graduates form United Students Against Sweatshops, whose protests persuaded a number of colleges and universities to impose fair labor standards on the manufacturers that supplied sports uniforms and other clothing bearing school logos; published handbooks for both students and faculty members committed to labor activism; and sponsored the establishment of Scholars, Artists and Writers for Social Justice, which rallied professors, journalists, and kindred groups to champion labor's cause. AFL-CIO headquarters also began to finance Jobs with Justice, founded in the late 1980s to mobilize working-class communities in support of strikes, organizing drives, and other campaigns for workers' rights. Pride at Work—the national association of lesbian, gay, bisexual, transgender, and queer (LGBTQ) labor activists—joined the roster of AFL-CIO "constituency groups." Another of these groups, the Asian Pacific American Labor Alliance, became a leading national advocate for Asian American civil rights, especially active around legislative attacks on immigrants and affirmative action.

In February 2000, in a move carefully orchestrated by the New Voice faction, the AFL-CIO Executive Council broke with more than a century of nativist tradition, declaring that "the American union movement has been enriched by the contributions and courage of immigrant workers" and calling for amnesty and permanent legal status for undocumented immigrants.[9] Unions also mobilized around that issue. In September 2003, labor-community coalitions in Seattle, Los Angeles, Miami, Chicago, and five other major cities dispatched buses carrying more than 900 immigrants and their supporters to take part in the Immigrant Workers Freedom Ride that culminated in a mass rally in New York City's Flushing Meadow Park on October 4. As the buses wended their way to the rally, they stopped in more than 100 communities in forty-two states, where local coalitions had organized demonstrations and press conferences. These actions paved the way for a huge lobbying effort by the newly formed Coalition for Comprehensive Immigration Reform, in which both SEIU and HERE played central roles.

Though religious leaders had long been key supporters of labor struggles, the new AFL-CIO inspired more elaborate efforts on that front. The National Interfaith Committee for Worker Justice started in Chicago in 1996, and by 1998 had twenty-nine affiliates from coast to coast, including groups of Roman Catholics, Protestants, Muslims, and Jews. In Los Angeles, where HERE Local 11 was campaigning for better contracts for hotel workers, Clergy and Laity United for Economic Justice delivered sermons in hotel restaurants. In Minneapolis, ministers held silent vigils that persuaded hotels to rehire workers fired for union activities. During Labor Day weekend 1999, activists preached in 700 churches, synagogues, and mosques, speaking on workers' right to organize and earn a living wage. The next year the Interfaith Committee organized a public fast in support of New York State's migrant farmworkers, helping to convince the legislature to bring them under the protection of state law with regard to the minimum wage and collective bargaining.

Labor-community alliances took other forms too. Both Jobs with Justice and local unions recruited progressive educators, clergy, politicians, and other civic leaders to form "workers' rights boards" that held public inquiries into labor disputes. A single hearing sometimes sufficed to get an employer to the bargaining table. In May 1998, in New York City, the workers' rights board established by Jobs with Justice drew 200 people to a downtown church to hear testimony about the Aramark Corporation's yearlong refusal to bargain with workers at the cafeteria it ran at the Wall Street headquarters of Salomon Smith Barney, an investment bank involved in numerous financial scandals. The next day Salomon ordered Aramark to resolve the issue, and within a week the workers' union—HERE Local 100—had formal recognition. In other instances the boards shouldered lengthy campaigns. In 1998–99, Seattle's workers' rights board took charge of mobilizing community support for a 138-day strike that finally won a first contract for SEIU members at a local psychiatric hospital.

Labor-community initiatives also included a great many living wage campaigns, in which Jobs with Justice typically partnered with local unions and labor councils. There were fights for county ordinances requiring that businesses contracting with city or county governments pay a living wage. In some cases the ordinances also covered businesses operating for or owned by these governments or doing work for their contractors. As of 1995, only a few cities had such laws. By the end of 2001, seventy living wage ordinances had been passed—at the county level as well as in cities—and about seventy more campaigns were under way.

When it came to electoral politics, the New Voice administration backed Democrats, but following President Clinton's embrace of NAFTA, it was hard to see them as anything more than the lesser of two evils. AFL-CIO headquarters did not interfere, then, when affiliated unions such as the Oil, Chemical and Atomic Workers and the International Longshore and Warehouse Union joined with independents like the

United Electrical Workers and California Nurses Association to found the Labor Party in June 1996, at a Cleveland convention attended by close to 1,400 delegates and about 200 observers. Other unions represented at this gathering included the American Federation of Government Employees, the Farm Labor Organizing Committee, and the United Mine Workers. Joining them were delegates from community-based groups such as Black Workers for Justice in North Carolina and the Kensington Welfare Rights Union in Philadelphia, from several dozen local unions and labor councils, and from more than forty state and city chapters of Labor Party Advocates, formed in the early 1990s to promote independent politics within the labor movement. Unlike the Working Families Party of New York, which was founded with John Sweeney's blessing in 1998 and later spread to other states, the Labor Party did not endorse candidates nominated by Democrats or Republicans. Instead, it aimed to build the labor movement's strength to the point where it could run its own candidates and win.

Both the pull of politics-as-usual and the potential for something more than that came into especially sharp focus during the week that followed Thanksgiving 1999, when the World Trade Organization (WTO) held a summit meeting in Seattle to hammer out plans for the new millennium. Various groups of anti-corporate radicals in the Northwest coalesced to form the Direct Action Network to coordinate demonstrations against the WTO, including civil disobedience aimed at shutting down the meeting. To their surprise, labor unions mobilized too, not just the most militant and progressive sectors of the Seattle movement but a wide array of unionists from across the country, including John Sweeney and other leaders of the new AFL-CIO. On Tuesday, November 30, the WTO had to delay its opening ceremonies on account of a protest more than 50,000-strong in which 20,000 unionists rubbed elbows with allies ranging from the anarchist Ruckus Society to mainstream environmental organizations like the Sierra Club. The large turnout and spirit of unity elated one and all.

But the AFL-CIO's agenda differed fundamentally from that of the Direct Action Network's coalition—and quite a few rank-and-file unionists who joined the march. While they hoped to disrupt the WTO to the point where it could no longer operate, in Seattle or anywhere else, labor leaders aimed to secure a seat at the table where the operations took place. An international embarrassment for President Clinton, the AFL-CIO's participation in the march informed the Democratic Party that its friends in the labor movement were dead serious about altering global trade negotiations to include unions. That point having been made, labor officials and staffers spent the evening of November 30 at a celebratory dinner, while the Direct Action coalition continued efforts to stop the WTO from meeting.

By the next morning, police had attacked the demonstrators with tear gas, pepper spray and rubber bullets; the mayor had declared a state of emergency; the governor had sent in the National Guard; more than 600 protestors were in jail; and unionists were hotly debating what to do about all of this. On Friday, December 3, about 5,000 local labor activists—defying orders from the mayor, AFL-CIO headquarters, and several national unions—marched through downtown Seattle to join a mass sit-in in front of the city jail, and the International Longshore and Warehouse Union (ILWU) threatened to close West Coast ports unless the protestors in custody were released.

This time, police held back. Before the weekend was out, the WTO talks had collapsed and all who had been arrested were out of jail.

The "Battle in Seattle," as the press called it, was not the only occasion when the labor movement and the Direct Action Network (DAN) established some common ground. Now a national organization, DAN played a central role in organizing the Mobilization for Global Justice that gathered in Washington, D.C., in April 2000 to protest policies of the International Monetary Fund and World Bank. The AFL-CIO and several national unions endorsed the permit-protected march on Sunday, April 16, though not the many acts of civil disobedience scheduled for the preceding week— and, unlike the rest of the coalition, they focused their wrath on U.S. trade with China more than the IMF or World Bank. In May 2000, DAN's chapter in New York City formed a labor-support committee that made friends with several local unions by engaging in actions that NLRB-certified labor organizations could not legally undertake—stopping delivery trucks from crossing a picket line, for example. But while DAN strongly opposed both mainstream political parties, unions went all out to support the Democrats' Al Gore when he ran against the Republicans' George W. Bush in that year's presidential election.

In other respects as well, the new AFL-CIO clung to old habits that limited organized labor's partnerships with other progressive forces. Unwilling to do anything that might lessen working-class support for Bill Clinton's reelection in 1996, the federation's spokespeople said virtually nothing about the damaging impacts of the welfare reforms he signed into law. Since a number of its affiliates represented police or prison guards, the AFL-CIO did not take strong stands against police brutality, capital punishment, mass incarceration, mistreatment of inmates, or prison privatization— all burning issues for national organizations like the American Civil Liberties Union and local activists in black and Latino communities. While unions often sided with environmentalists on causes such as safe removal of hazardous waste and corporate disclosure of the use of toxic substances, they just as often endorsed employers' challenges to pollution controls, on the grounds that controls might cost jobs. Announcing its historic shift on immigration policy, the AFL-CIO Executive Council called for immediate legal status for Hondurans, Guatemalans, Salvadorans, and Haitians, who fled violent regimes in their home countries and were summarily denied refugee status in the United States; but unlike the global justice movement, the council remained silent about the ways the U.S. government and U.S. corporations propped up these regimes.

Though years of state and federal prosecutions of labor racketeers had dramatically reduced organized crime's presence in the labor movement, some unions still harbored gangsters or tolerated personal corruption. Even unions associated with the New Voice initiative occasionally made headlines on this front. In 1998, the president of the Hotel Employees and Restaurant Employees agreed to retire in order to avoid criminal prosecution. In 1999, in response to a lawsuit filed by dissident members, the SEIU forced the retirement of Gus Bevona, the president of New York City's building services Local 32B–J (John Sweeney's home local), who occupied a thirteen-room penthouse office and paid himself an annual salary that once topped $500,000. That same year, the New Voice supporter Arthur Coia agreed to resign as president of the

Laborers' International Union and to plead guilty to failing to pay taxes on several Ferrari racecars he had collected. All three of these scandals unfolded in national unions especially active in immigrant organizing, and although the scandals cleared the way for more effective leaders, they also undermined organized labor's reputation in the immigrants' rights movement.

Old habits notwithstanding, moreover, there was a fundamental flaw in the notion that partnerships with other progressive forces could rescue unionism. Although they could certainly help out with initiatives like living wage campaigns and strike support, allies such as students, clergy, and community organizations lacked the power and resources to have a decisive impact on the labor movement's fate. From their standpoint, in fact, one of the most attractive things about the new AFL-CIO was that it seemed to have the wherewithal to help *them*, by supplying them with jobs as union staffers, by funding campus and community projects, and by sharing political contacts and expertise at strategic organizing. For activists in the poorest communities, assistance as simple as access to a union meeting hall or photocopy machine could make a crucial difference. Also, as the closing scenes of the Battle in Seattle made clear, workers' centrality to the world economy gave at least some unions considerable leverage—if not always the will—to enforce justice irrespective of the law. At a labor conference in Washington State, a radical environmentalist who had been beaten in Seattle described the change that came over police when her organization began to stage joint demonstrations with the ILWU: "We stand side by side, the longshoremen tell the cops, 'They're with us,' and then no one lays a hand on us."[10] Labor's allies could very seldom return such favors.

Employers, on the other hand, found powerful allies at all levels of lawmaking and law enforcement, from local authorities to state governments to the full array of federal officeholders. In 1999, Richard Trumka observed that, "intimidation and interference by employers is such standard practice in today's workplaces the freedom to join a union doesn't really exist at all."[11] Although the National Labor Relations Act (NLRA) was supposed to protect workers from retaliation when they tried to unionize, a survey by the AFL-CIO revealed that employers resorted to firings in almost a third of organizing drives, and in four out of five cases they called in one of the thousands of consulting and law firms that specialized in "union avoidance."[12] These outfits used all manner of tactics—stalling, rumor-mongering, espionage, threats, bribes, and so on—to derail organizing and, if the union should win that round, to prevent it from achieving a first contract.

Strikebreaking became a big business as well. In 1938, the U.S. Supreme Court had ruled that employers could permanently replace strikers who stopped work over economic issues as opposed to unfair labor practices, but companies rarely exercised this option until after Ronald Reagan fired striking air traffic controllers in 1981. By the mid-1990s, it was a common procedure, and employers that did not hire permanent replacements almost always brought in scabs. National employment agencies such as Worldwide Labor Support headquartered in Pascagoula, Mississippi, and U.S. Nursing Corporation based in Denver had sprung up to meet the demand for scabs, raking in hundreds of millions every year. Another fast-growing industry supplied armed guards trained to bully strikers in hopes of provoking them to violence so that police and the criminal courts could step in. Advertising its services in business magazines, the Special Response Corporation, headquartered in Baltimore, featured a photograph of one of its operatives wearing jackboots, a helmet, night-vision goggles, and a gasmask and wielding an oversized club.

When workers' complaints about union busting and strikebreaking reached the courts, the National Labor Relations Board, or its state-level equivalents, the cases were typically tied up in red tape for many months if not years. Often, the verdicts went against the unions; when employers lost, the fines levied on them were too small to have a deterrent effect. In response to pressures from the AFL-CIO, President Clinton ordered in 1995 that federal contracts no longer go to companies that permanently replaced strikers, but those that engaged in union-avoidance campaigns or used rent-a-guards to harass strikers remained eligible for contracts—and, in any case, the president's order was overturned after he left the White House.

Time and again in the Clinton era, government agencies made things more difficult for labor unions. As organizing picked up in immigrant communities, deportations multiplied too, their number reaching a new high in 2000. In late August 1997, just days after the Teamsters concluded their victorious strike against UPS, federal officials overseeing the union's affairs voided the election that had returned Ron Carey to the presidency. In November these officials declared that he must have known about his reelection team's machinations and forever barred him from seeking elective office in the union. The following year, James Hoffa Jr. became the Teamsters' general president and UPS, smelling blood, went back on its agreement to create 10,000 new full-time jobs. The United Farm Workers meanwhile hit a wall in its flagship campaign of the late 1990s—a drive to unionize workers in California's strawberry fields. Employers illegally disrupted the drive by engineering the establishment of a fake union that slandered the UFW, strong-armed its supporters, and rivaled it in elections; and the state's agricultural labor relations board abetted the scheme by declining to step in. In 1997, the National Labor Relations Board finally rejected the UAW's six-year-old petition for a representation election among truck drivers and package handlers at Federal Express (FedEx) facilities in New Jersey, Pennsylvania, and Delaware. Although the vast majority of FedEx workers were by then ground employees, the company had begun as an air courier and the NLRB ruled that it should still be regarded as such. That placed FedEx employees under the jurisdiction of the Railway Labor Act, which required that representation elections take place simultaneously in *all* of a company's facilities, not shop by shop or district by district. When a nineteen-month strike against Detroit's newspapers went down to defeat in 1997, the NLRB ruled that the papers had deployed unfair labor practices against the six unions involved, but three years later a federal court overturned that ruling. When exotic dancers beyond San Francisco sought to unionize, club owners resorted to legal machinations, converting dancers from employees to independent contractors ineligible for protection under the federal labor law, and the NLRB let that stand. The same loophole stymied labor organizing among other sex workers, such as prostitutes and nude models. The criminal justice system assaulted unionism too. In January 2000, for example, police in Charleston, South Carolina, beat and teargassed stevedores belonging to the International Longshoremen's Association when they tried to prevent a nonunion company from unloading a ship's cargo, and the state's attorney general quickly selected five union activists for indictment on charges of felony riot.

The situation would grow worse following the presidential race of 2000, which furnished a stark reminder that elections do not necessarily equal democracy. Intense campaigns to turn out voters from union households paid off; they made up 26 percent of that year's electorate. Al Gore narrowly won the national popular vote but failed to carry enough states. The election came down to Florida, where George W. Bush's brother Jeb was governor. Before the election, Florida officials had purged the voter rolls of tens of thousands of people wrongly identified as convicted felons. Then, on Election Day, new voting machines misread numerous ballots and rejected many more: some 6,000 in Broward County, 19,000 in Palm Beach County, 22,000 in and around Jacksonville, and so on across the state. When the Republicans proclaimed Bush the winner, the Gore campaign filed a challenge, and the AFL-CIO sent dozens of its best organizers to Palm Beach and Broward counties to help out. By order of the Gore team, they did not mobilize demonstrations or even attend protest rallies pulled together by Jesse Jackson and local civil rights leaders. Instead, the organizers helped Democratic Party operatives go door to door to collect affidavits from voters who had seen their paper ballots misinterpreted or rejected by machines and wanted recounts by human beings. In December, the recounts finally got under way, but the U.S. Supreme Court soon halted them, and on December 12 issued a five-to-four ruling that Bush had won the state. As his administration settled in, unions and their allies came face-to-face with challenges they had not anticipated and were ill-equipped to meet.

War on Terror, War on Labor

Despite the election debacle, labor activism gained momentum in the opening months of 2001. In March, leaders of three militant health care unions—the California Nurses Association, the Massachusetts Nurses Association, and the Pennsylvania Association of Staff Nurses and Allied Professionals—began to lay plans for a national campaign to improve working conditions, advance patient care by legislating nurse-to-patient ratios, and establish a national health system on the single-payer model (in effect, Medicare for all). In early June, some 4,000 demonstrators converged on the South Carolina State House in Columbia to demand that the attorney general drop charges against the "Charleston Five"—the union stevedores accused of felony riot. Later that month, in Raleigh, North Carolina, Black Workers for Justice and the Farm Labor Organizing Committee held a joint march to commemorate "Juneteenth" (June 19, 1865), the day that victorious Union troops finally arrived in Texas and spread the word that the Civil War had ended and people enslaved under the Confederacy were now free. Calling out employers for violating workers' freedom to organize, the marchers declared their intention to build a Black-Latino alliance to enforce that right. On August 24, in Normal, Illinois, 2,900 members of UAW Local 2488 struck the city's Mitsubishi auto factory in the wee hours of the morning, as soon as their contract expired. By noon, a thousand workers were picketing the plant, and the following day the company folded, agreeing to a contract far better than the one it had offered before the strike. On September 3—Labor Day—600 members of Teamsters Local 890 ended a two-year strike at the Basic Vegetable Products processing plant in King City, California. Midway through this strike, the plant's owners had sold it to ConAgra, a corporate giant that had expected to crush Local 890 without half trying. But when the local expanded its bargaining team to include representatives of more than forty other Teamster units at ConAgra plants, the company rescinded demands for concessions, agreed to wage increases, and reinstated the strikers with full seniority. Across the country, organizing drives were doing well enough that union membership was on target to grow in 2001—not by as much as the movement had hoped, but grow nonetheless.

And since the AFL-CIO no longer worried about undermining a Democratic president, its relationship with groups like the Direct Action Network took on new life. In 2000, the federation had merely endorsed the April 16 march against the International Monetary Fund and World Bank, but when the Mobilization for Global Justice scheduled a second mass protest for September 30, 2001, labor became a central player, committing lots of money and staff to the effort and pledging to turn out a great many union members.

Before this historic protest could take place, however, the ground shifted in ways no one had anticipated. On September 11, 2001, nineteen young men from Saudi Arabia, the United Arab Emirates, Egypt, and Lebanon hijacked passenger airliners, flew them into the twin towers of the World Trade Center in New York City and the Pentagon outside Washington, D.C., and crashed a fourth plane in rural Pennsylvania. More than 3,000 people perished. The attacks capped three years of assaults on U.S. military and diplomatic facilities by Al Qaeda, a clandestine network of Islamic religious fundamentalists who opposed secular government and objected to U.S. penetration of the Muslim world.

Media coverage of 9/11 highlighted the heroism of firefighters, police officers, and other first responders who rescued people at the World Trade Center, but otherwise workers got stiffed. Exemplifying the corporate response, management at the Delphi auto parts plant in Coopersville, Michigan, invited workers to observe a moment of silence for the 9/11 victims, but immediately added, "Don't turn off your machines."[13] When Congress established a fund to compensate the families of the dead, the legislation dictated that payouts differ according to the earning potential of the deceased, so the families of executives received far more than the families of janitors, restaurant servers, and clerks. Outside labor newspapers, there was little coverage of the cleanup that went on for many months, the 50,000 construction and other workers who took part—often as volunteers—and the fact that most of them belonged to unions. As a woman who registered volunteers wrote in *Labor Notes*, "I had to ask for photo ID, and I've never seen so many union cards in my life."[14] Whatever their tasks, cleanup workers at the World Trade Center site, now known as "Ground Zero," paid a steep price for pitching in. The New York Committee for Occupational Safety and Health distributed a fact sheet about the dangers of the toxic dust and fumes that pervaded the site and the steps workers could take to protect themselves, but the recommended safety equipment was rarely available, so many thousands of workers were harmed. Together with Dr. Stephen Levin, who ran a clinic for Ground Zero workers, local unions crusaded tirelessly for government recognition that their members' health had been compromised and for a fund to cover the necessary treatment. It took more than nine years for Congress to do the job. In December 2010, it finally passed the James Zadroga 9/11 Health and Compensation Act, named for a young police officer who had worked in the rubble of the World Trade Center and later died of lung disease.

The aftershocks of 9/11 rippled through the national economy for more than a year. New York City lost 100,000 jobs and registered a record number of homeless families. The city's HERE locals reported that at least a third of their members were out of work, and taxi drivers saw their income fall by half. Congress bailed out the airline industry, which was devastated nationwide, but Republicans defeated a provision that would have compensated the tens of thousands of airline workers who got laid off. Some 50,000 airport security screeners lost their positions when a new federal law made U.S. citizenship a requirement of the job. By year's end it became clear that the business boom of the 1990s had rested largely on stock manipulation and fraudulent profit reports. In October a story broke about corrupt accounting practices at the Enron Corporation, a Houston-based energy company with 20,000 employees and a close relationship with the Bush administration. In early December, Enron collapsed and pulled down Arthur Andersen, one of the world's biggest accounting firms. This bankruptcy was the largest in history, but only until summer 2002, when WorldCom, a telecommunications giant, went under. Spectacular business failures precipitated a sharp decline in the stock market, ravaging pension funds all across the country.

President Bush declared a "War on Terror." The first international target was Afghanistan, where Osama bin Laden, the wealthy Saudi who directed Al Qaeda, had lived for several years. After a few thousand Afghans had been killed and a friendly regime installed in Kabul, Bush prepared to oust Iraq's Saddam Hussein, who had no visible connection to Al Qaeda but did control extensive oil reserves. By the end of March 2003, U.S. troops were in Iraq as well as Afghanistan. Annual military spending grew by two-thirds, from $304 billion in 2000 to $506 billion in 2005. On the home front, the Bush administration moved to expand executive powers; to limit civil liberties, especially for Muslim immigrants; and to encourage Americans to report suspect behavior by neighbors or co-workers to the new Department of Homeland Security.

In earlier times, massive government spending on war would have boosted the economy in communities across the country, but a wave of mergers in the 1990s had concentrated military production in a handful of locales, such as southern California, Seattle, and Dallas-Fort Worth. War appropriations thus did little to offset industrial decline in the Rust Belt. New jobs under the Department of Homeland Security were more widespread but not well paid except at the highest levels.

Military contractors made out like bandits, however. Well before the United States went to war in Iraq, federal officials were consulting with corporate executives about finding a rationale for the war and identifying business opportunities that would arise after the invasion. Lucrative no-bid contracts for Iraq's reconstruction later went to firms like Halliburton, an oilfield services company formerly headed by Vice President Dick Cheney; Bechtel, a construction firm with close ties to the State Department; and the aviation giant Lockheed Martin, whose former executives and lobbyists were sprinkled throughout the Bush administration. These companies and their subsidiaries also got multiple contracts from agencies overseen by the

Department of Homeland Security, and after Hurricane Katrina smashed into the Gulf Coast in August 2005, they found yet another goldmine: massive federal funding of cleanup efforts run by the private sector.

Working people paid a high price for these ventures. Wage earners carried a disproportionate share of the tax burden, all the more after the Bush tax reforms of 2001 and 2003 slashed the levy on recipients of unearned income such as inheritance, stock dividends, and capital gains. Employees of the Department of Homeland Security were exempted from whistleblower protections that shield civil servants from punishment for revealing managerial incompetence, waste, fraud, and abuse. Companies involved in the post-Katrina cleanup routinely violated laws regarding workers' wages, hours, and safety. By the end of 2005, more than 2,400 U.S. troops—overwhelmingly the sons and daughters of working-class communities—had died in Afghanistan and Iraq and tens of thousands had been disabled. The casualties included not only the regular military but also members of the National Guard and Reserve units, which made up half of American forces in Iraq as of 2005.

If the War on Terror gave working people more reasons to protest, it also made many labor leaders less willing to take risks. Immediately following 9/11 the AFL-CIO pulled out of the Mobilization for Global Justice, which called off the demonstration planned for September 30. Some union officials went an extra mile to back the Bush initiatives. Doug McCarron, president of the United Brotherhood of Carpenters, invited George W. Bush to attend the union's conventions. The Teamsters' James Hoffa volunteered his members to gather information for the Department of Homeland Security.

A countertrend arose. In January 2003, as U.S. troops got ready for the invasion of Iraq, representatives of over 100 labor-based antiwar groups gathered in Chicago—at the headquarters of the dissident Teamsters Local 705—and formed U.S. Labor Against the War (USLAW). Supporting the effort were three national unions—the United Electrical Workers, the Farm Labor Organizing Committee, and the National Writers Union—along with more than fifty locals of other unions and several municipal labor councils. By summer 2004, more national unions had come on board, including the ILWU, UNITE, AFSCME, and SEIU, whose national convention unanimously condemned the war in Iraq that June. In September, as the Republican National Convention met in New York to nominate George W. Bush for a second term, unionists from across the city took part in a series of antiwar demonstrations and the Central Labor Council organized its own anti-Bush rally with the war in Iraq a prominent theme.

In that fall's presidential election, however, antiwar unions joined the rest in going all out for the Democrats' John Kerry, who had voted in the U.S. Senate to authorize war in Iraq; and the AFL-CIO opposed the ILWU's plans for a pre-election march on Washington to demand reforms that neither Bush nor Kerry favored, including universal health care, national legislation for a living wage, and an end to the Iraq war. Although many local unions approved this march and African American activists from groups such as the Coalition of Black Trade Unionists and the Teamsters National Black Caucus worked hard on the project, most of the labor movement was preoccupied with canvassing for Kerry, and no more than 10,000 people showed up on October 17 for what had been billed as the "Million Worker March." Meanwhile, at the state and local levels, some union leaders backed Republicans who seemed unbeatable. In New York State, for example, the health care union District 1199—now part of SEIU—supported the Republican George Pataki when he ran for a third term as governor in 2002, and AFSCME's District Council 37 in New York City endorsed the Republican Michael Bloomberg in his race for a second term as mayor in 2005.

Employers and public officials used the War on Terror as a tool against labor, though not always with success. Defending his indictments of the Charleston Five, South Carolina's attorney general likened supporters of the union shop to perpetrators of the 9/11 attacks. Just weeks later, however, in November 2001, a growing campaign in solidarity with the accused persuaded authorities to drop felony charges and settle for $100 fines. Dockworkers on the West Coast got targeted as well. In the spring of 2002, Tom Ridge—head of Homeland Security for the Bush administration—issued a threat to the ILWU: any concerted action that slowed Pacific port traffic would be regarded as sabotage against the War on Terror. Rather than test that edict, the union's 10,500 dockworkers stayed on the job after their contract expired on June 30. Then, at the end of September, the Pacific Maritime Association (PMA)—an alliance of shippers, transport companies, and terminal operators—locked out the union, charging that its members' adherence to safety rules amounted to a slowdown. In early October, President Bush invoked the Taft-Hartley Act and got a federal judge to order that ILWU members go back to work "at a normal and reasonable rate of speed."[15] The PMA welcomed this move, believing that the ILWU would be found guilty of violating the president's order and debilitated by fines and arrests. As one former staffer observed, however, the union's militancy and close ties to counterparts overseas created a "wild-card situation that could turn into a potentially ugly and bloody confrontation on the West Coast and in ports around the world."[16] In the end, the U.S. Justice Department declined to charge the ILWU with Taft-Hartley violations, and by late November longshore workers emerged from this standoff with their union intact and a good new contract in hand.

The labor movement could point to other advances too. In October 2001, 28,000 state employees in Minnesota won the largest strike in state history, stopping work when contract negotiations stalled, standing firm for two weeks despite a conservative media campaign that dubbed the action unpatriotic, and finally convincing state officials to improve on the "final" offer they had made before the strike. The next few years saw strike victories by schoolteachers in several New Jersey towns; public employees in Santa Clara County, California; 6,000 casino workers in Atlantic City; 20,000 workers at forty-eight General Electric factories spread across twenty-three states; and 100,000 employees of the phone company SBC Communications, with operations in thirteen states. Organizing drives made some headway as well. In 2003 employees at the Borders bookstore in Ann Arbor, Michigan—the company's flagship operation—voted to join the United Food and Commercial Workers, and in January 2004 they got their first contract, after a seven-week strike. The United Electrical Workers unionized five small manufacturing shops in Chicago over the course of 2004. The following year, the CWA won organizing campaigns at AT&T stores and customer-service call centers.

Nurses emerged as an especially militant group. When employers stonewalled at the bargaining table, nurses' unions routinely threatened to strike; they made good on the threat often enough that one and all took it seriously. In 2004, the California Nurses Association (CNA) heartened labor activists across the country by going to war against Governor Arnold Schwarzenegger after he blocked implementation of a patient-safety law that improved nurse-to-patient staffing ratios in the state's hospitals. CNA members and supporters picketed the governor's speaking engagements, sneaked into the events to unfurl banners that called him to task, and chased him to fundraisers in New York City and Washington as well as a Hollywood movie premiere. His popularity plummeted, and in the fall of 2005 he gave up and let the new ratios go into effect.

More often than not, though, organizing drives failed to yield union contracts, strikers had to settle for far less than they had hoped for, and unions were hard pressed to take care of their own members let alone defend the general public from the likes of Governor Schwarzenegger. Although the Bush years saw a steady increase in the proportion of NLRB elections that ended in victories for unions, which won about 60 percent of the contests as of 2005, employers so adamantly resisted collective bargaining that the victories did not lead to contracts in most cases; and the president's anti-union appointees to the NLRB were not about to clamp down on the unfair labor practices that created this pattern. With regard to strikes, unions once known for militancy seemed to be throwing in the towel or were simply outgunned by employers. In March 2002, the United Auto Workers announced it was severing ties with Local 2036 at the Accuride wheel factory in Henderson, Kentucky, whose members had been on strike or locked out for four years during which they had voted down nine proposed contracts packed with concessions. That same month, at the Lockheed Martin plant in Marietta, Georgia, 2,700 members of the Machinists went on strike against subcontracting, and although they lost that battle, they showed tremendous cohesion, staying out for seven weeks during which just sixty-two workers crossed picket lines. Three years later, on the other hand, 400 workers at this same plant scabbed during a strike against concessions that lasted just one week. In mid-October 2003, when members of the United Food and Commercial Workers in southern California struck grocery stores owned by Safeway, two other chains immediately instituted lockouts, and 149 days later 70,000 exhausted grocery workers voted to accept contract terms their union had initially refused to consider.

An even sadder tale unfolded at Delphi Automotive, a gigantic auto parts manufacturer that had spun off from General Motors. Unbeknownst to the union members who ratified it, the UAW's 2003 contract with the "Big Three" auto manufacturers (GM, Ford, and Chrysler) included an agreement to decide later about wages for new hires at Delphi. When the decision was finally solidified in 2004, it took Delphi's starting wages from $24.00 to $14.00 an hour. Both company and union spokesmen promised this concession would save jobs, but nothing could have been further from the truth. In 2005, as top executives resigned amidst revelations of irregular accounting, Delphi filed for bankruptcy, announced that hourly wages for all workers, irrespective of seniority, would now range from $10.00 to $12.00, that workers would henceforth have to pay 27 percent of the health insurance costs formerly covered by the company, and that resistance to the new regime would prompt the company to void pensions. In 2006, UAW headquarters asked Delphi workers to authorize a strike, and they quickly obliged, but by then it was too late. Delphi had already closed more than twenty plants in the United States, and a bankruptcy court was about to void the company's contracts with the union. Before the year was out, Delphi announced plans to sell or shutter twenty-one of its twenty-nine remaining plants. Pension obligations were foisted off on the federal government's Pension Benefit Guaranty Corporation.

Public employee unions that rocked the boat were vulnerable too. In December 2005, when members of the Transport Workers Union Local 100 struck New York City's bus and subway systems for two and a half days, the business press labeled the walkout an act of terrorism, and the strike's causes—management's demands for concessions with respect to pensions and health insurance—got lost in the noise. Local 100 had "declared war on the public," cried *Investor's Business Daily*, and authorities needed to make them pay.[17] Months after the union's members returned to work, New York State levied penalties under a law that allowed but did not require punishments for public employees who went on strike. Local 100 was fined $2.5 million; its president went to jail for three days; every worker who took part in the walkout was docked two days' pay for each day on strike; and the checkoff system that automatically deducted union dues from workers' paychecks was suspended until early 2007.

Against this backdrop, union membership—which had slightly increased in 2001—entered a steady decline. Union density meanwhile decreased by every measure between 2001 and 2005, falling from 13.5 percent to 12.5 percent overall, from 9.1 percent to 7.9 percent in the private sector, from 18.6 to 13.1 percent among private-sector construction workers, and from 37.4 to 36.5 percent for public employees. The total number of union members fell too, from almost 16.3 million in 2001 to 15.7 million in 2005.

The losses were unevenly distributed, with some unions growing—or at least holding their own—while others shrank. Partly, this pattern stemmed from sectoral differences; compared to unions based in manufacturing, for example, building trades unions had an easier row to hoe. But different levels of commitment to organizing new members entered the picture too. While organizing campaigns never ceased in a handful of unions such as the CWA, SEIU, AFSCME, and HERE, many others lacked the resources or simply the will to reach out for new members.

Those that did organize debated methods of outreach. The CWA strongly advocated member-based campaigns in which rank-and-file unionists helped workers in nonunion shops to build in-house organizing committees. Other unions, like SEIU and AFSCME, relied on the electioneering model in which paid staff took charge of the campaign. Additionally, more and more unions deployed "salts," who got jobs in workplaces targeted for organizing and built campaigns from the inside. Proponents of all of these strategies could point to successes. Whatever the pros and cons of the various methods of organizing, it clearly worked better to do something instead of nothing.

As density fell and the movement contracted, dissidents gained ground in a host of unions, those that organized as well as those that seemed stuck. In the Teamsters, the UAW, the Laborers, SEIU, HERE, AFSCME, the American Federation of Teachers, the International Longshoremen's Association, the Carpenters, the Bricklayers, the Machinists, the Transport Workers, and the International Brotherhood of Electrical Workers among others, reformers set forth specific demands for changes in union governance and priorities. They all had in common the conviction that, if the labor movement as a whole did not soon remake itself, it would pass the point of no return. The question was, what to do?

A House Divided

In the fall of 2002, Stephen Lerner—head of SEIU's building service division and architect of the Justice for Janitors campaign—began to circulate a set of proposals for remaking the AFL-CIO and its affiliated unions. By summer 2003, the proposals had been published in several labor periodicals and become the subject of wide debate among union staffers and officials. To remain relevant, Lerner contended, the labor movement had to increase dramatically efforts to organize the unorganized, especially in the private sector. For this to occur, the AFL-CIO's sixty-six affiliates had to reorganize themselves into fifteen unions, each with jurisdiction over a specific sector of the U.S. economy—retail trade, services, health care, durable manufacturing, construction, hotels and entertainment, and so on. The first step toward implementing this plan was to build a new labor movement inside the old, with "organizing unions" coming together to execute as much of it as they could and to promote its universal adoption.[18] While this alliance's ultimate goal would be workers' empowerment on the job, in their industries, and in society at large, the immediate objective—and the key to all other progress—was to boost union density, at least to the level of the mid-1950s, when it had peaked at almost 35 percent.

Anticipating objections in the name of union democracy—a central concern of dissident movements that might otherwise embrace his proposals—Lerner put a new spin on the issue. Dissidents were framing the question too narrowly, he suggested: "If only 10% of workers in an industry are unionized it is impossible to have real union democracy because 90% of the workers are excluded. If unions are weak there is no democracy at the work site. If unions don't dominate industries, there is no power to challenge the dictatorial power of corporations. If unions don't represent a significant percent of the workforce workers won't have political power in our communities or nationally."[19] In short, democracy meant nothing absent higher density.

In August 2003, the alliance Lerner called for materialized under the name New Unity Partnership (NUP). Five unions took part: SEIU, HERE, UNITE, the Laborers, and the United Brotherhood of Carpenters. Although Stephen Lerner and the SEIU's president Andy Stern were the project's most prominent spokespeople, the Carpenters' Doug McCarron was in some respects its pioneer. Ascending to his union's presidency in 1995, McCarron had quickly centralized its governance, establishing a network of fifty-five regional councils that had wrested authority away from the locals and taken command of their financial assets. He had then used this new power structure to promote vigorous organizing, which had taken the union's membership from 349,000 in 1995 to about 550,000 in 2001. Despite this, McCarron had become a marginal figure in the upper reaches of the AFL-CIO, and not only because of his ardent support for

George W. Bush. He had also offended fellow labor leaders by arguing that other building trades unions should merge into his to make things more convenient for construction contractors. Then, as if to confirm suspicions that he intended to raid these other unions, he had taken the Carpenters out of the AFL-CIO in February 2001 and not long after had told a contractors' convention, "We're serious about reorganizing the industry. We're serious about customer service."[20] McCarron's involvement in the NUP thus raised doubts about its purposes.

Still, the NUP unions were growing as many others shrank, and that gave the project considerable momentum. Practicing what they preached with regard to union consolidation, UNITE and HERE announced a merger plan in February 2004 and executed it in July. Later that year, Andy Stern inaugurated a blog titled *Unite to Win* that made the NUP's program for change more specific and audacious. He proposed that the AFL-CIO designate up to three "lead unions" in every industry, require that these unions devote 20 percent of their budgets to organizing, and help them cover this expense by refunding half of their per capita dues to the federation. He also proposed that the AFL-CIO be authorized to compel its affiliates to merge or stop them from doing so; that it review its affiliates' charters with an eye to revoking the charters of unions that seemed unable or unwilling to organize; and that state federations take control of local councils lest they stand in the way of efforts to increase union density. Rumor had it that, if the AFL-CIO failed to institute these changes, SEIU, the Laborers, and UNITE HERE would all emulate the Carpenters and drop out.

The NUP initiative generated a lot of controversy, and the opposition was not confined to labor officials who wished to preserve their fiefdoms or union staffers hoping to hang on to their jobs. Some worried that a reduction in the AFL-CIO's income from per capita dues would undercut important projects, such as lobbying for more union-friendly federal labor laws. Calls for a more centralized power structure—increases in AFL-CIO's authority over its affiliates and decreases in central labor councils' autonomy—fell flat virtually everywhere outside the NUP. The notion that union mergers offered a solution to labor's woes struck many people as foolish since mergers had already reduced the number of AFL-CIO unions from 135 in 1955 to 64 in 2005, a half-century that saw union density decline by almost two-thirds. Jane Slaughter, a veteran writer for *Labor Notes*, spoke for multitudes of labor activists when she argued that density is "a central aspect of union power" but "not the only one" and that organizing drives focused on this one goal ran the risk of generating undemocratic locals with sweetheart contracts achieved through backroom deals with employers.[21] Visitors to Andy Stern's blog could post comments and respond to one another, but as the Association for Union Democracy observed, their conversations were "more like an audience discussing a performance in the lobby than joining the debate."[22] Some of the posts joked about this. When one regular visitor asked, "How long do we have to debate these proposals before there's a vote?," another replied, "VOTE?!?!?!? Hahahahahaha!!!"[23]

By summer 2005, the NUP had morphed into the Change to Win (CTW) coalition, which included the Teamsters and United Food and Commercial Workers as well as NUP members. At first it seemed that CTW might rally the AFL-CIO around a new program—or at least try to do so. On June 15, at the coalition's inaugural meeting, fifty top officials of its constituent unions vowed to carry their proposals to the AFL-CIO convention scheduled for late July and to work with any and all unions that supported the CTW agenda. The AFL-CIO's executive council meanwhile signaled its readiness to compromise, offering a 25 percent dues rebate to unions that would spend the money on organizing and announcing that it would finance a massive drive to unionize the retail chain Wal-Mart under the auspices of the United Food and Commercial Workers. At the eleventh hour, however, CTW leaders abandoned plans to win over the rest of the labor movement.

On July 25, just as AFL-CIO's fiftieth convention got under way in Chicago, Andy Stern and James Hoffa held a joint press conference to announce that the SEIU and the Teamsters were leaving the federation. UNITE HERE and the Food and Commercial Workers meanwhile boycotted the convention, and although the Laborers' Union and United Farm Workers took part, both refused to present their officers for election to AFL-CIO committees. In the days that followed all four of these unions exited the AFL-CIO, casting their lot with Change to Win. These defections took about 6 million workers out of the federation, reducing its ranks and its dues income by more than 40 percent. The loss stunned those left behind. "It was like someone tore my heart out," said the Steelworkers' president Leo Gerard.[24] State federations and local labor councils wondered how to preserve projects that involved both the AFL-CIO unions that funded these bodies and the unions now in Change to Win.

The exodus overshadowed aspects of the AFL-CIO convention that would otherwise have made headlines. Delegates endorsed the establishment of a national holiday in honor of César Chávez. They revised the AFL-CIO's constitution so that more women and people of color would join its executive bodies and every union's delegation to future conventions would have to reflect the racial and gender diversity of that union's rank and file. They approved a plan to mobilize 100,000 shop stewards to campaign for a new national labor law that would protect workers' right to organize. They mandated a series of measures in line with Change to Win's proposals: strategic mergers, joint organizing projects, and the formation of industry coordinating committees to oversee co-operation among unions organizing in the same sectors or with members working for the same employers. And, in a startling break from conservative tradition, the executive council presented and the delegates passed a resolution that called for a rapid end to the U.S. war in Iraq, cancellation of Iraq's foreign debt, and recognition of Iraqi workers' right to organize, as well as an increase in federal benefits for American veterans of the war. While U.S. veterans of foreign wars had always enjoyed the AFL-CIO's sympathy, this marked the first time it had come out against a war in progress. If the expansive agenda suggested confidence in the future, however, the departure of two giant unions and the imminent departure of others made the convention a somber affair.

A downright festive atmosphere prevailed at the Change to Win Federation's founding convention, held in St. Louis on September 27. It made labor history by placing CTW's leadership in the hands of a white woman and a black man, installing Anna Burger from the SEIU as national chair and Edgar Romney from UNITE HERE as secretary-treasurer. "We are committed to diversity throughout our ranks," Romney declared, "and there is no better place to start than the top."[25] In another historic move, the delegates adopted a constitution that earmarked 75 percent of the federation's budget for organizing. With per capita dues projected to bring in $750 million a year, this was a gigantic commitment—more than $560 million annually—and CTW's affiliated unions expected that organizing drives would get even more from their own treasuries. In some respects, however, the convention resembled a corporate gathering. Resolution after resolution passed by acclamation, without debate; the agenda steered clear of hot-button political issues such as the war in Iraq, nor did union democracy come up for discussion; and although rank-and-file workers were invited to relate personal stories that illustrated the convention's theme—that organizing means power— the proceedings were tightly controlled from the top.

Some people who spoke from the convention's floor likened Change to Win to the young CIO and a number of journalists echoed that comparison, but there were crucial differences between the two. In contrast to the CIO, whose organizing focused on the main engines of the industrial economy, Change to Win preferred safer targets such as building services, hotels, and other "landlocked" sectors in which unions seldom had to contend with runaway shops. Whereas the CIO was to a large degree built from the bottom up by local unions whose members charted their own course, Change to Win's affiliates were centralized organizations whose executives made virtually all of the important decisions. Finally, the language of worker solidarity and social justice that had suffused the young CIO was mostly missing from Change to Win. Andy Stern, CTW's premier founder and spokesperson, regarded a "class-struggle mentality" as hopelessly old fashioned and sought to replace it with unionism based on co-operation with employers. He was confident that "a working 'relationship' that can add value to the business and help improve performance will result in workers sharing fairly in their employers' success."[26]

The national press dubbed Andy Stern the prophet of a new day for labor. He became the subject of a flattering profile on CBS television's *60 Minutes*, whose reporter Lesley Stahl called his partnership with employers "brave."[27] His book *A Country That Works: Getting America Back on Track* created a media sensation when it came out in the fall of 2006. The president of the U.S. Chamber of Commerce called him "a breath of fresh air"; Arnold Schwarzenegger invited him to speak at a California summit meeting on health care; *Fortune* magazine heaped praise on the deals he negotiated with employers; the *Wall Street Journal* described him as "shrewd" and "perhaps the most successful modern labor leader."[28] Had they been consulted, some members of SEIU's rank and file would have told a different story. In pursuit of density, the union had accepted—even proposed—some egregious sweetheart contracts, but the festering resentments this caused had not yet come to a head.

A few years down the line, the Change to Win Federation would be wracked by division, but for now the alliance stayed intact, and relations between its unions and those they had left behind did not entirely go to the dogs. Although the AFL-CIO Executive Council initially ordered state federations and local labor councils to exclude CTW unions, that policy was soon reversed, and in all but a few states affiliates of the two federations worked together under the auspices of "solidarity charters."[29] They occasionally raided each other for members—especially SEIU and AFSCME in Illinois, Iowa, and California—but the all-out warfare some had feared did not materialize.

If the split in the labor movement was less harmful than it might have been, however, that did not make it a good thing. Optimists predicted that competition would so stimulate organizing that union density would rise, but that gain did not materialize. In virtually every occupational group for which the Bureau of Labor Statistics calculated the figures, union density was lower in 2010 than in 2005. The only exceptions to that pattern were federal and municipal employees, whose rates of union membership rose by less than 1 percentage point in each case.

Of course, numbers were not the only way to measure unionism's vitality, and a split of this magnitude might have revitalized the labor movement by igniting debate about its underlying principles and ultimate purposes. As it happened, though, the two sides focused their back and forth on technicalities such as the correct formula by which unions that organized would get rebates on per capita dues to the AFL-CIO. Jerry Tucker—a former regional director of the UAW who had earned a national reputation as a tireless opponent of concessions bargaining—suggested in *Labor Notes* that a thoroughgoing debate could not unfold inside the AFL-CIO or Change to Win because leaders of both federations embraced "partnership unionism," based on the notion that American workers and American employers ought to collaborate. To move forward, Tucker argued, rank-and-file unionists and their allies had to create alternate arenas for discussion of the labor movement's future. "Then," he concluded, "the real debate can begin."[30]

13

Workers of the World

In the mid-1980s, looking back on many battles as a union leader at Ford's River Rouge plant, Paul Boatin drew this lesson: "In a struggle with the corporations, you've got to fight every day, every hour, every minute, every second, because their promises don't mean anything. They have no country, they have no god, they have no flag, they have no heart."[1] That outlook, once mostly confined to leftists like Boatin, spread throughout the labor movement as the twentieth century drew to a close and companies that had once proclaimed themselves good citizens embraced an entirely different identity. As General Electric's CEO Jack Welch told an interviewer in 1998, "Ideally, you'd have every plant you own on a barge, to move with currencies and changes in the economy."[2]

Free trade agreements—which some analysts aptly described as "bills of rights for capital"—had vastly increased corporations' global power and prerogatives.[3] Trade across national borders was as old as capitalism itself, but it grew ever more voluminous in the decades following the Second World War. In 1948, the United States joined with twenty-two other nations to implement the General Agreement on Tariffs and Trade (GATT), whose signatories mutually lowered trade barriers such as tariffs and import quotas. This system steadily expanded, thanks largely to the lending policies of the World Bank and the International Monetary Fund (IMF). To get loans, needy countries were required to enter multilateral free-trade agreements and to relax restrictions on the inflow of foreign investment and outflow of profits. By the mid-1990s, GATT had 128 member nations, and in 1995 it transformed itself into the World Trade Organization (WTO)—not merely an agreement but an intergovernmental agency empowered to regulate international trade and stop national governments from imposing their own regulations. As of 2016, the WTO had 164 members and oversaw more than 95 percent of global trade. These were the central institutions of the new world order that critics dubbed "neoliberalism," a word translated into many different languages around the world.[4]

Within this order, workers' welfare was, at best, an afterthought. Nominally, the WTO assigned the supervision of labor standards to the International Labor Organization (ILO), an agency established in 1919 and affiliated with the United Nations since 1946. The ILO brought together national governments, employers and labor organizations to set international rules regarding labor conditions and workers' rights, but it lacked enforcement mechanisms, relying instead on voluntary compliance. The WTO's charter, on the other hand, granted it authority to punish member nations that broke its rules, which included the commandment that they not embargo each other's goods based on labor practices—the fact, for example, that the goods had been produced by children, enslaved labor, or workers routinely exposed to deadly toxins.

A dominant force behind the WTO's establishment and growth, the U.S. government also instituted free trade agreements of its own. The first was a deal with Canada that went into effect in 1989 and later provided the foundation for the North American Free Trade Agreement (NAFTA) that incorporated the United States, Canada, and Mexico into a trade bloc starting in 1994. A slew of similar agreements followed, including a multilateral pact between the United States and five Central American nations plus the Dominican Republic and bilateral U.S. deals with Jordan, Israel, Chile, Peru, Australia, South Korea, and six other countries. Sometimes free traders encountered roadblocks. In 2005, a plan to expand NAFTA to encompass virtually all of the Western Hemisphere ran aground when some Latin American nations refused to accept U.S. domination of the project. The general trend, however, was toward increasingly free transnational flows of commodities, investment, profits, and jobs.

For working-class communities in the United States, job loss in manufacturing was the most visible aspect of the new regime. Between 2000 and 2015, the country lost more than 5 million industrial jobs. By the 2010s, layoffs in this sector were so much a part of American life that the real estate industry peddled "job loss protection" insurance for homebuyers, greeting card companies marketed sympathy cards for the newly unemployed, and local newspapers warned readers that unemployment could trigger heart attacks.[5] In addition, deindustrialization meant wage stagnation, not only because displaced workers flooded the labor market but also because the job losses came disproportionately from unionized parts of the economy. In 2015, union contracts covered just 7.4 percent of U.S. workers in the private sector. Many blamed this state of affairs on American corporations' lack of patriotism—their readiness to move production from the United States to parts of the world where wages were lower, tax burdens lighter, and laws regarding industrial pollution and workplace safety and health more lax.

Corporate treason was indeed part of the problem, but other important factors entered the picture too. With very few exceptions, large corporations could no longer be described as having nationalities; they were owned and controlled by investors from all over the world, sometimes directly and other times indirectly through private equity firms or hedge funds. And just as investment moved from country to country in search of the best return, it jumped from product to product and industry to industry. In earlier eras, profitmaking had depended first and foremost on production and sales—making better or cheaper goods and capturing larger shares of the market. By the dawn of the twenty-first century, profits derived mainly from accounting tricks, the manipulation of tax loopholes, and investors' ability in the Internet age to reallocate gigantic amounts of money in the blink of an eye.

If this damaged working-class life in the United States and other countries at the helm of the free trade empire, it was nothing short of a catastrophe for the poorer nations that came to be known as the "Global South." The new regime transformed their economies without making provisions for people pushed out of family farming, herding, or other traditional livelihoods disrupted by unfettered trade and foreign investment. Lenders from the World Bank and IMF demanded not only open borders but also cutbacks in government spending on social safety nets. Desperately competing for investment, debtor nations thus engaged in a race to the bottom almost unimaginable in wealthier parts of the world. In 2013, the ILO estimated that more than 200 million wageworkers around the globe could not find jobs. Another 1.5 billion people were confined to the informal economy, piecing together a living as street vendors, as domestic workers, as prostitutes, and in other occupations that left them unprotected by labor law and often harassed by authorities.

In short, neoliberalism—the new world economy and the political arrangements that made it possible—enriched corporate capitalists at the expense of workers everywhere, not just the United States. That realization dawned slowly on the U.S. labor movement. The parochial spirit seen in the Buy American campaigns of the 1980s survived in many quarters, with China replacing Japan as the primary target of resentment. A countertrend steadily gained ground, however. As the AFL-CIO's Richard Trumka observed: "Global companies begat global problems for workers—global problems begat the need for global unions."[6] Just how global unions might be built was unclear to say the least, but it was hard to deny their necessity.

Globalization from Above

The new world order spawned some heartbreaking reversals of labor victories. Barely a year after workers voted to unionize the Fieldcrest Cannon textile mills in Kannapolis, North Carolina, in 1999, the Pillowtex Corporation that owned Fieldcrest Cannon declared bankruptcy. Competitors whose mills were overseas had usurped the company's contracts with Wal-Mart. In 2003, Pillowtex went out of business, permanently laying off all of the workers in its mills and selling the Fieldcrest Cannon brands to firms that supplied U.S. retailers with linens produced in the Global South. The mill complex in Kannapolis was torn down to make way for a biotechnology research center.

Another landmark plant shut down in Ravenswood, West Virginia, where United Steelworkers Local 5668 had prevailed against the eighteen-month lockout by the Ravenswood Aluminum Corporation (RAC) in 1990–92. In 2009, RAC's parent company, Century Aluminum, idled the plant to pressure state officials into subsidizing its electricity bill and soon upped the stakes by canceling health insurance coverage for the plant's retirees. Over the next six years, West Virginia's legislature and public service commission tried without success to come up with a subsidy large enough to please the company; the United Steelworkers went to court on behalf of the retirees; and the retirees themselves held multiple protests in Ravenswood, at the state capitol, at Century's headquarters in Chicago, at a shareholder meeting in California, and anyplace else they could publicize the company's wrongdoing. Finally, in 2015, Century permanently shuttered the Ravenswood plant, citing competition from aluminum producers in China. By that time the company had its own Chinese operation, plants in Iceland and the Netherlands, two facilities in rural Kentucky with utility bills that met Century's demands, and a plant in Mount Holly, South Carolina, that was laying off half its workforce as part of a campaign for cheaper electricity. In January 2017, the company finally agreed to fund the Ravenswood retirees' health insurance, including back payments for the years they had been left in the lurch. That same month Century sued South Carolina's state-owned utility company, seeking electricity bills as low as those Century enjoyed in Kentucky.

Stories like those that unfolded in Kannapolis and Ravenswood echoed across the country. Even before the worldwide recession of 2007–9, the Big Three auto companies were shuttering factories in town after town. The same was true of Maytag, Sony, Motorola, Hewlett Packard, General Electric, Weyerhaeuser, Goodyear Tire and Rubber, and scores of other industrial giants. In one way or another, plant closings virtually always involved offshoring—a corporation's decision to send its own operations overseas, to buy from overseas suppliers what used to be made in the United States, or to abandon a U.S.-based industry or product line and invest in another based elsewhere.

In a variation on this theme, some mega-corporations demanded such large price cuts on the part of suppliers that offshoring became a must. By 1999, General Electric was directing suppliers to Mexico and holding "supplier migration" conferences to help them with logistics.[7] In 2003, *BusinessWeek* reported that Wal-Mart had "wrung tens of billions of dollars in cost efficiencies out of the retail supply chain," becoming such a gigantic retail chain that manufacturers of mass-market consumer goods had little choice but to meet its demands for price reductions, which frequently meant transferring production overseas.[8]

Although workers in manufacturing were especially hard hit by offshoring, the trend penetrated other sectors too. By the 2010s, a great many insurance, finance, retail, and telecommunications companies had shifted customer service jobs and back-office clerical operations from the United States to Asia, especially India and the Philippines. White-collar workers with very high levels of skill could find themselves displaced as well. Exported jobs included positions in computer programming, software development, graphic design, and biomedical research.

The U.S. government facilitated offshoring through the Overseas Private Investment Corporation, a federal agency that helped companies transfer money across borders and offered them insurance against losses caused by political instability in their host countries. Tax policy supported offshoring too. Under federal law, the profits that U.S.-based multinationals generated overseas were not taxable until and unless the money was transferred into the United States. That created a powerful incentive for corporations to earn as much as possible in other countries and spend as little as possible at home. Meanwhile, the constant threat that jobs would be offshored persuaded many state governments to accede to corporate pressures for special deals to lower their taxes. The watchdog group Citizens for Tax Justice counted 265 corporations whose annual state tax bills on U.S. profits averaged just 3 percent from 2008 through 2010—less than half of what they would have paid absent the concessions they wrung from public officials. Vying to attract and hold onto jobs, states offered ever-sweeter deals, so that some very profitable corporations wound up paying no state taxes at all.

From the standpoint of displaced workers in the United States, offshoring was all about the corporate search for rock-bottom wages, and that was clearly a major factor. In the 1990s, for example, the Walt Disney Company allocated all of its production of clothing and toys to contractors in China, Haiti, Vietnam, and elsewhere in the Global South. In one contractor's factory—the Keyhinge facility in Da Nang, Vietnam—labor monitors from Hong Kong found a thousand workers, mostly very young women, who spent sixty to seventy hours a week making tiny Disney figures that the McDonald's fast food chain gave away with its Happy Meals for children. On average, the workers' pay amounted to $250 a year.

Low wages were not the only attraction of offshoring, however. Multinationals also looked overseas for generous tax codes, slipshod enforcement of labor law, and, especially, a union-free environment. If these arrangements could not be secured in one place, there was always another place to set up shop. In the mid-1980s, the Alcoa Corporation formed a joint venture with the Japanese firm Fujikura and acquired automotive wiring factories in the United States and Mexico. By the early 1990s, Alcoa-Fujikura was transferring jobs from its U.S. facilities to their counterparts south of the border, but workers in the Mexican plants proved less biddable than the company had anticipated. In 1996, they sent a delegation to Alcoa's annual shareholders' meeting in Pittsburgh, where Benedictine nuns joined with worker spokespeople to present grievances about low wages, poor sanitation and safety provisions, and illegal firings of workers who tried to establish a union. Shamed into making some improvements with regard to wages and safety, Alcoa-Fujikura still resisted unionism, firing hundreds of worker activists and finally deciding in 2003 to move most of its Mexican operations to an industrial park near El Progreso, Honduras. There lay a multinational's dream: a free-trade zone in which the company's four plants were entirely exempt from tariffs, corporate income tax, state and city taxes, and even the local sales tax. Nor did Honduran authorities require Alcoa-Fujikora's compliance with national labor laws that guaranteed paid breaks and free transportation to the workplace. Here too, though, workers organized, and when unlawful dismissals failed to derail the campaign, the company (now wholly owned by Alcoa) once again pulled up stakes, closing all of its El Progreso plants in 2008.

In some instances, U.S. corporations' treatment of workers overseas led to lawsuits under the federal Alien Tort Statute, which allows citizens of other countries to go to U.S. courts for redress of human rights violations that have taken place abroad. In 1996 Burmese villagers sued Unocal (owned by Union Oil of California), alleging forced labor, false imprisonment, assault, and other violations in connection with the construction of a gas pipeline. Nine years later, the company settled the suit out of court. In 2001 and again in 2006, workers at Coca-Cola bottling plants in Colombia charged the company with mobilizing right-wing paramilitary squads to intimidate, kidnap, torture, and murder activists from the National Union of Food Industry Workers (Sindicato Nacional de Trabajadores de la Industria de Alimentos), which sought to unionize the plants. In both cases, U.S. courts sided with the company. In 2010, workers at Coca-Cola facilities in Guatemala filed a similar suit; a federal judge tossed it out before the case was even heard. Stymied in the courts, Coca-Cola workers in these and other countries—including Turkey, Egypt, and Indonesia—joined with U.S. unions and labor-support groups to organize a consumer boycott.

U.S. corporations doing business abroad were sued for other kinds of wrongdoing too. In 1999, Nigerian plaintiffs filed an Alien Tort claim against the Chevron oil company for colluding with their country's military to lay waste to communities that protested the firm's pollution of the Niger Delta. Again, a U.S. court sided with a U.S. corporation. But complaints filed overseas sometimes fell on more sympathetic ears. In 2010, for example, the Indian state of Kerala established a tribunal empowered to process monetary claims against Coca-Cola for depleting and polluting the water supply in the Palakkad district. In 2011 the Supreme Court of India reopened a case in which Union Carbide had paid out $470 million to settle claims concerning some 10,000 deaths, 100,000 permanent injuries, and enduring pollution caused by toxic gas that leaked out of the company's pesticide factory in the city of Bhopal in 1984. Dow Chemical, which had since acquired Union Carbide, howled that the case should remain closed, and a federal judge in the United States concurred, refusing to recognize the Indian ruling. Revisiting another decades-old case, an Ecuadoran court ruled in 2011 that Chevron owed damages for an environmental calamity that its Texaco subsidiary had created by drilling for oil in a rainforest from the mid-1960s into the 1990s. In this case, a U.S. court let the ruling stand, but in 2017 the U.S. Supreme Court overturned that decision.

What may well be corporate America's biggest overseas crime spree to date was perpetrated by the Freeport-McMoRan mining company headquartered in New Orleans and, after Hurricane Katrina, in Phoenix. In the mid-1990s, when environmentalists identified the company as the largest industrial polluter within U.S. borders, its CEO, Jim Bob Moffett, took offense. "I can assure you we receive better treatment in some foreign countries than we do here," he sniffed.[9] The most accommodating host was Indonesia's dictator Muhammad Suharto, who came to power in 1967 and promptly cut a deal with Freeport. In return for generous payoffs to himself and his cronies, Suharto gave the company unfettered access to the rich mineral resources of the Western Papua province. There, Freeport opened the Grasberg Mine, a gigantic open-pit operation that extracted and smelted copper, silver, and more gold than any other mine in the world. When Suharto was ousted in 1998, Freeport retained its mineral rights, redirecting payoffs to the new regime. Military and police officials got especially hefty bribes, in return for which they violently suppressed resistance by tribal people displaced by the mine's construction, mass protests against the company's dumping of mine waste into local forests and rivers, union organizing among the miners, and at least five strikes over the years 2000–17.

Just as corporations chartered in the United States expanded operations abroad, foreign companies enlarged their footprints as U.S. employers. Those from western Europe, who usually had relatively friendly relations with labor unions in their home countries, proclaimed codes of ethics that included recognition of workers' right to organize. In the United States, however, these companies routinely adopted a when-in-Rome attitude, battling unionism just as fervently as the typical American firm.

One prime example of this pattern was the German telecommunications giant Deutsche Telekom (DT), owner of the wireless phone company T-Mobile USA. At home, DT worked so amicably with the union ver.di (short for Vereinte Dienstleistungsgewerkschaft, or German United Services Trade Union) that the Communications Workers of America (CWA) endorsed the company's entry into the U.S. market in 2001, expecting to organize it in short order. But T-Mobile did all it could to remain union free. Its managers across the country received manuals prepared by an anti-union consulting firm that explained how to practice "union avoidance" without violating the National Labor Relations Act. Instead of saying that unionization *will* cause layoffs, for example, say that it *could* cause them; and instead of querying job applicants as to their feelings about unions, simply ask them what clubs they belong to so that you can weed out the "joiners." When tactics like these failed, T-Mobile pulled out other weapons. In 2006 a committee of workers at the company's customer-service call center near Allentown, Pennsylvania, contacted the CWA and began to stand at the facility's gate, holding union signs and distributing leaflets. Managers tried unsuccessfully to get state police to disperse them, sent security guards to record the license plate of every person who accepted a flyer, and instituted mandatory meetings at which they regaled workers with stories about the dangers of unionization. The organizing drive continued nonetheless—until 2011, when T-Mobile shut down this call center and shipped the jobs overseas.

The National Labor Relations Board (NLRB) ruled T-Mobile guilty of unfair labor practices in its efforts to intimidate workers, but the penalties were too mild to have a deterrent effect. Other European firms that broke U.S. labor laws to undermine collective bargaining included the French multinational Saint-Gobain at its industrial abrasives factory in Worcester, Massachusetts, and its ceramics plant in Niagara Falls, New York; the British retail chain Tesco PLC at its Fresh & Easy convenience stores in California and Nevada; the Norwegian company Kongsberg Automotive at its drive-train factory in Van Wert, Ohio; and the Dutch corporation Gamma Holding at its wire-fabric plant in Star City, Arkansas. Among the tactics they deployed were lockouts, plant closings, dismissals of union activists, and prohibitions against workers' talking about unions. Although the NLRB recognized illegal tactics as just that, it seldom meted out a punishment beyond the requirement that an offending employer post a notice declaring that workers had the right to organize and bargain collectively without interference.

Sometimes a contest between an American union and a foreign-based multinational ended happily for the union. For four months starting in late January 2010, the Rio Tinto Group, a British-Australian mining and metals conglomerate, locked out 570 workers employed at its open-pit borax mine in Boron, California. The company's goal was to destroy their union, Local 30 of the International Longshore and Warehouse Union (ILWU), which had refused to accept a contract that would have ended the union shop, done away with seniority, and allowed Rio Tinto to outsource work and transform regular full-time jobs into temporary part-time positions. Despite the mismatch—a small local versus a company with billions in annual profits, tens of thousands of workers, operations on six continents, and replacement workers in Boron—Local 30 won the fight, thanks to nonstop mass picketing at the mine, financial support from the labor movement in southern California, shows of solidarity by mining and maritime unions around the globe, and protests at Rio Tinto's headquarters in London and Melbourne along with British consulates in the United States and Canada.

In most cases, however, foreign multinationals, like their U.S. counterparts, succeeded in trampling on American workers' rights under the law. Investigators from the international agency Human Rights Watch laid much of the blame for this on the

U.S. government, in particular Congress's failure to amend the National Labor Relations Act to address employers' many obstructions of workers' right to organize, and the Senate's failure for more than sixty years to ratify the ILO rules that had enshrined that right since 1949. In fact, the situation was worse than Human Rights Watch suggested. The government did not just fail to protect workers' rights on U.S. soil; it also promoted offshoring under arrangements that systematically abused workers overseas.

Nowhere was this more obvious than in Mexico under the North American Free Trade Agreement. Thirty years before NAFTA went into effect, the Mexican government had initiated a Border Industrialization Program (Programa de Industrialización Fronteriza, or PIF) to provide jobs for families left high and dry after the United States discontinued the Bracero Program that had brought in hundreds of thousands of Mexican guest workers from 1942 through 1964. To attract foreign investors, the PIF allowed foreign companies to import machinery and materials without paying much in the way of duties, and Mexico's government sweetened the pot by drastically relaxing its enforcement of national labor laws that proclaimed workers' right to organize, to bargain collectively, to go on strike, and to enjoy benefits such as the eight-hour day, paid leave for pregnancy and childbirth, and provisions for workplace safety and health. By the early 1990s, about a half-million Mexican workers were employed in some 2,000 PIF factories that had been established by firms based in Japan, Europe and, especially, the United States. These factories were known as *maquiladoras*.

Under NAFTA, *maquiladoras* would multiply and spread beyond the border, but first the treaty's advocates in the United States had to win over or outmaneuver skeptics who thought that it would accelerate American job loss. As in all negotiations about international commerce, big business dominated the U.S. agenda through a "trade advisory committee" whose members came mostly from multinational corporations.[10] One big advantage for them was that NAFTA's elimination of tariffs between member countries would apply to North American subsidiaries of multinationals based overseas—Honda's American Honda Motor Company, for example—as well as companies headquartered in the United States, Canada, or Mexico. And if that made it difficult to bill NAFTA as a special boon to North American firms, it also guaranteed vast and vociferous corporate support for the deal. More than 2,700 companies, trade associations, and business groups came together to form the USA-NAFTA coalition, which plugged NAFTA in newspapers coast to coast, ran television ads proclaiming it "Good for jobs, good for us," and sent an army of lobbyists to Capitol Hill.[11] Among this campaign's most ardent supporters was the newly elected president Bill Clinton, who entered office after NAFTA had been signed by his predecessor, George H.W. Bush, but before the treaty had been ratified by Congress. When both the House and Senate approved the deal by comfortable margins in November 1993, the business community thanked Clinton for his bravery in rallying a critical mass of Democratic votes for NAFTA. According to the CEO of American Express, "He stood up against his two prime constituents, labor and environment, to drive it home over their dead bodies."[12] An aide to Congressman Dick Gephardt of Missouri—a stalwart opponent of NAFTA—pointed instead to political corruption; the treaty was ratified, he explained, "because of money, because of gifts, because of special interests, goodies and everything else."[13] Gullibility perhaps entered the picture too. USA-NAFTA had promised that the treaty would quickly create about 200,000 new jobs in the United States and preserve another 700,000; an investigation at the end of 1994, NAFTA's first year, identified just 535 new jobs and counted several thousand lost.

NAFTA's defenders nonetheless touted it as a blessing to workers since it was the first U.S. trade agreement to include safeguards for labor standards. To help get NAFTA through Congress, the Clinton administration had added to it a pair of side agreements designed to appease critics from the environmental and labor movements. Environmentalists got the North American Agreement on Environmental Cooperation, and organized labor got the North American Agreement on Labor Cooperation (NAALC). Both permitted individuals, unions, employers, and nongovernmental organizations to lodge complaints about practices in any NAFTA country. Under the NAALC, each of NAFTA's three signatories established a national administrative office to adjudicate complaints about labor conditions. In 2005, the U.S. Department of Labor proudly described this system as a means "to ensure that labor laws are being enforced in all three countries."[14] In fact, violations of labor laws were commonplace throughout NAFTA's jurisdiction and especially in Mexico.

Most of these violations did not generate formal complaints to the NAALC, for it soon became apparent that the process generally led nowhere. As of 2017, the various national administrative offices had received just thirty-nine complaints, twenty-five of them concerning labor conditions in Mexico. In almost every instance, the latter charged that *maquiladoras* and Mexican authorities alike had ignored the national law that enshrined workers' right to organize into unions of their own choosing. Nominally, the vast majority of Mexico's industrial workers had union representation. More often than not, however, the union was affiliated with the Confederation of Mexican Workers (Confederación de Trabajadores Mexicanos, or CTM) or the Revolutionary Federation of Workers and Peasants (Confederación Revolucionaria de Obreros y Campesinos, or CROC): labor federations deeply corrupted by close ties to business-friendly political parties and public officials. Nicknamed *charro* ("cowboy") unions, CTM and CROC affiliates signed many a contract with *maquiladoras*, where their main job was to keep production going at a fast clip no matter how many labor laws got bent or broken in the process.[15] When workers bucked this system by forming their own independent unions or by rallying around one of the militant unions that belonged to the Authentic Workers' Front (Frente Auténtico del Trabajo, or FAT), *maquiladora* managers clamped down as hard as they could. The first complaints filed under the NAALC zeroed in on this problem. In mid-February 1994, when NAFTA was less than two months olds, the Teamsters and the United Electrical Workers joined forces to ask that the U.S. National Administrative Office stop Honeywell and General Electric from strong-arming *maquiladora* workers who were trying to win recognition for unions affiliated with the FAT. The case ended predictably; the investigating officers reported that there was insufficient evidence that Mexico's labor laws had been violated. That verdict would be replicated multiple times over the next twenty-plus years.

When a national administrative office found that labor laws had in fact been violated, it could do nothing more than refer the case to cabinet-level officials of the country in which the complaint had been lodged and the one it had been lodged against. If they saw fit, the commissioners would then hold a seminar to inform all interested parties as to the content of the laws that had been broken and, in some cases, follow up with a workshop to teach the offending employers how to comply. In short, the NAALC was a recipe for inaction.

Doing nothing could take a long time, moreover. Consider, for example, the NAALC case regarding the ITAPSA brake factory near Mexico City. By the end of each work-day, everything and everyone in this plant was coated with dust from the asbestos used to make brake pads, and fumes from toxic solvents regularly filled the building too. Seeking a change, ITAPSA's 350 workers attempted to trade their CTM union for one affiliated with the FAT. Managers retaliated by firing fifty of them; threatening the rest with assault, rape, and job loss; and hiring armed thugs to attend the election in which CTM and FAT squared off—an election by voice vote that required each worker to publicly state a preference. The FAT union naturally lost. In mid-December 1997, a coalition of unions and labor support groups from the United States, Mexico, and Canada filed an NAALC complaint against ITAPSA and its owner, the Echlin auto-parts conglomerate with headquarters in the United States and production facilities around the world. At the end of January 1998, the U.S. National Administrative Office agreed to investigate the complaint; at the end of July, it publicly reported that the complainants' charges accurately described events and recommended a cabinet-level consultation. Almost two years later, in mid-May 2000, the U.S. secretary of labor and Mexican secretary of labor and social welfare issued a joint statement that called for two seminars on workers' right to organize unions of their own choosing. The first took place that summer in Tijuana, more than 1,500 miles from where ITAPSA work-ers lived; it was attended by workers from various *maquiladoras* that had violated the right to organize and by thugs from the CROC, who beat up many of the workers. The second seminar took place in the summer of 2002 in Monterrey, about 600 miles from ITAPSA workers' homes. There was no seminar about protection against asbestos and solvents, merely an agreement that the U.S. and Mexican governments would exchange information on workplace health and safety.

Some cases that came before national administrative offices were even more drawn out. In 2008, the Canadian office accepted a complaint by more than forty unions and support groups that North Carolina's state law against collective bargaining by public employees violated NAALC principles. As of 2018, the case was still under review. The same was true of complaints filed with both the U.S. and Canadian offices in 2011, after Mexico's president issued a decree that dissolved the country's publicly owned electrical power company and summarily fired its 44,000 workers, all to destroy their militant union, Sindicato Mexicano de Electricistas.

Of all the labor struggles that took place in Mexico under the NAFTA regime, the one with the happiest ending did not involve the NAALC at all. In September 2005, Sights Denim Systems—a *maquiladora* in Morelo, Coahuila, that laundered stone-washed blue jeans for Levi Strauss—shut down the plant without first notifying its 950 employees. To protect the severance pay to which they were entitled under both Mexican law and Levi Strauss's widely advertised code of ethics, the workers stopped seven trailer trucks from leaving the facility and stored their cargo—260,000 pairs of jeans—inside the plant, guarding them around the clock. Early the next year, they received severance payments that averaged about $10,000 apiece and, with that, let the jeans go.

Happy endings were exceptions to the rule, however; for workers across North America, NAFTA meant trouble, and its ripple effects damaged working people in virtually every part of the globe. While statistical analysts differed as to how many jobs were lost or gained and how much wages rose or fell, one and all could see that the agreement did not even come close to meeting the rosy promises of its proponents. More important, as the economist Jeff Faux observed on the eve of NAFTA's twentieth birthday, it "was the template for rules of the emerging global economy, in which the benefits would flow to capital and the costs to labor."[16] The WTO, the modern-day World Bank and IMF, the gigantic grid of bilateral and multilateral trade deals that incorporated nearly all of the world's nations into the same economic system—each of these applied principles pioneered by NAFTA. In this sense, the U.S. Chamber of Commerce was quite correct when it celebrated NAFTA's first two decades by declaring it a "triumphant agreement."[17]

Globalization from Below

Perhaps in every country and certainly in the United States, economic nationalism was workers' first response to globalization from the top down. The Buy American campaign of the 1980s enjoyed something of a revival in the NAFTA era. "If you can't find union-made, at least buy American-made," urged the head of the AFL-CIO Union Label and Service Trades Department.[18] Nonunion manufacturers with operations in the United States readily agreed. Indeed, the slogan Buy American often functioned as nothing more than an advertising tool. For example, Starkey Hearing Technologies, headquartered in Minnesota, used the phrase to distinguish its Audibel brand of hearing aids from those marketed by rival companies based in Europe. Most Starkey hearing aids were manufactured in the Global South, however, and the same was true of the European brands. Even when the goods in question really were made in the United States, calls to "Buy American" rested on flawed logic. In an interview with *Labor Notes*, Dana Frank—author of a path-breaking book on the long history of Buy American initiatives—succinctly summarized the problem: "'Buy American' campaigns operate on the assumption that if you buy a product made in the United States, then the company making the profit off that sale is going to reinvest in good union jobs in the United States—but that is very rarely the case. The companies didn't agree to that partnership. They have instead used those profits to lobby for free-trade agreements that grease the skids for them to go overseas."[19]

Unions' lobbying and demonstrations against these agreements had mixed results. While the drive to stop NAFTA failed in its main objective, it did prompt the deal's proponents to institute the NAALC—toothless protection, to be sure, but beneficial insofar as it facilitated cross-border co-operation among unions in the United States, Mexico, and Canada. Eight years later, in 2001, the AFL-CIO exerted enough pressure on Capitol Hill to derail efforts to place NAFTA's geographical expansion on a "fast track," which would have prevented Congress from amending the deal or delaying it by means of a filibuster. In 2003, when trade officials from thirty-four countries met in Miami to negotiate the expansion—dubbed the Free Trade Area of the Americas (FTAA)—the thousands of demonstrators who showed up to oppose the project included contingents from the United Steelworkers, the Service Employees International Union, the United Food and Commercial Workers, and other unions as well as a number of immigrant worker centers. Undermining U.S. officials' authority at the meeting, these protests helped to set the stage for the FTAA's death at the hands of several Latin American countries in 2005. That same year, however, labor lost a close-fought battle to stop passage of the Central American Free Trade Agreement, which the House approved by a two-vote margin, despite many union demonstrations at congressional offices.

Increasingly, U.S. unions turned to alternate initiatives in coordination with workers' movements in other countries. Cross-border alliances were not by any means unprecedented, especially with respect to Mexico and Canada. U.S.-Mexican labor solidarity dated back at least to the early twentieth century, when the Industrial Workers of the World had chapters in Mexico and some IWW members in the United States volunteered to fight in the Mexican Revolution. Later that century, Mexican labor activists lent support to CIO organizing in the U.S. Southwest and to strikes by CIO unions, whose most effective organizers included immigrants from Mexico. And, although the Cold War undercut these alliances, cooperation across the border resurged in the half-decade preceding NAFTA's enactment. New initiatives in that period included coordination between the AFL-CIO Farm Labor Organizing Committee and an independent Mexican union of tomato pickers employed by contractors for Campbell's Soup; the establishment of a labor center in Ciudad Juárez jointly supported by the Teamsters, the United Electrical Workers (UE), and FAT; and an array of multi-union solidarity groups that ranged from local organizations like the Support Committee for Maquiladora Workers in San Diego, California, to continental projects like the North American Worker-to-Worker Network.

The U.S. and Canadian labor movements had a longstanding relationship too, though they were somewhat estranged by the time NAFTA came along. Starting in the mid-nineteenth century, a great many unions headquartered in the United States developed locals in Canada and began to call themselves "internationals." American concerns and viewpoints invariably held sway, however, and by the 1970s Canadians in some of these internationals had lost patience with the AFL-CIO's acceptance of the two-party political system, indifference to issues specific to Canada, and turn toward concessions bargaining. In 1979, the Canadian district of the Oil, Chemical and Atomic Workers (OCAW) became an independent union, taking with it the majority of OCAW's progressive leaders. In 1982, United Auto Workers (UAW) locals at Chrysler's Canadian plants successfully struck to get back the cost-of-living raise that negotiators from the union's U.S. headquarters had given away three years earlier. In 1984, a UAW strike at General Motors plants in Canada won the same special adjustment. At the end of that year, the UAW's Canadian locals left to form their own union, eventually known as the Canadian Auto Workers. Other AFL-CIO unions that experienced a Canadian exodus included the International Brotherhood of Electrical Workers, the Operating Engineers, and the Communications Workers of America. By the time NAFTA went into effect in 1994, just 26 percent of Canadian union members belonged to organizations headquartered in the United States, down from 67 percent in the late 1960s. While some of the break-ups were relatively friendly, others—such as the UAW-CAW split—were not.

Friction could occur even in U.S.-based unions whose Canadian locals stayed put. After the United Steelworkers' president Lloyd McBride died in office in late 1983, a special election to select his replacement pitted the Canadian Lynn Williams—McBride's handpicked successor—against the American Frank McKee, whose platform combined unabashed nationalism with calls for greater militancy and union democracy. "It's bad enough that Canadian imports are taking American jobs," he declared. "I don't intend to stand idly by while they take over our union."[20] Williams won 59 percent of the vote, but owed his margin of victory to ballots cast in Canada, and on both sides of the border resentments simmered for some time.

The new distance between the Canadian and U.S. labor movements precluded a unified response to the Canada–United States Free Trade Agreement, signed in 1987 and implemented in 1989. While the Canadian Labour Congress (CLC) vigorously opposed this deal, the AFL-CIO scarcely noticed it. Joint work against NAFTA and then under NAFTA provided ground for solidarity despite differences, however. Neither movement mourned the demise in 1997 of the Canadian Federation of Labour, which had been founded in 1982 by building trades unions that left the CLC in order to preserve close relations with the AFL-CIO.

Projects that brought together U.S., Canadian, and Mexican unions steadily multiplied in the NAFTA era. The Coalition for Justice in the Maquiladoras, founded in 1989 by religious activists concerned with labor conditions under Mexico's Border Industrialization Program, significantly expanded its work with labor unions across North America. Complaints filed under the NAALC were often submitted by cross-border combinations of unions—up to dozens of them—and the teamwork went beyond joint complaints. In 1994, the United Electrical Workers not only lodged a complaint about employer attacks on Frente Auténtico del Trabajo, but also entered a strategic partnership in which the UE backed FAT's organizing drives at General Electric and Honeywell plants in northern Mexico and FAT assisted a UE campaign at the Aluminum Casting and Engineering Company in Milwaukee, where Mexican immigrants made up the largest group of employees. In 1997, when workers at Hyundai's Han Young plant in Tijuana struck for union recognition, a small group of unions filed an NAALC complaint and pulled together a much larger strike-support network. Unionists in eight U.S. cities and Toronto, Canada, demonstrated on behalf of Han Young workers; national labor federations in Brazil, Bangladesh, Spain, and other countries sent formal protests to the Mexican government; and in Portland, Oregon, members of the International Longshore and Warehouse Union kept a Hyundai ship waiting for twenty-four hours before they would handle its cargo. In 2011, when the Sindicato Mexicano de Electricistas (SME) filed complaints about the mass firing that accompanied the privatization of central Mexico's electrical power system, more than ninety other unions, union federations, and labor support organizations signed on as co-complainants, and many of them had already sent delegations to strategize with the SME.

Solidarity's horizons expanded in other respects too. The National Labor Committee that labor progressives had established in 1981 to rally U.S. unions against the

Reagan administration's aggression in Central America now campaigned for work-ers' rights around the globe, becoming a major force in the anti-sweatshop movement and a crucial point of contact between overseas labor activists and unions such as the Communications Workers, the Steelworkers, and the Union of Needletrades, Indus-trial, and Textile Employees (UNITE). In sharp contrast to its conservative stand on Central America in the 1980s, AFL-CIO headquarters built relations with all sectors of the Colombian labor movement, including its left wing; lobbied Congress to defund Plan Colombia, which had poured hundreds of millions of U.S. dollars into a regime infamous for murdering labor activists; and brought endangered activists to the United States for yearlong stints with American unions. Local unions, labor councils, and antiwar committees meanwhile sponsored speaking tours of Palestinian labor activ-ists who challenged U.S. policy in the Middle East.

Internationalism was a two-way street; U.S. unions not only provided assistance but received it as well. A sterling example of this pattern was the global movement in support of workers at five U.S. tire factories operated by Bridgestone/Firestone, a subsidiary of the Bridgestone auto-parts conglomerate headquartered in Japan. In response to company demands for massive givebacks, these workers went on strike in July 1994. By the end of the year replacement workers were running the factories, the strikers' union—the United Rubber Workers (URW)—was nearing bankruptcy, hun-dreds of its members had crossed picket lines to return to work, and Bridgestone/Fire-stone's management had vowed that those who remained on strike would never be allowed to return to their jobs. Then, in July 1995, the Rubber Workers merged into the much larger United Steelworkers, who transformed the Bridgestone/Firestone fight into a global campaign. Fifty full-time organizers built an international boycott of Bridgestone products. Strikers and their families made multiple trips to Japan to meet with labor, religious, and civil rights groups. A delegation to Europe organized pickets at Bridgestone's regional headquarters in Brussels. A world conference of Bridgestone workers drew attendees from sixty-five countries to Nashville, Tennes-see, home to the conglomerate's U.S. headquarters, and a tent city that the strikers erected across the street hosted overseas visitors every day. In July 1996, unionists around the world observed the strike's second birthday with actions that included an international labor conference in Japan, an impromptu strike at a Bridgestone plant in Turkey, and a chain of work stoppages and rallies in Latin America, not only at Bridgestone plants but also at those operated by other tire companies. Finally, the company blinked, returning to the bargaining table in October 1996, setting aside most of its demands for givebacks, and allowing strikers to return to their jobs. This victory would have been impossible save of the assistance Bridgestone/Firestone workers received from unionists abroad.

The same could be said of the Charleston Five, from the International Longshore-men's Association in South Carolina. Their supporters around the world, from Sweden to Korea, planned forty shutdowns of major shipping ports for November 13, 2002, the day the five defendants were scheduled to go to trial on charges of felony riot. That, more than anything else, explains why on November 12 the state prosecutor reduced the charges to misdemeanors and took prison sentences off the table.

Increasingly, cross-border labor initiatives included ongoing projects as well as emergency efforts. Building on long histories of internationalism, the United Electrical Workers and the International Longshore and Warehouse Union were especially prominent on this front, each counting many allies around the world, but other unions started to get in on the action too. In 1997 Sindicato de Trabajadores de la Industria Metálica, Acero, Hierro Conexos y Similares—the metalworkers' union affiliated with FAT—spearheaded the establishment of a cross-border alliance of unions with contracts in Echlin's North American factories. Other participating unions included the Canadian Auto Workers, the Teamsters, the Steelworkers, and UNITE as well as the UE. In the twenty-first century, transnationalism expanded beyond North America. In 2006, the Steelworkers joined with ten other unions from North America, South America, and Europe to form the Gerdau Workers World Council to coordinate dealings with the Gerdau steel conglomerate based in Brazil. By the following year, the United Mine Workers of America and Australia's Construction Forestry Energy Mining Union were jointly campaigning to organize Peabody Energy's coal mines in their respective countries.

The most groundbreaking of all transnational developments involved Change to Win and the All-China Federation of Trade Unions (ACFTU). The largest national labor federation in the world—with 193 million members as of 2008—the ACFTU went unrecognized by the AFL-CIO, which labeled it nothing more than a tool of the Chinese government. Much like its own government, moreover, the AFL-CIO had long exhibited hostility to China, campaigning against its admission to the WTO, demanding that it revalue its currency, and boycotting the toys it exported to the United States. Change to Win took a different approach. In 2007 it sent a high-level delegation to meet with ACFTU officials, setting the stage for an agreement formalized in 2009. Under this pact, the two federations agreed to organize face-to-face exchanges between their members, undertake joint research on corporations operating in the United States and China, and promote trade policies beneficial to workers.

Another sign of changing times could be found in the special news sources most often consulted by labor activists in the United States. From union newspapers and independent periodicals like *Labor Notes* to websites such as LaborNet and labor studies journals including *New Labor Forum* and *WorkingUSA*, labor media aimed at U.S. readers grew more and more attentive to developments in other countries. The *Labor Notes* monthly, for example, had long covered news from Canada and, once NAFTA was in place, from Mexico too; but as time went on it expanded its scope to run articles on workers' movements in Colombia, Argentina, Brazil, Nigeria, Senegal, China, Korea, Vietnam, Iran, Iraq, Egypt, and elsewhere around the globe. The LaborNet web project in San Francisco not only expanded its international coverage but also set up satellite offices in Britain, Germany, Austria, Turkey, Korea, and Japan. In the Internet age, international labor news was also accessible on the websites maintained by organizations like the National Labor Committee, AlterNet, and other radical media projects based in the United States, and by overseas groups such as Students and Scholars Against Corporate Misbehavior headquartered in Hong Kong and the London-based LabourStart news service that began in 1998 with daily reports on South Korea and soon expanded to cover the world in more than thirty languages. Simply by reading, then, U.S. labor activists could learn more than ever before about their counterparts overseas, and that increased the likelihood they would attend international meetings, which made the lessons all the more palpable.

Although organized labor had lost ground virtually everywhere in the world, the news from other countries included inspiring stories, sometimes from unexpected places. In 2004, for example, members of the Canadian Auto Workers occupied an Alcan aluminum smelter in Saguenay, Quebec—not to stop production but instead to keep it going in order to demonstrate the viability of an aged plant that Alcan had slated for closure on the grounds that it was entirely obsolete. Although the Canadian government declared the occupation illegal, the action succeeded in proving the plant's value. When the Rio Tinto conglomerate took over Alcan in 2007, the Saguenay smelter got an upgrade and remained open. While this story raised the possibility of reversing corporate decisions about plant closings, some of the news from post-Soviet Russia illustrated the potential of unions run by the rank and file. Stifled by the Soviet regime and then by the capitalists who took over in the 1990s, democratic unionism seemed downright impossible in Russia by the early 2000s, but an uprising at a Ford assembly plant in Vsevolozhsk indicated otherwise. In 2006, a worker-run union whose members made up just half of the plant's labor force pulled off a strike that won pay increases, better overtime pay, and higher pensions. Again and again the courts declared the strike illegal and again and again the union complied with the order to shut it down but then, just minutes later, announced that a new strike had begun. In all, the Vsevolozhsk strike—or strikes—endured for twenty-five days. Labor movements also provided islands of hope in Honduras, where unions became centers of resistance to a government installed by a coup d'état in 2009; in Egypt, where strikes by textile workers helped to end Hosni Mubarak's dictatorial reign in 2011; in Zimbabwe, where the labor leader Morgan Tsvangirai repeatedly challenged Robert Mugabe's one-man rule; and in India, where sex workers, waste pickers, domestic workers, and others excluded from the formal economy were organizing their own unions.

When international labor news did not raise spirits, it at least offered food for thought. In South Africa, where the long struggle against apartheid had finally borne fruit in 1994, labor unions that had played central roles in the struggle were increasingly estranged from the new government led by the African National Congress (ANC). To attract foreign investment, the government followed rules promulgated by the IMF and World Bank, privatizing public enterprises, lowering corporate taxes, embracing free trade, and so on. By 2001, unions were mounting mass protests across the country. A decade later, the labor movement itself was badly split, sometimes violently so. In August 2012, during a wildcat strike at British-owned platinum mines, leaders of a mining union aligned with the ANC joined police and company guards in firing on strikers, killing thirty-four, wounding more than seventy, and touching off a national wave of miners' strikes. Here was an exceptionally gruesome illustration of the free-trade empire's power to undermine democracy in the Global South.

In April 2013 came news of another disaster, this time the collapse of an eight-story building in the Rana Plaza industrial complex near Dhaka, Bangladesh. The incident killed more than 1,100 people, almost all of them garment workers making goods for Wal-Mart, Benneton, and other large retailers headquartered in the United States or Europe. The complex's owner, the garment company's managers, and local officials all knew that cracks had appeared on the building's walls, but they sent the workers inside nonetheless. Writing about Rana Plaza, more than one labor journalist in the United States compared it to the explosion that killed twenty-nine miners at Massey Energy's Upper Big Branch coal mine in Raleigh County, West Virginia, in April 2010. In that case, too, management had flagrantly neglected workers' safety. In Bangladesh, however, forty-one people were indicted in connection with the collapse, and thirty-eight of them faced murder charges. The Upper Big Branch explosion led to four indictments on misdemeanors or low-level felonies; the defendants, all of whom pled guilty or were convicted after a trial, served sentences ranging from one to three and a half years. Contrasting the two sets of indictments, the labor activist and writer Jonathan Tasini offered this suggestion for revamping U.S. law with regard to workplace health and safety: "Put CEOs who kill workers in jail—and throw away the key. Do that a few times and see how quickly some of this murder stops."[21]

Perhaps the most provocative international labor news came from China, where events repeatedly defied the common American vision of Chinese workers as helpless prisoners of a system that stamped out all resistance. In fact, this system saw many thousands of worker uprisings, especially after China joined the WTO at the end of 2001. These included protests by workers in publicly owned enterprises slated for privatization and ceaseless rebellions against harsh living and working conditions experienced by rural migrants to industrial centers. In 2008 China's government responded with a new national labor law that set minimum wages, placed limits on overtime, instituted provisions for job security and severance pay, gave unions more authority to bargain collectively, and imposed harsher punishments on public officials who failed to enforce workers' rights. Using the new law as leverage, workers throughout China struck for higher pay in 2010. One such action was a seventeen-day work stoppage at the Nanhai Honda plant in Guangdong Province, which resulted in a 24 percent raise and the institution of collective bargaining. Labor officials from the All-China Federation of Trade Unions tried to stop this strike and many others, sometimes even assaulting the strikers. Still, the movement continued beyond 2010, with work stoppages numbering in the thousands every year. In some respects, moreover, the ACFTU itself moved toward confrontation with management. It had taken steps in that direction as early as 2004, when it began to organize workers at Wal-Mart stores, McDonald's fast-food restaurants, and other foreign businesses that initially refused to recognize Chinese unions. Then, in 2008, China's government assigned the ACFTU to facilitate workers' legal claims against employers who violated the new labor law; that, too, placed it at odds with management.

The missing piece was meaningful union democracy; though China's union leaders were elected in most shops, rank and filers played no direct role in the vital business of collective bargaining. In 2015, China Labour Bulletin—a monitoring group based in Hong Kong and headed by a former railroad worker who had led a short-lived independent labor federation in Beijing—observed the fifth anniversary of the Nanhai Honda strike by interviewing some of its veterans still employed at the plant. As one reported, "I know that the process is always more important than the result and I want to be part of the process. As a union member, I need more than just getting fed with information and giving useless feedback on a deal that has already been done."[22] Many an American union member would have added nothing more than an amen.

Global Unionism

The next step beyond joint campaigns across borders and transnational circulation of labor news was co-operation under the auspices of global union federations—an old organizational model that got a new lease on life as workers around the world confronted the same multinational corporations and institutions. In the past, the U.S. labor movement had generally kept its distance from global alliances that Americans could not control. In the early twentieth century, the American Federation of Labor refused to join the International Federation of Trade Unions (IFTU), established in 1913 by unions affiliated with European socialist and labor parties. Following the First World War, Samuel Gompers chaired an international commission that incorporated labor rights into the peace treaty, which created the International Labor Organization. In this initiative, the AFL and the IFTU momentarily united, in large part because both resolutely opposed the Communist-led labor organizations fostered by the new-born Soviet Union. Still, the AFL would not join the IFTU, whose members endorsed socialist reforms such as public ownership of major industries. As the Second World War drew to a close, the CIO made a bolder foray onto the international scene, combining with the British and Soviet labor federations to launch the World Federation of Trade Unions (WFTU), which absorbed the IFTU. In 1949, however, as the Cold War gathered momentum, the CIO, Britain's Trades Union Congress, and other labor federations from Western Europe peeled away from the WFTU and joined with the AFL to form the anti-communist International Confederation of Free Trade Unions (ICFTU), which closely aligned itself with U.S. foreign policy and eventually grew much larger than its pro-Soviet rival.

Although the ICFTU had grand aims—a global program of labor education, for example—it seldom did more than monitor violations of workers' right to organize, including violations in the United States. Every year, these infractions were publicized in a report to the ILO. But if the ICFTU had little clout beyond the power to shame, it did lay the groundwork for organizations that could do more than that. By 2006, when it formed the International Trade Union Confederation by merging with a smaller network of secular unions that had begun as Christian organizations, the ICFTU supported global alliances of unions based in the same industrial sectors.

During the Cold War, these alliances—then known as "international trade secretariats"—devoted virtually all of their energy to opposing unions aligned with the WFTU, but after the Soviet Union's collapse in the early 1990s, they grew more tolerant of political diversity and more attentive to workers' battles with multinational corporations. Most secretariats had originated as European networks in the late nineteenth or early twentieth century and later expanded their reach in service of the Cold War. In 2002, after they had turned their attention to multinationals, they renamed themselves "global union federations" (GUFs for short), and in 2007 they formed their own Council of Global Unions. As of the mid-2010s, the council included nine GUFS; their member unions represented workers in sectors ranging from journalism, entertainment, and public services to manufacturing, transportation, and the hospitality industry. Some GUFs were quite small by global standards; just 600,000 people belonged to unions in the International Federation of Journalists, for example. Other GUFs were giants; the largest, the IndustriALL Global Union, brought together unions with a total of 50 million members in the mining, manufacturing, and energy industries of more than 140 countries. Although each federation operated in its own way and faced its own challenges, they rested on several common conclusions: that the rise of global systems of production and distribution created the need for a global labor movement; that this movement could not depend on governments or intergovernmental agencies like the ILO, IMF, or WTO to defend workers' rights on a global scale; and that even the most powerful multinational corporations were susceptible to disruption by global union federations that zeroed in on their vulnerabilities—the fact, for example, that international cargo worth billions of dollars had to pass through certain seaports and intermodal terminals that move freight from ships to trains or trucks and vice versa.

While their member unions still sought legally enforceable contracts at the local and national levels, the global federations focused on achieving "global framework agreements" (GFAs), which numbered just five in the year 2000 and ninety-one by 2013. Under these agreements, GUFs and multinational corporations set basic rules regarding workers' treatment and established procedures for peacefully settling issues not covered by the rules. In 2002, for example, the auto manufacturer Volkswagen and the International Metalworkers' Federation signed a GFA titled "Declaration on Social Rights and Industrial Relationships" that committed the company to uphold the ILO's core labor standards, including recognition of workers' right to organize and bargain collectively, and endorsed "cooperative conflict management."[23] The agreement covered all of the company's divisions: Volkswagen, Audi, Seat, Skoda, Rolls-Royce Bentley, Lamborghini, and Auto-Europa.

This did not eliminate the many barriers to union building. Although Volkswagen officially welcomed UAW organizers to the plant it opened in Chattanooga, Tennessee, in 2011, lower-level managers and supervisors campaigned against the union, as did business associations, Republican politicians, and right-wing groups such as Americans for Tax Reform. In February 2014, workers voted down the union by a margin of 712 to 626. The UAW nonetheless established a new local at the plant, hoping that it would be recognized as a bargaining agent once it recruited enough members; but Volkswagen was now moving in the opposite direction. In 2015, when the local won an election confined to the plant's small unit of highly skilled workers, the company challenged the outcome in court and punished the unit's workers by arbitrarily changing their schedules and raising their premiums for health insurance. As these developments illustrated, global framework agreements were no panacea. Like NAFTA's labor side agreement, however, they facilitated labor solidarity across borders; and, more than that, they gave GUFs some leverage with regard to corporations. In the spring of 2017, IndustriALL (which had absorbed the International Metalworkers Federation) organized unionists from Volkswagen facilities in Poland, Germany, Britain, Brazil, Switzerland, Mexico, and South Africa to gather in Chattanooga for consultations with brothers and sisters from the UAW. Charging that Volkswagen had made a mockery of the Declaration on Social Rights, IndustriALL's executive committee warned that it would move to revoke the agreement if the company did not start bargaining in Chattanooga.

By the early twenty-first century, almost all U.S. unions had affiliated with at least one GUF and often more than that—the Teamsters, for example, belonged to six. Despite their limitations as instruments of power, they brought U.S. labor unions closer to counterparts overseas, helping both in the process. In 2003, the service-sector GUF—Union Network International (later renamed UNI Global Union)—launched a campaign to organize the Canadian multinational Quebecor, the world's largest commercial printer. The drive established unions at Quebecor plants in the United States, Canada, Peru, Chile, and Brazil and, in 2007, won a global-framework agreement covering all of the company's facilities. That same year, the International Metalworkers Federation organized global meetings of unions representing workers at Arcelor Mittal, the world's largest steelmaker, with headquarters in Luxembourg and 320,000 workers in sixty countries. The upshot was an ongoing global partnership "to advance workers' rights throughout the company."[24] UNI meanwhile facilitated co-operation between the Communications Workers of America and the German telecommunications union ver.di. In 2008, ver.di helped the CWA launch T-Mobile Workers United, not itself a union but an employee organization that wrung better benefits from the company and unionized some of its units. In 2016–17, UNI put CWA members at Verizon and AT&T in touch with workers at Dominican and Filipino call centers where unions had been organized but did not yet have contracts. Other GUF projects included a worldwide boycott of Hyatt Hotels in summer 2012, as UNITE HERE took on the company's practice in its U.S. properties of replacing housekeeping workers with casual employees supplied by temp agencies; crucial support for the International Longshore and Warehouse Union's successful battle against lockouts by U.S. subsidiaries of the Mitsui and Marubeni conglomerates based in Japan; and transatlantic meetings in which German unionists helped Americans develop strategies for organizing U.S. factories newly established by the European multinationals Airbus and Siemens.

The Service Employees International Union (SEIU) developed an especially large set of transnational projects under UNI's umbrella. In 1996, SEIU had decided that its department of international affairs was merely an extravagance and shut it down. Before the decade was out, however, the union began organizing workers at the U.S. subsidiaries of multinational corporations, and in that context internationalism became a must. As SEIU officers and staff reached out for assistance from service-sector unions in Britain, the Netherlands, Germany, and elsewhere, they found that European unions accustomed to partnerships with employers and governments had begun to encounter the hostility unions had long faced in the United States. If SEIU had something to gain from allies overseas, then, it also had something to offer: first-hand knowledge as to how unions could win organizing drives and decent contracts when both the boss and the law placed barriers in their way. As one SEIU organizer put it, "We went from begging for help to collaborating for change."[25] After UNI was established in 2000, it oversaw the collaboration, drawing on a budget for new organizing that came mostly from SEIU. This generated several successful organizing campaigns, among school bus drivers in the United States and Britain, security officers in Germany, janitors in the Netherlands, and other groups.

The largest of these initiatives, launched in 2006, targeted Group 4 Securicor (G4S), a security services company that dominated the field on every continent and employed more people worldwide than any other corporation save for Wal-Mart. Drives to unionize G4S employees—not only in the United States and Europe but also in Latin America, Africa, Asia, and Oceania—went hand in hand with a massive corporate campaign in which unions around the globe exerted pressure on firms doing business with G4S. In 2008, G4S and UNI signed a global framework agreement that resulted in union growth, wage increases, and other advances for security guards in Poland, South Africa, Malawi, Mozambique, India, and Indonesia, along with new unions for guards in Ghana, Nepal, and Congo. A separate agreement between G4S and SEIU brought 50,000 new members into the union.

In July 2008, the Steelworkers took an even bolder step toward global unionism by merging with the British union Unite to create Workers Uniting (WU), with 3 million members in the United States, Canada, the Caribbean, Britain, and Ireland. "We're going to chase global capital," declared the Steelworkers' president Leo Gerard, and in line with that aim, WU immediately began exploring possibilities for mergers with unions in Australia, Asia, Latin America, and Eastern Europe.[26] A decade later, no such mergers had taken place and the Steelworkers and Unite still maintained entirely separate internal structures, though they had begun to negotiate jointly with some of the many global corporations that employed members of both unions.

Global inequalities militated against the construction of truly global unions. Assessing the possibilities, Ruth Needleman, a labor educator who worked with steel unions in the United States and overseas, pointed out that, whereas a crane operator in a U.S. steel mill had to work about fifty hours to make the monthly rent on a modestly sized apartment or house, someone with the same job in Mexico had to work three times as long to reach that goal. Such disparities made it exceedingly difficult to define union priorities meaningful to workers around the world, even those employed in the same industry or by the same corporation. This doubtless goes a long way to explain why the United Steelworkers' exceptionally close relationship with Los Mineros—a union of Mexican metal miners—stopped short of a merger. In 2007 Los Mineros launched strikes over health and safety conditions at three mines owned by the Grupo Mexico conglomerate, which also owned the Asarco smelting and refining facilities in the U.S. Southwest. The Steelworkers played a leading role in financing these actions; provided sanctuary for Los Mineros' president after a military assault crushed the strikes in 2010 and forced him to flee Mexico; and supported Los Mineros' continued organizing, just as Los Mineros supported the Steelworkers' contract fights with Asarco. Along the way, the two unions began talking about amalgamation, but as of 2018 they had taken no concrete steps in that direction.

For U.S. unions, another hindrance to globalism was Americans' limited knowledge of the world beyond their own shores. As Ruth Needleman observed, it was "a major eye-opener" for United Steelworkers officials to discover at international meetings that, although Arcelor Mittal had certainly targeted its workers in the United States, they remained much better off than the company's workers in places such as Brazil,

Mexico, Macedonia, and South Africa.[27] Americans sometimes seemed utterly oblivious to other nations' perspectives on world history too. Never was this more evident than in 1995, when the Steelworkers were building the Bridgestone/Firestone campaign and one protestor at a demonstration at the Japanese embassy in Washington was photographed with a sign that read, "Enola Gay, one more time."[28] This flippant reference to the warplane that had dropped the atomic bomb on Hiroshima came close to derailing the union's efforts to enlist the aid of Japanese labor officials. The damage was undone only after one of its vice presidents sent them personal apologies, the campaign's lead organizers went out of their way to stifle anti-Japanese sentiments, and a Steelworkers delegation to Japan made a well-publicized visit to the Hiroshima Peace Memorial Park, which commemorates the bomb's tens of thousands of victims.

In other instances, American unionists came across as cynical or downright callous in their approach to international solidarity. In 2006, as the G4S campaign was getting under way, SEIU's president Andy Stern told a business magazine that global unionism offered a way to save money on strike benefits: "If workers are ready to go on strike in the United States, and we are ready to pay them to strike, it would be very costly. But paying workers in Indonesia or India or other places to go on strike against the same global employer isn't particularly expensive." Did he mean to say that American unions should outsource strikes? the interviewer asked. "Yes," Stern replied, "absolutely."[29] That strikers in the Global South often faced violent repression did not seem to give him pause. Plain old American arrogance could cause friction too, even in successful global partnerships. An SEIU staffer assigned to the G4S campaign admitted, "People say . . . that we don't listen to others, we come in and change everything around. There's some truth to that."[30] A European unionist active in the campaign described his SEIU comrades as both "role models" and "a huge pain in the ass."[31]

Most damaging of all perhaps was the AFL-CIO's association with the U.S. government's foreign policy. Labor activists around the world remembered the years when government agencies funded and orchestrated the federation's international projects. In 1997, John Sweeney's New Voice administration took a stab at overcoming this toxic legacy by dismantling the regional institutes that had supervised AFL-CIO contributions to the Cold War overseas.[32] In their place stood a new American Center for International Labor Solidarity (the Solidarity Center), which parted company with the government in several noteworthy ways. It opposed U.S. military aid to Colombia, whose soldiers were killing labor activists; it demanded an end to the School of the Americas (later known as the Western Hemisphere Institute for Security Cooperation), where the U.S. Army trained military personnel for Latin American regimes friendly to the United States and hostile to workers' movements; it endorsed cancellation of the Global South's disabling debt to international banks; and, in 2009, when the Honduran army ousted the democratically elected president Manuel Zelaya, the AFL-CIO called for his restoration to office while the U.S. State Department recognized a new government that came to power in a bogus election overseen by the coup's architects. In contrast to the Cold War era, when fighting communism had overridden all other international goals, the AFL-CIO now focused on defending the ILO's core labor standards, fighting for trade agreements that protected workers' rights, and promoting labor solidarity on a global scale.

While some aspects of the AFL-CIO's foreign policy changed, however, others remained the same. In 1999, when the U.S. State Department revived the Cold War practice of enlisting labor officials as advisers, the new AFL-CIO's executive staff readily signed on. More important, over 90 percent of the Solidarity Center's annual budget came from the federal government, mostly the executive branch's U.S. Agency for International Development or the congressionally funded National Endowment for Democracy. The center's programs reflected its funders' concerns; it focused on countries and regions especially important to Washington and befriended U.S. allies in these places.

The most controversial venture unfolded in Venezuela, where the Solidarity Center funneled money from the National Endowment for Democracy into the Confederation of Venezuelan Workers (Confederacion de Trabajadores de Venezuela, or CTV). Aligned with a political party that had failed to unseat the country's socialist president, Hugo Chávez, in the election of 2000, CTV leaders took part in an unsuccessful coup d'état in April 2002. Following this incident, American critics and defenders of the Solidarity Center squared off in the U.S. labor press, but no matter who won that argument at home, the new AFL-CIO lost stature on the international stage. However one interpreted events in Venezuela, they brought to mind the bad old days when AFL-CIO operations in Latin America were little more than façades for the Central Intelligence Agency. Another dubious venture focused on Haiti, where the Solidarity Center developed an on-again, off-again relationship with unions involved in the coup in 2004 that ousted the country's first democratically elected president, Jean-Bertrand Aristide. Meanwhile, in Iraq, whose unions overwhelmingly condemned the U.S. occupation, the Solidarity Center poured resources into the one labor federation that condoned it.

In the early 2000s, opposition to such initiatives steadily gained ground among labor activists in the United States. In California, the trend's epicenter, central labor councils in San Francisco, San Jose, and the Monterey Bay area called on the AFL-CIO to "clear the air" by admitting to past misdeeds such as helping to set the stage for the fascist coup that had toppled Chile's democratically elected government in 1973.[33] Similar calls soon emanated from the King County Labor Council in Greater Seattle, the Washington State AFL-CIO, and the AFL-CIO's constituency group Pride at Work. In June 2002, California's statewide labor federation passed a resolution demanding that emissaries from AFL-CIO headquarters meet with the Californians to explain its international policies, past and present. When the meeting finally took place fifteen months later, it settled nothing. In March 2004, the California Federation of Teachers resolved that the AFL-CIO ought to fund its own international projects since federal sources such as the National Endowment for Democracy could not be trusted to have workers' best interests at heart. That July, the California Labor Federation's biennial convention unanimously called on the AFL-CIO not only to fund its own international projects but also "to fully account for what was done in Chile (and Venezuela) and other countries where similar roles may have been played in our name, and to describe, country by country, exactly what activities it may still be engaged in abroad with funds paid by government agencies and renounce any such ties that could compromise our authentic credibility."[34] In July 2005, maneuvers by the program committee stopped the California resolution from getting to the floor of the AFL-CIO's national convention in Chicago, but about 100 unionists demonstrated on its behalf. The following March, these same forces gathered in Washington, D.C., to launch the Worker to Worker Solidarity Committee with a combination of protests and workshops attended by activists from AFSCME, the Machinists, the CWA, and several other unions.

Although the Worker to Worker project soon faded, U.S. Labor Against the War (USLAW) gained momentum. In addition to shepherding an antiwar resolution to passage at the AFL-CIO convention of 2005, it developed relationships with a cross-section of Iraqi unions and labor federations, whose spokespeople toured the United States in 2005 and again in 2007. USLAW also organized demonstrations; established state and local chapters active in politics as well as the labor movement; held conferences that featured sessions with unionists from Pakistan, Iran, and other countries whose labor movements were typically invisible to Americans; and widely publicized the costs of the U.S. wars in Afghanistan and Iraq—the fact, for example, that many a state could have wiped out its public debt had it been allowed to keep the tax dollars it contributed to these wars. By 2012, USLAW's affiliates included three national unions (the CWA, the UE, and the Amalgamated Transit Union), six of the AFL-CIO's state federations, Pride at Work, the Coalition of Labor Union Women, and a network of local unions and labor councils that stretched from coast to coast. If the Solidarity Center's association with U.S. foreign policy government hampered global unionism, U.S. Labor Against the War had the opposite effect—a much smaller effect, to be sure, but beneficial nonetheless. It helped too that, in contrast to a half-century earlier, when the CIO had amputated its left flank, there were no labor witch-hunts against individuals and organizations that vocally disagreed with the government on international affairs.

Even under the best of circumstances, however, global unionism was swimming upstream. Ron Oswald, chief officer of the global union federation in charge of food services and hospitality, hit the nail on the head when he told a journalist in 2007 that "International companies are clearly a reality. International unions have yet to become so."[35] In the United States and other countries around the world, employers typically bargained with unions only when national law required it and skirted the law as much as the government would allow. Global unionism operated under even less protective rules—not laws but recommendations proffered by the International Labor Organization and promises enshrined in global framework agreements. Until workers could rely on an international agency to enforce labor rights or build union federations powerful enough to enforce them on their own, global unionism would remain little more than an ideal.

14

Rising Tide

"*Si se puede!*" "Yes we can!"[1] This chant rang out across the United States on Monday, May 1, 2006, when well over a million immigrants abandoned work and school to protest against a proposed law that would have increased federal penalties for undocumented immigrants and any people or institutions that assisted them. Los Angeles saw two demonstrations that together drew close to 700,000 participants; in Chicago, 400,000 gathered; in Milwaukee, some 70,000 came out; and 35,000 demonstrated in Florida cities and towns. Protests also took place in Houston, Denver, Phoenix, Atlanta, New York, and a host of smaller cities, from Burlington, Vermont, and Asbury Park, New Jersey, to Sioux Falls, South Dakota, and Salem, Oregon. With immigrant workers gone, thousands of local businesses shut down for the day, and some large companies had to curtail operations. Tyson Foods, the world's premier meat producer, closed about a dozen plants, mostly in Iowa and Nebraska. Eight Perdue chicken-processing plants in seven states also closed, along with Gold Kist poultry plants in North Carolina and Georgia.

The protests encountered opponents. In Salem, a couple of retirees who had come out to challenge the demonstrators told a local journalist that undocumented immigrants were "burglars" who stole American jobs and aimed "to steal citizenship" too.[2] At the state capital in Austin, Texas, a group of counterdemonstrators held signs declaring, "Keep Texas for Texans."[3] In West Palm Beach, Florida, some people in passing cars made obscene gestures and hollered, "Go home."[4] In Alabama, the Ku Klux Klan announced plans for an anti-immigrant rally the following weekend. On May 1, however, immigrant protestors and their supporters vastly outnumbered the opposition; and on May 7, when the Klan held its rally in Russellville, Alabama, only about 50 participants showed up and at least 250 people came out to jeer.

While churches with immigrant congregations were the main force that mobilized the May Day protests, immigrant worker centers played important roles too, and in most locales labor unions lent a hand with funding and logistics—mapping parade routes, setting up first aid and water stations, organizing security marshals, and so on. Unions especially active in these efforts included the Service Employees International Union (SEIU), the United Electrical Workers, the Laborers' International Union, the United Steelworkers, the United Food and Commercial Workers, the Farm Labor Organizing Committee, Teamsters in California and Chicago, the UNITE HERE organization of hotel, restaurant, and garment workers, and the United Farm Workers, which supplied the slogan *"Si se puede!"* as well as material assistance. Just months after the protests, in August 2006, the AFL-CIO established a partnership with the National Day Labor Organizing Network (NDLON), an alliance of community groups that sought to improve the working and living conditions of immigrants hiring out by the day. By partnering with the Laborers, NDLON gained support from Change to Win too.

The labor movement's support for immigrants' rights constituted much more than assistance to community allies; in many cases, immigrants were unionism's lifeblood. As of 2007, foreign-born workers made up 16 percent of the U.S. labor force and much more than that in some states: about 35 percent in California, 27 percent in New York, 26 percent in New Jersey, and 20 percent or more in Florida, Texas, and Arizona. In addition, foreign-born workers were concentrated in the same sectors as the unions most committed to organizing: construction, manufacturing, food services, health care, and so on. Well over half of foreign-born workers came from Latin America, with Mexicans the largest nationality, and about a quarter came from Asia. Often, the foreign born were among the first to welcome union organizers. Unions reached out to immigrants for all of these reasons as well as for solidarity's sake. As Mike Garcia, leader of SEIU Local 1877 in Los Angeles, observed: "If labor is to save itself from decline, it has to have an active organizing effort among immigrants."[5]

Employers clearly understood this; they regularly used immigration law to derail union organizing. Although the Supreme Court had ruled in 2002 (*Hoffman Plastic Compounds, Inc. v. National Labor Relations Board*) that undocumented workers were entitled to protection under the National Labor Relations Act, this decision also stipulated that they were not entitled to remedies when their rights were violated—not entitled to back pay, for example, should the National Labor Relations Board (NLRB) find that they had been illegally fired for signing union cards. Employers took full advantage of that loophole. In December 2007, a couple of weeks before a union election was scheduled to take place at the Fresh Direct online grocery store in New York City, the company sent all 900 of its warehouse workers a letter announcing that federal agents from Immigration and Customs Enforcement (ICE) would soon arrive to inspect the documents that authorized Fresh Direct employees to hold jobs in the United States. The letter's recipients got the message that this was about the organizing drive. Several dozen immediately quit—afraid even to go in to retrieve their paychecks—and when the election rolled around, just 530 showed up to vote, casting 426 ballots against unionization. In Mississippi, the state legislature gave employers an additional weapon known as SB 2988: a law enacted in March 2008 that made undocumented jobholders liable to fines up to $10,000 and prison terms of one to five years. The NLRB undercut immigrant organizing, too, by ruling that workers could be fired for engaging in a political strike—a strike, that is, like the May Day protests of 2006. But ICE remained employers' favorite weapon against immigrant workers who sought to organize.

Sometimes unionists used that weapon too, ultimately to their own detriment. In the early morning of August 25, 2008, ICE agents swept into Laurel and Ellisville, Mississippi, and raided two electronics factories operated by Howard Industries. The International Brotherhood of Electrical Workers (IBEW) Local 1317, which had organized the factories in 1974, was midway through the latest round of contract negotiations and a drive to increase the proportion of Howard workers who belonged to the union in this open-shop state. The day ICE showed up, some native-born workers cheered as 595 of their immigrant co-workers were carted off to an immigrant detention center, and it soon came out that a tip from an IBEW member had precipitated the raid. Then, in his public comments on the incident, the president of the state AFL-CIO blamed undocumented workers for unions' decline. "They have no recourse under the law. . . ," he declared. "And because they don't have a voice, neither do workers who belong to a union if they want to keep their job."[6] The IBEW's national headquarters quickly distanced the union from these sentiments, vowing to organize both native- and foreign-born workers and portraying the raid as the brainchild of Republicans who wished to divide constituencies that supported the Democrats. But that could not undo the damage to worker solidarity at Howard Industries; instead of growing, Local 1317 shrank.

On the whole, however, alliances between unions and immigrant communities were on the rise in Mississippi. The state legislature's black caucus provided the catalyst for this development. In addition to championing workers' right to organize, it successfully maneuvered to defeat hundreds of anti-immigrant initiatives that arose after SB 2988 became law. One of the caucus's leaders, Representative Jim Evans from Jackson, was also a staff member at the state AFL-CIO and, unlike its president, an active supporter of immigrants' rights. In 2000, he became a founding officer of the Mississippi Immigrants Rights Alliance (MIRA), whose directors included officers and staffers from the Laborers, the United Auto Workers, the United Food and Commercial Workers, and the Mississippi Association of State Employees, affiliated with the Communications Workers. MIRA assisted the Laborers' International Union as it organized and won first contracts at several poultry-processing plants. By 2009, MIRA had also helped UNITE HERE, the Teamsters, and the International Union of Operating Engineers organize about 5,000 workers in gambling casinos in Tunica and Biloxi. In both the poultry plants and the casinos, immigrant workers were a central force for unionization.

In other states too, co-operation between unions and immigrants' rights organizations helped to put workplace organizing drives over the top. In Minneapolis-St. Paul, Minnesota, the worker center Centro Trabajadores Unidos en Lucha launched an organizing drive that brought janitors working in chain stores into SEIU. The worker center Arise Chicago helped Latinos employed at Golan's Movers in Skokie, Illinois, to organize a workplace committee, call in Teamsters Local 705, and win a sixth-month strike that yielded a first contract. In Los Angeles, the Community Labor Environmental Action Network launched an immigrant worker center that joined with the United Steelworkers to unionize the city's car washes.

Nor was Mississippi the only southern state where immigrants invigorated unionism. In Tar Heel, North Carolina, the United Food and Commercial Workers (UFCW) had been trying to organize the Smithfield Foods pork-processing plant—the world's largest pork plant—since the early 1990s and had lost NLRB elections in 1994 and

1997. In 2004 the union decided to try again. By then, the plant's labor force of 5,000 included about 3,000 Latino immigrants, mostly from Mexico, along with black, white, and Native American workers. One of the UFCW's first steps when it returned to Tar Heel was to establish a Spanish-language worker center, which coordinated local participation in the protests of May 1, 2006. When Latinos did not show up for work that day, the company retaliated by calling in ICE, whose raid on the plant reduced its immigrant workforce by half. But the protestors' display of courage had repercussions beyond Smithfield's control. In November 2006, it fired seventy-five undocumented immigrants and announced its intention to fire hundreds more, but a two-day strike by Latino and other workers forced it to back down. That inspired black workers at the plant to circulate a petition demanding that Martin Luther King Day become a paid holiday. Some 80 percent of the plant's workers signed, and in January 2007 several hundred did not come to work on that day, forcing the plant to shut down. By 2008, the UFCW had collected enough signatures to schedule a third NLRB election for union recognition, which the union won in December of that year.

In Houston, Texas, too, the protests of May 1, 2006 had a ripple effect. By the end of that year, some 5,300 of the city's janitors—almost all of them Latino immigrants—had joined SEIU and unleashed a wave of strikes and street protests that won them first contracts that provided substantial wage increases and low-cost family health care subsidized by the cleaning companies. Bread-and-butter issues were not the only ones at stake. As Austraberta Rodriguez, who had been cleaning the city's offices for twenty-seven years, explained, "we also want more respect and more dignity."[7] The contract represented a huge step in that direction.

Another inspiring story came from Immokalee, Florida, center of the state's gigantic tomato industry and for many years ground zero for the industry's multiple violations of workers' rights. In the mid-1990s Immokalee's harvest workers—black and white Americans together with larger numbers of migrants from Haiti, Mexico, and Central America—began to organize for a living wage. Out of this grew the Coalition of Immokalee Workers, a multi-ethnic worker center that coordinated strikes in 1995, 1997, and 1999. The wage increases that followed these actions encouraged the coalition to step up the pressure by launching a nationwide Campaign for Fair Food that called on large corporate purchasers of tomatoes to pay an extra penny per pound to fund additional raises for harvest workers. The first target was the Taco Bell fast-food chain, whose parent company Yum! Brands agreed to the deal in 2005, following a four-year consumer boycott widely publicized through social media and embraced by high school and college students, churches, worker centers, and eventually the AFL-CIO. Over the next decade, the coalition oversaw boycotts that yielded thirteen more agreements, with fast food chains including McDonald's and Subway, grocery chains including Trader Joe's and Giant, and food-service companies including Aramark and Sodexo. Unions, local labor councils, and the AFL-CIO's Labor Council for Latin American Advancement were among the boycotts' most avid supporters, and the Coalition of Immokalee Workers adopted a more union-like agenda along the way. It got the Florida Tomato Growers Exchange to sign a Fair Food Code of Conduct that increased wages, stipulated stricter health and safety provisions, outlined a grievance procedure, and pledged participating growers to zero tolerance for child labor, workers' abuse by supervisors, and compulsory labor in payment of debts to recruiters who transported migrant workers to Florida. In 2015, the agreement expanded to cover out-of-state tomato fields owned by members of the Florida exchange. Newspapers across the country cheered these developments, and quite a few articles told readers how to contact the coalition.

If the Coalition of Immokalee Workers got favorable press coverage, nothing matched the applause that erupted in December 2008, when 200 members of United Electrical Workers Local 1110 occupied the Republic Windows & Doors factory on Chicago's Near North Side. About 80 percent of these workers were Latinos, predominantly immigrants, and most of the others were African Americans. On Tuesday, December 2, their plant's manager announced that the company would permanently close three days later and that workers would get neither the severance pay to which they were entitled under federal law nor pay for the vacation days most of them had accumulated. Bank of America, the company's primary creditor, had recently received a $25 billion federal bailout to offset losses stemming from predatory loans to home-buyers; now it declined to extend credit that would enable Republic to stay in business or even shut down in a lawful manner. Chase Bank, partial owner of Republic, also rejected requests for assistance.

Layoffs, banks, greed: these elements of the Republic story had a familiar ring in the winter of 2008–9, when the United States and most of Europe entered the second year of the Great Recession—a steep economic downturn triggered by shady prac-tices on the part of financial institutions. As Local 1110 showed, however, there were alternatives to the narrative the bankers had written. When quitting time came on Fri-day, December 5, most of Republic's workers refused to leave the plant, and support-ers from unions, worker centers, churches, immigrant organizations, and civil rights groups rallied outside the gates. The occupation lasted six days as the mayor advised police not to intervene and labor-friendly politicians helped the union drag both Bank of America and Chase into funding not only severance and vacation pay but also two months of health insurance coverage. As cheers went up across the country the *Lawn-dale News*, greater Chicago's largest bilingual Hispanic newspaper, declared that the Republic workers had won "because the majority of ordinary people were on their side. It no longer matters what race, ethnic group or religion any given group of work-ers may be, but that an injustice has been committed against ordinary people in tough times is just plain unacceptable to most Americans."[8] Many millions happily shared that opinion in December 2008, but history would soon make it seem tragically naive.

Unreliable Allies

The workers' win at Republic Windows was not the only cause for optimism; the future looked bright for larger reasons too. The Democrat Barack Obama—U.S. sena-tor from Illinois—was now the nation's president-elect. In his time as a state senator as well as his years in Washington, he had earned a reputation as a friend of both organized labor and immigrants' rights, and during his presidential race against the Republicans' Senator John McCain, he had accumulated a very heavy debt to the labor movement. Legions of unionists had become Obama volunteers; unions and their members had contributed hundreds of millions of dollars to the cause; the AFL-CIO had established a Union Veterans Council, whose first order of business was to agitate against the notion that it would be disloyal for military veterans not to vote for the war hero McCain; and both the AFL-CIO and Change to Win had mobilized massive drives to get out the vote for the Democrats. Equally important, union spokespeople had directly addressed the racism Obama faced as the first African American to run for president as the nominee of a major party. Stumping for Democrats in battleground states, Richard Trumka had called on union members not just to vote for Obama but also to convert brothers and sisters hesitant to do so because of his race. As Trumka told the Steelworkers' convention in July 2008, "There's no evil that's inflicted more pain and more suffering than racism, and it's something that we in the labor movement have a very, very special responsibility to challenge . . . because we know better than anyone else how racism is used to divide working people." Once unionists defeated "race haters" and placed Obama in the White House, Trumka promised, "We're going to be able to say that 2008 was the year that we took back our country and built a government that embraced workers and loved unions."[9] That December, when President-Elect Obama publicly endorsed the sit-in at Republic Windows & Doors, it seemed that Trumka's prophecy would be fulfilled.

Democrats who supported unions on the way up the political ladder had often forsaken them in the end, however, and that made some labor leaders as cautious as they were encouraged. While Change to Win wholeheartedly embraced the new administration—White House visitor logs showed that Andy Stern stopped in more than any other individual—AFL-CIO headquarters preferred the more guarded approach recommended by the labor historian Nelson Lichtenstein in a widely discussed online article for the magazine *Dissent*. As this essay pointed out, Democratic presidents had generally been most attentive to the demands of social movements they regarded as "troublesome, unreliable, and unpredictable allies."[10] With that in mind, Richard Trumka, who succeeded John Sweeney as the AFL-CIO's president in fall 2009, hoped to position his wing of the labor movement as a friend the Obama administration could not take for granted. But powerful forces militated against this strategy.

The election of a black president made white racism more strident in national politics. As soon as Barack Obama began to run for the presidency, a chorus of right-wing columnists, television hosts, and radio personalities bellowed that his Kenyan heritage on his father's side rendered him un-American and that his accomplishments, such as a law degree from Harvard and election to the U.S. Senate, were merely gifts bestowed on him by affirmative action programs. His opponents in both the Democratic primary and the general election leveled similar charges, usually but not always in more subtle language. Once President Obama was in office, right-wing media steered his grassroots opposition into a movement known as the Tea Party, funded by billionaire businessmen such as the energy magnates Charles and David Koch. Tea Partiers mobilized all manner of racist stereotypes, carrying placards and distributing handbills that portrayed Obama as a dimwit, as a pimp, as a mugger, as Hollywood's version of an African witch doctor, or in one case, as himself hanging from a noose. By summer 2010, the House of Representatives had the Tea Party Caucus, and a conservative surge at the polls in that fall's elections expanded the caucus's ranks as it gave Republicans the majority of House seats. From that point onward, even after his reelection in 2012, Obama was unable to enact significant legislation, depending instead on executive actions that his successors in the White House could easily overturn through executive actions of their own. Meanwhile, right-wing politicians and media figures vilified Muslims, insisted that immigrants were ruining the country, and continuously stoked a rumor that Obama had been born in Kenya and was thus ineligible to serve as the U.S. president. To hold Obama at arm's length under these circumstances would have placed the AFL-CIO uncomfortably close to the most reactionary trends in American politics.

Throughout his two terms in office, then, Barack Obama could count on support from organized labor; but he did not always reciprocate. For five years between college and law school he had worked as a community organizer in Chicago, and one of his mentors in that period had been Addie Wyatt—a civil rights activist and labor leader who helped to found both the Coalition of Black Trade Unionists and the Coalition of Labor Union Women. Thanks to her tutelage, Obama grasped unions' priorities and could speak their language. His campaign slogan was "Yes we can!" On the campaign trail, he sought out labor audiences, declared himself "a labor guy," referred to his listeners as "brothers and sisters," and pledged that his administration would support a whole raft of worker-friendly reforms, including paid family leave, an increase in the federal minimum wage, stronger labor protections in international trade deals, massive federal spending on infrastructure projects that would create jobs, a federal law to stop employers from permanently replacing strikers, some form of universal health care, and passage of the Employee Free Choice Act designed to simplify and speed up the process by which workers unionized.[11] When he took office in January 2009, the first bill he signed into law made it easier for workers to sue employers for wage discrimination on the basis of sex, race, national origin, age, religion, or disability. After that, however, he delivered virtually nothing beyond pro-union appointments to the Department of Labor and the National Labor Relations Board, modest spending on infrastructure, more vigorous federal enforcement of workplace safety and health laws, a bailout that rescued General Motors and Chrysler from bankruptcy and saved about a million jobs in the auto industry, and a new set of health-insurance provisions and regulations that extended coverage to more than 20 million people previously uninsured but left in the lurch roughly the same number.

While the Tea Party's rise and the Republican Party's march to the right guaranteed a sizable gap between Obama's promises and what he delivered, Democrats were a big part of the problem too. Whether or not the president's personal convictions made him a genuine "labor guy," he governed for the most part as a neoliberal. Wall Street insiders dominated his council of economic advisers. His economic recovery advisory board was a who's who of corporate CEOs and chaired by Jeffrey Immelt of General Electric, a leading exporter of jobs. When it came to international trade, the Obama administration's policies were much like those of the Clinton and Bush administrations, the only significant difference being that displaced workers who applied for federally funded job training and extended unemployment benefits were now more likely to have their claims approved. The Obama program for recovery from the Great Recession combined the Bush policy of bailing out the nation's largest financial institutions with a few progressive elements—commitment to paying union-level wages on federal construction projects; the establishment of the Consumer Financial Protection Bureau, charged with curbing predatory lending; and the proviso that corporations bailed out by the government could not reward their executives with bonuses. With regard to public education, the Obama and Bush administrations were virtually indistinguishable; both facilitated privatization in the form of charter schools and favored the high-stakes testing promoted by corporations that sold testing services and test-preparation media to public school systems. Despite numerous promises to the contrary, the Obama health-insurance system did not include a public option such as Medicare for people younger than sixty-five. The administration's policy on immigration was disappointing too. Despite Obama's participation in the Chicago protest of May Day 2006 and his endorsement as president of immigration reform that would give the undocumented a path to citizenship, his administration oversaw more deportations than any of its predecessors. Opposition from Democrats in the Senate meanwhile scuttled the Employee Free Choice Act (EFCA) intended to streamline union organizing. "I will make it the law of the land," Obama had promised as he ran for the presidency, and in 2010 he vowed to "keep on fighting" for the EFCA.[12] But his own party prevented it from coming up for a vote until 2016, when Republicans controlled both chambers of Congress and all pro-labor initiatives were certain to lose. This was by no means the first time that the Democratic Party had jilted organized labor, but given Obama's charismatic outreach to unionists and the high hopes that attended his election, this time hurt more than the rest.

Most discouraging was that the recovery from the Great Recession did not make life better for most people. Instead, they experienced what can fairly be described as a circus of horrors—a downright dizzying array of assaults on the quality of working-class life in the United States. Thanks to a law signed by George W. Bush, the federal minimum wage rose to $7.25 an hour in July 2009, but it stayed put after that. While the years 2011–16 saw uninterrupted growth in the number of jobs added to the U.S. economy, plant closings continued, and the new jobs were largely confined to low-wage sectors in which most workers lacked union protection. In fact, many of the new jobs were not even jobs in the traditional sense. Increasingly, corporations misclassified workers as "independent contractors," robbing them of employee benefits as well as collective bargaining rights and shielding themselves from legal liability for poor health and safety conditions, for industrial accidents, and for violations of wage and hours laws. Another increasingly common practice was to categorize workers as temps ineligible for benefits and for union membership, no matter how many years they spent on a single job. Stagnant wages and deteriorating benefits meant that more and more people needed to work for two or even three employers; so when the rate of unemployment fell, the scramble for jobs remained intense. If the Department of Labor's statistics masked this phenomenon, everyday life made it crystal clear. In 2011, McDonald's restaurants held job fairs across the country and attracted about a million applicants; just 6.2 percent got hired, making the McDonald's acceptance rate lower than that of most Ivy League schools. By 2016, almost 40 percent of young adults lived with their parents, unable to find work that paid enough to support their moving out—and, for those who had gone to college or career schools, to pay off student debts that averaged more than $30,000. In other cases, workers from their teens into their seventies hit the road, traveling from place to place to harvest beets, sell Christmas trees, take summer jobs in state and national parks, and do seasonal work in the dozens of "fulfillment centers" where items sold online by the retail colossus Amazon were sorted, boxed, and shipped.

To make matters worse, local, state, and federal agencies cut spending in ways especially damaging to working people. Public housing, hospitals, and transit systems decayed. Boards of education enlarged class sizes, suspended art and music programs, and often closed schools in poor and working-class communities, sometimes repurposing the buildings to house charter schools. Public colleges and universities raised tuition to offset cuts in funding. As the Occupational Safety and Health Administration decreased the frequency of workplace inspections, the number of on-the-job fatalities began to edge upward, after falling almost every year since the early 1970s. More than sixty local governments and public agencies such as sanitation districts filed for bankruptcy, discontinuing services, laying off workers, and slashing retirees' pensions. The largest municipal bankruptcy in U.S. history took place in 2013 in Detroit, which had once enjoyed a higher per capita income than any other big American city and now held the record for unemployment, tax delinquency, abandoned homes, and crumbling infrastructure. In Flint, Michigan, another city devastated by plant closings in the auto industry, local authorities saved money by using the Flint River as the public water source and by neglecting to treat the water with chemicals that would safeguard against pipe corrosion. The plan exposed some 30,000 families to toxic levels of lead.

And yet there always seemed to be enough money for war. Although Obama ran for the presidency as an antiwar candidate and continued the Bush administration's phased withdrawal of combat troops from Iraq, he more than tripled the U.S. military presence in Afghanistan, which did not return to Bush-era levels until 2015. His administration also sent troops into Libya; deployed special forces in more than 130 other countries; launched hundreds of drone strikes on suspected terrorists in Pakistan, Yemen, and Somalia; and outspent the Bush administration's budget for military operations. For labor leaders, Obama's military policies were a mixed bag. They approved of the drop in U.S. war casualties that attended the increase in drone warfare and applauded along with the rest of America when special forces sneaked into Pakistan and assassinated Osama bin Laden in May 2011. But they condemned the military aid extended to brutally anti-labor regimes in Honduras, Bahrain, and other countries, and by 2013 the AFL-CIO was calling on both Obama and Congress to withdraw troops from Afghanistan, reduce military spending, and use the savings to repair social safety nets and create civilian-sector jobs that paid a living wage.

Politics were moving ever further from these goals, however, and not just at the federal level. In state capitals across the country, the momentum belonged more and more to initiatives favored by corporate mouthpieces such as the National Chamber of Commerce, the National Association of Manufacturers, and the Koch brothers' Americans for Prosperity. Most influential of all was the American Legislative Exchange Council (ALEC), which supplied legislators and governors with model language for laws whose enactment would advance conservative causes. Founded in 1973, ALEC had at first reached out to Democrats as well as Republicans, but by the time Obama took office, it was staunchly aligned with the Republican Party and largely in control of its agenda at the state level. In January 2010, the Supreme Court opened the door to even more corporate influence by ruling in the case of *Citizens United v. Federal Election Commission* that any restriction on political advertising by individual citizens or groups of citizens violated the Constitution's guarantee of free speech. This decision applied to unions, nonprofits, and grassroots organizations as well as corporations, but corporate investments in politics outstripped what anyone else could muster.

State law now grew all the more reflective of corporate priorities. ALEC stepped up its promotion of "right to work" laws under which union contracts could not require that workers join the union, pay dues, or reimburse the union for the costs of representing them. As of 2011, twenty-two states had such laws, and just one of them (Oklahoma's) had been enacted more recently than the 1980s. By 2017, six more states had joined the right-to-work column, and they included states like Michigan and Wisconsin that had once been union strongholds. Another corporate objective was to curtail democracy by revising election law in ways that made it harder for poor and working people to vote—by requiring that voters present photographic identification, for example—and by redrawing electoral districts so that people likely to vote for Democrats were either confined to just one district or scattered across so many that they lost clout at the polls. Thanks in part to suppressive redistricting, the Republican Party entirely controlled thirty-two state legislatures by 2017, even in some places—Wisconsin, for example—where most of the statewide vote went to Democrats.

At the federal level, the National Labor Relations Board (NLRB) offered some respite from the drubbing that unionism and democracy took in the states, but the relief was not automatic. When George Bush left office, just two of the NLRB's five seats were occupied, and Senate Republicans blocked confirmation of Obama's nominees to fill the vacancies. He countered by making recess appointments that did not require Senate approval, but federal courts found these appointments invalid, and it was not until July 2013 that a compromise finally solidified a five-person board. Though Obama held office for eight years, his NLRB was fully operative for just three and a half. Several of its decisions significantly benefitted workers who sought to organize. It revised procedures so that workers who had signed enough union cards to trigger an NLRB election did not have to wait so long for that election to take place. It ruled that corporations that tried to shield themselves from labor law by hiring workers through temp agencies or franchisees were in fact "joint employers" and could be found liable for unfair labor practices. It declared that employers could not permanently replace strikers if the move was even partially aimed at abrogating their rights under the National Labor Relations Act. In sum, though, the Obama presidency fell far short of unions' expectations, let alone their best hopes.

That the AFL-CIO remained loyal nonetheless was hardly surprising; it had steadfastly backed Democratic administrations for more than thirty years. That Change to Win proved even more loyal did surprise some observers since one of its main rationales for leaving the AFL-CIO in 2005 had been that the federation had grown too cozy with Democrats, giving them far more than it got in return. With respect to Obama, Andy Stern—SEIU's president and Change to Win's principal spokesperson—expected to get just as much as he gave; and he gave a great deal, spending so heavily on Obama's presidential race that SEIU had to borrow money and reduce its staff by 10 percent to make ends meet. Taking stock 100 days into Obama's first term, Stern assured SEIU members that this investment was paying off. "SEIU is on the field, it's in the White House, it's in the administration," he declared, and Obama had indeed appointed or nominated several SEIU officials or former officials to serve in his administration.[13] In addition to advising the president on labor affairs, moreover, Andy Stern himself would help to draft Obama's signature legislation, the Affordable Care Act (ACA) of March 2010. This was enough to buoy Change to Win's hopes even after it became clear that the Employee Free Choice Act was a goner.

Things did not work out as anticipated. Whatever Andy Stern's input, the ACA that got signed into law was a compromise designed to please Senate Democrats who were definitely not friends of labor. They agreed to some popular reforms: a requirement that insurance companies cover medical expenses related to preexisting conditions; the elimination of lifetime limits on benefits; and a provision that young adults under age twenty-six be eligible for family coverage on a parent's insurance plan. But the law did not meet unionists' main goal for health reform. With SEIU in the vanguard and Obama cheering them on, the labor movement called in vain for an insurance system that included a publicly funded nonprofit option modeled on Medicare. Instead, the ACA funneled all but the very poorest Americans into the private insurance market, mandating that they buy coverage if they did not already have it and appropriating money to subsidize premiums paid by people with low to moderate incomes. To help pay for the subsidies, moreover, the law laid plans for a 40 percent "Cadillac tax" on the most generous employer-provided health insurance—the kinds of insurance plans unions often negotiated, or at least tried to win. Originally scheduled to start in 2018, this tax was later put off until 2020. Despite the ACA's deficiencies, SEIU vigorously pushed for its passage, defending it against critics on both the right and the left. In April 2010, just weeks after the ACA became law, Andy Stern resigned from SEIU's presidency, leaving it to his successors to retire the debt he had run up.

A month later, with the Tea Party gaining momentum and the Employee Free Choice Act hopelessly stalled, Sal Rosselli, president of the National Union of Health-care Workers, offered this reading of national politics: "Labor put so much money into electing the Democrats and Barack Obama, and look what the result is. It was a huge opportunity, at our position of greatest strength—theoretically. And we got no labor law reform and a shitty health care plan. And now the Democrats are going to lose it all." The only way forward, he concluded, was to build "a bottom-up movement that forces government to level the playing field, just like the civil rights movement in the '60s."[14] Some parts of the labor movement were wholly on board with this plan; others, not so much.

Disunity and Decline

Sal Rosselli's lament was not only a comment on Democrats' reliability as allies; it also reflected deep divisions within the Change to Win coalition. One center of conflict was UNITE HERE, a symbol of labor unity when it formed in 2004 but a site of internecine warfare just a few years later. In some respects the merger that created UNITE HERE was a match made in heaven. The Union of Needletrades, Industrial and Textile Employees (UNITE) had considerable assets—including a twenty-eight-story office building in the heart of Manhattan and the Amalgamated Bank valued at more than $4 billion as of 2010—but runaway shops in the garment and textile industries had decimated the union's membership and curtailed its prospects for new organizing. The Hotel Employees and Restaurant Employees Union (HERE) was financially strapped but larger than UNITE, and the hospitality industry offered plenty of opportunities for organizing. The two unions had very different cultures, however. UNITE was a highly centralized union that tended to organize from the top down by seeking deals with employers rather than mobilizing workers. HERE relied on militant worker-to-worker organizing drives and pressed members to play active roles in the daily life of the union. It did not take very long for these disparate cultures to clash. By 2008 Bruce Raynor, former president of UNITE and now general president of UNITE HERE, was secretly engineering a mass defection. The following year, local and regional bodies that had formerly belonged to UNITE broke away from UNITE HERE to form Workers United, which promptly affiliated with SEIU. In the summer of 2010, after two years of legal wrangling, condemnations back and forth, and failed efforts at mediation, the two sides reached a settlement. UNITE HERE got the Manhattan office building, where it is still headquartered, and exclusive jurisdiction to organize hotels, casinos, and private-sector food services. SEIU got the Amalgamated Bank and jurisdiction over food services in the public sector. That ended the fight, but not the ill feeling it caused.

As UNITE HERE fractured, so did SEIU. From outside the labor movement, no other American union seemed more dynamic than this one. Over one-fifth of all U.S. workers who joined unions in 2008 became members of SEIU, which was larger by far than any other affiliate of Change to Win or the AFL-CIO. It included workers of all sorts and fielded many of the country's most effective union organizers. Some of its units—most notably 1199 NE, which organized health care workers in southern New England—were models of labor solidarity and rank-and-file empowerment, recalling the young CIO at its very best. No other union was more deeply tied to the immigrants' rights movement than the SEIU; no other union launched more global initiatives; and since no other union devoted more money and energy to electing Obama, it was uniquely well positioned to influence the White House. When unions took part in mass marches and demonstrations, SEIU usually had the largest turnout. Wearing T-shirts, jackets and hats in the union's signature purple, its members looked like an army whose size and singlemindedness guaranteed victory.

From inside the movement, however, SEIU often looked more like a business than a labor organization. Leadership was highly centralized, even dictatorial. Applying corporate principles to union administration, national officers cut costs and consolidated power by merging multiple locals with elected leaders into gigantic units with leaders appointed by SEIU headquarters. Call centers ("member resource centers") run by paid staff increasingly replaced elected stewards as members' first line of defense against employers' violations of union contracts.[15]

With regard to organizing, SEIU had become quite businesslike too. In the public sector, it achieved contracts for hundreds of thousands of childcare providers and home health aides by striking deals with elected officials rather than organizing workers. In the private sector, it favored organizing through a neutrality agreement: a compact under which the union pledges not to strike, picket, or boycott and the employer pledges not to attack the organizing drive and, in most cases, to recognize the union if over half the employees sign membership cards. By the early 2000s, many unions sought such arrangements, which increased the rate at which organizing drives led to contracts. But SEIU's neutrality agreements typically included an extra element negotiated in secret: the union's promise to ignore some workers in exchange for free access to others. In 2006, for example, SEIU organizers abruptly and inexplicably dropped a Philadelphia drive to unionize guards employed by the security services company AlliedBarton. It later came to light that the union had traded the effort in Philadelphia for unrestricted access to AlliedBarton guards in Washington, Boston, Seattle, and Los Angeles. The workers abandoned under this deal went on to form their own organization, the Philadelphia Security Officers Union (PSOU), built with assistance from Jobs with Justice. Then, in 2012, SEIU organizers came back to town with AlliedBarton's blessing and tried unsuccessfully to poach on PSOU's campaign to unionize the company's unit at the University of Pennsylvania. This was one of many instances in which SEIU squared off against another union. In addition to UNITE HERE and PSOU, its antagonists in various raids and in some cases counterraids included the California Nurses Association, the American Federation of State, County and Municipal Employees (AFSCME), and the Federación de Maestros de Puerto Rico (the Federation of Puerto Rican Teachers), whose members SEIU tried unsuccessfully to steal after the island's government decertified the Federación for daring to strike.

Unsurprisingly, this brand of unionism generated internal opposition. In January 2008, dissidents in California formed SEIU Member Activists for Reform Today (SMART); by that spring it had spread to eleven more states and Canada. In Nevada, a group called Members for Union Democracy demanded the ouster of a staff member that Andy Stern had placed in charge of a statewide local. At the University of Massachusetts, 3,000 SEIU members fled into the Massachusetts Teachers Association rather than submit to the heavy hand of another Stern appointee. This was not simply an insurgency against Stern, however; it kept going after he left SEIU and Mary Kay Henry, a longtime member of the union's executive board, took his place at the helm.

Sal Rosselli's National Union of Healthcare Workers grew out of the dissidents' movement. The union was founded in January 2009, shortly after SEIU's executive board imposed a trusteeship on United Healthcare Workers-West (UHW), a 150,000-member mega-local headquartered in Oakland, California. Ostensibly, the trusteeship stemmed from a dispute over jurisdiction and governance. The executive board had ordered that 65,000 union members employed in nursing homes or home care leave UHW for a new statewide local of long-term care workers; UHW had insisted that these members stay put unless a majority voted to move. Beneath this conflict lay much deeper differences. Six years before the board trusteed UHW, Andy Stern had negotiated a secret bargain with several nursing home chains doing business in California. They recognized SEIU in return for promises that it would unionize just some of their facilities, that it would not challenge company control of wages and benefits, that its members would not go on strike, that they would not speak publicly about inadequate staffing, and that the union would promote the industry's legislative goals, such as more state funding for long-term health care and stricter limits on patients' right to sue. In 2007, *San Francisco Weekly* published a scorching exposé of this agreement, and UHW simultaneously issued a blueprint for vigorous organizing for better wages, benefits, and standards of patient care. Progressing from words to action, the local also played a central role in the formation of SMART, set up an "education fund" to finance lobbying for a health care system that would cover all Californians, and in September 2008 led a two-day strike in which nursing home workers in Salinas and Monterey demanded better pay, pensions, and health care benefits, and complained to the press that the staffing in their facilities was too sparse to meet patients' needs. The trusteeship's purpose was to shut down these deviations from corporate-style unionism as well as to consolidate the executive board's power. Instead of coming to heel, though, the dissidents founded the National Union of Healthcare Workers, whose membership soon rose from about 350 to 10,000, though SEIU furiously vied with the upstart in every organizing drive it conducted.

As observers often pointed out, the money unions poured into competing with one another—over $140 million in this case—could have been better spent on organizing in the many workplaces that no union had yet reached. At its founding convention in September 2005, Change to Win had envisioned "a groundbreaking organizing crusade," and some had expected that it would spur AFL-CIO unions to organize more vigorously too, much as the CIO's birth had taken the lead out of the AFL's shoes in the 1930s.[16] Whatever the case back then, however, competition was not the key to organized labor's revival in the early twenty-first century. Union membership in the United States fell from 15.7 million in 2005 to 14.8 million a decade later. The AFL-CIO tightened its belt, laying off staff and closing the National Labor College. The original Change to Win coalition meanwhile disintegrated. The Carpenters dropped out in 2009 rather than sign on to a no-raiding agreement. That same year UNITE HERE abandoned Change to Win and returned to the AFL-CIO, as did the Laborers' International Union in 2010 and the United Food and Commercial Workers in 2013.

Change to Win remained relevant by operating a Strategic Organizing Center whose services were available to any union that sought its assistance. By 2015, two AFL-CIO affiliates—the Communications Workers of America (CWA) and the United Auto Workers (UAW)—had signed on, the CWA for help with its drive to unionize T-Mobile's cell phone system across the United States and the UAW for help with its efforts at the Nissan auto assembly plant in Canton, Mississippi. The Strategic Organizing Center furnished support in the form of the Calling Out T-Mobile campaign, which both publicized the company's deceptive consumer advertising and filed a formal complaint that prompted the Federal Communications Commission to levy a $48 million fine, and the Coalition for Rights at Nissan that took aim at the company's lawbreaking to suppress worker organizing. It was one thing to expose corporate wrongdoing, however, and another to win union recognition. As of 2017, CWA had won contracts for just a few dozen T-Mobile employees at the company's facilities in New York and Connecticut, and the UAW had hit a brick wall in Mississippi.

The Nissan campaign targeted a plant that employed more than 5,000 workers, counting both regular employees and temps. The game plan was to win union recognition through an election conducted by the NLRB. These facts alone made it a highly unusual organizing drive. In the late 1990s, the annual number of NLRB elections had topped 3,000. By the mid-2010s, the figure was less than half that, and most of the elections took place in shops with fewer than fifty eligible voters. The portion of elections won by unions had expanded, from 51 percent in 1997 to 66 percent in 2015; but this was because unions had grown more hesitant to launch a drive they might not win. Commendably, the UAW went out on a limb, announcing in 2011 that it aimed to organize auto manufacturing in the South, where foreign-owned companies operated a dozen nonunion assembly plants in Kentucky, Tennessee, South Carolina, Georgia, Alabama, and Mississippi. Following the union's loss at the Volkswagen plant in Chattanooga in 2014 (discussed in chapter 13), attention turned to Nissan's facility in Canton, where an organizing drive had gone public in 2012.

The UAW mounted a multifaceted effort. It built a dedicated organizing committee, held rallies, ran ads, forged a strong partnership with the NAACP, staged a mass March on Mississippi to underscore the parallels between union rights and civil rights, publicized the $1.3 billion in tax breaks and other state and local subsidies that Nissan had received, lined up appearances by celebrity supporters like Senator Bernie Sanders and the actor Danny Glover, and tried to get the French government—the largest shareholder in Nissan's corporate partner Renault—to demand that Nissan stop fighting the union. In Nashville and a few other southern cities, labor and community activists converged on Nissan dealerships to hold informational pickets. Change to Win's Coalition for Rights at Nissan drew public attention to the company's violations of health and safety standards and laws against racial discrimination as well as the National Labor Relations Act. In the end, though, the Canton plant's workers voted against the UAW by a margin of 2,244 to 1,307.

Perhaps there were just too many obstacles in the union's path. Unlike Volkswagen, Nissan did not present itself as a neutral party; it fought the drive tooth and nail. In addition to subjecting workers to mandatory meetings with supervisors, the plant's managers waged psychological warfare by predicting that a union victory would trigger layoffs, temporarily firing a high-profile UAW supporter, threatening to shut down the low-cost auto leasing program that made workers' long commutes affordable, incessantly playing songs like Evilution's "Road to Destruction" on the public-address system, looping videos that smeared the UAW, and fostering an anti-union workers' group (Nissan Technicians for Truth and Jobs) whose members wore T-shirts that read "Want a union? Move to Detroit."[17] Across Mississippi, talk radio spewed racist opposition to the drive, telling white workers that the UAW hated their southern heritage and warning black workers—about 80 percent of the plant's workforce—that Nissan would respond to a union victory by sending them back to "picking cotton and digging ditches."[18] State chapters of the Chamber of Commerce, National Association of Manufacturers, and Americans for Prosperity lent the company a hand, as did the anti-labor public relations group the Center for Union Facts. While Congressman Bennie Thompson and other black legislators endorsed the UAW, all of the state's white political machine backed Nissan. Governor Phil Bryant ran his own vote-no initiative on Facebook, posting scary photographs of abandoned auto factories in Detroit. Describing the net effect, one worker told *Labor Notes*, "They were in our heads 24–7."[19] Then, just a week before the NLRB election took place on August 3–4, 2017, national news outlets broke the story that a UAW vice president had helped himself to $1.2 million in federal funds earmarked for the retraining of auto workers who lost their jobs during the Great Recession. It might have been impossible for any union to overcome all of this.

But the UAW faced additional challenges of its own making. First, it did not seek to organize the 40 percent of workers classified as temps, despite the recent NLRB ruling that made it possible to include them. As the labor journalist Chris Brooks pointed out, moreover, "UAW limited its campaign to talking union rather than acting union."[20] Its ground game did not involve in-plant petitions, slowdowns or other shop-floor actions to build solidarity and demonstrate the power of concerted action. The UAW's co-operation with Detroit's Big Three automakers posed a problem too. In 2011, when it announced its plan to organize southern auto plants, the union proposed "Principles for Fair Union Elections"—a neutrality agreement—whose preamble described the union as "fundamentally and radically different" from the old UAW that used to challenge employers. "We are moving on a path that no longer presumes an adversarial work environment with strict work rules, narrow job classifications or complicated contract rules," the document declared.[21] Not a single automaker signed on to the agreement; instead, the union's record of labor-management partnerships came back to bite the drive in Canton by feeding suspicions that the union aimed to hurt Nissan. The Facebook page maintained by Technicians for Truth and Jobs drew the connection. It featured a news-video clip in which a Ford executive thanked the UAW for helping the company beat the competition; an accompanying message proclaimed, "THAT COMPETITION WAS US!"[22] Finally, the UAW carried the baggage of concessions bargaining since the 1980s, including massive givebacks during the Great Recession. By the 2010s, quite a few U.S. auto-assembly workers at the nonunion plants operated by Nissan and other foreign-owned companies enjoyed wages higher than those of UAW members on the lower rungs of multitiered contracts the union had negotiated with the Big Three. If the UAW could not win in Canton in 2017, it was at least partly because it had conceded so much ground in the past.

Not that a different history on the UAW's part would have guaranteed a victory. In February 2017, at the Boeing aircraft plant in North Charleston, South Carolina, the International Association of Machinists (IAM) decisively lost an election in which one big issue was the union's record of militancy at Boeing's plant in Everett, Washington. At the end of 2009, the company had transferred much of its production of airliners from Everett to North Charleston, and workers in both plants had seen the move for exactly what it was: a punishment to the unionists in Everett for striking rather than agreeing to givebacks and a reward to the North Charleston workers for decertifying the IAM in September 2009, less than two years after they voted it in. When the union set out to reorganize the North Charleston plant, the drive's opponents told this story many times and so persuasively connected unionism with job loss and the open shop with job security that the IAM did not stand a chance. As developments at Boeing exemplified, moreover, failed organizing drives were not the only reason the labor movement shrank; decertification elections—which unions lost more than two-thirds of the time—took a toll too, as did the transfer of jobs from one place or corporate entity to another. Even the gigantic SEIU felt the pinch. Although it took in legions of new recruits year after year, its membership stood at 1.9 million as of 2017—just 100,000 more than when Change to Win was born twelve years earlier.

Roads to Renewal

As in the past, crisis encouraged creative thinking about the labor movement's future. Proposals came from many quarters: not only union staff and officers but also lawyers, scholars, journalists, and activists in labor and community-based organizations of every stripe. Some zeroed in on a purely operational matter, arguing for example, that unions needed to lower top officers' salaries, make more use of social media platforms like Facebook and Twitter, take better advantage of loopholes in the Taft-Hartley Act's ban on secondary boycotts, or train staff members in strategic research. Once it became clear that the Employee Free Choice Act was dead, new ideas for revising unionism's legal environment poured forth. Some thought the best bet was to strive for domestic applications of international treaties that recognized workers' right to organize; others believed U.S. workers might enforce that right by deploying the First Amendment's provisions for free assembly and free speech; and still others called for an effort to outlaw the hiring of permanent replacements for strikers or to establish an absolute right to strike by invoking the Thirteenth Amendment's ban on involuntary servitude. The biannual conferences hosted by *Labor Notes* magazine grew from 900 participants in 2006 to 3,000 in 2018, with activists gathering to trade viewpoints on everything from handling grievances, negotiating contracts, and mobilizing unions for political action to worker co-operatives, the relationship between labor rights and LGBTQ rights, and the labor movement's responsibility to promote the public good. In 2016, the magazine gathered much of the practical wisdom that had emerged at its conferences into *Secrets of a Successful Organizer*, a 265-page handbook for workplace organizing with or without a collective bargaining agreement. As the Labor Notes conferences swelled, labor activists were also a growing presence at conferences sponsored by scholarly groups like the Labor and Working Class History Association and on the pages of university-based journals like *New Labor Forum*. Union gatherings meanwhile addressed an ever-wider range of issues: climate change, criminal justice reform, Islamophobia, police violence against African Americans, and the possibilities for third-party politics, to name a few.

Out of this came the outlines of a general consensus in the movement's most progressive and action-oriented sectors: to survive, let alone grow, unions had to expand their agenda far beyond wages, hours, and working conditions and become organizations that closely linked day-to-day efforts to empower workers on the job with longer-range struggles for justice in society at large. Many called this "social justice unionism."[23] Others used different terms, such as "whole worker organizing," "civic unionism," or "class struggle unionism."[24] Practically speaking, all of these phrases meant much the same thing: instead of building labor-community alliances on a quid pro quo basis, unions would define community concerns as their very own. This was hardly the first time U.S. labor activists had embraced such an agenda, which called to mind the Knights of Labor, the Industrial Workers of the World, and the young CIO. It was, however, the first time since the dawn of the Cold War that a critical mass of labor leaders was so disheartened by the outcomes of business as usual that they thought it sensible to adopt a genuinely radical program.

Social justice unionism took multiple forms. Often it was a piecemeal affair involving a single local, a single event, a single cause, or a project in a single city, state, or shop. Unions in the entertainment industry—the Screen Actors Guild, the American Federation of Television and Radio Artists and the Actors Equity Association—launched a joint effort to get their industry to include people with disabilities, portray them accurately, and guarantee their access to facilities. Multiple unions joined the movement for a federal law to ban discrimination on the basis of sexual orientation and gender identity, and unionists were among the first to insist on explicit protections for transgender people. In Philadelphia, the UAW staffed Women Against Abuse, a shelter for women and children fleeing domestic violence, and the local Coalition of Labor Union Women partnered with Project Safe, which provided support services for sex workers. In southern California, IBEW Local 11 worked with community organizations to recruit men of color and women into its apprenticeship program and partnered with environmentalists to promote clean energy. At Sarah Lawrence College in Yonkers, New York, Local 30 of the Operating Engineers kicked off negotiations for a first contract for facilities maintenance workers with a teach-in in honor of Martin Luther King that featured the radical filmmaker Michael Moore. In Jacksonville, Florida, two shop stewards from Teamsters Local 512 joined with a community activist to host the *Worker Power Hour* podcast, which offered radical working-class views on labor issues and other national and international affairs. In St. Louis, Missouri, progressives from several unions came together with community organizations to establish the Workers' Education Society, which trained black youth for entry into historically segregated trades; fostered leadership skills among women, young workers, and people of color; offered classes and workshops on connections between workers' rights and struggles around race, gender, and disability; and countered Missouri's passage of a right-to-work law with a successful petition drive to subject the law to a statewide referendum (scheduled for November 2018). In New York State, where the LGBTQ movement had twice failed to win marital rights for same-sex couples, unions put the cause over the top by sending their own expert organizers to lead the charge. In North Carolina, the state AFL-CIO became an integral part of the Moral Mondays movement in which religious progressives led protests around issues like voter suppression, prisoners' rights, LGBTQ equality, universal health care, workers' right to organize, and inadequate funding for social programs and public schools. On September 12, 2016, Moral Mondays went national, and unions in thirty states took part in the Higher Moral Ground Day of Action in support of progressive change.

In 2011, social justice unionism swept the United States as mass uprisings for political and economic democracy enveloped the globe, spreading from North Africa—where the movement began in December 2010—to the Middle East, southern Africa, Europe, Asia, Oceania, and the Americas. The first U.S. manifestation of this movement emerged in Madison, Wisconsin, in February 2011, when the Tea

Party's newly elected governor Scott Walker announced plans to eliminate collective bargaining for public employees and about 1,000 members of the teaching assistants' union at the University of Wisconsin's Madison campus took to the streets for a Valentine's Day protest. Tens of thousands of public employees and their supporters turned out the following day. Several thousand poured into the Wisconsin capitol building to offer testimony against Walker's plan. Hundreds occupied the building overnight, staying on for ten days as crowds as large as 70,000 gathered outside and sympathy demonstrations popped up in Los Angeles, Chicago, and other cities. While the sympathy actions petered out once the state legislature enacted Walker's plan that March, crowds of thousands continued to demonstrate in Madison until the state's supreme court validated the new law in mid-June.

By then, things were heating up across the country. In March 2011 progressive union activists in Cleveland formed the Emergency Labor Network (ELN) in response to developments in Madison and to rumors that President Obama intended to reduce spending on Social Security and Medicare. By June, labor radicals across the country had endorsed the ELN, which called for movement-wide discussions on "what it will take to build a Labor Party in this country."[25] That year's May Day demonstrations had the largest union contingents in decades; in Milwaukee, where the gathering was organized by an immigrant worker center, Richard Trumka spoke, telling the crowd, "It's the same fight . . . immigrants' rights, workers' rights, student rights, voting rights."[26] In mid-June, just as the demonstrations in Madison wound down, student, community, and labor activists in New York City began a three-week occupation of City Hall Park, where they established a "Bloombergville" tent colony to protest the billionaire Mayor Michael Bloomberg's cuts in public services.[27] In August, some 45,000 members of the CWA and IBEW struck Verizon communications rather than submit to demands for concessions. Along with the usual picnics and parades, Labor Day events that September included protests of the neoliberal trade policies embraced by both the Democratic and Republican parties. Then, on Saturday, September 17, several hundred young radicals pitched tents in Zuccotti Park in New York City's downtown financial district. Calling the action Occupy Wall Street, they set forth grievances on behalf of "the 99 percent"—the masses of people steadily losing ground as wealth and power grew ever more concentrated in the 1 percent at the very top.[28]

Occupy Wall Street electrified activists around the world; within weeks, the Occupy movement spread to some 600 U.S. communities and thousands more overseas. An array of labor unions nurtured the movement in the United States, supporting it with marches, rallies, donations of food and blankets, legal assistance, and training in first aid. In return for these gifts, unionists received inspiration; Occupy's militant idealism was contagious, at least in the short term. In November 2011, rhetoric borrowed from Occupy Wall Street helped public employees in Ohio win a voter referendum on their right to engage in collective bargaining. That same month, at US Foods distribution centers from New York to Colorado, more than 2,000 Teamster truck drivers and package handlers staged sympathy strikes in solidarity with a pair of janitors unfairly treated by the company's branch in Streator, Illinois.

Close on the heels of the Occupy movement came the Fight for $15 campaign to win a living wage for workers in retail sales, fast food restaurants, and other notoriously low-paying industries. In November 2012, on the day after Thanksgiving, Walmart workers in 100 cities across the country picketed their stores; six days later several hundred fast food workers in New York City demonstrated for raises and the right to organize without interference from the boss. In 2013, one-day strikes in support of these same demands rolled across the United States, mobilizing low-wage workers from multiple industries. In 2014, the strikes became global events (and as of this writing, April 2018, they continue to take place around the world). The U.S. strikes went hand in hand with political efforts to establish $15 as the minimum hourly wage under local ordinances and state laws. By 2016, fourteen cities and counties had adopted such measures, and sixteen states had raised their minimums well above the federal floor. While SEIU coordinated both the strikes and the political initiatives, the campaign's energy spilled far beyond organizational borders. A great many unions, worker centers, labor councils, and civil rights organizations took part, and the movement had a major impact on public opinion. In a national poll conducted in January 2015, 63 percent of respondents said they favored a minimum wage of $15 an hour.

As social justice unionism advanced, experiments with worker co-operatives multiplied. The United Steelworkers took the lead in 2009, partnering with the Mondragon federation of worker co-ops in Spain's Basque region to explore possibilities for establishing union co-ops in the United States and Canada. Whereas Mondragon co-operatives were run by worker councils, the union co-op model called for management by union bargaining committees, making the enterprise more fully accountable to its workers. As one of the new model's architects explained, "Workers engaging in collective bargaining with their employer may appear to be drastically different from and incompatible with workers co-operating as owners, but the underlying approach is the same: workers supporting each other to improve their livelihood."[29] He might have added that it served the surrounding communities to establish an enterprise whose purpose was to provide safe, stable jobs—much more than private industry was doing in most cases. The Republic Windows & Doors factory that UE members had occupied in 2008 wound up as the union co-op New Era Windows, founded after a company that bought the Republic plant in 2009 abandoned it just three years later. Other union co-ops in operation by 2016 included the Steelworkers' WorX Printing Cooperative, an eco-friendly producer of custom T-shirts in Worcester, Massachusetts; taxi drivers' co-ops affiliated with the Communications Workers in Denver, San Jose, and Portland, Oregon; the SEIU's Cooperative Home Care Associates in the Bronx borough of New York City; and, in southwestern Ohio, produce farms, a grocery store, and a home-insulation company backed by the Cincinnati Union Co-op Initiative.

As the line between unions and workers co-ops faded, unions and workers centers moved toward each other too. In 2005, a survey of 137 worker centers across the country found that only 15 percent had ongoing relationships with labor unions. Ten years later they numbered about 250, some with multiple branches and membership in the thousands, and projects in tandem with unions were becoming the norm. Commitments to social justice made unions more like worker centers: more attentive to workers' lives beyond the job, less apt to see union recognition as the sole purpose of worker organizing, and readier to stay in touch should efforts to win recognition initially fail. "It can't always be about collective bargaining," explained a Steelworker organizer in Los Angeles. "It's about worker power. If we've learned anything from the worker center movement, it's that power can look like a lot of different things."[30] That insight enabled the Retail, Warehouse, and Department Store Union (by then a branch of the United Food and Commercial Workers) to help hundreds of immigrant workers achieve collective bargaining at car washes and grocery stores in New York City. At the same time, worker centers grew more like unions: less exclusively focused on advocacy and service delivery and more adept at workplace organizing and even collective bargaining. Workers' Dignity in Nashville, Tennessee, gathered labor unions and community organizations into citywide drives to improve the working conditions of hotel housekeepers and commercial cleaners. Although the Coalition of Immokalee Workers was not a certified union—and did not seek to become one lest this limit its ability to run boycotts—it nonetheless became a bargaining agent for tens of thousands of tomato harvesters and armed them with the rough equivalent of a union contract. In other instances worker centers organized workplace committees to take advantage of the National Labor Relations Act's Section 7, which recognizes workers' right to take part in "concerted activities for the purpose of collective bargaining or other mutual aid or protection," whether or not a certified union is part of the mix.[31] Among the worker centers that made use of this provision was Somos Un Pueblo Unido (We Are One People) in Santa Fe, New Mexico, which assisted the formation of some fifty committees of hotel and restaurant workers, car washers, landscapers, and housecleaners.

By 2014, sixteen worker centers had formally affiliated with local labor councils, and a great many more had partnered with unions on an ad hoc basis. One affiliate was the Workers' Defense Project/Proyecto Defensa Laboral (WDP), a member of the Austin Area AFL-CIO Council in Texas. An outgrowth of the immigrants' rights movement, the WDP had no relationship with unions in 2007, the year it began to study the labor conditions of immigrant construction workers, many of them undocumented; and when it approached building trades unions in connection with this investigation, it got snubbed in almost every case. In 2009, however, its public report about widespread violations of wage and safety laws prompted these same unions to apologize for the rejections and offer partnerships. In 2015, a WDP founder told an interviewer, "One of the things I'm most proud of is that we have burly white construction workers, who are thought of as the most Texan guys you could be, standing up and fighting with us for immigration reform, and standing with a bunch of undocumented immigrant workers and seeing their struggle as one."[32] In 2017, the Texas AFL-CIO mobilized against a new state law banning "sanctuary cities" that provided safe haven for the undocumented. Sounding every bit like a worker center, the state federation urged union members "to answer not just to the law, but to a higher power."[33]

At the national level the AFL-CIO developed closer relations with workers historically excluded from the labor movement by virtue of occupation or immigration status. A leader on this front was the Farm Labor Organizing Committee (FLOC), which received a full-fledged AFL-CIO charter in 2006, by which time it had been organizing farmworkers for almost forty years and won contracts for over 23,000 tomato harvesters, cucumber pickers, and other agricultural workers in the Midwest and North Carolina. Among those FLOC recruited in North Carolina were about 6,000 guest

THE LAST GASP?

workers in the United States on temporary H2-A visas; this marked the first time guest workers became members of a U.S. union. FLOC's inaugural campaign as a full affili-ate of the AFL-CIO focused on tobacco harvesters working for farmers who supplied the cigarette company R.J. Reynolds. Here, as in all of FLOC's organizing, labor-community alliances played a central role since neither federal nor state labor laws recognized farmworkers' right to organize. FLOC's community organizing was more than an addendum to organizing on the job, however. It also reflected the union's com-mitment to addressing workers' needs beyond the fields and their families' needs as well. In Toledo, Ohio, for example, FLOC established the Homies Union, which invit-ed Latino youth to build leadership skills and devise collective ways to improve life in their neighborhoods. In North Carolina's tobacco country the FLOCMigos youth group devised a similar program and took part in the Moral Mondays movement.

Another organization that helped the conventional labor movement break out of its shell was the Excluded Workers Congress, established in 2010 by organizations of domestic workers, guest workers, day laborers, ex-convicts, and others that unions had long neglected. Responding to its public calls for attention to the excluded, Rich-ard Trumka attended the congress's national meeting in 2011 and signed partnership agreements with two of its member groups: the National Domestic Workers Alli-ance and the National Guestworker Alliance. That same year, a third member of the Excluded Workers Congress—the National Taxi Workers Alliance (NTWA)—joined the AFL-CIO as an affiliated union, the first affiliate to represent workers classified as independent contractors. In 2013, the NTWA's executive director Bhairavi Desai was elected to the AFL-CIO Executive Council.

If partnership with the AFL-CIO was no panacea, it did give an organization greater access to financial resources, political backing, and other essential support. In Cali-fornia, unions helped the Domestic Workers Alliance finally win a long struggle for a state law protecting domestic workers' rights. In Pennsylvania, Jobs with Justice helped the Guestworker Alliance end a scam in which McDonald's restaurants trapped inter-national students in jobs that paid less than the minimum wage. With assistance from the AFL-CIO, the Taxi Workers Alliance added branches in San Francisco, Austin, and Montgomery County, Maryland, to its founding chapters in Philadelphia and New York.

Change to Win reached out to excluded workers too. In 2010, it inaugurated a drive to organize more than 75,000 workers driving trucks at the Los Angeles and Long Beach seaports, typically for companies that purposely misclassified them as indepen-dent contractors. Unprotected by labor law and ineligible for employee benefits, the drivers—virtually all of them people of color and most of them foreign born—were also compelled to lease the trucks they drove and take full responsibility for vehicle main-tenance, fuel, and insurance. Change to Win's organizing drive, which relied heavily on strikes and slowdowns, sought to get the drivers properly classified and win union recognition. Moving from company to company, it had made significant headway on both fronts by 2018. While Teamsters Local 848 spearheaded the effort, vital support came from a whole family of unions, churches, and social justice groups, including the Steelworkers, UNITE HERE, and other AFL-CIO affiliates as well as SEIU and the Los Angeles Poor People's Campaign, modeled on the Moral Mondays movement.

Labor activists took up the issue of sexual harassment and assault well before the fall of 2017, when high-profile women in the entertainment industry began to publicize their experience with sexual abuse at the hands of powerful men, inspired women working in media and politics to do the same, and made the hashtag #MeToo (a slogan they borrowed from the black community activist Tarana Burke) a sensation on the Internet. By that time, SEIU, UNITE HERE, and AFSCME had all begun to push for laws and contract provisions to shield women workers from sexual predators. The Coalition of Immokalee Workers had meanwhile tried to shame Wendy's fast food chain into taking action against assaults on women farmworkers. And, as the #MeToo movement spread online, UAW women at two Ford Motor factories in Chicago launched the hashtag #WhatAboutUs to draw attention to the fact that most working women who confronted sexual abuse on the job were not entertainers, media personalities, or congressional aides but industrial workers, hotel housekeepers, office cleaners, and so on.

While unions' commitments to social justice were fleeting or one dimensional in many instances, some walked the walk all day every day, year in and year out. This had long been the case with the United Electrical Workers and the International Longshore and Warehouse Union. Now they were joined by others, including the United Steelworkers and various locals in SEIU, the Teamsters, and the United Food and Commercial Workers. One exemplar of the trend was National Nurses United (NNU), born when the California Nurses Association merged with other unions in 2009. In the workplace, few unions were more militant than the NNU, whose affiliates had launched more than twenty major strikes by the end of 2016—mostly to enforce demands for better staffing of medical facilities. But Nurses United was also deeply involved in lobbying, electoral politics, and direct action in support of a Medicare-for-all health care system, stricter environmental protection, a much higher minimum wage, and tax laws that would compel corporations and the rich to pay their fair share. The Communications Workers of America (CWA) followed a similar path, combining workplace militancy—including multi-state strikes against telecommunications giants that pressed for concessions—with exceptionally strong support for worker-to-worker organizing by the union's rank and file. Financial donations and, more important, members' sustained involvement in community-based projects made CWA a mainstay of Jobs with Justice coalitions across the United States as well as local and national campaigns in defense of democracy and human rights.

UNITE HERE was another standout. In 2008 it became the first U.S. union to pass a comprehensive resolution in support of equal rights for all LGBTQ people, and it incorporated the issue into its political agenda in addition to its contracts. Its locals in New Haven, Connecticut, engineered a labor takeover of the board of alders (city council) in the elections of 2009. They then used that platform to establish a job training and placement program designed first and foremost to serve black and Latino communities with high unemployment. In Boston, UNITE HERE won a five-year struggle to get compensation for ninety-eight housekeepers summarily fired by a Hyatt hotel where the union did not have a contract. In Phoenix, UNITE HERE was the main mover behind Central Arizonans for a Sustainable Economy, whose voter registration drives so changed the political landscape that Joe Arpaio, Maricopa County's infamously xenophobic sheriff, was finally ousted from office in 2016.

The Chicago Teachers Union (CTU) offered yet another beacon. Although it had earned a reputation for militancy in the 1980s—when it took members out on strike on four different occasions—the CTU had not distinguished itself as a champion of the city's public school system. That changed in 2010, when a slate put forward by the dissident Caucus of Rank and File Educators was elected to lead the union. The new president was Karen Lewis, an African American teacher of high school chemistry with a devastatingly on-the-mark assessment of education "reforms" long endorsed by both the Democratic and Republican parties. As she told the crowd at the press conference following her election:

> Corporate America sees K-12 public education as a $380 billion trust that, up until the last ten or fifteen years, they haven't had a sizeable piece of. So this so-called school reform is not an education plan; it's a business plan. . . . Fifteen years ago, this city purposely began starving our lowest-income neighborhood schools of greatly needed resources and personnel. Class sizes rose; schools were closed. Then standardized tests, which in this town alone is a $60-million business, measured that slow death by starvation. These tests labeled our students, families and educators failures, because standardized tests reveal more about a student's zip code than it does about academic growth.[34]

That the CTU was at last taking on these issues laid the foundation for a citywide movement of teachers, students, parents, and community activists in defense of public education. In bargaining for the next contract, the union set forth demands that addressed both working conditions and learning conditions: higher pay, better job protections, less testing, smaller class sizes, and money for music, art, and physical education programs as well as the hiring of social workers, counselors, and school nurses. When bargaining stalled and the CTU struck for nine days in September 2012, tens of thousands of supporters joined the teachers' marches, rallies, and picket lines. Mayor Rahm Emanuel, a neoliberal Democrat, tried and failed to turn public opinion against the striking teachers, who won a contract that met most of their demands.

CTU leaders later toured nine cities to hold town hall meetings on the social justice model of teacher unionism, which swiftly gained ground. In 2015, a network of twenty caucuses formed the United Caucuses of Rank and File Educators to promote a social justice agenda in the National Education Association and the American Federation of Teachers. In spring 2018, teachers in West Virginia, Kentucky, Oklahoma, and Arizona staged statewide strikes to force lawmakers to stop starving public schools.

Despite the advances scored by social justice unionism, constraints, shortcomings, and disappointments were a big part of the landscape too. The AFL-CIO's partnerships with organizations of day laborers, domestic workers, and guest workers did not usher in an entirely new day for workers traditionally excluded from labor unions. In right-to-work states, new immigrants hired into plants that were already unionized often chose not to sign up, which encouraged old-timers to blame the newcomers for unions' declining strength. While the Day Labor Organizing Network, the Domestic Workers Alliance, and the National Guestworkers Alliance could count on unions for some assistance, worker centers remained their closest partners. While building trades unions in Texas made common cause with undocumented workers, quite the opposite occurred in some places. In Buffalo, New York, for example, the Northeast Regional Council of Carpenters proudly told the press that its member locals were matchlessly "proactive" in reporting the undocumented to immigration authorities.[35] Sex workers were the most marginalized of all. The union co-operative movement led by the United Steelworkers never developed a relationship with San Francisco's Lusty Lady union co-op founded by members of SEIU Local 790 in 2003. Although the Coalition of Labor Union Women endorsed union organizing among exotic dancers, they and other workers in the U.S. sex industry—which employed about 3 million by the 2010s—were hard pressed to find a welcoming union beyond the Retail, Warehouse and Department Store Union, which established several units at sex toy stores in New York City in 2017.

Progressive causes embraced by some parts of the labor movement were neglected or even opposed by others. Many unions merely tolerated the struggle for LGBTQ rights instead of supporting it. Although union rules forbade hate speech, the insults strikers hurled at scabs included homophobic, misogynist, and racist slurs. While many unions got behind environmental initiatives such as the BlueGreen Alliance jointly founded by Steelworkers and the Sierra Club, the Emerald Cities Collaborative in which SEIU played a central role, and the People's Climate Marches that took place in New York City in 2014 and Washington, D.C., in 2017, it remained relatively easy for dirty industries to get labor in their corner when it seemed that jobs were at stake. In 2015, the United Mine Workers and the International Brotherhood of Boilermakers joined coal companies in a lawsuit to stop the Environmental Protection Agency from phasing in stricter emissions standards at power plants. In the fall of 2016, a handful of unions[36] joined a coalition of Native American and environmental groups whose members assembled in North Dakota to stop construction of an oil pipeline that threatened to pollute water sources and desecrate sacred land; but other unions either ignored the protest or, like AFL-CIO headquarters, endorsed the pipeline on the grounds that it would create union jobs.

If narrow self-interest overshadowed principle with respect to the pipeline, it limited social justice unionism in other respects too. The local ordinances that raised minimum wages, thanks to the Fight for $15, routinely included exemptions for employers with union contracts that stipulated wages below the new floors. In 2015, after a decade of efforts to unionize low-wage workers at Wal-Mart, the United Food and Commercial Workers decided that the drive was too expensive to continue. Union leaders devoted to democracy in the world at large could be as dictatorial as any other inside their own organizations. While some unions strove to protect women workers from sexual abuse by managers or customers, the labor movement generally preferred to look the other way when the abusers were union members, officers, or staff. The UAW women who launched the #WhatAboutUs campaign had been mistreated by union brothers as well as supervisors, and testimony from women in the building trades made clear that the same patterns prevailed in the construction industry. As the #MeToo campaign gained momentum, AFL-CIO headquarters fired a high-level staffer known to mistreat women, and SEIU fired three such men. But this housecleaning was by no means exhaustive.

Sometimes, entirely uncontroversial causes just plain got lost amidst competing priorities. Inspired by the entertainment unions' initiatives in support of people with disabilities, the AFL-CIO convention of 2009 committed the federation to establishing a new constituency group for workers with disabilities. As of 2018, however, no such group had materialized.

Nowhere were social justice unionism's momentum and limitations more evident than in organized labor's reactions to Black Lives Matter. This movement grew out of an Internet meme that spread in summer 2013 after a Florida jury acquitted George Zimmerman for the murder of Trayvon Martin, an unarmed black teenager accosted by Zimmerman and fatally shot in the ensuing scuffle. In this case the killer was a civilian, and Black Lives Matter was an online campaign, confined to platforms such as Twitter and Facebook. In 2014, however, the campaign's founders—three young black women working as community organizers in California—began to mobilize street demonstrations against police killings of African Americans, and a national movement quickly sprang to life. The first street actions took place in August 2014 in Ferguson, Missouri, with Black Lives Matter rallying activists from across the country to reinforce local protests of a police officer's fatal shooting of Michael Brown, another unarmed teenager. In the years that followed, the Black Lives Matter network organized thousands of protests targeting both police brutality—multiple murders of black men, women, and even a twelve-year-old child—and violence perpetrated by white-supremacist vigilantes. Although black bloodshed was hardly a new phenomenon in American history, Black Lives Matter made it virtually impossible for the larger society simply to look the other way, and this posed new challenges for labor unions.

Some quickly embraced Black Lives Matter. Among the protestors in Ferguson were local contingents from the Coalition of Black Trade Unionists, the Amalgamated Transit Union, the Communications Workers, SEIU, and the Fight for $15 network. But the United Food and Commercial Workers (UFCW)—the union to which Michael Brown's mother belonged—merely called for "a fair investigation and justice under the law" and issued no statement when both a local grand jury and the U.S. Justice Department failed to indict Brown's shooter.[37] So it went time after time, with a sliver of the local labor movement actively supporting Black Lives Matter, other locals declining to hit the streets, and national unions loath to criticize law enforcement. If this testified to excessive caution on the part of labor leaders, it also reflected the fact that a great many police officers belonged to unions affiliated with the AFL-CIO or Change to Win. Some belonged to the AFL-CIO's International Union of Police Associations (IUPA), which represented the officers in Ferguson; but at least as many were members of mixed organizations such as SEIU, the Teamsters, the United Auto Workers, the UFCW . . . the list went on. The only union to express misgivings about this situation was a UAW local of graduate student employees at the University of California, which publicly urged the AFL-CIO to demonstrate solidarity with black communities by expelling the IUPA. The federation did not even acknowledge this proposal.

But it did respond to Black Lives Matter, establishing a Commission on Racial and Economic Justice charged with devising ways to make commitments to racial justice a cornerstone of labor solidarity. Hearings held in six cities—Cleveland, Oakland, Boston, St. Louis (a stone's throw from Ferguson), Minneapolis, and Birmingham—generated a long list of recommendations that began with the suggestion that all unions emulate those that "have engaged in tough conversations about criminal justice reforms, internal practices that support racial inequities and whether or how to support the Black Lives Matter movement."[38] To facilitate such conversations, the commission also developed an elaborate toolkit of resources to spark and guide discussions of Black Lives Matter and other aspects of racial justice along with women's equality, LGBTQ issues, and immigrants' rights.

That unions most in need of these discussions were the least likely to have them frustrated labor progressives, not only because they rejected narrow unionism on principle but also because it threatened the movement's future. Analyzing the UAW's defeat at Nissan, Tiffany Flowers, organizing director for one of the UFCW's southern locals and a young leader of efforts to merge labor activism with Black Lives Matter, assessed unions' prospects for penetrating the South:

> We need to build community before we can build campaigns. . . . [L]abor needs to do a very good and hard assessment of itself and right its wrongs before it's too late. Labor is silent when Black people are killed by the police. Labor is silent as millions of undocumented folks suffer through this evil regime. Labor is silent as our Muslim brothers and sisters come under attack. Labor is silent when transgender rights are under attack. Labor unions are failing to demonstrate the values that they purport to hold.[39]

That a rising generation of labor activists aimed to resolve these issues boded well for social justice unionism over the long run. For the present, though, the glass was only half full.

15

Tipping Points

Even if they recognized that time was on their side, labor progressives were in a grim mood in 2017, when the 1 percent gained a firmer grip on national politics than at any time since the Gilded Age. Hopes had soared in spring of 2015 when Vermont's U.S. senator Bernie Sanders announced that he would run for the Democratic Party's presidential nomination. The announcement came just weeks after Hillary Clinton—former first lady, U.S. senator from New York, and secretary of state under Obama—had declared her candidacy and party insiders had so quickly rallied behind her that pundits predicted she would win the nomination in a walk. That was bad news for unions. Clinton was a neoliberal through and through, and if she really was a shoo-in for the nomination, she would, to quote one syndicated columnist, "feel no compulsion to accede to the demands of organized labor."[1] It seemed that this would be yet another presidential election in which movements for social justice would have to choose between supporting a corporate Democrat or supporting a third-party nominee who could not possibly win. Then Bernie Sanders entered the race, and everything changed.

An independent socialist who caucused with Senate Democrats, Sanders owed virtually nothing to the party establishment or to corporate backers. Of his top twenty donors over the course of his career in Washington, nineteen were labor unions and the twentieth an organization of lawyers who specialized in suing corporations for negligence. His platform read like a working-class wish list. Its planks included, among other things, federal protection of workers' right to organize; universal health care through a Medicare-for-all system; tuition-free public colleges and universities; a federal minimum wage of $15; immigration reform that provided the undocumented with a path to citizenship; campaign finance reform to remove corporate money from the political process; and criminal justice reform to reduce the nation's prison population and end police abuse of black and Latino communities. Sanders knew how to listen too. Though he entered the race with a platform that did not explicitly address racism, the agenda soon expanded in response to criticisms from Black Lives Matter activists, who more than once took over the stage at his campaign events. By the time the Democratic primaries and caucuses began in February 2016, the Sanders race had become a gathering place for people from a wide range of social justice movements, among them a Labor for Bernie initiative launched in June 2015. As he vied for the nomination, Sanders got endorsements from just a handful of national unions: the Communications Workers, National Nurses United, the International Longshore and Warehouse Union, the United Electrical Workers, the American Postal Workers Union, and the Amalgamated Transit Union. The rest backed Clinton or, like the AFL-CIO Executive Council, backed no one until the party had an official nominee. Labor for Bernie had tremendous momentum at the grassroots, however. More than 100 local unions and labor councils endorsed Sanders, as did state federations of labor in Vermont and South Carolina, and many thousands of unionists organized rallies, made phone calls, and knocked on doors to get out the vote on his behalf.

The sense of determination and possibility spilled over into other quarters. Labor activists got behind insurgent Democrats and independents at the local and state levels, sometimes in tandem with the Sanders campaign and other times in separate efforts. The Working Families Party spread to new places, including Ferguson, Missouri, and Albuquerque, New Mexico. Labor candidates recently elected to city councils in Seattle, Richmond, California, and New Haven, Connecticut, expanded their base. There was also an uptick in worker militancy on the job. Despite their employer's recruitment of replacements, 1,000 Steelworkers on strike at the Marathon Oil refinery in Galveston Bay, Texas, held out for five months, finally forcing the company to meet demands for better health and safety. In May 2015, teachers in sixty-five districts across Washington State struck for one day to protest inadequate funding of public schools. In September teachers in Seattle returned to the streets for five days, demanding and winning a raise not only for themselves but also for support staff, who had been left behind in the past. That same month 40,000 UAW members at Chrysler defied their union officers by rejecting a proposed contract that would have maintained a two-tier system of wages, and they soon won an agreement that began to dismantle the tiers. In February 2016, more than 2,000 Steelworkers at Allegheny Technologies plants in Pennsylvania, Ohio, and West Virginia emerged victorious from a six-month lockout triggered by their refusal to agree to a contract laden with concessions. In March, 1,200 members of the California Nurses Association staged a weeklong strike to raise wages and staffing levels at the Kaiser Medical Center in Los Angeles. For two weeks that April, 36,500 members of the Communications Workers and the Brotherhood of Electrical Workers struck Verizon's East Coast operations to beat back its demands for concessions.

By the time the primary season ended in June 2016, Sanders had carried the day in twenty-two states, lost by a nose in several others, and accumulated 45 percent of the regular delegates to the nominating convention. It was a better showing than party insiders had anticipated and all the more impressive since, as was later revealed, the Democratic National Committee's campaign-funding arrangements unfairly favored Clinton. She had more delegates than Sanders, however, and that was that. In mid-July, with all conceivable paths to the nomination foreclosed, he dropped out of the race and endorsed his rival. Instead of giving up, the movement that had gathered in support of Sanders morphed into the network known as Our Revolution, which worked for progressive candidates and ballot measures at the state and local levels and scored victories in more than half of these contests in November 2016.

Hillary Clinton meanwhile squared off against the Republicans' Donald Trump, a real estate magnate and reality-TV star who had insinuated himself into national politics by promulgating the false claim that Barack Obama had been born in Kenya. That Trump became the party's nominee shocked the Republican establishment. Instead of sticking to the subtle expressions of bigotry that the party elite favored, Trump held forth like a drunk on a barstool, spewing contempt for Mexicans, Muslims, LGBTQ communities, people with disabilities, and anyone who dared to challenge his opinions. Unlike other candidates for the Republican nomination, moreover, Trump also presented himself as a critic of U.S. military adventures overseas and a champion of working-class communities laid low by corporate America's scramble to move operations offshore. The Clinton campaign assumed that these positions would alienate legions of voters, and the Trump campaign made the same assumption about Clinton's neoliberal affection for free trade.

It turned out that both campaigns judged correctly. As numerous pundits pointed out, Trump and Clinton were the two most disliked presidential candidates in recorded history; and to this day it is hard to say who was disliked more. While Hillary Clinton won the popular vote by almost 3 million, Donald Trump carried the Electoral College and became the forty-fifth president of the United States. Almost every U.S. labor union had supported Clinton, the only exceptions being the Fraternal Order of Police and the National Border Patrol Council in the American Federation of Government Employees. But it was one thing for a union to endorse a candidate and another thing for union members to support that candidate at the polls. While most cast their ballots for Clinton, a critical mass chose a third-party candidate, stayed home on Election Day, or voted for Trump. His margin of victory boiled down to very narrow wins in Wisconsin, Michigan, and Pennsylvania, where labor's get-out-the-vote efforts had guaranteed Obama's victories in 2008 and 2012. If Trump lacked a clear mandate, however, he wielded considerable power since the election gave Republicans the majority of seats in both the House and the Senate.

Two weeks after the election, a coalition of progressive organizations sent Donald Trump an open letter that called on him to set a good example by denouncing bigotry. Signatories included the AFL-CIO, Change to Win, a number of their affiliated unions, and constituency groups such as the Asian Pacific American Labor Alliance and Pride at Work as well as a wide range of community-based civil rights groups. The question was whether this coalition could hold firm as the Trump administration courted organized labor.

"Full Employment Isn't Enough"

The new administration's bid for unions' support started and ended with jobs. Trump himself had an unsavory reputation as an employer. In 1998 he spent $1.4 million to buy his way out of a lawsuit by undocumented Polish workers who had received sub-minimum wages for clearing the site for his Trump Tower on New York City's Fifth Avenue; when union contractors worked on his construction projects, they frequently got paid late and sometimes not at all; his Trump International Hotel in Las Vegas later ran afoul of the National Labor Relations Board for refusing to bargain with the union

(UNITE HERE) its employees had duly elected. In 2004 he tried unsuccessfully to get a trademark for the phrase "You're fired," the words with which he gleefully dismissed contestants on his TV show *The Apprentice*. As a candidate for the White House, however, he repeatedly pledged to punish U.S. corporations that fired Americans in order to ship jobs overseas.

His first initiative on this front was a shameless publicity stunt involving the Carrier Corporation's plans to transfer production of gas furnaces from a plant in Indianapolis to a facility in Mexico. In late November 2016, as president-elect, Trump proclaimed that he had persuaded Carrier to keep 1,100 jobs in Indianapolis in exchange for a decade's worth of state tax breaks engineered by his running mate Mike Pence, the governor of Indiana. In fact, the deal preserved just 800 jobs, leaving at least 550 on the chopping block. When Chuck Jones, president of United Steelworkers (USW) Local 1999, dared to point this out, Trump immediately attacked him on Twitter, advising USW members at the plant to "spend more time working—less time talking."[2] Unionists quickly sprang to Jones's defense. Brett Voorhies, a steelworker who headed the Indiana AFL-CIO, accused Trump of orchestrating a "dog and pony show," and time proved Voorhies correct in that assessment.[3] In July 2017, 340 workers at Carrier's Indianapolis plant lost their jobs, and 215 more were laid off in January 2018. The company meanwhile shuttered its furnace-parts factory in Huntington, Indiana, eliminating another 700 jobs.

As president, Trump touted virtually all of his actions as efforts to preserve and create jobs. On January 23, 2017—his first day in the Oval Office—he withdrew the United States from the Trans-Pacific Partnership (TPP), a massive free-trade agreement brokered by the Obama administration and widely regarded as a job killer. He then met with corporate executives, promising to slash government regulation of their industries, cut taxes, facilitate the opening of new factories, and impose high tariffs on imports produced by U.S. companies that sent production offshore. Next came a sit-down with leaders of building trades unions, to bask in their thanks for his withdrawal from the TPP and confirm their support for energy projects opposed by progressives. The next day, Trump issued executive orders that cleared the way for the Keystone XL and Dakota Access oil pipelines, both of which had been delayed by the Obama administration.

The new jobs that Trump promised did not always materialize. He often spoke of big plans to create jobs by rebuilding the country's crumbling infrastructure, but his first year in office brought no action on that front—or even a concrete proposal. In April 2017, he issued an executive order titled "Buy American and Hire American" that was advertised as a guarantee that federal agencies and federally funded projects would buy only American-made goods and that corporations would no longer use guest workers to undercut wages in fields requiring high levels of education and expertise. In actuality, the order did nothing more than mandate studies of the status quo and call for suggestions for change. As of the end of 2017, construction of the Keystone XL pipeline had not resumed; state courts were still considering the project, whose future grew all the more uncertain that November when another section of the Keystone pipeline leaked over 200,000 gallons of oil into agricultural land in South Dakota. Time and again, the president declared a commitment to building up the U.S.

steel industry by imposing quotas or high tariffs on imported steel, but he took neither step in 2017, and instead of shrinking, the volume of steel imports grew 19 percent larger than in the preceding year. In September 2017, Arcelor-Mittal announced that it would soon eliminate three-quarters of the jobs at its Conshohocken steel mill outside Philadelphia. The workers affected by this decision were hardly alone. Over the course of 2017, the U.S. Labor Department's Office of Trade Adjustment Assistance—the agency in charge of services for workers displaced by free trade agreements—received claim after claim, from workers losing their jobs at small companies like Henry Technologies, which manufactured refrigeration components in Marion, Illinois, to those being laid off by giants such as United Technologies, Xerox, and Boeing.

Finally, in March 2018, the president imposed a 25 percent tariff on foreign steel and a 10 percent tariff on foreign aluminum, in both cases temporarily exempting imports from Canada, Mexico, and a few other countries. The United Steelworkers loudly commended the move, as did AFL-CIO headquarters, but unions based in industries that consume steel and aluminum quietly worried that higher production costs could trigger layoffs. The European Union, China, and other U.S. trading partners meanwhile threatened to impose retaliatory tariffs on American exports, raising the specter of even more layoffs. Workers Uniting—the global steel union that included the United Steelworkers—did not immediately issue a statement, but there was evidence that the tariffs would set back the advance of global union federations. In São Paulo, Brazil, for example, steelworkers gathered outside the U.S. consulate to protest the same tariffs that the United Steelworkers applauded. In short, the tariffs' net effect on workers and their movements was impossible to predict.

The Republicans' signal achievement during the Trump administration's first year was the Tax Cuts and Jobs Act, which the president signed into law on December 22, 2017. Written for the most part by lobbyists for corporations and the super-rich, the act won the approval of both the House and Senate without receiving a single vote from Democrats. It permanently lowered corporate tax rates from 35 percent to 21 percent, and temporarily lowered personal rates with a formula that gave the biggest breaks to those with the biggest incomes. Republican press releases insisted that windfalls for corporations and the very rich would benefit the rest of the country by generating an abundance of new jobs. But that same recipe for economic growth failed when the Reagan administration tried it in the early 1980s, when the George W. Bush administration tried it in the early 2000s, and when Republican lawmakers in Kansas tried it a decade later; and there was no reason to imagine that it would now live up to the hype. Indeed, more than one of the lawmakers who voted for the Tax Cuts and Jobs Act admitted that the jobs they had utmost in mind were their own; wealthy donors had threatened to stop funding Republican candidates unless corporate taxes were drastically reduced. As one congressman explained, "My donors are basically saying get it done or don't ever call me again."[4]

The U.S. economy added jobs every month during President Trump's first year in office, just as it had added jobs every month since late 2010. As in the past, wage growth was sluggish, except at moments, such as in January 2018, when new minimum-wage ordinances won by the Fight for $15 movement kicked in. As had been the case since the mid-1970s, low-paying jobs multiplied more quickly than others and union density continued to fall. The situation called to mind something Jesse Jackson used to say on the campaign trail in 1988: *"Full employment isn't enough! In slavery, everyone had a job!"*[5]

However sincere or cynical its commitment to job creation, the new administration displayed no interest in working conditions or simple justice on the job. When building trades leaders met with the president in January 2017, he refused to commit himself to preservation of the Davis-Bacon Act, which required federally funded construction projects to pay union-level wages, and just days later Republican senator Jeff Flake of Arizona introduced a bill to overturn the act. The White House press secretary meanwhile told reporters that the president favored "right-to-work" laws, and Republicans in Congress soon introduced bills to amend the National Labor Relations Act and the Railway Labor Act to outlaw the union shop nationwide and override any state or local legislation to the contrary. It quickly became clear, moreover, that the Trump administration would do as little as possible to enforce federal protections of workers. The president's choice to head the Occupational Safety and Health Administration was Scott Mugno, a FedEx executive active in the U.S. Chamber of Commerce's lobbying against government oversight of workplaces. He immediately declared a moratorium on new regulations, including proposed rules about exposure to silica, noise, and combustible dust during construction. Once Trump's appointees made Republicans the majority on the National Labor Relations Board (NLRB), it overturned or reversed a slew of worker-friendly decisions, from the Obama-era ruling that had made it easier for temp workers to unionize to the requirement that settlements of unfair labor practices fully compensate aggrieved workers for their losses.

Most damaging to workers over the long run, Trump nominated and the Senate confirmed the arch-conservative judge Neil Gorsuch to serve on the U.S. Supreme Court. One of the first cases he heard there was *National Labor Relations Board v. Murphy Oil*, which concerned among other things workers' right to engage in collective action to improve labor conditions when they are not represented by a union. Trump's Justice Department weighed in with a brief insisting that this right hinged on the presence of a certified union, taking a position that if accepted by the court would severely limit what worker centers could accomplish. Another labor case on the docket was *Janus v. American Federation of State, County and Municipal Employees*, in which a plaintiff recruited by the anti-union Center for Individual Rights argued that public employees who do not belong to a union that negotiates on their behalf should not have to pay a fee to cover the costs of negotiations. As the winter of 2017–18 drew to a close, the court had not yet issued a decision in *Murphy* or *Janus*, but labor activists expected that neither case would go their way, and there was certainly no question as to how Gorsuch would weigh in. As a management-side labor law firm assured its clients, his opinions were highly unlikely to "contain any unpleasant surprises for employers."[6]

With the exception of Fox News—a right-wing outlet that praised virtually everything the president did—mainstream news media ceaselessly attacked Trump, whose administration supplied them with plenty of ammunition. He pulled the United States out of the Paris Climate Accord, a global agreement to reduce emission of greenhouse gases. He placed the Environmental Protection Agency (EPA) in the hands of Scott Pruitt, who had repeatedly sued the EPA as Oklahoma's attorney general and now gutted its programs related to the Safe Drinking Water Act of 1972. The billion-aire Betsy DeVos became secretary of education, although her confirmation hearing revealed that the only thing she knew for sure about public education was that she supported its privatization. Tom Price, the new secretary of health and human ser-vices, lasted less than eight months, leaving in disgrace after the press caught him spending more than $1 million in public funds to finance personal travel on charter jets and military planes. Anthony Scaramucci, a financier who served for just ten days as White House director of communications, telephoned a reporter to share astonish-ingly vulgar assessments of other members of the president's senior staff. Almost every day brought a new scandal; and an ongoing story about Russian interference in the presidential election steadily gained momentum after mid-February 2017, when Michael Flynn, Trump's national security adviser, resigned in response to revelations that he had lied about communications with Russia's ambassador to the United States.

While mainstream media covered all of this ad nauseam, they routinely ignored the administration's impact on workers and their organizations. When these topics did attract attention, it was typically in the context of a good-news story that did not probe beneath the surface. The president's cozy relationship with building-trades leaders—his assurance that they would "always find an open door with Donald Trump"—got wide coverage; not so the unanswered questions about the future of Davis-Bacon.[7] Nor did reporters look closely at what came of Trump's pledge that he would compel federal agencies to buy American. His vows to restore domestic manufacturing and coal production made headlines, but not the relaxation of safety standards in factories and mines. What workers experienced could not simply be erased, however. Donald Trump had garnered more votes from union members than any Republican presiden-tial candidate since Ronald Reagan in 1984, and at the end of his first year in office, much of that support remained intact, residing not only in the building trades but also in some industrial unions. Like their counterparts in the trades, leaders of the United Mine Workers and United Auto Workers avoided criticizing the notoriously thin-skinned president in hopes that he would revive their industries. But the clock was ticking. The administration had made promises it could not or at least would not keep, and it had queued up anti-union initiatives that no part of the labor movement would accept without a fight.

Reviewing the Trump administration's first year, some pundits joked that its main achievement had been to galvanize the opposition. There was much truth to that assertion. January 21, 2017, the day after the president's inauguration, saw Women's Marches in hundreds of U.S. cities and towns and 130 more overseas (including two in Antarctica!). In the United States at least 3.2 million turned out in support of wom-en's rights, immigrants' rights, Black Lives Matter, environmental protection, work-ers' right to organize, LGBTQ equality, tolerance for religious diversity, and other progressive causes opposed by Donald Trump. A week later, thousands of protestors amassed at more than fifteen international airports across the United States in an effort to stop implementation of a presidential order that barred people from seven Muslim-majority countries from entering the United States. On February 16 came A Day Without Immigrants, with tens of thousands of immigrants boycotting work, school, and stores to protest the Trump administration's plans to build a wall along the

U.S.-Mexican border and deport millions of undocumented immigrants. On April 29, People's Climate Marches took place in ten states and the District of Columbia, where 200,000 rallied on the Washington Mall in opposition to Trump's environmental policies. That summer and fall, when Republicans lawmakers set out to repeal the Affordable Care Act, they encountered hundreds of angry protests at town-hall meetings in their home states and districts, at their state and district offices, and on Capitol Hill. Three times repeal came up for a vote in the Senate, and every time it failed. On January 20, 2018, the first anniversary of Trump's inauguration, Women's Marches even bigger than the first round took place across the United States and in several cities overseas.

Labor activists took part in all of these actions, and some unions played central roles. Core sponsors of the Women's March movement included the American Federation of Teachers (AFT) and 1199SEIU: United Healthcare Workers East. In New York City, the Taxi Workers Alliance protested Trump's ban on Muslims' entry into the country by staging a strike at Kennedy International Airport. SEIU, UNITE HERE, and various worker centers threw their weight behind A Day Without Immigrants. The Climate Marches' national steering committee included the Communications Workers, SEIU, the Amalgamated Transit Union, the American Postal Workers, and the BlueGreen Alliance created by the United Steelworkers and the Sierra Club. The AFT, SEIU, and other unions became mainstays of the movement to defend the Affordable Care Act. The Our Revolution network that grew out of Bernie Sanders's presidential campaign survived beyond the elections of 2016, remaining a gathering place for social justice unionists and their allies, continuing to promote the causes addressed in Sanders's platform, and helping to elect more than forty people to state and local offices in 2017.

In August of that year, multiple unions condemned President Trump's insistence that some "very fine people" had been among the neo-Nazis, neo-Confederates, and other white supremacists who converged on Charlottesville, Virginia, for a Unite the Right rally, chanted Nazi slogans as they staged a torchlight parade, and the next day clashed with counterdemonstrators, one of whom was killed when a Nazi sympathizer from Ohio drove his car into a crowd.[8] In the wake of these events, Richard Trumka announced the AFL-CIO's departure from the president's advisory council on domestic manufacturing, letting loose about Trump's economic policies as well as his defense of racists:

> We cannot sit on a council for a president who tolerates bigotry and domestic terrorism. . . . It's clear that President Trump's manufacturing council was never an effective means for delivering real policy that lifts working families and his remarks today were the last straw. We joined this council with the intent to be a voice for working people and real hope that it would result in positive economic policy, but it has become yet another broken promise on the president's record. From hollow councils to bad policy and embracing bigotry, the actions of this administration have consistently failed working people.[9]

The Alliance for American Manufacturing, in which the United Steelworkers partnered with domestic manufacturers, left the president's council too, as did several corporate CEOs. As the defections mounted, Trump saved face by disbanding the group.

These developments had no discernable effect on the administration's relationship to the building trades, whose leaders did not make public statements on Charlottesville. The United Mine Workers ignored it too. The United Auto Workers, the Teamsters, and the International Association of Machinists played things down the middle in statements that condemned bigotry but did not mention the president. By December, however, the Machinists were calling out Trump's failure "despite all the tough bravado" to stop the outflow of union jobs with good wages and benefits.[10]

Back to the Future

If the Trump administration tested unions' principles and nerve, the labor movement faced more significant challenges too. Most of the issues that confronted working people had been there before Donald Trump entered the White House and would persist after he made his exit. Odds are, they persist as you read these words.

Capitalism has always been characterized by periodic crises, but today it is hard to escape the conclusion that it is reaching the end of its rope. In the United States and around the globe, debt plagues the vast majority of people, and the concentration of wealth at the top has reached mind-boggling proportions. According to yearly tallies by the anti-poverty organization Oxfam, in 2010 there were 388 individuals whose combined wealth equaled that of the poorest half of humanity; by January 2017, that number had dwindled to eight. What we have in effect is a new feudalism. The super-rich have already begun to dig moats around their castles, hiding money in secret offshore bank accounts, investing in cryptocurrency, purchasing "apocalypse insurance," buying real estate in out-of-the-way places and building compounds equipped with generators, solar panels, and weaponry.[11] The Armageddon they fear may never arrive, but we are nonetheless caught up in an economy made listless by the maldistribution of wealth.

Eco-disasters offer another testament to capitalism's growing fragility. When corporate balance sheets are the measure by which a system gauges its own health, long-term thinking becomes virtually impossible, and nature does not forgive shortsightedness. Climate change will raise sea levels, generate wildfires and hurricanes, dry up fresh water, and strain food supplies whether or not we care to notice that there is a pattern to these things. And in the face of eco-disasters—along with the political catastrophes they help to generate—many millions will lose their homes. By the 2010s, more than 200 million of the world's people were living outside their countries of origin, and this number will surely rise in years to come.

It turns out, moreover, that capitalism is not an adequate generator of jobs. On the one hand, it renders most people dependent on wages. On the other hand, it constantly seeks to reduce labor costs, most recently through computer-assisted automation, which has killed more jobs worldwide than any free trade agreement.

In addition, Americans face issues peculiar to, or especially pronounced in, the United States. Slavery combined with the country's colonial origins to bake racism into our national culture and make it exceptionally difficult to build solidarity across color lines. Our country consumes massive amounts of pornography, and yet we are reluctant to talk frankly about sex—as if things we do not discuss will simply go away. That reticence along with deference to power encourages men to feel entitled to women's bodies and fosters violence against LGBTQ people, sex workers, and others who are perceived to violate norms of sexual propriety. We lead the world in the murder rate per capita and the rate of incarceration, mass shootings take place with sickening regularity, and police kill almost 1,000 civilians a year. Our health care system is a mess. Although poll after poll shows strong majority support for expanding Medicare to cover one and all, what we have is a for-profit system that does not serve most people well. The pharmaceutical industry's promotion of pain medication set off an epidemic of addiction to opioids that has laid waste to families and whole communities. Our political system is a cesspool of corruption. The Trump administration may have carried self-dealing to new heights, but neoliberalism had already encouraged kleptocracy—rule by thieves—by insisting that, when an opportunity for private profit is identified, it must to be exploited. The claim that the free market provides the best approach to any worthwhile project fails the reality test, yet most politicians treat it as gospel. While hunger and homelessness remain a part of the American landscape, our government finds the money to station troops on every continent and maintain a gigantic arsenal of nuclear and conventional weapons that can surely not do the world any good. Certainly, that money could be better spent on other things.

Generations have passed since the nation made a significant investment in infrastructure. In 2016, the American Society of Civil Engineers estimated that it would take about $1 trillion simply to repair and upgrade the surface-transportation system; to do the same for water systems, the electrical power grid, airports, and seaports would cost at least $225 billion more. None of the infrastructure plans floated by Republicans or Democrats comes close to meeting these needs. The government's programs for rescue and recovery in the wake of natural disasters need upgrading too. Never was that more evident than when Puerto Rico struggled to cope with the effects of Hurricane Maria, a Category 5 storm that raged across the island on September 20, 2017. Three months later, much of the island still lacked electricity, the government did not know how many deaths had been caused by the storm, tens of thousands of Puerto Ricans had fled to the U.S. mainland, and the Federal Emergency Management Agency was overwhelmed.

As history demonstrates, the Republican and Democratic parties do not have solutions to these problems. Neither do the authors of this book. But history tells us that the labor movement offers the best vehicle for progress.

Despite many flaws—and sometimes utter failure to look out for the common good—labor unions remain the strongest civic institutions dedicated to advancing the interests of workers and their families; and when working people advance, so does the rest of society. Are American unions up to the task? In many respects, yes. That much is evident in the growth of social justice unionism; the commitments to solidarity that hold unions together day to day and prompt them to support each other's struggles; the pride and readiness to take risks that sustain workers through organizing drives and strikes; and the generosity that inspires union members to volunteer for service in their communities and in distant disaster zones, as when nurses, electricians, carpenters, and others from the U.S. mainland poured into Puerto Rico in the wake of Hurricane Maria. And to the degree that unions fall short of their potential or need to change and keep up with the times, they merit renovation and renewal because, whatever their imperfections, they are the best we have.

The labor movement may not require the union density of the 1950s to make an impact. In France, three different labor federations represent about 11 percent of workers—about the same percentage as unions in the United States—but the right to strike is in the French constitution, and unions can and do use strategic strikes to force employers and the government to negotiate labor and social issues. And even with their diminished numbers, unionists in the United States can be a real force. Richard Trumka has observed, "We punch way beyond our weight. But think about this, even if we only punched our weight, that's 13 percent, what other group in the United States . . . has 13 percent of the population?" AFL-CIO staffer Ana Avendaño adds, "If the metric is density, then things look grim, but if you look at the way that the Federation has changed since 1995, in terms of the role it plays in civil society, it's made huge advances."[12]

The history of American labor is one of constant struggle—against enslavement, impoverishment, and repression; for democratic rights, economic security, and dignity. The struggle has accomplished much. From the hours and conditions of labor to the regulation of occupational safety and health, to social welfare like minimum living standards for old and young or equal opportunity, even to the democratic franchise itself, many aspects of everyday life show the results of working people's organizing around common interests. Despite progress, the struggles never seem to end. Working people have returned again and again to the same issues of economic security and political democracy, though under different conditions.

While conditions have changed, U.S. society's basic structure has remained constant. Whether called "commerce" or "free enterprise," capitalism—the economic system based on profit and private property—has dominated American life from the colonial era to the present day. The quest for private profit is by nature exclusive, expansive, and unstable, reducing all value to profit, seeking always the highest rate of return, ever prone to speculation, overproduction, disinvestment, and crisis. For people who must work for a living, the struggle to defend and advance themselves, their families, and their communities either leads to organizing for some level of democracy or stays confined to individual efforts, heroic and admirable but limited and precarious.

The struggle for democracy depends on solidarity. America has always been multicultural, from indigenous peoples to wave after wave of newcomers, both enchained and free. Each native or newly arrived group has developed its own relationship to the common culture, and different groups have fared better or worse at one time or another. But their welfare has depended on their relationship to the economy. For most people, whether they work for a boss or for themselves, this relationship has been characterized by dependency, subordination, and insecurity. Though the remedy for these circumstances has always been co-operation and unity in action, securing solidarity has always been difficult.

When working people's solidarity has been limited in scope and vision, the privileged classes have set the rules. When restricted by democratic controls, elites have changed the rules to restore "balance" to their advantage. Working people and their movements have suffered historic defeats, from the expansion of slavery to the impoverishment of the Gilded Age to the suppression of modern movements for social justice to the devastation of deindustrialization. The stakes are higher now. Wealth and privilege are more powerful than ever. Out of the one hundred largest economies in the world, only thirty-one are sovereign nations—the rest are transnational corporations, and the ten largest corporations have more wealth than most countries in the world combined.

If no victory has ever been final, neither has any defeat. The hope for a better life and the impulse to resist injustice always revive. Workers' cardinal role in this historic drama comes from the fact that work is the engine of the system. Labor really does create all wealth. Many kinds of people can organize to maintain their rights and advance their interests; only working people can also organize to abolish the system altogether. When the final conflict comes—as come it will—working people will have to be ready; the world will hang in the balance.

In an interview in the 1970s, veteran organizer Stella Nowicki summed up the still-relevant lessons of her experience with the young CIO: "There's some tremendous potential in people—in labor people, in working people, and union people—and . . . there's a tremendous militancy that's sometimes below the surface and it'll rise and come up. I don't think the American working people are going to let down this country."[13] Amen, sister. Amen.

List of Abbreviations

1199	Hospital and Health Care Workers Union 1199
AAFLI	Asian American Free Labor Institute
AAPL	Alliance of Asian Pacific Labor
ACA	Affordable Care Act
ACORN	Association of Community Organizations for Reform Now
ACFTU	All-China Federation of Trade Unions
ACTWU	Amalgamated Clothing and Textile Workers Union
AFL	American Federation of Labor
AFL-CIO	American Federation of Labor and Congress of Industrial Organizations
AFSCME	American Federation of State, County and Municipal Employees
AFT	American Federation of Teachers
AIFLD	American Institute for Free Labor Development
AIM	American Indian Movement
ALEC	American Legislative Exchange Council
ANC	African National Congress
AOH	Ancient Order of Hibernians
ARU	American Railway Union
AWO	Agricultural Workers Organization
AWOC	Agricultural Workers Organizing Committee
B&O	Baltimore and Ohio Railroad
BAGL	Bay Area Gay Liberation
BIA	Bureau of Indian Affairs

CAW   Canadian Auto Workers

CBTU   Coalition of Black Trade Unionists

CEO   chief executive officer

CFI   Colorado Fuel & Iron

CFUN   Committee for a Unified Newark

CIA   Central Intelligence Agency

CIO   Committee for Industrial Organization; later, Congress of Industrial Organizations

CIO-PAC CIO Political Action Committee

CLC   Canadian Labour Congress

CLUW   Coalition of Labor Union Women

CNA   California Nurses Association

COF   Congreso Obrero de Filipinas

COINTELPRO Counterintelligence Program of the Federal Bureau of Investigation

COLA   cost of living adjustment

COPE   Committee on Political Education

CORE   Congress on Racial Equality

COSH   Committee on (or Coalition for) Occupational Safety and Health

CP   Communist Party

CROC   Confederación Revolucionario de Obreros y Campesinos

CTM   Confederación de Trabajadores Mexicanos

CTU   Chicago Teachers Union

CTV   Confederación de Trabajadores de Venezuela

CTW   Change to Win

CUA   Chinese Unemployed Alliance

CWA   Communications Workers of America

DAN   Direct Action Network

DT   Deutsche Telekom

EEOC   Equal Employment Opportunity Commission

EFCA   Employee Free Choice Act

ELN	Emergency Labor Network
ENA	Experimental Negotiations Agreement
EPA	Environmental Protection Agency
ERP	employee representation plan
FAT	Frente Auténtico del Trabajo
FBI	Federal Bureau of Investigation
FEPC	Fair Employment Practice Committee
FLOC	Farm Labor Organizing Committee
FLT	Federación Libre de Trabajadores
FLU	federal labor union
FOTLU	Federation of Organized Trades and Labor Unions
FLSA	Fair Labor Standards Act
FTA	Food, Tobacco, Agricultural, and Allied Workers of America
FTAA	Free Trade Area of the Americas
FTUI	Free Trade Union Institute
FWIU	Food Workers Industrial Union
G4S	Group 4 Securicor (security services corporation)
GATT	General Agreement on Tariffs and Trade
GE	General Electric Corporation
GFA	global framework agreement
GM	General Motors Corporation
GUF	global union federation
HERE	Hotel Employees and Restaurant Employees
IAM	International Association of Machinists
IBEW	International Brotherhood of Electrical Workers
ICC	Interstate Commerce Commission
ICE	Immigration and Customs Enforcement
ICFTU	International Confederation of Free Trade Unions
IFTU	International Federation of Trade Unions
ILA	International Longshoremen's Association

ILGWU	International Ladies' Garment Workers Union
ILO	International Labor Organization
ILWU	International Longshore and Warehouse Union
IMF	International Monetary Fund
IUE	International Union of Electrical, Radio, and Machine Workers
IUPA	International Union of Police Associations
IWW	Industrial Workers of the World
JMLA	Japanese-Mexican Labor Association
JfJ	Justice for Janitors
K of L	Knights of Labor
LBGTQ	lesbian, gay, bisexual, transgender, and queer
LCFO	Lowndes County Freedom Organization
LCLAA	Labor Council for Latin American Advancement
LFLRA	Lowell Female Labor Reform Association
MFDP	Mississippi Freedom Democratic Party
MFLU	Mississippi Freedom Labor Union
Mine Mill	Mine, Mill and Smelter Workers' Union
MIRA	Mississippi Immigrants Rights Alliance
MOU	Movimiento Obreros Unidos
NAACP	National Association for the Advancement of Colored People
NAALC	North American Agreement on Labor Cooperation
NAFTA	North American Free Trade Agreement
NAM	National Association of Manufacturers
NCF	National Civic Federation
NDLON	National Day Laborer Organizing Network
NFWA	National Farm Workers Association
NIRA	National Industrial Recovery Act
NLC	National Labor Committee (originally National Labor Committee in Support of Democracy and Human Rights in El Salvador)
NLRA	National Labor Relations Act (Wagner Act)

NLRB	National Labor Relations Board
NLU	National Labor Union
NNU	National Nurses United
NRA	National Recovery Administration
NTU	National Trades Union
NTU	National Typographical Union
NTWA	National Taxi Workers Alliance
NUP	New Unity Partnership
NWLB	National War Labor Board
NWRO	National Welfare Rights Organization
OAAU	Organization of Afro-American Unity
OCAW	Oil, Chemical and Atomic Workers
OPA	Office of Price Administration
OPM	Office of Production Management
ORIT	Inter-American Regional Organization of Workers (Organización Regional Interamericana de Trabajadores)
OSHA	Occupational Safety and Health Administration
PAFL	Pan-American Federation of Labor
PASSO	Political Association of Spanish-Speaking Organizations
PATCO	Professional Air Traffic Controllers Organization
PIF	Programa de Industrialización Fronteriza
PMA	Pacific Maritime Association
PSOU	Philadelphia Security Officers Union
PSP	Partido Socialista Puertorriqueño
RAC	Ravenswood Aluminum Corporation
RUM	Revolutionary Union Movement
SCLC	Southern Christian Leadership Conference
SEIU	Service Employees International Union
SFWR	Stewardesses for Women's Rights
SMART	SEIU Member Activists for Reform Today

SME	Sindicato Mexicano de Electricistas
SNCC	Student Non-Violent Coordinating Committee
SP	Socialist Party of America
SWOC	Steel Workers' Organizing Committee
SWP	Socialist Workers Party
TANF	Temporary Assistance for Needy Families
TPP	Trans-Pacific Partnership
TSEU	Texas State Employees Union
TUEL	Trade Union Educational League
TUUL	Trade Union Unity League
UAW	United Auto Workers
UCAPAWA	United Cannery, Agricultural, Packing, and Allied Workers of America
WDP	Workers Defense Project/Proyecto Defensa Laboral
UE	United Electrical, Radio and Machine Workers
UFCW	United Food and Commercial Workers
UFW	United Farm Workers
UHW	United Healthcare Workers-West
UMW	United Mine Workers
UNI	Union Network International
UNIA	Universal Negro Improvement Association
UnionWAGE	Union Women's Alliance to Gain Equality
UNITE	Union of Needletrades, Industrial and Textile Employees
UOPWA	United Office and Professional Workers of America
UPS	United Parcel Service
UPW	United Public Workers
URW	United Rubber Workers
USLAW	U.S. Labor Against the War
USWA	United Steelworkers of America
UTW	United Textile Workers

VVAW   Vietnam Veterans Against the War

Wash/Tech   Washington Alliance of Technology Workers

WFM   Western Federation of Miners

WFTU   World Federation of Trade Unions

WMC   War Manpower Commission

WPA   Works Progress Administration

WTO   World Trade Organization

WU   Workers Uniting

YLP   Young Lords Party

Notes and Selected Bibliographies

Preface to the Revised Edition

1. Stuart Silverstein, "Mixed Report Card for AFL-CIO Leader," *Los Angeles Times*, September 24, 1997, D15.

1: Labor in Colonial America: The Bound and the Free

1. "Christopher Columbus Reports to Ferdinand and Isabella: First Voyage, 1492–1493," in Kupperman, *Major Problems*, 5.

2. "Arthur Barlowe Sees America as the Garden of Eden, 1584," in Kupperman, *Major Problems*, 17.

3. "Thomas Harriot Forecasts Indian-Colonist Relationships, 1588," in Kupperman, *Major Problems*, 13.

4. "Christopher Columbus Reports . . . : First Voyage," in Kupperman, *Major Problems*, 6.

5. Fernando Colón, *The Life of the Admiral Christopher Columbus by his Son, Ferdinand*, ed. and trans. Benjamin Keen (1956; repr., New Brunswick, NJ: Rutgers University Press, 1992), 234; Pedro Mártir de Anglería, *Decadas del Nuevo Mundo* (Buenos Aires: Bajel, 1944), 198–201, translated and quoted in Forbes, *Africans and Native Americans*, 16.

6. Spanish Archives of New Mexico, microfilm, reel 8, 1033–34, 1045, translated and quoted in Gutiérrez, *When Jesus Came*, 185.

7. Forbes, *Africans and Native Americans*, 239–64.

8. "Canassatego's Speech, 1742," in Kupperman, *Major Problems*, 493.

9. Elizabeth Sprigs to John Sprigs, September 22, 1756, reprinted in Page Putnam Miller, *Landmarks of American Women's History* (Oxford, UK: Oxford University Press, 2003), 30.

10. Richard Frethorne to his parents, April 2, 1623, quoted in *The Records of the Virginia Company of London*, ed. Susan Myra Kingsbury (Washington: Library of Congress, 1905), 62.

11. Gottlieb Mittelberger, *Journey to Pennsylvania* (Cambridge: Belknap Press of Harvard University Press, 1960), quoted in Van der Zee, *Bound Over*, 255, 254.

12. Equiano, *The Interesting Narrative*, 58.

13. Ibid., 60–61.

14. Ibid., 62.

15. John Saffin, *A Brief and Candid Answer to a Late Printed Sheet, Entitled* The Selling of Joseph (1701; repr., [Boston]: Publications of the Colonial Society of Massachusetts, [1895]), 1:112, quoted in Foster, *Witnessing Slavery*, 31.

16. Moraley, *The Infortunate*, 94.

17. Henry Moore, *The Life of the Rev. John Wesley, M.A.* (1793; repr. Auburn, NY: John E. Beardsley, [1844]), 86.

18. Josiah Quincy, "Journal of Josiah Quincy, Jr., 1773," *Massachusetts Historical Society, Proceedings* 49 (June 1916): 463.

19. Satchell, "Only Remember Us."

20. Rediker, *Between the Devil and the Deep Blue Sea*, 93.

21. "ADVERTISEMENTS," *New-York Weekly Journal,* January 28, 1733, [4].

22. "To the Authors and others who were active in procuring the late Dissent," *South Carolina and American General Gazette*, September 23–30, 1774, [4].

23. Benjamin Franklin, "Poor Richard's Preface, 1758," in Franklin, *Poor Richard's Almanac and Other Writings*, ed. Bob Blaisdell (Mineola, NY: Dover Publications, 2013), 137.

24. *Acts and Laws of the State of Connecticut in America* (Hartford: Hudson and Goodwin, 1796), 293.

25. James Annesley, *Memoirs of an Unfortunate Young Nobleman, Return'd from a Thirteen Years Slavery in America, Where He Had Been Sent by the Wicked Contrivances of His Cruel Uncle* (London: J. Freeman, 1743), 77.

26. "An account of the Negroe Insurrection in South Carolina," in *COLONIAL RECORDS OF THE STATE OF GEORGIA*, vol. 22, pt. 2, *ORIGINAL PAPERS, CORRESPONDENCE: TRUSTEES, GENERAL OGLETHORPE AND OTHERS, 1737–1740*, comp. Allen D. Candler, William J. Northern, and Lucian Lamar Knight (Atlanta: Chas P. Byrd, 1913), 234.

27. Countryman, *The American Revolution*, 87.

28. Richard B. Morris, "The Emergence of American Labor," in Morris, *The History of the American Worker*, 22.

29. *Massachusetts Records* II (November 4, 1646), 180, reprinted in Massachusetts and William Henry Whitmore, *The Colonial Laws of Massachusetts* (Boston: Rockwell and Churchill, city printers, 1889), 13.

30. *Pennsylvania Gazette* (Philadelphia), May 29, 1776, quoted in Nash, "Poverty and Poor Relief," 4.

31. Edmond Wingate, *Maximes of Reason: or, the Reason of the Common Law of England* (London: R. & W.L. 1658), 771.

32. [John Oxendine, advertisement], *South Carolina Gazette*, May 25–June 1, 1765, [2]. In an advertisement printed just beneath this one, the runaway "wife" announced that she and John Oxendine were not legally married, that he was a lazy man, and that she intended henceforth to go by her maiden name, Mary Marshall, and "get my livelihood in an honest way" (idem). As a rule, however, notices placed by abandoned husbands went unanswered by the women in question.

33. "Charles-Town, November 5," *South Carolina Gazette*, October 29–November 5, 1763, [3].

34. Daniel Defoe, *A General History of the Pyrates*, ed. Manuel Schonhorn (1724, 1972; repr. Mineola, NY: Dover Publications, 1999), 587.

Aptheker, Herbert. *American Negro Slave Revolts.* New York: Columbia University Press, 1944.

Axtell, James. *The European and the Indian: Essays in the Ethnohistory of Colonial North America.* Oxford, UK: Oxford University Press, 1981.

Berlin, Ira. *Many Thousands Gone: The First Two Centuries of Slavery in North America.* Cambridge, MA: Harvard University Press, 1998.

Brooks, Thomas R. *Toil and Trouble: A History of American Labor.* New York: Delacorte Press, 1971.

Bushman, Richard L. *The Refinement of America: Persons, Houses, Cities.* New York: Knopf, 1992.

Casas, Bartolomé de Las. *The Devastation of the Indies: A Brief Account.* Baltimore: Johns Hopkins University Press, 1992.

Countryman, Edward. *The American Revolution.* 1985. Rev. ed. New York: Hill and Wang, 2003.

Creighton, Margaret S., and Lisa Norling. *Iron Men, Wooden Women: Gender and Seafaring in the Atlantic World, 1700–1920.* Baltimore: Johns Hopkins University Press, 1996.

Eldridge, Larry D., ed. *Women and Freedom in Early America.* New York: New York University Press, 1997.

Emory University. *Voyages: The Trans-Atlantic Slave Trade Database.* www.slavevoyages.org.

Equiano, Olaudah. *The Interesting Narrative and Other Writings.* Edited by Vincent Carretta. Rev. ed. New York: Penguin Books, 2003.

Foner, Philip S. *History of the Labor Movement in the United States.* Vol. 1, *From Colonial Times to the Founding of the American Federation of Labor.* New York: International Publishers, 1947.

Forbes, Jack D. *Africans and Native Americans: The Language of Race and the Evolution of Red-Black Peoples.* Urbana: University of Illinois Press, 1993.

Foster, Frances Smith. *Witnessing Slavery: The Development of Ante-Bellum Slave Narratives.* Westport, CT: Greenwood Press, 1979.

Gutiérrez, Ramón A. *When Jesus Came, the Corn Mothers Went Away: Marriage, Sexuality, and Power in New Mexico, 1500–1846.* Stanford, CA: Stanford University Press, 1991.

Kessler-Harris, Alice. *Out to Work: A History of Wage-Earning Women in the United States.* New York: Oxford University Press, 1982.

Kupperman, Karen Ordahl, ed. *Major Problems in American Colonial History: Documents and Essays.* Lexington, MA: D.C. Heath and Company, 1993.

Linebaugh, Peter, and Marcus Rediker. *The Many-Headed Hydra: Sailors, Slaves, Commoners, and the Hidden History of the Revolutionary Atlantic.* Boston: Beacon Press, 2000.

Littlefield, Alice, and Martha C. Knack. *Native Americans and Wage Labor: Ethnohistorical Perspectives.* Norman: University of Oklahoma Press, 1996.

Loewen, James W. *Lies My Teacher Told Me: Everything Your American History Textbook Got Wrong.* New York: The New Press, 1995.

Moraley, William. *The Infortunate: The Voyage and Adventures of William Moraley, an Indentured Servant.* Edited and annotated by Susan E. Klepp and Billy G. Smith. University Park: Pennsylvania State University Press, 1992.

Morgan, Edmund S. *American Slavery, American Freedom: The Ordeal of Colonial Virginia.* New York: W.W. Norton & Co., 1975.

Morris, Richard B., ed. *A History of the American Worker.* Princeton, NJ: Princeton University Press, 1983.

Nash, Gary B. "Poverty and Poor Relief in Pre-Revolutionary Philadelphia." *William and Mary Quarterly* 33, no. 1 (January 1976): 3–30.

———. *Red, White, and Black: The Peoples of Early America.* Englewood Cliffs, NJ: Prentice-Hall, 1974.

Núñez Cabeza de Vaca, Alvar, and Enrique Pupo-Walker. *Castaways: The Narrative of Alvar Núñez Cabeza De Vaca.* Berkeley: University of California Press, 1993.

Rediker, Marcus. *Between the Devil and the Deep Blue Sea: Merchant Seamen, Pirates, and the Anglo-American Maritime World, 1700–1750.* Cambridge, UK: Cambridge University Press, 1987.

Rorabaugh, W.J. *The Craft Apprentice: From Franklin to the Machine Age in America*. New York: Oxford University Press, 1986.

Satchell, Michael. "Only Remember Us." *U.S. News & World Report*, July 28, 1997, 51.

Spruill, Julia Cherry. *Women's Life and Work in the Southern Colonies*. Chapel Hill: University of North Carolina Press, 1938.

Stannard, David E. *American Holocaust: Columbus and the Conquest of the New World*. New York: Oxford University Press, 1992.

Thomas, Hugh. *Conquest: Montezuma, Cortés, and the Fall of Old Mexico*. New York: Simon & Schuster, 1993.

Van der Zee, John. *Bound Over: Indentured Servitude and American Conscience*. New York: Simon & Schuster, 1985.

Van Sertima, Ivan. *They Came Before Columbus*. New York: Random House, 1976.

Weber, David J. *The Spanish Frontier in North America*. New Haven, CT: Yale University Press, 1992.

———, ed. *What Caused the Pueblo Revolt of 1680?* Boston: Bedford/St. Martin's, 1999.

Wood, Peter H. *Black Majority: Negroes in Colonial South Carolina from 1670 Through the Stono Rebellion*. New York: Knopf, 1974.

2: The American Revolution

1. The Declaration of Independence's entire transcript can be found at www.archives.gov/founding-docs/declaration-transcript.

2. Richard B. Morris, "The Emergence of American Labor," in Morris, ed., *The History of the American Worker*, 27.

3. "NEW-YORK, May 12," *New-York Gazette*, May 12, 1766, [3].

4. "It IS BETTER TO WEAR A Homespun COAT THAN TO LOSE OUR LIBERTY," *New-York Gazette*, January 6, 1766, [2].

5. Commissioners of the Customs to Lords of the Treasury, February 12, 1768, reproduced in "The Seizure of John Hancock's Sloop 'Liberty,'" *Proceedings of the Massachusetts Historical Society* 55 (1921–22): 265.

6. Kayashuta, in George Morgan Letterbook, July 24, 1776, Pennsylvania Historical and Museum Collection, Carnegie Library, Pittsburgh, PA, 38, quoted in Calloway, *The American Revolution in Indian Country*, 29–30.

7. Thomas Jefferson, *Autobiography of Thomas Jefferson* (1821; repr., Mineola, NY: Dover Publications, 2005), 31.

8. Thomas Paine, *Rights of Man, Part the Second: Combining Principles and Practice* (1792), in Paine, *Common Sense, the Rights of Man, and Other Essential Writings*, 225.

9. "To the Honorable Coun[ci]l & House of [Representa]tives for the State of Massachusetts Bay in General Court assembled, January 13, 1777, reprinted in Aptheker, *A Documentary History*, vol. 1, 10.

10. Richard B. Morris, "The Emergence of American Labor," in Morris, *A History of the American Worker*, 37.

11. John Laurens to George Washington, May 19, 1782, quoted in Quarles, *The Negro in the American Revolution*, 67.

12. Persifor Frazer to Mary Worrall Frazer, July 25, 1776, reproduced in Persifor Frazer, *General Persifor Frazer: a Memoir Compiled Principally from His Own Papers by His Great-Grandson* (Philadelphia: n.p., 1907), 99.

13. [Public notice], *Independent Gazette*, January 24, 1784, reproduced in Charles M. Haar, "White Indentured Servants in Colonial New York," *Americana* 36, no. 3 (July 1940): 390.

14. Amos Singletary at the Massachusetts Ratifying Convention, Boston, January 25, 1788, quoted in William C. Rives, *History of the Life and Times of James Madison* (Boston: Little Brown and Company, 1870), 523.

15. Preamble to the Joint Resolution of Congress Proposing 12 Amendments to the US Constitution, 1st Cong., 1st sess. (September 25, 1789), 1 Stat. 97 (1845).

16. Sedition Act, ch. 74, 1 Stat. 596 (1798).

17. *American Citizen*, May 23, 1810, quoted in Howard B. Rock, *Artisans of the New Republic: The Tradesmen of New York City in the Age of Jefferson* (New York: New York University Press, 1984), 281.

18. Harriet H. Robinson, *Loom and Spindle: Or, Life Among the Early Mill Girls* (New York: Thomas Y. Crowell & Co, 1898), 70.

19. Loriman S. Brigham, "An Independent Voice: A Mill Girl from Vermont Speaks her Mind," *Vermont History* 41 (Summer 1973): 144, quoted in Dublin, *Women at Work*, 37.

20. *Boston Transcript*, March 6, 1834, quoted in Andrews and Bliss, *History of Women in Trade Unions*, 25.

21. Testimony of Prosser's Ben at trial of Prosser's Gabriel, October 6, 1800, Executive Papers, Negro Insurrection, Virginia State Library, Richmond, VA, quoted in Egerton, *Gabriel's Rebellion*, 51.

22. Quoted in Robert Sutcliff, *Travels in Some Parts of North America in the Years 1804, 1805, and 1806* (Philadelphia: B. and T. Kite, 1812), 50.

23. *An Account of the Late Intended Insurrection among a Portion of the Blacks of This City: Published by the Authority of the Corporation of Charleston*, 3rd ed. (Charleston: A.E. Miller, 1822), 38.

24. William Watkins Jr., "ADDRESS," *Genius of Universal Emancipation*, August 1825, 168.

25. David Walker, *Walker's Appeal, in Four Articles: Together with a Preamble, to the Coloured Citizens of the World, but in Particular, and Very Expressly, to Those of the United States of America* (1829; repr., Chapel Hill: University of North Carolina Press, 2011), 75.

26. Thomas E. Skidmore, *The Rights of Man to Property!: Being a Proposition to Make it Equal among the Adults of the Present Generation and to Provide for its Equal Transmission to Every Individual of Each Succeeding Generation, on Arriving at the Age of Maturity* (1828; repr., New York: Burt Franklin, 1964), 158.

27. Ibid., 311.

28. Ibid., 146.

Andrews, John B., and William Dwight Porter Bliss. *History of Women in Trade Unions*. 1911. Reprint, New York: Arno Press, 1974.

Aptheker, Herbert. *American Negro Slave Revolts*. New York: Columbia University Press, 1944.

———, ed. *A Documentary History of the Negro People in the United States*. Vol. 1, *From Colonial Times Through the Civil War*. New York: Citadel Press, 1962.

Armstrong, Virginia Irving, comp. *I Have Spoken: American History Through the Voices of the Indians*. Chicago: Sage Books, 1971.

Berlin, Ira. *Many Thousands Gone: The First Two Centuries of Slavery in North America*. Cambridge, MA: Harvard University Press, 1998.

Berlin, Ira, and Ronald Hoffman. *Slavery and Freedom in the Age of the American Revolution.* Urbana: University of Illinois Press, 1986.

Brooks, Thomas R. *Toil and Trouble: A History of American Labor.* New York: Delacorte Press, 1971.

Calloway, Colin G. *The American Revolution in Indian Country: Crisis and Diversity in Native American Communities.* New York: Cambridge University Press, 1995.

Countryman, Edward. *The American Revolution.* 1985. Rev. ed. New York: Hill and Wang, 2003.

De Pauw, Linda Grant. "The American Revolution." In De Pauw, *Battle Cries and Lullabies: Women in War from Prehistory to the Present.* Norman: University of Oklahoma Press, 2000, 115–31.

———. *Four Traditions: Women of New York During the American Revolution.* Albany: New York State American Revolution Bicentennial Commission, 1974.

———. "Land of the Unfree: Legal Limitations on Liberty in Pre-Revolutionary America." *Maryland Historical Magazine* 68, no. 4 (Winter 1973): 355–68.

Dinnerstein, Leonard, and Kenneth T. Jackson, eds. *American Vistas.* New York: Oxford University Press, 1995.

Dublin, Thomas. *Women at Work: The Transformation of Work and Community in Lowell, Massachusetts, 1826–1860.* New York: Columbia University Press, 1979.

Egerton, Douglas R. *Gabriel's Rebellion: The Virginia Slave Conspiracies of 1800 and 1802.* Chapel Hill: University of North Carolina Press, 1993.

———. *He Shall Go Out Free: The Lives of Denmark Vesey.* Madison, WI: Madison House, 1999.

Foner, Eric. *Tom Paine and Revolutionary America.* New York: Oxford University Press, 1976.

Foner, Philip S. *History of the Labor Movement in the United States.* Vol. 1, *From Colonial Times to the Founding of the American Federation of Labor.* New York: International Publishers, 1947.

———, ed. *We, the Other People: Alternative Declarations of Independence by Labor Groups, Farmers, Woman's Rights Advocates, Socialists, and Blacks, 1829–1975.* Urbana: University of Illinois Press, 1976.

Franki, M., and J. Hillstrom. *America's First Unfinished Revolution: The Untold Story of the True Creators of Independence—the Workers, Yeomanry, Blacks, and Women.* Detroit, MI: News and Letters Committees, 1976.

Frey, Sylvia R. *Water from the Rock: Black Resistance in a Revolutionary Age.* Princeton, NJ: Princeton University Press, 1991.

Gilbert, Amos. *A Sketch of the Life of Thomas Skidmore.* Chicago: C.H. Kerr, 1984.

Gross, Robert A. *The Minutemen and Their World.* New York: Hill and Wang, 1976.

Hoerder, Dirk. *Crowd Action in Revolutionary Massachusetts, 1765–1780.* New York: Academic Press, 1977.

Kerber, Linda K. *Women of the Republic: Intellect and Ideology in Revolutionary America.* Chapel Hill: University of North Carolina Press, 1980.

Kessler-Harris, Alice. *Out to Work: A History of Wage-Earning Women in the United States.* New York: Oxford University Press, 1982.

Ketcham, Ralph, ed. *The Anti-Federalist Papers and the Constitutional Convention Debates.* New York: New American Library, 1986.

Kneib, Martha. *Women Soldiers, Spies, and Patriots of the American Revolution.* New York: Rosen Publishing Group, 2004.

Morris, Richard B., ed. *A History of the American Worker.* Princeton, NJ: Princeton University Press, 1983.

Nash, Gary B. *Race and Revolution.* Lanham, MD: Rowman and Littlefield, 1990.

———. *The Urban Crucible: Social Change, Political Consciousness, and the Origins of the American Revolution.* Cambridge, MA: Harvard University Press, 1979.

Norton, Mary Beth. *Liberty's Daughters: The Revolutionary Experience of American Women, 1750–1800.* Boston: Little, Brown, 1980.

Paine, Thomas. *Common Sense, the Rights of Man, and Other Essential Writings of Thomas Paine; with an Introduction by Sidney Hook.* New York: New American Library, 1969.

Quarles, Benjamin. *Black Abolitionists.* New York: Oxford University Press, 1969.

———. *The Negro in the American Revolution.* Chapel Hill: University of North Carolina Press, 1961.

Rorabaugh, W.J. *The Craft Apprentice: From Franklin to the Machine Age in America.* New York: Oxford University Press, 1986.

Stewart, Maria W. *Maria W. Stewart, America's First Black Woman Political Writer: Essays and Speeches.* Edited by Marilyn Richardson. Bloomington: Indiana University Press, 1987.

Van der Zee, John. *Bound Over: Indentured Servitude and American Conscience.* New York: Simon & Schuster, 1985.

Young, Alfred F. *The American Revolution.* Dekalb: Northern Illinois University Press, 1976.

———, ed. *Beyond the American Revolution: Explorations in the History of American Radicalism.* DeKalb: Northern Illinois University Press, 1993.

———. *The Shoemaker and the Tea Party: Memory and the American Revolution.* Boston: Beacon Press, 1999.

3: Slavery and Freedom in the New Republic

1. Fisk University, Social Science Institute, *Unwritten History of Slavery: Autobiographical Accounts of Negro Ex-Slaves* (Washington: Microcard Editions, 1968), 143.

2. "Hannah Crasson: Age 84 when interviewed by T. Pat Matthews," in Belinda Hurmence, ed., *My Folks Don't Want Me to Talk about Slavery: Twenty-One Oral Histories of Former North Carolina Slaves* (Winston Salem, NC: John F. Blair, 1984), 18.

3. "Mary Reynolds: Louisiana," in Botkin, *Lay My Burden Down*, 121.

4. "Jenny Proctor, Alabama," in Botkin, *Lay My Burden Down*, 91.

5. "Rules in the Management of a Southern Estate," *De Bow's Review*, April 1857, 376.

6. Solomon Northup, *Twelve Years a Slave: Narrative of Solomon Northrup* (1853; repr., New York: Miller, Orton & Mulligan, 1855), 179.

7. Helen Tunnicliff Catterall, ed., *Judicial Cases Concerning American Slavery and the Negro*, vol. 2, *Cases from the Courts of North Carolina, South Carolina, and Tennessee* (1929; repr., New York: Octagon Books, 1968), 168.

8. Douglass, *Narrative*, 58.

9. Henry Stewart interviewed by Samuel Gridley Howe, November 8, 1863, in American Freedmen's Inquiry Commission Records, File No. 10: Canadian Testimony, in U.S. Department of War, Letters Received by the Office of the Adjutant General, Main Series, 1861–1870 (microfilm frame 500, reel 201, M619), RG 94 (National Archives, Washington, DC) (unpublished transcription by Matthew Furrow).

10. Betty Jones, Fluvanna County, interviewer unknown, *The Negro in Virginia* (1940; repr., New York: Arno Press, 1969), 147.

11. Laura S. Haviland, *A Woman's Life-Work: Labors and Experiences of Laura S. Haviland* (1881; repr., Chicago: C.V. Waite and Company, 1887), 301.

12. Eric J. Sundquist, *Empire and Slavery in American Literature, 1820–1865* (Jackson: University Press of Mississippi, 2006), 230.

13. Charles C. Jones, *The Religious Instruction of the Negroes. In the United States* (Savannah: Thomas Purse, 1842), 130.

14. Thomas R. Gray, *The Confessions of Nat Turner, the Leader of the Late Insurrection in Southampton, Va.* (Baltimore: T.R. Gray, 1831), 11.

15. R. Emmet Kennedy, *Mellows: A Chronicle of Unknown Singers* (1925; repr., Westport, CT: Greenwood Press, 1979), 14.

16. [Advertisement], *The Sun* (Baltimore), December 31, 1851, 3.

17. *Mechanics Free Press* (Philadelphia), August 16, 1828, quoted in Whitman, *Labor Parties*, 24.

18. "Journeymen Cordwainers. (LADIES BRANCH)," *Public Ledger*, June 10, 1836, 3.

19. Lemuel Shaw, in *Commonwealth v. Hunt* 45 Mass. 111, quoted in Leonard Levy, *The Law of the Commonwealth and Chief Justice Shaw* (1957; repr., New York: Oxford University Press, 1987), 189.

20. "Temperance Rally," *The Sun* (Baltimore), May 7, 1842, 2.

21. Adin Ballou and William S. Heywood. *Autobiography of Adin Ballou, 1803–1890: Containing an Elaborate Record and Narrative of His Life from Infancy to Old Age, with Appendixes* (Lowell, MA: Vox Populi Press, 1896), 342.

22. "New-York City Industrial Congress," *New-York Daily Tribune*, January 1, 1851, 7.

23. "The Pledge," *Working Man's Advocate*, April 6, 1844, in John R. Commons, ed., *Labor Movement, 1840–1860*, vol. 1, vol. 7 of *A Documentary History of American Industrial Society*, ed. Commons et al. (1910; repr., New York: Russell & Russell, 1958), 312.

24. "The Rights of Women," *Voice of Industry*, May 8, 1846, 2.

25. "New England Workingmen's Association," *Voice of Industry*, June 5, 1845, 2.

26. Julianna, *The Evils of Factory Life, Number I* (Lowell, MA: Lowell Female Reform Association, 1845), Factory Tracts, The Voice of Industry, http://www.industrialrevolution.org/factory-tracts.html.

27. Rheta Child Dorr, "The Eternal Question," *Colliers: The National Weekly*, October 30, 1920, 6.

28. "Declaration of Sentiments and Resolutions, by the Woman's Rights Convention, July 1848," in Foner, ed., *We, the Other People*, 78.

29. *New-York Daily Sentinel*, March 5, 1831, quoted in Stansell, *City of Women*, 133.

30. *Pittsburgh Journal*, reprinted in "Capital Against Labor: Factory Strike at Pittsburgh, " *Young America!*, October 18, 1845, 1.

31. National Trades Union (New York), The Convention of 1935, *Proceedings*, in John R. Commons and Helen L. Sumner, eds., *Labor Movement, 1820–1840*, vol. 2, vol. 6 of *A Documentary History of American Industrial Society*, ed. Commons et al. (1919; repr. New York: Russell & Russell, 1958), 251.

32. *Radical Reformer*, August 1, 1835, reprinted in Andrews and Bliss, *History of Women in Trade Unions*, 48.

33. "Report of the Committee on Female Labor," *National Laborer*, November 12, 1836, in Commons and Sumner, *Labor Movement, 1820–1840*, vol. 2, 281–91; quotations are on 290, 284, 281, 284.

34. "The Ladies' Procession at Lynn: from the *Boston Courier*, March 8," *Detroit Free Press*, March 13, 1860, 4.

35. *Beverly Citizen*, March 30, 1860, quoted in Blewett, *Men, Women and Work*, 120.

36. [Eliza Jane Cate], "Rights and Duties of Mill Girls," Chapter X, "Reduction of wages for Factory Labor," *The New England Offering: A Magazine of Industry*, 2 (July 1849), 156–57.

37. "The Slave Power and the Money Power," *The Liberator* (Boston), January 2, 1852, 4.

38. "The Working Classes," *The Liberator*, January 29, 1831, 3.

39. "Vigilance Committee," *The Liberator*, November 17, 1837, 4.

40. "New York and Brooklyn News," *Frederick Douglass' Paper*, February 2, 1855, 1.

41. "Meeting of the Hotel and Saloon Waiters," *New York Herald*, March 31, 1853, in Foner and Lewis, *The Black Worker to 1869*, 192.

42. "Reformatory: National Reform" [letter from William West], *The Liberator*, August 28, 1846, 4.

43. B. Gratz Brown, *Speech of the Hon. B. Gratz Brown, of St. Louis, on the Subject of Gradual Emancipation in Missouri: Delivered in the House of Representatives, February 12, 1857* (St. Louis: Missouri Democrat Book and Job Office, 1857), 25.

44. Proclamation signed by Juan Nepomuceno Cortina, Rancho del Carmen, County of Cameron, November 23, 1859, quoted and translated in Rosenbaum, *Mexicano Resistance*, 44.

45. William Henry Seward, "Irrepressible Conflict Speech," in *The Civil War and Reconstruction*, ed. Stanley Harrold (Malden, MA: Blackwell Publishing, 2008), 36.

46. [Editorial], *Hartford Daily Courant*, October 28, 1856, 2.

47. Charles Sumner, *The Crime Against Kansas: The Apologies for the Crime, the True Remedy* (1856; repr. New York: Arno, 1969), 9.

48. [Letter to the editors, September 19, 1856], *Semi-Weekly Standard* (Raleigh, NC), e, September 27, 1856, 3.

49. *Address of the Working Men of Pittsburgh*, 3–4.

50. *Dred Scott v. Sandford*, 60 US 393 (1857).

51. "Meeting at New Bedford," *The Liberator*, December 16, 1859, 3.

52. John Brown, Charlestown, Virginia, December 2, 1859, John Brown Papers, Chicago Historical Society, reprinted in Oates, *To Purge This Land*, 351.

Address of Working Men of Pittsburgh to Their Fellow Working Men in Pennsylvania. Pittsburgh: W.S. Haven, 1856.

Andrews, John B., and William Dwight Porter Bliss. *History of Women in Trade Unions*. 1911. Reprint, New York: Arno Press, 1974.

Aptheker, Herbert. *American Negro Slave Revolts*. New York: Columbia University Press, 1944.

———, ed. *A Documentary History of the Negro People in the United States*. Vol. 1, *From Colonial Times Through the Civil War*. New York: Citadel Press, 1962.

Armstrong, Virginia Irving, comp. *I Have Spoken: American History Through the Voices of the Indians*. Chicago: Sage Books, 1971.

Berlin, Ira. *Many Thousands Gone: The First Two Centuries of Slavery in North America*. Cambridge, MA: Harvard University Press, 1998.

———. *Slaves Without Masters: The Free Negro in the Antebellum South*. 1975. Reprint, New York: The New Press, 1992.

Berlin, Ira, Marc Favreau, and Steven F. Miller, eds. *Remembering Slavery: African Americans Talk About Their Personal Experiences of Slavery and Freedom.* New York: The New Press, 1998.

Blewett, Mary H. *Men, Women, and Work: Class, Gender, and Protest in the New England Shoe Industry, 1780–1910.* Urbana: University of Illinois Press, 1988.

Botkin, Benjamin Albert, ed. *Lay My Burden Down: A Folk History of Slavery.* Chicago: University of Chicago Press, 1945.

Dawley, Alan. *Class and Community: The Industrial Revolution in Lynn.* Cambridge, MA: Harvard University Press, 1976.

De León, Arnoldo. *Mexican Americans in Texas: A Brief History.* Arlington Heights, IL: Harlan Davidson, 1993.

Douglass, Frederick. *Narrative of the Life of Frederick Douglass, An American Slave, Written by Himself.* Edited by John W. Blassingame et al. 1845. Reprint, New Haven, CT: Yale University Press, 1999.

———. *My Bondage and My Freedom.* 1855. Reprint, New York: Dover Publications, 1969.

Dublin, Thomas. *Women at Work: The Transformation of Work and Community in Lowell, Massachusetts, 1826–1860.* New York: Columbia University Press, 1979.

Fields, Barbara Jeanne. *Slavery and Freedom on the Middle Ground: Maryland during the Nineteenth Century.* New Haven, CT: Yale University Press, 1985.

Foner, Philip S. *History of the Labor Movement in the United States.* Vol. 1, *From Colonial Times to the Founding of the American Federation of Labor.* New York: International Publishers, 1947.

———, ed. *We, the Other People: Alternative Declarations of Independence by Labor Groups, Farmers, Woman's Rights Advocates, Socialists, and Blacks, 1829–1975.* Urbana: University of Illinois Press, 1976.

———. *Women and the American Labor Movement: From the First Trade Unions to the Present.* New York: Free Press, 1982.

Foner, Philip S., and Ronald L. Lewis. *The Black Worker: A Documentary History from Colonial Times to the Present.* Vol. I, *The Black Worker to 1869.* Philadelphia: Temple University Press, 1978.

Genovese, Eugene D. *The Political Economy of Slavery.* New York: Vintage Books, 1967.

———. *Roll, Jordan, Roll; The World the Slaves Made.* New York: Pantheon Books, 1974.

González, Deena J. *Refusing the Favor: The Spanish-Mexican Women of Santa Fe, 1820–1880.* New York: Oxford University Press, 1999.

Harding, Vincent. *There Is a River: The Black Struggle for Freedom in America.* New York: Harcourt Brace Jovanovich, 1981.

Hurtado, Albert L. *Indian Survival on the California Frontier.* New Haven, CT: Yale University Press, 1988.

Juravich, Tom, William F. Hartford, and James R. Green. *Commonwealth of Toil: Chapters in the History of Massachusetts Workers and Their Unions.* Amherst: University of Massachusetts Press, 1996.

Kessler-Harris, Alice. *Out to Work: A History of Wage-Earning Women in the United States.* New York: Oxford University Press, 1982.

Laurie, Bruce. *Artisans into Workers: Labor in Nineteenth-Century America.* Urbana: University of Illinois Press, 1997.

Mellon, James. *Bullwhip Days: The Slaves Remember.* New York: Weidenfeld & Nicolson, 1988.

Menchaca, Martha. *Recovering History, Constructing Race: The Indian, Black, and White Roots of Mexican Americans.* Austin: University of Texas Press, 2001.

Montgomery, David. *Citizen Worker: The Experience of Workers in the United States with Democracy and the Free Market During the Nineteenth Century.* Cambridge: Cambridge University Press, 1993.

Morris, Richard B., ed. *A History of the American Worker.* Princeton, NJ: Princeton University Press, 1983.

Oates, Stephen B. *To Purge This Land with Blood: A Biography of John Brown.* New York: Harper & Row, 1970.

Quarles, Benjamin. *Black Abolitionists.* New York: Oxford University Press, 1969.

Roediger, David R. *The Wages of Whiteness: Race and the Making of the American Working Class.* London: Verso, 1991.

Rorabaugh, W.J. *The Craft Apprentice: From Franklin to the Machine Age in America.* New York: Oxford University Press, 1986.

Rosenbaum, Robert J. *Mexicano Resistance in the Southwest: "The Sacred Right of Self-Preservation."* Austin: University of Texas Press, 1981.

Saxton, Alexander. *The Rise and Fall of the White Republic: Class Politics and Mass Culture in Nineteenth-Century America.* London: Verso, 1990.

Stansell, Christine. *City of Women: Sex and Class in New York, 1789–1860.* New York: Knopf, 1986.

Wertheimer, Barbara M. *We Were There: The Story of Working Women in America.* New York: Pantheon Books, 1977.

White, Deborah G. *Ar'n't I a Woman?: Female Slaves in the Plantation South.* New York: Norton, 1985.

Whitman, Alden. *Labor Parties, 1827–1834.* New York: International Publishers, 1943.

Wilentz, Sean. *Chants Democratic: New York City & the Rise of the American Working Class, 1788–1850.* New York: Oxford University Press, 1984.

4: Civil War and Reconstruction

1. Abraham Lincoln, "First Inaugural Address—Final Text," March 4, 1861, in *The Collected Works of Abraham Lincoln*, ed. Roy P. Basler, Marion Dolores Pratt, and Lloyd A. Dunlap (New Brunswick, NJ: Rutgers University Press, 1953), vol. 4, 263.

2. Abraham Lincoln, "Emancipation Proclamation," in Basler, Pratt, and Dunlap, *The Collected Works*, vol. 6, 29.

3. "President Lincoln's Letter," *New York Tribune*, August 25, 1862, 4.

4. Lydia Maria Child to John G. Whittier, January 25, 1862, in *Letters of Lydia Maria Child*, comp. Harriet Winslow Sewall (Boston: Houghton, Mifflin and Co., 1883), 161.

5. "Speech of John S. Rock, Esq.," *The Liberator*, February 14, 1862, 3.

6. "Confiscation and Emancipation of Contrabands," *The Liberator*, April 4, 1862, 3.

7. Du Bois, *Black Reconstruction*, 55.

8. *The Boston Commonwealth*, July 10, 1863, reprinted in Darlene Clark Hine and Kathleen Thompson, *A Shining Thread of Hope: The History of Black Women in America* (New York: Broadway Books, 1998), 132.

9. G.P. Touson, "Letter from Folly Island," *The Christian Recorder*, November 12, 1864, 1.

10. "Refuge of Oppression: The Democracy of Pennsylvania," *The Liberator*, August 8, 1862, 1.

11. This was not the only time that officialdom refused to recognize Tubman's service in the war. Her claim to a veteran's pension—first filed in 1865—was denied until 1899, when Congress passed a special bill on her behalf. See Larson, *Bound for the Promised Land*, 277–79, 383n33.

12. "Convention of Colored Iowa Soldiers," *The Christian Recorder*, November 18, 1865, 1.

13. Story told by Marjorie Lawson and recorded by Susan Morgan, n.d., reprinted in Kathryn L. Morgan, "Caddy Buffers: Legends of a Middle Class Negro Family in Philadelphia," *Keystone Folklore Quarterly* 11, no. 2 (Summer 1966): 75.

14. U.S. Constitution, amend. 14, sec. 1.

15. U.S. Constitution, amend. 15, sec. 1.

16. Henry Blake, interview with Samuel Taylor, n.d., in *Arkansas Narratives:* Part 1, vol. 7 of *Slave Narratives: A Folk History of Slavery in the United States, from Interviews with Former Slaves*, prepared by the Federal Writers' Project ([1936–1938]; repr., St. Clair Shores, MI: Scholarly Press, 1976), 178.

17. The Klan specialized in labor discipline. Its founder, Nathan Bedford Forrest—who had been the largest slave trader in Memphis, Tennessee, before the war and had served as a Confederate general (and commander of the troops who committed the Fort Pillow massacre)—became a railroad executive who used convict labor to construct his Selma, Marion, and Memphis line. See Gao, *African Americans in the Reconstruction Era*, 231–33, and Matthew J. Mancini, *One Dies, Get Another: Convict Leasing in the American South, 1866–1928* (Columbia: University of South Carolina Press, 1996), 133–34.

18. Testimony of J.R. Holliday, Atlanta, GA, October 21, 1871, in *Testimony Taken by the Joint Select Committee to Inquire into the Condition of Affairs in the Late Insurrectionary States: Georgia*, vol. 1, vol. 6 of *Report of the Joint Select Committee to Inquire into the Affairs of the Late Insurrectionary States*, 42nd Congress, 2nd sess., 1872, S. Rep. 41, 420.

19. Testimony of Augustus R. Wright, Washington, D.C., July 13, 1871, ibid., 140.

20. "Proceedings of the Alabama Labor Union Convention: Tuesday, January 3, 1871," in Foner and Lewis, *The Black Worker*, vol. 2, 122.

21. "The Exodusters," *Atchison Daily Champion*, May 10, 1879, 1.

22. *Boston Daily Evening Voice*, November 3, 1865, in John R. Commons and John B. Andrews, eds., *The Labor Movement, 1860–1880*, vol. 1, vol. 9 of *A Documentary History of American Industrial Society*, ed. Commons et al. (1910; repr., New York: Russell & Russell, 1958), 304–5.

23. *Boston Daily Evening Voice*, October 5, 1865, in Foner and Lewis, *The Black Worker*, vol. 1, 391.

24. Sylvis, *Life, Speeches, Labors*, 280.

25. Ibid., 414.

26. Ibid., 80.

27. Ibid., 186.

28. *Proceedings of the National Labor Union* (1868), 23, quoted in Andrews and Bliss, *History of Women in Trade Unions*, 87.

29. "Workingwomen's Association," *The Revolution* 2, no. 12 (September 24, 1868): 181.

30. Augusta Lewis, report to the convention of the International Typographical Union, Baltimore, 1871, quoted in George A. Stevens, *New York Typographical Union No. 6: Study of a Modern Trade Union and Its Predecessors* (Albany, NY: J.B. Lyon, 1913), 437. In 1872, Lewis married Alexander Troup, the Typographical Union's national secretary-treasurer and an avid supporter of women's integration into the organization. The two soon moved to New Haven,

Connecticut, where they raised seven children and published the *Daily Union*, a labor newspaper, as Mrs. Troup agitated for woman suffrage. See Stevens, 432, and Cavanagh, *Augusta Lewis Troup*.

31. Andrew C. Cameron, *The Address of the National Congress to the Workingmen of the United States* (Chicago: Hazlitt and Quinton, 1867), in Commons and Andrews, *The Labor Movement, 1860–1880*, vol. 1, 158–9.

32. *Mariposa Gazette*, July 13, 1867, quoted in Ping Chiu, *Chinese Labor in California, 1850–1880* (Madison: State Historical Society of Wisconsin, 1963), 47.

33. "Address: The Relations of the Colored People to American Industry," *The New Era*, January 13, 1870, 1.

34. "Telegraphic: Domestic News," *Daily Phoenix* (Columbia, SC), July 29, 1869, 3.

35. "Organization Among the Colored People," *National Anti-Slavery Standard*, November 6, 1869, 2.

36. "Address: The Relations of the Colored People to American Industry," *The New Era*, January 13, 1870, 1.

37. "Newport (R.I.) Labor Meeting," *National Anti-Slavery Standard*, October 30, 1869, 1.

38. Aurand, *From the Molly Maguires to the United Mine Workers*, 25.

39. Dacus, *Annals of the Great Strikes*, 75.

40. Ibid., 308, 378, 387.

41. F.S., McComb City, Mississippi, "The Working Man's Vision," *The International Journal* (November 1876), reprinted in *Rhyme and Reason: Molders Poetry From Sylvis to the Great Depression*, ed. James E. Cebula and James E. Wolfe (Cincinnati, OH: Sylvis Society, 1984), 98.

Andrews, John B., and William Dwight Porter Bliss. *History of Women in Trade Unions*. 1911. Reprint, New York: Arno Press, 1974.

Aptheker, Herbert. *American Negro Slave Revolts*. New York: Columbia University Press, 1944.

———, ed. *A Documentary History of the Negro People in the United States*. 1951. Reprint, New York: Citadel Press, 1969.

Aurand, Harold W. *From the Molly Maguires to the United Mine Workers: The Social Ecology of an Industrial Union, 1869–1897*. Philadelphia: Temple University Press, 1971.

Balser, Diane. *Sisterhood & Solidarity: Feminism and Labor in Modern Times*. Boston: South End Press, 1987.

Botkin, Benjamin Albert, ed. *Lay My Burden Down: A Folk History of Slavery*. Chicago: University of Chicago Press, 1945.

Brecher, Jeremy. *Strike!* Rev. ed. Boston: South End Press, 1997.

Cavanagh, Joan, comp. and ed. *Augusta Lewis Troup: Worker, Activist, Advocate*. New Haven, CT: Greater New Haven Labor History Association, 2008. https://issuu.com/lwberndtsonjr/docs/gussie.

Dacus, J.A. *Annals of the Great Strikes in the United States: A Reliable History and Graphic Description of the Causes and Thrilling Events of the Labor Strikes and Riots of 1877*. 1877. Reprint, New York: Burt Franklin, 1969.

DuBois, Ellen Carol. *Feminism and Suffrage: The Emergence of an Independent Women's Movement in America, 1848–1869*. Ithaca, NY: Cornell University Press, 1978.

Du Bois, W.E.B. *Black Reconstruction in America, 1860–1880*. 1935. Reprint, New York: Atheneum, 1992.

Foner, Eric. *Reconstruction: America's Unfinished Revolution, 1863–1877.* New York: Harper & Row, 1988.

Foner, Philip S. *History of the Labor Movement in the United States.* Vol. 1, *From Colonial Times to the Founding of the American Federation of Labor.* New York: International Publishers, 1947.

———. *Organized Labor and the Black Worker, 1619–1973.* 1974. Reprint, New York: International Publishers, 1976.

Foner, Philip S., and Ronald L. Lewis, eds. *The Black Worker: A Documentary History from Colonial Times to the Present.* Vol. 1, *The Black Worker to 1869.* Philadelphia: Temple University Press, 1978.

———. *The Black Worker: A Documentary History from Colonial Times to the Present.* Vol. 2, *The Black Worker During the Era of the National Labor Union.* Philadelphia: Temple University Press, 1978.

Gao, Chunchang. *African Americans in the Reconstruction Era.* New York: Garland, 2000.

Harding, Vincent. *There Is a River: The Black Struggle for Freedom in America.* New York: Harcourt Brace Jovanovich, 1981.

Jaynes, Gerald David. *Branches Without Roots: Genesis of the Black Working Class in the American South, 1862–1882.* New York: Oxford University Press, 1986.

Kenny, Kevin. *Making Sense of the Molly Maguires.* New York: Oxford University Press, 1998.

Larson, Kate Clifford. *Bound for the Promised Land: Harriet Tubman, Portrait of an American Hero.* New York: Ballantine, 2004.

McPherson, James M. *The Negro's Civil War: How American Negroes Felt and Acted During the War for the Union.* Urbana: University of Illinois Press, 1982.

———. *Ordeal by Fire: The Civil War and Reconstruction.* New York: McGraw-Hill, 1993.

Montgomery, David. *Beyond Equality: Labor and the Radical Republicans, 1862–1872.* New York: Knopf, 1967.

———. *Citizen Worker: The Experience of Workers in the United States with Democracy and the Free Market During the Nineteenth Century.* Cambridge, UK: Cambridge University Press, 1993.

Norton, Lee. *War Elections, 1862–1864.* New York: International Publishers, 1944.

Painter, Nell Irvin. *Exodusters: Black Migration to Kansas After Reconstruction.* New York: Knopf, 1977.

Redkey, Edwin S., ed. *A Grand Army of Black Men: Letters from African-American Soldiers in the Union Army, 1861–1865.* Cambridge: Cambridge University Press, 1992.

Roediger, David R. *The Wages of Whiteness: Race and the Making of the American Working Class.* London: Verso, 1991.

Saxton, Alexander. *The Indispensable Enemy: Labor and the Anti-Chinese Movement in California.* Berkeley: University of California Press, 1971.

Schwalm, Leslie A. *A Hard Fight for We: Women's Transition from Slavery to Freedom in South Carolina.* Urbana: University of Illinois Press, 1997.

Sylvis, James C. *The Life, Speeches, Labors and Essays of William H. Sylvis, Late President of the Iron-Moulders' International Union; And Also of the National Labor Union.* Philadelphia: Claxton, Remsen & Haffelfinger, 1872.

Takaki, Ronald T. *Strangers from a Different Shore: A History of Asian Americans.* Boston: Little, Brown, 1989.

Yellen, Samuel. *American Labor Struggles: 1877–1934.* 1936. Reprint, New York: Monad Press, 1974.

5: Labor Versus Monopoly in the Gilded Age

1. "Too Much of Most Everything," *Chicago Tribune*, August 14, 1884, 4.

2. Vega, *Memoirs*, 59.

3. Walt Whitman, "Our Real Culmination," in *Specimen Days & Collect* (Glasgow, UK: Wilson and McCormick, 1883), 337.

4. Hofstadter, *Social Darwinism*, 24.

5. Andrew Carnegie, "Wealth," *North American Review*, June 1889, 657.

6. Quoted in William J. Ghent, *Our Benevolent Feudalism* (New York: Macmillan, 1902), 29.

7. William Graham Sumner, *The Challenge of Facts and Other Essays*, ed. Albert Galloway Keller (New Haven, CT: Yale University Press, 1914), 90.

8. McNeill, *The Labor Movement*, 455.

9. Yellow Wolf, *Yellow Wolf*, 60.

10. Coleman, *Voices of Wounded Knee*, xxi.

11. Jerry Green, ed., *After Wounded Knee: Correspondence of Major and Surgeon John Vance Lauderdale While Serving With the Army Occupying the Pine Ridge Indian Reservation, 1890–1891* (East Lansing: Michigan State University Press, 1996), 38–39.

12. John M. Carroll, ed., "Extracts from Letters Written by Lieutenant Alexander R. Piper . . . during the Sioux Campaign, 1890–1891," *The Unpublished Papers of the Order of Indian Wars* (New Brunswick, NJ: privately published, 1977), 10:1, quoted in Coleman, *Voices of Wounded Knee*, 173.

13. See, for example, "Wages and Cheapness," *National Labor Tribune*, June 9, 1877, 1.

14. Adamic, *From Many Lands*, 59.

15. Colorado Bureau of Labor Statistics, *First Biennial Report of the Bureau of Labor Statistics of the State of Colorado 1887–1888*, comp. James Rice and C.J. Driscoll (Denver: Collier & Cleaveland, 1888), 342.

16. Marie Hall Ets, *Rosa, The Life of an Italian Immigrant*, 2nd ed. (Madison: University of Wisconsin Press, 1999), 204.

17. Lucy Warner, "Why Do People Look Down on Working Girls?: How It Looks from a Working Girl's Standpoint," *Far and Near*, January 1891, 37.

18. B.P. Wilcox, "Anti-Chinese Riots in Washington," *Washington Historical Quarterly* 20, no. 3 (July 1929): 206.

19. John Swinton, *Striking for Life: Labor's Side of the Labor Question: The Right of the Workingman to a Fair Living* ([New York]: American Manufacturing and Pub. Co., 1894), 38.

20. William Roscoe Thayer, *Life and Letters of John Hay* (Boston: Houghton Mifflin, 1915), 2: 7.

21. Reprinted in [untitled], *Tiffin (Ohio) Tribune*, September 6, 1877, 2.

22. See Ezra Asher Cook, *Knights of Labor Illustrated: "Adelphon Kruptos," The Full, Illustrated Ritual Including the "Unwritten Work" and an Historical Sketch of the Order* (Chicago: Ezra A. Cook, 1886), 37.

23. "Labor in Line," *The Times* (Philadelphia), June 18, 1882, 1.

24. Reprinted in Jelley, *Voice of Labor*, 197; for the entire Preamble and Declaration of Principles, see 197–210.

25. McNeill, *The Labor Movement*, 460.

26. Ibid., 460.

27. Ibid., 459.

28. Jelley, *Voice of Labor*, 198.

29. "Assemblies of Colored Men," *Journal of United Labor*, August 15, 1880, 49.

30. Thomas Barry, quoted in "Repulsive Tyranny," *The Frankfort (Kansas) Sentinel*, January 27, 1888, [4].

31. *Memphis Watchman*, January 15, 1887, quoted in *The Memphis Diary of Ida B. Wells: An Intimate Portrait of the Activist as a Young Woman*, ed. Miriam DeCosta-Willis (Boston: Beacon Press, 1995), 126.

32. Quoted in Terence Powderly, *Thirty Years of Labor, 1859–1889* (Columbus, OH: Excelsior Publishing House, 1889), 653.

33. "The Knights of Labor," *The Sun* (Baltimore), October 16, 1886, 5.

34. "Color Line in Society," *Topeka Daily Capital*, October 17, 1886, 3.

35. [Untitled], *Cleveland Gazette*, October 23, 1886, 2.

36. "Eight Hours," *The Sun* (New York), January 23, 1889, 4.

37. "Fourth Annual Session of the Federation of Organized Trades and Labor Unions of the United State and Canada, 1884," in American Federation of Labor, *Proceedings of the American Federation of Labor, 1881, 1882, 1883 . . . 1888* (Bloomington, IL: Pantagraph Printing and Stationery, 1905), 14.

38. "Eight Hours for Labor," *The Sun* (Baltimore), April 30, 1886, 1.

39. The full text of Altgeld's pardon can be found in Linder, "The Haymarket Riot Trial."

40. John Brown to D.R. Tilden, November 28, 1859, quoted in John Brown Jr. to Franklin Sanborn, November 11, 1887, reprinted in Louis Ruchames, ed., "John Brown, Jr. and the Haymarket Martyrs," *Massachusetts Review* 5, no. 4 (Summer 1964): 768.

41. Samuel Gompers, "Annual Report to the A.F. of L. Convention, Detroit, Michigan, December 1890," excerpted in Gompers, *Labor and the Common Welfare*, 3.

42. Laurie, *Artisans into Workers*, 177.

43. R.P. Fleming to Samuel Gompers, November 6, 1892, excerpted in Foner and Lewis, *The Black Worker*, vol. 4, 23.

44. Samuel Gompers to A.D. Bauer, June 13, 1892, quoted in Foner, *History of the Labor Movement*, vol. 2, 196.

45. "Homestead Occupied by Militia," *Philadelphia Inquirer*, July 13, 1892, 1.

46. G.W. Howard to Samuel Gompers, September 5, 1892, quoted in Foner, *History of the Labor Movement*, vol. 2, 255.

47. "Statement from the Pullman Strikers," in "Exhibit 4—Motions, Resolutions, and Reports of the American Railway Union, June 12 to 23, inclusive, 1994," in Testimony of Sylvester Keliher, August 16–17, 1894, in *Report on the Chicago Strike of June–July 1894, by the United States Commission, Appointed by the President July 26, 1894, under the Provisions of Section 6 of Chapter 1063 of the Laws of the United States Passed October 1, 1888, with Appendices Containing Testimony, Proceedings, and Recommendations*, 53rd Cong., 3rd sess., 1895, Ex. Doc. 7, 88.

48. *Globe*, 8; *Times*, 3; *Post*, 8.

49. Foner and Lewis, *The Black Worker*, vol. 3, 272.

50. Thomas E. Watson, "The Negro Question in the South," *The Arena* 6, October 1892, 548.

51. Samuel Gompers, *Seventy Years of Life and Labor: An Autobiography*, ed. Nick Salvatore (Ithaca, NY: ILR Press, 1984), 123.

52. Eugene V. Debs, *Unionism and Socialism; a Plea for Both* (Terre Haute, IN: Standard Publishing Company, 1904), 29.

53. George E. McNeill, "The Trade Unions and the Monopolies," *American Federationist*, December 1896, 208.

Adamic, Louis. *From Many Lands*. New York: Harper & Brothers, 1940.

Brown, Dee. *Bury My Heart at Wounded Knee: An Indian History of the American West*. New York: Holt, Rinehart & Winston, 1970.

Burgoyne, Arthur Gordon. *The Homestead Strike of 1892*. 1893. Reprint, Pittsburgh: University of Pittsburgh Press, 1979.

Coleman, William S.E., comp. *Voices of Wounded Knee*. Lincoln: University of Nebraska Press, 2000.

Diner, Hasia R. *Erin's Daughters in America: Irish Immigrant Women in the Nineteenth Century*. Baltimore: Johns Hopkins University Press, 1983.

Fink, Leon. *Workingmen's Democracy: The Knights of Labor and American Politics*. Urbana: University of Illinois Press, 1983.

Foner, Philip S. *History of the Labor Movement in the United States*. Vol. 1, *From Colonial Times to the Founding of the American Federation of Labor*. New York: International Publishers, 1947.

———. *History of the Labor Movement in the United States*. Vol. 2, *From the Founding of the American Federation of Labor to the Emergence of American Imperialism*. 2nd ed. New York: International Publishers, 1975.

Foner, Philip S., and Ronald L. Lewis, eds. *The Black Worker: A Documentary History from Colonial Times to the Present*. Vol. 3, *The Black Worker During the Era of the Knights of Labor*. Philadelphia: Temple University Press, 1978.

———. *The Black Worker: A Documentary History from Colonial Times to the Present*. Vol. 4, *The Black Worker During the Era of the American Federation of Labor and the Railroad Brotherhoods*. Philadelphia: Temple University Press, 1978.

Freifeld, Mary Ellen. "The Emergence of the American Working Classes: The Roots of Division, 1865–1885." PhD diss., New York University, 1980.

Geronimo. *Geronimo: His Own Story*. Transcribed by S.M. Barrett. Edited by Frederick W. Turner. Rev. ed. New York: Meridian, 1996.

Gompers, Samuel. *Labor and the Common Welfare*. Compiled and edited by Hayes Robbins. New York: E.P. Dutton, 1919.

Green, James R. *Death in the Haymarket: A Story of Chicago, the First Labor Movement, and the Bombing That Divided Gilded Age America*. New York: Pantheon Books, 2006.

Greene, Victor R. *The Slavic Community on Strike: Immigrant Labor in Pennsylvania Anthracite*. Notre Dame, IN: University of Notre Dame Press, 1968.

Hofstadter, Richard. *Social Darwinism in American Thought*. Rev. ed. Boston: Beacon Press, 1955.

Jelley, S.M. *The Voice of Labor*. Philadelphia: H.J. Smith & Co, 1888.

Laurie, Bruce. *Artisans into Workers: Labor in Nineteenth-Century America*. 1989. Reprint, Urbana: University of Illinois Press, 1997.

Levine, Susan. *Labor's True Woman: Carpet Weavers, Industrialization, and Labor Reform in the Gilded Age*. Philadelphia: Temple University Press, 1984.

Limerick, Patricia Nelson. *The Legacy of Conquest: The Unbroken Past of the American West*. New York: Norton, 1987.

Linder, Douglas O. "Haymarket Trial (1886)." Famous Trials. n.d. www.famoustrials .com/Haymarket.

McNeill, George E., ed. *The Labor Movement: The Problem of Today*. Boston: A.M. Bridgman, 1886.

Miner, Claudia. "The 1886 Convention of the Knights of Labor." *Phylon* 44, no. 2 (2nd Quarter, 1983): 147–59.

Montgomery, David. *The Fall of the House of Labor: The Workplace, the State, and American Labor Activism, 1865–1925*. Cambridge, UK: Cambridge University Press, 1987.

———. *Workers' Control in America: Studies in the History of Work, Technology, and Labor Struggles*. Cambridge, UK: Cambridge University Press, 1979.

Rachleff, Peter J. *Black Labor in Richmond, 1865–1890*. 1984. Reprint, Urbana: University of Illinois Press, 1989.

Roediger, David R., and Franklin Rosemont, eds. *Haymarket Scrapbook*. Chicago: C.H. Kerr, 1986.

Saxton, Alexander. *The Indispensable Enemy: Labor and the Anti-Chinese Movement in California*. Berkeley: University of California Press, 1971.

———. *The Rise and Fall of the White Republic: Class Politics and Mass Culture in Nineteenth-Century America*. London: Verso, 1990.

Takaki, Ronald T. *Strangers from a Different Shore: A History of Asian Americans*. Boston: Little, Brown, 1989.

Vapnek, Lara. *Breadwinners: Working Women and Economic Independence, 1865–1920*. Urbana: University of Illinois Press, 2009.

Vega, Bernardo. *Memoirs of Bernardo Vega: A Contribution to the History of the Puerto Rican Community in New York*. Translated by Juan Flores. Edited by César Andreu Iglesias. New York: Monthly Review Press, 1984.

Verrill, A. Hyatt. *The Real Americans*. New York: Putnam, 1954.

Ware, Norman. *The Labor Movement in the United States, 1860–1895: A Study in Democracy*. New York: D. Appleton, 1929.

Weir, Robert E. *Beyond Labor's Veil: The Culture of the Knights of Labor*. University Park: Pennsylvania State University Press, 1996.

———. *Knights Unhorsed: Internal Conflict in a Gilded Age Social Movement*. Detroit: Wayne State University Press, 2000.

Yellen, Samuel. *American Labor Struggles: 1877–1934*. 1936. Reprint, New York: Monad Press, 1974.

Yellow Wolf. *Yellow Wolf: His Own Story*. [Translated by Thomas Hart.] Transcribed and edited by L.V. McWhorter. Rev. ed. Caldwell, ID: Caxton Printers, 1986.

6: Labor and Empire

1. Samuel Gompers, "Should Hawaii Be Annexed?" *American Federationist*, November 1897, 216.

2. John Hay to Theodore Roosevelt, July 27, 1898, in William Roscoe Thayer, *The Life and Letters of John Hay* (Boston: Houghton Mifflin, 1915), 2: 337.

3. J.J. Henna and M. Zeno Gandia, *The Case of Puerto Rico* (Washington: Press of W.F. Roberts, 1899), 8–9.

4. Ibid., 33.

5. Carroll D. Wright, "The Relation of Production to Productive Capacity,—II," *Forum,* February 1898, 671.

6. Brooks Adams, *America's Economic Supremacy* (New York: Macmillan Company, 1900), 32.

7. "The War with Spain, and After," *Atlantic Monthly,* June 1898, 726.

8. Franklin H. Giddings, "Imperialism?" *Political Science Quarterly* 13, no. 4 (December 1898): 590.

9. Rudyard Kipling, "The White Man's Burden," *McClure's Magazine,* February 1899, 290.

10. Theodore Roosevelt, "America's Part of the World's Work," in *The Works of Theodore Roosevelt: National Edition,* vol. 14, *Campaigns and Controversies,* ed. Hermann Hagedorn (New York: Charles Scribner's Sons, 1926), 317.

11. "Reconstruction and Disfranchisement," *Atlantic Monthly,* October 1901, 435.

12. John W. Galloway, 24th Infantry, to editor, *Richmond Planet,* December 30, 1899, 1.

13. Editorial, *American Federationist,* July 1901, 261.

14. Charles A. Conant, "The Struggle for Commercial Empire," *The Forum,* June 1899, 433.

15. Montgomery, *The Fall of the House of Labor,* 174.

16. John H. Patterson (speech at the Dayton Centennial, Dayton, OH, March 19, 1896), quoted in Chester E. Rightor, with Don C. Sowers, and Walter Matscheck, *City Manager in Dayton; Four Years of Commission-Manager Government, 1914–1917; and Comparisons with Four Preceding Years Under the Mayor-Council Plan, 1910–1913* (New York: Macmillan, 1919), 2.

17. "Is the Constitution Obsolete?" *Commercial West,* May 30, 1908, 8.

18. Frank Munsey to Theodore Roosevelt, February 13, 1912, quoted in *Letters of Louis D. Brandeis: Volume II 1907–1912: People's Attorney,* ed. Melvin I. Urofsky and David W. Levy (Albany: State University of New York Press, 1972), 727.

19. Edgar Gardner Murphy, *Problems of the Present South; A Discussion of Certain of the Educational, Industrial, and Political Issues in the Southern States* (New York: Longmans, Green, and Co, 1909), 17.

20. Arthur C. Johnson, "To Prod Diplomats," *Washington Post,* February 11, 1910, 1.

21. "Force to Land in Cuba Again," *New York Times,* September 23, 1906, 1.

22. Smedley D. Butler, "'In Time of Peace': The Army," *Common Sense,* November 1935, 8.

23. Elbert Hubbard, *A Message to Garcia* (East Aurora, NY: Roycroft Shop, 1899), 3.

24. Ibid., 8.

25. Ibid., 11.

26. "Organization, High Dues, and Success," *American Federationist,* April 1897, 33.

27. Samuel Gompers, "Organization of the Unskilled" (excerpted from report to the annual convention of the American Federation of Labor, Nashville, Tennessee, December 1897), in Gompers, *Labor and the Employer,* 161.

28. "President Gompers' Report," *Report of Proceedings of the Twenty-Second Annual Convention of the American Federation of Labor, held at New Orleans, Louisiana, November 13 to 22, 1902* (Washington: Law Reporter Company, 1902), 21.

29. Henry White, general secretary, United Garment Workers of America, quoted in "Industrial Peace and Progress: Views of Labor's Advocates," *American Federationist,* March 1902, 109.

30. "James Duncan, First Vice-President of the A.F. of L., Addresses the Workers on Labor Day," *American Federationist*, October 1903, 1051.

31. Taylor, *Principles of Scientific Management*, 106.

32. "Call It by Its Right Name," *American Federationist*, March 1921, 226.

33. *Speech of William Howard Taft: Accepting the Republican Nomination for President of the United States; Together with the Speech of Notification by Senator Elihu Root*, 62nd Cong., 2nd sess., 1912, S. Doc. 902, 10.

34. U.S. Department of Justice, *Annual Report of the Attorney General of the United States for the Year 1913* (Washington: Government Printing Office, 1913), 16.

35. Clayton Antitrust Act, Public Law 63–212 §§ 6 and 20, 38 *Stat* 731, 738, codified at 15 *US Code* §17 and 29 US Code §52.

36. Samuel Gompers, "Labor Provisions of the Clayton Antitrust Law," *American Federationist*, November 1914, 971–72.

37. Jack London, *War of the Classes* (New York: Macmillan, 1905), 30.

38. "Platform of the Socialist Party, Adopted at Chicago, Ill., May 5, 1904," in *The World Almanac and Encyclopedia 1905, s.v. "National Party Platforms of 1904"* (New York: Press Publishing Company, 1904), 107.

39. Joseph Ettor, "I.W.W. versus A.F. of L.," *New Review*, May 1914, 283.

40. Unpublished circular to general executive board, November 19, 1915, quoted in Mark Perlman, *The Machinists: A New Study in American Trade Unionism* (Cambridge, MA: Harvard University Press, 1961), 45.

41. "Negroes Endorse Socialist Ticket," *Chickasha Daily Express*, October 15, 1919, 1.

42. Industrial Workers of the World, *Proceedings of the First Convention of the Industrial Workers of the World, Founded at Chicago, June 27–July 8, 1905* (New York: New York Labor News Company, 1905), 1.

43. Ibid., [viii].

44. Justus Ebert, *The Trial of a New Society* (Cleveland: I.W.W. Publishing Bureau, 1913), 61.

45. See W.E. Trautmann, *One Big Union: An Outline of a Possible Industrial Organization of the Working Class, with Chart* (Chicago: Charles H. Kerr & Company, 1911).

46. James Fair, in Bird, Georgakas, and Shaffer, *Solidarity Forever*, 184.

47. [*Colored Workers of America: Why You Should Join the I.W.W.*, n.d.], excerpted in "The I.W.W. and the Negro," *Bloomfield's Labor Digest*, December 6, 1919, 60.

48. Quoted in "Hillstrom Executed," *Ogden Standard*, November 19, 1915, 10.

49. Samuel Gompers, "Editorial," *American Federationist*, February 1912, 139.

50. Samuel Gompers, "Editorial," *American Federationist*, July 1913, 534.

51. "Socialist Politics," *The Public*, September 23, 1919, 899; Eugene V. Debs, *Unionism and Socialism: A Plea for Both* (Terre Haute, IN: Standard Publishing, 1904), 14.

52. Oscar Ameringer, *Union Scabs and Others* (Cleveland: I.W.W. Publishing Bureau, 1910), 1.

53. "American Labor's Position in Peace or in War," reprinted in Samuel Gompers, *President Gompers on Labor, the Courts and the Law: Being the Testimony of Mr. Gompers Before the United States Senate Committee on Manufactures, in Its Hearing on Production and Profits in Coal* (Washington: American Federation of Labor, 1921), 58.

54. "President Wilson's War Address, delivered to the Congress, April 2, 1917," reprinted in *Americanism: Woodrow Wilson's Speeches on the War*, ed. Oliver Marble Gale (Chicago: Baldwin Syndicate, 1918), 43.

55. Freda Maurer, "Fifteen Years at Topping," reprinted in Gladys L. Palmer, *Union Tactics and Economic Change: A Case Study of Three Philadelphia Textile Unions* (Philadelphia: University of Pennsylvania Press, 1932), 150.

56. "The Socialist Party and the War," reprinted in *The American Labor Yearbook, 1917–18*, ed. Alexander Trachtenberg (New York: Rand School of Social Science, 1918), 52.

57. Eugene V. Debs, "The November Elections," *Social Revolution*, December 1917, 5.

58. *Investigation Activities of the Department of Justice*, 66th Cong., 1st sess., 1919, S. Doc. 153, serial 7607, 172.

59. William Haywood, Circular Letter, 1919, vol. 86, American Civil Liberties Union Records, Microfilm, Reel 121, ACLU Archives, quoted in Chester, *The Wobblies in Their Heyday*, 201.

60. Edward F. Mason to the Delegates to the Central Trades and Labor Union, May 23, 1917, reprinted in "The Massacre of East St. Louis," *The Crisis*, September 1917, 221.

61. "Labor Is Entitled To A Fair Standard Of Living," *Railroad Trainman*, February 1919, 139.

62. Central Labor Council of Seattle and Vicinity, *The Seattle General Strike: An Account of What Happened in Seattle, and Especially in the Seattle Labor Movement, during the General Strike, February 6 to 11, 1919* (Seattle: Seattle Union Record Publishing Company, 1919), 63.

63. Partido Socialista, *Programa, constitución territorial, y actuaciones del PS*, fourth convention, May 1919 (San Juan: Justicia, 1919), excerpted and translated in Quintero Rivera, *Workers' Struggle in Puerto Rico*, 105.

64. "What the Japanese Agitators Want," *Honolulu Star Bulletin*, February 13, 1920, 6.

65. "Labor Party Launched—Its Aims," *Brooklyn Eagle*, January 16, 1919.

66. J. Charles Laue, "A.F.L. Parley Swept for Negro Equality: Convention Demands Railway Clerks Delete Clauses Barring Them . . . ," *New York Call*, June 11, 1920, 3.

67. Rev. Patrick Molyneux, St. Brendan's Roman Catholic Church, Braddock, Pennsylvania, sermon September 21, 1919, excerpted in Interchurch World Movement, *Public Opinion and the Steel Strike*, 279.

68. Interchurch World Movement, *Public Opinion and the Steel Strike*, 99.

69. "Whose Country Is This?" *Los Angeles Times*, November 7, 1919, 20.

70. John E. Edgerton, president, National Association of Manufacturers, [untitled statement], *Open Shop Review*, August 1921, [296].

71. "Open Shop Idea Endorsed by Prominent Men of Our Nation," *Chamber of Commerce and State Manufacturers Journal*, September 1921, 14.

72. W.E.B. Du Bois, "The Negro Mind Reaches Out," in *The New Negro*, ed. Alain Locke (New York: Albert & Charles Boni, 1925), 386.

Almaguer, Tomás. *Racial Fault Lines: The Historical Origins of White Supremacy in California*. Berkeley: University of California Press, 1994.

Bernstein, Irving. *The Lean Years: A History of the American Worker, 1920–1933*. Boston: Houghton Mifflin, 1972.

Bird, Stewart, Dan Georgakas, and Deborah Shaffer. *Solidarity Forever: An Oral History of the IWW*. Chicago: Lake View Press, 1985.

Brecher, Jeremy. *Strike!* Rev. ed. Boston: South End Press, 1997.

Brissenden, Paul F. *The I.W.W.: A Study of American Syndicalism*. New York: Columbia University, 1919.

Brody, David. *Steelworkers in America: The Nonunion Era*. New York: Russell & Russell, 1970.

———. *Workers in Industrial America: Essays on the Twentieth Century Struggle*. 2nd ed. New York: Oxford University Press, 1993.

Buhle, Mari Jo. *Women and American Socialism, 1870–1920*. Urbana: University of Illinois Press, 1981.

Chaplin, Ralph. *Wobbly: The Rough-and-Tumble Story of an American Radical*. Chicago: University of Chicago Press, 1948.

Chester, Eric Thomas. *The Wobblies in Their Heyday: The Rise and Destruction of the Industrial Workers of the World During the World War I Era*. Santa Barbara, CA: Praeger, 2014.

Cole, Peter, David Struthers, and Kenyon Zimmer, eds. *Wobblies of the World: A Global History of the IWW*. London: Pluto Press, 2017.

Copeland, Tom. "Wesley Everest, IWW Martyr." *Pacific Northwest Quarterly* 77, no. 4 (October 1986): 122–29.

Dunn, Robert W., ed. *The Palmer Raids*. New York: International Publishers, 1948.

Dye, Nancy Schrom. *As Equals and As Sisters: Feminism, the Labor Movement, and the Women's Trade Union League of New York*. Columbia: University of Missouri Press, 1980.

Flynn, Elizabeth Gurley. *The Rebel Girl: An Autobiography, My First Life (1906–1926)*. New York: International Publishers, 1973.

Foner, Philip S. *History of the Labor Movement in the United States*. Vol. 2, *From the Founding of the American Federation of Labor to the Emergence of American Imperialism*. 2nd ed. New York: International Publishers, 1975.

———. *History of the Labor Movement in the United States*. Vol. 3, *The Policies and Practices of the American Federation of Labor, 1900–1909*. New York: International Publishers, 1964.

———. *History of the Labor Movement in the United States*. Vol. 4, *The Industrial Workers of the World, 1905–1917*. New York: International Publishers, 1965.

———. *History of the Labor Movement in the United States*. Vol. 5, *The AFL in the Progressive Era*. New York: International Publishers, 1980.

———. *History of the Labor Movement in the United States*. Vol. 6, *On the Eve of America's Entrance into World War I, 1915–1916*. New York: International Publishers, 1982.

———. *History of the Labor Movement in the United States*. Vol. 7, *Labor and World War I, 1914–1918*. New York: International Publishers, 1987.

———. *History of the Labor Movement in the United States*. Vol. 8, *Postwar Struggles, 1918–1920*. New York: International Publishers, 1988.

———. *Organized Labor and the Black Worker, 1619–1973*. New York: International Publishers, 1976.

Foner, Philip S., and Ronald L. Lewis, eds. *The Black Worker: A Documentary History from Colonial Times to the Present*. Vol. 5, *The Black Worker from 1900 to 1919*. Philadelphia: Temple University Press, 1980.

Gómez-Quiñones, Juan. *Mexican American Labor, 1790–1990*. Albuquerque: University of New Mexico Press, 1994.

Gompers, Samuel. *Labor and the Common Welfare*. Compiled and edited by Hayes Robbins. New York: E.P. Dutton, 1919.

———. *Labor and the Employer*. Compiled and edited by Hayes Robbins. New York: E.P. Dutton, 1920.

———. *Seventy Years of Life and Labor: An Autobiography.* Edited by Nick Salvatore. Ithaca, NY: ILR Press, 1984.

Gorn, Elliott J. *Mother Jones: The Most Dangerous Woman in America.* New York: Hill and Wang, 2001.

Green, James R. *Grass-Roots Socialism: Radical Movements in the Southwest, 1895–1943.* Baton Rouge: Louisiana State University Press, 1978.

———. *The World of the Worker: Labor in Twentieth-Century America.* New York: Hill and Wang, 1980.

Greenwald, Maurine Weiner. *Women, War, and Work: The Impact of World War I on Women Workers in the United States.* Westport, CT: Greenwood Press, 1980.

Grigsby, Daryl Russell. *For the People: Black Socialists in the United States, Africa, and the Caribbean.* San Diego: Asante Publications, 1987.

Hall, Greg. *Harvest Wobblies: The Industrial Workers of the World and Agricultural Laborers in the American West, 1905–1930.* Corvallis: Oregon State University Press, 2001.

Huberman, Leo. *The Labor Spy Racket.* New York: Modern Age Books, 1937.

Huyssen, David. *Progressive Inequality: Rich and Poor in New York, 1890–1920.* Cambridge, MA: Harvard University Press, 2014.

Interchurch World Movement of North America. *Public Opinion and the Steel Strike: Supplementary Reports of the Investigators to the Commission of Inquiry, the Interchurch World Movement.* New York: Harcourt, Brace and Company, 1921.

James, Winston. *Holding Aloft the Banner of Ethiopia: Caribbean Radicalism in Early Twentieth-Century America.* London: Verso, 1999.

Kornbluh, Joyce L., ed. *Rebel Voices: An I.W.W. Anthology.* Ann Arbor: University of Michigan Press, 1964.

Kornweibel, Theodore. *"Investigate Everything": Federal Efforts to Compel Black Loyalty During World War I.* Bloomington: Indiana University Press, 2002.

———. *Seeing Red: Federal Campaigns against Black Militancy, 1919–1925.* Bloomington: Indiana University Press, 1998.

McCoy, Alfred W. *Policing America's Empire: The United States, the Philippines, and the Rise of the Surveillance State.* Madison: University of Wisconsin Press, 2009.

Miller, Stuart Creighton. *"Benevolent Assimilation": The American Conquest of the Philippines, 1899–1903.* New Haven, CT: Yale University Press, 1982.

Montgomery, David. *The Fall of the House of Labor: The Workplace, the State, and American Labor Activism, 1865–1925.* Cambridge: Cambridge University Press, 1987.

———. *Workers' Control in America: Studies in the History of Work, Technology, and Labor Struggles.* Cambridge: Cambridge University Press, 1979.

Okihiro, Gary Y. *Cane Fires: The Anti-Japanese Movement in Hawaii, 1865–1945.* Philadelphia: Temple University Press, 1991.

Perry, Jeffrey Babcock. *Hubert Harrison: The Voice of Harlem Radicalism, 1883–1918.* New York: Columbia University Press, 2009.

Quintero Rivera, A.G., ed. *Workers' Struggle in Puerto Rico: A Documentary History.* Translated by Cedric Belfrage. New York: Monthly Review Press, 1976.

Salvatore, Nick. *Eugene V. Debs: Citizen and Socialist.* Urbana: University of Illinois Press, 1982.

Sellars, Nigel Anthony. *Oil, Wheat & Wobblies: The Industrial Workers of the World in Oklahoma, 1905–1930.* Norman: University of Oklahoma Press, 1998.

Shannon, David A. *The Socialist Party of America; A History*. 1955. Reprint, Chicago: Quadrangle Books, 1967.

Shulman, Harry. "Labor and the Anti-Trust Laws." *Illinois Law Review of Northwestern University* 34, no. 7 (1940): 769–87.

Smith, Robert Michael. *From Blackjacks to Briefcases: A History of Commercialized Strikebreaking and Unionbusting in the United States*. Athens: Ohio University Press, 2003.

Taylor, Frederick Winslow. *The Principles of Scientific Management*. 1911. Reprint, New York: W.W. Norton, 1967.

Vapnek, Lara. *Breadwinners: Working Women and Economic Independence, 1865–1920*. Urbana: University of Illinois Press, 2009.

Vega, Bernardo. *Memoirs of Bernardo Vega: A Contribution to the History of the Puerto Rican Community in New York*. Translated by Juan Flores. Edited by César Andreu Iglesias. New York: Monthly Review Press, 1984.

Wakstein, Allen M. "The Origins of the Open-Shop Movement, 1919–1920." *Journal of American History* 51, no. 3 (December 1964): 460–75.

Weyforth, William O. *The Organizability of Labor*. Baltimore: Johns Hopkins Press, 1917.

Williamson, Joel. *The Crucible of Race: Black-White Relations in the American South Since Emancipation*. New York: Oxford University Press, 1985.

Woodward, C. Vann. *The Strange Career of Jim Crow*. New York: Oxford University Press, 1955.

Yellen, Samuel. *American Labor Struggles, 1877–1934*. 1936. Reprint, New York: Monad Press, 1980.

7: America, Inc.

1. Donner, *Protectors of Privilege*, 30.

2. William Green to Paul Smith, June 17, 1929, quoted in Bernstein, *The Lean Years*, 143.

3. Stuart Chase, *Prosperity: Fact or Myth* (New York: C. Boni, 1929), 40.

4. C. Coapes Brinley, "Shall We Let Down the Bars?" *Industrial Management* 65, no. 4 (April 1923): 248.

5. E.K. Hall, "The Spirit of Cooperation Between Employer and Employee," *Law and Labor* 11, no. 3 (March 1929): 53.

6. Speech before the American Iron and Steel Institute, quoted in "Record Era in Steel Surveyed by Schwab," *New York Times*, May 25, 1929, 7.

7. C.B. Seger, "Employee Representation and Personnel Work in a Large-Scale Organization with Many Plants," *Proceedings of the Academy of Political Science in the City of New York* 9, no. 4 (January 1922): 7.

8. William M. Leiserson to Morris L. Cooke, March 28, 1929, quoted in Bernstein, *The Lean Years*, 170.

9. Benjamin M. Selekman and Mary Van Kleeck, *Employes' Representation in Coal Mines: A Study of the Industrial Representation Plan of the Colorado Fuel and Iron Company* (New York: Russell Sage Foundation, 1924), 185.

10. Quoted in Arthur Pound and Samuel Taylor Moore, eds., *They Told Barron: Conversations and Revelations of an American Pepys in Wall Street; the Notes of the Late Clarence W. Barron[,] Publisher of* The Wall Street Journal, The Boston News Bureau, *Etc.* (New York: Harper & Bros, 1930), 82.

11. Ernest T. Trigg, quoted in Wainwright Evans, "A Business Man of the New Day," *Nation's Business*, April 1929, 90.

12. "The 'Yellow Dog' Device as a Bar to the Union Organizer," *Harvard Law Review* 41, no. 6 (April 1928): 770–75.

13. *Adkins v. Children's Hospital*, 261 U.S. 558 [1923], quoted in Thomas Reed Powell, "The Judiciality of Minimum-Wage Legislation," *Harvard Law Review* 37, no. 5 (March 1924): 564.

14. Calvin Coolidge, "The Press Under a Free Government," in *Foundations of the Republic: Speeches and Addresses* (New York: Charles Scribner's Sons, 1926), 187.

15. "Text of William Allen White's Address," *The Courier-Journal* (Louisville, KY), April 10, 1927, 10.

16. Bruce Barton, "The New Business World: Number Five in a Series" (transcript of a radio talk, November 30, 1929), in Bruce Barton Papers, Wisconsin State Historical Society, Madison, WI, quoted in Lears, *Fables of Abundance*, 227.

17. Bruce Barton, *The Man Nobody Knows* (Indianapolis: Charter Books, 1925), 13.

18. "Easter Sun Finds the Past in Shadow at Modern Parade," *New York Times*, April 1, 1929, 3.

19. "Coolidge Rated Conservative But An Enigma," *The Sun* (Baltimore), August 7, 1923, 4.

20. "Complete Text of Herbert Hoover's New York Address," *Detroit Free Press*, October 23, 1928, 10.

21. W.S. Killingsworth, "Better Housing for Orchard Help," *Pacific Rural Press*, March 13, 1920, 422.

22. "Green Follows Gompers' Trail; Motto: Caution," *Chicago Daily Tribune*, December 31, 1924, 7.

23. In 1936, Congress extended the act's coverage to airlines. See "Airlines Labor Bill Passed by the House," *New York Times*, April 7, 1936, 18.

24. Adamic, *Dynamite*, 192.

25. Adamic, *Dynamite*, 214.

26. Vega, *Memoirs*, 170–71.

27. Dave Moore, interview by Judith Stepan-Norris, January 1984, excerpted in Stepan-Norris and Maurice Zeitlin, *Talking Union* (Urbana: University of Illinois Press, 1996), 43.

28. Marvel Cooke, "I Was Part of the Bronx Slave Market," *Daily Compass* (New York), January 8, 1950, 1. See also "Jobless Domestics Form Virtual 'Slave Block' in New York," *The Afro- American* (Baltimore), August 31, 1935, 11.

29. V.C. French to William Green, March 29, 1933, International Association of Machinists, National Union File No. 6, AFL-CIO Headquarters, Washington, D.C., quoted in Brody, *Workers in Industrial America*, 77.

30. "Dearborn Chief Appeals for Federal Aid in Tracking Leaders of River Rouge Riot," *Detroit Free Press*, March 9, 1932, 3.

31. Robert Gottlieb and Robert Kimball, eds., *Reading Lyrics* (New York: Pantheon Books, 2000), 259.

Adamic, Louis. *Dynamite: A Century of Class Violence in America, 1830–1930*. 1931, 1934. Rev. ed. [London]: Rebel Press, 1984.

Allen, Frederick Lewis. *Only Yesterday: An Informal History of the Nineteen-Twenties*. New York: Harper & Row, 1957.

Bakke, E. Wight, and Clark Kerr, eds. *Unions, Management, and the Public.* New York: Harcourt, Brace, 1948.

Barrett, James R. *The Irish Way: Becoming American in the Multiethnic City.* New York: Penguin Press, 2012.

Bernstein, Irving. *The Lean Years: A History of the American Worker, 1920–1933.* Boston: Houghton Mifflin, 1972.

Blee, Kathleen M. *Women of the Klan: Racism and Gender in the 1920s.* Berkeley: University of California Press, 1991.

Brandes, Stuart D. *American Welfare Capitalism, 1880–1940.* Chicago: University of Chicago Press, 1976.

Bremner, Robert H. *From the Depths: The Discovery of Poverty in the United States.* New York: New York University Press, 1964.

Brody, David. *Workers in Industrial America: Essays on the Twentieth Century Struggle.* 2nd ed. New York: Oxford University Press, 1993.

Cherniak, Martin. *The Hawk's Nest Incident: America's Worst Industrial Disaster.* New Haven, CT: Yale University Press, 1986.

Chernow, Ron. *The House of Morgan: An American Banking Dynasty and the Rise of Modern Finance.* New York: Atlantic Monthly Press, 1990.

Donner, Frank J. *Protectors of Privilege: Red Squads and Police Repression in Urban America.* Berkeley: University of California Press, 1990.

Foner, Philip S. *History of the Labor Movement in the United States.* Vol. 9, *The T.U.E.L. to the End of the Gompers Era.* New York: International Publishers, 1991.

———. *History of the Labor Movement in the United States.* Vol. 10, *The T.U.E.L. 1925–1929.* New York: International Publishers, 1991.

Frank, Dana. *Purchasing Power: Consumer Organizing, Gender, and the Seattle Labor Movement, 1919–1929.* Cambridge: Cambridge University Press, 1994.

Galbraith, John Kenneth. *The Great Crash, 1929.* Boston: Houghton Mifflin, 1979.

Gómez-Quiñones, Juan. *Mexican American Labor, 1790–1990.* Albuquerque: University of New Mexico Press, 1994.

Higham, John. *Strangers in the Land: Patterns of American Nativism, 1860–1925.* 1955. Reprint, New York: Atheneum, 1970.

Lears, T.J. Jackson. *Fables of Abundance: A Cultural History of Advertising in America.* New York: Basic Books, 1994.

MacLean, Nancy. *Behind the Mask of Chivalry: The Making of the Second Ku Klux Klan.* New York: Oxford University Press, 1994.

McElvaine, Robert S. *The Great Depression: America, 1929–1941.* New York: Times Books, 1984.

McWilliams, Carey. *Factories in the Field: The Story of Migratory Farm Labor in California.* 1939. Reprint, Hamden, CT: Archon Books, 1969.

Mikhailov, B.Y. et al. *Recent History of the Labor Movement in the United States, 1918–1939.* Moscow: Progress Publishers, 1977.

Montgomery, David. *The Fall of the House of Labor: The Workplace, the State, and American Labor Activism, 1865–1925.* Cambridge: Cambridge University Press, 1987.

———. *Workers' Control in America: Studies in the History of Work, Technology, and Labor Struggles.* Cambridge: Cambridge University Press, 1979.

Pycior, Julie Leininger. *Democratic Renewal and the Mutual Aid Legacy of US Mexicans.* College Station: Texas A&M University Press, 2014.

Saposs, David J. "Labor." *American Journal of Sociology* 36, no. 6 (May 1931): 913–22.

Vega, Bernardo. *Memoirs of Bernardo Vega: A Contribution to the History of the Puerto Rican Community in New York*. Translated by Juan Flores. Edited by César Andreu Iglesias. New York: Monthly Review Press, 1984.

Yung, Judy. *Unbound Feet: A Social History of Chinese Women in San Francisco*. Berkeley: University of California Press, 1995.

8: Labor on the March

1. "Unfair Practices Defined by NRA," *New York Times*, October 29, 1933, 24.

2. Franklin D. Roosevelt, "The Second 'Fireside Chat'—'What We Have Been Doing and What We Are Planning to Do.' May 7, 1933," in *The Public Papers and Addresses of Franklin D. Roosevelt, with a Special Introduction and Explanatory Notes by President Roosevelt*, vol. 2, *The Year of Crisis, 1933*, comp. Samuel I. Rosenman (New York: Random House, 1938), 164.

3. "National Industrial Recovery Act" in United States, National Archives and Records Administration, *Our Documents: 100 Milestone Documents from the National Archives* (Oxford: Oxford University Press, 2003), 160.

4. Byron Price, "Causes Are Outlined for Industrial Strife," *Palladium-Item* (Richmond, IN), August 9, 1934, 8.

5. Paul Comly French, "Children on Strike," *The Nation*, May 31, 1933, 611.

6. J.W., "The Textile Strike," *The Nation*, September 5, 1934, 273.

7. Karl Lore, "Labor Faces the Company Union," *The Nation*, April 4, 1934, 406.

8. American Federation of Labor, *Report of Proceedings of the Fifty-Fourth Annual Convention of the American Federation of Labor: Held at San Francisco, California, October 1 to 12, Inclusive, 1934* (Washington, D.C.: Judd & Detweiler, n.d.), 453.

9. Harry Anderson to E.S. Cowdrick, June 1936, quoted in Albert Kahn, *High Treason: The Plot Against the People* (New York: Lear Publishers 1950), 166.

10. Quoted in Blaine Owen, "Night Ride in Birmingham," *New Republic*, August 28, 1935, 67.

11. "'No Work, No Eat,' Dole Takers Told," *Oakland Tribune*, September 5, 1937, 1.

12. "Text of Wagner Labor Disputes Bill as Sent to the President for Signature," *New York Times*, July 2, 1935, 15.

13. De Caux, *Labor Radical*, 214.

14. Minton and Stuart, *Men Who Lead Labor*, 86

15. Preis, *Labor's Giant Step*, 42.

16. "Lewis Drive Urges Industrial Unions," *New York Times*, November 27, 1935, 38.

17. McKenney, *Industrial Valley*, 358.

18. "Industrial Steel Union Drive Begins," *Pittsburgh Post-Gazette*, June 18, 1936, 1–2.

19. Philip Murray, interview by Frederick Harbison, n.d., quoted in Harbison, "Labor Relations in the Iron and Steel Industry, 1936 to 1939" (PhD diss., Princeton University, 1940), 30.

20. Bob Stinson, in Terkel, *Hard Times*, 132.

21. De Caux, *Labor Radical*, 239.

22. Alfred P. Sloan Jr., *My Years with General Motors* (Garden City, NY: Doubleday, 1964), 406.

23. Jean Collier Brown, *Concerns of Household Workers: Program with Household Workers in the Y.W.C.A.* (New York: The Womans Press, 1941), 139.

24. Mrs. Violet Baggett to *The United Auto Worker*, February 25, 1937, reprinted in Vorse, *Labor's New Millions*, 80–81.

25. "Status of the Negro in Labor Unions," *Des Moines Register*, April 23, 1944, 12; Levinson, *Labor on the March*, 209.

26. *People's World*, December 4, 1939, quoted in Douglas Monroy, *Rebirth: Mexican Los Angeles from the Great Migration to the Great Depression* (Berkeley: University of California Press, 1999), 258.

27. McKenney, *Industrial Valley*, 379.

28. "Leonard Lyons: Dubinsky and Lewis Meet," *Detroit Free Press*, February 16, 1942, 20.

29. Paul Y. Anderson, "How Mohawk Valley 'Formula' for Breaking Industrial Strikes Was Conceived; How It Operates," *St. Louis Post-Dispatch*, August 29, 1937, part 7, page 1.

30. "Dubinsky Back in AFL," *Philadelphia Inquirer*, June 9, 1940, B9.

31. "A.F. of L. Leader Strikes Anti-Semitic Note In Letter Attacking the C.I.O.," *Wisconsin Jewish Chronicle* (Milwaukee), June 4, 1937, 1.

32. "Democrats Put on Pressure to End Trade Fear," *Chicago Tribune*, October 18, 1937, 1.

33. "'Aristocratic Anarchy' Laid to New Deal Foes," *Pittsburgh Press*, December 29, 1937, 1.

34. Carlson, *Under Cover*, 194–95; "We Prefer Democracy," *The Gazette and Daily* (York, PA), September 13, 1939, 6.

35. "Streamlined Klan to Fight C.I.O. Planned," *Courier-Journal* (Louisville, KY), December 16, 1938, section 3, page 6.

36. "Elliott Roosevelt Raps Coughlin; Priest's Spokesman Makes Reply," *Minneapolis Tribune*, July 17, 1939, 5.

37. *Labor Advocate*, April 24, 1937, quoted in Kelley, *Hammer and Hoe*, 140.

38. "Communists Rule the C.I.O., Frey of A.F.L. Testifies; He Names 284 Organizers," *New York Times*, August 14, 1938, 1.

39. De Caux, *Labor Radical*, 242–43.

40. *Party Platforms, 1940: Republican, Democratic, Socialist, Communist* (New York: Harper & Brothers, 1940), n.p.

41. Bulosan, *America Is in the Heart*, 188.

42. Paul Robeson, "Ballad for Americans," recorded February 9, 1940, New York City, with American People's Chorus and Victor Symphony Orchestra, conducted by Nathaniel Shilkret, on *The Original Recording of Ballad for Americans and Great Songs of Faith, Love and Patriotism*, Vanguard (MP3), 1989.

43. Bulosan, *America Is in the Heart*, 189.

44. Mark Naison, *Communists in Harlem During the Depression* (1984; repr. Urbana: University of Illinois Press, 2005), 174.

45. Paul Robeson, "Speech at National Maritime Union Convention," July 8, 1941, reprinted in Philip Foner, ed., *Paul Robeson Speaks: Writings, Speeches, Interviews, 1918–1974* (New York: Brunner/Mazel, 1978), 138.

Badger, Anthony J. *New Deal/New South: An Anthony J. Badger Reader.* Fayetteville: University of Arkansas Press, 2007.

Bernstein, Irving. *Turbulent Years: A History of the American Worker, 1933–1941.* Boston: Houghton Mifflin, 1970.

Brody, David. *Workers in Industrial America: Essays on the Twentieth Century Struggle.* 2nd ed. New York: Oxford University Press, 1993.

Bulosan, Carlos. *America Is in the Heart: A Personal History.* 1946. Reprint, Seattle: University of Washington Press, 1973.

Carlson, John Roy. *Under Cover: My Four Years in the Nazi Underworld of America.* New York: E.P. Dutton & Company, 1943.

Clark, Paul F., Peter Gottlieb, and Donald Kennedy, eds. *Forging a Union of Steel: Philip Murray, SWOC, and the United Steelworkers.* Ithaca, NY: ILR Press, 1987.

Cohen, Lizabeth. *Making a New Deal: Industrial Workers in Chicago, 1919–1939.* Cambridge: Cambridge University Press, 1990.

De Caux, Len. *Labor Radical: From the Wobblies to CIO, a Personal History.* Boston: Beacon Press, 1970.

Denning, Michael. *The Cultural Front: The Laboring of American Culture in the Twentieth Century.* London: Verso, 1998.

Fichtenbaum, Myrna. *The Funsten Nut Strike.* New York: International Publishers, 1992.

Fine, Sidney. *Sit-Down: The General Motors Strike of 1936–1937.* Ann Arbor: University of Michigan Press, 1969.

Foner, Philip S. *Organized Labor and the Black Worker, 1619–1973.* New York: International Publishers, 1976.

Foner, Philip S., and Ronald L. Lewis, eds. *The Black Worker: A Documentary History from Colonial Times to the Present.* Vol. 7, *The Black Worker from the Founding of the CIO to the AFL-CIO Merger, 1936–1955.* Philadelphia: Temple University Press, 1983.

Frank, Dana. *Women Strikers Occupy Chain Store, Win Big: The 1937 Woolworth's Sit-Down.* Chicago: Haymarket Books, 2012.

Fraser, Steve. *Labor Will Rule: Sidney Hillman and the Rise of American Labor.* New York: Free Press, 1991.

Harris, Herbert. *Labor's Civil War.* New York: Knopf, 1940.

Huberman, Leo. *The Labor Spy Racket.* New York: Modern Age Books, 1937.

Kelley, Robin D.G. *Hammer and Hoe: Alabama Communists During the Great Depression.* Chapel Hill: University of North Carolina Press, 1990.

Kraus, Henry. *The Many and the Few: A Chronicle of the Dynamic Auto Workers.* 2nd ed. Urbana: University of Illinois Press, 1985.

Kwong, Peter. *Chinatown, New York: Labor and Politics, 1930–1950.* New York: Monthly Review Press, 1979.

Levinson, Edward. *Labor on the March.* New York: Harper & Brothers, 1938.

Lichtenstein, Nelson. *The Most Dangerous Man in Detroit: Walter Reuther and the Fate of American Labor.* New York: Basic Books, 1995.

Lynd, Staughton, ed. *"We Are All Leaders": The Alternative Unionism of the Early 1930s.* Urbana: University of Illinois Press, 1996.

McKenney, Ruth. *Industrial Valley.* 1939. Reprint, Ithaca, NY: ILR Press, 1992.

Minton, Bruce, and John Stuart. *Men Who Lead Labor.* New York: Modern Age Books, 1937.

Preis, Art. *Labor's Giant Step: Twenty Years of the C.I.O.* New York: Pathfinder Press, 1964.

Pycior, Julie Leininger. *Democratic Renewal and the Mutual Aid Legacy of US Mexicans.* College Station: Texas A&M University Press, 2014.

Serrin, William. *The Company and the Union: The "Civilized Relationship" of the General Motors Corporation and the United Automobile Workers.* New York: Knopf, 1973.

Stepan-Norris, Judith, and Maurice Zeitlin. *Talking Union.* Urbana: University of Illinois Press, 1996.

Terkel, Studs. *Hard Times: An Oral History of the Great Depression*. 1970. Reprint, New York: Pantheon Books, 1986.

Vargas, Zaragosa. *Labor Rights Are Civil Rights: Mexican American Workers in Twentieth-Century America*. Princeton, NJ: Princeton University Press, 2005.

Vega, Bernardo. *Memoirs of Bernardo Vega: A Contribution to the History of the Puerto Rican Community in New York*. Translated by Juan Flores. Edited by César Andreu Iglesias. New York: Monthly Review Press, 1984.

Vorse, Mary Heaton. *Labor's New Millions*. New York: Modern Age Books, 1938.

Weber, Devra. *Dark Sweat, White Gold: California Farm Workers, Cotton, and the New Deal*. Berkeley: University of California Press, 1994.

Yung, Judy. *Unbound Feet: A Social History of Chinese Women in San Francisco*. Berkeley: University of California Press, 1995.

Zieger, Robert H. *The CIO, 1935–1955*. Chapel Hill: University of North Carolina Press, 1995.

9: Hot War, Cold War

1. "War Is NOT Inevitable," *Akron Beacon Journal*, August 1, 1940, 6.

2. "Hillman Says Labor's Gains Will Be Kept," *Pittsburgh Press*, August 1, 1940, 8.

3. De Caux, *Labor Radical*, 363, 380.

4. "Biddle's Intervention Asked in Plot Trial," *Minneapolis Star Journal*, September 19, 1941, 25.

5. "6 Workers Always on Time, Lose Only 2 Days During War," *Detroit News*, March 14, 1943, part 1, page 18.

6. Arthur Huff Fauset, "I Write As I See," *Philadelphia Tribune*, February 7, 1942, 4.

7. Walter White, *A Rising Wind* (Garden City, NY: Doubleday, Doran and Company, 1945), 18.

8. U.S. Bureau of Labor Statistics, *Maintenance-of-Membership Awards of National War Labor Board* (Washington: U.S. Government Printing Office, 1943), 1.

9. Sylvia Woods, "You Have to Fight for Freedom," in Lynd and Lynd, *Rank and File*, 126.

10. Ibid., 129.

11. "Union Dispute at Shipyard Called Smoldering Volcano," *Los Angeles Times*, June 5, 1943, 15.

12. Arthur Sears Henning, "New Deal Hears the Echo: Clear It with Sidney," *Chicago Tribune*, September 26, 1944, 2.

13. Stella Nowicki, "Back of the Yards," in Lynd and Lynd, *Rank and File*, 88.

14. Norman Bully, interview by Jack W. Skeels, October 12, 1961, UAW Oral Histories, 1959–1963, Walter P. Reuther Library, Archives of Labor and Urban Affairs, Wayne State University, Detroit, MI, 23.

15. George W. Mawhinney, "All Penna. Pits Are Closed, With 200,000 Men Idle," *Philadelphia Inquirer*, May 2, 1943, 1.

16. Current, "The Detroit Elections," 332.

17. Lawrence Resner, "Stamford Tied Up 3 Hours In Demonstration by Labor," *New York Times*, January 4, 1946, 4.

18. "32 Pickets Seized in Camden Strike," *New York Times*, November 23, 1946, 4.

19. "The General Strike," *Hartford Courant*, December 7, 1946, 6.

20. "'Wartime Pay During Peace' Lacks Backing," *Nevada State Journal* (Reno), October 17, 1945, 4.

21. "Ryan Issue In Dock Strike," *Plain Speaker* (Hazleton, PA), October 17, 1945, 1.

22. Congress of Industrial Organizations, *Final Proceedings*, 171.

23. Ibid., 278.

24. Ibid., 113–14.

25. E.C. Kreutzberg, "Windows of Washington," *STEEL: The Magazine of Metalworking and Metalproducing*, November 4, 1946, 72.

26. "Would Business Men Like to Do Business Under a Law Written by the CIO?" *Akron Beacon Journal*, May 2, 1947, 30.

27. Revels Cayton, interview by Allan Bérubé, September 23, 1994, quoted in Bérubé, *My Desire for History: Essays in Gay, Community, and Labor History* (Chapel Hill: University of North Carolina Press, 2011), 310.

28. Edwin H. Sutherland, "The Sexual Psychopath Laws," *Journal of Criminal Law and Criminology* 40, no. 5 (January–February 1950): 543.

29. Harry Hay, interview by Christian Arthur Bain, September 1998, quoted in Bain, "A Short History of Lesbian and Gay Labor Activism in the United States," in Hunt, *Laboring for Rights*, 60.

30. Brief for the United States as Amicus Curiae, *Brown v. Board of Education*, 347 U.S. 483 (1954), quoted in Dudziak, *Cold War, Civil Rights*, 100–1. In these passages, the brief quotes a letter to the U.S. Attorney General from Secretary of State Dean Acheson; see Dean Acheson to James P. McGranery, November 28, 1952, reprinted at David Langbart, "Foreign Policy and Domestic Discrimination," *The Text Message Blog, National Archives*, last modified March 5, 2015, https://text-message.blogs.archives.gov/2015/03/05/foreign-policy-and -domesticdiscrimination.

31. Dudziak, *Cold War, Civil Rights*, 142.

32. An act to establish an uniform Rule of Naturalization, ch. 3, 1 Stat 103 (1790).

33. "CIO Wants No Outside Help In Organization Drive In South," *Baltimore Sun*, April 19, 1946, 17.

34. Quoted in Matles and Higgins, *Them and Us*, 201.

35. Elaine Fogg, "Recommendations For Labor Board Made By CIO Union," *Honolulu Advertiser*, July 31, 1945, 5.

36. Juan Sáez Corales, "Twenty-Five Years of Struggle: My Reply to Persecution," in Quintero Rivera, *Workers' Struggle in Puerto Rico*, 160.

37. Serrin, *The Company and the Union*, 156–57.

38. William Jacobs, "CIO Approves Merger with Former Rival," *Pittsburgh Press*, December 2, 1955, 1.

39. "Meany-Reuther Statement," *New York Times*, February 10, 1955, 20.

40. "Text of the AFL-CIO Merger Agreement," 428.

41. Quoted in AFL-CIO, *Problems of Working Women: Summary Report of a Conference* (Washington: Industrial Union Department, AFL-CIO, 1961), 49.

42. "Text of the AFL-CIO Merger Agreement," 428.

43. Gus Tyler, *Labor Revolution: Trade Unions in a New America* (New York: Viking Press, 1967), 243.

44. The text of the Union Member's Bill of Rights can be found on the website of the Association for Union Democracy: https://uniondemocracy.org/legal-rights-and-organizing/about-the-lmrdaand-the-union-members-bill-of-rights/union-members-bill-of-rights.

45. James Reston, "Washington: Big Steel, Big Labor, and Big Politics," *New York Times*, October 18, 1959, E8.

46. Fiszman, "The Development of Administrative Roles."

47. Testimony of William C. Doherty Jr. on May 11, 1967, in *Hearings Before the Committee on Foreign Affairs [of the] House of Representatives*, HR 7099, the Foreign Assistance Act of 1967, 90th Cong., 1st sess., May 8–11, 1967, part 5, 1098.

Bernstein, Irving. *Turbulent Years: A History of the American Worker, 1933–1941*. Boston: Houghton Mifflin, 1970.

Brody, David. *Workers in Industrial America: Essays on the Twentieth Century Struggle*. 2nd ed. New York: Oxford University Press, 1993.

Buhle, Paul. *Taking Care of Business: Samuel Gompers, George Meany, Lane Kirkland, and the Tragedy of American Labor*. New York: Monthly Review Press, 1999.

Burk, Robert F. *The Corporate State and the Broker State: The Du Ponts and American National Politics, 1925–1940*. Cambridge, MA: Harvard University Press, 1990.

Calavita, Kitty. *Inside the State: The Bracero Program, Immigration, and the I.N.S.* New York: Routledge, 1992.

Carlson, John Roy. *The Plotters*. New York: Dutton, 1946.

Chapman. Gordon W. "Labor and International Affairs." *World Affairs* 125, no. 1 (Spring 1962): 25–29.

Congress of Industrial Organizations. *Final Proceedings of the Eighth Constitutional Convention of the CIO*. n.p.: [Congress of Industrial Organizations], 1946.

———. *Official Reports on the Expulsion of Communist Dominated Organizations from the CIO*. Washington: Congress of Industrial Organizations, 1954.

Current, Gloster B. "The Detroit Elections: Problem in Reconversion." *The Crisis*, November 1945, 319–21, 332.

De Caux, Len. *Labor Radical: From the Wobblies to CIO, a Personal History*. Boston: Beacon Press, 1970.

Dower, John W. *War Without Mercy: Race and Power in the Pacific War*. New York: Pantheon Books, 1993.

Dudziak, Mary L. *Cold War Civil Rights: Race and the Image of American Democracy*. Princeton, NJ: Princeton University Press, 2000.

Fiszman, Joseph R. "The Development of Administrative Roles: The Labor Attaché Program of the U. S. Foreign Service." *Public Administration Review* 25, no. 3 (September 1965): 203–12.

Foner, Jack D. *Blacks and the Military in American History: A New Perspective*. New York: Praeger Publishers, 1974.

Foner, Philip S. *Organized Labor and the Black Worker, 1619–1973*. New York: International Publishers, 1976.

Foner, Philip S., and Ronald L. Lewis, eds. *The Black Worker: A Documentary History from Colonial Times to the Present*. Volume VII, *The Black Worker from the Founding of the CIO to the AFL-CIO Merger, 1936–1955*. Philadelphia: Temple University Press, 1983.

Fraser, Steve. *Labor Will Rule: Sidney Hillman and the Rise of American Labor*. New York: Free Press, 1991.

Glaberman, Martin. *Wartime Strikes: The Struggle Against the No-Strike Pledge in the UAW During World War II.* Detroit: Bewick Editions, 1980.

Gluck, Sherna Berger. *Rosie the Riveter Revisited: Women, the War, and Social Change.* Boston: Twayne, 1987.

"The Great Train Strike," *Life*, June 3, 1946, 27–33.

Griswold del Castillo, Richard. *World War II and Mexican American Civil Rights.* Austin: University of Texas Press, 2008.

Halpern, Martin. *UAW Politics in the Cold War Era.* Albany: State University of New York Press, 1988.

Haverty-Stacke, Donna T. *Trotskyists on Trial: Free Speech and Political Persecution Since the Age of FDR.* New York: New York University Press, 2015.

Holland, Max. "Private Sources of U.S. Foreign Policy: William Pawley and the 1954 Coup d'État in Guatemala.*" Journal of Cold War Studies* 7, no. 4 (Fall 2005): 36–73.

Honey, Michael K. *Southern Labor and Black Civil Rights: Organizing Memphis Workers.* Urbana: University of Illinois Press, 1993.

Hunt, Gerald, ed. *Laboring for Rights: Unions and Sexual Diversity Across Nations.* Philadelphia: Temple University Press, 2009.

Isserman, Maurice. *Which Side Were You On?: The American Communist Party During the Second World War.* Middletown, CT: Wesleyan University Press, 1982.

Johnson, David K. *The Lavender Scare: The Cold War Persecution of Gays and Lesbians in the Federal Government.* Chicago: University of Chicago Press, 2004.

Jones, William Powell. *The March on Washington: Jobs, Freedom, and the Forgotten History of Civil Rights.* New York: W.W. Norton, 2013.

Katznelson, Ira. *When Affirmative Action Was White: An Untold History of Racial Inequality in Twentieth-Century America.* New York: W.W. Norton, 2005.

Klinkner, Philip A., and Rogers M. Smith. *The Unsteady March: The Rise and Decline of Racial Equality in America.* Chicago: University of Chicago Press, 1999.

Kovel, Joel. *Red Hunting in the Promised Land: Anticommunism and the Making of America.* New York: Basic Books, 1994.

Leeds, Morton. "The AFL in the 1948 Elections." *Social Research* 17, no. 2 (June 1950): 207–18.

Lichtenstein, Nelson. *A Contest of Ideas: Capital, Politics, and Labor.* Urbana: University of Illinois Press, 2013.

———. *Labor's War at Home: The CIO in World War II.* Cambridge: Cambridge University Press, 1982.

Lipsitz, George. *Rainbow at Midnight: Labor and Culture in the 1940s.* Urbana: University of Illinois Press, 1994.

Lynd, Staughton, and Alice Lynd, eds. *Rank and File: Personal Histories by Working-Class Organizers.* Boston: Beacon Press, 1973.

Matles, James J., and James Higgins. *Them and Us: Struggles of a Rank-and-File Union.* Englewood Cliffs, NJ: Prentice-Hall, 1974.

Milkman, Ruth. *Gender at Work: The Dynamics of Job Segregation by Sex During World War II.* Urbana: University of Illinois Press, 1987.

Ngai, Mae M. *Impossible Subjects: Illegal Aliens and the Making of Modern America.* Princeton, NJ: Princeton University Press, 2004.

Prickett, James R. "Communist Conspiracy or Wage Dispute?: The 1941 Strike at North American Aviation." *Pacific Historical Review* 50, no. 2 (May 1981): 215–33.

Quintero Rivera, A.G., ed., *Workers' Struggle in Puerto Rico: A Documentary History.* Translated by Cedric Belfrage. New York: Monthly Review Press, 1976.

Ross, Irwin. *The Loneliest Campaign: The Truman Victory of 1948.* New York: New American Library, 1968.

Serrin, William. *The Company and the Union: The "Civilized Relationship" of the General Motors Corporation and the United Automobile Workers.* New York: Knopf, 1973.

Sims, Beth. *Workers of the World Undermined: American Labor's Role in U.S. Foreign Policy.* Boston: South End Press, 1992.

"Text of the AFL-CIO Merger Agreement." *Monthly Labor Review* 78, no. 4 (April 1955): 428–30.

Vargas, Zaragosa. *Labor Rights Are Civil Rights: Mexican American Workers in Twentieth-Century America.* Princeton, NJ: Princeton University Press, 2005.

Windmuller, John P. "Foreign Affairs and the AFL-CIO." *Industrial and Labor Relations Review* 9, no. 3 (April 1956): 419–32.

Zieger, Robert H. *The CIO, 1935–1955.* Chapel Hill: University of North Carolina Press, 1995.

10: The Sixties

1. "Excerpts from Addresses at Lincoln Memorial During Capital Civil Rights March," *New York Times*, August 29, 1963, 21.

2. Joseph Azbell, interview by Blackside, Inc., October 31, 1985, for *Eyes on the Prize: America's Civil Rights Years (1954–1965)*, Henry Hampton Collection, Film and Media Archive, Washington University Libraries, http://digital.wustl.edu/e/eop/eopweb/azb0015 .0570.005josephazbell.html.

3. Max Lerner, "Alabama Fires," *Pittsburgh Courier*, June 15, 1963, 25.

4. Sheyann Webb, interview by Blackside, Inc., December 6, 1985, for *Eyes on the Prize*, http://repository.wustl.edu/concern/videos/v692t789g.

5. "State Troopers Block Convention Hall Entry," *Asbury Park (New Jersey) Press*, August 26, 1964, 2.

6. Fannie Lou Hamer, "It's in Your Hands," in *Black Women in White America: A Documentary History*, ed. Gerda Lerner (1972; repr., New York: Vintage Books, 1992), 611. Originally titled as "The Special Plight and the Role of Black Woman" (speech at NAACP Legal Defense Fund Institute, New York City, May 7, 1971).

7. James Forman, *The Making of Black Revolutionaries: A Personal Account* (New York: Macmillan, 1972), 352; Harvard Sitkoff, *The Struggle for Black Equality, 1954–1980* (1981; repr., New York: Hill and Wang, 2008), 186.

8. Jack Shepherd, "A Worker Hits the Freedom Road," *Look*, November 16, 1965, M22.

9. "Excerpts From Addresses at Lincoln Memorial During Capital Civil Rights March," *New York Times*, August 29, 1963, 21.

10. Fannie Lou Hamer, "Nobody's Free Until Everybody's Free" (speech, National Women's Political Caucus, Washington, D.C., July 10, 1971), in *The Speeches of Fannie Lou Hamer: To Tell It Like It Is*, ed. Maegan P. Brooks and Davis W. Houck (Jackson: University Press of Mississippi, 2011), 137.

11. Director, FBI, to SAC [Special Agent in Charge], Albany, "Counterintelligence Program, Black Nationalist-Hate Groups, Internal Security," August 25, 1967, 1–2, reproduced in *Federal Bureau of Investigation (FBI), Freedom of Information and Privacy Acts, Subject: (COINTELPRO) Black Extremist,* 1.00-448006, Section 1, https://vault.fbi.gov/cointelpro /cointel-pro-black-extremists/cointelpro-black-extremists-part-01-of.

12. Floyd McKissick, "From a Black Point of View: Cry 'Power to the People,'" *New York Amsterdam News*, November 8, 1969, 15.

13. "The Black Panthers' 10-Point Program," *Detroit Free Press*, January 18, 1970, 4B.

14. "El Plan de Aztlán" (First National Chicano Youth Liberation Conference, Denver, CO, March 1969), reprinted by Movimiento Estudiantil Chicana/o de Aztlán, Arizona State University, last modified February 12, 2006, http://clubs.arizona.edu/~mecha/pages/PDFs/ElPlanDeAtzlan.pdf.

15. "National Preamble and Principles of La Raza Unida Party" (adopted at El Congreso de Aztlán, Albuquerque, New Mexico), November 24–26, 1972, series "La Raza Unida Political Party," sub-series: "National City Chapter," folder: "Correspondence, incoming," Herman Baca Papers, 1964–2013 (MSS 0649), Special Collections and Archives, University of California at San Diego, 32–33, http://library.ucsd.edu/dc/object/bb5393826p/_1.pdf.

16. Everett R. Holles, "Convicts Seek to Form a National Union," *New York Times*, September 26, 1971, 74.

17. Indians of all Nations, "Alcatraz Proclamation," 1969, in Brian Ward, ed., *The 1960s: A Documentary Reader* (Chichester, UK: Wiley-Blackwell, 2010), 194.

18. Vine Deloria Jr., *Behind the Trail of Broken Treaties: An Indian Declaration of Independence* (Austin: University of Texas Press, 1985), 34.

19. James Tracy, "The Original Rainbow Coalition: An Interview with Bobby Lee," *James Tracy: Writings on Cities, Hidden Histories & Social Movements. Author Dispatches Against Displacement & Hillbilly Nationalists*, January 3, 2007, https://jamestracybooks.org/2007/01/03/the-original-rainbow-coalition-an-interview-with-bobbylee.

20. Fort Hood Three Defense Committee, *The Fort Hood Three: The Case of the Three G.I.'s Who Said "No" to the War in Vietnam* (New York: Published by Fort Hood Three Defense Committee, 1966), 10–11.

21. National Welfare Rights Organization, "Mrs. Johnnie Tillmon Succeeds George Wiley as Head of NWRO," press release from NWRO, Washington, D.C., January 12, 1973, quoted in West, *National Welfare Rights Movement*, 122.

22. Iris Morales, "¡Palante, Siempre Palante!: The Young Lords," in Torres and Velázquez, *The Puerto Rican Movement*, 218.

23. "What is Gay Liberation Front?" flyer, spring 1970, Gay Liberation Front file, Lesbian Herstory Archives, [Brooklyn], quoted in Kissack, "Freaking Fag Revolutionaries," 107.

24. "Handicapped [Movement] Says Protest Could Go On Indefinitely," *Santa Cruz (CA) Sentinel*, April 27, 1977, 33.

25. "Malcolm X Labor's Ally?" *1199 News*, Winter 1993, 27, quoted in Opie, *Upsetting the Apple Cart*, 47.

26. "Port City Hospital Strike State's Top News Story," *Aiken (South Carolina) Standard*, December 24, 1969, 13.

27. "Abernathy to Organize Working Poor with 'Soul Power, Union Power,'" *Greenville (SC) News*, August 15, 1969, 32.

28. Roy McHugh, "Press Box: Putting the Squeeze on Grapes," *Pittsburgh Press*, August 24, 1969, section 4, page 2.

29. Quoted in Ellen Cantarow, "Jessie Lopez De La Cruz: The Battle for Farmworkers' Rights," in Cantarow, O'Malley, and Strom, *Moving the Mountain*, 151.

30. Marion K. Sanders, "James Haughton Wants 500,000 More Jobs," *New York Times Sunday Magazine*, September 14, 1969, 124.

31. Philip Shabecoff, "Black Unionists Form Coalition," *New York Times*, October 3, 1972, 33.

32. Ricki Fulman, "Get Off My Back, Don't 'Fly' Me," *New York Daily News*, September 13, 1974, final edition, 58.

33. Mike LaVelle, "Blue Collar Views: Stewardesses Recoil Over Ads," *Chicago Tribune*, August 22, 1974, 18.

34. "Playboy Bunny Bites Back," *Kansas City (MO) Times*, October 23, 1972, 2A.

35. "We Move Forward!" *Union W.A.G.E.*, January–February 1972, 1.

36. Labor Leadership Assembly for Peace, policy statement, reprinted in "Labor Leaders Split With Johnson On Vietnam War," *Gazette and Daily* (York, PA), December 14, 1967, 25.

37. Gary Kapanowski, interview by Miriam Frank, February 12, 2001, quoted in Frank, *Out in the Union*, 69.

38. Hobson, *Lavender and Red*, 89.

39. Coyle, Hershatter, and Honig, "Women at Farah," 258.

40. Ibid., 260–61.

41. Crystal Lee Sutton, oral history, n.d., in Victoria Byerly, *Hard Times Cotton Mill Girls: Personal Histories of Womanhood and Poverty in the South* (Ithaca, NY: ILR Press, 1986), 206–7.

42. Gary Bryner, interview by Studs Terkel, in Terkel, *Working: People Talk About What They Do All Day and How They Feel About What They Do* (1974; repr., New York: The New Press, 1997), 193.

43. John Carson Parker, "Commentary: The Options Ahead for the Debt Economy," *Business Week*, October 12, 1974, 120.

44. Samuel P. Huntington, "The United States," in Michael J. Crozier, Samuel P. Huntington, and Joji Watanuki, *The Crisis of Democracy: Report on the Governability of Democracies to the Trilateral Commission* (New York: New York University Press, 1975), 113.

45. Steven Rattner, "Volcker Asserts U.S. Must Trim Living Standard," *New York Times*, October 18, 1979, A1.

46. "UAW Chief Quitting 'Useless' Price Panel," *Chicago Tribune*, July 20, 1978, section 4, page 7.

47. "104 Labor, Minority Groups Organize to Battle 'Right-Wing Corporate Power,'" *Los Angeles Times*, October 18, 1978, part 1, page 16.

Balser, Diane. *Sisterhood & Solidarity: Feminism and Labor in Modern Times*. Boston: South End Press, 1987.

Barnard, John. *American Vanguard: The United Auto Workers During the Reuther Years, 1935–1970*. Detroit: Wayne State University Press, 2004.

Brecher, Jeremy. *Strike!* Rev. ed. Boston: South End Press, 1997.

Brody, David. *Workers in Industrial America: Essays on the Twentieth Century Struggle*. 2nd ed. New York: Oxford University Press, 1993.

Buhle, Paul. *Taking Care of Business: Samuel Gompers, George Meany, Lane Kirkland, and the Tragedy of American Labor*. New York: Monthly Review Press, 1999.

Cantarow, Ellen, with Susan Gushee O'Malley, and Sharon Hartman Strom. *Moving the Mountain: Women Working for Social Change*. Old Westbury, NY: Feminist Press, 1980.

Carmichael, Stokely, and Michael Thelwell. *Ready for Revolution: The Life and Struggles of Stokely Carmichael (Kwame Ture)*. New York: Scribner, 2003.

Carson, Clayborne. *In Struggle: SNCC and the Black Awakening of the 1960s*. Cambridge: Harvard University Press, 1995.

Cobble, Dorothy Sue. *The Other Women's Movement: Workplace Justice and Social Rights in Modern America*. Princeton, NJ: Princeton University Press, 2004.

———. "'A Spontaneous Loss of Enthusiasm': Workplace Feminism and the Transformation of Women's Service Jobs in the 1970s," *International Labor and Working-Class History*, no. 56 (Fall 1999): 23–44.

Coyle, Laurie, Gail Hershatter, and Emily Honig. "Women at Farah: An Unfinished Story." In *A Needle, a Bobbin, a Strike: Women Needleworkers in America*, edited by Joan M. Jensen and Sue Davidson, 227–77. Philadelphia: Temple University Press, 1984.

Dittmer, John. *Local People: The Struggle for Civil Rights in Mississippi*. Urbana: University of Illinois Press, 1994.

Donner, Frank J. *The Age of Surveillance: The Aims and Methods of America's Political Intelligence System*. New York: Knopf, 1980.

Fletcher, Bill, and Fernando Gapasin. *Solidarity Divided: The Crisis in Organized Labor and a New Path Toward Social Justice*. Berkeley: University of California Press, 2008.

Foner, Philip S. *Organized Labor and the Black Worker, 1619–1973*. New York: International Publishers, 1976.

———. *Women and the American Labor Movement: From World War I to the Present*. New York: Free Press, 1980.

Foner, Philip S., and Ronald L. Lewis, eds. *The Black Worker: A Documentary History from Colonial Times to the Present*. Vol. 7, *The Black Worker Since the AFL-CIO Merger, 1955–1980*. Philadelphia: Temple University Press, 1984.

Frank, Miriam. *Out in the Union: A Labor History of Queer America*. Philadelphia: Temple University Press, 2014.

Ganster, Paul, ed. *The Maquiladora Program in Tri-National Perspective: Mexico, Japan, and the United States*. San Diego, CA: Institute for Regional Studies of San Diego State University, 1987. http://irsc.sdsu.edu/docs/pubs/border_issue/BIS2.PDF.

García, Ignacio M. *Chicanismo: The Forging of a Militant Ethos Among Mexican Americans*. Tucson: University of Arizona Press, 1997.

Georgakas, Dan, and Marvin Surkin. *Detroit, I Do Mind Dying: A Study in Urban Revolution*. 1975. Updated ed. Cambridge, MA: South End Press, 1998.

Green, James R. *The World of the Worker: Labor in Twentieth-Century America*. New York: Hill and Wang, 1980.

Hampton, Henry. *Collection. Film and Media Archive*. Washington University Libraries, St. Louis, MO.

Hampton, Henry, Steve Fayer, and Sarah Flynn. *Voices of Freedom: An Oral History of the Civil Rights Movement from the 1950s Through the 1980s*. New York: Bantam Books, 1990.

Harris, William Hamilton. *The Harder We Run: Black Workers Since the Civil War*. New York: Oxford University Press, 1982.

Hobson, Emily K. *Lavender and Red: Liberation and Solidarity in the Gay and Lesbian Left*. Oakland: University of California Press, 2016.

Hollibaugh, Amber. "Sexuality and the State: Defeat of the Briggs Amendment." [Interview of Hollibaugh by Diane Ehrensaft and Ruth Milkman]. *Socialist Review* no. 45 (May/June 1979): 55–72.

Jones, Charles E., ed. *The Black Panther Party (Reconsidered)*. Baltimore: Black Classic Press, 1998.

Kc, Diwas. "Of Consciousness and Criticism: Identity in the Intersections of the Gay Liberation Front and the Young Lords Party." Master's thesis, Sarah Lawrence College, 2005.

Kissack, Terence. "Freaking Fag Revolutionaries: New York's Gay Liberation Front, 1969–1971." *Radical History Review* no. 62 (Spring 1995): 104–34.

Lee, Chana Kai. *For Freedom's Sake: The Life of Fannie Lou Hamer.* Urbana: University of Illinois Press, 1999.

Levy, Peter B. *The New Left and Labor in the 1960s.* Urbana: University of Illinois Press, 1994.

Lichtenstein, Nelson. *State of the Union: A Century of American Labor.* Princeton, NJ: Princeton University Press, 2002.

McGuire, Danielle L. *At the Dark End of the Street: Black Women, Rape, and Resistance—a New History of the Civil Rights Movement from Rosa Parks to the Rise of Black Power.* New York: Alfred A. Knopf, 2010.

Moody, Kim. *An Injury to All: The Decline of American Unionism.* London: Verso, 1988.

Muñoz, Carlos. *Youth, Identity, Power: The Chicano Movement.* London: Verso, 2007.

Nadasen, Premilla. *Welfare Warriors: The Welfare Rights Movement in the United States.* New York: Routledge, 2005.

Opie, Frederick Douglass. *Upsetting the Apple Cart: Black-Latino Coalitions in New York City from Protest to Public Office.* New York: Columbia University Press, 2015.

Payne, Charles. *I've Got the Light of Freedom: The Organizing Tradition and the Mississippi Freedom Struggle.* Berkeley: University of California Press, 1995.

Seifer, Nancy. *Nobody Speaks for Me!: Self-Portraits of American Working Class Women.* New York: Simon & Schuster, 1976.

Sidel, Ruth. *Urban Survival: The World of Working-Class Women.* Boston: Beacon Press, 1978.

Shockley, John S. *Chicano Revolt in a Texas Town.* Notre Dame, IN: University of Notre Dame Press, 1974.

Sonnie, Amy, and James Tracy. *Hillbilly Nationalists, Urban Race Rebels, and Black Power: Community Organizing in Radical Times.* Brooklyn: Melville House, 2011.

Theoharis, Jeanne. *The Rebellious Life of Mrs. Rosa Parks.* Boston: Beacon Press, 2013.

Thompson, Heather Ann. *Blood in the Water: The Attica Prison Uprising of 1971 and Its Legacy.* New York: Pantheon Books, 2016.

Torres, Andrés, and José E. Velázquez. *The Puerto Rican Movement: Voices from the Diaspora.* Philadelphia: Temple University Press, 1998.

West, Guida. *The National Welfare Rights Movement: The Social Protest of Poor Women.* New York: Praeger, 1981.

Whalen, Carmen Teresa, and Víctor Vázquez-Hernández. *The Puerto Rican Diaspora: Historical Perspectives.* Philadelphia: Temple University Press, 2005.

Woodard, Komozi. *A Nation Within a Nation: Amiri Baraka (LeRoi Jones) and Black Power Politics.* Chapel Hill: University of North Carolina Press, 1999.

11: Hard Times

1. Donald John Devine, *Reagan's Terrible Swift Sword: Reforming & Controlling the Federal Bureaucracy* (Ottawa, IL: Jameson Books, 1991), 84.

2. AFL-CIO press release, quoted in Furr, "The AFT, the CIA, and *Solidarność*," 32.

3. Karen J. Hossfeld, "Hiring Immigrant Women: Silicon Valley's 'Simple Formula,'" in *Women of Color in U.S. Society*, ed. Maxine Baca Zinn and Dill Bonnie Thornton (Philadelphia: Temple University Press, 1994), 75.

4. Clyde H. Farnsworth, "Washington Raises Level of Criticism," *New York Times*, March 27, 1982, 29; Patrick D. Hazard, "Days of Bashing Toyotas in Protest Are Over," *The Press Democrat* (Santa Rosa, CA), July 29, 1983, 27.

5. A federal prosecutor later charged both men with violating Vincent Chin's civil rights. The older of the two defendants, Ronald Ebens, was convicted and sentenced to twenty-five years. His stepson, Michael Nitz, was acquitted, and Ebens's conviction was overturned on appeal. See Darden and Thomas, *Detroit*, 155–80.

6. Bill Parker, "Plant Closings and the Alternatives: The Chrysler Experience" (mimeo, April 1982), 17, quoted in Moody, *An Injury to All*, 166.

7. "Concessionary Bargaining: Will the New Cooperation Last?" *BusinessWeek*, June 14, 1982, 66.

8. Steven Greenhouse, "The Corporate Assault on Wages," *New York Times*, October 9, 1983, F1.

9. Gregory Stricharchuk, "Tying the Knot: With Ranks Thinning, Unions Seek Mergers to Retain Their Clout," *Wall Street Journal*, January 18, 1985, Eastern edition, 1.

10. William Serrin, "Labor's Changing Outlook: Can Unions Achieve a Comeback?" *New York Times*, February 22, 1986, 8.

11. William Serrin, "Labor's New Militants are Getting More Pushy," *New York Times*, August 31, 1986, E5.

12. Jack Metzgar, "'Running the Plant Backwards' in UAW Region 5," *Labor Research Review*, no. 7 (Fall 1985): 35.

13. Drummond Ayres Jr., "Coal Strike: Armageddon for U.M.W. and Leader?" *New York Times*, August 15, 1989, A17.

14. Kwong, *The New Chinatown*, 152.

15. Delgado, *New Immigrants, Old Unions*, 22. Delgado identifies the company, its proprietor, its workers, and their union by pseudonyms, but local press coverage of the story reveals the real names. See Harry Bernstein, "Illegal Alien Issue Raised in East L.A. Dispute," *Los Angeles Times*, September 18, 1985, part IV, 1.

16. J.F. Otero, "Immigration Policy Drifting toward Disaster," *AFL-CIO American Federationist*, February 1981, 2.

17. Macario Camorlinga, testimony in Milkman and Wong, *Voices from the Front Lines*, 36.

18. McKibben, "New Believers," 52.

19. "Happy 30th Anniversary, Clean Water for North Carolina!" *Clean Currents* (Summer 2014): 3, www.cwfnc.org/documents/CleanCurrents-Summer-2014.pdf.

20. Hoerr, "Solidaritas at Harvard," n.p.

21. *AFL-CIO News*, quoted in Carolyn J. Jacobson and Susan L. Phillips, "Women and the Labor Press: Emerging from the Shadows," in *The New Labor Press: Journalism for a Changing Union Movement*, ed. Sam Pizzigati and Fred J. Solowey (Ithaca, NY: ILR Press, 1992), 114.

22. Eisenberg, *We'll Call You if We Need You*, 78.

23. John T. Scally, "Winning Through Staff Unionism," in Shostak, *For Labor's Sake*, 296.

24. Voss and Sherman, "Breaking the Iron Law of Oligarchy," 321.

25. Greg Tarpinian, quoted in Stephen Franklin, "Steelworkers' Victory an Ending Labor Likes," *Chicago Tribune*, May 29, 1992, section 3, 4.

26. Bronfenbrenner, "We'll Close!," 9.

Bass, G. Nelson, III. "Organized Labor and U.S. Foreign Policy: The Solidarity Center in Historical Context." PhD diss., Florida International University, 2012.

Battista, Andrew. "Unions and Cold War Foreign Policy in the 1980s: The National Labor Committee, the AFL-CIO, and Central America." *Diplomatic History* 26, no. 3 (July 2002): 419–51.

Brecher, Jeremy, and Tim Costello, eds. *Building Bridges: The Emerging Grassroots Coalition of Labor and Community.* New York: Monthly Review Press, 1990.

Bronfenbrenner, Kate. "We'll Close! Plant Closings, Plant-Closing Threats, Union Organizing and NAFTA." *Multinational Monitor* 18, no. 3 (March 1997): 8–13.

Buhle, Paul. *Taking Care of Business: Samuel Gompers, George Meany, Lane Kirkland, and the Tragedy of American Labor.* New York: Monthly Review Press, 1999.

Clark, Paul F. "Organizing the Organizers: Professional Staff Unionism in the American Labor Movement." *ILR Review* 42, no. 4 (July 1989): 584–99.

Cohen, Sheila. *Ramparts of Resistance: Why Workers Lost Their Power, and How to Get It Back.* London: Pluto Press, 2006.

Cobble, Dorothy Sue, ed. *Women and Unions: Forging a Partnership.* Ithaca, NY: ILR Press, 1993.

Darden, Joe T., and Richard W. Thomas. *Detroit: Race Riots, Racial Conflicts, and Efforts to Bridge the Racial Divide.* East Lansing: Michigan State University Press, 2013.

Delgado, Héctor L. *New Immigrants, Old Unions: Organizing Undocumented Workers in Los Angeles.* Philadelphia: Temple University Press, 1993.

Dones, Nicola, and Netsy Firestein. "Labor's Participation in Work/Family Issues: Successes and Obstacles." In *Learning from the Past—Looking to the Future*, edited by Christopher Beem and Jody Heymann, 1–24. Racine, WI/Boston: Work, Family and Democracy Project, 2002. www.working-families.org/publications/labor_participation.pdf.

Dunn, Geoffrey. "*Watsonville on Strike*: Reflexivity and Conflict." *Jump Cut*, no. 35 (April 1990): 117–20. www.ejumpcut.org/archive/onlinessays/JC35folder/WatsonvilleStrike.html.

Eisenberg, Susan. *We'll Call You If We Need You: Experiences of Women Working Construction.* Ithaca, NY: ILR Press, 1998.

Frank, Dana. *Buy American: The Untold Story of Economic Nationalism.* Boston: Beacon Press, 1999.

Frank, Miriam. *Out in the Union: a Labor History of Queer America.* Philadelphia: Temple University Press, 2014.

Furr, Grover C. "The AFT, the CIA, and *Solidarność*." *Comment* [Montclair State College, NJ] 1, no. 2 (Spring 1982): 31–34. https://msuweb.montclair.edu/~furrg/furraft82.pdf.

Gilpin, Toni, et al. *On Strike for Respect: The Clerical & Technical Workers' Strike at Yale University (1984–85).* Chicago: C.H. Kerr, 1988.

Green, Hardy. *On Strike at Hormel: The Struggle for a Democratic Labor Movement.* Philadelphia: Temple University Press, 1990.

Halley, Patrick S. *Wimpy.* Charleston, SC: BookSurge Publishing, 2008.

Hatch, Julie, and Angela Clinton. "Job Growth in the 1990s: A Retrospect." *Monthly Labor Review* 123, no. 12 (December 2000): 3–18.

Hathaway, Dale A. *Can Workers Have a Voice?: The Politics of Deindustrialization in Pittsburgh.* University Park, PA: Pennsylvania State University Press, 1993.

Hirsch, Barry T., and David A. Macpherson. *Union Membership and Coverage Database.* Last modified January 21, 2018. www.unionstats.com.

Hoerr, John. "Solidaritas at Harvard." *The American Prospect*, no. 14 (Summer 1993). http:// prospect.org/article/solidaritas-harvard.

———. *We Can't Eat Prestige: The Women Who Organized Harvard*. Philadelphia: Temple University Press, 1997.

Holcomb, Desma, and Nancy Wohlforth. "The Fruits of Our Labor: Pride at Work." *New Labor Forum*, no. 8 (Spring/Summer 2001): 9–20.

International Centre for Trade Union Rights. *Trade Unions of the World*. 6th ed. London: John Harper Publishing, 2005.

Juravich, Tom, and Kate Bronfenbrenner. *Ravenswood: The Steelworkers' Victory and the Revival of American Labor*. Ithaca, NY: ILR Press, 1999.

Kingsolver, Barbara. *Holding the Line: Women in the Great Arizona Mine Strike of 1983*. Ithaca, NY: ILR Press, 1989.

Kwong, Peter. *The New Chinatown*. New York: Hill and Wang, 1987.

Labor Notes (published monthly by the Labor Education and Research Project, Detroit). 1993–96.

Labor Research Review (published irregularly by the Midwest Center for Labor Research, Chicago). 1982–96.

Lichtenstein, Nelson. *State of the Union: A Century of American Labor*. Princeton, NJ: Princeton University Press, 2002.

Louie, Miriam Ching Yoon. *Sweatshop Warriors: Immigrant Women Workers Take on the Global Factory*. Cambridge, MA: South End Press, 2001.

MacLean, Nancy. *Freedom Is Not Enough: The Opening of the American Workplace*. Cambridge, MA: Harvard University Press, 2006.

Mantsios, Gregory, ed. *A New Labor Movement for the New Century*. New York: Monthly Review Press, 1998.

Martin, Molly, ed. *Hard-Hatted Women: Stories of Struggle and Success in the Trades*. Berkeley, CA: Seal Press, 1988.

McCartin, Joseph Anthony. *Collision Course: Ronald Reagan, the Air Traffic Controllers, and the Strike That Changed America*. New York: Oxford University Press, 2011.

McKibben, Bill. "New Believers." *Mother Jones*, April 1989, 38–41, 52.

Milkman, Ruth, and Kent Wong. *Voices from the Front Lines: Organizing Immigrant Workers in Los Angeles* [*Voces desde la lucha: la organización de los trabajadores inmigrantes en Los Angeles*]. Translated by Luis Escala Rabadán. Los Angeles, CA: Center for Labor Research and Education, UCLA, 2000.

Moccio, Francine A. *Live Wire: Women and Brotherhood in the Electrical Industry*. Philadelphia: Temple University Press, 2009.

Moody, Kim. *An Injury to All: The Decline of American Unionism*. London: Verso, 1988.

———.*Workers in a Lean World: Unions in the International Economy*. London: Verso, 2001.

Park, Valerie Anastasia. "United Tradeswomen: The Nuts and Bolts of Women's Grassroots Activism in the New York City Construction Industry, 1979–1984." Master's thesis, Sarah Lawrence College, 2001.

Payne, Richard J. "Black Americans and the Demise of Constructive Engagement." *Africa Today* 33, nos. 2–3 (2nd –3rd Quarter 1986): 71–89.

Quan, Katie. "Memories of the 1982 ILGWU Strike in New York Chinatown." *Amerasia Journal* 35, no. 1 (2009): 76–91.

Rachleff, Peter J. *Hard-Pressed in the Heartland: The Hormel Strike and the Future of the Labor Movement*. Boston: South End Press, 1993.

Ryan, Francis. *AFSCME's Philadelphia Story: Municipal Workers and Urban Power in the Twentieth Century*. Philadelphia: Temple University Press, 2011.

Scipes, Kim. *AFL-CIO's Secret War against Developing Country Workers: Solidarity or Sabotage?* Lanham, MD: Lexington Books, 2010.

Shabecoff, Philip. "Dispute Rises on Working at Home for Pay." *New York Times*, March 10, 1981, A1.

Shostak, Arthur B., ed. *For Labor's Sake: Gains and Pains as Told by 28 Creative Inside Reformers*. Lanham, MD: University Press of America, 1995.

Sims, Beth. *Workers of the World Undermined: American Labor's Role in U.S. Foreign Policy*. Boston: South End Press, 1992.

Tait, Vanessa. *Poor Workers' Unions: Rebuilding Labor from Below*. Cambridge, MA: South End Press, 2005.

Voss, Kim and Rachel Sherman. "Breaking the Iron Law of Oligarchy: Union Revitalization in the American Labor Movement." *American Journal of Sociology* 106, no. 2 (September 2000): 303–49.

Wilkerson, Jessie. "Out Front and Strong: Local Women of the Tennessee Committee on Occupational Safety and Health." Master's thesis, Sarah Lawrence College, 2006.

Ziedenberg, Jason, and Vincent Schiraldi. *The Punishing Decade: Prison and Jail Estimates at the Millennium*. Washington, D.C.: Justice Policy Institute, 1999.

12: One Step Forward, Two Steps Back

1. Sweeney and Kusnet, *America Needs a Raise*, 56.

2. Ibid., 5.

3. Alexander G. Higgins, "World Leaders Put on Guard about Global Financial Crisis," *Indianapolis Star*, January 31, 1999, A12.

4. Kate Shaughnessy, personal communication, July 2000.

5. We are indebted to the veteran organizer Daisy Anarchy for much of the information in this paragraph.

6. David Firestone, "Union Victory at Plant in South Is Labor Milestone," *New York Times*, June 25, 1999, A16.

7. "Face Value: Mother Jones Meets the Microchip," *The Economist*, June 12, 1999, 64.

8. Bob Herbert, "A Workers' Rebellion," *New York Times*, August 7, 1997, A31.

9. AFL-CIO Executive Council, Statement on Immigration, February 16, 2000, in *The United States Since 1945: A Documentary Reader*, ed. Robert P. Ingalls and David K. Johnson (Oxford, UK: Wiley-Blackwell, 2009), 203.

10. Kim Marks, Alliance for Sustainable Jobs and Environment, remarks during the panel discussion "Community-Labor Alliances" (at the conference "A Declaration of Solidarity: The ILWU Struggle and the Future of Labor," Olympia, WA, December 14, 2002).

11. Quoted in Hall, "7 Days in June," 14.

12. Paul Osterman, "New Rules for the New Economy," *Boston Globe*, September 5, 1999, D7.

13. "Labor and the War," *Labor Notes*, November 2001, 9.

14. Jo Cagan, "A Volunteer's Story," *Labor Notes*, October 2001, 5.

15. U.S. District Judge William Alsup, Plaintiff's Temporary Restraining Order, October 8, 2002, quoted in "No Contempt of Court Charges in West Coast Port Battle," *Oakland Post*, November 20, 2002, 2.

16. Peter Olney, "On the Waterfront: Analysis of ILWU Lockout," *New Labor Forum* 12, no. 2 (Summer 2003): 36.

17. "High Noon in NYC," *Investor's Business Daily*, December 21, 2005, A10.

18. Stephen Lerner, "An Immodest Proposal: A New Architecture for the House of Labor," *New Labor Forum* 12, no. 2 (Summer 2003): 28.

19. Ibid., 25.

20. Quoted in Harry Kelber, "Construction Unions Face Dilemma as Carpenters Bolt from AFLCIO," *Labor Educator*, April 3, 2001, www.laboreducator.org/inside3.htm.

21. Jane Slaughter, "Sweetheart Contracts Are No Answer," *New Labor Forum* 12, no. 3 (Fall 2003): 75.

22. Matt Noyes, "Making a Splash: SEIU's Unite to Win and the 'Free and Open Debate' on Labor's Future," *Union Democracy Review*, n.d., Internet exclusive, www.uniondemocracy.org /UDR/83SEIU's%20Unite%20to%20Win.htm.

23. Ibid.

24. Quoted in Roberta Wood, "Break in Labor Unity Challenges AFL-CIO Delegates; but Convention Adopts Sweeping Leadership Diversity Plan, Call to Bring Troops Home," *People's Weekly World*, July 30, 2005, 1.

25. Change to Win Strategic Organizing Center, "New Labor Federation Pledges to Carry Out Most Aggressive Organizing Campaign in 50 Years," Change to Win, September 27, 2005, www.changetowin.org/news/new-labor-federation-pledges-carry-out-most-aggressive organizing-campaign-50-years.

26. Stern, *A Country That Works*, 70–71.

27. "Andy Stern: The New Boss," Lesley Stahl, *60 Minutes*, aired May 12, 2006, on CBS, transcript (www.cbsnews.com/news/andy-stern-the-new-boss), 2.

28. Kirkland, "The New Face of Labor," 126; "Hot Topic: The UAW's Awakening," *Wall Street Journal*, Eastern edition, September 29, 2007, A8.

29. Hurd, "U.S. Labor 2006," 316.

30. Jerry Tucker, "A New Labor Federations Claims Its Space," *Labor Notes*, November 2005, 11.

Allen, Joe. "When Big Brown Shut Down: The UPS Strike Ten Years On." *International Socialist Review*, no. 55 (September-October 2007). http://isreview.org/issues/55/bigbrown .shtml.

American Federation of State, County and Municipal Employees. "AFSCME Poll Shows Doctors Fed Up with Healthcare System, Want Collective Bargaining." Press release, June 16, 2001. www.afscme.org/news/press-room/press-releases/2001/afscme-poll-shows-doctors -fed-up-with-healthcare-system-want-collective-bargaining.

Beachy, Ben. *NAFTA's 20-Year Legacy and the Fate of the Trans-Pacific Partnership*. Washington, D.C.: Public Citizen's Global Trade Watch, 2014.

Brooks, Siobhan. "Organizing from Behind the Glass: Exotic Dancers Ready to Unionize." *Z Magazine*, January 1997, 11–14.

Cummings, Richard. "US: Lockheed Stock and Two Smoking Barrels." CorpWatch: Holding Corporations Accountable. January 16, 2007. www.corpwatch.org/article.php?id=14307.

Day, Mark. "A Brief History of the UPS Teamsters and the Communication Techniques Leading Up to the 1997 UPS Strike." Unpublished paper in possession of the author, 2011.

Dudzic, Mark, and Derek Seidman. "What Happened to the Labor Party?: An Interview with Mark Dudzic. *Jacobin*, October 11, 2015. www.jacobinmag.com/2015/10/tony-mazzochi -mark-dudzic-us-labor-party-wto-nafta-globalization-democrats-union.

"Editorial: Toward a New Washington Consensus," *Multinational Monitor*, September 2001, 5.

Feeley, Dianne. "U.S. Unions & the War." *Against the Current*, no. 113 (November 2004): 4.

Fine, Janice. "Building Community Unions." *The Nation*, January 1, 2001: 18–22.

Fletcher, Bill, and Fernando Gapasin. *Solidarity Divided: The Crisis in Organized Labor and a New Path Toward Social Justice*. Berkeley: University of California Press, 2008.

Francia, Peter L. *The Future of Organized Labor in American Politics*. New York: Columbia University Press, 2006.

Hall, Mike. "7 Days in June." *America @ Work*, August 1999, 13–15.

Hartung, William D. *Prophets of War: Lockheed Martin and the Making of the Military-Industrial Complex*. New York: Nation Books, 2011.

Hirsch, Barry T., and David A. Macpherson. *Union Membership and Coverage Database*. Last modified January 21, 2018. www.unionstats.com.

Hurd, Richard W. "U.S. Labor 2006: Strategic Developments Across the Divide." *Journal of Labor Research* 28, no. 2, (Spring 2007): 313–25.

Kirkland, Rik. "The New Face of Labor." *Fortune*, October 16, 2006, 122–32.

Labor Notes (published monthly by the Labor Education and Research Project, Detroit). 1995–2006.

Leadership Conference on Civil and Human Rights. *Railroaded Out of Their Rights: How a Labor Law Loophole Prevents FedEx Express Employees from Being Represented by a Union*. Washington, Leadership Conference on Civil and Human Rights, 2010. https://web .archive.org/web/20100626131136/http://civilrights.org/publications/fedex-rla-loophole/rla -fedex-loophole.pdf.

Loprest, Pamela. "How Are Families that Left Welfare Doing? A Comparison of Early and Recent Welfare Leavers." *New Federalism: National Survey of America's Families; An Urban Institute Program to Assess Changing Social Policies*. Series B, No. B-36. Washington: Urban Institute, April 2001. http://files.eric.ed.gov/fulltext/ED452329.pdf.

Mantsios, Gregory, ed. *A New Labor Movement for the New Century*. New York: Monthly Review Press, 1998.

McAlevey, Jane, and Bob Ostertag. *Raising Expectations (and Raising Hell): My Decade Fighting for the Labor Movement*. London: Verso, 2012.

Minchin, Timothy J. *Labor Under Fire: A History of the AFL-CIO Since 1979*. Chapel Hill: University of North Carolina Press, 2017.

Moberg, David. "Union Cities." *American Prospect*. September 11, 2000, 35–37.

Moffitt, Robert, and Jennifer Roff. *The Diversity of Welfare Leavers. Welfare, Children & Families: A Three City Study*. Policy Brief 00-2. Baltimore: Welfare, Children & Families Study, Johns Hopkins University, [2000]. http://files.eric.ed.gov/fulltext/ED450180.pdf.

Moody, Kim. *US Labor in Trouble and Transition: The Failure of Reform from Above, the Promise of Revival from Below*. London: Verso, 2007.

Mort, Jo-Ann, ed. *Not Your Father's Union Movement: Inside the AFL-CIO*. London: Verso, 1999.

New Labor Forum (published three times a year by the Murphy Institute for Worker Education and Labor Studies of the City University of New York). 1997–2006.

Page, Leonard R. "The NLRA at 70: Perspectives from the Office of the General Counsel." *Labor Law Journal* 56, no. 3 (Fall 2005): 186–91.

Rosenblum, Jonathan, "The Battle in Seattle, 15 Years On: How an Unsung Hero Kept the Movements United." *YES! Magazine*, December 1, 2014. www.yesmagazine.org/people-power/battle-in-seattle-wto-15-years-on-unsung-hero-tyree-scott.

Scott, Robert E. "NAFTA's Impact on the States." Economic Policy Institute, April 10, 2001. www.epi.org/publication/briefingpapers_nafta01_impactstates.

Smith, Robert Michael. *From Blackjacks to Briefcases: A History of Commercialized Strikebreaking and Unionbusting in the United States*. Athens: Ohio University Press, 2003.

Stern, Andy. *A Country That Works: Getting America Back on Track*. New York: Free Press, 2006.

Sweeney, John J., and David Kusnet. *America Needs a Raise: Fighting for Economic Security and Social Justice*. Boston: Houghton Mifflin, 1996.

"Toward a New Washington Consensus." *Multinational Monitor*, September 2001, 5.

US Bureau of Labor Statistics. *National Labor Relations Board (NLRB) Union Representation Elections, 1997–2009*, by Drew M. Simmons. June 30, 2010.www.bls.gov/opub/mlr/cwc/national-labor-relations-board-nlrb-union-representation-elections-1997-2009.pdf.

Wilson, Joseph, Manning Marable, and Immanuel Ness. *Race and Labor Matters in the New U.S. Economy*. Lanham, MD: Rowman & Littlefield, 2006.

Wright, Carter. "A Clean Sweep: Justice for Janitors." *Multinational Monitor*, January–February 2001, 12–14.

13: Workers of the World

1. Baul Boatin, interview by Judith Stepan-Norris [September 1983 or August 1984], quoted in Stepan-Norris and Maurice Zeitlin, *Talking Union* (Urbana: University of Illinois Press, 1996), 6.

2. CNN *Moneyline*, December 8, 1998, quoted in Janet Lowe, *Welch: An American Icon* (New York: John Wiley & Sons, 2001), 140

3. Roman and Arregui, *Continental Crucible*, 58.

4. Harvey, *Brief History of Neoliberalism*, 2–4.

5. "Purchase Confidently with Long & Foster," *Courier-Post* (Camden, NJ), April 12, 2009, 2E.

6. Richard Trumka, untitled remarks at the conference "Global Companies—Global Unions—Global Research—Global Campaigns," New York City, February 9, 2006, quoted in Bronfenbrenner, ed., *Global Unions*, 1.

7. Aaron Bernstein, "Welch's March to the South," *BusinessWeek*, December 6, 1999, 74.

8. Anthony Bianco and Wendy Zellner, "Is Wal-Mart Too Powerful?" *BusinessWeek*, October 6, 2003, 102.

9. Eyal Press, "Freeport-McMoRan at Home and Abroad," *The Nation*, July 31, 1995, 126.

10. Charles Lewis, "The Treaty No One Could Read: How Lobbyists and Business Quietly Forged NAFTA," *Washington Post*, June 27, 1993, 2.

11. "30-Second Politics," *Washington Post*, October 13, 1993, A14.

12. James Robinson, quoted in MacArthur, *The Selling of Free Trade*, 275.

13. Michael Wessell, quoted in MacArthur, *The Selling of Free Trade*, 275.

14. U.S. Department of Labor, Bureau of International Labor Affairs, U.S. National Administrative Office, *North American Agreement on Labor Cooperation: A Guide* (Washington, D.C.: U.S. Department of Labor, 2005), www.dol.gov/ilab/trade/agreements/naalcgd.htm.

15. *"Charro"* became the popular adjective for do-nothing unions in the late 1940s, when Mexico's government placed sellouts in charge of traditionally militant unions and railroad workers found themselves under the thumb of Jesús Diaz de León, known as El Charro because he enjoyed dressing up like a traditional cowboy. See Robert F. Alegre and Elena Poniatowska, *Railroad Radicals in Cold War Mexico: Gender, Class, and Memory* (Lincoln: University of Nebraska Press, 2013), 57.

16. Jeff Faux, "NAFTA's Impact on U.S. Workers," *Working Economics Blog*, Economic Policy Institute, December 9, 2013, www.epi.org/blog/naftas-impact-workers.

17. U.S. Chamber of Commerce, *NAFTA Triumphant: Assessing Two Decades of Gains in Trade, Growth and Jobs* (Washington, D.C.: U.S. Chamber of Commerce, 2015), www.uschamber.com /sites/default/files/documents/files/nafta_triumphant_updated_2015.pdf.

18. Charles E. Mercer, quoted in Gregory Chancelada and Jack Naudi, "Look for the Union Label—If You Can Find It," *Lansing (MI) State Journal*, Business Weekly, May 31, 2004, 14.

19. Dana Frank, interview by Chris Brooks, "When 'Buying American' Is Selling Out," *Labor Notes*, May 2017, 6.

20. Quoted in John P. Moody, "USW Split," *Pittsburgh Post-Gazette*, March 12, 1984, 9.

21. Jonathan Tasini, "Murder Charges Against Rana Plaza Owners Who Killed 1,137 Human Beings," *Working Life*, June 1, 2015, www.workinglife.org/general-interest/murder -chargesagainst-rana-plaza-owners-who-killed-1137-human-beings.

22. "Five Years On, Nanhai Honda Workers Want More from Their Trade Union," *China Labour Bulletin*, May 15, 2015, www.clb.org.hk/en/content/five-years-nanhai-honda-workers -wantmore-their-trade-union.

23. "Declaration on Social Rights and Industrial Relationships at Volkswagen," June 6, 2002, 1, IndustriALL Global Union, www.industriallunion.org/sites/default/files/uploads /documents/GFAs/Volkswagen/vweng.pdf.

24. Ruth Needleman, "The Steelworkers Union Goes Global," *New Labor Forum* 17, no. 2 (Summer 2008): 85.

25. Anonymous organizer, interview by Jamie K. McCallum, 2010, quoted in McCallum, *Global Unions*, 57.

26. Quoted in Lynn Williams, *One Day Longer: A Memoir* (Toronto: University of Toronto Press, 2011), 263.

27. Needleman, "The Steelworkers Union Goes Global," 86.

28. Juravich and Bronfenbrenner, "Out of the Ashes," 260.

29. Lenny T. Mendonca, "Shaking Up the Labor Movement: An Interview with the Head of the Service Employees International Union," *McKinsey Quarterly* 1 (March 2006): 56.

30. Anonymous organizer, interview by Jamie K. McCallum, 2010, quoted in McCallum, *Global Unions*, 69.

31. Anonymous activist, interview by Jamie K. McCallum, 2010, quoted in McCallum, *Global Unions*, 150.

32. These were the American Institute for Free Labor Development, the African-American Labor Center, the Asian American Free Labor Institute, and the Free Trade Union Institute, all discussed in previous chapters.

33. Resolution No. 6, California Labor Federation Convention, San Diego, July 13, 2004, reprinted in Fred Hirsch, "Build Unity and Trust Among Workers Worldwide," *LabourNet*, July 29, 2004, www.labournet.net/world/0407/hirsch.html.

34. Ibid.

35. Quoted in Moberg, "Solidarity Without Borders," 48.

Adams, Roy J. "Canada-U.S. Labor Link Under Stress." *Industrial Relations* 15, no. 3 (October 1976): 295–312.

Bacon, David. *Building a Culture of Cross-border Solidarity*. Institute for Research on Labor and Employment Reports. Los Angeles: Institute for Transnational Social Change, University of California at Los Angeles Labor Center, 2011. http://www.escholarship.org/uc/item/05f6g6s7.

———. *The Children of NAFTA: Labor Wars on the U.S./Mexico Border*. Berkeley: University of California Press, 2004.

———. *The Right to Stay Home: How US Policy Drives Mexican Migration*. Boston: Beacon Press, 2013.

Bass, G. Nelson, III. "Organized Labor and U.S. Foreign Policy: the Solidarity Center in Historical Context." PhD diss., Florida International University, 2012.

Bronfenbrenner, Kate, ed. *Global Unions: Challenging Transnational Capital Through Cross-Border Campaigns*. Ithaca, NY: ILR Press/Cornell University Press, 2007.

Caulfield, Norman. *NAFTA and Labor in North America*. Urbana: University of Illinois Press, 2010.

Erem, Suzan, and E. Paul Durrenberger. *On the Global Waterfront: The Fight to Free the Charleston 5*. New York: Monthly Review Press, 2008.

Frank, Dana. *Buy American: The Untold Story of Economic Nationalism*. Boston: Beacon Press, 1999.

Goethem, Geert van. *The Amsterdam International: The World of the International Federation of Trade Unions (IFTU), 1913–1945*. Aldershot, UK: Ashgate, 2006.

——— and Robert Anthony Waters. *American Labor's Global Ambassadors: The International History of the AFL-CIO During the Cold War*. New York: Palgrave Macmillan, 2013.

Goldfield, Michael, and Bryan D. Palmer. "Canada's Workers Movement: Uneven Developments." *Labour/Le Travail* 59 (Spring 2007): 149–77.

Harvey, David. *A Brief History of Neoliberalism*. Oxford, UK: Oxford University Press, 2000.

Hennessy, Rosemary. *Fires on the Border: The Passionate Politics of Labor Organizing on the Mexican Frontera*. Minneapolis: University of Minnesota Press, 2013.

Human Rights Watch. *A Strange Case: Violations of Workers' Freedom of Association in the United States by European Multinational Corporations*. New York: Human Rights Watch, 2010.

Institute on Taxation and Economic Policy and Citizens for Tax Justice. *Corporate Tax Dodging in the Fifty States, 2008–2010*. Washington: Citizens for Tax Justice and Institute on Taxation and Economic Policy, 2011. www.ctj.org/corporatetaxdodgers50states/CorporateTaxDodgers50StatesReport.pdf.

Juravich, Tom, and Bronfenbrenner, Kate. "Out of the Ashes: The Steelworkers' Global Campaign at Bridgestone/Firestone." In *Multinational Companies and Global Human Resource Strategies*, edited by W.N. Cooke, 249–67. Westport, CT: Quorum Books, 2001.

Labor Notes (published monthly by the Labor Research and Education Project, Detroit). 1994–2017.

MacArthur, John R. *The Selling of Free Trade: NAFTA, Washington, and the Subversion of American Democracy.* Berkeley: University of California Press, 2001.

McCallum, Jamie K. *Global Unions, Local Power: The New Spirit of Transnational Labor Organizing.* Ithaca, NY: ILR Press/Cornell University Press, 2013.

McIntyre, Robert S., Matthew Gardner, and Richard Phillips. *The Sorry State of Corporate Taxes: What Fortune 500 Firms Pay (or Don't Pay) in the USA and What They Pay Abroad—2008 to 2012.* Washington: Citizens for Tax Justice and Institute on Taxation and Economic Policy, 2014. www.ctj.org/corporatetaxdodgers/sorrystateofcorptaxes.pdf.

McKillen, Elizabeth. *Making the World Safe for Workers: Labor, the Left, and Wilsonian Internationalism.* Champaign: University of Illinois Press, 2013.

Moberg, David. "Solidarity Without Borders." *In These Times,* February 2007, 48–51.

Mokhiber, Russell, and Robert Weissman. *Corporate Predators: The Hunt for Mega-Profits and the Attack on Democracy.* Monroe, ME: Common Courage Press, 1999.

National Labor Committee Education Fund in Support of Worker and Human Rights in Central America U.S. and Comunicación Comunitaria. *The Wal-Martization of Alcoa: Alcoa's High Tech Auto Parts Sweatshop in Honduras Rocked by Corruption & Human Rights Scandal.* New York: National Labor Committee, 2007.

New Labor Forum (published three times a year by the Murphy Institute for Worker Education and Labor Studies of the City University of New York). 1997–2017.

Ojeda, Martha A., and Rosemary Hennessy. *NAFTA from Below: Maquiladora Workers, Farmers, and Indigenous Communities Speak Out on the Impact of Free Trade in Mexico.* San Antonio, TX: Coalition for Justice in the Maquiladoras, 2006.

Roman, Richard, and Edur Velasco Arregui. *Continental Crucible: Big Business, Workers and Unions in the Transformation of North America.* 2nd ed. Oakland, CA: PM Press, 2015.

Scipes, Kim. *AFL-CIO's Secret War Against Developing Country Workers: Solidarity or Sabotage?* Lanham, MD: Lexington Books, 2011.

———. "Labor Imperialism Redux? The AFL-CIO's Foreign Policy Since 1995." *Monthly Review* 57, no. 1 (May 2005): 8–15.

United States Department of Labor, Bureau of International Labor Affairs. Submissions under the North American Agreement on Labor Cooperation (NAALC). www.dol.gov/ilab/trade/agreements/naalc.htm.

United States International Trade Commission. *Economic Impact of Trade Agreements Implemented Under Trade Authorities Procedures, 2016 Report.* USITC publication 4614. June 2016. www.usitc.gov/publications/332/pub4614.pdf.

Williams, Lynn. *One Day Longer: A Memoir.* Toronto: University of Toronto Press, 2011.

14: Rising Tide

1. Victor Calderon, "Thousands Protest: Salinas Police Estimate 13,000 Turned Out," *The Californian* (Salinas, CA), May 2, 2006, 3A.

2. Thelma Guerrero, "'Silent Population' Shouts Its Values, Goals in Salem," *Statesman Journal* (Salem, OR), May 2, 2006, 2A.

3. Elizabeth Pierson, "Crowds Take to Austin's Streets to Push for Migrant Rights," *The Monitor* (McAllen, TX), May 2, 2006, 6.

4. Alan M. Valdez and Pilar Ulibarri de Rivera, "On 'Day Without,' Many Speak Out, Take to the Street," *Palm Beach Post* (West Palm Beach, FL), May 2, 2006, 4A.

5. Teresa Watanabe and Joe Mathews, "Unions Helped to Organize 'Day Without Immigrants,'" *Los Angeles Times* (Ventura County Edition), May 3, 2006, B9.

6. Elizabeth Crisp, "Raids Shake Up Community," *Hattiesburg (MS) American*, August 31, 2008, 10A.

7. "Striking Houston Workers Seek Higher Wages, Dignity," *Longview (TX) News-Journal*, November 5, 2006, 15A.

8. Daniel Nardini, "Victory for the Republic Workers," *Lawndale (IL) Bilingual News*, December 25, 2008, 22.

9. "AFL-CIO's Richard Trumka on Racism and Obama," July 1, 2008, YouTube, www .youtube.com/watch?v=7QIGJTHdH50.

10. Nelson Lichtenstein, "Labor's Role in the Obama Era: A Troublesome and Unreliable Ally?" *Dissent* (online), June 7, 2010, www.dissentmagazine.org/online_articles/labors-role-in -the-obama-era-a-troublesome-and-unreliable-ally.

11. Corey Williams, "Obama Speaks at End of Detroit Labor Day Parade," *Battle Creek (MI) Enquirer*, September 2, 2008, 4A.

12. "Remarks for Senator Barack Obama: AFL-CIO; Philadelphia, PA, April 2, 2008," Organizing for America, https://web.archive.org/web/20090707085244/http://www.barackobama .com/2008/04/02/remarks_for_senator_barack_oba_3.php; Michael O'Brien, "Obama Says He'll 'Keep On Fighting' to Pass 'Card Check' Bill," *The Hill*, August 4, 2010, http://thehill .com/blogs/blog-briefingroom/news/112613-obama-says-hell-keep-on-fighting-to-pass-card -check-bill.

13. Kris Maher, "U.S. News: SEIU Campaign Spending Pays Political Dividends—Service Union Wins Top Administration Posts and Backing on Legislation, but Outlays to Boost Obama Strain Its Finances," *Wall Street Journal*, Eastern edition, May 16, 2009, A2.

14. Lee Sustar, "Interview: Sal Rosselli: NUHW and the Fight for Union Democracy," SocialistWorker.org, May 27, 2010, https://socialistworker.org/2010/05/27/nuhw-and-fightunion -democracy.

15. Steve Early, "SEIU's Dial 1-800-Solution Runs into Trouble," *Labor Notes*, June 2011, 5.

16. Change to Win Strategic Organizing Center, "New Labor Federation Pledges to Carry Out Most Aggressive Organizing Campaign in 50 Years," Change to Win, September 27, 2005, www.changetowin.org/news/new-labor-federation-pledges-carry-out-most-aggressive -organizing-campaign-50-years.

17. Sid Salter, "Worker Benefits of Unionizing Nissan Plant Remain Unclear," *Clarion-Ledger* (Jackson, MS), February 3, 2013, 9A.

18. Lucy Pasha-Robinson, "Nissan: Mississippi Radio Warns Workers They'll Go Back to 'Picking Cotton' If They Unionise as Plant Rejects UAW in Vote," *Independent*, U.S. edition (online), August 5, 2017, www.independent.co.uk/news/business/news/nissan-mississippi -radio-workers-picking-cotton-unionise-uaw-reject-vote-a7878236.html.

19. Chris Brooks, "Why Did Nissan Workers Vote No?" *Labor Notes*, September 2017, 3.

20. Brooks, "Why Did Nissan Workers Vote No?" 4.

21. *UAW Principles for Fair Union Elections* (Detroit: UAW, 2011), reproduced online at The Truth About Cars, http://images.thetruthaboutcars.com/2011/01/C416852713.pdf.

22. Nissan Technicians for Truth and Jobs, Facebook page, August 2, 2017 (10:52 a.m.), www .facebook.com/search/top/?q=nissan%20technicians%20for%20truth%20and%20jobs%20 competition%20was%20us.

23. Bill Fletcher Jr. "A New Brand of Unionism," *New Labor Forum* 25, no. 1 (Winter 2016): 16.

24. McAlevey, *Raising Expectations*, 14; Mariya Strauss, "Building a Multiracial Working-Class Movement Through Civic Unionism and Potluck Dinners," *New Labor Forum* 26, no. 2 (Spring 2017): 101; Ness, *New Forms of Worker Organization*, 5.

25. "Action Program Adopted by the Emergency Labor Network Conference (Kent, Ohio—June 24–26, 2011)," ELN: Emergency Labor Network, http://laborfightback.org/eln /conference_action_program.htm.

26. Dinesh Ramde, "Workers Demand Better Jobs, Pay," *Stevens Point (WI) Journal*, May 2, 2011, 5A.

27. Mark Brenner, "Reform Teachers Meet to Assess Damage, Defend Public Education," *Labor Notes*, August 2011, 11.

28. Mark Landler, "Protests Offer Obama Opportunity to Gain, and Room for Pitfalls," *New York Times*, October 7, 2011, A15.

29. Witherell, "An Emerging Solidarity," 252.

30. Sonia Singh, "Car Washers Build Pressure," *Labor Notes*, May 2016, 15.

31. National Labor Relations Act of 1935, Sec. 7, U.S. Code 29, §157.

32. Draut, *Sleeping Giant*, 182.

33. "Call Your Texas Senator Today! Vote No on SB4—Sanctuary Cities Bill," Texas AFL-CIO, February 7, 2017, www.texasaflcio.org/blog/2017/2/6/call-your-texas-senator-today-vote -no-on-sb4-sanctuary-cities-bill.

34. "Labor Beat: Karen Lewis Election Victory Press Conference," June 12, 2010, YouTube, www.youtube.com/watch?v=42TtWpO9vf0.

35. Lou Michel, "Union Tips Off Border Patrol in Immigration Crackdown," *Buffalo News* (online), March 9, 2017, http:// buffalonews.com/2017/03/09/ice-border-patrol-not-ones-seeking -removal-undocumented-workers.

36. SEIU, the American Postal Workers Union, the Amalgamated Transit Union, the United Electrical Workers, the Longshore and Warehouse Workers Union, the Communications Workers of America, and National Nurses United.

37. "UFCW President Hansen Statement on the Mother of Michael Brown," UFCW: A Voice for Working America, August 22, 2014, www.ufcw.org/2014/08/22/ufcw-president-hansen -statement-on-mother-of-michael-brown.

38. AFL-CIO, *AFL-CIO Labor Commission on Racial and Economic Justice Report*, 33.

39. Chris Brooks, "After Nissan: Can We Organize the South?" *Labor Notes* (online), September 1, 2017, www.labornotes.org/2017/09/after-nissan-can-we-organize-south.

AFL-CIO. *Death on the Job: The Toll of Neglect: A State-by-State Profile of Worker Safety and Health in the United States.* Washington, D.C.: AFL-CIO, 2016.

———. *Talking About Racial and Economic Justice: Tools to Move a Constructive Conversation Within Your Union and Within Your Community.* Washington: AFL-CIO, 2016. https://racial-justice.aflcio.org/system/files/final_racecommission_toolkit2016_1.pdf.

Bobo, Kim, and Marién Casillas Pabellón. *The Worker Center Handbook: A Practical Guide to Starting and Building the New Labor Movement.* Ithaca, NY: ILR Press/Cornell University Press, 2016.

Bradbury, Alexandra, Mark Brenner, and Jane Slaughter. *Secrets of a Successful Organizer.* Detroit: Labor Notes, 2016.

Bruder, Jessica. *Nomadland: Surviving America in the Twenty-First Century.* New York: W.W. Norton, 2017.

Burns, Joe. *Reviving the Strike: How Working People Can Regain Power and Transform America.* Brooklyn: Ig Publishing, 2011.

Court, Jamie. "Internal Memos Show How Andy Stern and Union Sold Workers Out." *Huff-Post.* April 11, 2007; updated May 25, 2011. www.huffingtonpost.com/jamie-court/internal -memos-show-how-a_b_45596.html.

Delman, Edward. "Obama Promised to End America's Wars—Has He?: The President's Military Record, by the Numbers." *The Atlantic* (online). March 30, 2016. www.theatlantic.com /international/archive/2016/03/obama-doctrine-wars-numbers/474531.

Draut, Tamara. *Sleeping Giant: How the New Working Class Will Transform America.* New York: Doubleday, 2016.

Early, Steve. *Civil Wars in U.S. Labor: Birth of a New Workers' Movement or Death Throes of the Old?* Chicago: Haymarket Books, 2011.

Early, Steve. *Save Our Unions: Dispatches from a Movement in Distress.* New York: Monthly Review Press, 2013.

Fine, Janice. *Worker Centers: Organizing Communities at the Edge of the Dream.* Ithaca, NY: ILR Press/Cornell University Press, 2006.

Fletcher, Bill, Jr., and Fernando Gapasin. *Solidarity Divided: The Crisis in Organized Labor and a New Path Toward Social Justice.* Berkeley: University of California Press, 2008.

Getman, Julius G. *Restoring the Power of Unions: It Takes a Movement.* New Haven, CT: Yale University Press, 2010.

Labor Notes (published monthly by the Labor Education and Research Project, Detroit). 2005–17.

Lafer, Gordon. *The One Percent Solution How Corporations Are Remaking America One State at a Time.* Ithaca, NY: ILR Press/Cornell University Press, 2017.

Larson, Eric, ed. *Jobs with Justice: 25 Years, 25 Voices.* Oakland, CA: PM Press, 2013.

Lydersen, Kari. *Revolt on Goose Island: The Chicago Factory Takeover and What It Says About the Economic Crisis.* Brooklyn: Melville House, 2014.

Macías-Rojas, Patrisia. *From Deportation to Prison: The Politics of Immigration Enforcement in Post-Civil Rights America.* New York: New York University Press, 2016.

McAlevey, Jane. *No Shortcuts: Organizing for Power in the New Gilded Age.* New York: Oxford University Press, 2016.

McAlevey, Jane, and Bob Ostertag. *Raising Expectations (and Raising Hell): My Decade Fighting for the Labor Movement.* London: Verso, 2012.

Milkman, Ruth, and Ed Ott, eds. *New Labor in New York: Precarious Workers and the Future of the Labor Movement.* Ithaca, NY: ILR Press/Cornell University Press, 2014.

Milkman, Ruth, Joshua Bloom, and Victor Narro. eds. *Working for Justice: The L.A. Model of Organizing and Advocacy.* Ithaca, NY: ILR Press/Cornell University Press, 2010.

Minchin, Timothy J. *Labor Under Fire: A History of the AFL-CIO Since 1979.* Chapel Hill: University of North Carolina Press.

Ness, Immanuel. *Guest Workers and Resistance to U.S. Corporate Despotism.* Urbana: University of Illinois Press, 2011

————. *New Forms of Worker Organization: The Syndicalist and Autonomist Restoration of Class-Struggle Unionism*. Oakland, CA: PM Press, 2014.

Newburger, Eric C., and Thomas Gryn. *The Foreign-Born Labor Force in the United States: 2007*. [Washington, D.C.]: U.S. Dept. of Commerce, Economics and Statistics Administration, U.S. Census Bureau, 2009. www.census.gov/content/dam/Census/library/publications /2009/acs/acs-10.pdf.

New Labor Forum (published three times a year by the Murphy Institute for Worker Education and Labor Studies of the City University of New York). 2005–17.

Nichols, John. *Uprising: How Wisconsin Renewed the Politics of Protest, from Madison to Wall Street*. New York: Nation Books, 2012.

Quigley, Fran. *If We Can Win Here: The New Front Lines of the Labor Movement*. Ithaca, NY: ILR Press/Cornell University Press, 2015.

Rolf, David. *The Fight for Fifteen: The Right Wage for a Working America*. New York: The New Press, 2016.

Smith, Matt. "Union Disunity." *SF Weekly* (online), April 11, 2007. https://archives.sfweekly .com/sanfrancisco/union-disunity/Content?oid=2162525.

Uetricht, Micah. *Strike for America: Chicago Teachers against Austerity*. London: Verso Books, 2014.

Winslow, Calvin. *Labor's Civil War in California: The NUHW Healthcare Workers' Rebellion*. 2nd ed. Oakland, CA: PM Press, 2012.

Witherell, Rob. "An Emerging Solidarity: Worker Cooperatives, Unions, and the New Union Cooperative Model in the United States." *International Journal of Labour Research* 5, no. 2 (July 2013): 251–68.

15: Tipping Points

1. David Shribman, "How Will Hillary Clinton Handle Interest Groups?" *Star-Democrat* (Easton, MD), April 29, 2015, A7.

2. Joseph Pete, "Union Boss Supported After Trump's Tweet," *The Times* (Munster, IN), December 6, 2016, A1.

3. Ibid., A1.

4. Patricia Cohen, "Haste on Tax Measures Risks Trail of Loopholes," *New York Times*, November 14, 2017, A18.

5. Art Harris, "The Reflowering of Bert Lance," *Washington Post*, June 13, 1988, D1.

6. Ilyse Schuman and Michael J. Lotito, "Who Is Neil Gorsuch and Where Does He Stand on Labor and Employment Issues?" January 31, 2017, *Littler*, www.littler.com /publicationpress/publication/who-neil-gorsuch-and-where-does-he-stand-labor-and -employment-issues.

7. Laurie Kellman, "White House Welcomes Some Unions Over Others," *Baltimore Sun*, May 8, 2017, 5.

8. Michael D. Shear, Glenn Thrush, and Maggie Haberman, "Trump Response to Violent Rally Shocks His Allies," *New York Times*, August 17, 2017, A1.

9. "AFL-CIO Representatives Resign from Presidential Council on Manufacturing" (press release), AFL-CIO: America's Unions, August 15, 2017, https://aflcio.org/press/releases/afl-cio -representatives-resign-presidential-council-manufacturing.

10. "Despite President Trump's Tough Talk, Jobs Are Still Bleeding to Mexico," International Association of Machinists and Aerospace Workers, December 14, 2017, www.goiam.org/news

/territories/tcu-union/legislative-outlook/despite-president-trumps-tough-talk-jobs-still
-bleeding-mexico.

11. Evan Osnos, "Doomsday Prep for the Super-Rich," *The New Yorker* (online), January 30, 2017, www.newyorker.com/magazine/2017/01/30/doomsday-prep-for-the-super-rich.

12. Minchin, *Labor Under Fire*, 312.

13. *Union Maids* (1976), directed and produced by James Klein, Miles Mogulescu, and Julia Reichert, June 5, 2011, YouTube, www.youtube.com/watch?v=74gvcvXlgnM.

Bernal, Karen, et al. *Autopsy: The Democratic Party in Crisis*. n.p., 2017. https://
democraticautopsy.org/wp-content/uploads/Autopsy-The-Democratic-Party-In-Crisis.pdf.

Bivens, Josh. "Adding Insult to Injury: How Bad Policy Decisions Have Amplified Globalization's Costs for American Workers." Economic Policy Institute. July 11, 2017. www
.epi.org/publication/adding-insult-to-injury-how-bad-policy-decisions-have-amplified
-globalizations-costs-for-american-workers.

———, et al. "How Today's Unions Help Working People: Giving Workers the Power to
Improve Their Jobs and Unrig the Economy." Economic Policy Institute. August 24, 2017.
www.epi.org/publication/how-todays-unions-help-working-people-giving-workers-the
-power-to-improve-their-jobs-and-unrig-the-economy.

———, and Hunter Blair. "A Public Investment Agenda That Delivers the Goods for American Workers Needs to Be Long-lived, Broad, and Subject to Democratic Oversight." Economic Policy Institute. December 8, 2016. www.epi.org/publication/a-public-investment
-agenda-that-delivers-the-goods-for-american-workers-needs-to-be-long-lived-broad-and
-subject-to-democratic-oversight.

Colvin, Alexander J.S. "The Growing Use of Mandatory Arbitration: Access to the Courts
Is Now Barred for More Than 60 Million American Workers." Economic Policy Institute.
September 27, 2017. www.epi.org/publication/the-growing-use-of-mandatory-arbitration.

Cook, Christopher D. "Trumping Labor: The Republican Plan to Gut Workers' Rights." *The
Progressive* (online), February 14, 2017. http://progressive.org/magazine/trumping-labor
-the-republican-plan-to-gut-workers'-rights.

Davis, Mike. "The Great God Trump & the White Working Class." *Catalyst: A Journal of
Theory and Strategy* 1, no. 1 (Spring 2017): 151–71.

Desmond, Matthew. *Evicted: Poverty and Profit in the American City*. New York: Crown
Publishers, 2016.

Fletcher, Bill. *"They're Bankrupting Us!": And 20 Other Myths About Unions*. Boston: Beacon Press, 2012.

Grossman, Elizabeth. "House Republicans Vow to Do 'Everything We Can' to Roll Back
Labor Law Gains." *In These Times* (online), March 1, 2017. http://inthesetimes.com
/working/entry/19933house_republicans_vow_to_do_everything_we_can_to_roll
_back_labor_law_gains.

Harris, Malcolm. *Kids These Days: Human Capital and the Making of Millennials*. New
York: Little, Brown, 2017.

Hedges, Chris. *Wages of Rebellion: The Moral Imperative of Revolt*. New York: Nation
Books, 2015.

———, and David Talbot. *Unspeakable: Chris Hedges on the Most Forbidden Topics in America*. New York: Hot Books, 2016.

Hill, Marc Lamont. *Nobody: Casualties of America's War on the Vulnerable, from Ferguson
to Flint and Beyond*. New York: Atria Books, 2016.

Hirsch, Barry T., and David A. Macpherson. *Union Membership and Coverage Database.* Last modified January 21, 2018. www.unionstats.com.

Klein, Naomi. *No Is Not Enough: Resisting Trump's Shock Politics and Winning the World We Need.* Chicago: Haymarket Books, 2017.

Labor Notes (published monthly by the Labor Education and Research Project, Detroit). 2016–17.

McChesney, Robert W., and John Nichols. *People Get Ready: The Fight Against a Jobless Economy and a Citizenless Democracy.* New York: Nation Books, 2016.

Miller, Justin. "Trump Stacks Labor Department with Friends of Big Business." *The American Prospect* (online). September 19, 2017. http://prospect.org/article/trump-stacks-labor-department-friends-big-business.

Minchin, Timothy J. *Labor Under Fire: A History of the AFL-CIO since 1979.* Chapel Hill: University of North Carolina Press, 2017.

New Labor Forum (published three times a year by the Murphy Institute for Worker Education and Labor Studies of the City University of New York). 2017.

Nichols, John. "Donald Trump's Dangerously Coherent Agenda." Rosa Luxemburg Stiftung. October 2017. http://www.rosalux-nyc.org/donald-trumps-dangerously-coherent-agenda.

———. *Horsemen of the Trumpocalypse: A Field Guide to the Most Dangerous People in America.* New York: Nation Books, 2017.

Richman, Shaun. "How Bosses Use 'Open Shop' Campaigns to Crush Unions." *In These Times* (online), December 5, 2017. http://inthesetimes.com/working/entry/20728/open-shops-right-to-work-union-busting-organizing-labor-movement.

Scott, Robert E. "Currency Manipulation and Manufacturing Job Loss: Why Negotiating 'Great Trade Deals' Is Not the Answer." Economic Policy Institute. July 21, 2016. www.epi.org/publication/why-negotiating-great-trade-deals-is-not-the-answer.

Tirado, Linda. *Hand to Mouth: Living in Bootstrap America.* New York: Berkley Books, 2015.

Yeselson, Rich. "Can Trump Break the Democrats' Grip on the Union Movement?" *Politico Magazine* (online), February 8, 2017. www.politico.com/magazine/story/2017/02/trump-building-trades-unions-labor-support-history-republicans-214752.

Index

About the Authors

Priscilla Murolo teaches history at Sarah Lawrence College. **A.B. Chitty** works as a librarian systems officer at Queens College. Murolo and Chitty live in Yonkers, New York. Comics journalist **Joe Sacco** is the author of *Palestine, Safe Area Goražde*, and *The Great War*. He lives in Portland, Oregon.

Publishing in the Public Interest

Thank you for reading this book published by The New Press. The New Press is a nonprofit, public interest publisher. New Press books and authors play a crucial role in sparking conversations about the key political and social issues of our day.

We hope you enjoyed this book and that you will stay in touch with The New Press. Here are a few ways to stay up-to-date with our books, events, and the issues we cover:

- Sign up at www.thenewpress.com/subscribe to receive updates on New Press authors and issues and to be notified about local events
- Like us on Facebook: www.facebook.com/newpressbooks
- Follow us on Twitter: www.twitter.com/thenewpress

Please consider buying New Press books for yourself; for friends and family; or to donate to schools, libraries, community centers, prison libraries, and other organizations involved with the issues our authors write about.

The New Press is a 501(c)(3) nonprofit organization. You can also support our work with a tax-deductible gift by visiting www.thenewpress.com/donate.